OXFORD READINGS IN FEMINISM

FEMINISM AND RENAISSANCE STUDIES

Published in this series:

OXFORD READINGS IN FEMINISM

Feminism and Renaissance Studies

Edited by
Lorna Hutson

OXFORD
UNIVERSITY PRESS

OXFORD
UNIVERSITY PRESS

Great Clarendon Street, Oxford OX2 6DP

Oxford University Press is a department of the University of Oxford.
It furthers the University's objective of excellence in research, scholarship,
and education by publishing worldwide in

Oxford New York

Athens Auckland Bangkok Bogotá Buenos Aires Calcutta
Cape Town Chennai Dar es Salaam Delhi Florence Hong Kong Istanbul
Karachi Kuala Lumpur Madrid Melbourne Mexico City Mumbai
Nairobi Paris São Paulo Singapore Taipei Tokyo Toronto Warsaw

and associated companies in Berlin Ibadan

Published in the United States
by Oxford University Press Inc., New York

First published 1999

British Library Cataloguing in Publication Data

Data available

Library of Congress Cataloging in Publication Data

ISBN 0-19-878244-6
ISBN 0-19-878243-8 (pbk)

1 3 5 7 9 10 8 6 4 2

Typeset by Best-set Typesetter Ltd., Hong Kong
Printed in Great Britain
on acid-free paper by
Bookcraft Limited
Midsomer Norton, Somerset

Contents

Notes on Contributors

SHARON ACHINSTEIN teaches at the University of Maryland. She edited *Gender, Literature and the English Revolution* (*Women's Studies*, 24; 1994). Her book *Milton and the Revolutionary Reader* won the Milton Society of America prize. Her current work is on dissent, gender, and politics in Restoration England.

TIM CARTER is Professor of Music at Royal Holloway and Bedford New College, University of London. He is the author of *Jacopo Peri (1561–1633): His Life and Works*, *Music in Late Renaissance and Early Baroque Italy* and the Cambridge Opera Handbook on Mozart's *Le Nozze di Figaro*. Current research projects include theoretical and analytical issues in the music of Claudio Monteverdi.

NATALIE ZEMON DAVIS is Henry Charles Lea Professor of History Emeritus from Princeton University and Adjunct Professor of History at the University of Toronto. Her most recent book is *Women on the Margins: Three Seventeenth Century Lives*.

LAURA GOWING is Senior Lecturer at the University of Hertfordshire. Her book, *Domestic Dangers: Women, Words and Sex in Early Modern London* was published by Oxford University Press in 1996.

LORNA HUTSON is Professor of English Literature at the University of Hull. She is author of *Thomas Nashe in Context* (1989) and of *The Usurer's Daughter: Male Friendship and Fictions of Women in Sixteenth Century England* (1994).

FREDRIKA H. JACOBS is Associate Professor of Art History at Virginia Commonwealth University. She is the author of *Defining the Renaissance Virtuosa: Women Artists and the Language of Art History and Criticism*, and has contributed articles to journals such as *Master Drawings*, *The Art Bulletin*, and *Renaissance Quarterly*.

LISA JARDINE is Professor of Renaissance Studies at Queen Mary and Westfield College, University of London, and an Honorary Fellow of King's College, Cambridge. Her books include: *Still Harping on Daughters* (1983), *Erasmus, Man of Letters* (1993), and *Worldly Goods* (1996). The essay included in this volume is based on primary research by Lisa Jardine from a book co-authored with Anthony Grafton entitled *From Humanism to the Humanities* (1986).

STEPHANIE H. JED is Associate Professor of Italian and Comparative Literature at the University of California, San Diego. She is author of *Chaste*

Thinking: The Rape of Lucretia and the Birth of Humanism (1989) and other essays in Renaissance Studies. She is working on a book project entitled, 'Reorganising Knowledge: Feminist Librarians and the Italian Nation'.

ANN ROSALIND JONES is Esther Clouman Dunn Professor of Comparative Literature at Smith College, Northampton, Massachusetts. She is the author of *The Currency of Eros: Women's Love Lyric in Europe 1540–1620*, and translator, with Margaret Rosenthal, of *The Poems and Selected Letters of Veronica Franco*.

VICTORIA KAHN is Professor of Rhetoric and Comparative Literature at the University of California at Berkeley, and the author of *Rhetoric, Prudence and Skepticism in the Renaissance* (1985) and *Machiavellian Rhetoric* (1995). The essay included in this volume, which won the 1998 prize for Best Article from the Society of Early Modern Women, is part of a book in progress entitled *The Romance of Contract, 1640–74*.

JOAN KELLY (1928–82) was Professor of History at City College of New York, University of New York. She was the author of *Leon Battista Alberti: Universal Man of the Early Renaissance* (1969). Her collected essays on feminist theory and the study of the Renaissance appeared posthumously, edited by friends and colleagues, after her early death in 1982.

CHRISTIANE KLAPISCH-ZUBER has since 1962 researched and taught the demography and historical anthropology of medieval Italy at the École des Hautes Études en Sciences Sociales, Paris, where she is currently Director of Studies. She is the author of more than a hundred articles and of several books on the history of the family and kinship in the Middle Ages, and on women in the fourteenth and fifteenth centuries in Italy.

IAN MACLEAN is titular Professor of Renaissance Studies at Oxford University and a Senior Research Fellow of All Souls College. He is the author of *Women Triumphant: Feminism in French Literature 1610–52* (1977), *Interpretation and Meaning in the Renaissance: The Case of Law* (1992), and of *Montaigne Philosophe* (1996).

PATRICIA PARKER taught at the University of East Africa (Dar es Salaam), the University of Toronto, and Berkeley, California, before becoming Professor of English and Comparative Literature at Stanford University. Her recent books include: *Shakespeare from the Margins* (1996) and (with Margo Hendricks) *Women, 'Race' and Writing in the Early Modern Period* (1994). She is currently editing the new Arden *Midsummer Night's Dream*.

LYNDAL ROPER is Reader in History at Royal Holloway, University of London. She is currently researching witchcraft and witchcraft interrogations in Southern Germany. Her *Oedipus and the Devil: Witchcraft, Sexuality and Religion in Early Modern Europe* appeared in 1994; *The Holy Household: Women and Morals in Reformation Augsburg* in 1989.

NANCY J. VICKERS is President of Brynmawr College. She has taught French and Italian at Dartmouth College, and at the University of Southern California. She has published numerous articles on Renaissance poetry, and is co-editor of *Rewriting the Renaissance: the Discourses of Sexual Difference in Early Modern Europe* and *A New History of French Literature*.

MERRY E. WIESNER (-HANKS) is Professor and Chair of the Department of History at the University of Wisconsin–Milwaukee. She is one of the editors of *Sixteenth Century Journal* and the author or editor of eight books, including monographs and source collections, and over 40 articles on various aspects of women's lives and gender structures in early modern Europe, especially Germany.

Introduction

Lorna Hutson

FEMINISM AND THE 'RENAISSANCE'

'Women', wrote Jacob Burckhardt in 1860, 'stood on a footing of perfect equality with men' in the culture of the Italian Renaissance. There was, he went on to claim, 'no question of "woman's rights" or female emancipation, simply because the thing itself was a matter of course. . . . The same intellectual and emotional development which perfected the man was demanded for the perfection of the woman.'[1] In 1928 Virginia Woolf, writing of the English Renaissance (the age of Shakespeare), expressed a rather different view of its relation to the emancipation of women. 'Woman' in Shakespeare's age, Woolf wrote, 'pervades poetry from cover to cover; she is all but absent from history. . . . Some of the most inspired words, some of the most profound thoughts in literature fall from her lips; in real life she could hardly read, could scarcely spell, and was the property of her husband.'[2] This 'queer, composite being' of poetry and social history expresses all the contradictions in the idea of 'Feminism and Renaissance Studies'. For the 'Renaissance' is not so much a historical *period*—after all, Burckhardt is talking about Italy from the fourteenth to the sixteenth centuries, Woolf about England in the sixteenth and seventeenth—as it is a statement of belief in the civilizing power of certain forms of culture, specifically literature and the fine arts. Yet, as Woolf says, 'in real life' the women who were so full of wit and genius in Shakespeare's plays could scarcely read and write. So how are we to work out the relationship between the poetry and the reality, how are we to judge what women were capable of? The answer Woolf gave lay outside the province of 'Renaissance Studies' as conceived by Burckhardt and his followers. What she called for was more *social history*:

What one wants, I thought—and why does not some brilliant student at Newnham or Girton supply it?—is a mass of information; at what age did she marry; how many children had she as a rule; what was her house like; had she

1

a room to herself; did she do the cooking; would she be likely to have a servant? All these facts lie somewhere, presumably, in parish registers and account books; the life of the average Elizabethan Woman must be scattered about somewhere, could one collect it and make a book of it.[3]

The work which Woolf asked for in 1928 has been, and continues to be done. Indeed, Merry Wiesner has recently spoken of 'a flood of research' in which 'studies of women and gender in early modern England vastly outweigh those of any other European country, and perhaps those of all the countries of Europe taken together'.[4] Nevertheless, the problem of Woolf's 'queer, composite being', persists in the notion of 'Feminism and Renaissance Studies' itself. For, in academic terms, 'Renaissance Studies' are located in departments not just of history, but of literature in different languages, art history, and music. Moreover, the term 'Renaissance' implies, as 'early modern' does not, a process of cultural evaluation, and a consensus about the evaluative criteria being used.[5] When Erasmus wrote of good letters as having been 'reborn' in his own time, evaluative criteria were clearly being brought into play. The evaluative language in which he and other humanists expressed these criteria, however, was deeply implicated in definitions of sexual difference. At the beginning of his rhetorical handbook, *On the Copia of Words and Ideas*, for example, Erasmus described, in a double sexual analogy, the contrast between a man's aspirations towards performance of a successful oration and his risk of failing. 'Just as there is nothing', he writes, 'more admirable or splendid than a speech with a rich copia of words overflowing in a golden stream, so it is, assuredly, that such a thing may be striven for at no slight risk, because, according to the proverb: "Not every man has the luck to go to Corinth." '[6] The successful oration—a 'rich copia of words overflowing in a golden stream'—invokes Jove's insemination of Danaë in a shower of gold, a fantasy of affluent potency, while not having 'the luck to go to Corinth' alludes to the cost of sex with the courtesan, Lais of Corinth, thus inverting the shower of gold (a wealthy orgasm) in the identification of poverty with failure to use a woman for sex. It hardly needs pointing out that these are not metaphors which would encourage girls with Latin enough to open Erasmus's book to read on, though the book was, in fact, recommended for the use of school*boys*. In other words, it is not just that the recovery of the cultural activities of the average European woman of the fifteenth or sixteenth centuries (cooking, housework, managing servants, childbirth, prayer, and so forth) would seem beside the point to 'Renaissance Studies' in the Burckhardtian tradition; it is that, traditionally, Burckhardtian 'Renaissance Studies' uncritically takes over (and, indeed, abstracts and makes universal) a set of evaluative languages and conceptual frameworks which, in Renaissance texts, explicitly exclude women from significant cultural activity, or align them with an inferior type of creativity. This volume provides examples both of the feminist social history which Woolf called for, and of the literary and linguistic work required to expose the ideological work of gender in traditional Renaissance historiography. Indeed, most of the articles contain elements of both social history and deconstructive analyses of the discursive constitution of gender. In Fredrika Jacobs's article in Part IV, we learn how the print-maker, Diana Scultori, was denied full membership to the artisans' confraternity of San Guiseppe in Rome, when she and her husband moved there in 1575. This lack of material and institutional support, Jacobs writes, was compounded in a critical language 'rife with gender-based evaluative opposites' codified by the institutions in question. Similarly, Lisa Jardine's article in Part I, revealing the lack of any practical career-structure for women humanists in fifteenth-century Italy, simultaneously exposes and subjects to analysis the gendered language deployed by male humanists which ingeniously both praised women's achievements, and rendered them insignificant, subordinate to the possession of the virtue of chastity.

Nor, in the work of feminist social historians exemplified here, do we have merely the 'mass of facts' which Virginia Woolf called for. Feminist social history is now as alive to the semiotics of culture as feminist literary and art history have become to the social, material, and linguistic conditions of literary and artistic genius. In an article written in the 1970s, and reprinted here in Part II, Natalie Zemon Davis turns to Bakhtin's theories of carnivalesque practices of symbolic inversion as a way of reconsidering the meaning of women's inferior position in a social order modelled on a metaphysical hierarchy of gender. If women were, like children and fools, 'naturally' inferior, then did they not, like children and fools, enjoy a ritualized licence that might be appropriated for radical forms of action and thought? Reviewing the implications of her own practice, Davis notes that feminist social history, learning from anthropology and cultural history, has begun to take into account the question of sex roles, sexual symbolism, and sexual behaviour as a serious factor in the analysis of pre-industrial economic and social structures.[7] To Woolf's 'mass of facts' has been added the recognition that symbolic practices, involving honour (especially sexual honour) are material in analysing the economic and social position of women in the past.

'HUMANISM' AFTER FEMINISM

Woolf's observations notwithstanding, Renaissance scholars continued for the most part throughout the twentieth century to accept Burckhardt's view that the humanist classical revival improved the lot of women both in Italy and in the Northern Renaissance. Northern Europe, moreover, was blessed by the Reformation, which was thought to have enhanced the status of women through its rejection of a misogynist cult of virginity, and its promotion of a more affectionate model of conjugal relations.[8] When the feminist movement first impinged on literary studies of the Renaissance, this sanguine view of the liberating effects of Renaissance humanism and reformed religion was still in the ascendant, and not only Erasmus and St Thomas More, but Shakespeare and even Ben Jonson were all congratulated for their 'feminism'.[9] Yet the Burckhardtian narrative of a Renaissance humanism which was also liberating to women is, in itself, a misleading one. To take Burckhardt's own remarks about the liberated behaviour of women as a starting point, it is striking that most of these occur in the context of his discussions of the novelist Matteo Bandello (c.1480–1562) whose stories of domestic adultery and ingenious revenge were translated into French and English, and subsequently supplied the plots of much English Renaissance drama, including Shakespeare's. To Burckhardt, for whom the Italian Renaissance serves as the cradle of modern self-consciousness, the birth of the modern 'individual', Bandello's novels are statements about the freedom of Italian domestic morality, the private-life counterpart of the political individualism that characterizes his famous view of 'the state as a work of art'. Burckhardt sums up the Italian moral character as one in which 'the individual first inwardly casts off the authority of a state' after which, 'his love . . . turns mostly for satisfaction to *another individuality, equally developed*, namely, to his neighbour's wife' (italics mine). The adulteries and revenges that Burckhardt found so 'thrillingly' described in Bandello thus take on the heroic colouring of the Italian political individualism which he elsewhere celebrates. The 'individuality' of this fictional type of Renaissance woman helps to support Burckhardt's argument that Italy was the first culture in Europe to produce an internalization of personal morality—'a modern standard of good and evil—a sense of moral responsibility—which is essentially different from that which was familiar to the Middle Ages'.[10]

'Renaissance Woman' plays a very minor part within the larger Burckhardtian drama in which the political and religious naivety of the Middle Ages was exchanged, via the revival of learning and the arts fostered by Italian republics and despotisms, for the spirit of enquiry and scepticism that was henceforth to characterize modern Europe. Yet what feminist criticism calls into question is not just the accuracy of the Burckhardtian image of women, but the larger historical drama itself. For the 'Renaissance' as Burckhardt conceived it (and as his conception was given popular currency by John Addington Symonds and Matthew Arnold) underwrites what Tony Davies has called 'the myth of essential and universal Man', that is, the idea that there can be a human essence (ungendered but implicitly masculine, and unaffected by history or culture, but implicitly European or North American and 'civilized') the condition of which it is the job of great art and literature to express.[11] As Davies points out, the retrospective attribution of this nineteenth-century universalizing humanism to the fifteenth- and sixteenth-century classical scholars who called themselves 'humanists' is an anachronism. However, the influence of the Burckhardtian narrative of the Renaissance as the beginning of a new age of liberated self-discovery for 'Man' can scarcely be overemphasized. The first essay in this collection is a famously direct assault on that narrative by the erstwhile Burckhardtian Renaissance scholar, Joan Kelly. In her first book on Leon Battista Alberti (written under the name of Joan Gadol) Kelly actually defended Burckhardt against a recent scholarly attack, citing as 'brilliant' an essay by the distinguished Renaissance scholar, Ernst Cassirer which argued that in sixteenth-century literature, 'The consideration of individuality acquires an entirely new value.'[12] Later on, when Kelly was very ill with cancer and knew that she would not live to see the completion of the feminist work she had begun, she described the revolution that feminism had brought to her thinking as a decentring of Renaissance Man from her mental universe:

I knew now that the entire picture I had of the Renaissance was partial, distorted, limited . . . Leonardo had said that 'the earth is not the center of the sun's orbit nor at the center of the universe . . . and anyone standing on the moon, when it and the sun are both beneath us, would see this our earth and the element of water upon it just as we see the moon . . . ' All I had done was to say, with Leonardo, suppose we look again at this dark, dense immobile earth from the vantage point of the moon? Suppose we look again at this age, the Renaissance, reputed for its liberation from old conforming forms, renowned for its revival of classical and republican ideas? Suppose we look at the Renaissance from the vantage point of women?[13]

In the essay reprinted here, Kelly integrates Marxism and feminism to argue that in economic, social, and ideological terms, the developments which Burckhardt celebrated as constituting the liberating forces of the Renaissance—the development of modern states, the abandonment of feudal relations, the diffusion of Latin literacy and with it classical models of the division between household and politics, public and private—were far from liberating for women. In doing so, she also implicitly challenges the liberal humanist reading that identifies (as Cassirer did) the compellingly individualized voices of canonical Renaissance texts with a 'universally human' point of view. She shows that Baldesar Castiglione's dialogue, *The Courtier*, for all its attractive illusion of spontaneity (which, according to Burckhardt would bespeak the emergence of a more self-conscious individuality) articulates for women a position of considerably less social power and sexual freedom than that granted them by the less individualized poetic texts of the medieval tradition of *amor courtois*. She argues, moreover, that feminists need to read canonical Renaissance texts, such as Castiglione's or Leon Battista Alberti's (who wrote a dialogue on household life, as Castiglione wrote a dialogue on life at court) in the context of analysing the wider social, economic, and discursive constitution of femininity. Thus, where Burckhardt saw expressed in Alberti's works, including his treatise on domestic economy, the sensibility of their author, in particular the 'sympathetic intensity with which he entered into the whole of life around him', Kelly rather observes the way in which Alberti's treatise borrowed from Aristotelian political and economic writings in order to identify women with the *oikos* or household, rather than the *polis* or the city, the sphere of 'politics'. Some feminists have argued that Kelly reads canonical authors too literally, failing to register the play of meaning opened up by the dialogue form.[14] Nevertheless, Kelly's contrast between the freedoms enjoyed by two types of courtly lady—the twelfth-century Eleanor of Aquitaine and the sixteenth-century Elizabetta Gonzaga as humanistically portrayed by Castiglione—remains a striking refutation of the Burckhardtian idealization of the necessarily liberating effects on women of Renaissance court culture and humanist learning. Her conclusions remain controversial, too, in the light of the way in which a Burckhardtian emphasis on reading Renaissance canonical texts as a key site for the 'emergence of individuality' has been given a new lease of life in Stephen Greenblatt's particular version of the new historicist criticism.[15]

Lisa Jardine's essay is taken from a book co-authored with Anthony Grafton on the legacy of Renaissance humanist propaganda for the self-image of the humanities in schools and universities in the late twentieth century. Nineteenth-century historiography of the Renaissance assimilated to the notion of the Renaissance 'humanist'—the scholar concerned with the revival of Greek and Latin literature—the associations of the German word '*Humanismus*' (translated as 'humanism') which suggested, quite inaccurately, that the humanists of the fifteenth and sixteenth centuries were concerned with 'an essential humanity, unconditioned by time or place'.[16] Historians of education in the Burckhardtian tradition, influenced by this idea, tended to idealize the educational aims of the humanists, often citing as both exceptional and 'characteristic' of the humanists' lofty aims the achievements of a small minority of women who were favoured with the same education in Latin and Greek as their male kin.[17] Jardine and Grafton's general argument against taking at face value the inflated claims for the ethical worth of Latin literacy made by fifteenth-century humanists and exaggerated by their nineteenth-century historians is given point by their analysis of the practical uselessness of a humanist education for women. Active civic virtue—the professed goal of a humanist education—being, as Kelly also pointed out, denied to women, the humanist celebrants of learned women (like their nineteenth-century historians) fall back on insisting on the learned woman's iconic chastity.

My own essay in this collection develops Kelly's and Jardine's suggestions about the way in which the humanist classical revival actually reinforced the idea that man's destiny as a deliberative 'political animal' (in Aristotle's formulation) was dependent on a prior definition of the household as the non-political sphere to which women were confined. It shows how the *Oeconomicus* of Xenophon was read by Northern humanists as a text which offered an image—in the figure of the 'good husband' sitting outside in the 'agora', or political arena—of the potential of humanist eloquence as a form of learning the true value of which could only be realized *outside* the cloisters and the universities, in the public, negotiating spheres of politics and commerce. Women, then, became figuratively associated, through the wide diffusion of the *Oeconomicus* via Erasmus, Shakespeare, and others, with a domestic resource which has a capacity to err, and which therefore must (like the errant resources of eloquence itself) be mastered by the 'good husband'.

Stephanie Jed's article, though not, ostensibly, concerned with humanism as such, implicitly rethinks the assumptions behind a famous chapter of Burckhardt's *Civilisation of the Renaissance in Italy* entitled 'On the Discovery of the World and Man', in which the nineteenth-century conception of humanism as the study of 'Man' is yoked to the European 'discovery' of America in such a way as to suggest that the emergence of European self-consciousness is intrinsically bound up with the growth of a spirit of enquiry fostered by the rational observation and exploration of the natural world. Borrowing from the 'standpoint theory' of feminist sociologist Dorothy Smith, Jed wittily exposes the ostensible 'rationality' of European taxonomies of the New World marvels—iguanas which live on dirt, and women who are also poets—as a form of knowledge indissociable from the pragmatic, concrete relationships in which it is produced.

HISTORICIZING FEMININITY

Definitions of 'femininity' vary historically and across cultures. Early feminist criticism of Shakespeare, for example, by referring to the 'nature of women', implied that women's nature was transhistorical, rather than suggesting that the 'femininity' which we think we recognize is not only historically derived from Shakespeare, but from nineteenth- and twentieth-century humanist traditions of reading Shakespeare. Recent criticism of Shakespeare which takes into account, for example, the transvestism of Shakespeare's theatre, and the medical theory of sexual difference in the Renaissance (as discussed in this volume by Ian Maclean, and in a book-length study by Thomas Laqueur[18]) is able to cast a quite different light on questions of gender as constructed by Renaissance drama. Ian Maclean's work reprinted here was originally part of an innovative investigation of 'woman' as a theoretical discursive construct over a range of academic disciplines in a period when the scholasticism that dominated the medieval universities was being overtaken by Renaissance humanism. The present chapter is concerned with the female body as conceived in Renaissance medical discourse. On the whole, Maclean demonstrates that Renaissance medicine continues to follow Galen's model of the structural identity of the male and female sex organs, and continues to believe, with Galen and Aristotle, in the female's being made of colder and moister humours than the man, so that her sex organs remain internal, and she is unable to 'concoct' perfect semen from blood. Falloppio's description of the female genitalia in 1561 marks the beginning of the end, argues Maclean, of the Galenic parallelism of male and female sex organs.[19]

As Maclean shows, intellectual disciplines were not isolated from one another, authoritative statements being transmitted from one to the other in the form of *loci communes*, or 'commonplaces'. Natalie Davis's essay, 'Women on Top' demonstrates the truth of this in her assembly of commonplaces drawn from medical, ethical, and political discourses in the Renaissance, all of which authoritatively align femininity with disorder and inversion. Davis's argument, however, develops the idea that these associations, in conjunction with the persistence, throughout pre-industrial Europe, of the *topos* of the world-upside-down both as a conceptual tool and as a festive practice, may have offered possibilities for new ideas about sex-roles, and even innovative political action. A complex licence, Davis argues, was afforded the unruly women, a licence which has been interpreted as reinforcing their subjection, but which may, conversely, be seen as a conceptual resource.

The last two essays in this Part use archival material in order to interpret historical and cultural variants in attitudes towards and fantasies about maternal femininity. Christiane Klapisch-Zuber finds in the marital and dotal practices in fifteenth-century Florence an explanation for the attribution of coldness and cruelty towards widowed mothers who left their marital family, taking their dowry with them, in order to remarry or return to their natal kin. A general social intolerance of married widows obliged women to make a choice between these courses of action; there could be no 'good mother', Klapisch-Zuber therefore concludes, under the contradictory prescriptions of virtuous femininity in the Florentine patrilineal system. It has been argued, however, that Klapisch-Zuber's exclusive focus on marriage as a lineage strategy has led to a neglect of the question of marriage as an affective bond. In a series of articles, Stanley Chojnaki has used testamentary evidence to argue for a more positive view of women's autonomy and power as beloved and propertied wives in the Venetian republic.[20] However, the Venetian phenomenon of massive dowry inflation in the late sixteenth century and the consequent remedial policy of marriage limitation has also been argued to be the motivating force behind a new feminist sensibility among single women in seventeenth-century Venice.[21]

Lyndal Roper's essay argues for the validity of using psychoanalytic theory in order to interpret archival documents relating to witchcraft trials in the seventeenth century. The evidential status of witchcraft documents has always been a problem for historians, she argues. However, rather than seeing accusations of witchcraft as deriving from the misogyny of post-Reformation culture, Roper reads them as complex psychic documents, expressive of pre-Oedipal fantasies of a malevolent maternity and giving imaginative form to the ambivalent feelings of women towards other women. Roper's work attempts to get beyond the anthropological social history that would seek the explanation for the phenomenon of witch-hunting in collective beliefs and symbols. In exploring the psychic world of both the accusers and those who confessed, she investigates what our subjectivities have in common with those of women and men in the seventeenth century.

GENDER AND GENRE

The humanist pedagogy that characterized both the Italian and the Northern Renaissance distinguished itself from its scholastic antecedent chiefly through its emphasis on the value of the *literature* of the classical past. A practitioner's knowledge of a wide range of literary genres—declamation, verse epistle, comic and tragic drama, and so forth—became, therefore, widely diffused among educated men in this period. Paying attention to the place of the 'feminine' as it was constructed in literary genres, then, is another way of rewriting intellectual history and the history of gendered subjectivity (as opposed to Burckhardtian 'individuality') in the past. Two of the essays (those by Nancy Vickers and Patricia Parker) examine the figure of femininity in men's writing, while the other two (by Ann Jones and Victoria Kahn) look at texts by women.

Nancy J. Vickers adapts Laura Mulvey's psychoanalytic analysis of the simultaneous promise of pleasure and threat of castration embodied in the image of woman in narrative cinema. She uses this to account for one of the most idiosyncratic (and yet subsequently most imitated and formulaic) characteristics of the lyric poetry of the first great humanist, Petrarch. Petrarch's persistent representation of Laura, his beloved, as a body fragmented and dispersed represents, argues Vickers, a neutralization of the threat of textual dismemberment (the failure to achieve a poetic 'corpus') elsewhere acknowledged in Petrarch's fictive assumption of the identity of Acteon. Petrarchism—the legacy of this technique of describing an absent beloved in a series of ingenious analogies—is thus said to enable men to speak poetically by silencing women. However, as Ann Jones shows in this volume and elsewhere, women were able to adapt the strategies of Petrarchism for their own poetic purposes (Jones does, however, argue that women tended to use the technique of descriptive enumeration—*blason*—less visually than men).[22]

Patricia Parker's essay deals with Renaissance literary culture's ambivalence towards the very textuality it so assiduously cultivates. Humanists, engaged in the educational promotion of literature as the foundation of a masculine capacity to deliberate and persuade effectively in the public sphere, were both committed to rhetorical amplification and haunted by the spectre of ineffectual or redundant speech. Parker shows how these ambivalences are acknowledged by the presence, in a range of plays by Shakespeare and other texts, of female figures who embody, in their corpulence and volubility, the text's hazardous deferrals.

Ann Jones's essay comes back, initially, to the themes of Lisa Jardine's discussion of women humanists. Jardine and Jones both observe how humanist educators, while stressing the identity of eloquence and moral virtue for men, tend, when addressing women, to associate public speaking and writing with sexual promiscuity. However, Jones offers three examples of sixteenth-century women poets—the French Pernette du Guillet and Catherine des Roches, and the Italian Tullia d'Aragona—who used different poetic strategies to negotiate a position from which to write. Interestingly, in view of Vickers's reading of Petrarch, Jones finds Pernette du Guillet adapting the Acteon myth when writing to Maurice Scève. Catherine des Roches appropriates for herself Renaissance domestic ideology, while the courtesan Tullia d'Aragona exploits her clients' rivalry, publishing a collection of verse epistles that constructs her as the member of a prestigious group.

Victoria Kahn's essay marries the history of literary genre to the history of political thought, revising the latter as it does so. Kahn's phrase, 'the romance of contract', is almost an oxymoron; in established contract theory, the parties to contract are moved, not by romantic passion, but by rational self-interest. Carole Pateman's feminist critique of modern contract theory argues that the triumph of Lockean political theory at the end of the seventeenth century excluded women (bound within the unequal sexual contract of marriage) from being rational participants in the political contract. Kahn examines how the seventeenth-century genre of romance—and in particular, its modification in a novella by the royalist Margaret Cavendish—invokes contemporary analogies between political and marital contracts in ways which make problematic any distinction between 'rational' and 'passionate' contractual obligation. A revised history of political theory in the period, and one which views differently the contribution of women, and the ideology of marriage, is thereby called for.

WOMEN'S AGENCY

Sharon Achinstein's essay makes a bridge between the penultimate and final parts of this collection, linking up with the topic of Victoria Kahn's essay, and particularly with Kahn's desire to revise unexamined assumptions about the constitution of rationality in the history of political thought in this period. Borrowing her title, 'Women on Top in the Pamphlet Literature of the English Revolution' from Natalie Davis's classic essay 'Women on Top' (reprinted in Part II) Achinstein considers how far the festive *topos* of the disorderly woman can be said to account for the explosion of mysogynistic sexual satire in the political pamphlet literature of the interregnum. Rather than explaining Royalist and Parliamentarian representations of disruptive, orgiastic women in terms of exclusively male political concerns, Achinstein sees the period as one in which women's real political and destabilizing interventions were contributing to new definitions of intentionality and rationality, and thus to the establishment of rationality as the predominant means of expression in the public sphere.

The allocation of the essays in this collection to different sections, while meant to facilitate the book's use by students and teachers, are clearly not representative of hard and fast distinctions. Although this, the last section of the book, is ostensibly devoted to the topic of recovering the historical agency of women, such a project of recovery can depend, as I have tried to show, on dismantling the established critical and evaluative languages which Burckhardtian cultural history itself inherited from the Renaissance. The title of Fredrika Jacobs's essay, 'La Donnesca Mano' ('the womanly hand') comes from a book-length study which examines critical fortunes of sixteenth-century Italian women artists. Sixteenth-century Italy saw, of course, the publication of Giorgio Vasari's *Lives of the Artists* (1568) which, while it provides valuable comments on paintings by women (many of which are now lost) more significantly established the genre of modern art criticism, with its exclusions and gendered hierarchies. Jacobs's book invokes the adoption, by Vasari and other art critics, of a habit of thought in which the notion of the 'female' is incorporated into a scheme of polarized opposites, one pole of which acquires superior value (including 'male', 'one', 'right'), while the other is rendered inferior (thus, 'woman', 'plural', 'left'). (Readers can find a discussion of this influential Pythagorean mode of argumentation in Ian Maclean's essay in this volume, pp. 127–155.) Jacobs's question, which recalls a theme in both Jardine's and Jed's essays, is whether exceptions which challenge the taxonomies possible within this structuring principle—exceptions such as the 'woman artist'—alter or reaffirm the principle. Her title, 'the womanly hand', invokes such an exception, as it refers to the poet Torquato Tasso's distinction between 'feminine' (*feminile*) and womanly (*donnesco)* virtue, the latter marking the exceptional woman, who inhabits a median point between the negatively valorized adjective '*feminile*' and the positively valorized '*virile*' (masculine).

Although women artists were, by definition, such 'exceptional women', Jacobs shows how the language of art criticism as it evolved between the time of Alberti and that of Vasari, tended towards the realization of a two-tiered structure of critical evaluation, in which *artigiano* (craftsman) became the negative pole of *artista* (artist), thus helping to distinguish the *pittrice* (woman artist) who displayed *diligenza* (diligence) from the *pittore* (male artist) capable of *sprezzatura* (skilful improvisation). Jacobs's findings corroborate Svetlana Alpers's argument that the Italian Renaissance tradition, based on such elements as perspective, the privileging of fresco, the priority of the viewer over the object viewed, and the aspiration of the painting to the status of poetry, has impoverished the language of modern art criticism when confronted by works which do not conform to this tradition, including work in the Flemish tradition and work by women.[23]

Elements of Jacobs's work anticipate the themes of Merry Wiesner's now classic essay on male bonding and women's work in sixteenth- and seventeenth-century Germany. Wiesner begins with the orthodox narrative of economic history: increasingly, capitalistic divisions between masters and journeymen within the crafts guilds point to the decline of those medieval institutions within economic life in the sixteenth and seventeenth centuries in Europe. Yet, as she points out, this narrative underestimates the real economic power wielded by the ritual function of guilds as centres of male bonding. Just as Jacobs observes how women lacked full access to the artisans' confraternities that would codify the theoretical language of art criticism in sixteenth-century Italy, so Wiesner shows how crafts guilds in Germany in the same period began to devalue occupations which maintained their link with household production. Journeymen who once could have expected to marry and become mastercraftsmen were now obliged to face a lifetime of bachelorhood and wage-labour. They compensated, argues Wiesner, by defining their honour—their symbolic capital—as dependent on their dissociation from women, and from the taint of women's work.

The symbolic capital of honour is also a concern of Laura Gowing's essay on women's activities as suitors in cases of defamation in the ecclesiastical courts in London in the sixteenth and seventeenth centuries. Noting women's lack of political and common law agency, Gowing finds, in the ecclesiastical courts' jurisdiction over sexual matters, a space in which women were directly engaged in contesting their symbolic capital—their sexual honour. Her findings paradoxically reveal that the official, homiletic language of mutual responsibility for sexual sin was not the idiom adopted by litigants themselves, whether male or female. Rather, the language of sexual slander, as revealed by depositions in the ecclesiastical courts, while testifying to women's social agency as litigants, also reveals their bondage within the conceptual framework of the double sexual standard.

It is appropriate that a section on the recovery of women's agency should end with the problem of the inaudible voices of the past. We are so bound by textual traces in interpreting past cultural activity (and literary critics frequently use the term 'voice' to mean textual traces, the achievement of a subject position in writing) that Tim Carter's attempt to recover, in the history of the emergence of a new musical style, the contribution made by a particular woman's musical taste as expressed by her *voice*, seems to stretch the powers of scholarship to its limits. Carter invokes the work of Anthony Newcomb and Suzanne Cusick, musicologists who have both drawn attention to the inadequacy of investigating the actvities of women as singers and composers by looking for masculine markers of authorial signature and professional status.[24] Carter's analysis of the position of the Florentine singer, Vittoria Archilei, among the proprietorial interests and professional rivalries of composers Guilio Caccini and Jacopo Peri, asks us to rethink our assumptions about the relation of performance to composition, and the originating claims of each. From the evidence of printed texts and private letters, and from records of musical performance, Carter hypothesizes that Archilei may have been more innovative in bringing into existence the unembellished, expressive style of the Florentine 'new music' than a gender-blind musicology had previously thought.

These essays are by no means a definitive collection on the subject of 'Feminism and Renaissance Studies'. By far the largest body of work to emerge in this area—the study of individual women writing in English in the sixteenth and seventeenth centuries—has, for the very reason of its dominance of the field, not been represented here. There are other, more serious omissions—Spain only comes in via the New World, and there is nothing directly on race, nor directly on the question of women and religion. No collection of this kind can be comprehensive, and my decision not to abridge any of the essays has limited the selection still further. Nevertheless, there is a rationale here. Every discipline centred on the study of the Renaissance has its favoured narratives of the emergence of modernity, though the emphases of these narratives (and what they admit as evidence) obviously varies in ways which have defined the disciplines. The writings in this volume disrupt those narratives either by subjecting their language and argumentative strategies to feminist critique, or by offering alternative accounts of women's and men's agency, or both. They thus give readers access, via their own original and provocative contributions to specific disciplinary debates, both to the range of disciplines and methodologies in question, and to the creative force of feminist writing as a challenge to the policing of disciplinary boundaries.

I would like to thank the general editors of this series, Susan James and Teresa Brennan, for supporting the idea of this collection, as well as the editors at Oxford University Press, Tim Barton and Angela Griffin, for their helpfulness throughout its production. I am grateful to all the contributors for giving permission for their work to appear in a collection which brings together an extraordinary wealth of different forms of expertise to bear on the question of women and gender in the history of Western culture, and I hope it will be a stimulus to teachers, students, and readers whatever section of the library they frequent.

Notes

1. Jacob Burckhardt, *The Civilization of the Renaissance in Italy*, trans. S. G. C. Middlemore (Harmondsworth: Penguin, 1990), 250–1. I would like to thank Angela Leighton, Alan Stewart, and Cathy Sprent for reading the introduction, and Laura Gowing and Virginia Cox for help and advice with the collection.
2. Virginia Woolf, *A Room of One's Own* [1928] (Harmondsworth: Penguin, 1945), 45.
3. Ibid. 46–7.
4. Merry Wiesner, *Gender, Church and State in Early Modern Germany* (London and New York: Longman, 1998), 2.
5. See W. K. Ferguson, *The Renaissance in Historical Thought* (Cambridge, Mass.:

Houghton Mifflin Co., 1948), 19–64. For discussions of what is at stake in the choice between the terms 'Renaissance' and 'early modern', see Leah S. Marcus, 'Renaissance/Early Modern Studies', in Stephen Greenblatt and Giles Gunn (eds.), *Redrawing the Boundaries: The Transformation of English and American Studies* (New York: The Modern Language Association of America, 1992), 41–63 and Wiesner, *Gender, Church and State*, 208–12.

6. Desiderius Erasmus, *On Copia of Words and Ideas*, ed. and trans. D. B. King and H. D. Rix (Milwaukee: Marquette University Press, 1963), 11. For Erasmus's use of the metaphor of 'renaissance' or 'rebirth', see Ferguson, *The Renaissance*, 37.

7. Natalie Zemon Davis, '"Women's History" in Transition: The European Case', *Feminist Studies*, 3 (1976), 83–103, reprinted in Joan Wallach Scott (ed.), *Feminism and History* (Oxford: Oxford University Press, 1996), 79–104.

8. See W. and M. Haller, 'The Puritan Art of Love', *Huntington Library Quarterly*, 5 (1942), 235–72. For a bibliography of recent work in English and German which deals with the effect of the Reformation on women's lives, see Wiesner, *Gender, Church and State*, 215–19.

9. See e.g. Juliet Dusinberre, *Shakespeare and the Nature of Women* (London: Macmillan, 1975), 40–75.

10. Burckhardt, *Civilization of the Renaissance in Italy*, 252, 279–83, 289.

11. See Tony Davies, *Humanism* (London: Routledge, 1997), 10–25.

12. Ernst Cassirer, 'Some Remarks on the Question of Originality in the Renaissance', *Journal of the History of Ideas*, 4 (1943), 54. See Joan Gadol's introduction to *Leon Battista Alberti: Universal Man of the Renaissance* (Chicago and London: Chicago University Press, 1969).

13. Joan Kelly, 'author's preface', *Women, History and Theory* (Chicago and London: University of Chicago Press, 1984), xiii.

14. See Pamela Benson, *The Invention of the Renaissance Woman* (University Park: Pennsylvania State University Press, 1992), 33.

15. See e.g. Stephen Greenblatt's *Renaissance Self-Fashioning* (Chicago: University of Chicago Press, 1980), 1, where he states that his interests lie 'in the perception, as old in academic writing as Burckhardt and Michelet—that there is in the early modern period a change in the intellectual, social and psychological, and aesthetic structures that govern the generation of identities', and *Shakespearean Negotiations* (Oxford: Clarendon Press, 1988), 88, where he assumes that Shakespeare's characters of women are fully realized 'individuals'. For a feminist critique of New Historicism, see Ros Ballaster, 'New Hystericism: Aphra Behn's *Oronooko*: The Body, the Text and the Feminist Critic', in Isobel Armstrong (ed.), *New Feminist Discourses* (London: Routledge, 1992), 283–95.

16. See Davies, *Humanism*, 25.

17. Contrast the accounts in the Burckhardtian William Harrison Woodward, *Vittorino da Feltre and Other Humanist Educators* (Cambridge: Cambridge University Press, 1897), 119–121 and Margaret L. King, 'Book-Lined Cells: Women and Humanism in the Early Italian Renaissance', in Patricia Labalme (ed.), *Beyond their Sex: Learned Women of the European Past* (New York: New York University Press, 1980).

18. Thomas Laqueur, *Making Sex: The Body and Gender from the Greeks to Freud* (Cambridge, Mass.: Harvard University Press, 1990).

19. Readers interested in this topic should also consult Katherine Park, 'The

Rediscovery of the Clitoris', in David Hillman and Carla Mazzio (eds.), *The Body in Parts* (London: Routledge, 1997), 171–95.

20. See Stanley Chojnaki, 'The Power of Love: Wives and Husbands in Late Medieval Venice', in Mary Erler and Maryanne Kowalski (eds.), *Women and Power in the Middle Ages* (Athens and London: University of Georgia Press, 1988), 126–48 and 'Patrician Women in Early Renaissance Venice', *Studies in the Renaissance*, 21 (1974), 176–203.

21. See Virginia Cox, 'The Single Self: Feminist Thought and the Marriage Market in Early Modern Venice', *Renaissance Quarterly*, 48 (1995), 513–81.

22. Ann Rosalind Jones, *The Currency of Eros: Women's Love Lyric in Europe 1540–1620* (Bloomington: Indiana University Press, 1990), 7.

23. Svetlana Alpers, 'Art History and its Exclusions', in Norma Broude and Mary D. Garrard (eds.), *Feminism and Art History* (New York: Harper and Row, 1982), 183–200.

24. See Anthony Newcomb, 'Courtesans, Muses or Musicians? Professional Women Musicians in Sixteenth Century Italy', in Jane Bowers and Judith Tick (eds.), *Women Making Music: The Western Art Tradition 1150–1950* (London: Macmillan: 1986) and Suzanne Cusick, '"Thinking from Women's Lives": Francesca Caccini after 1627', in Kimberly Marshall (ed.), *Rediscovering the Muses: Women's Musical Traditions* (Boston: Northeastern University Press, 1993), 206–25. See also Anne Macneil, 'The Divine Madness of Isabella Andreini', *Journal of the Royal Musical Association*, 120 (1995), 195–215.

Part I. Humanism after Feminism

1 Did Women Have a Renaissance?

Joan Kelly

One of the tasks of women's history is to call into question accepted schemes of periodization. To take the emancipation of women as a vantage point is to discover that events that further the historical development of men, liberating them from natural, social, or ideological constraints, have quite different, even opposite, effects upon women. The Renaissance is a good case in point. Italy was well in advance of the rest of Europe from roughly 1350 to 1530 because of its early consolidation of genuine states, the mercantile and manufacturing economy that supported them, and its working out of postfeudal and even postguild social relations. These developments reorganized Italian society along modern lines and opened the possibilities for the social and cultural expression for which the age is known. Yet precisely these developments affected women adversely, so much so that there was no renaissance for women—at least, not during the Renaissance. The state, early capitalism, and the social relations formed by them impinged on the lives of Renaissance women in different ways according to their different positions in society. But the startling fact is that women as a group, especially among the classes that dominated Italian urban life, experienced a contraction of social and personal options that men of their classes either did not, as was the case with the bourgeoisie, or did not experience as markedly, as was the case with the nobility.

Before demonstrating this point, which contradicts the widely held notion of the equality of Renaissance women with men,[1] we need to

Reprinted from *Becoming Visible: Women in European History*, edited by Renate Bridenthal and Claudia Koonz, © 1977 by Houghton Mifflin Co. Used by permission.

I first worked out these ideas in 1972–1973 in a course at Sarah Lawrence College entitled "Women: Myth and Reality" and am very much indebted to students in that course and my colleagues Eva Kollisch, Gerda Lerner, and Sherry Ortner. I thank Eve Fleisher, Martin Fleisher, Renate Bridenthal, and Claudia Koonz for their valuable criticism of an earlier version of this paper.

21

consider how to establish, let alone measure, loss or gain with respect to the liberty of women. I found the following criteria most useful for gauging the relative contraction (or expansion) of the powers of Renaissance women and for determining the quality of their historical experience: (1) the regulation of *female sexuality* as compared with male sexuality; (2) women's *economic* and *political roles*, i.e., the kind of work they performed as compared with men, and their access to property, political power, and the education or training necessary for work, property, and power; (3) the *cultural roles* of women in shaping the outlook of their society, and access to the education and/or institutions necessary for this; (4) *ideology* about women, in particular the sex-role system displayed or advocated in the symbolic products of the society, its art, literature, and philosophy. Two points should be made about this ideological index. One is its rich inferential value. The literature, art, and philosophy of a society, which give us direct knowledge of the attitudes of the dominant sector of that society toward women, also yield indirect knowledge about our other criteria: namely, the sexual, economic, political, and cultural activities of women. Insofar as images of women relate to what really goes on, we can infer from them something about that social reality. But, second, the relations between the ideology of sex roles and the reality we want to get at are complex and difficult to establish. Such views may be prescriptive rather than descriptive; they may describe a situation that no longer prevails; or they may use the relation of the sexes symbolically and not refer primarily to women and sex roles at all. Hence, to assess the historical significance of changes in sex-role conception, we must bring such changes into connection with all we know about general developments in the society at large.

This essay examines changes in sex-role conception, particularly with respect to sexuality, for what they tell us about Renaissance society and women's place in it. At first glance, Renaissance thought presents a problem in this regard because it cannot be simply catego-rized. Ideas about the relation of the sexes range from a relatively complementary sense of sex roles in literature dealing with courtly manners, love, and education, to patriarchal conceptions in writings on marriage and the family, to a fairly equal presentation of sex roles in early Utopian social theory. Such diversity need not baffle the attempt to reconstruct a history of sex-role conceptions, however, and to relate its course to the actual situation of women. Toward this end, one needs to sort out this material in terms of the social groups to which it responds: to courtly society in the first case, the nobility of the petty despotic states of Italy; to the patrician bourgeoisie in the second, particularly of republics such as Florence. In the third case, the relatively equal position accorded women in Utopian thought (and in those lower-class movements of the radical Reformation analogous to it) results from a larger critique of early modern society and all the relations of domination that flow from private ownership and control of property. Once distinguished, each of these groups of sources tells the same story. Each discloses in its own way certain new constraints suffered by Renaissance women as the family and political life were restructured in the great transition from medieval feudal society to the early modern state. The sources that represent the interests of the nobility and the bourgeoisie point to this fact by a telling, double index. Almost all such works—with certain notable exceptions, such as Boccaccio and Ariosto—establish chastity as the female norm and restructure the relation of the sexes to one of female dependency and male domination.

The bourgeois writings on education, domestic life, and society constitute the extreme in this denial of women's independence. Suffice it to say that they sharply distinguish an inferior domestic realm of women from the superior public realm of men, achieving a veritable "renaissance" of the outlook and practices of classical Athens, with its domestic imprisonment of citizen wives.[2] The courtly Renaissance literature we will consider was more gracious. But even here, by analyzing a few of the representative works of this genre, we find a new repression of the noblewoman's affective experience, in contrast to the latitude afforded her by medieval literature, and some of the social and cultural reasons for it. Dante and Castiglione, who continued a literary tradition that began with the courtly love literature of eleventh- and twelfth-century Provence, transformed medieval conceptions of love and nobility. In the love ideal they formed, we can discern the inferior position the Renaissance noblewoman held in the relation of the sexes by comparison with her male counterpart and with her medieval predecessor as well.

LOVE AND THE MEDIEVAL LADY

Medieval courtly love, closely bound to the dominant values of feudalism and the church, allowed in a special way for the expression of

23

sexual love by women. Of course, only aristocratic women gained their sexual and affective rights thereby. If a knight wanted a peasant girl, the twelfth-century theorist of *The Art of Courtly Love*, Andreas Capellanus, encouraged him "not [to] hesitate to take what you seek and to embrace her by force."[3] Toward the lady, however, "a true lover considers nothing good except what he thinks will please his beloved"; for if courtly love were to define itself as a noble phenomenon, it had to attribute an essential freedom to the relation between lovers. Hence, it metaphorically extended the social relation of vassalage to the love relationship, a "conceit" that Maurice Valency rightly called "the shaping principle of the whole design" of courtly love.[4]

Of the two dominant sets of dependent social relations formed by feudalism—*les liens de dépendence*, as Marc Bloch called them— vassalage, the military relation of knight to lord, distinguished itself (in its early days) by being freely entered into. At a time when everyone was somebody's "man," the right to freely enter a relation of service characterized aristocratic bonds, whereas hereditability marked the servile work relation of serf to lord. Thus, in medieval romances, a parley typically followed a declaration of love until love freely proffered was freely returned. A kiss (like the kiss of homage) sealed the pledge, rings were exchanged, and the knight entered the love service of his lady. Representing love along the lines of vassalage had several liberating implications for aristocratic women. Most fundamental, ideas of homage and mutuality entered the notion of heterosexual relations along with the idea of freedom. As symbolized on shields and other illustrations that place the knight in the ritual attitude of commendation, kneeling before his lady with his hands folded between hers, homage signified male service, not domination or subordination of the lady, and it signified fidelity, constancy in that service. "A lady must honor her lover as a friend, not as a master," wrote Marie de Ventadour, a female troubadour or *trobairitz*.[5] At the same time, homage entailed a reciprocity of rights and obligations, a service on the lady's part as well. In one of Marie de France's romances, a knight is about to be judged by the barons of King Arthur's court when his lady rides to the castle to give him "succor" and pleads successfully for him, as any overlord might.[6] Mutuality, or complementarity, marks the relation the lady entered into with her *ami* (the favored name for "lover" and, significantly, a synonym for "vassal").

This relation between knight and lady was very much at variance with the patriarchal family relations obtaining in that same level of society. Aware of its incompatibility with prevailing family and marital relations, the celebrants of courtly love kept love detached from marriage. "We dare not oppose the opinion of the Countess of Champagne who rules that love can exert no power between husband and wife," Andreas wrote (p. 175). But in opting for a free and reciprocal heterosexual relation outside marriage, the poets and theorists of courtly love ignored the almost universal demand of patriarchal society for female chastity, in the sense of the woman's strict bondage to the marital bed. The reasons why they did so, and even the fact that they did so, have long been disputed, but the ideas and values that justify this kind of adulterous love are plain. Marriage, as a relation arranged by others, carried the taint of social necessity for the aristocracy. And if the feudality denigrated marriage by disdaining obligatory service, the church did so by regarding it not as a "religious" state, but an inferior one that responded to natural necessity. Moreover, Christianity positively fostered the ideal of courtly love at a deep level of feeling. The courtly relation between lovers took vassalage as its structural model, but its passion was nourished by Christianity's exaltation of love.

Christianity had accomplished its elevation of love by purging it of sexuality, and in this respect, by recombining the two, courtly love clearly departed from Christian teaching. The toleration of adultery it fostered thereby was in itself not so grievous. The feudality disregarded any number of church rulings that affected their interests, such as prohibitions of tournaments and repudiation of spouses (divorce) and remarriage. Moreover, adultery hardly needed the sanction of courtly love, which, if anything, acted rather as a restraining force by binding sexuality (except in marriage) to love. Lancelot, in Chrétien de Troyes's twelfth-century romance, lies in bed with a lovely woman because of a promise he has made, but "not once does he look at her, nor show her any courtesy. Why not? Because his heart does not go out to her. . . . The knight has only one heart, and this one is no longer really his, but has been entrusted to someone else, so that he cannot bestow it elsewhere."[7] Actually, Lancelot's chastity represented more of a threat to Christian doctrine than the fact that his passion (for Guinevere) was adulterous, because his attitudes justified sexual love. Sexuality could only be "mere sexuality" for the medieval church, to be consecrated and directed toward procreation by Christian marriage. Love, on the other hand, defined as passion for the good, perfects the individual; hence love, according to Thomas Aquinas, properly directs itself toward God.[8] Like the churchman, Lancelot spurned mere sexuality— but for the sake of sexual love. He defied Christian *teaching* by reattaching love to sex; and experiencing his love as a devout vocation,

25

as a passion, he found himself in utter accord with Christian *feeling*. His love, as Chrétien's story makes clear, is sacramental as well as sexual:

> ... then he comes to the bed of the Queen, whom he adores and before whom he kneels, holding her more dear than the relic of any saint. And the Queen extends her arms to him and, embracing him, presses him tightly against her bosom, drawing him into the bed beside her and showing him every possible satisfaction. . . . Now Lancelot possesses all he wants. . . . It cost him such pain to leave her that he suffered a real martyr's agony. . . . When he leaves the room, he bows and acts precisely as if he were before a shrine. (p. 329)

It is difficult to assess Christianity's role in this acceptance of feeling and this attentiveness to inner states that characterize medieval lyric and romance, although the weeping and wringing of hands, the inner troubles and turmoil of the love genre, were to disappear with the restoration of classical attitudes of restraint in the Renaissance. What certainly bound courtly love to Christianity, however, aside from its positive attitude toward feeling, was the cultivation of decidedly "romantic" states of feeling. In Christian Europe, *passion* acquired a positive, spiritual meaning that classical ethics and classical erotic feeling alike denied it. Religious love and courtly love were both suffered as a destiny, were both submitted to and not denied. Converted by a passion that henceforth directed and dominated them and for which all manner of suffering could be borne, the courtly lovers, like the religious, sought a higher emotional state than ordinary life provided. They sought ecstasy; and this required of them a heroic discipline, an ascetic fortitude, and single-mindedness. Love and its ordeals alike removed them from the daily, the customary, the routine, setting them apart as an elite superior to the conventions of marriage and society.

Religious feeling and feudal values thus both fed into a conception of passionate love that, because of its mutuality, required that women, too, partake of that passion, of that adulterous sexual love. The lady of medieval romance also suffered. She suffered "more pain for love than ever a woman suffered" in another of Marie de France's romances. As the jealously guarded wife of an old man, ravished by the beauty of her knight when she first saw him, she could not rest for love of him, and "*franc et noble*" (i.e., free) as she was, she granted him her kiss and her love upon the declaration of his—"and many other caresses which lovers know well" during the time she hid him in her castle.[9] So common is this sexual mutuality to the literature of courtly love that one cannot take seriously the view of it as a form of Madonna worship in which a remote and virginal lady spurns consummation. That stage came later, as courtly love underwent its late medieval and Renaissance transformation. But for the twelfth century, typical concerns of Provençal *iocs-partitz*, those poetic "questions" on love posed at court (and reflecting the social reality of mock courts of love played out as a diversion) were: "Must a lady do for her lover as much as he for her?"; or, "A husband learns that his wife has a lover. The wife and the lover perceive it—which of the three is in the greatest strait?"[10] In the same vein, Andreas Capellanus perceived differences between so-called "pure" and "mixed" love as accidental, not substantial. Both came from the same feeling of the heart and one could readily turn into the other, as circumstances dictated. Adultery, after all, required certain precautions, but that did not alter the essentially erotic nature even of "pure" love, which went "as far as the kiss and the embrace and the modest contact with the nude lover, omitting the final solace" (p. 122).

The sexual nature of courtly love, considered together with its voluntary character and the nonpatriarchal structure of its relations, makes us question what it signifies for the actual condition of feudal women. For clearly it represents an ideological liberation of their sexual and affective powers that must have some social reference. This is not to raise the fruitless question of whether such love relationships actually existed or if they were mere literary conventions. The real issue regarding ideology is, rather, what kind of society could posit *as a social ideal* a love relation outside of marriage, one that women freely entered and that, despite its reciprocity, made women the gift givers while men did the service. What were the social conditions that fostered these particular conventions rather than the more common ones of female chastity and/or dependence?

No one doubts that courtly love spread widely as a convention. All ranks and both sexes of the aristocracy wrote troubadour poetry and courtly romances and heard them sung and recited in courtly gatherings throughout most of medieval Europe. But this could happen only if such ideas supported the male-dominated social order rather than subverted it. The love motif could, and with Gottfried of Strasbourg's *Tristan* (c1210) did, stand as an ideal radically opposed to the institutions of the church and emerging feudal kingship. But in its beginnings, and generally, courtly love no more threatened Christian feeling or feudalism than did chivalry, which brought a certain "sacramental" moral value and restraint to the profession of warfare. While courtly love celebrated sexuality, it enriched and deepened it by means of the Christian notion of passion. While the knight often betrayed his lord

27

to serve his lord's lady, he transferred to that relationship the feudal ideal of freely committed, mutual service. And while passionate love led to adultery, by that very fact it reinforced, as its necessary premise, the practice of political marriage. The literature of courtly love suppressed rather than exaggerated tensions between it and other social values, and the reason for this lies deeper than literature. It lies at the institutional level, where there was real agreement, or at least no contradiction, between the sexual and affective needs of women and the interests of the aristocratic family, which the feudality and church alike regarded as fundamental to the social order.

The factors to consider here are property and power on the one hand, and illegitimacy on the other. Feudalism, as a system of private jurisdictions, bound power to landed property; and it permitted both inheritance and administration of feudal property by women.[11] Inheritance by women often suited the needs of the great landholding families, as their unremitting efforts to secure such rights for their female members attest. The authority of feudal women owes little to any gallantry on the part of feudal society. But the fact that women could hold both ordinary fiefs and vast collections of counties—and exercise in their own right the seigniorial powers that went with them—certainly fostered a gallant attitude. Eleanor of Aquitaine's adultery as wife of the king of France could have had dire consequences in another place at another time, say in the England of Henry VIII. In her case, she moved on to a new marriage with the future Henry II of England or, to be more exact, a new alliance connecting his Plantagenet interests with her vast domains centering on Provence. Women also exercised power during the absence of warrior husbands. The lady presided over the court at such times, administered the estates, took charge of the vassal services due the lord. She *was* the lord—albeit in his name rather than her own—unless widowed and without male children. In the religious realm, abbesses exercised analogous temporal as well as spiritual jurisdiction over great territories, and always in their own right, in virtue of their office.

This social reality accounts for the retention of matronymics in medieval society, that is, a common use of the maternal name, which reflects the position of women as landowners and managers of great estates, particularly during the crusading period.[12] It also accounts for the husband's toleration of his wife's diversions, if discreetly pursued. His primary aim to get and maintain a fief required her support, perhaps even her inheritance. As Emily James Putnam put it, "It would, perhaps, be paradoxical to say that a baron would prefer to be sure that his tenure was secure than that his son was legitimate, but it is certain that the relative value of the two things had shifted."[13] Courtly literature, indeed, reveals a marked lack of concern about illegitimacy. Although the ladies of the romances are almost all married, they seldom appear with children, let alone appear to have their lives and loves complicated by them. Much as the tenet that love thrives only in adultery reflected and reinforced the stability of arranged marriage, so the political role of women, and the indivisibility of the fief, probably underlies this indifference to illegitimacy. Especially as forms of inheritance favoring the eldest son took hold in the course of the twelfth century to preserve the great houses, the claims of younger sons and daughters posed no threat to family estates. Moreover, the expansive, exploitative aristocratic families of the eleventh and twelfth centuries could well afford illegitimate members. For the feudality, they were no drain as kin but rather a source of strength in marital alliances and as warriors.

For all these reasons, feudal Christian society could promote the ideal of courtly love. We could probably maintain of any ideology that tolerates sexual parity that: (1) it can threaten no major institution of the patriarchal society from which it emerges; and (2) men, the rulers within the ruling order, must benefit by it. Courtly love surely fits these requirements. That such an ideology did actually develop, however, is due to another feature of medieval society, namely, the cultural activity of feudal women. For responsive as courtly love might seem to men of the feudality whose erotic needs it objectified and refined, as well as objectifying their consciousness of the social self (as noble), it did this and more for women. It gave women lovers, peers rather than masters; and it gave them a justifying ideology for adultery which, as the more customary double standard indicates, men in patriarchal society seldom require. Hence, we should expect what we indeed find: women actively shaping these ideas and values that corresponded so well to their particular interests.

In the first place, women participated in creating the literature of courtly love, a major literature of their era. This role they had not been able to assume in the culture of classical Greece or Rome. The notable exception of Sappho only proves the point: it took women to give poetic voice and status to female sexual love, and only medieval Europe accepted that voice as integral to its cultural expression. The twenty or more known Provençal trobairitz, of whom the Countess Beatrice of Die is the most renowned, celebrated as fully and freely as any man the love of the troubadour tradition:

Handsome friend, charming and kind,
when shall I have you in my power?
If only I could lie beside you for an hour
and embrace you lovingly—
know this, that I'd give almost anything
to see you in my husband's place,
but only under the condition
that you swear to do my bidding.[14]

Marie de France voiced similar erotic sentiments in her *lais*. Her short tales of romance, often adulterous and always sexual, have caused her to be ranked by Friedrich Heer as one of the "three poets of genius" (along with Chrétien de Troyes and Gautier d'Arras) who created the *roman courtois* of the twelfth century.[15] These two genres, the romance and the lyric, to which women made such significant contributions, make up the corpus of courtly love literature.

In addition to direct literary expression, women promoted the ideas of courtly love by way of patronage and the diversions of their courts. They supported and/or participated in the recitation and singing of poems and romances, and they played out those mock suits, usually presided over by "queens," that settled questions of love. This holds for lesser aristocratic women as well as the great. But great noblewomen, such as Eleanor of Aquitaine and Marie of Champagne, Eleanor's daughter by her first marriage to Louis VII of France, could make their courts major cultural and social centers and play thereby a dominant role in forming the outlook and mores of their class. Eleanor, herself granddaughter of William of Aquitaine, known as the first troubadour, supported the poets and sentiments of Provence at her court in Anjou. When she became Henry II's queen, she brought the literature and manners of courtly love to England. When living apart from Henry at her court in Poitiers, she and her daughter, Marie, taught the arts of courtesy to a number of young women and men who later dispersed to various parts of France, England, Sicily, and Spain, where they constituted the ruling nobility. Some of the most notable authors of the literature of courtly love belonged to these circles. Bernard of Ventadour, one of the outstanding troubadours, sang his poems to none other than the lady Eleanor. Marie de France had connections with the English court of Eleanor and Henry II. Eleanor's daughter, Marie of Champagne, was patron both of Andreas Capellanus, her chaplain, and Chrétien de Troyes, and she may well be responsible for much of the adulterous, frankly sexual behavior the ladies enjoy in the famous works of both. Chrétien claimed he owed to his "lady of

Champagne" both "the material and treatment" of Lancelot, which differs considerably in precisely this regard from his earlier and later romances. And Andreas's *De remedio*, the baffling final section of his work that repudiates sexual love and women, may represent not merely a rhetorical tribute to Ovid but a reaction to the pressure of Marie's patronage.[16]

At their courts as in their literature, it would seem that feudal women consciously exerted pressure in shaping the courtly love ideal and making it prevail. But they could do so only because they had actual power to exert. The women who assumed cultural roles as artists and patrons of courtly love had already been assigned political roles that assured them some measure of independence and power. They could and did exercise authority, not merely over the subject laboring population of their lands, but over their own and/or their husbands' vassals. Courtly love, which flourished outside the institution of patriarchal marriage, owed its possibility as well as its model to the dominant political institution of feudal Europe that permitted actual vassal homage to be paid to women.

THE RENAISSANCE LADY: POLITICS AND CULTURE

The kind of economic and political power that supported the cultural activity of feudal noblewomen in the eleventh and twelfth centuries had no counterpart in Renaissance Italy. By the fourteen century, the political units of Italy were mostly sovereign states that regardless of legal claims, recognized no overlords and supported no feudatories. Their nobility held property but no seigniorial power, estates but not jurisdiction. Indeed, in northern and central Italy, a nobility in the European sense hardly existed at all. Down to the coronation of Charles V as Holy Roman Emperor in 1530, there was no Italian king to safeguard the interests of (and thereby limit and control) a "legitimate" nobility that maintained by inheritance traditional prerogatives. Hence, where the urban bourgeoisie did not overthrow the claims of nobility, a despot did, usually in the name of nobility but always for himself. These *signorie*, unlike the bourgeois republics, continued to maintain a landed, military "class" with noble pretensions, but its members increasingly became merely the warriors and ornaments of a court. Hence, the Renaissance aristocrat, who enjoyed neither the independent political powers of feudal jurisdiction nor legally guaranteed status in the ruling estate, either served a despot or became one.

In this sociopolitical context, the exercise of political power by women was far more rare than under feudalism or even under the traditional kind of monarchical state that developed out of feudalism. The two Giovannas of Naples, both queens in their own right, exemplify this latter type of rule. The first, who began her reign in 1343 over Naples and Provence, became in 1356 queen of Sicily as well. Her grandfather, King Robert of Naples—of the same house of Anjou and Provence that hearkens back to Eleanor and to Henry Plantagenet—could and did designate Giovanna as his heir. Similarly, in 1414, Giovanna II became queen of Naples upon the death of her brother. In Naples, in short, women of the ruling house could assume power, not because of their abilities alone, but because the principle of legitimacy continued in force along with the feudal tradition of inheritance by women.

In northern Italy, by contrast, Caterina Sforza ruled her petty principality in typical Renaissance fashion, supported only by the Machiavellian principles of *fortuna* and *virtù* (historical situation and will). Her career, like that of her family, follows the Renaissance pattern of personal and political illegitimacy. Born in 1462, she was an illegitimate daughter of Galeazzo Maria Sforza, heir to the Duchy of Milan. The ducal power of the Sforzas was very recent, dating only from 1450, when Francesco Sforza, illegitimate son of a condottiere and a great condottiere himself, assumed control of the duchy. When his son and heir, Caterina's father, was assassinated after ten years of tyrannous rule, another son, Lodovico, took control of the duchy, first as regent for his nephew (Caterina's half brother), then as outright usurper. Lodovico promoted Caterina's interests for the sake of his own. He married her off at fifteen to a nephew of Pope Sixtus IV, thereby strengthening the alliance between the Sforzas and the Riario family, who now controlled the papacy. The pope carved a state out of papal domains for Caterina's husband, making him Count of Forlì as well as the Lord of Imola, which Caterina brought to the marriage. But the pope died in 1484, her husband died by assassination four years later—and Caterina made the choice to defy the peculiar obstacles posed by Renaissance Italy to a woman's assumption of power.

Once before, with her husband seriously ill at Imola, she had ridden hard to Forlì to quell an incipient coup a day before giving birth. Now at twenty-six, after the assassination of her husband, she and a loyal castellan held the citadel at Forlì against her enemies until Lodovico sent her aid from Milan. Caterina won; she faced down her opponents, who held her six children hostage, then took command as regent for her young son. But her title to rule as regent was inconsequential. Caterina ruled because she mustered superior force and exercised it personally, and to the end she had to exert repeatedly the skill, forcefulness, and ruthless ambition that brought her to power. However, even her martial spirit did not suffice. In the despotisms of Renaissance Italy, where assassinations, coups, and invasions were the order of the day, power stayed closely bound to military force. In 1500, deprived of Milan's support by her uncle Lodovico's deposition, Caterina succumbed to the overwhelming forces of Cesare Borgia and was divested of power after a heroic defense of Forlì.

Because of this political situation, at once statist and unstable, the daughters of the Este, Gonzaga, and Montefeltro families represent women of their class much more than Caterina Sforza did. Their access to power was indirect and provisional, and was expected to be so. In his handbook for the nobility, Baldassare Castiglione's description of the lady of the court makes this difference in sex roles quite clear. On the one hand, the Renaissance lady appears as the equivalent of the courtier. She has the same virtues of mind as he and her education is symmetrical with his. She learns everything—well, almost everything—he does: "knowledge of letters, of music, of painting, and . . . how to dance and how to be festive."[17] Culture is an accomplishment for noblewoman and man alike, used to charm others as much as to develop the self. But for the woman, charm had become the primary occupation and aim. Whereas the courtier's chief task is defined as the profession of arms, "in a Lady who lives at court a certain pleasing affability is becoming above all else, whereby she will be able to entertain graciously every kind of man" (p. 207).

One notable consequence of the Renaissance lady's need to charm is that Castiglione called upon her to give up certain "unbecoming" physical activities such as riding and handling weapons. Granted, he concerned himself with the court lady, as he says, not a queen who may be called upon to rule. But his aestheticizing of the lady's role, his conception of her femaleness as centered in charm, meant that activities such as riding and skill in weaponry would seem unbecoming to women of the ruling families, too. Elisabetta Gonzaga, the idealized duchess of Castiglione's *Courtier*, came close in real life to his normative portrayal of her type. Riding and skill in weaponry had, in fact, no significance for her. The heir to her Duchy of Urbino was decided upon during the lifetime of her husband, and it was this adoptive heir—not the widow of thirty-seven with no children to compete for her care and attention—who assumed power in 1508. Removed from any direct exercise of power, Elisabetta also disregarded the pursuits and pleasures associated with it. Her letters express none of the sense of freedom and daring Caterina Sforza and Beatrice d'Este experienced in riding and the hunt.[18] Altogether, she lacks spirit. Her correspondence shows her to be as docile in adulthood as her early teachers trained her to be. She met adversity, marital and political, with fortitude but never opposed it. She placated father, brother, and husband, and even in Castiglione's depiction of her court, she complied with rather than shaped its conventions.

The differences between Elisabetta Gonzaga and Caterina Sforza are great, yet both personalities were responding to the Renaissance situation of emerging statehood and social mobility. Elisabetta, neither personally illegitimate nor springing from a freebooting condottiere family, was schooled, as Castiglione would have it, away from the martial attitudes and skills requisite for despotic rule. She would not be a prince, she would marry one. Hence, her education, like that of most of the daughters of the ruling families, directed her toward the cultural and social functions of the court. The lady who married a Renaissance prince became a patron. She commissioned works of art and gave gifts for literary works dedicated to her; she drew to her artists and literati. But the court they came to ornament was her husband's, and the culture they represented magnified his princely being, especially when his origins could not. Thus, the Renaissance lady may play an aesthetically significant role in Castiglione's idealized Court of Urbino of 1508, but even he clearly removed her from that equal, to say nothing of superior, position in social discourse that medieval courtly literature had granted her. To the fifteen or so male members of the court whose names he carefully listed, Castiglione admitted only four women to the evening conversations that were the second major occupation at court (the profession of arms, from which he completely excluded women, being the first). Of the four, he distinguished only two women as participants. The Duchess Elisabetta and her companion, Emilia Pia, at least speak, whereas the other two only do a dance. Yet they speak in order to moderate and "direct" discussion by proposing questions and games. They do not themselves contribute to the discussions, and at one point Castiglione relieves them even of their negligible role:

When signor Gasparo had spoken thus, signora Emilia made a sign to madam Costanza Fregosa, as she sat next in order, that she should speak; and she was

34

making ready to do so, when suddenly the Duchess said: "Since signora Emilia does not choose to go to the trouble of devising a game, it would be quite right for the other ladies to share in this ease, and thus be exempt from such a burden this evening, especially since there are so many men here that we risk no lack of games." (pp. 19–20)

The men, in short, do all the talking; and the ensuing dialogue on manners and love, as we might expect, is not only developed by men but directed toward their interests.

The contradiction between the professed parity of noblewomen and men in *The Courtier* and the merely decorative role Castiglione unwittingly assigned the lady proclaims an important educational and cultural change as well as a political one. Not only did a male ruler preside over the courts of Renaissance Italy, but the court no longer served as arbiter of the cultural functions it did retain. Although restricted to a cultural and social role, she lost dominance in that role as secular education came to require special skills which were claimed as the prerogative of a class of professional teachers. The sons of the Renaissance nobility still pursued their military and diplomatic training in the service of some great lord, but as youths, they transferred their non-military training from the lady to the humanistic tutor or boarding school. In a sense, humanism represented an advance for women as well as for the culture at large. It brought Latin literacy and classical learning to daughters as well as sons of the nobility. But this very development, usually taken as an index of the equality of Renaissance (noble) women with men,[19] spelled a further decline in the lady's influence over courtly society. It placed her as well as her brothers under male cultural authority. The girl of the medieval aristocracy, although unschooled, was brought up at the court of some great lady. Now her brothers' tutors shaped her outlook, male educators who, as humanists, suppressed romance and chivalry to further classical culture, with all its patriarchal and misogynous bias.

The humanistic education of the Renaissance noblewoman helps explain why she cannot compare with her medieval predecessors in shaping a culture responsive to her own interests. In accordance with the new cultural values, the patronage of the Este, Sforza, Gonzaga, and Montefeltro women extended far beyond the literature and art of love and manners, but the works they commissioned, bought, or had dedicated to them do not show any consistent correspondence to their concerns as women. They did not even give noticeable support to women's education, with the single important exception of Battista da Montefeltro, to whom one of the few treatises advocating a humanistic education for women was dedicated. Adopting the universalistic outlook of their humanist teachers, the noblewomen of Renaissance Italy seem to have lost all consciousness of their particular interests as women, while male authors such as Castiglione, who articulated the mores of the Renaissance aristocracy, wrote their works for men. Cultural and political dependency thus combined in Italy to reverse the roles of women and men in developing the new noble code. Medieval courtesy, as set forth in the earliest etiquette books, romances, and rules of love, shaped the man primarily to please the lady. In the thirteenth and fourteenth centuries, rules for women, and strongly patriarchal ones at that, entered French and Italian etiquette books, but not until the Renaissance reformulation of courtly manners and love is it evident how the ways of the lady came to be determined by men in the context of the early modern state. The relation of the sexes here assumed its modern form, and nowhere is this made more visible than in the love relation.

THE RENAISSANCE OF CHASTITY

As soon as the literature and values of courtly love made their way into Italy, they were modified in the direction of asexuality. Dante typifies this initial reception of courtly love. His *Vita Nuova*, written in the "sweet new style" (*dolce stil nuovo*) of late-thirteenth-century Tuscany, still celebrates love and the noble heart: "*Amore e 'l cor gentil sono una cosa.*" Love still appears as homage and the lady as someone else's wife. But the lover of Dante's poems is curiously arrested. He frustrates his own desire by rejecting even the aim of union with his beloved. "What is the point of your love for your lady since you are unable to endure her presence?" a lady asks of Dante. "Tell us, for surely the aim of such love must be unique [*novissimo*]!"[20] And novel it is, for Dante confesses that the joy he once took in his beloved's greeting he shall henceforth seek in himself, "in words which praise my lady." Even this understates the case, since Dante's words neither conjure up Beatrice nor seek to melt her. She remains shadowy and remote, for the focus of his poetry has shifted entirely to the subjective pole of love. It is the inner life, *his* inner life, that Dante objectifies. His love poems present a spiritual contest, which he will soon ontologize in the *Divine Comedy*, among competing states of the lover poet's soul.

This dream-world quality expresses in its way a general change that came over the literature of love as its social foundations crumbled. In the north, as the *Romance of the Rose* reminds us, the tradition began to run dry in the late-thirteenth-century period of feudal disintegration—or transformation by the bourgeois economy of the towns and the emergence of the state. And in Provence, after the Albigensian Crusade and the subjection of the Midi to church and crown, Guiraut Riquier significantly called himself the last troubadour. Complaining that "no craft is less esteemed at court than the beautiful mastery of song," he renounced sexual for celestial love and claimed to enter the service of the Virgin Mary.[21] The reception and reworking of the troubadour tradition in Florence of the late 1200s consequently appears somewhat archaic. A conservative, aristocratic nostalgia clings to Dante's love poetry as it does to his political ideas. But if the new social life of the bourgeois commune found little positive representation in his poetry, Florence did drain from his poems the social content of feudal experience. The lover as knight or trobairitz thus gave way to a poet scholar. The experience of a wandering, questing life gave way to scholastic interests, to distinguishing and classifying states of feeling. And the courtly celebration of romance, modeled upon vassalage and enjoyed in secret meetings, became a private circulation of poems analyzing the spiritual effects of unrequited love.

The actual disappearance of the social world of the court and its presiding lady underlies the disappearance of sex and the physical evaporation of the woman in these poems. The ladies of the romances and troubadour poetry may be stereotypically blond, candid, and fair, but their authors meant them to be taken as physically and socially "real." In the love poetry of Dante, and of Petrarch and Vittoria Colonna, who continue his tradition, the beloved may just as well be dead—and, indeed, all three authors made them so. They have no meaningful, objective existence, and not merely because their affective experience lacks a voice. This would hold for troubadour poetry too, since the lyric, unlike the romance, articulates only the feelings of the lover. The unreality of the Renaissance beloved has rather to do with the *quality* of the Renaissance lover's feelings. As former social relations that sustained mutuality and interaction among lovers vanished, the lover fell back on a narcissistic experience. The Dantesque beloved merely inspires feelings that have no outer, physical aim; or, they have a transcendent aim that the beloved merely mediates. In either case, love casts off sexuality. Indeed, the role of the beloved as mediator is asexual in a double sense, as the *Divine Comedy* shows. Not only does the beloved never respond sexually to the lover, but the feelings she arouses in him turn into a spiritual love that makes of their entire relationship a mere symbol or allegory.

Interest even in this shadowy kind of romance dropped off markedly as the work of Dante, Petrarch, and Boccaccio led into the fifteenth-century renaissance of Graeco-Roman art and letters. The Florentine humanists in particular appropriated only the classical side of their predecessors' thought, the side that served public concerns. They rejected the dominance of love in human life, along with the inwardness and seclusion of the religious, the scholar, and the lovesick poet. Dante, for example, figured primarily as a citizen to his biographer, Lionardo Bruni, who, as humanist chancellor of Florence, made him out as a modern Socrates, at once a political figure, a family man, and a rhetor: an exemplar for the new polis.[22] Only in relation to the institution of the family did Florentine civic humanism take up questions of love and sexuality. In this context, they developed the bourgeois sex-role system, placing man in the public sphere and the patrician woman in the home, requiring social virtues from him and chastity and motherhood from her. In bourgeois Florence, the humanists would have nothing to do with the old aristocratic tradition of relative social and sexual parity. In the petty Italian despotisms, however, and even in Florence under the princely Lorenzo de' Medici late in the fifteenth century, the traditions and culture of the nobility remained meaningful.[23] Castiglione's *Courtier*, and the corpus of Renaissance works it heads, took up the themes of love and courtesy for this courtly society, adapting them to contemporary social and cultural needs. Yet in this milieu, too, within the very tradition of courtly literature, new constraints upon female sexuality emerged. Castiglione, the single most important spokesman of Renaissance love and manners, retained in his love theory Dante's two basic features: the detachment of love from sexuality and the allegorization of the love theme. Moreover, he introduced into the aristocratic conception of sex roles some of the patriarchal notions of women's confinement to the family that bourgeois humanists had been restoring.

Overtly, as we saw, Castiglione and his class supported a complementary conception of sex roles, in part because a nobility that did not work at all gave little thought to a sexual division of labor. He could thus take up the late medieval *querelle des femmes* set off by the *Romance of the Rose* and debate the question of women's dignity much to their favor. Castiglione places Aristotle's (and Aquinas's) notion of woman as a defective man in the mouth of an aggrieved misogynist, Gasparo; he criticizes Plato's low regard for women, even though he did permit them to govern in *The Republic*; he rejects Ovid's theory of love as not "gentle" enough. Most significantly, he opposes Gasparo's bourgeois notion of women's exclusively domestic role. Yet for all this, Castiglione established in *The Courtier* a fateful bond between love and marriage. One index of a heightened patriarchal outlook among the Renaissance nobility is that love in the usual emotional and sexual sense must lead to marriage and be confined to it—for women, that is.

The issue gets couched, like all others in the book, in the form of a debate. There are pros and cons; but the prevailing view is unmistakable. If the ideal court lady loves, she should love someone whom she can marry. If married, and the mishap befalls her "that her husband's hate or another's love should bring her to love, I would have her give her lover a spiritual love only; nor must she ever give him any sure sign of her love, either by word or gesture or by other means that can make him certain of it" (p. 263). *The Courtier* thus takes a strange, transitional position on the relations among love, sex, and marriage, which bourgeois Europe would later fuse into one familial whole. Responding to a situation of general female dependency among the nobility, and to the restoration of patriarchal family values, at once classical and bourgeois, Castiglione, like Renaissance love theorists in general, connected love and marriage. But facing the same realities of political marriage and clerical celibacy that beset the medieval aristocracy, he still focused upon the love that takes place outside it. On this point, too, however, he broke with the courtly love tradition. He proposed on the one hand a Neo-Platonic notion of spiritual love, and on the other, the double standard.[24]

Castiglione's image of the lover is interesting in this regard. Did he think his suppression of female sexual love would be more justifiable if he had a churchman, Pietro Bembo (elevated to cardinal in 1539), enunciate the new theory and had him discourse upon the love of an aging courtier rather than that of a young knight? In any case, adopting the Platonic definition of love as desire to enjoy beauty, Bembo located this lover in a metaphysical and physical hierarchy between sense ("below") and intellect ("above"). As reason mediates between the physical and the spiritual, so man, aroused by the visible beauty of his beloved, may direct his desire beyond her to the true, intelligible source of her beauty. He may, however, also turn toward sense. Young men fall into this error, and we should expect it of them, Bembo explains in the Neo-Platonic language of the Florentine philosopher Marsilio Ficino. "For finding itself deep in an earthly prison, and deprived of spiritual contemplation in exercising its office of governing the body, the soul of itself cannot clearly perceive the truth; wherefore, in order to have knowledge, it is obliged to turn to the senses . . . and so it believes them . . . and lets itself be guided by them, especially when they have so much vigor that they almost force it" (pp. 338–339). A misdirection of the soul leads to sexual union (though obviously not with the court lady). The preferred kind of union, achieved by way of ascent, uses love of the lady as a step toward love of universal beauty. The lover here ascends from awareness of his own human spirit, which responds to beauty, to awareness of that universal intellect that comprehends universal beauty. Then, "transformed into an angel," his soul finds supreme happiness in divine love. Love may hereby soar to an ontologically noble end, and the beauty of the woman who inspires such ascent may acquire metaphysical status and dignity. But Love, Beauty, Woman, aestheticized as Botticelli's Venus and given cosmic import, were in effect denatured, robbed of body, sex, and passion by this elevation. The simple kiss of love-service became a rarefied kiss of the soul: "A man delights in joining his mouth to that of his beloved in a kiss, not in order to bring himself to any unseemly desire, but because he feels that that bond is the opening of mutual access to their souls" (pp. 349–350). And instead of initiating love, the kiss now terminated physical contact, at least for the churchman and/or aging courtier who sought an ennobling experience—and for the woman obliged to play her role as lady.

Responsive as he still was to medieval views of love, Castiglione at least debated the issue of the double standard. His spokesmen point out that men make the rules permitting themselves and not women sexual freedom, and that concern for legitimacy does not justify this inequality. Since these same men claim to be more virtuous than women, they could more easily restrain themselves. It that case, "there would be neither more nor less certainty about offspring, for even if women were unchaste, they could in no way bear children of themselves . . . provided men were continent and did not take part in the unchastity of women" (pp. 240–241). But for all this, the book supplies an excess of hortatory tales about female chastity, and in the section of the dialogue granting young men indulgence in sensual love, no one speaks for young women, who ought to be doubly "prone," as youths and as women, according to the views of the time.

This is theory, of course. But one thinks of the examples: Eleanor of Aquitaine changing bedmates in the midst of a crusade; Elisabetta Gonzaga, so constrained by the conventions of her own court that she would not take a lover even though her husband was impotent. She, needless to say, figures as Castiglione's prime exemplar: "Our Duchess who has lived with her husband for fifteen years like a widow" (p. 253). Bembo, on the other hand, in the years before he became cardinal, lived with and had three children by Donna Morosina. But however they actually lived, in the new ideology a spiritualized noble love *supplemented* the experience of men while it *defined* extramarital experience for the lady. For women, chastity had become the convention of the Renaissance courts, signaling the twofold fact that the dominant institutions of sixteenth-century Italian society would not support the adulterous sexuality of courtly love, and that women, suffering a relative loss of power within these institutions, could not at first make them responsive to their needs. Legitimacy is a significant factor here. Even courtly love had paid some deference to it (and to the desire of women to avoid conception) by restraining intercourse while promoting romantic and sexual play. But now, with cultural and political power held almost entirely by men, the norm of female chastity came to express the concerns of Renaissance noblemen as they moved into a new situation as a hereditary, dependent class.

This changed situation of the aristocracy accounts both for Castiglione's widespread appeal and for his telling transformation of the love relation. Because *The Courtier* created a mannered way of life that could give to a dependent nobility a sense of self-sufficiency, of inner power and control, which they had lost in a real economic and political sense, the book's popularity spread from Italy through Europe at large in the sixteenth and seventeenth centuries. Although set in the Urbino court of 1508, it was actually begun some ten years after that and published in 1528—after the sack of Rome, and at a time when the princely states of Italy and Europe were coming to resemble each other more closely than they had in the fourteenth and fifteenth centuries. The monarchs of Europe, consolidating and centralizing their states, were at once protecting the privileges of their nobility and suppressing feudal power.[25] Likewise in Italy, as the entire country fell under the hegemony of Charles V, the nobility began to be stabilized. Throughout sixteenth-century Italy, new laws began to limit and regulate membership in a hereditary aristocratic class, prompting a new concern with legitimacy and purity of the blood. Castiglione's demand for female chastity in part responds to this particular concern. His theory of love as a whole responds to the general situation of the Renaissance nobility. In the discourse on love for which he made Bembo the spokesman, he brought to the love relation the same

41

psychic attitudes with which he confronted the political situation. Indeed, he used the love relation as a symbol to convey his sense of political relations.

The changed times to which Castiglione refers in his introduction he experienced as a condition of servitude. The dominant problem of the sixteenth-century Italian nobility, like that of the English nobility under the Tudors, had become one of obedience. As one of Castiglione's courtiers expressed it, God had better grant them "good masters, for, once we have them, we have to endure them as they are" (p. 116). It is this transformation of aristocratic service to statism, which gave rise to Castiglione's leading idea of nobility as courtiers, that shaped his theory of love as well. Bembo's aging courtier, passionless in his rational love, sums up the theme of the entire book: how to maintain by detachment the sense of self now threatened by the loss of independent power. The soul in its earthly prison, the courtier in his social one, renounce the power of self-determination that has in fact been denied them. They renounce *wanting* such power; "If the flame is extinguished, the danger is also extinguished" (p. 347). In love, as in service, the courtier preserves independence by avoiding desire for real love, real power. He does not touch or allow himself to be touched by either. "To enjoy beauty without suffering, the Courtier, aided by reason, must turn his desire entirely away from the body and to beauty alone, [to] contemplate it in its simple and pure self" (p. 351). He may gaze at the object of his love-service, he may listen, but there he reaches the limits of the actual physical relation and transforms her beauty, or the prince's power, into a pure idea. "Spared the bitterness and calamities" of thwarted passion thereby, he loves and serves an image only. The courtier gives obeisance, but only to a reality of his own making: "for he will always carry his precious treasure with him, shut up in his heart, and will also, by the force of his own imagination, make her beauty [or the prince's power] much more beautiful than in reality it is" (p. 352).

Thus, the courtier can serve and not serve, love and not love. He can even attain the relief of surrender by making use of this inner love-service "as a step" to mount to a more sublime sense of service. Contemplation of the Idea the courtier has discovered within his own soul excites a purified desire to love, to serve, to unite with intellectual beauty (or power). Just as love guided his soul from the particular beauty of his beloved to the universal concept, love of that intelligible beauty (or power) glimpsed within transports the soul from the self, the particular intellect, to the universal intellect. Aflame with an utterly spiritual love (or a spiritualized sense of service), the soul then "understands all things intelligible, and without any veil or cloud views the wide sea of pure divine beauty, and receives it into itself, enjoying that supreme happiness of which the senses are incapable" (p. 354). What does this semimystical discourse teach but that by "true" service, the courtier may break out of his citadel of independence, his inner aloofness, to rise and surrender to the pure idea of Power? What does his service become but a freely chosen Obedience, which he can construe as the supreme virtue? In both its sublimated acceptance or resignation and its inner detachment from the actual, Bembo's discourse on love exemplifies the relation between subject and state, obedience and power, that runs through the entire book. Indeed, Castiglione regarded the monarch's power exactly as he had Bembo present the lady's beauty, as symbolic of God: "As in the heavens the sun and the moon and the other stars exhibit to the world a certain likeness of God, so on earth a much liker image of God is seen in . . . princes." Clearly, if "men have been put by God under princes" (p. 307), if they have been placed under princes as under His image, what end can be higher than service in virtue, than the purified experience of Service?

The likeness of the lady to the prince in this theory, her elevation to the pedestal of Neo-Platonic love, both masks and expresses the new dependency of the Renaissance noblewoman. In a structured hierarchy of superior and inferior, she seems to be served by the courtier. But this love theory really made her serve—and stand as a symbol of how the relation of domination may be reversed, so that the prince could be made to serve the interests of the courtier. The Renaissance lady is not desired, not loved for herself. Rendered passive and chaste, she merely mediates the courtier's safe transcendence of an otherwise demeaning necessity. On the plane of symbolism, Castiglione thus had the courtier dominate both her and the prince; and on the plane of reality, he indirectly acknowledged the courtier's actual domination of the lady by having him adopt "woman's ways" in his relations to the prince. Castiglione had to defend against effeminacy in the courtier, both the charge of it (p. 92) and the actuality of faces "soft and feminine as many attempt to have who not only curl their hair and pluck their eyebrows, but preen themselves . . . and appear so tender and languid . . . and utter their words so limply" (p. 36). Yet the close-fitting costume of the Renaissance nobleman displayed the courtier exactly as Castiglione would have him, "well built and shapely of limb" (p. 36). His clothes set off his grace, as did his nonchalant ease, the new manner of those "who seem in words, laughter, in posture not to care" (p. 44).

To be attractive, accomplished, and seem not to care; to charm and do so coolly—how concerned with impression, how masked the true self. And how manipulative: petitioning his lord, the courtier knows to be "discreet in choosing the occasion, and will ask things that are proper and reasonable; and he will so frame his request, omitting those parts that he knows can cause displeasure, and will skillfully make easy the difficult points so that his lord will always grant it" (p. 111). In short, how like a woman—or a dependent, for that is the root of the simile.

The accommodation of the sixteenth- and seventeenth century courtier to the ways and dress of women in no way bespeaks a greater parity between them. It reflects, rather, that general restructuring of social relations that entailed for the Renaissance noblewoman a greater dependency upon men as feudal independence and reciprocity yielded to the state. In this new situation, the entire nobility suffered a loss. Hence, the courtier's posture of dependency, his concern with the pleasing impression, his resolve "to perceive what his prince likes, and . . . to bend himself to this" (pp. 110–111). But as the state overrode aristocratic power, the lady suffered a double loss. Deprived of the possibility of independent power that the combined interests of kinship and feudalism guaranteed some women in the Middle Ages, and that the states of early modern Europe would preserve in part, the Italian noblewoman in particular entered a relation of almost universal dependence upon her family and her husband. And she experienced this dependency at the same time as she lost her commanding position with respect to the secular culture of her society.

Hence, the love theory of the Italian courts developed in ways as indifferent to the interests of women as the courtier, in his self-sufficiency, was indifferent as a lover. It accepted, as medieval courtly love did not, the double standard. It bound the lady to chastity, to the merely procreative sex of political marriage, just as her weighty and costly costume came to conceal and constrain her body while it displayed her husband's noble rank. Indeed, the person of the woman became so inconsequential to this love relation that one doubted whether she could love at all. The question that emerges at the end of *The Courtier* as to "whether or not women are as capable of divine love as men" (p. 350) belongs to a love theory structured by mediation rather than mutuality. Woman's beauty inspired love but the lover, the agent, was man. And the question stands unresolved at the end of *The Courtier*—because at heart the spokesmen for Renaissance love were not really concerned about women or love at all.

Where courtly love had used the social relation of vassalage to work out a genuine concern with sexual love, Castiglione's thought moved in exactly the opposite direction. He allegorized love as fully as Dante did, using the relation of the sexes to symbolize the new political order. In this, his love theory reflects the social realities of the Renaissance. The denial of the right and power of women to love, the transformation of women into passive "others" who serve, fits the self-image of the courtier, the one Castiglione sought to remedy. The symbolic relation of the sexes thus mirrors the new social relations of the state, much as courtly love displayed the feudal relations of reciprocal personal dependence. But Renaissance love reflects, as well, the actual condition of dependency suffered by noblewomen as the state arose. If the courtier who charms the prince bears the same relation to him as the lady bears to the courtier, it is because Castiglione understood the relation of the sexes in the same terms that he used to describe the political relation: i.e., as a relation between servant and lord. The nobleman suffered this relation in the public domain only. The lady, denied access to a freely chosen, mutually satisfying love relation, suffered it in the personal domain as well. Moreover, Castiglione's theory, unlike the courtly love it superseded, subordinated love itself to the public concerns of the Renaissance nobleman. He set forth the relation of the sexes as one of dependency and domination, but he did so in order to express and deal with the political relation and its problems. The personal values of love, which the entire feudality once prized, were henceforth increasingly left to the lady. The courtier formed his primary bond with the modern prince.

In sum, a new division between personal and public life made itself felt as the state came to organize Renaissance society, and with that division the modern relation of the sexes made its appearance,[26] even among the Renaissance nobility. Noblewomen, too, were increasingly removed from public concerns—economic, political, and cultural—and although they did not disappear into a private realm of family and domestic concerns as fully as their sisters in the patrician bourgeoisie, their loss of public power made itself felt in new constraints placed upon their personal as well as their social lives. Renaissance ideas on love and manners, more classical than medieval, and almost exclusively a male product, expressed this new subordination of women to the interests of husbands and male-dominated kin groups and served to justify the removal of women from an "unladylike" position of power and erotic independence. All the advances of Renaissance Italy, its protocapitalist economy, its states, and its humanistic culture, worked to mold the noblewoman into an aesthetic object: decorous, chaste, and doubly dependent—on her husband as well as the prince.

Notes

1. The traditional view of the equality of Renaissance women with men goes back to Jacob Burckhardt's classic, *The Civilization of the Renaissance in Italy* (1860). It has found its way into most general histories of women, such as Mary Beard's *Women as Force in History* (1946), Simone de Beauvoir's *The Second Sex* (1949), and Emily James Putnam's *The Lady* (1910), although the latter is a sensitive and sophisticated treatment. It also dominates most histories of Renaissance women, the best of which is E. Rodocanachi, *La femme italienne avant, pendant et après la Renaissance*, Hachette, Paris, 1922. A notable exception is Ruth Kelso, *Doctrine for the Lady of the Renaissance*, University of Illinois Press, Urbana, 1956, who discovered there was no such parity.
2. The major Renaissance statement of the bourgeois domestication of women was made by Leon Battista Alberti in Book 3 of *Della Famiglia* (*c*1435), which is a free adaptation of the Athenian situation described by Xenophon in the *Oeconomicus*.
3. Andreas Capellanus, *The Art of Courtly Love*, trans. John J. Parry, Columbia University Press, New York, 1941, pp. 150–151.
4. Maurice Valency, *In Praise of Love: An Introduction to the Love-Poetry of the Renaissance*, Macmillan, New York, 1961, p. 146.
5. "*E il dompna deu a son drut far honor/Cum ad amic, mas non cum a seignor.*" Ibid., p. 64.
6. Lanval (Sir Launfal), *Les lais de Marie de France*, ed. Paul Tuffrau, L'Edition d'Art H. Piazza, Paris, n.d., p. 41. English ed., *Lays of Marie de France*, J. M. Dent and E. P. Dutton, London and New York, 1911.
7. Excellent trans. and ed. by W. W. Comfort, *Arthurian Romances*, Dent and Dutton Everyman's Library, London and New York, 1970, p. 286.
8. Thomas Aquinas, *Summa Theologiae*, pt. 1–2, q. 28, art. 5.
9. Lanval, *Les lais*, p. 10.
10. Thomas Frederick Crane, *Italian Social Customs of the Sixteenth Century*, Yale University Press, New Haven, 1920, pp. 10–11.
11. As Marc Bloch pointed out, the great French principalities that no longer required personal military service on the part of their holders were among the first to be passed on to women when male heirs were wanting. *Feudal Society*, trans. L. A. Manyon, University of Chicago Press, Chicago, 1964, p. 201.
12. David Herlihy, "Land, Family and Women in Continental Europe, 701–1200," *Traditio*, 18 (1962), 89–120. Also, "Women in Medieval Society," *The Smith History Lecture*, University of St. Thomas, Texas, 1971. For a fine new work on abbesses, see Joan Morris, *The Lady Was a Bishop*, Collier and Macmillan, New York and London, 1973. Marie de France may have been an abbess of Shaftesbury.
13. Emily James Putnam, *The Lady*, University of Chicago Press, Chicago and London, 1970, p. 118. See also the chapter on the abbess in the same book.
14. From *The Women Troubadours*, trans. and ed. by Meg Bogin, Paddington Press, New York/London, 1976.

15. Friedrich Heer, *The Medieval World: Europe 1100–1350*, Mentor Books, New York, 1963, pp. 167, 178–179.
16. This was Amy Kelly's surmise in "Eleanor of Aquitaine and Her Courts of Love," *Speculum*, 12 (January 1937), 3–19.
17. From *The Book of the Courtier*, by Baldesar Castiglione, a new translation by Charles S. Singleton (New York: Doubleday, 1959), p. 20. Copyright © 1959 by Charles S. Singleton and Edgar de N. Mayhew. This and other quotations throughout the chapter are reprinted by permission of Doubleday & Co., Inc.
18. Selections from the correspondence of Renaissance noblewomen can be found in the biographies listed in the bibliography.
19. An interesting exception is W. Ong's "Latin Language Study as a Renaissance Puberty Rite," *Studies in Philology*, 56 (1959), 103–124; also Margaret Leah King's "The Religious Retreat of Isotta Nogarola (1418–1466)," *Signs*, Summer 1978.
20. Dante Alighieri, *La Vita Nuova*, trans. Barbara Reynolds, Penguin Books, Middlesex, England and Baltimore, 1971, poem 18.
21. Frederick Goldin, trans., *Lyrics of the Troubadours and Trouvères*, Doubleday, New York, 1973, p. 325.
22. David Thompson and Alan F. Nagel, eds. and trans., *The Three Crowns of Florence: Humanist Assessments of Dante, Petrarca, and Boccaccio*, Harper & Row, New York, 1972.
23. For Renaissance humanistic and courtly literature, Vittorio Rossi, *Il quattrocento*, F. Vallardi, Milan, 1933; Ruth Kelso, *Doctrine for the Lady of the Renaissance*, University of Illinois Press, Urbana, 1956. On erotic life, interesting remarks by David Herlihy, "Some Psychological and Social Roots of Violence in the Tuscan Cities," *Violence and Civil Disorder in Italian Cities, 1200–1500*, ed. Lauro Martines, University of California Press, Berkeley, 1972, pp. 129–154.
24. For historical context, Keith Thomas, "The Double Standard," *Journal of the History of Ideas*, 20 (1959), 195–216; N. J. Perella, *The Kiss Sacred and Profane: An Interpretive History of Kiss Symbolism*, University of California Press, Berkeley, 1969; Morton Hunt, *The Natural History of Love*, Funk & Wagnalls, New York, 1967.
25. Fernand Braudel, *The Mediterranean World*, Routledge & Kegan Paul, London, 1973; A. Ventura, *Nobiltà e popolo nella società Veneta*, Laterza, Bari, 1964; Lawrence Stone, *The Crisis of the Aristocracy, 1558–1641*, Clarendon Press, Oxford, 1965.
26. The status of women as related to the distinction of public and private spheres of activity in various societies is a key idea in most of the anthropological studies in *Women, Culture, and Society*, eds. Michelle Zimbalist Rosaldo and Louise Lamphere, Stanford University Press, Stanford, 1974.

2 Women Humanists: Education for What?

Lisa Jardine

Somewhere between 1443 and 1448 the distinguished teacher Lauro Quirini,[1] a former pupil of Guarino Guarini of Verona (1374–1460), addressed a letter of advice to the humanist Isotta Nogarola of Verona.[2] He was responding to a request from her brother for guidance on appropriate reading for an advanced student of the *studia humanitatis* in the technical disciplines of dialectic and philosophy:

Your brother, Leonardo . . . asked me some time ago if I would write something to you, seeing that at this time you are devoting extremely zealous study (as he terms it) to dialectic and philosophy. He was anxious for me to impress upon you, in most solid and friendly fashion, which masters above all you ought to follow in these higher disciplines.[3]

Quirini prefaces his detailed suggestions for study with an elaborately dismissive paragraph in which he is at pains to point out that to the learned humanist with a real command of classical Latin (among whom he numbers Isotta, some of whose writing he has been shown), all study of dialectic and philosophy must appear uncouth and clumsy:

For you, who have been thoroughly instructed in the most polished and excellent art of discourse, and who find that elegance in orating and suavity of speech come naturally, you are able of your own accord to expect the greatest perfection in eloquent speech. But we semi-orators and petty philosophers have most of the time to be content with mean speech—generally inelegant.[4]

He insists, however, that Isotta Nogarola should not therefore be misled by difficulty for its own sake, even though 'now especially we pursue that philosophy which in no way concerns itself with felicity of expression' (*eam enim hoc potissimum tempore philosophiam sequimur, quae nullum sequitur florem orationis*).[5] Technical scholastic dialectic is to be vigorously avoided:

From Anthony Grafton and Lisa Jardine, *From Humanism to the Humanists* (Duckworth, 1986), 29–57. © Anthony Grafton and Lisa Jardine. Reprinted with permission.

I absolutely insist, and I place the weight of my authority behind this, that you avoid and shun the new philosophers and new dialecticians as men minimally schooled in true philosophy and true dialectic, and that furthermore you harden your heart against all their writings. For they do not teach the approach to the old tried and tested discipline of dialectic, but they obscure the clear and lucid path of this study with goodness knows what childish quibbles, inextricable circuities and pedantic ambiguities. And while seeming to know a great deal, they distort the most readily intelligible matters with a kind of futile subtlety. So that, as the comedian would say, 'they find a knot in a bullrush' ['make difficulties where there are none' (Plautus, Terence)]. On which account, having been diverted by these obstacles, they are unable to aspire to the true philosophy, in which indeed, although they wish to seem sagacious debaters, they let slip the truth, as the old saying goes, with excessive cross-examination.[6]

According to Quirini the source of genuine understanding of dialectic and philosophy remains Aristotle (whose texts *veram et elegantem philosophiam continent* 'contain true and elegant philosophy'). And for a clear grasp of the sense of Aristotle's philosophical works he directs Isotta away from the newfangled, towards less pretentious expositors:

Let me instruct you which authors you *should* follow. Read studiously the celebrated works of learned Boethius, easily the most acute of men, and fully the most knowledgeable. Read, that is, all those treatises which he composed with erudition on the art of dialectic, and the dual commentaries he published on Aristotle's *Categories* and *De interpretatione*, the first for understanding the texts, the second as an examination of the higher art. In these you will be able to find the pronouncements of almost all the most relevant and reliable of the Greek commentators.[7]

Having mastered dialectic with Boethius, Isotta should proceed to Aristotle's moral philosophy, and thence to mathematics, natural philosophy and metaphysics. Since she has no Greek, Quirini suggests the Arab commentators (in their Latin versions), as providing the best access to the nuances of Aristotle's texts. In spite of their 'barbarity', Averroes and Avicenna are preferable in this respect to any of the 'new' philosophers— a sign, incidentally, that Quirini takes Isotta's intellectual aspirations entirely seriously.[8] To these he adds Thomas Aquinas. However, Quirini concludes, in the end the Roman historians and moralists, and supremely Cicero himself, will add the final gloss and lustre to Isotta's grasp of higher learning, and the lessons in life it provides.

This leads him to round off his letter with a eulogy of philosophy as the supreme guide to virtuous conduct—*bonae artes* and right living go hand in hand:

For nothing is more seemly than philosophy, nothing more lovely, nothing more beautiful, as our Cicero was wont to say; and I may perhaps add, more properly, nothing more divine in matters human. For this is the single, most sacred discipline, which teaches true wisdom and instructs in the right manner of living. Whence it comes about that to be ignorant of philosophy is not simply to go through life basely, but also ruinously. Accordingly, throw yourself wholeheartedly, as they say, into this one matter. For I wish you to be not semi-learned, but skilled in all the liberal arts (*bonae disciplinae*), that is, to be schooled in the art of discourse, and in the study of right debating, and in the science of things divine and human.[9]

Quirini's letter articulates a mature humanistic position on the type of rigorous study of language and *scientia* appropriate to *eloquentia*. But although the advice is standard, even commonplace, the circumstances in which it is given are unusual. It was not customary for a woman to pursue advanced humanistic studies. Indeed Leonardo Bruni's well-known letter to Battista Malatesta of some forty years earlier explicitly states that while the *bonae artes* are an appropriate occupation for a noblewoman (the favourite analogy is that it keeps their fingers out of mischief, like spinning or needlework),[10] public proficiency in advanced studies is indecorous:

There are certain disciplines which while it is not altogether seemly to be entirely ignorant of, nevertheless to ascend to the utmost heights of them is not at all admirable. Such are geometry and arithmetic, on which if too much time and energy is expended, and every subtlety and obscurity pursued to the utmost, I shall restrain you by force. And I shall do the same in the case of Astronomy, and perhaps in the case of Rhetoric. I have said this more reluctantly in the case of this last, since if ever there was anyone who has bestowed labour on that study I profess myself to be of their number. But I am obliged to consider many aspects of the matter, and above all I have to bear in mind who it is I am addressing here. For why exhaust a woman with the concerns of *status* and *epichiremata*, and with what they call *crinomena* and a thousand difficulties of rhetorical art, when she will never see the forum? And indeed that artificial performance which the Greeks call *hypocrisis*, and we call *pronuntiatio* (which Demosthenes maintained to rank first, second and third, such was its importance), as it is essential to performers, so it ought not to be pursued by women at all. For if a woman throws her arms around while speaking, or if she increases the volume of her speech with greater forcefulness, she will appear threateningly insane and requiring restraint. These matters belong to men; as war, or battles, and also contests and public controversies. A woman will not, therefore, study any further what to speak either for or against witnesses, either for or against torture, either for or against hearsay evidence, nor will she busy herself with *loci communes*, or devote her attention to dilemmatic questions or to cunning answers; she will leave, finally, all public severity to men.[11]

'Cultivation' is in order for a noblewoman; formal competence is positively unbecoming. Presumably it is because encouraging her higher studies might be considered improper that Quirini insists at the beginning of his letter of advice to Isotta that it is specifically at the request of her brother (her father being dead) that he offers such advice.

So in the case of Quirini's letter to Isotta Nogarola we have familiar sentiments about the moral desirability of humanistic education, addressed to an unusual student—one of whom it can be said with certainty that full competence as a humanist would probably be construed as unbecoming, if not *immoral*. It is because this particular conjunction must concentrate our minds so remarkably well on the question of what 'moral' might possibly mean in the context of humanistic education that we choose it as the focus for this second chapter. It gives us striking additional information to bring to the general question (in relation to students of either sex): What was humanist education envisaged as an education *for*?

Propaganda documents issued by humanists on behalf of their emerging educational programme (epistles of advice, introductions and prefaces to texts and translations, epideictic orations for deceased humanist pedagogues) consistently (like Quirini's exhortation above) make the identity of humanist eloquence and moral integrity—right living—automatic and self-evident. Ludovico Carbone's funeral oration for Guarino is a masterly example of the form, and is particularly pertinent to the present consideration of the humanism of Isotta Nogarola, which moves very much in the shadow of the great teacher's influence:[12]

It was shameful how little the men of Ferrara knew of letters before the arrival of Guarino. There was no one who even understood the basic principles of grammar, who understood the propriety and impact of words, who was able to interpret the poets, let alone who was learned in the art of oratory, who professed rhetoric, who was competent to speak gravely and elegantly and dared to do so in public. Priscian was lost in oblivion, Servius was unheard of, the works of Cicero were unknown, and it was considered miraculous if someone mentioned Sallust, or Caesar, or Livy, or if anyone aspired to understand the ancient authors. At forty our citizens were still occupied with childish studies, still struggling and embroiled with the rudiments, until the liberal arts had been reduced entirely to ruins. But after a propitious star had brought this divine individual to Ferrara, there followed an extraordinary transformation in competence . . . From all quarters they came to listen to that most felicitous voice, so that one might call him another Theophrastus (of whom it is said that his teaching attracted at least two thousand scholars). No one was considered noble, no one as leading a blameless life, unless he had followed Guarino's courses. So that in a short space of time our citizens were led out of the deepest shadows into a true and brilliant light, and all suddenly became eloquent, learned, elegant and felicitous of speech.[13]

The equation is unashamedly explicit: Guarino brought literary studies to Ferrara; literary studies transformed men overnight into paragons of virtue. All the detail is about grammar and oratory, all the evaluations concern 'leading a blameless life'. Good grammarians lead blameless lives.

Quirini's letter of advice to Isotta Nogarola is heavily ornamented with this assumed equivalence of proficiency in humane letters and personal virtue. What makes his insistence on this conventional humanist equation interesting is that, as applied to advanced studies in relation to a *woman*'s life, it lacks the comfortably self-evident quality of equivalent set-pieces addressed to men. Leonardo Bruni's view, in the passage we cited, that the virtuous woman should not pursue indecorously advanced studies, is typical not just of the humanist educators, but of generations of scholars and historians of humanism. Garin's footnote to this passage in his Italian abridgement of the text states firmly that 'the exaltation of ethico-political studies (which are concerned with the *vita civile*) evidenced in Bruni's treatise is the keynote in all early humanist pedagogy'; he then adds that Bruni would obviously not advocate pursuit of rhetorical studies to a noble *woman*, since she clearly ought not to be concerned with its 'excessive use, above all in a practical sphere'.[14]

The Latin letters which make up the two volumes of Isotta Nogarola's *Opera* testify eloquently to the intriguing social and practical difficulties which arise when it comes to extolling the virtue inseparable from eloquence of a female humanist. In 1436 Guarino was sent some of the Nogarola sisters' compositions (Isotta's and her sister Ginevra's) by Jacopo Foscari. Guarino replied with a letter of studied and effusive praise for their scholarly achievement and their manifest virtuousness. Their learning and their virtue brought glory to their native city, Verona (which happened also to be Guarino's):

On this above all I bestow my admiration: such is the likeness of each sister's expression, such the similarity of style, such the sisterhood of writing and indeed the splendour of both their parts, that if you were to remove the names Ginevra and Isotta you would not easily to be able to judge which name you should place before which; so that anyone who is acquainted with either knows both together. Thus they are not simply sisters in birth and nobility of stock, but also in style and readiness of speech.

Oh the glory indeed of our State and our Age! Oh how rare a bird on earth, like nothing so much as a black swan! If earlier ages had borne these proven virgins, with how many verses would their praises have been sung, how many deserved praises from truly unstinting authors would have consigned them to immortality! We see Penelope consecrated in the verses of the poets because she wove so well, Arachne because she spun a most fine thread, Camilla and Penthesilea because they were female warriors. Would they not have honoured these modest, noble, erudite, eloquent women, would they not sing their praises to the skies, would they not rescue them from the clutches of oblivion, by whatever means they please, and preserve them for posterity?[15]

Here the virtue of the Nogarola sisters is characterised in two ways, neither of them 'civic': first, the sisters are indubitably virgins (Ginevra in fact fades from the scene when she marries);[16] secondly, they are represented as sisters in spirit to various magnificent women of classical antiquity. Humanists—male humanists—praising the Nogarola sisters liken them routinely to Sappho, Cornelia, Aspasia, Portia:[17] figures also invoked in defence of the education of women by Bruni in his epistle to Battista Malatesta.[18] Guarino's figurative selection of 'active' virtuous women is a particularly elegant literary ploy: Penelope and Arachne, spinners of exquisitely fine yarns, Camilla and Penthesilea, seductive Amazons and conquerors of entire male armies, deflect his compliments from any awkwardness over the public visibility of (real) women! The strategy of all such compliments is the same: they shift the focus of praise away from the engaged and civic (women speaking publicly), making figurative purity and iconic Amazon valour the object of attention. These are what brings glory to humanism, and to Verona for nurturing such distinction.

This method of celebrating the Nogarolas' virtue is essentially an evasion of the conventional humanist tactic of identifying the virtue of humanism with morality in the market place. And—as in the case of Bruni—this evasion in the sources is compounded in the scholarly secondary literature. In his *Vita di Guarino Veronese*, Sabbadini describes how Guarino chose to send Leonello d'Este copies of the pieces he had been sent by Foscari, during an absence from Ferrara, as follows:[19]

How should he spend his time away? In correspondence. But Guarino did not want to send an empty vessel, so he included some fruits of the Verona school—not those which nourish the body, but rather those which provide fruit for the soul. And those fruits issued from the intellects of two Veronese virgins, the Nogarola sisters, Isotta and Ginevra . . . These two women are among the most characteristic products of the Renaissance. In them for the first time, humanism was married with feminine gentility, especially in the case of Isotta, who remained in this respect unsurpassed. With the Nogarola sisters the Guarinian strain of humanist pedagogy reached its culmination.[20]

Sabbadini takes it for granted that the glory bestowed by Isotta and Ginevra on the school of Guarino derives from their *figurative* presence (as emblems of virtue rather than as real female performers on the public and professional stage). This is touchingly revealed in a later comment. Discussing abusive attacks on Isotta (to which we shall come shortly), he says that these were probably the work of jealous women, rather than of men, since 'envy is a peculiarly feminine passion'.[22] Real women are not the shining examples into which Guarino transforms the Nogarola sisters.

It proved almost impossible in practice, as it turns out, to sustain the equivalence of Isotta Nogarola's humanistic competence and her supreme virtuousness as a woman. Two exchanges of letters make this clear. The first is the exchange between Isotta and Guarino, preluded by the letter of praise from which we have just quoted (the exchange for which Isotta is remembered in histories of humanist education). Guarino's enthusiasm for Isotta's and Ginevra's compositions, expressed in a number of letters to male humanist colleagues and pupils, encouraged Isotta to write to him directly. Guarino failed to answer the letter.[22] At this point the social precariousness of Isotta's position as a humanist scholar becomes evident. Isotta was driven to write a second letter to Guarino, in which she positively begged for a response from the master. And the reason she gives is that her unanswered letter (publicly sent, publicly unanswered) compromises her as a woman. A woman of marriageable age has written an articulate (even pushy) letter, unsolicited, to a man of distinction. He has ignored her, and by so doing has exposed as illusory the notional 'equality' and 'free scholarly exchange' between them. In her first letter Isotta had expressed in entirely conventional terms her anxiety that, coming from a woman, her writing might be considered presumptuous—garrulous, a woman speaking out of turn:

Do not hold it against me, if I have transgressed those rules of silence especially imposed on women, and seem scarcely to have read that precept of Vergerio's, which warns against encouraging articulateness in the young, since in plentiful speech there is always that which may be censured. And Sophocles too called silence a woman's greatest ornament.[23]

In the absence of a reply from Guarino, convention has become a reality. Guarino's silence confirms Isotta's forwardness:

'You have treated me wretchedly, and have shown as little consideration for me as if I had never been born. For I am ridiculed throughout the city, those of my own condition deride me. I am attacked on all sides: the asses inflict their bites on me, the oxen attack me with their horns' [Plautus]. Even if I am most deserving of this outrage, it is unworthy of you to inflict it. What have I done to be thus despised by you, revered Guarino?[24]

'S[a]epissime . . . venit in mentem queri fortunam meam, quoniam femina nata sum' (How often . . . does it occur to me to lament my fortune, because I was born a woman), exclaims Isotta.[25]

The second epistolary exchange of interest to us here involved Isotta and Damiano Borgo.[26] Borgo had apparently challenged Isotta with the familiar claim that women outdo men above all in talkativeness. Isotta responded by claiming that to make such an accusation was to condemn all women on the strength of a few, and she challenged Borgo to maintain this view once he had considered the many examples of women who outdo both other women and all men 'in every kind of virtue and distinction':

Consider Cornelia, mother of the Gracchi, for eloquence; Amesia, who publicly pleaded to packed assemblies with most prudent speech; Afrania, wife of the senator Lucinius Buco, who argued the same kind of cases in public. Did not Hortensia do the same? Did not Sappho overflow with the perfection of her verses? Portia, Fannia and the rest are celebrated in the verses of countless most learned men. Take note of Camilla, whom Turnus, so the poet tells, supported with such honour. Did not Tamyris, Queen of the Scythians, massacre Cyrus, King of the Persians, and his entire army, so that indeed no witness survived to tell of so great a defeat? Did not the Amazons build a state without men? Did not Marpesia, Lampedo and Orithia conquer most of Europe and some states in Asia too, without men? For they were so strongly endowed with virtus [valour/virtue] and with remarkable military skill, that to Hercules and Theseus it seemed impossible to bring the forces of the Amazons under their rule. Penthesilea fought manfully in the Trojan wars in amongst the strongest Greeks, as the poet testifies:
    Penthesilea in fury in the midst of her thousands, rages.
Since this is so, I ask you whether you will grant that rather than women exceeding men in talkativeness, in fact they exceed them in eloquence and virtue?[27]

Here improper talkativeness is replaced by proper 'eloquence and virtue', and Isotta maintains that it is in these latter that women outdo men. But the rhetorical means to this end is an appeal once again to ancient female figurative *virtus* to displace social improprieties. Once again, also, the actual precariousness of Isotta's own position is the most obvious feature of such an argument. 'Virile' argumentative ability and 'Amazon-like' independence from men may make nice points in arguing for the appropriateness of female humanistic education. But they can all too readily be seen in a 'real-life' context as a socially indecorous absence of modesty and due deference, if not as a real social threat—the proverbial husband-beating shrew.[28] Isotta's Amazon citations are taken almost verbatim from Justin, and it is striking that in incorporating the example of Tamyris she herself tacitly acknowledges the awkwardly threatening possibilities of such illustrations—she stops short where Justin embellishes the story of Cyrus' defeat (exacted by Tamyris to avenge the death of her only son at Cyrus' hands):

Having hacked off Cyrus' head, Queen Tamyris hurled it into a vat filled with human blood, at the same time exclaiming with cruel venom: 'Sate yourself with blood, you who were always thirsty and insatiable for it.'[29]

Triumphant warrior-women all too easily become voracious, man-eating monsters.

As it happens, Isotta's own fortunes poignantly illustrate the awkward 'moral' predicament of the unusually able, educated woman. (And once again, that awkwardness is common to her personal history and to the secondary literature upon it.) In 1438, a year after Isotta's difficult exchange of letters with Guarino, an anonymous pamphleteer addressed an invective against the vices of Veronese women (a popular brand of formal *vituperatio*). In it, having lashed out in conventionally Juvenalian fashion at female immodesty, vanity and promiscuity, he singled out the women of the Nogarola family for special blame. In a passage now much-quoted by feminist historians, he imputes to Isotta a sexual deviancy to match (according to his account) the grotesqueness of her public intellectual self-aggrandisement:

She who has acquired for herself such praise for her eloquence behaves in ways utterly inconsistent with so much erudition and such a high opinion of herself: although I have believed the saying of numerous very wise men, 'the woman of fluent speech [*eloquentem*] is never chaste', which can be supported by the example of the greatest number of learned women . . . And lest you are inclined to condone even in the slightest degree this exceedingly loathsome and obscene misconduct, let me explain that before she made her body generally available for uninterrupted intercourse, she had first submitted to, and indeed earnestly desired, that the seal of her virginity should be broken by none other than her brother, to make yet tighter her relationship with him. By God! . . . [What inversions will the world tolerate], when that woman, whose most filthy lust knows no bounds, dares to boast of her abilities in the finest literary studies.[30]

The charge of incest is, of course, pure libellous invention, although, unfortunately, male scholars since the contemporary Veronese human-ist Barbo have seen fit to leap to Isotta's defence as if the accusations might possibly be in earnest. The charge that she is *unchaste* challenges the view that as a woman she can be a prominent humanist and remain a right-living person ('the woman of fluent tongue is never chaste'). It is a studied part of the pamphleteer's contention that in Verona women regularly step out of line (are domineering), and that this is evidence of Verona's general decadence and erosion of morals. When Sabbadini maintains, in his account of the Nogarola sisters' importance, that 'the fruits of the Verona school . . . issued from the intellects of two Veronese virgins . . . In them for the first time, humanism was married with feminine gentility, especially in the case of Isotta, who remained in this respect unsurpassed', we cannot help thinking that he too bonds Isotta's *chastity* with her acceptability as a humanist. Isotta is 'unsur-passed', her hymen intact until death; the bastions of Ginevra's human-ist competence were penetrated at her marriage.

When a woman becomes socially visible—visible within the power structure—Renaissance literary convention makes her a sexual preda-tor. We need only compare, for example, Boccaccio's influential Renais-sance rendering of the story of Semiramis, the ancient Queen of the Assyrians. Boccaccio celebrates Semiramis among 'illustrious' women for successfully ruling in her son's place during his minority, thus pre-serving his patrimony:

It was almost as if she wanted to show that in order to govern it is not necessary to be a man, but to have courage. This fact heightened that woman's glorious majesty as much as it gave rise to admiration in those who looked upon her.[31]

Then he deftly topples her manly valour into predatory sexuality:

But with one wicked sin this woman stained all these accomplishments worthy of perpetual memory, which are not only praiseworthy for a woman but would be marvellous even for a vigorous man. It is believed that this unhappy woman, constantly burning with carnal desire, gave herself to many men.[32]

As in the case of Isotta, the heinousness of the sexual offence is intensified by its involving incest: Semiramis, it is claimed, had sexual intercourse with that very son whose power interests she had substituted for (one might remark that as Semiramis seized priority over her first-in-line son, so Isotta publicly obtrudes over her technically 'prior' brother).

So the charge against Isotta Nogarola is conventional. But that charge—and the public humiliation of Isotta it effected—does direct our attention to the *problem* of a mature woman who obtrudes herself, in her own right, beyond the bounds of social decorum. Her rank might have entitled her to be a modest patron of learning; it did not entitle her to participate actively within the public sphere.[33] When female patrons of this period write to female humanists it is striking how insistently they dwell on the celebratory and decorative nature of their scholarly aptitude—female patron and female scholar alike add lustre (they argue) to male achievement.[34]

Isotta and her family were away from Verona for three years from 1439 to 1441. After their return, Isotta no longer corresponds with other scholars as brilliant student of secular learning (*virilis animi*, learned 'beyond her sex'). Instead she is 'most learned and most religious'; *doctissima* becomes *sancta virgo, dignissima virgo, pia virgo*.[35] Her correspondents extol her for her Christian piety, her deep commitment to sacred letters. And they celebrate her celibacy, rather than her chaste purity. Not surprisingly, the 'illustrious women' with whom she is now compared are Mary and her mother Anna, the loved woman of the Song of Songs ('*Pulchra es amica mea et macula non est in te*').[36] Indeed Isotta's later male correspondents insist in a rather depressing and unhealthy way on the special importance in God's eyes (or perhaps their own) of her celibate state as confirmation of the admirable nature of her studiousness.[37] Isotta withdrew entirely from public view and became a virtual recluse in her family home (there are signs that her brothers were not entirely delighted with having to support a deliberately celibate sister as well as an aged mother).[38]

According to her nineteenth-century biographer Abel, Isotta totally renounced her secular studies, became a mystic and a saint, and devoted the remainder of her life to God. This is a version of events which feminist historians embrace, because it suggests 'thwarted ambitions', and the poignancy of a potentially brilliant career stifled by oppressive patriarchal intervention. But we need to be just as cautious at this point in Isotta's history as at earlier points at which critical prejudice obviously biased its telling. The letter of advice from Quirini on the advanced secular studies of logic and philosophy with which we opened this chapter dates from well after the return to Verona. The letters testifying to Isotta's asceticism, on the other hand, are all those of her 'mentor', Ludovico Foscarini (Isotta's letters to him do not survive).[39] Foscarini's correspondence with Isotta certainly depends for its propriety on the assumption that there could be no carnal involvement intended, so his insistence on Isotta's saintliness and spirituality is part of the strategy for 'coping' with a female scholar (even so, Abel claims a passionate love affair between the two).[40] The point is, whatever her continuing interest in the *studia humanitatis*, there was no public outlet for Isotta's secular training once she became a mature woman, and there never had been, even before the libel of 1438.

Can we sustain historically the humanist propaganda claim that virtue and right living are the direct products of fifteenth-century humanist studies? The current view of the English-speaking scholarly community is that they were not, that a work like Vergerio's *De ingenuis moribus* 'does not lend itself readily to a civic interpretation as formulated by Saitta and Garin, and followed by many recent historians of humanism'.[41] But the critics of Saitta and Garin go on to say that if humanism provided an education in grammar and rhetoric which did *not* prepare its students morally for civic life, then it must have been a 'pure' intellectual training. When Vergerio writes that liberal studies are a preparation 'for every life' and 'for every kind of man', they argue, he means that studies are an end in themselves, a way of each individual's realising his full potential as a human being.

Isotta Nogarola's life shows us that this is not in fact the case. Certainly educators like Vergerio (and remember Isotta shows knowledge of Vergerio's treatise in one of the letters we used above) insist on the general civilising effect of the *bonae artes* without specifying either a moral or a civil context to which their training is attached. In other words, the educational programme of the humanist pedagogues is not job-specific. But the *value* attached to humanist studies does depend upon a particular ideology, and in this important sense it is firmly tied to its civic context. It is for precisely this reason that Isotta Nogarola failed to 'achieve', in spite of having access to humanist studies, as did others who failed to notice the tight inter-connectedness between the status of the *bonae artes* as a training and the political establishment and its institutions (other women, and those of inappropriate rank).[42] *Ad omne genus hominum*, 'for every type of person', has to be read out as 'for every appropriately well-placed male individual'. 'Opportunity', that is, is a good deal more than having ability, and access to a desirable programme of study. It is also being a good social and political fit for the society's assumptions about the purpose of 'cultivation' as a qualifying requirement for power.

If humanism has been of its nature tightly 'civic', then as a woman Isotta Nogarola would never have had the support of the community of distinguished humanist scholars and teachers in her pursuit of humanist studies. But equally, if humanism had really set as its highest goal the pursuit of learning for its own sake, she would not have disappeared so decisively from secular scholarly view in the mature years of her life—years in which she continued to excel in those studies. She could continue an excellent student of humanism in private, but she could not be publicly supported as 'virtuous' in doing so.

What we are stressing is that the independence of liberal arts education from establishment values is an illusion. The individual humanist is defined in terms of his relation to the power structure, and he is praised or blamed, promoted or ignored, to just the extent that he fulfils or fails to fulfil those terms. It is, that is, a condition of the prestige of humanism in the fifteenth century, as Lauro Martines stresses, that 'the humanists, whether professionals or noblemen born, were ready to serve [the ruling] class. The most apolitical of them could be drawn into the political fray'.[43] The fortunes of a gifted woman embarked on the humanist training show vividly how a programme with no explicit employment goals nevertheless presupposes those goals, and how the enterprise of pursuing secular humanist studies can be regarded as morally laudable (a 'virtuous' undertaking) only where achieving that goal is socially acceptable. A woman, as Bruni so eloquently insisted, was not available to be drawn into the public fray to marshal the morality of humanism in the service of the State in the fifteenth century. She could not argue politically in public without appearing indecorous; she could not even *pronounce* publicly without risking appearing 'threateningly insane and requiring restraint'.[44] Study, for her, consigned her to marginality, relegated her to the cloister. Because she could not enter the public arena, by virtue of her sex, Isotta Nogarola withdrew, figuratively and emotionally, from public intellectual intercourse to the nearest thing she could contrive to a secular cloister—her 'book-lined cell'.[45]

Isotta Nogarola, striking as her case is, is by no means unique among female pupils for whom the great fifteenth-century humanists served as teachers or mentors, and whose femaleness set them (and, in the eyes of historians of humanism, has continued to set them) awkwardly apart from their male counterparts. To consolidate our argument that the careers of such women are illuminating for our understanding of humanism as a movement in fifteenth-century Italy, let us turn to another surviving correspondence, this time between the learned Cassandra Fedele of Venice and the distinguished male humanist Politian.

In about 1491[46] Angelo Poliziano began a correspondence with Cassandra Fedele, a learned young woman already noted in humanist circles for her ability as a Latinist.[47] Fedele initiated this exchange of letters by addressing to Politian a letter of admiration—a suit for the great man's attention, and the established way of laying a claim to a place in the circle of erudite humanist scholars in the period. That letter is now lost, but an equivalent one addressed to Pico in 1489 survives, and gives us a good idea of the tone of Fedele's bid for intellectual recognition:[48]

Although I had for a long time had the intention of writing to you, yet I was almost deterred by the renown of your divine gifts (described by many, and above all by Lactantius Thedaldus, most distinguished herald of your praises) and had rather determined to remain speechless than to appear deficient in brilliance and merely femininely pleasing when celebrating your achievements. But after your *Lucubrationes*, most rich in words and ideas, had been brought to me recently by that best of men, Salviatus, and I had often read them avidly, and had become acquainted with your intellectual skill and singular learning from them, I feared lest I might be reproved by many unless I celebrated your unheard-of gifts to the best of my feeble ability to all men, by whom you are held to be a miracle, you are praised and you are revered, especially as a result of the dissemination of your works. Because in those works are contained fine phrasing, most serious meaning, brilliance, divine sublimity of interpretation, and finally, all things cohere harmoniously by divine influence.[49]

Fedele here combines a display of Latinity with an indication of her serious and informed scholarship—she has already read Pico's latest theological work—and an extravagantly flattering exclamation of praise (which continues for a further half page), for the virtue, glory and honour of the age which Pico's intellect represents. We may take it she wrote similarly to Pico's friend and colleague Politian.

Politian, who claims already to be familiar with Fedele's work and reputation (he had probably seen the letter Pico had received, and heard of her widely acclaimed performance in a public oration in 1487),[50] replied with an extended, set-piece panegyric on her peculiarly womanly achievement. This letter was followed by a visit to the Fedele household in June 1491,[51] during a trip to Venice with Pico. In public terms, the attention meant that Fedele's accomplishment was recognised in the Florentine humanist community, to which she was admitted, notionally, as a member.[52]

What was this group of which she had become a member? Well, essentially, it was a gentlemen's club of noble or nobly-connected scholar-courtiers, who depended upon the patronage of Lorenzo de' Medici.[53] When Politian reported back to Lorenzo, after the visit to Fedele's family home, he did so in terms of Fedele's gracious and courtier-like acceptance of an invitation to become part of his entourage (or at least to be associated with his court), an invitation extended by *Lorenzo* in the form of a greeting:

Item. Yesterday evening I visited that learned Cassandra Fedele, and I greeted her, Excellency, on your part. She is a miraculous phenomenon, Lorenzo, whether in the vernacular or in Latin; most modest, and to my eyes also beautiful. I departed stupefied. She is a great admirer of yours, and speaks of you most knowledgeably, as if she knew you intimately. She will come to Florence one day, in any case, to see you; so prepare yourself to honour her.[54]

Most historians broadly agree that by the later decades of the fifteenth century the continuing support for humanism of the increasingly totalitarian Florentine ruling house tended to push scholarly energies to the margins of real political debate, and into 'contemplative' rather than 'active' studies—providing ornamental and propaganda proof of the civility and moral probity of the regime, rather than technical expertise in politics and government. Lauro Martines, who on the whole takes issue with those Italian historians of the school of Baron and Garin who characterise humanism as 'civic' and politically influential in the late trecento and early quattrocento, points out that on the late decades of the quattrocento he and they are in broad agreement. Pooling his own and Garin's views, he comments on Politian himself:

'He lives and works in a time when the new [humanistic] culture is no longer an operative force in the city, in that very Florence of humanistic merchants and chancellors, now transformed into mere courtiers and professors, often courtier-professors'. The new type of chancellor, still a humanist, lost his political influence during the middle decades of the fifteenth century and became 'a solemnly haughty administrator like Bartolomeo Scala'.[55]

In this setting, the rhetoric of humanism represents the power of Latinity and eloquence as actual power—as meshed with civic activity in a close and influential relationship. But individual humanists are increasingly pursuing the recondite and arcane in scholarship as an end in itself. We might instance Politian's own dedication to Greek studies and textual problems in the last years of his life as evidence of this increasing tendency of humanists retained in official posts by those in power to busy themselves with erudition for its own sake.

The point of drawing attention to this unsignalled flight from political engagements to grateful courtiership at the time of the exchange of letters between Politian and Cassandra Fedele is that Fedele gained admission to a club which could not afford to recognize the implications of the fact that a woman *could* become a member. In a period which afforded no power to a woman in her own right, a woman's achievement in a sphere which supposedly stood in some active relation to power could not be allowed to stand *as* woman's achievement.[56] This, at least, is the explanation we offer for the fact that Politian assiduously *mythologises* Fedele into 'not-woman': into an emblem of humanistic achievement which avoids confronting her sex as a problem.

Politian's first letter to Fedele, his *laudatio* of female scholarly accomplishment, opens with a passage from Virgil's *Aeneid* (a passage which becomes, fascinatingly, a virtual synecdoche for the whole of Fedele's surviving reputation in later secondary literature on her):[57]

> *O decus Italiae virgo, quas dicere gratis*
> *quasve referre parem*

(O virgin, glory of Italy, what thanks shall I try to utter or repay).[58]

In the *Aeneid* this exclamation of rapt admiration is addressed to Camilla, supremely virtuous Amazon warrior-maiden, whose appearance at the end of the procession of protagonists rallied against Aeneas fills Turnus with rapture:[59]

A warrior-maid, never having trained her woman's hands to Minerva's distaff or basket of wool, but hardy to bear the battle-brunt and in speed of foot to outstrip the winds. She might have flown o'er the topmost blades of unmown corn, nor in her course bruised the tender ears . . .[60]

Politian's celebration of Cassandra proceeds self-consciously to sustain the same tone of wonder. This accomplished practitioner of the *studia humanitatis* is a latter-day paragon of 'manly' virtue (manly because active and productive; virtuous because employed in those studies associated with probity of character):

What an astonishing impact it must make upon us, truly, that it was possible for such [letters] to be produced by a woman—what do I say, a woman? By a girl, rather, and a virgin. It shall therefore no longer be the exclusive privilege of antiquity to boast of their Sybils and their Muses, the Pythagoreans of their female philosophers, the Socratics of their Diotima, of Aspasia; and neither will the relics of Greece proclaim those female poets, Telesilla, Corinna, Sappho, Anyte, Erinna, Praxilla, Cleobulina and the others. Now we shall readily believe the Roman account of the daughters of Laelius and Hortensius, of Cornelia, mother of the Gracchi, as matrons of surpassing eloquence. Now we know, truly by this we know, that your sex has not after all been condemned to slowness and stupidity.[61]

And still in the vein of Camilla he exclaims:

But truly in our age, in which few men indeed raise their head to any height in letters, you, however, stand forth as the sole girl who handles books in place of wool, a reed pen instead of vegetable dye, a quill pen instead of a needle, and who instead of daubing her skin with white lead, covers paper with ink.[62]

Politian's enthusiasm culminates in an outburst of personal desire actually to confront this paragon of female virtue—a passion which, remember, precedes his ever having set eyes upon her. So vividly has he conjured up the warrior-maiden from her literary productions that her physical person, like her intact virginity, is vividly present to him in them:

O how I should like to be transported where I might actually contemplate your most chaste visage, sweet virgin; if I might admire your appearance, your cultivation, your refinement, your bearing; if I might drink in your pronouncements, inspired into you by your Muses, as it were with thirsty ears; so that, finally, infused with your spirit and inspiration I might become most consummate Poet,
    Not Thracian Orpheus, not Linus shall vanquish me in song though his mother be helpful to the one, and his father to the other, Calliope to Orpheus and fair Apollo to Linus.[63]

Here the personal homage—the cult of the virgin goddess—culminates in the final invocation of the Fates/the poet to the harbinger of the Golden Age (the return of the virgin Astraea, the age of the infant king):

> aspice venturo laetentur ut omnia saeclo!
> o mihi tum longae maneat pars ultima vitae,
> spiritus et quantum sat erit tua dicere facta

(Behold, how all things exult in the age that is at hand! O that then the last days of a long life may still linger for me, with inspiration enough to tell of thy deeds!)

From Camilla, warrior-maiden, Cassandra Fedele (practising Latinist) has become virgin Muse, object of poetic cult, herald of the Golden Age.[64]

Encouraged by the significant amount of attention accorded by Politian to herself as a female scholar, and on the strength of some verbal commitment made by Politian during his visit to pursue the intellectual contact they had established, Fedele again wrote to Politian. This time he failed to reply. Perhaps the *actual* exchange of letters and views with the *real* girl ranked rather low on his list of intellectual priorities.[65] After a suitable wait she wrote again, this time a poignant letter of reproach; and in 1493 Politian replied, with a letter which keeps perfect decorum with the topos of 'lament' (woman abandoned) of her second letter.[66] Politian claims as his excuse that her intellectual performance on the occasion of his visit has left him absolutely tongue-tied—incapable of utterance. He makes this state allusively vivid with another quotation from the *Aeneid*, this time a passage from Book Three. Aeneas recounts to Dido the tale of his encounter with Andromache, whom he found passionately weeping and lamenting on her dead husband Hector's tomb. Aeneas' appearance further intensifies her grief, since it reminds her of the Troy that was, and she exclaims passionately to him. Confronted with this spectacle of majestic female fortitude in adversity, Aeneas is struck speechless:

> 'Hector ubi est?' dixit lacrimasque effudit et omnem
> implevit clamore locum. vix pauca furenti
> subicio et raris turbatus vocibus hisco.

('Where is Hector?' she spake, and shedding a flood of tears, filled all the place with her cries; to her frenzy scarce can I make a brief reply, and deeply moved gasp for broken words).[67]

Aeneas' reaction to Andromache's lament is particularly poignant, since it will soon be followed by Dido's own passionate lament when Aeneas himself abandons her. The passage encapsulates male admiration 'deeply moved with broken words', faced with the enormity of female grief 'manfully' endured.

In Politian's case it is, supposedly, awe and a sense of his own inadequacy at Fedele's superb Latinity and general cultivation which have left him thus rapt, but the implicit tone of contrition is elegantly appropriate as a response to female reproach.[68] Supposedly, because we must surely feel that the choice of excuse is a choice of literary *topos*. As we saw, in an exactly similar situation (having made the same social gaffe of failing to reply to a letter), Guarino chose another plausible *topos*—the exhortation to the woman beset with adversity to remain *virilis animi*: it was Isotta Nogarola's 'manliness of mind' which persuaded him he could treat her *as* a man. And even if the vulgar crowd abuses her as a woman, her manly fortitude of spirit should allow her to rise above it:

This evening I received your letters, full of complaints and accusations, in which you render me uncertain as to whether I should feel pain for you or congratulate myself. For when I saw fit to give my attention to that outstanding intellect of yours, with its attendant embellishments of learning, I was accustomed besides to express strongly my opinion that you were manly of spirit, that nothing could happen which you would not bear with a courageous and indomitable spirit. Now, however, you show yourself so cast down, humiliated and truly womanish that I am able to perceive nothing which accords with my previous magnificent opinion of you.[69]

This *topos* allowed Guarino to reprove Nogarola for allowing social convention (femaleness) any place in her scholarly life—how could a mere intermission in their correspondence threaten her womanly honour?[70]

Like Guarino's with Nogarola, Politian's relationship with Fedele is established entirely within the world of letters; confronted (physically) with her ability, he responds with the awe appropriate to a Muse or Goddess:

For when some time ago I had come to your house for the purpose of seeing and greeting you (which was the chief reason for my visit to Venice), and you had presented yourself after a long wait, clothed beautifully, yourself most beautiful, like a nymph emerging from the woods before me, and when then you had addressed me compellingly with ornate and copious words, and, truth to tell, with a kind of echo of the divine about them, then my soul was of a sudden (as I think you remember) struck senseless at such a miracle and such rarity, so that, as Aeneas reports of himself, 'I gasped with broken words', and could scarcely even apologise for my inability to speak . . . When therefore I returned to Florence, full of these impressions and totally overwhelmed by it all, I received from you your spectacular letters, to which I often tried to reply, but I know not how, my very writing fingers faltered, the very pen dropped from my hands. For I did not dare to submit to the unequal contest, whereby I was obliged to fear more the charge of insolence and baseness if I replied, than that of idleness or lack of courtesy if I remained silent. My failure to reply has not therefore come about out of negligence, but out of bashfulness, not from contempt, but reverence.[71]

At this point Politian intensifies the 'literary' quality of his celebration of the woman of letters. He introduces the figure of *another* young, beautiful and learned woman, the Florentine Alessandra Scala.[72] Too awestruck to answer Fedele's letters, Politian tells her, he took them instead to Alessandra Scala, and recreated the experience of Fedele's combination of learning and loveliness by having Scala read them aloud to the assembled company. Bartolomeo Scala, Marsilio Ficino and Pico della Mirandola praised their accomplishment.

This effects the metamorphosis of the individual talented woman into a *genus* of representatives of female worth, and it brings Politian to the substantial part of his letter, the offering, as it were, to Cassandra. On the occasion of a previous visit to the Scala household, he had joined the audience for a private performance, in Greek, of Sophocles' *Electra*, in which Alessandra Scala took the title role.[73] The central set-piece in Politian's letter is a description of the impression her performance made upon him:

But let me return to Alessandra. She busies herself day and night with the study of both Latin and Greek. And the other day, when the Greek tragedy of Sophocles was performed in her father's house, for which the greatest number of learned men had been assembled . . . she took the part of Electra, one virgin playing another, and performed with such talent, art and grace, that all fastened their eyes and minds upon her. There was in her words that Attic charm, utterly genuine and native, her gestures everywhere so prompt and effective, so appropriate to the argument, so covering the range of the various feelings, that they added greatly to the truth and believableness of the fiction. Nor was she so mindful of Electra that she forgot Alessandra. Altogether humbly and modestly, her eyes were not simply downcast to the ground, but firmly fixed there at all times. To see her you would have said she felt the difference between an actress and a virgin. For though she satisfied the requirements of the stage, yet she was in no way theatrical, as if she produced her gestures not for just anyone, but only for the learned and the upright.[74]

Once again, more than Alessandra's competence in Greek is at stake. What Politian celebrates is the *spectacle* of Alessandra performing as antique womanhood of supreme virtue (as his Greek epigram addressed to Alessandra herself on the occasion of this performance confirms).[75] It is the symbolic impact of the woman *verecunde omnia et pudenter, non modo ad terram demissis sed pene in terram semper defixis oculis* ('With shame and modesty in everything, her eyes not only constantly cast down to the ground, but fixed upon it'). The ideal nature of her performance does not derive from her impeccable Greek grammar and pronunciation (hardly at all, as Politian describes it), but almost entirely from her modesty, the probity of her person, her 'chastity' (that predictable invoking of virginity).[76] Alessandra/Electra is beauty/purity itself, a figure talismanic of the revival of Greek learning and culture which Politian and his colleagues are undertaking. And Politian closes his letter to Fedele by joining her and Scala in a single image of the exemplary learned woman:

Alessandra Scala alone, therefore, is now talked of here, the Florentine Electra, a girl undoubtedly worthy for you, most learned Cassandra, to call sister, inasmuch as she alone of all our age, I shall not say, attains to your stature, but certainly follows in your footsteps.[77]

His letter here comes, as it were, full circle. From an encounter with a learned female Latinist, whose reproach allows him to applaud her typical pose of virtuous grief (whether or not expressed in impeccable Latin), he passes to the claim that Alessandra the Hellenist and Cassandra the Latinist are sisters in learning, and thereby sidesteps again the need to assess their *real* intellectual achievement, while for the time being celebrating 'female humanism' as a phenomenon worthy of the age.[78]

Now, like Alessandra Scala, Cassandra Fedele *was*, on the evidence of her published letters and orations, an accomplished humanist and scholar. And the problem which Politian's letters appear both to raise, and astutely to evade, is: What could such accomplishment be *for* in a woman?

The women humanists are accomplished; their accomplishment is celebrated by their male correspondents in terms of an abstract intellectual ideal (warrior-maiden, *virilis animi*; grieving spouse, majestic in suffering), or in terms of a social ideal (chastity, obedience, modesty, constancy, beauty). Guarino combines the two when he writes of the Nogarola sisters, Isotta and Ginevra (whom he has never met), on the strength of their display pieces of Latin prose:

Why do the poets not honour these modest, noble, erudite, eloquent women? ... What are you doing, you noble young men of our city? ... Do you not fear that common outburst against you:

for indeed you young men display a womanish mind; while that virgin displays a virile one [*De officiis* 1].[79]

On the other hand, humanistic accomplishment in the quattrocento is notionally the means of access to humanism as a *profession*, leaving aside for a moment whether what is envisaged is a political career, or a teaching career, or even a courtier's. When Isotta Nogarola writes to Guarino and receives a eulogy in reply, or when Fedele succeeds in eliciting a congratulatory response from Politian, they have apparently crossed the threshold from promising student to accomplished practitioner. The same might be said to be the implication of Politian's Greek epigram addressed to Alessandra Scala on the occasion of her performance as Electra: 'You have made it into the ranks of those honoured by society for their achievement as Latinists and Hellenists, those, that is, to whom our society looks as civic leaders and figure-heads of the civilised community.' All three women certainly reacted to the great men's attention *as if* this had happened: Scala replied (as any male humanist would have done) with a competent Greek epigram praising Politian in his turn;[80] Nogarola and Fedele wrote letters in response to their mentors, which assume that an active and fully par-ticipating correspondence will now ensue. Fedele and Nogarola reacted to the subsequent *rebuff* with a personal and passionate intensity which suggests that they themselves had been well and truly deceived—that they had really expected to be treated from now on as equal intellec-tuals, not as forward women, or amorous encounters.[81]

It is this confusion on their part that we find deeply suggestive for our assessment of quattrocento Italian humanism as a whole. Within the humanist confraternity (sic) the accomplishment of the educated woman (the 'learned lady') is an end in itself, like fine needlepoint or the ability to perform ably on lute or virginals. It is not viewed as a training for anything, perhaps not even for virtue (except insofar as all these activities keep their idle hands and minds busy).[82] As signs of *cul-tivation* all such accomplishments satisfactorily connote a leisured life, a background which regards the decorative as adding lustre to rank and social standing, and the ability to purchase the services of the best available teachers for such comparatively useless skills. And there is supposed to be an evident discontinuity between such accomplishment and the world of the professional humanist, be he teacher, advisor or holder of public office. But that discontinuity is in practice, it appears, precariously established—sufficiently precariously for it to cause mis-understanding, puzzlement, uneasiness, textual difficulty in the letters exchanged between accomplished women and professional men, as the one strives for recognition, the other to evade it. Following receipt of Scala's Greek epigram, for instance, Politian addresses a succession of Greek epigrams to 'Alessandra poetess' which transform the exchange from one between Greek virtuosi into a series of formalized lover's addresses to an absent beloved, hoping for some substantial sign of favour ('To me who desire fruit you, however, send only flowers and leaves, signifying that I labour in vain').[83] Scala is thus eff-ectively excluded from the exchange altogether, in spite of Politian's continuing protestations of admiration.[84] Only if mythologized can the woman humanist be celebrated without causing the male humanist professional embarrassment.

But if the gap between accomplishment (the ability of the noble, leisured pupil) and profession (the learned training of the active civic figure) is problematic in the case of women, might it not be so for men in a comparable position? That is to say, do the exchanges of letters between Guarino and Leonello d'Este or between Politian and Lorenzo de' Medici prove anything more about the noble pupil-patron than that he is accomplished, in currently validating social terms? It seems that for the nobleman also, who did not in practice earn a living or pursue a career, humanist learning provided the male equivalent of fine needlepoint or musical skill: it provided the fictional identity of rank and worth on which the precarious edifice of the fifteenth-century Italian city state's power structure depended. It read out as 'valour', 'manliness', 'fortitude', 'benevolence', the male equivalents of 'modesty' and 'chastity', but less readily discernible to our modern eye as culturally constructed 'moral' attributes—that, at least, is what we seem to begin to see when we 'look to the ladies' in the humanist case.

Notes

1. On Quirini see *Lauro Quirini umanista*, ed. V. Branca (Florence, 1997); *Isotae Nogarolae Veronensis opera quae supersunt omnia*, ed. E. Abel, 2 vols (Budapest, 1886), I, xliv, xccii; R. Sabbadini, 'Briciole umanistiche', *Giornale storico della letteratura italiana* 43 (1904), 247–50; L. Martines, *The Social World of the Florentine Humanists* (Princeton, 1963), 97–8.
2. Isotta Nogarola (1418–1466): see most recently M. L. King, 'The religious retreat of Isotta Nogarola (1418-1466); sexism and its consequences in the fifteenth century', *Signs* 3 (1978), 807–22, which contains a full bibliography in an appendix. See also Abel's introductory essay in the *Opera*; M. L. King, 'Book-lined cells: women and humanism in the early Italian Renaissance', in *Beyond their Sex; Learned Women of the European Past*, ed. P. H. Labalme (New York and London, 1980), 66–90; P. O. Kristeller' 'Learned women of early modern Italy: humanists and university scholars', ibid., 91–116; D. M. Robathan, 'A fifteenth-century bluestocking', *Medievalia et humanistica*, fasc. 2 (1944), 106–11.
3. All passages are quoted from Abel's edition of Nogarola's works (hereafter 'Abel'). '*Leonardus germanus tuus . . . iam pridem me rogarat, ut nonnihil ad te scriberem, nam quoniam hoc tempore dialecticae et philosophiae acrem, ut is aiebat, operam das, voluit, ut ipse fidelissime ac amicissime te commonerem, quos praecipue magistros in his altioribus disciplinis sequi deberes*' (Abel, II, 10).
4. '*Tu enim, quae politissima et exquisitissima arte dicendi edocta es assueta in eleganti oratione, suavitateque dicendi, tuo iure perornatissimum exposcere potes eloquium, at nos semioratores minutique philosophi parvo et illo ineleganti persaepe contenti sumus*' (Abel, II, 11).
5. Ibid.
6. '*Cupio, inquam, idque meo iure iubeo, ut novos hos philosophos novosque dialecticos tamquam homines minime verae philosophiae veraeque dialecticae instructos non modo evites et fugias, verum etiam omnia eorum scripta stomacheris, nam dialecticae quidem non viam disciplinae veteris iam probatae docent, sed*

nescio quibus puerilibus captionibus, inextricabilibus circuitibus et scrupulosis ambagibus huiusce disciplinae claram et dilucidam semitam obfuscarunt. Nam ut multa scire videantur, omnia etiam planissima futili quadam subtilitate corrumpunt et, ut inquit comicus, "nodum in scirpo quaerunt". Quapropter his impedimentis detenti nequeunt ad veram et solidam aspirare philosophiam, in qua etiam dum acuti disputatores videri cupiunt, veritatem nimium altercando, ut vetus sententia dicit, amiserunt' (Abel, II, 13–14).

7. *'[His ergo explosis] quos sequi debeas, breviter edocebo. Lege igitur studiose Boetii Severini, viri facile acutissimi abundeque doctissimi praeclara monumenta, id est tractatus omnes, quos in arte dialectica erudite confecit, et eius commentarios, quos in Aristotelis Cathegoriis et Periermenias duplices edidit, primos ad litterae intelligentiam, secundos ad altioris artis indaginem. In quibus cunctorum fere probatissimorum Graecorum commentatorum sententias videre poteris'* (Abel, II, 15–16).

8. For an account of the serious use of Averroes' commentaries on Aristotle's texts in the Renaissance which is entirely consistent with Quirini's advice to Isotta Nogarola, see C. B. Schmitt, 'Renaissance Averroism studied through Venetian editions of Aristotle–Averroes (with particular reference to the Giunta Edition of 1550–2)', *Convegno internazionale: l'Averroismo in Italia, Atti dei convegni Lincei* 40 (Rome, 1979), 121–42. Schmitt is, of course, concentrating largely on a later period.

9. *'Nihil enim philosophia formosius, nihil pulchrius, nihil amabilius, ut Cicero noster dicebat, ego vero forsan rectius, nihil philosophia in rebus humanis divinius. Haec enim unica, sanctissima disciplina est, quae veram sapientiam edocet et rectum vivendi modum instruit, ex quo fit, ut ignari huius non modo turpiter sed etiam perniciose per vitam obirent. Proinde huic uni rei, toto, ut aiunt, pectore incumbe, volo enim te non semidoctam esse, sed cunctarum bonarum disciplinarum peritiam habere, id est et bene dicendi artem et recte disputandi disciplinam et humanarum atque divinarum rerum scientiam noscere'* (Abel, II, 21–2).

10. See, for example, Erasmus: 'The distaff and spindle are in truth the tools of all women and suitable for avoiding idleness . . . Even people of wealth and birth train their daughters to weave tapestries or silken cloths . . . It would be better if they taught them to study, for study busies the whole soul . . . It is not only a weapon against idleness but also a means of impressing the best precepts upon a girl's mind and of leading her to virtue.' *Christiani matrimonii institutio* (Basle, 1526), ch. 17, unpaginated, cit. *Not in God's Image: Women in History*, ed. J. O'Faolain and L. Martines (London, 1979), 194. Politian, writing in praise of another woman humanist, Cassandra Fedele, commends her for having exchanged 'her spinning wool for her books, her vegetable dye for a reed pen, her needle for a quill pen'. See *Clarissimae feminae Cassandrae Fidelis Venetae epistolae et orationes . . .* ed. I. P. Tomasinus (Padua, 1636), 156.

11. *'Sunt enim disciplinarum quaedam, in quibus ut rudem omnino esse non satis decorum, sic etiam ad cacumina illarum evadere nequaquam gloriosum; ut geometria et arithmetica, in quibus, si multum temporis consumere pergat et subtilitates omnes obscuritatesque rimari, retraham manu atque divellam. Quod idem faciam in astrologia, idem fortasse et in arte rhetorica. Invitior de hac postrema dixi, quoniam, si quisquam viventium illi affectus fuit, me unum ex eo numero esse profiteor. Sed multarum rerum habenda mihi ratio est et in primis,*

cui scribam, videndum. Quid enim statuum *subtilitates et* epicherematum *curae et illa, quae appellantur* crinomena, *et mille in ea arte difficultates mulierem conterant, quae forum numquam sit aspectura? Iam vero actio illa artificiosa, quam Graeci* hypocrisim, *nostri* pronuntiationem *dixere, cui Demosthenes primas et secundas et tertias tribuit, ut actori necessaria, ita mulieri nequaquam laboranda, quae, si brachium iactabit loquens aut si clamorem vehementius attollet, vesena coercendaque videatur. Ista quidem virorum sunt; ut bella, ut pugnae, sic etiam fori contentiones atque certamina. Non igitur pro testibus neque contra testes dicere addiscet mulier, neque pro tormentis aut contra tormenta, neque pro rumoribus aut contra rumores, nec se communibus locis exercebit, neque interrogationes bicipites neque responsiones veteratorias meditabitur; totam denique fori asperitatem viris relinquet.' Leonardo Bruni Aretino Humanistisch-Philosophische Schriften mit einer Chronologie seiner Werke und Briefe,* ed. H. Baron (Leipzig, 1928), 11–12. In spite of Bruni's warning, Battista Malatesta delivered a public oration in Latin to the Emperor Sigismund. See Kristeller, 'Learned women of early modern Italy', 93–4.

12. The Nogarola sisters were tutored in humanistic studies by Martino Rizzoni, one of Guarino's old pupils. This allows Sabbadini to claim them as members of Guarino's 'school'. In addition to corresponding with Guarino himself, Isotta Nogarola exchanged letters with a number of humanists of his circle, and received scholarly advice from Quirini, another graduate of Guarino's school.

13. *Ludovici Carbonis Ferrariensis, artium doctoris et comitis palatini apostolici, oratio habita in funere praestantissimi oratoris et poetae Guarini Veronensis,* in *Prosatori latini del quattrocento,* ed. E. Garin (Milan and Naples, 1952), 381–417. *'Pudendum erat quam parumper litterarum sciebant nostri [Ferrarienses] homines ante Guarini adventum. Nemo erat, non dicam qui oratoriam facultatem nosceret, qui rhetoricam profiteretur, qui graviter et ornate diceret et in publico aliquo conventu verba facere auderet, sed qui veram grammaticae rationem cognosceret, qui vocabulorum proprietatem vimque intelligeret, qui poetas interpretari posset. Iacebat Priscianus, ignorabatur Servius, incognita erant opera Ciceronis, miraculi loco habebatur, si quis Crispum Sallustium, si quis C. Caesarem, si quis T. Livium nominaret, si quis ad veterum scriptorum intelligentiam aspiraret. Quadagesimus fere annus cives nostros in ludo puerili occupatos inveniebat in iisdem elementis semper laborantes, semper convolutos. Usque adeo bonarum litterarum ruina facta erat. Postea vero quam divinus hic vir dextro sidere Ferrariam ingressus est, secuta est mirabilis quaedam ingeniorum commutatio . . . Currebatur undique ad vocem incundissimam, ut alterum Theophrastum diceres, ad quem audiendum legimus perrexisse discipulos ad duo milia. Nemo putabatur ingenuus, nemo in lauta vitae parte, nisi Guarini esset auditor. Unde brevi de obscurissimis tenebris educti sunt nostri homines in veram et clarissiman lucem, omnes repente diserti, omnes eruditi, omnes limati, omnes in dicendo suaves extiterunt'* (390–2).

14. E. Garin, *L'educazione umanistica in Italia* (Bari, 1953), 32.

15. Abel, II, 58–9. There is in fact a better text of this exchange of letters in *Epistolario di Guarino Veronese,* ed. R. Sabbadini, 3 vols (Venice, 1915–19), II, 292–309, and we have taken the Latin text from there. Sabbadini wrote a magisterial review of Abel's edition of Isotta Nogarola's works, in which he helpfully points out a large number of discrepancies between his versions of the

letters and Abel's: 'Isotta Nogarola', *Archivio storico italiano*, 18 (1886), 435–43. He also redates some of the letters. '*Quodque praecipua admiratione prosequor, tanta est in utriusque dictione paritas, tanta stili similitudo, tanta scribendi germanitas et quidem utrobique magnifica, ut si Zinebrae nomen auferas et Isotae, non facile utri utram anteponas iudicare queas, adeo ut "qui utramvis norit, ambas noverit"* [Terence]: *ita sunt non modo creatione et sanguinis nobilitate sorores, sed etiam stilo atque facundia. O civitatis, immo et aetatis nostrae decus! O "rara avis in terris nigroque simillima cygno!"* [Juvenal]. *Si superiora saecula hasce probandas creassent virgines, quantis versibus decantatae, quantas, modo non malignis scriptoribus, laudes assecutae immortalitati traditae fuissent. Penelopen quia optime texuit, Aragnen quia tenuissima fila deduxit, Camillam et Penthesileam quia bellatrices erant, poetarum carminibus consecratas cernimus; has tam pudicas, tam generosas, tam eruditas, tam eloquentes non colerent, in astra laudibus non eveherent, non ab oblivionis morsibus quavis ratione vendicarent et sempiterno donarent aevo?*'

16. There is a striking letter from Damiano Borgo to Isotta Nogarola describing how much changed Ginevra is for the worse since her marriage. The letter is preoccupied with virginity and defloration, and one can only take as the sense of the letter that Isotta's purity preserves for her a transcendent beauty which could not survive loss of virginity. Abel takes this quite naturally as an indication that Ginevra had lost her 'flair' for humanistic letters. See Abel, I, 261–7 for the letter, dated the last day of November 1440; Abel, I, xxxi-iii for Abel verdict on Ginevra's 'Fall'.

17. See Robathan, 'A fifteenth-century bluestocking', for some references to such compliments: Abel, I, 114, 125, 160, 180. Isotta also uses them of herself, for example, Abel, I, 256; I, 76.

18. *Leonardo Bruni . . . Schriften*, ed. Baron, 5–6. See below for a comparable letter from Politian to Cassandra Fedele, written in 1494, which opens with Virgil's *O decus Italiae virgo* (*Cassandrae Fidelis epistolae*, ed. Tomasinus, 155).

19. Guarino's noble pupil replied exactly as he knew he was expected to. He praised the two sisters' work in the same figurative terms as his master: *Hos igitur ingenii et studiorum fructus quos e duabus tuae civitatis virginibus collegisti collectosque ad me misisti non admirari non possum et summis prosequi laudibus eoque magis quod abs te, qui huiusce rei non negligendus testis es, mirum in modum probantur extollunturque . . . Illud equidem non parvi facio quod id mulierum genus etsi antea perrarum fuit, hoc tamen tempore perrarissimum esse consuevit*' (*Epistolario*, ed. Sabbadini, II 298).

20. R. Sabbadini, *Vita di Guarino Veronese* (Catania, 1896), 122.

21. Ibid., 126.

22. For Sabbadini's observations on the dating of this series of letters, as Abel presents it, see Sabbadini, 'Isotta Nogarola', 440.

23. '*Neque hoc mihi vitio dare, si tacendi leges mulieribus praesertim impositas praegressa sum illudque Vergerii praeceptum haud legisse videar, qui adolescentibus monet parum loqui proedesse, cum in multo sermone semper sit quod reprehendi possit. Et Sophocles quoque taciturnitatem in feminis singularem ornatum appellavit*' (Abel, I, 77: not in Sabbadini).

24. '"*Usa sum te nequiore meque magis haud respectus es quam si nunquam gnata essem. Per urbem enim irrideor, meus me ordo deridet, neutrobi habeo stabile stabulum, asini me mordicus scindunt, boves me incursant cornibus*"

[Plautus]. *Nam si ego hac contumelia digna eram maxime, tu tamen indignus qui faceres. Quodnam ob factum ita abs te contemnor, Guarine pater?'* (Abel, I, 80).

25. Abel, I, 79. Eventually Guarino replied at length, and rebuked Isotta for panicking. A strikingly similar incident occurs in the correspondence between Politian and Cassandra Fedele, see below.

26. On Borgo see Sabbadini, 'Briciole umanistiche', 250–1.

27. '*Volumus in eloquentia aspice Corneliam Grachorum matrem; Amesiam, quae Romano coram populo frequenti concursu prudentissima oratione causam dixit; Affraniam Lucinii Buconis senatoris coniugem, quae easdem causas in foro agitavit. Hortensia nonne hoc idem factitavit? Nonne Sapho mira carminis suavitate manavit? Portiam, Fanniam et reliquas quantis doctissimorum virorum versibus decantatas legimus? Volumus in bello aspice Camillam, quam Turnus, ut ait poeta, tanto honore prosequebatur. Nonne Thomiris regina Scytarum Cirum Persarum regem cum universo exercitu trucidavit, ut ne nuntius quidem tantae cladis superfuerit? Amazones nonne sine viris auxere rem publicam? Marpesia, Lampedo, Orithia maiorem partem Europae subiecerunt, nonnullas quoque sine viris Asiae civitates occupaverunt? Tantum enim virtute et singulari belli scientia pollebant, ut Herculi et Theseo impossibile videretur Amazonum arma regi suo afferre. Pantasilea bello Troiano inter fortissimos Graecos viriliter dimicavit; testis est poeta: "Pantasilea furens mediisque in milibus ardet"* [Virgil]. *Quod cum ita sit, te rogo, ut me certiorem reddas, si mulieres loquacitate vel potius eloquentia et virtute viros superent?'* (Abel, I, 256–7).

28. For a general discussion of the way in which Renaissance literature transformed the 'forward' woman into insatiate man-eater and indomitable shrew, see L. Jardine, *Still Harping on Daughters: Women and Drama in the Age of Shakespeare* (Brighton, 1983), ch. 4.

29. Justinus, *Epitome of Trogus*, I.8.

30. For the text of this invective see A. Segarizzi, 'Niccolo Barbo patrizio veneziano del sec. XV e le accuse contro Isotta Nogarola', *Giornale storico della letteratura italiana* 43 (1904), 39–54; 50–4. '*[Ea] que sibi tantam ex dicendi facultate laudem acquisierit, ea agat, que minime cum tanta eruditione et tanta sui existimatione conveniant, quamvis hoc a multis longe sapientissimis viris acceperim: nullam eloquentem esse castam, idque etiam multarum doctissimarum mulierum exemplo comprobari posse . . . Nisi vero hoc nimium sane tetrum atque obscenum scelus sit aliquantulum a te comprobatum quod ante quam corpus suum assiduis connubiis divulgaret primo fuerit passa atque etiam omnino voluerit virginitatis sue specimen non ab alio nisi a fratre eripi hocque modo vinclo propiore ligari. Proh deum atque hominum fidem, "quis celum terris non misceat et mare celo"* [Juvenal], *cum illa, que in tam spurcissima libidine modum sibi non inveniat, audeat se tantum in optimis literrarum studiis iactare'* (53). See also Jardine, op. cit., 57.

31. *De claris mulieribus*, transl. G. A. Guarino (New Brunswick, 1963), cit. Jardine, op. cit., 182.

32. *De claris mulieribus*, cit. Jardine, op. cit., 99.

33. The issue of female patrons is an interesting one, and ripe for investigation. Where women were accidentally in control of *wealth* (through quirks in inheritance law), there appears to have been considerable social encouragement for their directing that wealth towards culture rather than towards

power. On the unexpected prominence of noble women with charge of their own wealth in this period see Jardine, op. cit., ch. 3. On Mary Sidney, Countess of Pembroke, as exemplar of the wealthy woman directing that wealth to cultural manifestations of family power, see M. Brennan, *Aristocratic Patronage and Literature 1550–1650: The Herbert Family, Earls of Pembroke* (in press); M. E. Lamb, 'The Countess of Pembroke's patronage', *English Literary Renaissance* 12 (1982), 162–79.

34. W. L. Gundersheimer is mistaken in thinking that a patron like Eleonora of Aragon did not correspond with female humanists ('her surviving correspondence with nonrelatives is with men', *Beyond their Sex*, ed. Labalme, 56). Cassandra Fedele made a point of corresponding with a number of female heads of state, including Eleonora, and the letters received are to be found in Tomasinus' edition of her letters. See below.

35. Abel, II, 181; II, 96; II, 39; II, 105.

36. Id., II, 25.

37. Id., II, 23–7; 96–7; 98–100.

38. Id., II, 73–87.

39. Id., I, lvii.

40. Id., I lvii–lviii. Isotta Nogarola's one major published work was an epistolary dialogue between herself and Ludovico Foscarini entitled *De pari aut impari Evae atque Adae peccato* (a set-piece debate on whether Adam or Eve was the more culpable in the Fall). This, however, does not mean that the case for Isotta's later spirituality and asceticism is proven, since the letters of Heloise and Abelard provide an impeccable model for an exchange of letters between a senior man and a secluded woman strenuously debating the relative culpability of mankind and womankind. It is therefore an eminently suitable form for the single public appearance of the work of a female scholar otherwise debarred on grounds of decorum from public display of her intellectual virtuosity. Although the Renaissance *fortuna* of the Abelard and Heloise letters is cloudy, we do know that Petrarch owned a copy of the medieval 'canon' of their exchange. Abel takes it for granted (a) that the dialogue between Isotta and Ludovico testifies to the repressed passion between them and (b) that it represents the core of Isotta's later preoccupation with spiritual as opposed to secular learning. But it is just as appropriate to regard the exchange as a virtuoso exercise by an exceptionally talented woman, in a suitably 'literary' context. For a discussion of some of these problems of 'reading' the exchange between Heloise and Abelard, see P. Dronke, *Abelard and Heloise in Medieval Testimonies* (Glasgow, 1976); P. Dronke, 'Heloise and Marianne: some reconsiderations', *Romanische Forschungen* 72 (1960), 223–56; P. Dronke, *Women Writers of the Middle Ages; A Critical Study of Texts from Perpetua (†203) to Margaret Porete (†1310)* (Cambridge, 1984), ch. 5, 'Heloise'; M. M. McLaughlin, 'Peter Abelard and the dignity of women: twelfth-century "feminism" in theory and practice', in *Peter Abelard—Pierre le Vénérable, Colloques Internationaux du CNRS no. 546* (Paris, 1975). On Isotta Nogarola's dialogue, see P. Gothein, 'L'amicizia fra Lodovico Foscarini e l'umanista Isotta Nogarola', *La Rinascita* 6 (1943), 394–413. As well as describing some of the central arguments of the Adam and Eve dialogue and the further exchanges of letters between Isotta and Ludovico to be found in Abel, Gothein also provides a perfect example of how ready a traditional critic can be to read spirituality

and intense emotional involvement into every line of an exchange between a distinguished public man and a dependent secluded woman.

41. D. Robey, 'Vittorino da Feltre e Vergerio', in *Vittorino da Feltre e la sua scuola: umanesimo, pedagogia, arti*, ed. N. Giannetto (Florence, 1981), 241–53; 252.

42. Lauro Martines has been at particular pains to point out the close correlation between social rank and public prominence of the Florentine humanists. See Martines, *The Social World of the Florentine Humanists*, passim; L. Martines, *Power and Imagination: City-States in Renaissance Italy* (London, 1980), passim.

43. Martines, *Power and imagination*, 295.

44. Having looked at the careers of a number of other fifteenth-century educated women, including Cassandra Fedele and Laura Cereta (see below), it appears that all celebrated public performances by women humanists (orations before Emperors and prelates, disputations in the universities, invited lectures and so forth) are 'occasional' rather than professional. That is, an able woman might be afforded the unusual honour of a public appearance to 'show off' her talent, but it was on the strict understanding that this would not become a regular event. It is striking that we have not come across a single scholar, either of the fifteenth century or of the nineteenth or twentieth, who has suggested that any of these performances by exceptional women were other than outstanding (to us they seem competent but ordinary). *That* the woman performs is remarkable; *what* she performs is not the point. For Fedele's orations, see *Cassandrae Fidelis epistolae*, ed. Tomasinus. For Laura Cereta's formal pieces see *Laurae Ceretae Brixiensis feminae clarissimae epistolae . . .* ed. I. P. Tomasinus (Padua, 1640).

45. See King, 'Book-lined cells', for references to both Matteo Bosso's and Ludovico Foscarini's representations of Isotta Nogarola's study as a 'cell' (74).

46. G. Pesenti, 'Alessandra Scala: una figurina della rinascita fiorentina', *Giornale storico della letteratura italiana* 85 (1925), 241–67; 248; see also W. P. Greswell, *Memoirs of Angelus Politianus, Joannes Picus of Mirandula*, etc. (London, 1 805), 309.

47. Cassandra Fedele (*c.*1465–1558). Although this is the date of birth which stands in the standard works, it is clearly incorrect. G. Pesenti, in a footnote to his seminal article on Alessandra Scala, cites Cesira Cavazzana as responsible for suggesting 1465 as Fedele's birth date, and indicates that this is a correction for the even less plausible 1456: 'Cesira Cavazzana, *Cassandra Fedele, erudita veneziana del Rinascimento*, Venezia, 1906 (estr. dall' *Ateneo Veneto*). C'é chi crede che la F. nascesse nel 1456; ma la data più plausibile è il 1465; certa è invece la data della morte [1558]: cfr. ibid., 13 sg.' (G. Pesenti, 'Alessandra Scala: una figurina della rinascenza fiorentina', *Giornale storico della letteratura italiana* 85 (1925), 241–67; 248). In a letter of 1488, Eleonora of Aragon calls Cassandra 'femina adolescens'; she was regarded as extraordinarily precocious when she performed publicly in an oration and disputation in 1487. 1470 is a more plausible birth date. It still leaves her five years older than Alessandra Scala, who certainly treats Fedele as senior to her in their correspondence (Politian also refers pointedly to Fedele's seniority over Scala). See Pesenti, 'Alessandra Scala', 243, for similar comments on the implausibility of the birthdate of 1450 proposed in the earlier literature for Alessandra Scala (see below). For Fedele's extant works, see I. P. Tomasinus, *Clarissimae*

feminae Cassandrae Fidelis venetae epistolae et orationes . . . (Padua, 1636); Pesenti, 'Alessandra Scala' (fn. 1), 266–7 (transcription of an unpublished letter from Fedele to Pico, 1489). On Fedele, see most recently King, 'Book-lined cells'; Kristeller, 'Learned women', passim; see also C. Cavazzana, 'Cassandra Fedele, erudita veneziana del Rinascimento', *Ateneo Veneto* 29 (1906), 2: 73–91, 249–75; Greswell *Memoirs*, 135–6; Pesenti, 'Alessandra Scala', 248–52.

48. Pesenti, 'Alessandra Scala', 266–7. Politian mentions his close friend Pico in both his extant letters to Fedele.

49. *'Etsi ad te iamdiu scribere proposueram, tuis tamen divinis virtutibus pene deterrita, perceptis a multis et maxime a Lactantio Thedaldo ornatissimo tuarumque acerrimo praecone laudum, potius obmutescere destinaveram, quam parum luculenter et femine(e) admodum tuas perlibare virtutes. Sed postquam his proximis diebus ab optimo viro Salviato tuae ad me lucubrationes ornatae verborum sententiarumque copiosissimae delatae essent, quas cum saepius lectitassem, ex his tui ingenii dexteritatem ac singularem doctrinam cognovissem, a multis reprehendi posse verebar nisi pro mei viribus ingenioli tuas inauditas dotes celebrarem, quibus ut miraculum teneris, laudaris ac veneraris, praesertim tuo opere edito; cui quoniam insunt dilucida verba, sensus gravissimi, splendor, sublimitas interpretandi divina, omnia denique divinitus quadrant. [Nec mirum; nam in omni disciplinarum genere fulges ac splendes, virtutes ornas, homines ad litteras capessendas incendis, quin immo inflammas]'* (267).

50. See King, 'Book-lined cells', 69. For the text of this oration see *Cassandrae Fidelis epistolae*, ed. Tomasinus, 193–200.

51. The date is fixed by the account of the visit given by Politian to Lorenzo de' Medici in a letter written the following day. See below.

52. Just as Isotta Nogarola's fame was established in the humanist circle around Leonello d'Este at Ferrara by the exchange of letters between herself and Guarino. See above.

53. For the characterization of the Florentine humanists of this period as scholar-courtiers, see Martines, *The Social World of the Florentine Humanists*, 5–6.

54. *'Item*: visitai iersera quella Cassandra Fidele litterata, e salutai ec., per vostra parte. È cosa, Lorenzo, mirabile, nè meno in vulgare che in latino; discretissima, *et meis oculis etiam bella*. Partìmi stupito. Molto è vostra partigiana, e di Voi parla con tanta pratica, *quasi te intus et in cute norit*. Verrà un di in ogni modo a Firenze a vedervi; sicche apparecchiatevi a farli onore' (I. Del Lungo, *Prose volgari inedite e poesie latine e greche edite e inedite di Angelo Ambrogini Poliziano* (Florence, 1867), 81). '*Quasi te intus et in cute norit*' is surely only decorous as a courtierly comment.

55. E. Garin, 'L'ambiente del Poliziano', *Il Poliziano e suo tempo, atti del IV convegno internazionale di studi sul rinascimento* (Florence, 1957), 24; Garin, 'I cancellieri umanisti della repubblica fiorentina da Coluccio Salutati a Bartolomeo Scala', *Rivista storica italiana* 71 (1959), 204; cit. Martines, *The Social World of the Florentine Humanists*, 5–6.

56. Female heirs *substitute* for absent men; they do not hold power in their own right, and the male line is reinstated as soon as possible. See Jardine, *Still Harping on Daughters*, ch. 3.

57. See, for instance, Del Lungo's footnote against her name in the letter to Lorenzo quoted above.

58. *Aeneid* 11. 508–9.

59. If *O decus Italiae virgo* became a catch-phrase for a female representation of learning or chaste wisdom, that might explain the fact that Botticelli's 'Pallas and the Centaur' was known as 'Camilla' in the fifteenth century.

60. *Aeneid* 7. 803–17; 805–8. This passage is picked out by Auerbach as the acme of Virgilian 'sublime'—female valour sublimely idealized. E. Auerbach, *Literary Language and its Public in Late Latin Antiquity and in the Middle Ages*, transl. R. Manheim (London, 1965), 183–6.

61. '*Mira profecto fides, tales proficisci a femina (quid autem a femina dico?) imo vero a puella, et Virgine potuisse. Non igitur iam Musas, non Sibyllas, non Pythias obijciant vetusta nobis secula, non suas Pythagorei Philosophantes feminas, non Diotimam Socratici, nec Aspaciam, sed nec poetrias illas Graeca iactent monimenta, Telesillam, Corinnam, Sappho, Anyte(m), Erinnem, Praxiham, Cleobulinam, et caeteras: credamusque facile Romanis iam Laelij, et Hortensij filias, et Corneliam Gracorum matrem fuisse matronas quantumlibet eloquentissimas. Scimus hoc profecto scimus, nec eum sexum fuisse a natura tarditatis, aut hebetudinis damnatum'* (*Cassandrae Fidelis epistolae*, ed. Tomasinus, 155–6). Guarino's celebratory letter in praise of Isotta and Ginevra Nogarola which gave rise to the correspondence between himself and Isotta is similarly extravagant in invoking ancient prototypes of outstanding female accomplishment; see above. For further comment on the routineness of such clusters of 'exemplary' women in compliments to living women see Robathan, 'A fifteenth-century bluestocking', 106–11.

62. '*At vero aetate nostra, qua pauci quoq(ue) virorum caput altius in literis extulerunt, unicam te tamen existere puellam, quae pro lana librum, pro fuco calamum, stylum pro acu tractes, et quae non cutem cerussa, sed atramento papyrum linas*' (ibid.). See King, 'Book-lined cells', 76.

63. '*O, quis me igitur statim sistat istic, vt faciem virgo tuam castissimam contempler, vt habitum, cultum, gestumq(ue) mirer, vt dictata, instillata tibi a Musis tuis verba quasi sitientibus auribus perbibam, deniq[ue] vt afflatu instin(c)tuq(ue) tuo consum(m)atissimus repente Poeta euadam,*

    nec me carminibus vincat, aut Thracius Orpheus,
    aut Linus: huic mater quamvis, atque huic pater adsit,
    Orpheo Calliopea, Lino formosus Apollo. (Eclogues 4.55–7)'
    (*Cassandrae Fidelis epistolae*, ed. Tomasinus, 157).

64. For an interesting footnote on such 'becomings', see M. R. Lefkowitz, 'Patterns of women's lives in myth', in her *Heroines and Hysterics* (London, 1981), 41–7.

65. Just as Guarino's correspondence with Isotta Nogarola rated sufficiently low on *his* list of priorities for him also to overlook replying to her in good time. See above.

66. This is the same pattern as that followed in the exchange of letters between Guarino and Nogarola. Both women claim to have been publicly shamed by their male correspondent's prolonged silence, although undoubtedly such men habitually failed to reply to letters from less distinguished male colleagues. The shame is clearly *social*—the woman's overture if ignored is deemed forward. Later, in 1494, when she herself failed to answer a letter of Politian's promptly, Fedele wrote a humorous letter excusing her tardiness (*tibi debeo, ecce persoluo sero. tamen; sed melius sero quam nunquam*). *Cassandrae Fidelis epistolae*, ed. Tomasinus, 159–60.

67. *Aeneid* 3. 312–14.

68. It should be remarked that contrition was not a character trait in evidence anywhere else in Politian's public career aside from his studied dealings with female scholars; he was renowned for his ability to quarrel with other humanists, for example, with Alessandra Scala's father Bartolomeo and her future husband Marullus. On Politian's life, see F. O. Mencken, *Historia vitae et in literas meritorum Angeli Politiani* . . . (Lipsiae, 1736). On his relations with Bartolomeo Scala see A. Brown, *Bartolomeo Scala, 1430–1497, Chancellor of Florence: the Humanist as Bureaucrat* (Princeton, 1979), 211–19.

69. '*Hoc vesperi tuas accepi litteras querimoniae plenas et accusationis, quibus incertum me reddidisti tibine magis condoleam an mihi ipsi gratular. Nam cum tuum istud perspexisse viderer ingenium adiunctis doctrinae ornamentis insigne, te adeo virili animo et opinari et praedicare solebam, ut nihil accidere posset quod non forti et invicto ferres pectore. Nunc autem sic demissam abiectam et vere mulierem tete ostentas, ut nihil magnifico de te sensui meo respondere te cernam'* (*Epistolario di Guarino Veronese*, ed. Sabbadini, vol. II (Venice, 1916), 306–7).

70. There is, we think, a distinctly hollow ring to Guarino's protestations that Isotta's 'virility' of temperament precludes the possibility of attaching social blame to her actions. '*Cum enim intelligeres tuum in me pro litteraria inter nos necessitudine officium fecisse scriptis ad me tam suavibus tam ornatis tam laudatissimis litteris (nam sicut ex studiis arrogans esse non debes, ita bonorum tuorum aestimatrix non ingrata fias oportet) quid tibi obiectari potuit quod matronalem constantiam labefactaret?'* (ibid.)

71. '*Nam cum te olim domi visurus salutaturusque venissem, qua maxime causa profectus Venetias fueram, tuque te diutus* [sic] *expectanti habitu quodam pulchro pulcherrima ipsa quasi nympha mihi de silvis obtulisses, mox ornatis copiosisque verbis atque ut verissime dicam divinum quiddam sonantibus compellasses, ita mihi animus repente (quod te arbitror meminisse) miraculo illo tanto et rei novitate obstupuit, ut quod de se ait Aeneas, "raris tubatus vocibus hiscerem", vixque illud saltem meam tibi excusare infantiam potueram . . . Harum igitur imaginum plenus, atque hac undique rerum facie circumfusus, ut Florentiam sum reversus, litteras abs te mirificas accepi; quibus cum respondere saepius tentassem, nescio quo pacto digiti ipsi scribentes haesitabant, ipse de manibus calamus excidebat; nec enim subire impar certamen audebam, quasi magis mihi timendum crimen esset arrogantis et improbi, cum respondissem, quam desidis ac parum officiosi, cum tacuissem. Non igitur neglegentia factum est ut non rescripserim, sed verecundia, non contemptu, sed reverentia'* (G. B. Pesenti, 'Lettere inedite del Poliziano', *Athenaeum* 3 (1915), 284–304; 299–300).

72. Alessandra Scala (1475–1506). See Pesenti 'Alessandra Scala'. Pesenti's article is a good starting point for work on Scala, in spite of its thoroughgoing sentimentalizing of her relationships with all the men among her colleagues and tutors. Naturally all men become Scala's suitors in Pesenti's reconstruction of her life.

73. An ostentatious display of learning on her father's part. He, according to Pesenti, knew no Greek. This performance also provided the occasion for Politian's first Greek epigram addressed to Alessandra Scala. See below.

74. '*Sed revertor ad Alexandram. Dies ea noctesque in studiis utriusque linguae versatur. Ac superioribus diebus, cum graeca tragoedia Sophoclis in ipsius paternis aedibus maximo doctorum conventu virorum exhiberetur . . . ipsa Electrae*

79

virginis virgo suscepit, in qua tantum vel ingenii vel artis vel gratiae adhibuit, ut omnium in se oculos atque animas una converteret. Erat in verbis lepos ille atticus prorsus genuinus et nativus, gestus ubique ita promptus et efficax ita argumento serviens, ita per affectus varios decurrens, ut multa inde veritas et fides fictae diu fabulae accederet. Nec tamen Electrae sic meminit ut Alexandrae sit oblita. Verecunde omnia et pudenter, non modo ad terram demissis sed pene in terram semper defixis oculis: sentire illam diceres quid ludiae alicui et mimae, quid ingenuae rursus ac virgini conveniret; nam cum scaenae satisfaceret nihil de scaena tamen sumebat, quasi non cuilibet, sed doctis tantummodo et probis ederet gestum' (Pesenti, 'Lettere inedite', 300–1).

75. For the epigram see *Poliziano: Epigrammi greci*, ed. A. Ardizzoni (Florence, 1951; reprinted in A. Politianus, *Opera omnia*, Turin, 1970), 20 (Italian transl., 56): 'When the girl Alessandra took the part of Electra, she, virgin, the Sophoclean virgin girl, all were struck with utter amazement . . .'

76. Quentin Skinner has suggested to us that in their somewhat bizarre insistence on the virginity of the women humanists, the male humanists are 'doing the best that their moral vocabulary allowed them' by way of praising their *virtus*—for which chastity is the strict female equivalent. *Virtus*, the supposed product of the *studia humanitatis*, is a quality of a *vir*; in substituting the more appropriately female 'chastity' in the case of a woman we have gender creating a clear case of textual difficulty.

77. *'Sola igitur nunc in ore omnibus apud nos Alexandra Scala, hoc est florentina Electra, digna nimirum puella quam tu, doctissima Cassandra, sororem voces, utpote quae sola omnium nostra aetate, non dicam tecum contendat, sed tuis certe vestigiis insistat'* (Pesenti, 'Lettere inedite', 301).

78. Guarino encouraged a correspondence between Isotta Nogarola and Costanza Varano, as Politian does one between Fedele and Scala, thus actually effecting a kind of merging of the female scholars into a composite figure of intellectual 'worth', Similarly, women humanists exchanged complimentary letters with women in positions of civic prominence or power (confirming their mutual 'worth'). Fedele corresponded with Queen Isabella of Spain (*Cassandrae Fidelis epistolae*, ed. Tomasinus, letters 11 (Cassandra to Isabella, n.d.), 12 (Isabella to Cassandra, 1488), 13 (Cassandra to Isabella, 1487), 60 (Cassandra to Isabella, 1492), 66 (Cassandra to Isabella, 1495)); with Beatrice, Queen of Hungary (sister of Eleonora of Aragon and d'Este) (letters 21, 1488; 71, 1497; 78, n.d.); with Beatrice Sforza (letter 57 (Cassandra to Beatrice, n.d.), 58 (Beatrice to Cassandra, 1493)); and with Beatrice Sforza's mother, Eleonora of Aragon, Duchess of Ferrara, letter 105 (Eleonora to Cassandra, 1488). All these women were notable patrons of the arts, and Fedele presumably approached them with an eye to possible patronage (she was invited to Spain in 1488). Kristeller comments that on the whole patronage was sought for *vernacular* works from these female patrons. See Kristeller, 'Learned women', 93–4.

79. *Epistolario di Guarino Verones*, ed. Sabbadini, II, 293–4. Guarino used this same passage from the *De officiis* in his complimentary letter to Varano (see R. Sabbadini, *Vita di Guarino Veronese* (Catania, 1896; reprinted in *Guariniana*, ed. M. Sancipriano, Turin, 1964), 157–8).

80. See above.

81. See above, and King, 'Religious retreat' and 'Book-lined cells'.

82. A point regularly made in favour of education of girls by Erasmus and More.

See, for example, More's letter to his daughter Margaret: '*Quaeso te, Margareta, fac de studiis vestris quid fit intelligam. Nam ego potius quam meos patiar inertia torpescere, profecto cum aliguo fortunarum mearum dispendio valedicens aliis curis ac negociis, intendam liberis meis et familiae*' ('I beg you, Margaret, tell me about the progress you are all making in your studies. For I assure you that, rather than allow my children to be idle and slothful, I would make a sacrifice of wealth, and bid adieu to other cares and business, to attend to my children and my family'. *The Correspondence of Sir Thomas More*, ed. E. F. Rogers (Princeton, 1947), letter 69 (134), transl. E. F. Rogers, *St. Thomas More: Selected Letters* (New Haven and London, 1961), 109. More makes the explicit point, in writing to Margaret after her marriage, that her learning is intended for *no other audience* than her father and her husband: '*Sed tu, Margareta dulcissima, longe magis eo nomine laudanda es, quod quum solidam laboris tui laudem sperare non potes, nihilo tamen minus pergis cum egregia ista virtute tua cultiores literas et bonarum artium studia coniungere; et conscientiae tuae fructu et voluptate contenta, a populo famam pro tua modestia nec aucuperis nec oblatam libenter velis amplecti, sed pro eximia pietate qua nos prosequeris satis amplum frequensque legenti tibi theatrum simus, maritus tuus et ego*' (But, my sweetest Margaret, you are all the more deserving of praise on this account. Although you cannot hope for an adequate reward for your labour, yet nevertheless you continue to unite to your singular love of virtue the pursuit of literature and art. Content with the profit and pleasure of your conscience, in your modesty you do not seek for the praise of the public, nor value it overmuch even if you receive it, but because of the great love you bear us, you regard us—your husband and myself—as a sufficiently large circle of readers for all that you write). Rogers, *Correspondence*, letter 128 (302), transl. Rogers, *St. Thomas More*, 155.

83. Ardizzoni, *Epigrammi greci*, epigram XXXII (22) (Italian transl. 58).
84. A number of humanists wrote Greek 'love' poems addressed to Alessandra. One of them, Marullus, eventually married her.

The Housewife and the Humanists

Lorna Hutson

THE ABSENT DOMESTIC WOMAN

In 1541 Miles Coverdale published an English translation of the humanist Heinrich Bullinger's guide to matrimony, *Der Christlich Eestand* (1540). It was to be, in English, an extremely influential text. It went through nine editions by 1575 and was the model for subsequent treatments of the subject.[1] As early as 1543, Thomas Becon had reissued Coverdale's translation under his own name, with the addition of an elaborate preface, imitative of Erasmus' *Encomium Matrimonii*, included 'for the more readie sale'. In 1591, the preacher Henry Smith remarketed it under his name, with a dedication to Lord Burghley. A most popular manual of the seventeenth century, John Dod and Robert Cleaver's *A Godlie Forme of Householde Government* (1610) 'used whole paragraphs at a time' of Coverdale's Bullinger, and the metaphors of the latter 'crop up again and again' in other guides to marriage.[2]

Chapter 19 of Coverdale's Bullinger, entitled, 'Of Covenient Carefulnes and just keping of the house lyke Christen folke' offers what seems to us a predictable enough division of conjugal labour:

What so ever is to be done without the house, that belongeth to the man & the woman to studye for thinges within to be done, and to se saved or spent conveniently whatsoever he bringeth in. As the bird fleeth to and fro to bring to the nest, so becommeth it the man to apply his outward busines, And as the damme kepeth the nest, hatcheth the egges, & bringeth forth the frute, so let them both lern to do of the unreasonable fowles or bestes created of God naturally to observe theyr sondrye propertyes.[3]

Extract from 'The Housewife and the Humanist', in *The Usurer's Daughter* (Routledge, 1994). © Lorna Hutson. Reprinted with permission.

There is, as John Winkler remarked in another context, 'a *lot* of culture packed into this one exemplum from nature'.[4] By the time of Dod and Cleaver's *Godlie Forme of Household Government*, the formula had been enlarged and improved:

This is also a Dutie (not to bee forgotten) Namely, that Husbands be diligent and Carefull to make provision for their Houses . . . The dutie of the Husband is to get goods: and of the Wife to gather them together, and save them. The dutie of the Husband is to travell abroad, to seeke living: and the Wives dutie is to keepe the house. The dutie of the Husband is to get money and provision: and of the Wives, not vainely to spend it. The dutie of the Husband is to deale with many men: and of the Wives to talke with few. The dutie of the Husband is, to be entermedling: and of the wife, to be solitary and withdrawne. The dutie of the man is, to be skilfull in talke: and of the wife, to boast of silence. The dutie of the husband is to be a giver, and of the Wife, to be a saver. The dutie of the Man is, to Apparell himselfe as he may: and of the Woman, as it becommeth her. The dutie of the husband is, to dispatch all things without dore: and of the wife, to oversee and give order for all things within the house.[5]

So striking is the symmetry of the Dod and Cleaver formulation, that, in her influential article surveying sixteenth- and seventeenth-century guides to marriage, the social historian Kathleen Davies reproduced it in the form of a binary scheme:

Husband	*Wife*
Get goods	Gather them together and save them
Travel, seek a living	Keep the house
Get money and provisions	Do not vainly spend it
Deal with many men	Talk with few
Be 'entermedling'	Be solitary and withdrawn
Be skilful in talk	Boast of silence
Be a giver	Be a saver
Apparel yourself as you may	Apparel yourself as it becomes you
Be Lord of all	Give account of all
Dispatch all things outdoor	Oversee and give order within.[6]

Yet there is, for all its predictability, a puzzle about the very symmetry of this formulation of conjugal interdependence. It is, simply, too symmetrical to be anything other than a fiction. Nancy Armstrong, contrasting Davies' schematization of Dod and Cleaver with the discursively amplified role of the 'domestic woman' in eighteenth-century household literature, observes that the seventeenth-century model articulates only one gender: 'the Puritan household consisted of a male and female who were structurally identical, positive and negative versions of the attributes.[7] Catherine Belsey, likewise, finds a contradiction between Dod and Cleaver's explicit delineation of spheres of responsibility (outdoors for husband, indoors for wife) and the actual allocation of responsibilities that would, in practice, make the household the woman's sphere:

> The husband's responsibilities occupy twenty-nine pages and the wife's, with some repetition, rather less than two. In essence, the wife's responsibilities are to provide a visible model of submission, and not to get in the way, unless her husband is absent . . . the attempt to find a place of authority for the wife results in the renewed insistence on her submission. She is subsumed under the will of her husband . . . a woman is to govern and not to govern, present as example . . . but absent from the place where decisions are made.[8]

The division comes to appear very nearly meaningless: the husband occupies both spheres after all, is both 'indoors' and 'outdoors' all at once, negotiating in the marketplace, and governing the godly household. The woman, as good wife, is merely the example of his ability to govern.

What, then, made this 'natural history' of the conjugal household—the model of husband as hunter-gatherer, and the wife as saver and keeper—so indispensable to humanist moral philosophy? Its provenance is not far to seek: the exemplum as Bullinger uses it derives from a text entitled *Oeconomicus*, written by the Socratian philosopher Xenophon, and from its derivative, a pseudo-Aristotelian text of the same name, but inferior composition.[9] So popular was the Xenophonic formulation with the northern humanists that it inevitably makes an appearance whenever matters pertaining to the household or to women are being discussed in a humanist text of moral philosophy. Thus, in Richard Hyrde's translation of Vives' *Instruccion of a Christen Woman*, the section on 'shamefastness' requires that women should be sober and sparing in their diet, since the cultivation of habits of thrift,

> 'be in householdyng the womans party as Plato and Aristotle say full well. The man getteth, the woman saveth and kepeth. Therfore he hath stomake gyven him to gether lustily & she hath hit taken from her, that she may warely kepe.'[10]

The division of household labour according to the 'natural' properties of the sexes ('stomach' meaning courage or boldness in hunting) in turn dictates their natural properties in other contexts (the man's courageous 'stomach' legitimating his stomach in its other sense as appetite for food and sex).

Versions of Xenophon's natural history of the division of household labour according to the scheme of husband 'outdoors' and wife 'indoors' seem, then, to have been relevant to the humanist project in a variety of ways. What made the model so compelling? Nothing, surely, to do with the the production of a sphere of influence for the 'wife'. For the cultural significance of this natural history concerns men: its function in the sixteenth century was not to legitimate a new version of femininity, but a new version of masculinity. The point of it was not, primarily, to guarantee *in reality* the husband's governance of his wife, but to prove, through a persuasive fiction of the well-governed wife, the legitimate and responsible contribution of a Christian humanist education to the secular and practical spheres of masculine activity. For it was only through the definition of conjugal femininity as the symbolic boundary of 'good husbandry' (the displaced marker of the husband's accountability as head of the household) that good husbandry could come to claim as its sphere nothing less than 'out of bounds-ness' itself—the time/space of opportunity, both for negotiation and for the production of rhetorically persuasive fictions.

XENOPHON'S SUCCESSFUL DISAPPEARING ACT: HOUSEKEEPING LITERATURE AND THE 'BANALITY' OF ECONOMICS

It is actually an effect of the persistence of a hierarchy of values which conforms to that established by Xenophon's gendered division of economic labour that the cultural centrality of an ostensibly gynaecological text (Xenophon's *Oeconomicus*), and its seventeenth-century 'marriage guidance' derivatives has not been taken seriously by critics and historians of change in economic thought. Thus, in a careful and sceptical critique of claims made for the originality of Aristotle's economic thinking, M. I. Finley dismisses in passing the contribution of that second-rate thinker, Xenophon, arguing that although 'the model that survived and was imitated was Xenophon's *Oikonomikos*' yet, 'it was not from *Hausvaterliteratur* that modern economic thinking arose'.[11] For rather different reasons, Kathleen Davies in her article on English *Hausvaterliteratur* or books of 'the art of household', likewise devalues the genre, refusing to allow it any creative cultural force. Davies is, of course, concerned to refute the argument that the Protestant, or, as it is misleadingly called, 'Puritan' doctrine of marriage was liberal in its effects on the position of women in society. In demonstrating the doctrine's far from liberal implications, however, she makes the mistake of underestimating its novelty and prescriptive force, and this is simply because she, like Finley, has been duped by the hierarchizing rhetoric of a gendered division of economic labour which manages, by associating economic prudence with the penny-pinching of good housewives, to make the topic of thrift seem familiar and beneath our notice. The household order prescribed by Dod and Cleaver is, Davies decides 'in fact a picture of a household built on the firm economic base of bourgeois endeavour, whether of the fourteenth, fifteenth or sixteenth centuries'. Marriage guidance literature is, therefore 'a collection of descriptive rather than prescriptive texts, written by authors who were not advocating new ideals for marriage but were describing the best form of bourgeois marriage as they knew it'.[12] Davies can decide that the sixteenth-century humanistic texts derived from Xenophon and pseudo-Aristotle are no different from English fifteenth-century antecedents untouched by Xenophonic influence because she has already dismissed the practical economic advice contained in the humanistic household literature as familiar and unnecessary:

Many of the more peripheral characteristics assumed to be peculiar to Puritan writings on marriage are also to be found in earlier works. Careful prudence and foresight are common features of both; Whytforde's advice to householders to keep a year's rent or income in store 'for chances' is an example of capitalistic caution, and his remedy for poverty—to spend less—is typical of the rather banal quality of the advice offered by all these conduct book writers . . . Vives, too, was much exercised about the prudent governing of the house-hold . . . the sobriety and prudence described in Roper's *Life* of More are very like the characteristics advised by Bullinger as a means to material prosperity.[13]

And yet, if Vives and Whitford (the latter was, like the former, a humanist and a friend of More and Erasmus) were so concerned about thrift and prudence, would it not be as logical to assume that this is in itself a sign that their texts were not *descriptive* of existing practices, but advocative of practices currently ignored, undervalued or even actively disdained by their readers? It would seem that the humanists valued the moral philosophy of the ancient world for its provision of exemplary authority for the changes in social practice they advocated. Citing the proverb, 'the steppe of the husbande maketh the fatte donghyll', Whitford is drawing on the pseudo-Aristotelian *Economics*, a text which, as Josef Soudek has shown, was widely read between 1420 and 1520 in Leonardo Bruni's humanistic Latin translation.[14] It is a mistake, moreover, to assume that the readership at whom the humanists aimed this literature was confined to the 'bourgeois' householders imagined by Davies. Erasmus recommended the reading of the Aristotelian *Economics* to the duke to whom he dedicated his *Apophthegmata*; Lawrence Humphrey argued in his *Of Nobilitye*, that 'It behoveth also, a Noble man bee skild in house Phylosophie: and be not ignoraunte, in governmente of housholde. Thereof wrate *Xenophon*, and *Aristotle*. Whiche also *Paule* touched, wrytynge to the *Ephesians*.' Leonardo Bruni dedicated his translation of the Aristotelian *Economics* to Cosimo de Medici for, 'to whom else can advice more appropriately be given than to one who owns ample means and desires to preserve them with praise and to increase them with dignity?', while Johannes Herrold, translator of Erasmus, dignified his gift of one such translation to George and Anna Fugger by associating it with the household philosophy of Aristotle and Xenophon.[15]

It is furthermore wrong to assume that 'example[s] of capitalistic caution' typical of householding texts, were already 'banal' to sixteenth-century readers. Indeed, Whitford's advice to have a year's rent in store for chances is *immediately* qualified by reassurance to the reader that such prudence 'is nat contrary unto christianyte, where extreme or very strayte nede is nat perceyved in the neighbour.' Clearly, as Whitford affirms elsewhere, it was more usual to regard surplus in prosperity as bound, both for reasons of charity and in guarantee of future friendship, to be extended to neighbours rather than stored against mischance, for 'thou canst have none so sure castel or garde of thy lyfe: as is love and frendshyppe of thy neyghboure.'[16] One of the great ideological conflicts of Northern Europe in the sixteenth-century—the conflict over credit extension to friends and neighbours, and the legitimacy of exacting interest payments as assurance for the honouring of debts—may be invoked briefly here to demonstrate just how far from 'banal' were the issues raised by the householding texts in terms of the beliefs and practices of their sixteenth-century readers.

It is common knowledge that, as the business operations of northern European merchants expanded during the fifteenth and sixteenth centuries, so they became more reliant on systems of credit which would ensure the honouring of assurances of their wealth at a temporal and geographical distance.[17] In the second half of the fifteenth century, Antwerp overtook Bruges as a business centre. Antwerp's quarterly markets enabled an unprecedented year-round liquidation of debts and credits; previously the end of a fair had marked the ritual closing of exchange, and required the settling of all accounts. As a result of the year-round liquidity of transaction, Antwerp became a centre for the permanent establishment of foreign exchanges, places where 'bills of exchange' might be drawn on reserves held abroad.[18] A practical merchants' guide to account-keeping, translated into English in 1547, makes the Antwerp exchange analagous to what

we in England . . . use in Markettes, [where] there are Goldsmithes which either if we have money will take it to the Market and make a bill to paie it againe at London or where ye will to have it paied, or els will lend you so much in the Market, and take your bill to be paied againe at London or els where, for a reasonable profite'.[19]

There was however, as the same writer notes, a great deal of ideological opposition to this unprecedented increase in the incidence of transferable, profit-making credit relations between men. 'Marchantes who deliver their money by exchange are called usurers and worse then infidels', he wrote, by an 'ignorant and rude sort of people' who 'neyther knowe what exchange is, neither yet how necessary . . . it is for the Marchant, that like as a ship cannot passe the seas without saile and rudder, no more can the marchaunt travaile Countrees without exchange'.[20] If the voice of the non-mercantile population—which this author dismissed as 'ignorant and rude' was one source of opposition, another was the voice of scholastic theology: canon law prohibited as usurious any gain made over the mere principal in any credit transaction. In England in 1487, a statute was passed against so-called 'dry exchange'—considered to be a mere cover for usury—and in 1531 Thomas Cromwell revived a proclamation to forbid exchanges and rechanges; a letter from Richard Gresham (father of Thomas Gresham) to Thomas Cromwell dated July 1538 protests against the measure on the grounds that the prohibition of exchange tends to result in the exporting of specie:

there is diverse merchants that will shortly prepare th[emselves] towards Borduus for provision of wines, and f[or lacke of] exchanges I do suppose that there will be some convey[ance] of gold amongst them. I am sure, my Lord, that such exchanges and rechanges do much to the stay of the said gold in England, which would else be conveyed [away].[21]

The issue of credit in commercial relations, of which foreign exchange was one aspect, remained in dispute. Despite the credit crisis and the high incidence of bankruptcy in London in the 1560s, conscience prevailed against the legalization of interest in the Parliament of 1571.[22]

If we want evidence of how both popular and theological opposition hindered capitalistic enterprise outside England, we have only to look at the fortunes of the Fuggers in Germany. Lyndal Roper has explained how, in his declining years, Anton Fugger took to consulting a female sorcerer, a crystal ball gazer. Roper deduces from this that Fugger himself was not immune to the feelings of ambivalence with which people of sixteenth-century Augsburg regarded the pursuit of wealth in general, and the activities of merchant capitalists in particular:

For sixteenth-century people, wealth was a malignant force. People got rich only by making others poorer. Only by finding treasure . . . could one become harmlessly rich. Within the city [of Augsburg], wealth was inherently limited, goods were finite and the crucial economic issue was perceived as being the *division* of resources, not the creation of wealth. When Augsburg craftsmen of the 1560s diagnosed the city's ills they laid the blame at the door of newcomers, people who clogged up the crafts . . . But popular opinion might also . . . identify the wealthy capitalists as the source of the problem, because they had cornered supplies and taken an unfair share . . . In the weaving industry, the town's foremost employment . . . guild protectionism won the day in a triumph of the belief that wealth was finite and that the common good ought to take precedence over individual gain.[23]

Earlier in the century, the Fugger enterprise had felt the force of opposition in the form of the canon law prohibition on interest-bearing loans. In 1515 the magnate Jacob Fugger paid the expenses of the Ingolstadt Professor Johann Eck to go to Bologna to hold a disputation on the practice of collecting interest. At issue, as the historian Heiko Oberman writes,

was the legitimacy of profit-making commerce with capital, a practice long accepted in international banking and financial circles but still encountering organised resistance in Germany, especially among humanists. Thus the practice urgently needed the protective rationale of a new theology of capital. A new interpretation of the church's prohibition of usury was required, an interpretation that would permit smooth financing of investments, especially the rapidly expanding long-distance commerce, without the restrictive overhead of a guilty conscience.[24]

Although Eck and others attempted to shift discussion from a canon law question of permissibility (centring on the prohibition stipulated in Deuteronomy 23 : 20 and Luke 6 : 35, and theoretically supported by the Aristotelian conception of money as sterile) towards one of pastoral care (the magisterial discrimination between honest and dishonest exactions of interest), debates in Germany, France and England over the legitimacy of interest were to go on for another fifty years.[25]

Ideological battles are never fought, however, upon a single front, still less upon a single front which is also legislative. Norman Jones, in his study of the usury debate in England, opens with the observation that, whereas the 1571 Parliamentary discussion of usury was dominated by the idea of God, the Parliamentary debate which legalized interest-bearing loans in 1624 treated the issue as purely economic, a purely secular matter.[26] Evidently, the battle had already been fought elsewhere. The question is, where?

One answer for England might be the conceptual space created, in the circulation of economic projects involving the utilization of interest-bearing loans, by such formulae as 'every man is rather borne to profit his . . . common weale, in revealynge . . . hidden treasure . . . then to seeke after his owne private gaine' or the Ciceronian equivalent, 'nihil est utile, quod non sit honestum' ('nothing is expedient or profitable which is not honest').[27] The latter, taken from Cicero's *De Officiis*, implies the former, for the *De Officiis* is, itself, a sustained philosophical inquiry into the possibility of reconciling, in any situation, the pursuit of what is expedient or profitable (*utilis*) with the pursuit of what is morally right (*honestus*). As the practical value of any moral virtue depends on its being appropriate or fitting (*decorus*) to the contigencies of time and place (*occasio*), the only rule of thumb that Cicero can offer for instant recognition of a clash between the demands of the expedient and the morally honest is the rule of 'common' before 'private weal', the dictum that a man should never pursue his private good at the expense of the whole community.[28] 'The selfe same profyte that is of every private persone is commen profyte', one sixteenth-century translation ran, 'whiche profyte if any man plucke to hym selfe all comforte is dissolved a sondre . . . in lyke manner it is ordayned that it shulde not be lawfull for any man to hurt an other bycause of his private welthe'.[29] As wealth was conceived as finite, and bargaining a struggle for advantage in the disposition of finite resources, we would expect Cicero's representation of *utilitas* or 'profit', even before its philosophical reconciliation with the pursuit of *honestas*, to be ethically circumscribed, dissociated from the pure pragmatics of the marketplace. And, as we expect, the ethical circumscription of the pursuit of material gain takes the form of its translation into an art of household provision, for instruction in which Cicero refers the reader to Xenophon:

But a mannes substance muste bee gotten, by those thinges, which be farre from dishonestye: and must be saved by diligence, and honest sparinge: and by those same meanes also, it must be encreased. Xenophon the Socratian hathe gone throroughe these thynges very handsomely in that booke which is intituled Economicus: the which we tourned oute of Greeke into latine when we were the same age in a maner, as you are nowe.[30]

Xenophon turns up everywhere. And yet historians of economic and social thought continue to dismiss the efficacy of his text, to deny that it made, through its humanistic revival, a conceptual space for changes in practice. This, as I suggested before, is a measure of the success of the text's complex strategy of simultaneously elevating and deprecat-ing the element of prudential *calculation* which is practically all that the ancient sense of *oikonomia* has in common with the present-day sense in which 'economics' is a science. That Davies and Finley can so easily dismiss the much imitated Xenophonic model in spite, or perhaps because, of the frequency of its imitation attests to the partic-ular importance of its self-effacement, or self-displacement. For what the humanists perceived to be the value of Xenophon's text was pre-cisely its capacity to offer pragmatic counsel in the prudential and cal-culating conduct of household affairs in the form of a rhetorical fiction which displaced the ethical stigma of the calculating outlook from the centre to the periphery of the text: from the governing husband to the governed wife. We may cite an article exploring issues in the history of economic thought, published in 1958, for evidence of the enduring power of Xenophon's rhetoric in this respect. The author argues that historians have been mistaken in seeking the origins of economic thought in the utilitarian figment known as 'Economic Man':

Is it not rather in the *mulier economica* in whom we have to recognize the ancestress of those peculiar frames of mind which modern economists have been rashly disposed to regard as the birthright of Economic Man in general or as the offspring of the spirit of capitalism? Commerce and trade have been in ancient Greece too deeply intertwined with warfare . . . to be suspect of fos-tering a spirit of thriftiness . . . Such propensities are much more likely to arise in the interior of the house and as an object of womanly worries. From the stone age onwards, man's proper attitude towards wealth has been a tendency to spend generously . . . Women, on the other hand, by inborn feelings driven to provide food for hungry mouths of children, were bound early to learn not to rely too confidently on what their male partners may, or may not, bring home from their sylvan hunting excursions. They must have developed a much stronger propensity to think in terms of scarce means; of distribution according to needs; and of provision for an uncertain future by economising and thriftiness. It is significant that even in the fourth century B.C. Xenophon, keeping an elegant and uncertain balance between the aristocratic tradition of *insouciance* and nascent utilitarianism, allows his Isomachus, a model gentleman (kalokagathos) to leave the spending department of his oikonomia entirely to his wife, after having educated her.[31]

Xenophon may have been a second-rate philosopher but he was, as Philip Sidney pointed out, a first-rate composer of persuasive fictions. In the final section of this chapter, I shall examine some of the ways in which the rhetorical emplotment of the *Oeconomicus* was imitated in humanist texts whose influence in the spheres of economic, social or cultural history cannot be denied. Before I go on to do that, however, I want to look at the form of Xenophon's text itself.

ECONOMICS AS EXEMPLARITY: XENOPHON'S RHETORIC OF HUSBANDRY

Xenophon's *Oeconomicus* was a text that lent itself, as M. I. Finley noted, to imitation. Cicero, recommending it to his son in the *De Officiis*, linked the practical instructiveness of the text with the eloquence that moved him to turn it from Greek into Latin. The cultural significance of Xenophon's art of household, then, is bound up with the exemplarity of its textual ordering. It follows that any exploration of the 'influence' of Xenophon on social thought or practice is also a case study of the extent to which such practical and social knowledge bears the imprint of the rhetorical medium in which it is conveyed.

Sixteenth-century humanism was, in its pedagogical manifestation, associated with an activity of reading which Victoria Kahn has called 'a practice of examples, or an exemplary practice'.[32] The faculty of interpretation, or skill in understanding the meaning of a text was tied in with the exercise of the reader's judgement and invention in the selection and transformation of elements of the text into *exempla* applicable to future occasions for the production of persuasive discourse. Thus, as Terence Cave writes, this exemplary practice of reading, the principles of which are supremely expressed in Erasmus' *De Copia*, 'constitutes a major episode in the history of imitation theory' by means of which

the activities of reading and writing become virtually identified. A text is read in view of its transcription as part of another text; conversely, the writer as imitator concedes that he cannot entirely escape the constraints of what he has read. In this respect, imitation is also germane to interpretation, since the interpretative act can only become visible in a second discourse which claims to be a reconstitution of the first.[33]

Some texts, of course, are more 'exemplary', richer in imitative potential than others, because, as Kahn explains, they educate the reader's judgement in the faculty of *decorum*, that is, the art of knowing where and when and how a certain example might be appropriately adapted. Decorum is both a textual and a life skill; a facility in the persuasive structuring of discourse, and a practical capacity for the discovery of resources for action within the contingencies of a particular occasion. So Cicero notes in the *De Officiis* that for poets to observe decorum is to achieve persuasive verisimilitude, while in moral philosophy, decorum, linked to the art of good timing, becomes identical to the strategic virtue of prudence.[34] Texts that enable the reader's sense of decorum, by offering a model of the invention and disposition of examples to greatest persuasive effect within the discourse, might be said to embody an 'economic' or generative principle within an aesthetics which thus values form as potentially transformative, and identifies knowledge with the future uses of imitation. Xenophon's might be said to be one such text, and the science of 'husbandry' that it disclosed to the understanding of a humanist scholar might therefore seem to contribute as much to an identification of masculine power with the economics of using and ordering a discourse, or the contingencies of a particular situation, as with that of using and ordering a wife and household.

We can follow the moves of Xenophon's text as they appeared to a sixteenth-century reader if we use an English translation made in 1534 (and frequently reissued) by the French humanist Gentian Hervet, at the request of Geoffrey Pole, brother to Reginald.[35] Hervet had been one of Thomas Lupset's pupils at Corpus Christi before becoming a tutor in the Pole household, so it may be that the translation published under his name was one to which Thomas Lupset refers, in his *Exhortacion to yonge men* (1531), as being by himself.[36] Whatever the case, it seems certain that there was an interest being taken in this text by a group of humanists connected both with the Pole household and with Erasmus.[37] Indeed, Hervet's translation opens with a note to the reader praising Xenophon 'for his swete eloquence' which caused him to be 'surnamed *Musa Attica*, that is to say, the songe of Athens'; the phrase renders a tribute to Xenophon made by Erasmus in a footnote to his edition of Cicero's *De Senectute*.[38]

Xenophon's text opens with Socrates and Critobolus engaged in an attempt to define the 'art of household' or *oikonomia*. 'I harde', Hervet's translation begins, 'vpon a time the wyse Socrates commone of the ordring of an house.'[39] In the ensuing dialogue, Socrates engages Critobolus in dispute as to whether the art of 'household' (*oikonomia*) is a kind of knowledge (*epistēmēs tinos onoma*—translated by Hervet as 'the name of a science') such as medicine or carpentry. Critobolus affirms that it is, but Socrates problematizes this too facile answer by probing the definition of 'house' and 'household'. Both agree that a man's 'house' means more than the physical enclosure of his possessions within one fixed space; 'a mans house' (*oikos*) they decide must extend to all 'that a man hath' (sig. A2^v). This is already an interesting argumentative move, for it means that the science of ordering one's 'house' will henceforward be taken to include strategies to maximize the advantages, or transform into 'goods and substance' contingencies that contribute to one's well-being but are beyond the sphere of the 'household' in a physical sense. So indeed, Socrates tests Critobolus by asking him if enemies which a man might 'possess' are therefore to be included in his house, as being 'goods' and 'substance'? Critobolus demurs, but Socrates proves that whatever is possessed is defined as a 'good' not by any intrinsic quality, but by whether or not its possessor knows how to 'use and order' (*chrēsthai*) it to advantage. So the man who knows how to profit by his enemies may indeed call them 'goods and substance': 'it is a point than of a good husband, and a good order of an house, to haue a waye, to vse his enemies too, that he may get some profit by them' (sigs A4^{r-v}). The art to 'use and order' is thus fundamental to the definition of *oikonomia*, or 'household' as a kind of knowledge, and that kind of knowledge bears a startling resemblance to what we would define as 'economy' in a liberal sense, such as when we speak of the 'economy' of a well-made artefact, or of a text. *Oikonomia* is thus the science which defines itself as the effective use of the possession (*oikos*).

The next phase of the dialogue concerns the exemplarity of the knowledge called *oikonomia*: it is a skill attained by example and practice, not subject to theoretical transmission. So Socrates insists that he cannot teach Critobolus about *oikonomia* because, being a philosopher, he (Socrates) has no household. This is, of course, disingenuous, but the meaning of alerting the reader to the issue of exemplarity will not become clear until a later section in the text. In the meantime, Socrates asks Critobolus to master the art of household by looking at examples of households known to him. Critobolus cannot do this, however, until he has proved his capacity to learn by example: 'Ye must prove your selfe, if ye shalbe able to knowe it, whan ye see them' (sig. B1ᵛ). Critobolus assumes the position of the naive 'reader' of these exemplary households: 'I have seen theim', he says, 'and I know them both, but I have never the more vantage for that' (sig. B2ʳ). The cause is, says Socrates, that he has looked upon examples of good and bad households

as ye loke vpon the players of enterludes (*tous tragōdous kai kōmōdous*), not to thintent that ye may be a poete, but for a pastime & a recreation. And peradventure ye do well in that, for ye bee not mynded to be a poete: but where ye be compelled to kepe & fynde horses, will ye not judge your selfe a foole, if ye goe not about to study a remedy, that ye be not ignorant in that behalfe[?]

(sig. B2ʳ)

The idea of learning by *looking* at a household is transposed through the analogy with looking at a play into a concept of understanding which resembles the humanists' practice of exemplary reading; to consider a play from the point of view of the poet-dramatist is to gain a practical knowledge of its persuasive economy of representation. But Critobolus is 'not minded to be poet', so he never considers the practical architecture of a play. Nor, in fact, is he minded to keep horses. He expresses surprise at the sudden turn of the conversation: 'your mynd is that I shoulde breke horses?', he asks. The horse-breaking example is not, as it turns out, relevant to the discussion of *oikonomia*, except as the analogy which transposes the theme of exemplary learning to the topic which will be all-important: the training of the wife. Socrates declares:

I canne shewe you some men, the which have so vsed and ordered their wives, that they comfort them and help them toward the increasyng of their house: and some that have suche wives, the which vtterly destroi the hous, and so for the moste part of men have . . . a horse, most commonly, if he be skittishe, and do some displesure, we blame the breker. And a wyfe likewise . . . if he do not teache hir, if she be rude, vnwomanly, and wytles, is not he to be blamed?

(sig. B2ᵛ)

Exemplarity does not, after all, mean learning by example; it means learning by *teaching* by example. The art of household is exemplary because it involves the man practising his own histrionic exemplarity

95

in the training that will transform a 'rude' and 'wytles' partner into a womanly helpmeet. And it is hardly surprising to learn from Kathleen Davies that among 'Puritan' books of domestic conduct, 'the metaphor of horse-breaking was a familiar one—it occurs in Bullinger, Smith, Gouge, and Dod and Cleaver, but Whatley was particularly fond of it, and uses it several times'.[40]

Curious, however, is the turn taken by the text after the concepts of horse-breaking and wife-training have been introduced. For the expected gynaecology is not immediately forth-coming; it is deferred through an extended episode full of double analogies involving military activity and 'husbandry' in the sense of tilling the soil. What seems to be taking place in this section is a deliberate form of mystification. Its final objective is to define the man who has mastered the art of household as the most honourable and necessary of citizens in any state. The occupations of farming and of war, carrying associations of honesty and honour respectively, and traditionally conceded as vital to any state, function as means of legitimizing this new form of 'science' or 'occupation' (more properly, perhaps, an 'art of existence') as something that should be practised by the noblest men of the community.

Xenophon's deferral of the expected amplification and explication of Socrates' introduction of the theme of wife-training also serves to defer any conclusion over the meaning of 'husbandry' itself; by thus opening out a space of suspended definition, Xenophon expands and dignifies husbandry's signifying possibilities until these are quite uncontainable by any one definition of the term. By this process, the prudential practice of husbandry is dissociated from the physical interior of the household; by the time the text relocates 'husbandry' in the supervision of the household and the wife, the term already exceeds supervision of wife and household to the extent that these tasks function like synecdoches, mere parts by which the whole may be recognized.

To motivate the deferral in question, Xenophon has Socrates express a desire to define the noblest and most beneficial occupation in the commonweal (*to koinon*—the community). Craftsmen, Socrates finds, cannot qualify as the noblest citizens since they have 'small leysure to sette theyr mind and diligence to doe theyr friendes any good, nor also the commonwelth,' and their labours 'destroy the bodies of them that do occupy those' (sig. B3ᵛ). Xenophon's concern to equate male beauty and leisure as signs of nobility has, *pace* Foucault, a rhetorical purpose here.[41] For the leisure to serve friends and commonwealth that defines the nobleman places him symbolically 'outdoors' in the sense of being unconfined by a narrowing daily routine. It is this sense of patrician freedom that is realized symbolically in the 'outdoors' complexion of men who are not bound to labour as craftsmen. The virtue of symbolism is its transferability; thus other 'outdoor' occupations which do involve routine labour, but are required by Xenophon for the rhetorical purposes of the next phase of his argument (the occupations of farming and warfare) may become impressionistically assimilated to the definition of nobility through their association with health and good looks.

In using farming and warfare as analogies for the art of household, Xenophon's next purpose appears to be to endow his definition of *oikonomia* with the physical dignity and ethical integrity of the one, and the glamour and honour of the other. Thus, when Critobolus has been persuaded of the inferiority of all handicrafts, Socrates proves by the overwhelming authority of the example he offers that 'husbandry' is beyond doubt the fittest occupation for the good citizen:

Let not vs thynke scorne, nor be ashamed to folow [in Greek *mimēsasthai*— imitate] the kyng of the Persis [Persians]. For they saye, that he, supposing the science of warre, and also of housebandry to be most honourable, and also necessary among other faculties, doth regarde and exercise theym wonderfly.

(sig. B4^r)

Critobolus expresses our incredulity: 'Do ye thynke', he asks Socrates witheringly, 'that the kyng of Persia careth any thynge for housebandry?' (sig. B4^r). Socrates then details the means by which Cyrus retains control of his vast empire; by maintaining garrisons in tributary realms under the surveillance of lieutenants and by rewarding those who cultivate and invest in their lands. As James Tatum has explained, we see in the *Oeconomicus* a thumbnail sketch of the 'economy of empire' by which Cyrus the great rules in the *Cyropaedia*. Tatum argues that 'Cyrus's creation of a court and an empire is essentially an exercise in persuasion . . . however, he does not aim for technical perfection in the ordinary manner of orators. The entire *Cyropaedia*, and not only Cyrus's discourse . . . invites rhetorical study.'[42] Cyrus' imperial economy is plotted as the narrative of a life devoted to the achievement of control over other people by the rhetorical exploitation of their affections. Such exploitation simultaneously displaces itself: by winning the affection of lieutenants, the exemplary ruler diffuses and makes paradigmatic his absolute authority, rendering it the more secure.[43] For readers familiar (as sixteenth-century readers would be) with the *Cyropaedia*, Xenophon's invocation of Cyrus the younger in the context of the *Oeconomicus* detaches the concept of 'husbandry' from the sense of subsistence farming and prepares it for a new and enlarged sense of a rhetorical economy, or a 'use and ordering' of subordinates through persuasion and imitation.

The symbolic husbandry of Cyrus' empire is exquisitely worked by Xenophon in the *Oeconomicus* into a final exemplum which I want to pause over, because it was to become a favourite of sixteenth-century humanists. Lawrence Humphrey's *The Nobles, or Of Nobilitye* (1563), for example, is a polemic arguing for the reformation of the aristocracy through a programme of humanistic learning comparable to that elaborated by Thomas Elyot in *The Boke named the Governour*. In setting out the arguments in favour of a liberal education, however, Humphrey charges the English nobility not with ignorance but with idleness, and launches into a set piece in praise of the 'husbandry' practised by ancient rulers. Pre-eminent among his examples is Xenophon's anecdote of Cyrus in his garden at Sardis:

That the practise of husbandry was also familyer to kynges, the example of *Cirus* the younger proveth. Who accounted it no stayne, paynefully with hys owne handes to sowe whole fyeldes, to graffe in his Orchardes, cut & border flowers and herbes in hys Garden, and curyously to plant hys trees in seemly order. Nay when *Lisander*, the *Lacedemonian Legate* came to him with presentes, vaunted to hym, that all he saw, him selfe had sowed and set. Whereat he wondring, and viewinge hys purple Roabes, hys bodies beautie, the sumptuous Persian ornamentes, embrawderyes of golde and pearle, amazed cryed out, Justly *O Cierus*, men deame thee happy, sith in thee vertue and Fortune meets. For so almoste translated it Cicero out of *Xenophon*. Wherefore learned men, for they see this labour greatly accepted and honoured of the *Consuls* and lords of *Roome*, and the ancient grekes and kinges, thinke it not unmeete or unfitting for oure Nobles.[44]

Through his deployment of Cicero's imitation of the Cyrus exemplum in the context of an education programme for England's governors, Humphrey has produced a reading of Xenophon's *oikonomia* or 'husbandry' as a form of cultural production which enables the government of peoples.

Humphrey's use of Xenophon's example to sum up the potential transformation of the English nobility's 'meane invention and judgement'[45] through a humanist reading programme parallels the persuasiveness with which Socrates' invocation of Cyrus' 'economy of empire' extends and elevates Xenophon's definition of husbandry. As the very strongest form of proof (*tekmērion*) of the effectiveness of Cyrus' rule, Xenophon's Socrates relates how none of the emperor's soldiers ever desert him. Such a proof of persuasive or charismatic virtue testifies implicitly to Cyrus' incessant labour in the art of cultural production—the labour of ensuring the loyalty of a colonized people through the strategic innovation and reordering of customs and codes of living. This cultural work is subsequently stylized as 'husbandry' in the anecdote, made famous by Cicero, of the bejewelled and perfumed Cyrus in the garden, explaining to an astonished Lysander that he did all the gardening himself:

Doe ye mervaile of this Lysander? By the feyth that I owe to god when I am well at ease, I never go to diner, vnto the time I have done somewhat, eyther in feates of armes or some poynt of housebandry, tyl I sweate.

(sig. B7^{r–v})

'Sweat' here is the synecdochic detail which, for readers of the *Cyropaedia*, invokes all the Spartan practices of physical endurance—the hunting, the military exercises, the diet of cresses or bread—that mark out the virtuous Persians in contrast to the 'effeminate' Medes who drink wine and banquet, and adorn themselves with jewels and cosmetics. As Tatum points out, it is a sign of the purely rhetorical, rather than ethical value of these differences of *nomoi* or mores for Cyrus that he should, having exploited the chance to expose the 'effeminacy' of the Medes in earlier contexts, finally choose to adapt their practice of using cosmetics to increase his spellbinding power as a ruler.[46] 'Sweat', in other words, is no less rhetorical here, in its setting out and adorning of this textual exemplum of the king with the signs of honest good health, than jewels and kohl would be in the setting out and adorning of his actual presence. The purpose of the Sardis anecdote, as Cicero and Lawrence Humphrey appreciated, is to replace the notion of husbandry as necessary toil with the notion of husbandry as an art of existence which is both the sign and essence of the most fortunate, the rulers of the commonwealth. As Cicero puts it, 'in you virtue and fortune meet' ('virtuti tuae fortuna coniuncta est'[47]); it is not exactly that Cyrus is fortunate *because* of his virtuous activity, but that his eminence, which may be considered partly due to fortune, does not exempt him from labour, but rather dignifies the continual prudential labour (which is virtue) of preserving itself. As Xenophon has Socrates explain to Critobolus, the anecdote is told, 'for this cause, that ye may see, that thei that be riche and fortunate, cannot well kepe theim from housebandry' (sig. B7ᵛ).

After a set piece on the praises of rural life, Critobolus agrees that Socrates has sufficiently proved that husbandry is the most honourable occupation in a commonweal. Socrates sums up the argument so far, reminding Critobolus that they have defined the house to be a man's goods, and 'goods' to be all that a man could 'use and order', and that having discovered that most crafts keep men indoors and destroy their bodies, they further decided that husbandry 'semed to be most honourable, and best estemed in cities and common welthes, because it maketh good men, well disposed and well mynded to do good for the common welthe' (sig. C4ᵛ). The shift between defining the art of household as an exemplary knowledge, to be learned by imitation, and the art of 'husbandry' as a dignified 'outdoors' state of being, signifier of patrician good health, sub-stantial leisure and means, and charismatic and surveillant visibility, is marked in the Greek by the movement from *oikonomia* to *georgeon*; in English this distinction is effaced through the homology of 'household' and 'housebandry', emphasizing the conceptual link the text is clearly concerned to make. What finally constructs that link is the use of an exemplary figure—the good husband himself—who is sought under the rubric of the 'good and beautiful man' (*to kalos kagathos aner*) which Hervet translates as 'good and honest man'. In this phase Socrates relates to Critobolus how he has been searching among craftsmen and citizens for the *kalos te kagathos aner*, the true gentleman, in vain, until he heard by reputation of one Ischomachus,

And for bycause I hard, that Ischomachus was generally, bothe of men, woman [sic], citizines and strangers, called and taken for a good and honest man, methoughte I coulde do no better, than to prove howe I myghte commune with hym. And vppon a tyme, whan I sawe hym sitting in a porche of a churche, for bycause me thought he was at leyser, I came to hym, and sette me downe by hym, and said: What is the cause, good Ischomachus, that ye, which be wont to be ever more occupied, sytte here nowe after this manner, for I have seene you for the most part evermore doing somewhat, and lyghtly never ydell . . . ? Nor ye shulde nowe have seen me, good Socrates, sayde he . . . if I had not apointed with certaine straungers to tary here for them. And if ye were not here, where wolde ye have bene, or howe wolde ye have ben occupied, said I to hym: for I wold knowe of you very fayne, what thynge you do, that maketh ye to be called a good and honest (*kalos te kagathos*) man? The good complection of your body sheweth well ynoughe, that ye byde not alway slouggynge at home.

(sig. C4^v)

Ischomachus, the ideal citizen, is linked with the honourable occupation of husbandry-as-farming (*georgeon*) by the sign of his complexion; his is an 'outdoors' occupation, unlike that of a craftsman. But his being out of doors signifies not physical labour but readiness for negotiation in the public sphere—Socrates finds him at the temple of Zeus in the *agora* or marketplace (Hervet's substitution of a 'chuche porche' would convey to a sixteenth-century reader this sense of a public place for the transacting of business). Xenophon is careful to define Ischomachus' market-place activity as patrician obligation rather than commerce or trading—'taxes, preastes or subsidies' translates Hervet—but the point is, nevertheless, that the discovery of Ischomachus in the text as 'being outdoors' signifies a state of apparent leisure which is actually preparedness-for-business, a state of being furnished, or possessed, of the means to speak and act to advantage in the public domain. If this quality of 'being outdoors', simultaneously at leisure and 'occupied', is what defines the gentleman, the next question is, how is it achieved? What, in other words, is Ischomachus' gentlemanly 'occupation'? 'I wolde know of you very fayne, what thynge ye do . . .?' asks Socrates. Ischomachus does not answer directly. He does not limit to any profession the perfection of his suspension between leisure and business, the 'beauty' of his timely discovery, awaiting an appointment in the marketplace. Instead he answers, simply: 'in dede, good Socr[ates], I do not alwaye byde at home, for my wyfe can order wel inough suche thynges as I have there' (sig. C5^r).

Thus, by deferral through the intervening definition of 'husbandry' (*georgeon*) as the most noble and necessary occupation in the commonweal, this *topos* of the well-ordering of the wife comes to acquire a special symbolic and political significance. The wife becomes the displaced marker of all that resists definition in the art of 'husbandry'—all that, by definition, would close off husbandry's potent identification with the practical mastery of temporal and spatial contingency and the rhetorical transformation of propriety. 'Husbandry' as Xenophon defines it, is dignified by being identified with the acquisition of a practical, exemplary knowledge resembling the humanist concept of 'decorum'—that is, the capacity of invention and judgement to order speech and action to meet the demands of the occasion. This practical knowledge is, in turn, elevated by association

LORNA HUTSON

with the imperial economy of persuasion practised by Cyrus the Great, and discovered as the potential of every man who has a wife at home. Xenophonic husbandry is the new masculine ideal of the sixteenth century, the textually acquired but practical art of existence that identifies the man of liberal education, good birth and reasonable means as the most necessary member for the defence and maintenance of a commonweal.

Notes

1. Miles Coverdale, *The Christen State of Matrimonye* (London, 1541); Heinrich Bullinger, *Der Christlich Eestand* (Zurich: Christoffel Froschower, 1579); see John K. Yost, 'The value of married life for the social order in the early English Renaissance', *Societas* 6 (1976), 25–39.
2. See Kathleen M. Davies, 'The sacred condition of equality—how original were Puritan doctrines of marriage?', *Social History* 5 (1977), 579–80, 564n.; see also Derrick S. Bailey, *Thomas Becon and the Reformation of the Church in England* (London: Oliver and Boyd, 1952), p. 22.
3. Coverdale, *Christen State*, sig. J2^v.
4. John Winkler, *The Constraints of Desire: the Anthropology of Sex and Gender in Ancient Greece* (London: Routledge, 1990), p. 23.
5. John Dod and Robert Cleaver, *A Godlie Forme of Household Government: for the ordering of private families* (London: Thomas Marshe, 1612), sig. L4^r.
6. Davies, 'Sacred condition of equality', p. 570.
7. Nancy Armstrong, *Desire and Domestic Fiction: a Political History of the Novel* (Oxford: Oxford University Press, 1987); pp. 18–19; see also p. 110.
8. Catherine Belsey, *The Subject of Tragedy: Identity and Difference in Renaissance Drama* (London: Methuen, 1985), pp. 159–60.
9. Xenophon, *Oeconomicus*, tr. E. C. Marchant (London: Heinemann, 1929) vii. 23–35, pp. 420–5. For the derivation of the pseudo-Aristotelian *Oeconomia* from Xenophon, see Aristotle, *Economics*, tr. E. S. Forster in vol. X of *The Works of Aristotle*, ed. J. A. Smith and W. D. Ross (Oxford: Clarendon Press, 1921), p. x.
10. Richard Hyrde, tr. of Juan Luis Vives, *A very frutefull and pleasant boke, called the instruction of a Christien woman* (London: T. Berthelet, 1541), sig. M1^r.
11. M. I. Finley, 'Aristotle and economic analysis', *Past and Present* 47 (1970), 3–25, 22.
12. Davies, 'Sacred condition of equality', p. 577.
13. *Ibid.*, pp. 576–7.
14. Richard Whitford, *A Werke for Householders* (London: R. Redman, 1537), sig. F5^v; see Aristotle, *Economics*, 1345^a, and Josef Soudek, 'Leonardo Bruni and his public: a statistical and interpretative study of his annotated Latin version of the (Pseudo-) Aristotelian *Economics*', *Studies in Medieval and Renaissance History* 5 (1968), 51–136.
15. Erasmus, *Apopthegmatum Opus* (Paris: Johannes Roigny, 1533), sig. A2^r; Lawrence Humphrey, *The Nobles, or of Nobilitye* (London: Thomas Marshe,

1563), sig. Y5^v; Bruni is cited by Soudek, 'Leonardo Bruni and his public', 66; for Johannes Herrold, see J. Margolin, introduction to Erasmus' *Encomium Matrimonii* in *Opera Omnia Desiderii Erasmi Roterdami* (Amsterdam: North Holland Publishing Co., 1975), V: 364.

16. Whitford, *A Werke for Householders*, sigs F5^r and F6^v; see also below, p. 63.
17. De Roover, *Money, Banking and Credit in Medieval Bruges* (Cambridge, Mass.: Harvard University Press, 1948), p. 11; for a provocative interpretation of the anxieties faced by early modern capitalists on this account, see Lyndal Roper, 'Stealing manhood: capitalism and magic in early modern Germany', *Gender and History* 3 (1991), 4–22, 14.
18. Abbot Paynton Usher, *The Early History of Deposit Banking in Mediterranean Europe* (Cambridge, Mass.: Harvard University Press, 1943), pp. 12–34; on foreign exchange as a credit system, see Raymond de Roover, *Gresham on Foreign Exchange* (Cambridge, Mass.: Harvard University Press, 1949), pp. 94–106.
19. Jan Ympyn Christoffels, *A notable and very excellent woorke, expressing and declaryng the maner and forme how to kepe a boke of accomptes or reconynges, verie expedient and necessary to all Marchantes* (London, 1547), sig. C2^r.
20. Christoffels, *A notable woorke*, sig. C2^r; see also Thomas Wilson, *A Discourse uppon Usurye by waye of Dialogue and oracions* (London: Richard Tottel, 1572); sigs P6^r–7^v; de Roover, *Foreign Exchange*, p. 177.
21. J. S. Brewer, J. Gairdner and R. S. Brodie (eds), *Letters and Papers, Foreign and Domestic, of the Reign of Henry VIII* (London: Eyre & Spottiswoode, 1862–1932), 21 vols, vol. 13, pt 1, p. 536; see J. L. Bolton, *The Medieval English Economy* (London: J. M. Dent and Sons, 1980), pp. 342–3.
22. R. H. Tawney, introduction to Thomas Wilson, *A Discourse Upon Usury* (London: Frank Cass, 1925), pp. 160–1 explains that while the Act repealed the 1552 Act under which persons taking any interest whatsoever were to forfeit interest and principle, reviving the Act of 1545 under which persons taking more than 10 per cent were to forfeit the treble value of their wares and profits, any transaction involving less than 10 per cent would give no legal security to the creditor. For the credit crisis, see G. D. Ramsay, *The City of London in International Politics at the Accession of Elizabeth Tudor* (Manchester: Manchester University Press, 1975), pp. 58–61; the effect of the 1571 Act, see Norman Jones, *God and the Moneylenders: Usury and Law in Early Modern England* (Oxford: Basil Blackwell, 1989), ch. 2.
23. Roper, 'Stealing manhood', pp. 10–11.
24. Heiko Oberman, *Masters of the Reformation: The Emergence of a New Intellectual Climate in Europe*, tr. Dennis Martin (Cambridge: Cambridge University Press, 1981), p. 130.
25. Oberman, *Masters of the Reformation*, p. 146; on Deuteronomy see Benjamin Nelson, *The Idea of Usury: From Tribal Brotherhood to Universal Otherhood* (Chicago: Chicago University Press, 1969).
26. Jones, *God and the Moneylenders*, pp. 1–5.
27. Richard Hitchcocke, *A Pollitique Platt* (London: John Kingston, 1580), sig. **1^r; for Hitchcocke's proposal to use interest on loans, see sig. A4^v and table. Cicero is cited by John Dee in his *Brytannicae Reipublicae Synopsis* for which see William Sherman, 'A reader's guide to the Elizabethan Commonwealth', *Journal of Medieval and Renaissance Studies* 20 (1990), 300n. For the

'commonweal' ideology of Elizabethan economic projects, see Joan Thirsk, *Economic Policy and Projects* (Oxford: Clarendon Press, 1978), pp. 33–50.

28. See Walter Nicgorski, 'Cicero's Paradoxes and his idea of utility', *Political Theory* 12 (1984), 557–78, 565–7.

29. Robert Whittinton, *The thre bookes of Tullyes offyces both in latyn tonge in englysshe* (London: Wynkyn de Worde, 1534), sig. Q3ᵛ, 'formula, qua officium cognoscitur', sigs Q5ʳ–Q6ᵛ.

30. Nicholas Grimald, *Marcus Tullius Ciceroes thre bookes of duties* (London: Richard Tottel, 1558), sigs O7ᵛ–O8ʳ.

31. Kurt Singer, 'Oikonomia: an inquiry into the beginnings of economic thought and language', *Kyklos* 11 (1958), 29–57, 40.

32. Victoria Kahn, 'Humanism and the Resistance to Theory' in Patricia Parker and David Quint (eds), *Literary Theory/Renaissance Texts* (Baltimore: Johns Hopkins University Press, 1986), p. 377; see also Terence Cave, *The Cornucopian Text* (Oxford: Clarendon Press, 1978).

33. Cave, *Cornucopian Text*, p. 35.

34. Cicero, *De Officiis*, tr. Walter Miller (London: Heinemann, 1913), I.xxvii–xxviii, pp. 95–103; see Whittinton, *Tullyes offyces*, sig. I1ʳ, 'So it is that this temperaunce that we interpretate so as I have sayd is a scyence of oportunitie of tyme to do any thynge, but this same selfe defynycion may be the defynicion of prudence'. See Victoria Kahn, *Rhetoric, Prudence and Skepticism in the Renaissance* (Ithaca and London: Cornell University Press, 1985), p. 35.

35. Gentian Hervet, *Xenophons Treatise of Householde* (London: T. Berthelet, 1534), sig. A1ʳ. There were further editions in 1544, 1557 and 1573. For comparing the Greek, I have used E. C. Marchant's parallel text; I have also benefited from Leo Strauss, *Xenophon's Socratic Discourse* (Ithaca and London: Cornell University Press, 1970).

36. See John Archer Gee, *The Life and Works of Thomas Lupset* (New Haven: Yale University Press, 1928), pp. 1–121.

37. For the associations of humanists such as Lupset, Starkey and Hervet both with the Poles and with Erasmus, see James McConica, *English Humanism and Reformation Politics* (Oxford: Clarendon Press, 1966); Gordon Zeeveld, *Foundations of Tudor Policy* (Cambridge, Mass.: Harvard University Press, 1948); Thomas F. Mayer, *Thomas Starkey and the Commonweal* (Cambridge: Cambridge University Press, 1989).

38. Compare, 'This boke of householde, full of high wisdome, written by the noble philosopher Xenophon, the scholer of Socrates, the which for his swete eloquence, and incredible facilitie, was surnamed Musa Attica, that is to sai, the songe of Athenes', Hervet, *Treatise of Householde*, sig. A1ʳ, with M. T. Ciceronis, *Cato Maior Seu de Senectute*, D. Erasmi annotationibus illustratus (Paris: Michael Vascosan, 1536) sig. I8ʳ: 'Xenophon Socratis discipulus ob elegantiem dulcedinem & incredibilem dicendi facilitatem, musa attica appellatus est.'

39. Hervet, *Treatise of Householde*, sig. A2ʳ. Henceforward all references to this edition will appear in the text.

40. Davies, 'Sacred condition of equality', p. 572.

41. Michel Foucault, *The Use of Pleasure*, vol. 2 of *The History of Sexuality*, tr. Robert Hurley (Harmondsworth: Penguin, 1984), p. 152.

42. James Tatum, *Xenophon's Imperial Fiction: On the Education of Cyrus* (Princeton, NJ: Princeton University Press, 1989), p. 192.

43. *Ibid.*, pp. 189–92; in the *Oeconomicus*, the 'Cyrus' figured is Cyrus the Younger, who never in fact became king, but as Tatum affirms, p. 41, 'the association between the older and the younger Cyrus later turned into a literary project in its own right'.
44. Humphrey, *The Nobles*, sig. I8[r–v].
45. *Ibid.*, sig. X2[r].
46. Tatum, *Xenophon's Imperial Fiction*, p. 197, pp. 98–106.
47. Cicero, *De Senectute*, tr. William A. Falconer (London: Heinemann, 1923), XVII: 59–60, pp. 70–3.

4 The Tenth Muse: Gender, Rationality, and the Marketing of Knowledge

Stephanie Jed

In 1650, Anne Bradstreet's brother-in-law published her poetry in London under the title *The Tenth Muse, Lately Sprung Up in America*. In 1657, the volume was annotated in William London's *Catalogue [of] the Most Vendible Books in England . . .* as "Mrs. Bradstreet. The 10. Muse, a Poem. 80." In 1668, a volume appeared in Mexico City celebrating and commemorating the completion of the cathedral. It included a sonnet of Juana Inés de Asbaje with an epigraph exalting her as "a glorious honor of the Mexican Museum" ("glorioso honor del Mexicano Museo"). In Madrid in 1689, the printer Juan García Infanzón published the first edition of the works of Sor Juana Inés de la Cruz, describing her on the title page as "the Tenth Muse . . . who in various meters, languages and styles fertilizes various issues" ("Musa Dézima . . . Que en varios metros, idiomas, y estilos, fertiliza varios assumptos"). Finally, in 1683, in Oxford, the Ashmolean Museum opened its doors to the public for the first time, charging admission to "peasants and women-folk who gaze at the library as a cow might gaze at a new gate with such noise and trampling of feet that others are much disturbed."[1]

My essay begins, against the background of this seventeenth-century compilation of "facts," to form an intuition and a question. The intuition is: that the category "Tenth Muse" was implicated in the European politics of constructing the "New World" as a museum. After all, institutions of knowledge and history-making, such as the Escorial, the British Museum, the Archivo de las Indias, the archives of the trading companies, "natural" histories and collections of travel narratives, were united by the common "museal" project of ruling new lands and peoples and making them "vendible."[2] The category "Tenth Muse," then, might provide an important interpretive key to the gender

From Patricia Parker and Margo Hendricks (eds.), *Women, 'Race' and Writing in the Early Modern Period* (Routledge, 1994), 195–207. Reprinted with permission.

fictions implicit in these sixteenth and seventeenth-century institutions of classifying, knowing, and ruling. Indeed, the "evidence" for connecting the "Tenth Muse" to sixteenth and seventeenth-century European taxonomic activities is abundant, but finding a rhetorical strategy for doing so is arduous. The question is: why?

THE "FACTS" OF THE TENTH MUSE

We might begin this investigation by looking at the fictional category "Tenth Muse" in the first published volumes of Anne Bradstreet and Sor Juana. In both cases, this fiction was the effect of social relations between men of letters and commerce for whom the idea of a woman writer made no sense. The epithet "Tenth Muse" thus provided a fiction to make sense of or explain the emergence of significant women writers in the colonial literature market. Taking on this explanatory function, the category "Tenth Muse" became a taxonomic "fact" which could account for the otherwise unintelligible appearance of women writers. As a fictional or constructed "fact," it provided a solution to the taxonomic impossibility of classifying Bradstreet and Sor Juana either as women or as writers. This "fact," moreover, had the function of commodifying these writers within a system of assumptions about authorship (men, inspired by Muses, did it) and gender (women did not write).[3] As a "fact" designed to account for and control any variance from the gender norm, the fictional classification "Tenth Muse" made these writers more intelligible, and thus more "vendible," in a taxonomic system which separated women from writers.

Anne Bradstreet's brother-in-law and promoter John Woodbridge carefully adhered to this taxonomic "fact," by introducing *The Tenth Muse* and her work of writing in the light of gender ambiguity. Fearing that the "excellency" of Bradstreet's poetry might make the (male) reader doubt that a woman wrote them, Woodbridge wrote: "the worst effect of his reading will be unbelief, which will make him question whether it be a woman's work, and ask, is it possible?" The two contradictory meanings of "whether it be a woman's work"—one being the question "could a woman have written such accomplished poetry?" and the other "should women be allowed to write poetry?"—were precisely those which characterized the difficulty of classifying the woman writer: if she were a writer, she could not be a woman, and if she were a woman, why wasn't she doing a woman's work? Given these two alternative taxonomies, Woodbridge chose them both: he classified Bradstreet as a woman "honoured and esteemed . . . [for] her exact diligence in her place," but he also classified her as a woman who wrote outside the time and space of "a woman's work," in the "few hours curtailed from her sleep and other refreshments." In this way, in Woodbridge's estimation, she was able to sustain the ambiguity of being both a woman and a writer. And so, she earned the classification "Tenth Muse," that "factual" category which marked her gender ambiguity. A "curious" kind of neutral, she occupied a category all her own.[4]

Bradstreet's own "Prologue" to her poetry adhered, in many ways, to this same taxonomic "fact." Citing the very convention that excluded women from writing, she excoriated the hypothetical critic "who says my hand a needle better fits." At the same time, however, she suggested that the Muse who inspired her poetry, unlike the female personifications who inspired male poets, was a neuter:

> My foolish, broken, blemished Muse so sings,
> And this to mend, alas, no art is able,
> 'Cause nature made it so irreparable.
>
> (ll. 18–20)[5]

The syntax here is ambiguous enough to allow the "it" (of l. 20) to refer to either the Muse's song or to the "Muse" herself, made neuter for the occasion of inspiring a female poet. By interrupting the paradigm of the female muse who inspires the male writer, Bradstreet created a third space for herself, representing the taxonomic "fact" of her gender ambiguity as a woman writer and "Tenth Muse."

Sor Juana articulated a similar "fact" in her response to a Peruvian gentleman who suggested she become a man. The Muses, she implied, in their traditional function of separating women from writers, had exempted themselves from helping her to respond to his suggestion ("para responderos / todas las musas se eximen"). But, in any case, Sor Juana was uninterested in the prospect. She came to the convent, precisely "because there is no one to verify if I am a woman" and because there, her body could be "neuter or abstract" ("sólo sé que mi cuerpo / . . . / es neutro, o abstracto"). Indeed, the term "virgin," describing her sex, could be applied to either woman or man ("es común de dos lo virgen").[6] Given Sor Juana's insistence on transgressing gender categories and creating a gender fiction for herself, it is no wonder that the taxonomic "fact" of the "Tenth Muse" was invoked to classify and circumscribe her works in the literary market.

There are other interesting gender contradictions implicit in the "fact" of the "Tenth Muse," contradictions that seem to be at the heart of national and colonial projects. The titles of the works of both "Tenth Muses" included metaphors of generation which exceeded gender norms. Bradstreet's title, *The Tenth Muse, Lately Sprung Up in America*, evoked an image of parthenogenesis: this muse was not born from any inseminated figure of Mother America, but she sprang rather from the soil of New England, seemingly without the help of English seed. Here, the category "Tenth Muse," which accounted for Bradstreet's deviation from the Puritan sanctions against women making public statements,[7] also played an important role in English colonization. If the nine classical Muses represented the power of English (and European) culture to dominate the world, a new category was required to assimilate new manifestations of this power in places far from London. The "Tenth Muse," a muse of commodification, incorporated Bradstreet's parthenogenetic verses into an English genealogy and continuity of power.

In like manner, Sor Juana was represented on her title page as "fertilizing" with her writings the colonial soil of New Spain. This title evoked an image of an androgynous muse, a female personification who could also perform the task of fertilization. In this case as well, the "fertilizing" verses, which accounted for Sor Juana's choice of the veil over marriage, illustrated the extent to which the "Tenth Muse," the muse of commodification, may have served Spanish colonial projects. Once again, the procreative capacity of her verses indicated the "Tenth Muse's" ability to reproduce Spanish and imperial power in places far removed from European museums.

Bradstreet and Sor Juana were constructed as "Tenth Muses" in a period in European cultural history which was dominated by the episteme of the museum.[8] And as Paula Findlen has so brilliantly shown, the museum, that dwelling-place sacred to the nine Muses, became the "axis through which all other structures of collecting, categorizing, and knowing intersected."[9] In addition to being the epistemological institution which collected the "New World" for the purposes of ruling it, the museum also represented a space of social relations and activities. Reports from the "New World," promotional literature, "natural" histories, editorial projects, and economic ventures provided the textual and relational ground for collecting, classifying, and knowing the "Tenth Muse" as a commodity and resource for cultural exploitation.[10] We might turn to this relational context to understand the production of the category "Tenth Muse."

"FACTS" PRODUCED IN THE CONTEXT OF RELATIONS

The construction of two eminent colonial poets as Tenth Muses in the latter half of the seventeenth century constitutes but one later episode in a long narrative of developing colonial economies. The earlier episodes of this narrative, I would like to suggest, may be found in the writings of collectors, natural historians, encyclopedists, and other culture brokers who were engaged in the separation of "knowledge" from colonial interests. In his book *The Old World and the New*, J. H. Elliott traces the route of New World objects and facts as they began to crowd the museums and studies of sixteenth-century European scholars.

At first, these objects and facts, collected indiscriminately and for curiosity's sake alone, were, Elliott says, "lumped together into an undifferentiated category of the marvellous or exotic." As such, they reinforced already existing European habits of thought and constructing knowledge. Later, as the desire to domesticate and appropriate the resources of the New World intensified, Europeans devised new methods to differentiate and rationalize the exotic in accordance with their goal of ruling and commodifying the new lands and peoples.[11] By the seventeenth century, questionnaires, travel narratives, encyclopedic compendia, museums, and libraries collected and classified "information" about places, plants, animals, and peoples, previously considered exotic, in such a way as to make them seem attractive to European investors and consumers. The construction of the category "Tenth Muse" can be understood in the context of this rationalizing program.

A "natural" historian's report about the iguana illustrates this relation between "facts," commodification, and reason. In Book 12, chapter 7 of his *Historia general y natural de las Indias*, Gonzalo Fernández de Oviedo (1478–1557), the official historiographer of Charles V and the military governor of the fortress of Santo Domingo, writes of the iguana, a creature then unknown in Europe.[12] He covers several points regarding the iguana, exemplifying the European concerns to classify New World knowledge and to exploit new commodities in commerce and trade. With regard to classification, Oviedo tells us that it is difficult to know if the iguana belongs to the category of animal or fish, and he warns us not to confuse the iguana with the crocodile, as many, including Pedro Martire, have done. He then goes on to treat the commodity side of knowledge, telling us that there are many ways to cook the iguana and its eggs, but that so far, the iguana's nourishment remains a mystery. In regard to this last point, the mystery of the iguana's nourishment, Oviedo writes:

It is such a quiet animal, that it neither screams nor moans nor makes any sound, and it will stay tied up wherever you put it, without doing any damage or making any noise, for ten or twenty days and more without eating or drinking anything. Some say, on the contrary, that if you give the iguana a little cassava or grass or something similar, it will eat it. But I have had some of these animals sometimes tied up in my house, and I never saw them eat, and I had them watched day and night, and in the end, I never knew nor was able to understand what they were eating in the house, and everything that you give them to eat remains whole.[13]

At the end of the chapter, Oviedo connects his commodification of this creature to another kind of commerce, the European trade in exotic specimens and facts, a commerce that would enable Europe to secure cultural, and not just economic, domination over the newly encountered civilizations. Oviedo writes:

Having written the above, two of the bigger iguanas were brought to me, and we ate part of one in my house, and the other I had put away, tied up, to send to Venice to the Magnificent Mr. Joan Baptista [Ramusio], chancellor of the Signoria, and it was tied to a post on the patio of this fortress of Santo Domingo for more than forty days, during which time, it never ate any of the many things it was given; and I was told that these animals ate only earth, and I had a hundred pounds of dirt put in a barrel as the iguana's provisions, so that there would be no lack of it at sea. And I hope that while I am correcting these treatises, ships will arrive to let us know if the iguana arrived alive in Spain and with what nourishment.

When I arrived in Spain in 1546, however, I found out from the one who took the animal that it had died at sea.[14]

I am interested and intrigued by the tale of this ill-fated expedition for what it can reveal about how "social relations of domination are frozen into the logics" of taxonomies in the colonial period.[15] Once we start to examine the "rationality" of Oviedo's decision to send an iguana to Venice in a barrel of dirt, a whole series of relations emerges—social, cultural, and economic—to support this concept of reason. An analysis of the episode of the iguana will thus reveal some aspects of social organization underlying the construction and commodification of knowledge about the "New World." It can also point us to methods for analyzing the role of colonial women writers in this social organization.

111

Oviedo's account of the iguana is structured as a collection of taxonomic statements. For example, the discussion of whether the iguana should be classified as a "terrestrial animal" or fish has the effect of reifying those categories confounded by Oviedo's own contradictory understanding of the iguana, which "lives in both rivers and trees." In this way, Oviedo introduces the iguana to the European public more as an effect of his taxonomic prowess than as an effect of his inadequate eye. More important, however, is the function of this taxonomic prowess in the construction of a certain kind of rationality in Oviedo's account. Oviedo's ability to classify the iguana, with confidence, under the category "animal" serves as evidence that he knew enough about the iguana to believe that sending one in a barrel of dirt to Venice was a "rational" project.[16] Perhaps a similar line of reasoning was used to classify our "Tenth Muses" and to transport them to Europe.

Statements like "I never saw them eat" or "everything that you give them to eat remains whole" are selected by Oviedo, the "teller of the tale," to convince us, from his imperial point of view, of the rationality of his project.[17] It is a rationality which refers both to the rationale for colonial ventures and the relations of inequality and domination required to sustain those ventures. And it is this concept of rationality which determines the selection and categorization of statements about the iguana's eating habits. Also informing this concept of rationality is Oviedo's relation to the Venetian statesman Ramusio; from the perspective of their common cultural and economic investment in New World taxonomies, this interested relation could indeed be seen as "rational." In his statements about the iguana, Oviedo, then, transposes a concept of rationality from his relations with Ramusio to the purported actuality of the iguana's nourishment. As we shall see later, a similar mechanism of transposed rationality might be investigated in relation to the construction of the Tenth Muse. It is important, in both cases, to examine how fictional categories and misguided observations can be generated from these "rational" relations.

Oviedo's relation with the Venetian Giovanni Battista Ramusio (1485–1557) was, in some ways, emblematic of the intercultural relations which sustained the dynamic of empire. This dynamic was characterized by a tension between the standardizing effects of the imperial bureaucracy and the economic and cultural differences within its jurisdiction. These cultural differences, rationalized and smoothed over by the bureaucratic structures of record-keeping and diplomatic networks, eventually produced the culture of national states. Ramusio's publication of Oviedo's works in Italian constitutes a chapter in that process. Oviedo informs us that when he sent off a live iguana to Venice in 1540, Ramusio was the secretary or chancellor of Venice's Council of Ten. He had come into contact with Oviedo through the official imperial network: Andrea Navagero, the official historiographer of the Venetian Republic, had established relations with Pietro Martire and with various members of the Council of the Indies in Seville and probably met Oviedo there in 1525 when Oviedo was preparing the abridged version of his *Historia natural*. Navagero, then, not only put Oviedo and Ramusio in contact with each other, but saw to it that Oviedo's *Sumario* or abridged version of his work would be published in Venice in Italian in 1534.[18]

The epistolary relation that ensued between Oviedo and Ramusio, who never met in person, was essentially one between an informant from the periphery and a metropolitan broker of knowledge. Because of his powerful position as knowledge-broker and important administrator of the Venetian State, Ramusio was sometimes better informed about New World developments than his informants and even provided information to Oviedo, at times, that helped him understand the "reality" he was living.[19] It is important to see Oviedo's production of facts about Hispaniola in relation to the interests of publishers like Ramusio who would market these facts in a particular ideological frame. And it is in this context of Ramusio's role as a broker of knowledge that the rationality involved in collecting facts about the iguana and sending one to Venice begins to emerge.

Ramusio had constructed and cornered a market of consumers of news about the New World which included not only traditional intellectuals but also merchants, bankers, and a general reading public in some way identified with the drama of New World encounters. In order to attract this general reading public, Ramusio organized his collection of New World accounts around the heroes and hopes of chivalry and conquest,[20] a cultural paradigm whose traditional function in European literature had always been to mystify the waging of war under the guise of epic poetry. Oviedo's literary talents and military role as governor of the fortress of Santo Domingo made him a perfect fit for this paradigm, whose function in the sixteenth century was to mystify the international economic partnerships, which would cause so much suffering throughout the world, under the guise of natural history. On January 1, 1538, two years before Oviedo attempted the expedition of the iguana, Oviedo and Ramusio entered into just such an economic partnership.

Signing a contract with Antonio di Priuli, the procurator of San Marco, Ramusio and Oviedo invested 400 gold ducats in an international business venture to which they committed themselves for six years. The 400 ducats were used to buy Italian and Venetian goods to send to Santo Domingo, where Oviedo sold them at a profit and used the money to buy liquors and sugars to sell in Cadiz, again, obviously, at a profit. This partnership, tracing the route of the infamous rum triangle, was among the first of its kind and provided a model for subsequent, larger-scale enterprises. Following this example, in 1560, the heirs of Tommaso Giunti, the publishers of Ramusio's collection *Navigazioni e viaggi*, invested a part of their publishing profits in a trading company that would take earnings from the selling of books and glass products and turn them into sugar and pepper for European markets.[21] If the trade in New World commodities and the trade in facts about natural resources had once served separate functions in the construction of imperial domination, now these two functions were completely intertwined. This network of economic/cultural relations constitutes a more pertinent signifier for Oviedo's descriptive statements about the iguana than any notion of what Oviedo may have actually observed. In the context of these relations, we can understand that it was reasonable and rational for Oviedo to ship off to Venice a live iguana in a barrel of dirt. Only by making visible and analyzing these relations are we able to challenge this concept of reason.

REORGANIZING KNOWLEDGE

The project of reconstructing an analogous context in which "facts" about the "Tenth Muse" were produced is a complex one. In the case of Anne Bradstreet, several circumstances surrounding the publication of *The Tenth Muse* point to a specific rhetorical context for her commodification as a poet.[22] Stephen Bowtell, for example, the publisher of *The Tenth Muse*, was a noted publisher of "political" materials.[23] In the context of England's civil wars, his investment in the commodity of a colonial "Tenth Muse" may be seen as a move to strengthen the image of the English nation in its Atlantic enterprise. William London's listing of *The Tenth Muse* in his 1657 *Catalogue [of] the Most Vendible Books in England* confirmed this function of Bradstreet's poetry as a "passive" item in an inventory of England's cultural merchandise.[24] Another London bookseller who collected and published Civil War books and pamphlets, George Thomason, included his copy of *The Tenth Muse*, purchased a few days after its issue, in a "secret" collection representing, in some sense, the interregnum state of the nation.[25] Here, the urgency with which Bradstreet's writings were acquired and collected may point to the crucial role played by cultural commodities in the formation of political ties. A further investigation of questions like these would put us on the path to interpreting the role of the "Tenth Muse" in constructing the "New World" as a museum.

The same kinds of textual relations might be researched in the case of Sor Juana. The political worlds which commodified her writings were those of the viceroys and the Church. It was the Countess of Paredes, wife of the Marquis de la Laguna (viceroy of New Spain from 1680 to 1686), who actually transported Sor Juana's writings to Madrid. And another imperial servant in New Spain, Juan Camacho Gayna, took the credit for preparing the first edition of Sor Juana's works. As Octavio Paz has suggested, it is likely that the Jesuit Diego Calleja had a more active role in the editing of this volume, as he had "a long-continuing interest" in Sor Juana.[26] For our purposes here, we might investigate rather what role these figures, and others associated with Sor Juana's writings, may have played in the administering of "New Spain" for a profit. What relations did these profits have to "facts" about the "New World" and categories for knowledge-making? The research and interpretation of texts representing these relations would provide a context for understanding the construction and promotion of Sor Juana as a "Tenth Muse."

My interest in these questions is twofold: first, I am interested in making the texts of publishers, bureaucrats, catalogue-makers, "natural" historians, investors, ethnographers, culture-brokers, and the like come together to tell us something about how the fiction of the "Tenth Muse" was produced as a "fact" within a particular concept of reason and taxonomy. The assembling of such texts would make visible, I believe, the way in which the "facts" of the "Tenth Muse" constituted a fiction related to the "I" who was ruling.[27] In the eyes of these producers of "facts," it would seem reasonable to make sense of a woman writer as a "Tenth Muse." The "Tenth Muse" was a packaging of knowledge that would sell, still another commodity to be exported and exploited in the metropolitan capitals of London and Madrid.

Second, I am interested in the "facts" of the "Tenth Muse" as a gender fiction, an "unreal" category which points to the constructed nature of all historical knowledge. Research libraries and archives, products of the same colonial relations which produced the "Tenth Muse," do not readily offer information about their own taxonomic fictions. The "Tenth Muse" and the various texts of culture-brokers, investors, "natural" historians, etc., which, coming together, construct her as a fiction, raise questions about the fictional structures in which we work. Perhaps Adrienne Rich was alluding to this fiction, when she wrote of Anne Bradstreet's place in a Women's Archive.

In her 1966 essay on the Puritan poet Anne Bradstreet, Adrienne Rich made a distinction between Bradstreet's earlier poems treating such themes as the Ages of Man and Assyrian monarchs and her later poems written "in response to the simple events in a woman's life." Characterizing Bradstreet's earlier poetry as "pedestrian, abstract, mechanical," Rich wrote: "Had she stopped writing after the publication of these verses, or had she simply continued in the same vein, Anne Bradstreet would survive in the catalogues of *Women's Archives*, a social curiosity or at best a literary fossil" (emphasis mine).[28] Rich went on to claim that the later, more personal poems "rescue Anne Bradstreet from the Women's Archives and place her conclusively in literature."[29] In her 1979 reflection on this essay, Rich regretted her "condescending references to 'Women's Archives,'" saying that such condescension exemplified "the limitations of a point of view which took masculine history and literature as its center and which tried from that perspective to view a woman's life and work."[30] No longer attempting to "rescue" Anne Bradstreet from the Women's Archives, Rich, in this reflection, rescues the Women's Archive as an important site of feminist research. To imagine a Women's Archive in which women writers share the shelf space in function of their relations with one another is to make visible the fictional categories and contradictions within which they wrote.

It is not clear, however, how we are to imagine this fictional Women's Archive and the fictional point of view which would take women's history and literature as its center. Are we to imagine a series of writings by individual women writers lying inert on a shelf in a vault, unable to be organized in the kind of organic relations from which most institutions of historical records were formed? Writers of the stature of Anne Bradstreet and Sor Juana, after all, never knew each other. Indeed, because the "facts" of conquest and colonialism implied a particular organization of social relations and knowledge, women writers in history could neither know each other nor form political or social ties. How then could a Women's Archive activate a relation which never existed in history? Would there be rearranging or more writing to be done?

In the histories of many archives and libraries, we find that generations of librarians and archivists have been arranging and rearranging historical materials to fit their own cultural needs. As the researcher walks into a library, archive, or museum, s/he is instantly aware of becoming part of this fiction. In a miscellany of sixteenth-century broadsheets in the Marciana Library in Venice, for example, we can read the notes of a nineteenth-century librarian who saw fit to extract materials pertaining to geography and the New World from their original context among chivalric verses and verses pertaining to European wars. We can see in these notes that in sixteenth-century Italy there was a social-historical connection between the literary *topoi* of chivalry and the conquest of the New World, a connection which, by virtue of the librarian's intervention, has been lost to the modern consciousness.[31] The feminist reader, reconstructing this connection, makes visible again the relations of sexual domination common to texts as diverse in time and kind as Ariosto's *Orlando furioso*, Vespucci's (in)famous letter of 1505, and the later abundance of English promotional literature highlighting the virgin, bride-like quality of the New World.[32] Understood as an intertext, these texts may be seen as one measure of the relation between women writers. Effecting a powerful relation of disconnection between women, this intertext can nonetheless be seen as one which bound women's writing together. In a Women's Archive, we might analyze the conditions under which this relation of disconnection in women's writing was produced instead of focusing on the images of disconnected women.

We might even rearrange materials to correspond to our interest in the appearance of women writers in relation to colonial representations of women. For how can we separate John Smith's representation of New England as a woman whose "treasures [have] yet never beene opened, nor her originalls wasted, consumed, nor abused" from the Muse who would soon after favor those treasures with her verses?[33] In the same way, it is difficult to separate the construction of Sor Juana as a "Tenth Muse" from the relations of ruling between Spain and New Spain and from the efforts of the Spanish kings to promote their cause of Christendom against the advance of Protestantism. The promotion of Bradstreet and Sor Juana as Muses in the literary marketplaces of London and Madrid, then, gives us some insight into the gendered construction of nationhood in these metropolitan capitals. These are some of the fictions whose records might be foregrounded in the

Women's Archive, activating relations between those colonial women writers who never did, because they never could, relate to one another in institutional ways.

Nor should this kind of rearrangement of materials be seen as particularly radical or disrespectful of existing taxonomies. In the State Archive in Milan, where I have worked, archival materials have been disordered and reordered, dismembered and reclassified, according to the whims, logics, bureaucratic requirements, and scholarly exigencies of successive generations of archivists. The scholar is often reminded that archival reorganizations correspond to the establishment of new relations between citizens and the State, as well as to developments in scientific methods. We find, for example, that at the turn of this century, archival work, including reorganizations of materials, filing, and the making of catalogues and inventories, had come to a halt. The historian Nicola Raponi did not see this as a necessarily negative development. "It was," he wrote, "not a period of inertia but a rich and intense period of *methodological disorientation* . . . which was reflected in a kind of *eclectic* activity."[34]

I would like to suggest that we are currently living through a similar moment of disorientation, one which would favor making visible the constructed or fictional nature of "facts" and their classifications. Analysis of the rhetorical organization of inventories and catalogues of libraries, archives, and museums formed in the sixteenth and seventeenth centuries would be one way of dramatizing the fictional nature of colonial documentation projects.[35] Another way of dramatizing these rhetorics would be, of course, to write new fictions.

THE "TENTH MUSE" AT SEA

In the course of my search to understand the "Tenth Muse" syndrome in relation to colonial epistemologies, I was delighted to come upon the following account of Anne Bradstreet and Sor Juana Inés de la Cruz in a late seventeenth-century "natural" history of literature from the "New World." The hypothetical author of this history, perhaps one of Charles II's correspondents in Mexico City, had some familiarity with these women writers—both published and promoted as "Tenth Muses" in the metropolitan capitals of London and Madrid—and seemed anxious to represent them as potentially useful to culture-brokers at home. I report the passage in its entirety for the remarkable light it shines upon the space of "Tenth Musedom" in colonial economies and constructions of knowledge.

BOOK XII, CHAPTER VII

Concerning the woman or poet called Tenth Muse and the many commodities of this kind which exist in the New World.

This is a kind of commodity or woman who may be found in New England as well as in New Spain. In the first edition of my *General and Natural Literary History*, I put her in Book XIII, Chapter III (which deals with male writers), and now it seemed to me more appropriate to put her in this chapter which deals with women, in spite of the opinion of many that she could belong in either chapter, because many men do not know how to determine if she is a woman or a poet and they treat her as a neutral thing, thinking of her both as a woman and as a poet, because she is both, and both as a woman and as a poet, she exercizes and continues her life. She is called Tenth Muse.

I repeat that she is reputed to be a neutral animal, because she knows not only how to cook and sew but also how to write poetry better than many men. But I have decided to put her here in the category of women, because readers should not confuse the two categories woman and poets, as many others have done.

I have visited Tenth Muses on several occasions, but I have never seen them write. The Tenth Muse is so quiet and diligent that she never neglects her womanly duties and so it is a mystery as to when she finds time to write. Perhaps she writes in the "few hours curtailed from her sleep and other refreshments," but I have never seen this happen. Moreover, she is content not to control the publication of her own work;[36] the vendibility of her writings, so favorable to the merchandizing of colonial projects, is completely out of her hands. Although the Tenth Muse performs many inspirational functions in culture and economy, the source of her own inspiration remains a mystery.

Having written the above, the published works of two Tenth Muses—Anne Bradstreet and Sor Juana—were brought to me, and we read part of the book by Sor Juana that afternoon, and the other I had put away, wrapped up, to send to London to the publishers of the Magnificent Thomas Heywood's *Generall History of Women* (1657) in the hopes that they would print an appendix regarding the Tenth Muse Anne Bradstreet. And I hope that while I am correcting these treatises, ships will arrive to let us know if the Tenth Muse's book arrived alive in London and in what condition.

When I arrived in London in 1700, however, I found out from the one who took the book that the Tenth Muse Anne Bradstreet would eventually end up in *The Norton Anthology of Literature by Women*.

Notes

I want to emphasize that this essay is a theoretical reflection on the construction of the "Tenth Muse" in relation to history and history-making institutions; it is not an essay on Anne Bradstreet and Sor Juana. I hope I will not seem arrogant by using and developing the construction of these writers as examples. For relevant bibliography, I refer the reader to Raymond F. Dolle, *Anne Bradstreet: A Reference Guide* (Boston: G. K. Hall & Co., 1990) and to the important collection of essays edited (and authored) by Stephanie Merrim, *Feminist Perspectives on Sor Juana Inés de la Cruz* (Detroit: Wayne State University Press, 1991).

Many people have helped me to work out the ideas in this essay. The students in my Gender Studies class (Spring 1991) explored the possibilities of a Women's Archive in their construction of a historicizing, fictive relationship between Sor Juana and Anne Bradstreet. Bett Miller's dissertation in progress on the works of Nicole Brossard has challenged me to explore alternative spatial constructions and genealogies of women's writing. I would like to express appreciation to Eduardo Garcia for his stimulating feedback and support. I would like to express special gratitude to my colleagues who have read and generously discussed with me countless drafts of this essay: Judith Halberstam, Nicole Tonkovich, Beth Holmgren, and Pasquale Verdicchio.

1. Concerning the early publication and promotion of Anne Bradstreet's works, see *The Tenth Muse (1650) and, From the manuscripts, Meditations Divine and Morall Together with Letters and occasional Pieces by Anne Bradstreet*, facsimile reproductions with an intro. by Josephine K. Piercy (Delmar: Scholars' Facsimiles & Reprints, 1978); Dolle, *Anne Bradstreet*, 1–4; Pattie Cowell, "The Early Distribution of Anne Bradstreet's Poems," in *Critical Essays on Anne Bradstreet*, ed. Pattie Cowell and Ann Stanford (Boston: G. K. Hall & Co., 1983), 270–9; Elizabeth Wade White, *Anne Bradstreet "The Tenth Muse"* (New York: Oxford University Press, 1971), 251–92. Concerning the early publication of the works of Sor Juana, see *Sor Juana Inés de la Cruz ante la historia*, A compilation by Francisco de la Maza (Mexico City: Universidad Nacional Autónoma de México, 1980), 35; Ludwig Pfandl, *Sor Juana Inés de la Cruz, La Décima Musa de México: Su vida, su poesía, su psique*, ed. Francisco de la Maza (Mexico City: Universidad Nacional Autónoma de México, 1983), 83–6. Pfandl notes that Lope de Vega, in 1624, had referred to Marcia Leonarda as the "tenth muse." Indeed, many other cases of "Tenth Muses" might be cited. Finally, the episode of the Ashmolean Museum is reported in Paula Findlen's important essay, "The Museum: Its Classical Etymology and Renaissance Genealogy," *Journal of the History of Collections* 1, no. 1 (1989), 72.
2. Findlen, "The Museum," 68.
3. I am indebted to my colleague Nicole Tonkovich for helping me to clarify these gender norms with respect to literary production. For an important

treatment of the same gender contradiction in the history of science, see Londa Schiebinger, "Feminine Icons: The Face of Early Modern Science," *Critical Inquiry* 14, no. 4 (1988), 661–91; and *The Mind Has No Sex? Women in the Origins of Modern Science* (Cambridge, Mass., and London: Harvard University Press, 1991).

4. John Woodbridge, "Epistle to the Reader," *The Works of Anne Bradstreet*, ed. Jeannine Hensley (Cambridge, Mass., and London: Harvard University Press, 1967), 3.

5. Anne Bradstreet, "The Prologue," ibid., 15–17.

6. *A Sor Juana Anthology*, trans. Alan S. Trueblood (Cambridge, Mass., and London: Harvard University Press, 1988), 26–33 (poem no. 48).

7. Susan Howe, "The Captivity and Restoration of Mrs. Mary Rowlandson," *Temblor*, no. 2 (n.d.), 118; Annette Kolodny, *The Land Before Her: Fantasy and Experience of the American Frontiers, 1630–1860* (Chapel Hill: University of North Carolina Press, 1984), 17.

8. The work of Michel Foucault has, of course, been fundamental to the understanding of this episteme. See, in particular, *The Order of Things: An Archeology of the Human Sciences* (New York: Vintage Books, 1973).

9. Findlen, "The Museum," 63.

10. Daniel Defert, "Collecting the World: Accounts of Voyages from the Sixteenth to the Eighteenth Centuries," *Dialectical Anthropology* 7, no. 1 (September 1982), 11–20. For a related study, may I refer the reader to my "Making History Straight: Collecting and Recording in Sixteenth-Century Italy," *Bucknell Review* 35, no. 2 (1992), 104–20.

11. J. H. Elliott, *The Old World and the New: 1492–1650* (Cambridge: Cambridge University Press, 1970), 32–8.

12. Gonzalo Fernández de Oviedo, *Historia general y natural de las Indias*, vols. 117–21 in the series Bibiloteca de Autores Españoles (Madrid: Ediciones Atlas, 1959), vol. 118 (vol. 2 of the *Historia general*), 32–5. Cf. Elliott's brief reference to the episode in *The Old World*, 37.

My own research (limited as it is to events and developments on or emanating from the Italian peninsula) has led me to think about the "Tenth Muse" in relation to Oviedo. Remote in time and place from the construction and promotion of the "Tenth Muse," this text nonetheless provides a jarring (and, I believe, productive) context for making visible the relation of taxonomies and "facts" to gender, rationality, and the marketing of knowledge. It is my hope that scholars who specialize in Sor Juana and Anne Bradstreet will think of other texts more pertinent to this argument.

13. Oviedo, *Historia*, 32. Translations are my own.

14. Ibid., 35.

15. Donna Haraway, "Teddy Bear Patriarchy: Taxidermy in the Garden of Eden, New York City, 1908–1936," *Social Text*, vol. 11 (Winter 1985), 52. See also Margaret Hodgen, "The Place of the Savage in the Great Chain of Being," in her *Early Anthropology in the Sixteenth and Seventeenth Centuries* (Philadelphia: University of Pennsylvania Press, 1964), 386–430.

16. My analysis of this episode is indebted to the feminist sociological methods articulated by Dorothy E. Smith in her books: *The Everyday World as*

Problematic: A Feminist Sociology (Boston: Northeastern University Press, 1987); The Conceptual Practices of Power: A Feminist Sociology of Knowledge (Boston: Northeastern University Press, 1990); Texts, Facts, and Femininity: Exploring the Relations of Ruling (London and New York: Routledge, 1990).

17. Smith, Texts, 21–8.
18. Marica Milanesi, "Introduzione," in Giovanni Battista Ramusio, Navigazioni e viaggi, 6 vols (Turin: Einaudi, 1978–85), vol. 1, xxi. (Oviedo's Sommario and Della naturale e generale istoria dell'Indie may be found in vol. 5 of this edition.)
19. Ibid., xix–xx.
20. Defert, "Collecting the World," 16.
21. Milanesi, introductory note to Ramusio's "Discorso sopra varii viaggi . . ." in Navigazioni, vol. 2, 961–2.
22. This section of my essay is especially indebted to Patricia Parker's essay "Rhetorics of Property: Exploration, Inventory, Blazon," in Literary Fat Ladies: Rhetoric, Gender, Property (London and New York: Methuen, 1987), 126–54. Parker's brilliant analysis of the figure of inventory illuminates the way in which the promotion of a woman writer can become a way of making her "a passive commodity in a homosocial discourse or male exchange in which the woman herself does not speak" (131).
23. White, Anne Bradstreet, 252.
24. Parker, "Rhetorics of Property," 131.
25. Cowell, "The Early Distribution," 272 n. 11; White, Anne Bradstreet, 251–2. The place of this copy of the 1650 edition of The Tenth Muse in Thomason's collection of Civil War and Commonwealth period books and pamphlets now residing in the British Museum is dramatically inviting of rhetorical analysis.
26. See bibliography in n. 1 and Octavio Paz, Sor Juana or, The Traps of Faith, trans. Margaret Sayers Peden (Cambridge, Mass.: Harvard University Press, 1988), 199. For an important analysis of the political context in which Sor Juana wrote, see Jean Franco, "Sor Juana Explores Space," in Plotting Women: Gender and Representation in Mexico (New York: Columbia University Press, 1989), 23–54.
27. Haraway, "Teddy Bear Patriarchy," 52.
28. Adrienne Rich, "Anne Bradstreet and Her Poetry," in The Works of Anne Bradstreet, xiii. This essay was written for the first printing of this edition in 1967.
29. Ibid., xvii.
30. Adrienne Rich, "Postscript," ibid., xxi.
31. Biblioteca Marciana, Misc. stampe 2088.
32. "Lettera di Amerigo Vespucci delle isole nuovamente trovate in quattro suoi viaggi" (Florence, 1505). On the subject of gender in English promotional literature, see Kolodny, Parker, 141–6, and especially the essay of Louis Montrose, "The Work of Gender in the Discourse of Discovery," Representations 33 (1991), 1–41.
33. John Smith, "The Description of New England," in Tracts and Other Papers relating principally to the Origin, Settlement and Progress of the Colonies in North America, collected by Peter Force (Gloucester, Mass.: Peter Smith, 1963) vol. 2, 9. Cited also by Parker, "Rhetorics of Property," 140.

34. Nicola Raponi, "Per la storia dell'Archivio di Stato di Milano: Erudizione e cultura nell' *Annuario* del Fumi (1909–1919)," *Rassegna degli Archivi di Stato* 31, no. 2 (1971), 316.
35. Here, I would like to suggest that Parker's analysis of the figure of inventory in literary and political texts might be transposed to the actual instruments of historical research.
36. Franco, "Sor Juana," 25.

Part II. **Historicizing Femininity**

5 The Notion of Woman in Medicine, Anatomy, and Physiology

Ian Maclean

3.0.1 What follows is extracted from an interdisciplinary study of the notion of woman in scholarly texts of the sixteenth and early seventeenth centuries. The various disciplines—theology, law, medicine, practical philosophy—all possess authoritative texts which attract commentary; the fact that nearly all of these are written in Latin and widely diffused through the mechanism of the book fairs makes them a coherent and accessible body of doctrine not only to scholars working within the individual disciplines but also those beyond them.

3.0.2 Three broad areas of enquiry are pursued in the context of this corpus of texts: the notion of woman itself; the idea of sex difference; the relationship between sex difference and other differences. From the earliest times, and in the most far-flung cultures, the notion of female has in some sense been opposed to that of male, and aligned with other opposites. The ways in which these opposites have been used in argumentation and related to each other are the subject of an illuminating investigation by G. E. R. Lloyd entitled *Polarity and analogy: two types of argumentation in early Greek thought* (Cambridge, 1971). The earliest stage in the use of polarity, in Lloyd's analysis, is represented by the related opposites attributed by Aristotle to the Pythagoreans in *Metaphysics* A.3 [986a 21ff]:

male	female
limit	unlimited
odd	even
one	plurality
right	left

square	oblong
at rest	moving
straight	curved
light	darkness
good	evil

Here there is no classification of the different sorts of opposites; nor is the alignment of male–limit–odd–one–right etc. justified by reasoning or empirical evidence. In the Renaissance, this set of opposites was known not only through Aristotle's account of it,[1] but also through the Hippocratic corpus, in which it is implicit.

3.0.3 Lloyd turns next to the use made of opposites by Eleatic philosophers, which is not relevant to this study; after this he considers Plato, whose interest in this topic is most clearly represented in the Renaissance by the theory of division, developed and resurrected principally by Ramus whose dichotomies are present in many texts of the late sixteenth and early seventeenth centuries.[2] Finally Lloyd examines Aristotle's own work, in which a more sophisticated analysis of these opposites and of modes of opposition is to be found, known to scholastic and Renaissance scholars alike.[3] Even in Jacopo Zabarella's innovative works on logic, this analysis is simply reproduced.[4] Its principal source is *Categories* x [11*b* 15ff]; there, opposites are divided into (1) correlative opposites (Zabarella's 'species relativa': e.g. double/half, father/son); (2) contraries, which can either admit an intermediate ('species contraria mediata': e.g. black/white) or not ('species contraria immediata': e.g. odd/even, health/sickness); (3) positive and privative terms ('species privata': e.g. sight/blindness); finally (4) contradictories ('species contradictoria': e.g. 'he sits'/'he does not sit'). The opposite male/female which is our concern here is sometimes an opposite of privation (see below, 3.3.3), sometimes a contrary either admitting or not admitting an intermediate (see below, 3.5.5); it can attract parallels with correlative opposites. The complexity of the notion of woman, and the dislocations which occur within that notion, arise in part, as will be seen, from the structures of thought inherited from Aristotle.

3.0.4 The problem is exacerbated by the presence in intellectual life of unexplained and unjustified Pythagorean related dualities, not only in ancient medical texts, but also in the works of Aristotle himself, who treats the opposites right/left, above/below, front/back in this primitive manner, as Lloyd has shown.[5] The notion of the historical development of thought—either applied to earlier and later texts of the Aristotelian corpus, or to the relationship between this and the earlier Hippocratic corpus—is not invoked by Renaissance thinkers to resolve this confusion, and it seems that concepts of difference, division, definition and opposition are problematic to them. The notion of woman, intimately involved with this area of speculation, reflects well the hesitancies and incoherences inherent in Renaissance modes of thought.

3.1.1 The subject of woman as seen by physiologists, anatomists and physicians is complex and multifaceted, because of its contiguity (and coincidence) with spermatology, hysterology, the science of the humours and theories of physical change. It is also very closely related to embryology, which exercises a deep influence on medical discussions about woman, and even determines to some degree the series of problems considered by medieval and Renaissance writers. In the excellent accounts of ancient embryology by Erna Lesky[6] and H. B. Adelmann,[7] this fact is pointed out, and the principal questions are listed: what is the origin of semen? do both sexes produce it? which part of the body develops first in the foetus? what determines sex and resemblance of children to parents? These questions give rise to a set of *loci classici* which are discussed by Renaissance doctors.

3.1.2 Renaissance medicine is distinct from the medieval discipline not only because of the work of humanists who produce the great editions, indices and commentaries of Aristotle, Hippocrates and Galen in the first half of the sixteenth century, but also because of the growth of experimental anatomy. The work of Andreas Vesalius, Gabriele Falloppio and Realdo Colombo is paralleled in the clinical sphere by the producers of *consilia* (case histories) and great writers on physiology, among them Jean Fernel. Although most doctors refer to ancient sects (the 'practici' who follow Averroes, the 'peripatetici', the 'Galenici', the 'methodici', the 'empirici'), the vast majority of them are, according to Adelmann, 'thoroughgoing Galenists at heart',[8] but influenced to different degrees by Aristotle, Avicenna and Hippocrates. It is this last for whom the greatest respect is shown. Where his texts are thought to be erroneous, interpolation is invoked (see below, 3.3.7); Aristotle is sometimes described as his vulgar plagiarist.[9] Peripatetic doctors, working on the new published texts of the Philosopher, set out to defend him, but differ in their interpretations, as will be seen (below, 3.4.2). The 'neoterici' (doctors of the modern school), working from observation and experiment, attack all ancient authorities, but are not altogether free from inherited beliefs and structures of thought.[10] The situation by the end of the sixteenth century is quite confused, but it may be said with a certain degree of confidence that the general context of medicine remains Galenist, while the work of Aristotle and the 'neo-terici' is in dispute, leading to accusations of incompetence and pla-giarism. Such accusations are found in the *De universa mulierum medicina* of Rodrigues de Castro (1546?–1627), published in 1603; he denounces the sixteenth-century collection of medical texts on woman entitled *Gynaecea* as 'an amalgam of excellent doctrine and wild speculation which could easily mislead students of medicine',[11] yet he himself relies heavily on some parts of it. The *Gynaecea*, which first appears in 1566, and is expanded in later editions (1577, 1586–7, 1597) is an extremely useful document for the purposes of this study. It assembles the major writings on woman not only of antiquity and the Middle Ages, but also of contemporaries.[12] It shows that the most prolific period of writing comes after the great editions of medical authorities and the publication of the findings of anatomists (*c.*1540–1600), and that such writing is undertaken in France, Spain, Germany and Italy.

3.1.3 This rather confused situation produces, in the case of medical disputes about woman, the curious combination of doctors claiming to be Galenists and feminists: that is, believing 'against Aristotle' that men and women are equally perfect in their sex (see below, 3.3.5). The combination is curious, because Galen himself does not claim this; it becomes even more bizarre, when theology in the form of the Aris-totelian Aquinas is invoked as further evidence of the equality of the sexes.[13] Many doctors at the end of the sixteenth and the beginning of the seventeenth centuries write eloquently against the wrong done to the honour of woman by Aristotle,[14] and it is possible to argue that there is a feminist movement in medical spheres, where in theology there is little evidence of one. The contradictions involved in this movement will emerge in the course of the chapter. But reliance on ancient authorities and deep structures of thought, such as the Pythagorean opposites which are strongly in evidence in ancient texts on woman, produce a matrix as inescapable as the scholastic synthe-sis. The problem unique to Renaissance doctors, 'to harmonize the received texts with a growing body of fresh knowledge that renewed and increasingly more intensive and extensive observations were every day bringing to their notice',[15] leads even conservative doctors such as Jean Riolan the Elder to state that 'it is absurd to combat observation and experience with reason out of respect for antiquity'.[16] But obser-vation can only affect the tenets of medical science if such instruments as the microscope make it possible; in embryology and gynaecology, the major developments are all post-1650 (Reinier de Graaf, Karl Ernst von Baer[17]). Until these breakthroughs, the questions asked of the evidence available were not necessarily the most profitable ones, as they emerge not so much from observation as from a conceptual framework inherited from the ancients.

3.1.4 It may be helpful at this point briefly to recapitulate Aristotle's and Galen's ideas on woman. According to the former's theory, a male animal is one that generates in another, whereas the female generates in herself.[18] She is further characterized by deprived, passive and material traits, cold and moist dominant humours and a desire for completion by intercourse with the male.[19] This is essentially the medieval understanding of Aristotle, as P. Diepgen has shown;[20] it has been seen how such notions are syncretized with Christian thought. Galen differs in one essential point (the existence and efficacy of female semen: see below 3.4.1–3.4.3); this idea was known in the medieval period, but not developed.[21] His account of woman in the *De usu partium corporis* (xiv) is otherwise in harmony with peripatetic teaching, which is enriched by him with a more extensive theory of the humours.[22] Arising from these accounts of woman, a series of problems arise which will be considered in turn here. Is she a monstrous creation? Is she an imperfect version of the male? Does she produce semen, and is this fertile? How is sex determined? What physiological features are unique to woman, and what effects are these thought to have? What are the psychological differences between the sexes?

3.2.1 Is woman a monstrous creation? This question has clear theological associations which have already been discussed elsewhere[23]. A monster is something created *praeter naturam*, not in the ordinary course of nature.[24] Although females are the result of a generative event not carried through to its final conclusion according to the Aristotelian theory, sex difference is necessary for the reproduction of the species, and so the female is not monstrous, but is according to the general tendency of nature (*intentio naturae universalis*). A text often invoked is Aristotle's *Metaphysics*, in which it is asserted that men and women are not of different species.[25] Sex difference is a feature of higher animals, but it is postulated in plants and even metals by alchemists, and is essential to mystical understandings of the universe.

3.2.2 None but satirical or facetious texts support the proposition of monstrosity. They do so often by referring to a sentence in Erasmus's *Praise of Folly*: 'Plato seems to doubt whether woman should be classed with brute beasts or rational beings'.[26] The Platonic text alluded to seems to be *Timaeus* 91A, although this could be applied to men as much as women (see below, 3.7.3). A related Platonic text, sometimes invoked, is from the same section of the *Timaeus*, and suggests that women incarnate the souls of men who in a previous life have behaved in a dissolute or debauched fashion.[27]

3.2.3 It is interesting that so many texts at the end of the sixteenth century contain refutations of this proposition; this may be attributed to the currency of Jacques Cujas's joke and the *Disputatio nova contra mulieres*, which are sometimes confused.[28] The arguments follow the same course: both man and woman are of the same species; sex difference is the material, formal and efficient cause of procreation; woman, in her own sex, is as perfect as man.[29] As the last argument suggests, opponents of Aristotle are able to use the proposition of monstrosity as a means of attacking peripatetic doctors,[30] even though some of the latter refute it as vehemently as Galenists.[31] Wherever monstrous conception and births are discussed, there is little to indicate that woman is considered as such or as responsible for such, except perhaps through the influence of her imagination on the foetus (see below, 3.7.5). It would seem safe to assume that this question was debated only for the sake of form, or to refute a specific satirical text, and that it reflects more on the surprising success of the *facetiae* of Cujas and the author of the *Disputatio nova contra mulieres* than anything else.

3.3.1 Is woman an imperfect version of the male, and are the anatomical and physiological differences between the sexes caused by a lack of some element or elements in woman? In Aristotelian and Galenic terms,[32] woman is less fully developed than man. Because of lack of heat in generation, her sexual organs have remained internal, she is incomplete, colder and moister in dominant humours, and unable to 'concoct' perfect semen from blood. Two axioms are implied here: that the hottest created thing is the most perfect, and that a direct comparison can be made between the genitalia of man and woman in function, number and form.

3.3.2 A group of peripatetic doctors justify the 'imperfect male' theory by reference to scholastic theology, often specifying Aquinas as the source;[33] those who distinguish *natura particularis* and *natura universalis* in this way include Francisco de Valles (Vallesius) (1542–92) in a syncretic work entitled *De iis quae scripta sunt physicè in sacris literis* (1582);[34] Gaspard Bauhin in his *Theatrum anatomicum* (1592),[35] and Bartholomäus Keckermann (1571?–1608?) in the *Systema physicum* (1610).[36] Such syncretism is not surprising in followers of Aristotle, although it is not common to all peripatetics. It is rare among Galenists, although at least one late example can be cited.[37]

3.3.3 Other physiologists defend the theory of imperfection without reference to theology. These include Kaspar Hofmann (1574–1648), a vigorous supporter of Galen and opponent of Harvey. In 1625 he published a commentary on Galen's *De usu partium corporis* which includes a general exposition of his views on woman; four years later, in a polemical work on embryology (see below, 3.4.3), he produces a coherent account of the axiom of heat and of the differences between hotter and colder creatures. From this account it becomes evident why heat is associated with perfection in physical terms. Heat is instrumental in the production of the most perfectly concocted semen from which the male will be born, which is produced in the right (hotter) testicle and deposited in the right (hotter) side of the uterus.[38] The male grows faster *in utero*, is of darker and harder flesh, more hirsute, more able to sustain extremes of temperature, has larger arteries and veins, a deeper voice, is less prone to disease, more robust, broader, comes to full maturity more slowly and ages less quickly than the colder female. He may be ambidextrous whereas she rarely is, and has mental characteristics which may also be attributed to body heat: courage, liberality, moral strength, honesty. The female on the other hand, being colder, is characterized by the deprivation or opposite of these features. The authorities quoted by Hofmann in establishing these differences based on body temperature are principally Hippocrates, Galen and Aristotle.[39]

3.3.4 An example of a latter-day orthodox peripatetic is provided by Cesare Cremonini (1550–1630), in whose polemical treatise *De calido innato et semine* (1634) is found an apology for Aristotle's theory of sex difference directed against the Galenists on the specific point of the efficacy and existence of female semen (see below, 3.4.3). According to Cremonini, woman is less perfect than man in the context of procreation (*in ordine ad generationem*), because it is she who carries the foetus and is the place of conception. Just as the seed is more noble and perfect than the earth in which it is planted and from which it draws nourishment, so also is the male more noble and perfect than the female.[40] Both Hofmann and Cremonini accept the Aristotelian and Galenic argument that the difference in sexual organs between male and female may be explained by the lack of heat in generation which, in the case of the female, causes the genitalia to remain internal. This leads both to accept comparability of form, number, and general function.

3.3.5 After 1600, the vast majority of doctors reject these axioms in favour of the argument from specific sexual function. Both sexes are

133

needed for reproduction; one sex begets in another, the other in itself, and each has an appropriately differentiated physiology. The earliest suggestion of such an approach is found in the writings of Julius Caesar Scaliger (see below, 3.3.6), although not in a medical context, nor necessarily proposed seriously. A more important influence is Gabriele Falloppio's description of the female genitalia in his *Observationes anatomicae* (1561), which is adduced by many writers,[41] and marks one of the most important changes brought about by experimental anatomy in this domain before 1670. Galen's comparison of male and female genitalia (uterus = inverted penis, ovaries (*testes mulierum*) = testes) is rejected by the *neoterici* in favour of a new alignment drawn from Falloppio (clitoris = penis, nymphae = praeputium, etc.); but although even Falloppio describes male and female genitalia as altogether comparable, it seems that the number, size and function of the specifically compared organs are difficult to establish and, by the end of the sixteenth century, most anatomists abandon this parallelism.[42] The Parisian doctor André Du Laurens writes a very coherent account of this medical dispute in 1593, concluding against comparability;[43] after this, the only asseverations in medical writing which are based on Galenic or Falloppian parallels are to be found in the long debate about female semen (examined below, 3.4.1–3.4.3); it might perhaps be added, however, that Descartes's anatomy makes a Galenic alignment of genitalia.[44] Du Laurens's position, which is that generally accepted after 1600, is consistent with thoroughgoing functionalism, for he rejects also the Aristotelian and Galenic argument of vestigial, non-functional organs in each sex (nipples in man, testes in woman)[45] (see below, 3.4.1–3.4.3). By 1600, in nearly all medical circles, the peripatetic claim that the female is an imperfect persun of the male[46] is banished from the textbooks, and one sex is no longer thought to be an imperfect and incomplete version of the other. Indeed, far from being described as an inferior organ, the uterus now evokes admiration and eulogy for its remarkable rôle in procreation.[47]

3.3.6 If woman is no longer an imperfect version of the male, is she yet colder and moister than he? Girolamo Cardano (1501–76) discusses this question as early as 1548 in his *Contradicentia medica*,[48] but it is Julius Caesar Scaliger's facetious attack on another of Cardano's works, the *De subtilitate*, which gives fresh impetus to the debate. In his *Exercitationes de subtilitate* of 1557, Scaliger sets out to demonstrate that Cardano's inflexible application of the theory of the humours is absurd; in doing this, he claims at one point that man and woman are of equal temperature, but that this is not apparent since woman, being more humid, appears to be colder, and man, the drier, seems to be hotter.[49] Such an argument is somewhat surprising as it comes from a known Aristotelian and anti-feminist,[50] and this may reinforce the suspicion that it is rehearsed paradoxically or as a joke. It is, however, widely quoted by serious doctors as well as feminists.[51]

3.3.7 The debate is made more confused by the fact that not all ancient authorities agree on this point. According to Maurice de la Corde's edition of the Hippocratic (or rather pseudo-Hippocratic) *De morbis mulierum* (1585), it seems that this school of medical thought believes woman's blood to be hotter than the male's, and that she is therefore altogether of a higher temperature.[52] The relevant passage is, however, declared to be an interpolation by Christóbal de Vega (1510?–1573?), the respected professor of medicine at Alcalá de Henares, in his commentary on Hippocrates's *Prognostic* (1552),[53] and most commentators thereafter accept this view.[54] Nearly all other ancient texts can be interpreted to indicate that woman is colder and moister in dominant humours, but after 1580 this is no longer assumed to be a sign of imperfection. Woman's temperature is functional; her colder metabolism causes her to consume ('burn up') food less fast, thus leaving residues of fat and blood which are necessary for the nutriment of the foetus and for the eventual production of milk.[55] When not required for the foetus or newborn child, these residues account for the physiological and anatomical features peculiar to woman (see below, 3.8.1). Such functionalism is, of course, subjacent or even sometimes explicit in ancient texts; but it had become overlaid by the conclusions it had engendered.

3.3.8 While all agree that the hottest male is hotter than the hottest female, it is not clear whether physiologists believe that the hottest female is colder than the coldest male. At least one scholastic source argues this,[56] but Galen in his treatise on the pulse, followed by some late Renaissance commentators, seems to suggest that an overlap is possible, arising from differences of style of life, climate and diet. This might help to account for the ethical problem which arises when some men are dominated by some women (see below, 3.5.2).[57] That women in general are of lower temperature than men is, however, not questioned, and this has important implications in ethics, in which physiology is invoked to justify the relegation of woman to the home.[58]

3.3.9 Other conclusions are also drawn from the coldness of woman, which are consistent with Aristotelian and Galenic doctrine, and indeed often explicitly stated in the writings of these authorities. The transfer of this material to the renewed theory of functionalism demonstrates the capacity of Renaissance doctors to salvage from ancient writings whatever details fit into their modified conceptual scheme, and, in using them, still to claim the authority of philosophers whose justificatory structures of thought they have rejected. Menstruation results from woman's colder metabolism; unlike female animals who do not menstruate, she cannot, for sociological reasons (*institutio*) use up excesses of blood in physical exercise, and does not produce bodily hair as does the male. Woman rarely goes bald (that is, 'burns up' her hair). Like boys and eunuchs, she has a high voice, denser, paler, fattier, softer flesh than the male, which burns better than does his on funeral pyres,[59] and is rarely ambidextrous. She takes longer to form in the womb, causes more pain at childbirth to her mother, being less able to help herself than the more active male; but she reaches puberty earlier, and ages more quickly because of the corrupting effect of her dominant humidity. Her physical shape (fatter hips and narrower shoulders than the male) is also the result of colder humours, which do not possess sufficient energy to drive matter up towards the head.[60] The psychological effects of coldness are often set out in ethical writings;[61] it is here that the most obvious dislocation of thought occurs, for it seems that physiologists retain the beliefs in the less perfect mental faculties of woman even after the abandonment of the 'imperfect male' theory: thus Galenists argue not only that woman is equally perfect in her sex as the male is in his, but also that she is inferior to him for physiological reasons.

3.4.1 Closely connected with the debates discussed above is that concerning the existence and efficacy of female semen.[62] The medieval opinion, that woman has testes (what are now known to be ovaries), but that these are residual and not functional, is attractive because of its possible syncretism with Gen. 2:23,[63] and because of its consistency with the dualities male/female, form/matter, act/potency, possession/deprivation. It can also be used as an argument against the enjoyment of coitus by woman, which austere religious moralists sometimes rehearse.[64] Renaissance anatomists expose many Aristotelian and indeed Galenic fallacies about the female genitalia which were authoritative in the Middle Ages,[65] but they have little observational evidence to bring to bear on this topic: indeed, Falloppio even adds some credence to the medieval view by stating in his *Observationes anatomicae* that he was unable to perceive anything resembling semen in the female testes.[66]

3.4.2 Before considering the clash of Galen and Aristotle on this point, it should be said that neoaristotelians of the Renaissance do not even agree as to what really is the opinion of Aristotle. Adelmann points out that this is not surprising, since the *De generatione animalium* is ambiguous on this topic.[67] Prominent among peripatetics who believe that woman has no semen are Julius Caesar Scaliger[68] and Cesare Cremonini;[69] Fortunio Liceti[70] and Joannes Magirus (d. 1596)[71] both represent neoaristotelians who argue that women have semen. To complete a rather confusing picture, one should add that at least one thoroughgoing Galenist, Kaspar Hofmann, argues that women do not have perfect and efficacious semen.[72] There are therefore among neoaristotelians those who declare that woman is imperfect and has no semen (Cremonini); others who argue that although imperfect, woman has a *virtus formatrix* (Liceti); and a third category denying that woman is imperfect or that she lacks semen (Magirus). Similarly, among Galenists, there are those who argue that woman is cold, imperfect and yet has semen (Mundinus Mundinius);[73] others who argue that woman is cold, but perfect in her sex and possessing a *virtus formatrix* (Du Laurens);[74] and a third category arguing that woman is cold, imperfect and lacks semen (Hofmann). No writer on physiology argues that woman possesses the material and formative faculties sufficient to procreate of herself, although it is argued that the *mola uteri* is a result of the conjunction of woman's (incomplete or imperfect) semen and menstrual blood.[75] One theory not represented above is that of Fabius Pacius of Vicenza (1547–1614), who wrote in his *Commentarius in Galeni libros methodi medendi pars prima* of 1597 that the heat of the uterus is the agent of procreation, and menstrual blood together with semen the matter:[76] this ancient theory had already been refuted by Aristotle, whose arguments are reproduced by Mercuriale against Pacius.[77]

3.4.3 The commonly accepted view is that expressed by Galen in the *De semine* (II. 2), which states that woman has semen which is colder and less active than that of the male.[78] The question remains whether it is efficient both formally and materially, or simply materially, or simply formally. The Galenic position, that it contributes to both the form and the matter of the embryo, is that which is most commonly adopted; it helps to explain the resemblance of children to their parents, which Aristotle attributes rather unsatisfactorily to menstrual blood. The rôle of menstrual blood, in both the Aristotelian and Galenic systems, is the provision of matter. This area of medical discussion, which Reinier de Graaf released from obtuseness by

his treatise on the female genitalia in 1672, is the subject of a pro-
tracted debate involving Mundinius, Parisano, Liceti, Cremonini and
Hofmann between 1609 and 1635 in which the orthodox Galenist and
Aristotelian positions, the heretical Galenist stance and an uncertain
and confused eclecticism (Parisano) are all rehearsed.[79] Although this
long debate must appear anachronistic and obscurantist today,[80] it represents nonetheless the last philological enquiry into the subject, and
reproduces the most advanced conceptual schemes based on traditional embryology. Modern histories of medicine concentrate on
the advances made by experimental anatomists and physiologists
(Fabricius ab Aquapendente, William Harvey, Marcello Malpighi),
which are indeed important, but more to posterity than to contemporaries. These still relied on a synthetic structure in which Galen and
Aristotle are indispensable.

3.5.1 The questions of imperfection and semen are naturally connected with that of sex determination *in utero*. Here a variety of ancient
theories known principally through Aristotle's *De generatione animalium* are discussed by Renaissance writers. Sex is said to be determined
at the moment of conception by the male semen alone, which may be
affected by diet, climate or physical constitution (Aristotle); sex is also
said to be determined by the conjunction of male and female semen
and their relative temperature (Galen). Another theory, influenced by
or influencing Pythagoras's dualities, attributes sex difference to the
position of the foetus in the uterus (left or right side), and the provenance of the semen from the left or right testicle.[81] This last hypothesis is widely commented upon and often found as part of recipes for
ensuring that children are of the desired sex (which in nearly all cases
is male).[82] Some physiologists, however, doubt it on the grounds of its
unprovability.[83] It is clear that most doctors accept the Galenic view
of sex determination after 1600.

3.5.2 For those who adopt a coherent Aristotelian position, and for
Paracelsus (who in this respect at least resembles an Aristotelian),[84]
there is a clear difference between the sexes, and between both sexes
and all forms of monstrous (unnatural) births. Among followers of
Galen and prearistotelian physiologists, other possibilities are discussed. Whereas, according to Aristotle, sex is a contrariety which does
not permit of true intermediaries (since it is based on the opposite of
privation), in Aristotle's account of Parmenides's theory, revived by
Levinus Lemnius (1505–68), there are two stages of intermediaries
between perfect men (the result of dominant male semen and a position in the right-hand side of the uterus) and perfect women (who are

born from dominant female semen in the left-hand side of the uterus). These are the effeminate male (dominant male semen, left-hand side of the uterus) and the virago (female semen, right-hand side of uterus);[85] of the latter Felix Platter, Jacques Dubois and Rodrigues de Castro all speak.[86] This does not mean that a perfectly ambiguous creature can be procreated (see below, 3.5.5); nor does it necessarily imply (although it is sometimes taken to mean this) that the hottest female is hotter than the coldest male. The ranges of humours and temperature are more commonly assumed to overlap, thus providing a rudimentary physiological framework by which ethical and political problems such as dominant wives and successful queens may be explained. An extreme statement of the theory that psychological variations in sex can be attributed to physical constitution is found in the preface to Theodorus Collado's *Adversaria seu commentarii medicinales* of 1615, where it is claimed that all men and women have 'diversae naturae', and that sex has no necessary relation to character (see below, 3.8.3).

3.5.3 Aristotle's account of sex differentiation *in utero* is widely rejected in favour of the Galenic theory by the end of the sixteenth century. This latter theory seems to allow for the production of a sexually ambiguous being, if the temperature of the male and female semen are at a crucial point; it has been seen, however, that a discontinuous spectrum of (normal) sex difference is generally preferred by the Renaissance. This preference may have influenced the debate concerning epigenesis and preformation which emerges from microscope observations in the second half of the seventeenth century. The belief that the individual spermatozoon incorporates a 'preformed' human being reflects the predisposition to find a clear differentiation of sex *ab initio*, which perhaps accounts in part for the popularity of this theory at that time, and the unattractiveness of the theory of epigenesis, although it should be added that this also had impressive adherents, among them William Harvey.[87]

3.5.4 One implication of the Galenist theory which intrigues Renaissance doctors is the question of sex change: there is a *locus classicus* on this topic in Pliny's *Natural History* (VII.4). Whether a woman can become male is a question related to the debate about the comparability of male and female genitalia (see above, 3.3.5). The few clinical cases attested in the Renaissance are all of women changing into men; this is what would have been expected, as what is perfect is unlikely to change into that which is less so (even though Ambroise Paré talks of women 'degenerating into men').[88] These cases are all recorded with great circumspection by physiologists, who prudently do not treat them as conclusive. Johann Schenck von Grafenberg produces a list of cases in his *Observationes* (1584–97) which is subsequently referred to by other writers on this topic.[89]

3.5.5 Hermaphrodites are also rare occurrences, but are much more fully documented, notably by Gaspard Bauhin.[90] A possible reason for the attention they receive is to be found in the importance of the notion of hermaphrodite or androgyne to occult and neoplatonist currents of thought in the Renaissance. It is generally agreed that hermaphrodites belong not at a mid point on the sexual spectrum between (normal) female and (normal) male births, but rather to the category of monster. Just as a firm distinction of sex is sought by Renaissance thinkers in theology and medicine, so also is a firm distinction of natural and unnatural adhered to (see below, 3.9.3). The causes of monstrous births (imbalance of blood, semen and heat; illness of one or other parent) clearly indicate that hermaphrodites belong to the category of unnatural.[91]

3.6.1 Next to be considered are the unique physiological features of woman which are relevant to her general notion.[92] Menstruation is one of these. In the Middle Ages this was firmly associated with the malediction (Gen. 3: 16), with uncleanness, and with certain deleterious physical effects, usually relating to the transmission of diseases (notably smallpox) by heredity or contagion. The malignity of menses is chronicled in ancient medical texts, notably in Aristotle, Columella, Pliny and Plutarch[93] and these opinions are reproduced by early Renaissance writers.[94] A debate on this topic occurs, in which Jean Fernel (1497–1558) and Jean Riolan the Elder (d. 1606) support the view that menses are malignant in a variety of ways,[95] whereas later writers, Bottoni, Mercuriale and Rodrigues de Castro, all argue that menses are only malignant when the whole female organism is ill.[96] It is true that some doctors argue that they possess curative powers or virtue, but closer examination of the texts reveals that these powers are attributed to them because of the sympathy between the disease and the menses, which far from being beneficial are in this system as noxious as the disease on which they act homeopathically.[97] For all this, there is far less stress on the noxious nature of menses at the end of the sixteenth century, and the majority of texts stress their harmless excremental nature. In doing so, they can be said to contrast with neoscholastic theological texts, in which the paradigm clean/unclean is upheld. There is, as might be expected, an abundant clinical literature on this subject.

3.7.1 A series of questions about the uterus, raised in antiquity and debated in the Renaissance, is also of interest here. Is the uterus an animal in its own right, endowed with powers of movement and a sense of smell? Is it eager to procreate (*avidum generandi*)? What illnesses does it cause in woman? Is it sympathetic to the moon and the imagination?

3.7.2 The conflicting ancient texts concerning the animality of the uterus are those of Plato (*Timaeus* 91A) where the uterus is described as a 'καθάπερ τι ζῷον παιδοποιΐας ἐπιθυμητικὸν' (*animal avidum generandi*) and Galen, who refutes the Platonic view that the uterus is animal because of its alleged powers of independent movement and its alleged sense of smell in several texts, notably the *De locis affectis* (IV. 5). Galen accounts for the movement of the uterus by claiming it is caused by the constriction or relaxation of muscles, and dismisses the alleged sense of smell as ridiculous. Early Renaissance anatomists consider the Platonic doctrine as a sort of metaphor, and pour scorn on the anatomical description of the uterus by Galen; this tentative sympathy for Platonic anatomy is taken up not only by certain doctors, including Jean Riolan the Elder, but also in popular literature by François Rabelais.[98] The overwhelming majority of physiologists seem, however, to accept Galen's criticism of Plato on this point, and refutations of the view that the uterus is an independent being living in woman may be found in many writings.[99]

3.7.3 A second question is whether the uterus makes woman eager to procreate, and desire the male. Such a view accords well with the Aristotelian concept by which the imperfect should desire the perfect: the comparison is found in *Physics* 1.9 [192*a* 22]: 'matter desires form as the female the male'. The jurist André Tiraqueau throws doubt on the reading of this passage,[100] but he seems to be alone in the Renaissance in doing so; certainly Falloppio accepted the authority of the text as quoted here (see n. 19). This argument is rehearsed by Riolan the Elder,[101] it is also reflected in Bonacciuoli's etymology of vulva from *volens*.[102] Scaliger, however, asserts in his *Exercitationes* (CXXXI.4) that the sexes desire each other mutually, and that no argument about perfection or imperfection can be made about the uterus's alleged avidity for coitus. The fact of mutual desire has, of course, never been in doubt psychologically; for this reason, perhaps, there is no late defence of this proposition. It is even enshrined in the *locus classicus* (*Timaeus* 91A–D) in which Plato refers to the unruly member in man which is equivalent to the uterus.

3.7.4 Women are sometimes said to be more prone to illness than men;[103] this is nearly always attributed to the influence of the uterus.[104]

The etymological association of hysteria with ὑστέρα (= uterus) is well known; many of its forms are psychological. Even woman's garrulity (see above, 2.7.2) is said to be one effect of hysteria;[105] *furor uterinus*, or excessive desire for coitus, is another which attracts much comment.[106] Mercado has an exhaustive list of hysterical illnesses, many of them inducing lovesickness, melancholia, listlessness and irrational behaviour.[107] This is evidently one reason why women are thought to possess weaker powers of mind compared to men, but there is no clear agreement as to which powers are in question. Another cause of irrationality cited is the supposed singularity of cranial suture (*sutura sagittalis*) in woman, which does not allow humours to escape and hence subjects their brains to 'perturbationes' (passions).[108] Thus although many of these doctors argue that woman is as perfect in her sex as is man in his, they do not accord to her equal possibilities for psychological control.

3.7.5 Two external forces are said to act on the uterus: the moon and the imagination. Most doctors record the ancient belief in the influence of the moon; Du Laurens doubts this, although there is little sign that his hesitation is known to many outside the anatomical sphere.[109] The alleged effect of the imagination (the 'power to generate mental images') on the uterus, especially during pregnancy, causing birthmarks and deformities, is also noted.[110] Paracelsus and other occult philosophers make much of this.[111] Some doctors comment on this belief; its most comprehensive refutation does not occur until 1727, written by J. A. Blondel (*The strength of imagination in pregnant women examined; and the opinion that marks and deformities arise from thence demonstrated to be a vulgar error*). It seems still to hold some credence in the popular mind today.

3.8.1 For the Renaissance, the physical characteristics of woman exclusive to their sex—colder and moister humours, menstruation, the womb and its diseases—have psychological implications. There are *loci classici* in which these are recorded: the most celebrated of these is found in the *Historia animalium* ix.1 [608*a* 21ff]:

In all genera in which the distinction of male and female is found, Nature makes a similar differentiation in the mental characteristics of the sexes. This differentiation is the most obvious in the case of human kind and in that of the larger animals and the viviparous quadrupeds. In the case of these latter, the female is softer in character, is the sooner tamed, admits more readily of caressing, is more apt in the way of learning . . . In all cases, excepting those of the bear and leopard, the female is less spirited than the male, . . . softer in disposition, more mischievous, less simple, more impulsive, and more attentive to the nurture of the young; the male, on the other hand, is more spirited than the female, more savage, more simple and less cunning . . . the nature of man is most rounded off and complete, and consequently in man the qualities or capacities above referred to are found in their perfection. Hence woman is more compassionate than man, more easily moved to tears, at the same time is more jealous, more querulous, more apt to scold and to strike. She is, furthermore, more prone to despondency and less hopeful than the man, more void of shame or self-respect, more false of speech, more deceptive, and of more retentive memory. She is also more wakeful, more shrinking, more difficult to rouse to action, and requires a smaller quantity of nutriment.

3.8.2 This *locus* is not exhaustive, nor is it necessarily systematic. Its scientific basis is the theory which relates bodily humours to mental characteristics; a combination of cold and moist produces a retentive memory because, like wax, impressions can be registered easily and remain fixed on cold and moist substances. The memory, which is sometimes linked to the 'intellectus passibilis', is also associated with woman (*vs* man) as is passive (*vs* active). Imagination is thought to be stronger in woman because cold and moist objects are subject to metamorphosis; another form of metamorphosis is found in mental changeability, manifesting itself in deceit, inconstancy, lack of stamina, infidelity, but also inventiveness.[112] Many inventions are traditionally associated with women in popular literature. The effect of the uterus on the mind weakens rationality and increases the incidence and violence of passions in women: hate, vengeance, fear, anger are all thought commonly to hold greater sway over the female sex; but also compassion, pity and love.[113] The softer flesh of woman predisposes her to psychological softness (*mollities*), which is described as a vice or defect in the *Nicomachean Ethics*; childbirth predisposes her to a greater tolerance of pain.[114] Such psychological assumptions are not systematized in the writings of either Aristotle or Galen, although the latter gives some indication of the relationship between the humours and psychology in the *De humoribus*. They are present in authoritative texts often in the form of incidental remarks; perhaps for this reason orthodox medical writings tend to make less reference to them than popular literature. Galen himself, after demonstrating the influence of extraneous factors (style of life, diet, climate) on humours in the male and the female, suggests that medical students should be careful to relate humours to their whole context (*totius rei naturam*).[115] By using Galen's example of a misleading case, Julius Caesar Scaliger is able to ridicule the inflexible application of the theory of the humours to psychology in his *Exercitationes* (CCLXXIV). Other arguments about sexual psychology based on physical phenomena are also attacked in the Renaissance; an example is the proof of natural modesty (*verecundia*) in woman—the fact that drowned female corpses float face down wards in the water—which is discredited by Bonacciuoli, and shown to result from purely anatomical causes.[116]

3.8.3 Some doctors, notably Martinus Akakia and Rodrigues de Castro, assert with vehemence that women are equal to men in the *operationes animi,* just as they are the equal of men in the perfection of their sex.[117] This argument has theological weight. Jerome asserts that sex is not of the mind [*animus*],[118] and Aquinas's argument that sex is not of the soul [*anima*] is similar, although not explicitly identical.[119] The operations of the mind referred to seem to be those associated with the image of God understood as *anima rationalis*: will, intellect and memory. This conflicts with the popular notion of woman's psychology (3.8.2) which makes her inferior in the first two operations and superior in the last. Another suggestion is made by Theodorus Collado, who puts forward the theory of a random distribution of mental strengths and weaknesses in both sexes.[120] There seems to be little support for this hypothesis, as might be expected, for it undermines both the difference of sex, which is an indispensable duality in Renaissance as in scholastic thought, and the theory of the humours, which is the dominant theory of psychological difference. Even to those doctors who argue that woman is equally perfect in her sex as is man in his, the fact of her coldness is accepted and with it the psychological implications mentioned above. Moreover, the psychological effects of the uterus are not denied by such doctors, who accept also that the 'passiones animi' can in turn affect the uterus, inducing sterility.[121] It is clear that psychological limitations must have a bearing on the ethical status of woman; her assumed frailty of body, which best befits her for the care of the young and makes her unsuited to exposure to the dangers of the outside world, is accompanied by mental and emotional weaknesses which are the natural justification for her exclusion from public life, responsibility and moral fulfilment.

3.9.1 From this discussion of medical commentaries and texts, it emerges that the Aristotelian notion of woman is abandoned by 1600 by most doctors in favour of a modified form of Galenism, in which some elements of the Aristotelian synthesis remain, and some tenets of Galenism are adapted to concord with the results of new anatomical studies and clinical observation. This eclectic approach leads to attempts to remove ambiguities and conflicting opinions in ancient authoritative writings. The popularity of the title *Contradicentia* *medica* is testimony to this, as well as indicating an underlying desire for synthesis and a continuing respect for ancient medical philosophy. While real advances are being made by patient observation and experiment in narrowly defined areas of study, the vast body of Renaissance medicine is struggling to maintain a synthetic outlook with the help of ingenious but sometimes makeshift strategies of interpretation.

3.9.2 By the end of the sixteenth century, many doctors are convinced that the notion of woman has changed, and that by the removal of the taint of imperfection she has attained a new dignity. But although she is thought to be equally perfect in her sex, she does not seem to achieve complete parity with man, or does so only at the expense of considerable dislocation in medical thought. Her physiology and humours seem to destine her to be the inferior of man, both physically and mentally; the doctors who argue that she is his equal in the *operationes animi* are either inconsistent with the general context of medical science to which they adhere in most cases, or, more rarely, have Paracelsian tendencies, as does Theodorus Collado. Woman, therefore, remains notionally the inferior of the male.

3.9.3 Two aspects of Aristotelian thought reinforce this notion of inferiority. The first is the metaphorical association of woman with mother earth, nutrition, fruitfulness and the fluctuations of the moon, which is deeply embedded in the substratum of ancient medical thought, and sometimes explicit there.[122] The implications of these metaphors—passivity, receptiveness, compassion, mutability—may account in part for the Renaissance view of female psychology. The second aspect is the primordial nature of sex difference. Sex difference is not only a feature of the higher animals; it is postulated in plants and stones. The difference is an example of the opposite of privation (the 'species privata'). Even after the arguments which make the female a deprived form of the male have been rejected, the *difference* of sex retains the associations of deprivation, and plays an important part in the infrastructure of Renaissance thought.

3.9.4 As well as bearing comparison in the 'species privata', woman is also compared with man in the 'species relativa'. To this potential source of confusion must be added the presence of prearistotelian dualities (left/right, even/odd, male/female etc.) which are sometimes culled from Aristotle himself, and sometimes quoted from texts of the Hippocratic corpus. Empirical data certainly cast doubts on these Pythagorean opposites, as does the revised understanding of functionalism, developed by Renaissance thinkers in a way which parallels the development of mechanism;[123] but they remain present in some degree in nearly all late Renaissance medical texts. They operate under the aegis of the pre-eminent duality of natural/unnatural. The force of this duality has been apparent throughout this chapter, but its exact sense is hard to define. It includes not only that which is part of nature, constituting a criterion of 'the natural', but also that which belongs to the process of nature defined by the Aristotelian da Monte as 'principium motus et quietis corporum naturalium'.[124] This definition implies intention or plan; Aristotle is eager to show purpose to be inherent in nature.[125] More powerful still than the *intentio naturae* (which Christian philosophers might wish to understand as 'the tendency of nature') is necessity: 'many things occur by natural necessity which are not part of nature's plan' declares the peripatetic aphorism.[126] Woman, in Aristotelian terms, is part of the general plan of nature, which effects procreation by the conjunction of the sexes; she is *necessarily* born female, because of the prevailing conditions at the moment of her conception. But as an individual, she is not planned by nature, whose *intention* is always to produce the most perfect being. By arguing that woman is 'equally perfect in her own sex' as the male is in his, late Renaissance Galenists resolve this anomaly, and thereby disunite the physiology and anatomy of male and female in matters of sex. The argument of 'equal perfection' marks thus a transition from the 'species privata' to a version of the 'species relativa', in which factors external to sex (temperature, physical and mental powers) promote comparisons. But this 'species relativa' still incorporates the notion of purpose in nature and the notion of hierarchy; and both still work to the disadvantage of woman's status *vis-à-vis* man.

3.9.5 One important factor which acts as a liberating force on medical philosophy is the absence of the paradigm of marriage. This is very influential in theology and, like the opposite clean/unclean, is one which belongs to the 'species contraria immediata'. Unfettered by these paradigms, Renaissance physiologists can conceive of a continuum rather than fixed states; in their eyes, all mankind is in a process of continual change linked to age and health; but in this process woman changes more, and more often, and within a shorter space of time.[127] Medical writers can proclaim that they have raised the status of woman in declaring her to be equally perfect in her sex; in removing from her physiological functions the taint of uncleanness; in describing her in terms which take account of the continuous change to which she is subject. It might even be claimed that the impressive bibliography of works concerning gynaecology and gynaecological diseases between 1540 and 1600 is some indication that more attention is being paid to the special problems of the female sex. For all this, woman is considered to be inferior to man in that the psychological effects of her cold and moist humours throw doubt on her control of her emotions and her rationality; furthermore, her less robust physique predisposes her, it is thought, to a more protected and less prominent rôle in the household and in society. Although apparently not bound by the authority of the divine institution of matrimony, doctors nonetheless produce a 'natural' justification for woman's relegation to the home and exclusion from public office, and provide thereby, as well as coherence with a central tenet of theology, an important foundation on which arguments in ethics, politics and law are based.

Notes

1. See, for example, *D. Thomae Aquinatis in Metaphysicorum Aristotelis Libros praeclarissima commentaria . . . cum defensionibus F. Bartholomaei Spinae super his commentariis . . .* , Venice, 1560, of. 11^{r-v}, for Aquinas's medieval paraphrase and Spina's Renaissance commentary.
2. See W. J. Ong, *Ramus, method and the decay of dialogue*, New York, 1974, pp. 199ff. Ong points out that dichotomies are not uniquely neoplatonic in origin. See also K. J. Höltgen, 'Synoptische Tabellen in der medizinischen Literatur und die Logik Agricolas und Ramus', *Sudhoffs Archiv*, XLIX (1965), 371–90.
3. For the anthropological and ancient background, see Lloyd, *Polarity and analogy*, pp. 15–17.
4. *In duos Aristotelis Libros Posteriores Analyticos commentarii* (1582), in *Opera logica*, Frankfurt, 1608, I. 669–70; *Tabulae logicae* (1579), in *Opera logica*, II.127.
5. *Polarity and analogy*, pp. 51–5.
6. *Die Zeugungs- und Vererbungslehre der Antike und ihr Nachwirken* (Abhandlungen der Geistes- und Sozialwissenschaftlichen Klasse, LXX (1950), Wiesbaden, 1951.
7. *Marcello Malpighi and the evolution of embryology*, Ithaca, New York, 1966, II.752ff.
8. *Ibid.* II.754.
9. e.g. by Girolamo Mercuriale (1530–1606), *De morbis muliebribus* (1582), II. 2, in *Gynaecea*, ed. Israel Spachius, Strasbourg, 1597, pp. 230–1.
10. See Adelmann, *Marcello Malpighi*, II. 755.
11. *De universa mulierum medicina* (1603), Hamburg, 1662, I. 19: 'una cum praestanti doctrina, similes fabellos et prodigiosa multa contineri, quae facile possint tyronibus fucum facere'.
12. Its editors are, respectively, Hans Kaspar Wolf, Gaspard Bauhin and Israel Spachius. Spachius's cumulative edition contains the following texts: Felix Platter (1536–1614), *De mulierum paribus generationis dicatis tabulae iconibus illustrae* (1583); Moschion, *De passionibus mulierum* (sixth cent. A. D.), ed. Konrad Gesner and Hans Kaspar Wolf; Trotula, *Muliebria* (eleventh

cent.); Nicolas de la Roche (Rocheus), *De morbis mulierum curandis* (1542); Luigi Bonacciuoli (Buonaccioli, Bonaciolus) (d. *c.*1540), *Enneas muliebris* (*c.*1480); Jacques Dubois (Sylvius) (1478–1555), *De mensibus mulierum et hominis generatione* (1555); Jakob Rüff (Ruffus) (1500–58), *De conceptu et generatione hominis* (1584); Mercuriale, *De morbis muliebribus;* Giovanni Battista da Monte (Montanus) (1498–1551), *De affectibus uterinis libellus, cum decem consiliis muliebribus* (1554); Vittore Trincavelli (1496–1568), *Consilia muliebria tria* (1586); Albertino Bottoni (d. *c.*1596), *De morbis muliebribus* (1585); Jean Le Bon (d. *c.*1583), *Therapia puerperarum* (1571); Ambroise Paré (1510?–90), *De hominis generatione* (1573); Albucasis, *De morbis muliebribus* (eleventh cent.); François Rousset, *De partu caesareo* (1581), trnas. Gaspard Bauhin; Bauhin (1560–1624), *Libellus variarum historiarum ea quae in libro de partu caesareo tractantur comprobantium* (1588); Maurice de la Corde (Cordaeus) (fl. 1569–74). *Commentarii in librum priorem Hippocratis de muliebribus* (1585); Martinus Akakia (1539–88), *De morbis muliebribus* (1579); Luis Mercado (Mercatus) (1525?–1611), *De mulierum affectionibus* (1579). I have included dates of birth and death where known in order to indicate that many works were published posthumously, although probably known during their authors' lifetime (cf. La Corde, below, 3.3.7). The dates following the title are those of the earliest recorded editions in Hirsch or Durling. *Gynaecea* is hereafter referred to as *G*, and the book and chapter number of the author's work alone are given.

13. e.g. by Mercado, I. 2, *G*, 805,807, who refers to *Summa*, 1*a* 92, 1 and *Summa contra gentiles*, xcv.

14. Notably Mercado, I. 1, *G*, 803–8; Mercuriale, I. 1, *G*, 209; Akakia, prolegomena, *G*, 745; Jean Varandal (Varandaeus) (d. 1617), *Tractatus therapeuticus de morbis mulierum* (1619), preface, in *Opera omnia*, Lyons, 1658, pp. 477–81; de Castro, *De universa mulierum medicina*, I. 126–31; André Du Laurens (Laurentius), *Anatomica humani corporis historia* (1593), VIII, cap. 1, Frankfurt, 1600, p. 280.

15. Adelmann, *Marcello Malpighi*, II. 757.

16. *Ad librum Fernelii de procreatione hominis commentarius*, Paris, 1578, fo. 17ᵛ, quoted by Adelmann, *Marcello Malpighi*, II. 753: 'cum ergo stultum sit ratione pugnare contra sensum et experientiam, pro antiquitatis reverentia'.

17. Reinier de Graaf, *De mulierum organis generatione inservientibus tractatus novus*, Leyden, 1672; on Karl Ernst von Baer, see Lesky, *Die Zeugungs-und Vererbungslehre*, p. 149.

18. *De generatione animalium*, I. 2 [716*a* 13]. Usually rendered into Latin as 'feminam in seipso, marem in alio gignere'. This is universally accepted ('ex confessa omnium hominum opinione', Kaspar Hofmann, *De generatione hominis*, Frankfurt, 1629, p. 2).

19. This commonplace from *Physics*, I. 9 [192*a* 22] is elegantly rendered by Gabriele Falloppio (1523–62), *Tractatus de metallis seu fossilibus*, XI, in *Opera omnia*, Frankfurt, 1600, I. 300: 'ea proportio quae est inter materiam et formam, est inter foeminam et marem. Nam foemina sustentatur mari, et appetit marem, tanquam perfectionem, quemadmodum et materia appetit formam, tanquam optatum et amatum'.

20. *Scientia*, LXXXIV, 53–8, 132–4.

21. See O. Temkin, *Galenism: rise and decline of a medical philosophy*, Cornell, 1973, p. 79; P. Diepgen, *Frau und Frauenheilkunde in der Kultur des Mittelalters*, Stuttgart, 1963, pp. 147–8. See also below, 3.4.1.

22. The theory of the humours is attributed by Aristotle to Empedocles (*Metaphysics*, A.6 [981*a* 25f]). Galen develops it in *De elementis*, II. 1 (see da Monte, 'doctrina de quatuor humoribus', in *Medicina universa*, ed. M. Weinrich, Frankfurt, 1587, pp. 159–61).

23. See *Renaissance notion of woman*, pp. 12–13.

24. On monsters and monstrosity, see Paré, *Des monstres et prodiges* (1573), ed. J. Céard, Geneva, 1971; Martin Weinrich (1548–1609), *De ortu monstruorum commentarius*, (Breslau), 1595.

25. I. 9 [1058*a* 31–2], usually latinized as 'mas et femina non differunt specie'.

26. 'Plato dubitare videtur, utro in genere ponat mulierem, rationalium animantium an brutorum', *Opera omnia*, IV. 418. Giovanni Nevizzano attributes this dictum to Eusebius, *De praeparatione evangelica*, XII. 12, but I have not been able to find it there (*see Sylvae nuptialis libri sex* (1521), Lyons, 1556, p. 22). Among satirical texts which refer to this quotation are Jacques Yver, *Le printemps*, Paris, 1572, fos. 102–3; anon. *Disputatio nova contra mulieres*, XLIII; Giuseppe Passi, *I donneschi diffetti*, Venice, 1599, p. 8; Trousset-Olivier, *Alphabet de l'imperfection et malice des femmes*, p. 418.

27. Referred to by Tiraqueau, *De legibus connubialibus*, I. 1.55, in *Opera omnia*, Frankfurt, 1616, II. 12; Montaigne, *Essais*, ed. Thibaudet and Rat, III. 5, p. 834; Pierre Grégoire, *De republica*, Frankfurt, 1597, VII. 11, p. 446; Paolo Zacchias (1584–1569), *Quaestiones medicolegales* (1624–50), Amsterdam, 1651, p. 470.

28. e.g. by Joachimus Eberartus, *Bonus mulier*, n.p., 1616, E3v, who assumes that Scaliger's *Exercitatio cxxxi* (see below, 3.7.3) was written 'contra Cujatium', and Johann Peter Lotz (Lotichius) (1598–1669), *Gynaicologia*, Rintheln, 1630, p. 30, who attributes the *Disputatio nova contra mulieres* to Cujas. See also *Renaissance notion of woman*, pp. 12–13, 70–71.

29. For an exemplary text, see Weinrich, *De ortu monstruorum*, II. 65–9.

30. e.g. Akakia, prolegomena, *G*, 745.

31. e.g. Bartholomäus Keckermann, *Systema physicum*, Hanau, 1617, pp. 593–601.

32. *De generatione animalium*, II. 3 [737*a* 27]; *De usu partium corporis*, XIV. 6.

33. According to Aristotle, the male principle in nature is associated with active, formative and perfected characteristics, while the female is passive, material and deprived, desiring the male in order to become complete. The duality male/female is therefore paralleled by the dualities active/passive, form/matter, act/potency, perfection/imperfection, completion/incompletion, possession/deprivation. In a celebrated passage of the *De generation animalium* (II. 3 [838*a* 27]; cf. IV. 6 [775*a* 15f]) Aristotle described the female as ἐστὶ πεπηρωμένον; the Latin formulations most frequently encountered are '[Quasi]mas laesus', 'animal occasionatum'.

The Philosopher's argument runs thus: nature would always wish to create the most perfect thing, which is the most completely formed, the best endowed with powers of procreation, and the hottest. Such a creature is the male, who implants his semen in the female to the end of procreating males. If, however, there is some lack of generative heat, or if climatic conditions are adverse, then creation is not perfected and a female results. Aristotle, according to Aquinas, does not mean by this that females are against the intention of nature, because both sexes are necessary to procreation; but that, as regards the individual females are the result of a generative event not carried through to its final conclusion. See also Aquinas, *Summa theologiae*, la 92, 1.

34. Lyons, 1588, pp. 50–8.
35. I. 32–3, Frankfurt, 1605, pp. 210–12.
36. Hanau, 1617, pp. 572–3.
37. Viz. Sebastian Meyer, *Augustae laudes Divinae Majestatis e divinis Galeni de usu partium libris selectae*, Freiburg, 1627, pp. 197–8.
38. On this point see de Valles, *In aphorismos Hippocratis commentarii* (1561), Cologne, 1589, p. 166.
39. *De generatione hominis*, pp. 3–4. The texts referred to by Hofmann are Hippocrates, *Aphorisms*, v. 38,48,62; *Epidemics*, III. 70, IV. 45–6, VII. 32; *Regimen*, I. 22; Aristotle, *De partibus animalium*, III. 1; *Historia animalium*, IV. 11, v. 10–11, VII. 1, 4–5, 11, IX. 1; *De generatione animalium*, I. 19–20, II. 3–6, IV. 1–3, 7, v. 3–4, IX. 2; Galen, *De usu partium corporis*, XIV. 1–6; *De semine*, II. 1–5; *De caussis pulsuum*, III. 2.
40. *De calido innato et semine pro Aristotele adversus Galenum*, Leyden, 1634, VII. 4, pp. 214–15. For the parallel with plant life (male–seed/woman–earth) see Plato, *Timaeus*, 91D, and Aristotle, *De generatione animalium*, I. 2 [716a 17]. Fortunio Liceti (1577–1657), *De perfecta constitutione hominis in utero*, Padua, 1616, XIII, p. 47, claims that to be the place of procreation is not ignoble, since all procreation is active (on activity being noble, see Chap. 2, n.21). Cremonini's views accord well with medieval discussions (e.g. Trotula, G, 42) and early Renaissance medicine (e.g. da Monte, 'De temperamentis ratione sexus', in *Medicina universa*, pp. 156–9).
41. *Observationes anatomicae*, in *Opera omnia*, pp. 420–2, cited by Du Laurens, *Anatomica humani corporis historia*, VII, cap. 12, p. 273, and Johann Schenk von Grafenberg (1530–1598), *Observationes medicae* (1584–97), Frankfurt, 1609, pp. 601–3.
42. A related question is that of sex change; see below, 3.5.4.
43. *Anatomica humani corporis historia*, VII, q. 8, pp. 274–5.
44. See P. Hoffmann, 'Féminisme cartésien', *Travaux de linguistique et de littérature*, VII. 2 (1969), 83–105.
45. The *loct classici* compare these organs to the eyes of a mole: see Aristotle, *Historia animalium*, I. 9 [491b 26], IV. 8 [533a 10], where these eyes are said to represent a case of the natural course of development congenitally arrested, and especially Galen, *De usu partium corporis*, XIV. 6, cited by Hofmann, *Commentarii in Galeni de usu partium corporis*, Frankfurt, 1625, p. 309, and Emilio Parisano (1567–1643), *De subtilitate*, Venice, 1623, pp. 147–8.
46. See above, note 33.
47. Parisano, *loc. cit.*: 'mulier seu foemina quatenus foemina perfecta est, nec perfectior esse potest: quoniam ad concipiendum, ad procreandam prolem, continendam, fovendam, aleandam, perficiendamque talibus instrumentis, talique temperatione opus habuit'; cf. Valladier, *La saincte philosophie de l'âme*, pp. 818–19.
48. II. 6, in *Opera omnia*, Lyons, 1663, VI. 645–54.

49. *Exercitationes*, CCLXXIV, Frankfurt, 1592, pp. 832–8: 'eundem viri, mulierisque calorem. In muliere non apparere, dilutum humore multo. In viro sentiri, quod acriatur siccitate'.

50. Scaliger is the editor of the *Historia animalium* and the peripatetic Theophrastus's *De causis plantorum* and the pseudo-Aristotelian *De plantis*. For his anti-feminist views, see *Electa Scaligerea, hoc est Julii Caesari Scaligeri sententiae, praecepta, definitiones, axiomata*, ed. Christophorus Freibisius, Hanau, 1634, pp. 308–13.

51. e.g. Akakia, *G*, 745; de Castro, *De universa mulierum medicina*, I. 131.

52. *G*, 506–7; but La Corde (fl. 1569–74) argues that, according to Hippocrates, woman is hotter only in blood temperature.

53. *Prognosticorum Hippocratis è Graeco in Latinum versio, cum expositionibus in Galeni commentaria*, Lyons, 1576, p. 1143.

54. e.g. Du Laurens, *Anatomica humani corporis historia*, VIII, q. 2, p. 283.

55. Classical authorities records that, in some animals, the female is the hotter, viz. bears, leopards, lions and falcons (Aristotle, *Historia animalium*, IX. 1 [608*a* 35]; Pliny, *Natural History*, XI. 110). According to de Valles (*Controversiae medicae*, I. 9, pp. 27–9, quoting Galen, *De caussis pulsuum*, III.2) this is because her function is different from that of the human female, which is 'concipere, lactare et educare foetus'.

56. Tostatus, *Opera omnia*, I. 232.

57. *De caussis pulsuum*, III.2; Giovanni Zecchi (1533–1601), *Tractatus de pulsibus* (1599), Frankfurt, 1650, pp. 933–5; de Castro, *De universa mulierum medicina*, I. 91–8. According to Aristotelian taxonomy, this would still mean that in general men were hotter than women, since the best of any class governs its relative position to other classes (see *Topics*, III. 2 [117*b* 32ff]).

58. See *Renaissance notion of woman*, pp. 57–8.

59. The *locus classicus* is in Macrobius, *Saturnalia*, VII. 7.5, quoted by Mercuriale, *G*, 257.

60. See above, note 39.

61. See ibid, pp. 657.

62. Although also closely linked to the debates, the controversy concerning the origin and concoction of semen is not relevant here, as it has no bearing on the difference of sex. For an informed Renaissance account, see Du Laurens, *Anatomica humani corporis historia*, VIII, q. 4, pp. 287–9.

63. According to Cajetan, the phrase 'caro de carne mea' indicates that woman does not possess a *virtus formatrix*, but merely provides matter in procreation (*Commentarii in quinque Mosaicos libros*, p. 25).

64. In the Aristotelian understanding of fertilization, only the male needs be aroused, as the female does not contribute to the generation of the foetus; for Galen, sexual pleasure in both male and female is functional (i.e. both woman and man must be aroused for them to be fertile and emit semen). Some Galenists not only prescribe means of arousing woman, but also go so far as to suggest that there is a further, non-functional, element in sexual pleasure which softens man's sad lot on this earth ('mulieribus [maribusque] videtur venerei coitus sensus à natura datus, non tantùm ad sobolis propagationem et speciei humanae conservationem, sed etiam ad humanae vitae miserias, voluptatis illius tanquam blandimentis leniendas et demulcendas': Paré, III, *G*, 405). The whole topic of sexual pleasure in marriage (or outside

it) is debated with varying degrees of obliquity and varying degrees of austerity; the analogy most often made is that with the pleasures of food and drink. Scaliger's aphorism 'sapientes bibunt ut ne bibant; nebulones bibunt ut bibant' (paralleled by 'appetit foemina ut impleatur; mas ut depleatur', *Exercitationes*, CXXXI. 4, p. 454) may be placed at one end of the spectrum; Francisco Barbaro's suggestion of moderate indulgence in sexual pleasure using the metaphor of eating and gluttony ('De coitus ratione', in *De re uxoria* (fifteenth cent.), Amsterdam, 1639, pp. 141–8, cf. Aquinas, *Summa*, suppl. 49,1, followed by St Francis of Sales, *Introduction à la vie dévote*, in (*Euvres*, ed. Ravier and Devos, pp. 240–4) may be placed at the other. Between these views falls Michel de Montaigne's suggestion that sexual pleasure is to be enjoyed with prostitutes and in illicit relationships, and dutiful but unpleasurable coitus undertaken with the wife (*Essais*, ed. Thibaudet et Rat, I. 30, pp. 197–8, and III. 5, *passim*; cf. Plutarch, *Conjugalia praecepta*, XVI).

65. e.g. Vesalius, *Humani corporis fabrica*, Basle, 1543, pp. 145, 520, 532, quoted by Screech, *The Rabelaisian marriage*, p. 92, and W. Wiegand, 'What about the *Fabrica* of Vesalius?', in *Three Vesalian essays*, New York, 1952, pp. 59–63.

66. *Opera omnia*, p. 421.

67. *Marcello Malpighi*, II. 739.

68. *Exercitationes*, VI. 7, pp. 33–5.

69. *De calido innato et semine, passim*.

70. *De perfecta constitutione hominis in utero*, XIII–XV, pp. 45–55.

71. *Physiologiae peripateticae libri sex* (1603), Geneva, 1629, V. 15, pp. 428–40; pp. 437–8 are plagiarized from Mercuriale (see *G*, 258), a Galenist.

72. Hofmann cites *De semine*, II. 4 and *De usu partium corporis*, XIV. 7 as Galenic *loci* which negate the suggestion made in *De semine*, II. 2 that woman possesses semen (*Apologiae pro Galeno libri sex*, Lyons, 1668, I. 189).

73. *Disputatio . . . in qua ea, quae de semine sunt controversa inter peripateticos et veteres medicos, et doctissimos quosdam neotericos accurantissime discutuntur*, Treviso, 1609.

74. *Anatomica humani corporis historia*, VIII, q. 5, pp. 289–91.

75. There is a controversy about the origin of the *mola uteri*: see de Valles, *Controversiae medicae* (1564), Frankfurt, 1582, II. 6, p. 67; Mercuriale, I. 3, *G*, 219–22; Du Laurens, *Anatomica humani corporis historia*, VIII, q. 5, p. 291; de Castro, *De universa mulierum medicina*, I. 45–8.

76. Vicenza, 1597, II. 3, pp. 538–66.

77. IV. 5, *G*, 273. The ancient theory derives from Empedocles according to Aristotle (*De generatione animalium*, I. 18 [723a 24f]).

78. Reproduced by Paré, *G*, 403; Rüff, *G*, 168; Mercuriale, IV. 5, *G*, 273; Akakia, II. 1, *G*, 774–7; de Castro, *De universa mulierum medicina*, I. 45–8.

79. The bibliography of this debate is somewhat confused; it appears to begin with Mundinius's *Disputatio . . . de semine* (1609); followed by Liceti, *De perfecta constitutione hominis in utero* (1616); Parisano, *De subtilitate* (1621); Mundinius, *De genitura pro Galeno adversus peripateticos et nostrae aetatis philosophos et medicos disputatio* (1622); Parisano, *De semine a toto proventu* (1623); Mundinius, *Ad disputationem de Genitura additamentum apologeticum, in quo Aemilii Parisani opinionem de semine a toto proventu et de stygmatum causis ab omni probabilitate alienam esse sustinetur* (1625);

Hofmann, *De generatione hominis contra Mundinum Mundinium* (1629); Cremonini, *De calido innato et semine, pro Aristotele adversus Galenum* (1634); Parisano, *De subtilitate pars altera* (1635).

80. Adelmann, *Marcello Malpighi*, II. 760ff.

81. See Aristotle, *De generatione animalium*, IV. 1 [765a 3ff].

82. e.g. Bonacciuoli, IV, *G*, 130; Levinus Lemnius, *Occulta naturae miracula* (1559), Antwerp, 1574, I. 9, pp. 39–45.

83. The doubts, based on empirical evidence, are already voiced by Aristotle (*De generatione animalium*, IV. 1 [765a 3ff]; see also Mercado, III. 6, *G*, 1003–4. Another aspect of Pythagorean thought is found in the supposed relationship between length of pregnancy, survival of foetus and sex determination; see Mercado, IV. 1, *G*, 1039–40, where the following diagram based on the association female–even, male–odd promotes certain predictions:

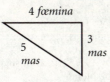

84. See Pagel, *Das medizinische Weltbild des Paracelsus*, pp. 62–70.

85. *Occulta naturae miracula*, I. 4, p. 15.

86. According to Platter, the virago does not menstruate, because she uses up her residues of fat and blood by a more active life (*G*. ***2v). Dubois defines the virago as 'mulier barbata, vegeta, virilis, voce gravi, infoecunda, quia calor multus sanguinem dissipat' (*G*, 163). See also de Castro, *De universa mulierum medicina*, I. 96.

87. On preformation *versus* epigenesis, see J. Needham, *A history of embryology*, revised by A. Hughes, Cambridge, 1959, esp. pp. 115–78.

88. *Des monstres et prodiges*, ed. Céard, pp. 29–30.

89. *Observationes*, pp. 575–6, referred to as authoritative by de Castro, *De universa mulierum medicina*, I. 11.

90. *De hermaphroditorum monstrosorumque partium natura* (1604), Oppenheim, 1614; also by Schenck von Grafenberg, *Observationes*. pp. 573–5.

91. See Mercado, III. 7, *G*, 1005–12; Akakia, II. 14, *G*, 793–4.

92. Although breasts are a secondary sexual characteristic considered at length in both anatomical and pathological studies, they are not of primary importance to the questions with which this study is concerned. They do, however, have a considerable metaphorical presence in iconology and in religious literature, representing humane or maternal feelings, nutritiousness and fecundity, and in iconography they are often the primary symbol of the difference of sex.

93. See Diepgen, in *Scientia*, LXXXIV, 132; Du Laurens, *Anatomica humani corporis historia*, VIII, q. 9, pp. 295–6, The *loci classici* are Aristotle, *Historia animalium*, III. 19 [521a 22ff]; Pliny, *Natural history*, VII. 15; Columella, *De re rustica*, XI. 3, 31,50,64; Plutarch, *Symposium*, III, q. 4.

94. e.g. Dubois, *G*, 148; see also Tiraqueau, *De legibus connubialibus*, I. 15.132, in *Opera omnia*, II. 235; Nevizzano, *Sylva nuptialis*, p. 82.

95. Fernel, *Physiologia* (1554), VI. 7, in *Universa medicina*, Hanau, 1610, pp. 166–8; Riolan, *Physiologia*, IV. 8. in *Universae medicinae compendia*, Paris, 1598, fo. 33.

96. Bottoni, XIII, *G*, 347; Mercuriale, IV. 1, *G*, 257–8; de Castro, *De universa mulierum medicina*, I. 78–80. See also Magirus, *Physiologia peripatetica*, v. 15, p. 437; Du Laurens, *Anatomica humani corporis historia*, VIII, q. 8, pp. 294–5.

97. See Cardano, *De subtilitate*, XI, in *Opera omnia*, III. 937; a *locus classicus* is Pliny, *Natural history*, XXVIII. 6.18.

98. For a fuller account see Screech, *The Rabelaisian marriage*, pp. 84–103; R. Antonioli, *Rabelais et al médecine*, Geneva, 1976, (*Etudes Rabelaisiennes*, XII), pp. 195ff, esp. 198–9.

99. Bottoni, XXXIX, *G*, 368; Mercuriale, IV. 20, *G*, 294; Akakia, I. 8, *G*, 760–3; Mercado, II. 9, *G*, 929; de Castro, *De universa mulierum medicina*, I. 17–19. Fernel criticizes both Galen and Plato on this topic (*Pathologia*, VII. 14, in *Universa medicina*, p. 327, referred to by La Corde, *G*, 545).

100. *De legibus connubialibus*, I. 9.92, in *Opera omnia*, II. 143.

101. *Physiologia*, VII. 5, in *Universae medicinae compendia*, fos. 73–4.

102. See *G*, 109.

103. One Aristotelian *locus* (*Historia animalium*, III. 19 [521a 27]) suggests, however, that they are less prone to diseases of the blood.

104. See Mercado, I. 2, *G*, 807–8. The Hippocratic *locus* which attributes all female illnesses to the uterus is in *Places in men, ad. fin.* (see Hippocrates, *Opera omnia*, ed. A. Foesius, Geneva, 1657, p. 423), referred to by Du Laurens, *Anatomica humani corporis historia*, VII, q. 11, p. 277.

105. Mercado, II. 10, *G*, 927; Cremonini, *Explanatio proemii librorum Aristotelis de physico auditu*, Padua, 1596, fo. 16v.

106. Mercado, II. 10, *G*, 925–6; this state is most common in widows deprived of coitus, according to La Roche, v, *G*, 74. See also Galen, *De locis affectis*, VI. 5.

107. II. 4–10, *G*, 896ff.

108. The *locus classicus* is in Aristotle, *De partibus animalium*, II. 7 (653b 1ff). See also Diepgen, in *Scientia*, LXXXIV, 55.

109. *Anatomica humani corporis historia*, VIII, q. 10, p. 297.

110. See Lemnius, *Occulta naturae miracula*, I. 4, pp. 15–16, and Mercado, III. 7, *G*, 1011.

111. See Pagel, *Paracelsus: an introduction to philosophical medicine in the era of the Renaissance*, Basle and New York, 1958, p. 122.

112. With moist humours specifically, Scaliger associates changeability, lack of stamina and excessive delicacy ('fluxus; enervis; laboris impotens; deliciarum amator', *Exercitationes*, CCLXXIV).

113. For the presence of these ideas in popular literature, see Maclean, *Feminism in French literature*, Oxford, 1977, pp. 46ff.

114. Cf. Seneca, *Epistolae*, XCV: 'pati natae'.

115. *De caussis pulsuum*, III. 2.

116. I, *G*, 110.

117. Akakia, *G*, 745; de Castro, *De universa mulierum medicina*, I. 131. Du Laurens even accords them superior powers of mind ('memoria felicior, inventio subtilior, verborum quae animi conceptus experimunt copia maior', *Anatomica humani corporis historia*, VIII, q. 2, p. 282).

118. *Epistolae*, cxxii, *PL*, xii. 1016: a Renaissance commonplace (see Caelius Rhodiginus, *Lectiones antiquae* (1517), Geneva, 1630, xiii. 33, col. 718).
119. *Summa*, 1a 93,4.
120. *Adversaria seu commentarii medicinales*, Cologne, 1615, ¶3r–5r.
121. See Mercado, ii. 2, *G*, 882, where he claims that malfunction of the uterus can make women 'imbecilliores, ineptae ad actiones obeundas, tristes, taediosae'; and Mercuriale, i.2, *G*, 213: 'passiones animi quod mirifice sterilitatem inducant, certum est: memini me legere apud quendam mulierem si in coitu ploret non posse concipere, sic etiam faciunt nimis timor, moeror et ira immodica'.
122. e.g. Plato, *Timaeus*, 91D; Aristotle, *De generatione animalium*, i. 2 [716a 15]; *Historia animalium*, vii. 2 [582a 33]; Plutarch, *Symposium*, iii, q. 4.
123. See R. Lenoble, *Mersenne ou la naissance du mécanisme*, Paris, 1943.
124. *Medicina universa*, p. 355. See also *Metaphysics*, Δ.4 [1014b 16ff].
125. See *Physics*, ii. 8–9 [198b 10ff], and *De generatione animalium*, v. 1 [778a 29ff].
126. 'Multa fiunt ex necessitate naturae, quae non fiunt ex eius intentione', quoted by Henning Arnisaeus (d. 1635), *De iure connubiorum*, Frankfurt, 1613, p. 150, attributed to *Physics*, ii. 9.
127. It was commonly believed after Aristotle that the normal lifespan of a woman was shorter than that of a man; the *locus classicus* is *Historia animalium*, vii. 3 [583b 28].

6 Women on Top

Natalie Zemon Davis

From Natalie Zemon Davis, *Society and Culture in Early Modern France* (Polity Press, 1965), 124–51. © Natalie Zemon Davis. Reprinted with permission.

I

The female sex was thought the disorderly one par excellence in early modern Europe. "*Une beste imparfaicte*," went one adage, "*sans foy, sans loy, sans craincte, sans constance.*" Female disorderliness was already seen in the Garden of Eden, when Eve had been the first to yield to the serpent's temptation and incite Adam to disobey the Lord. To be sure, the men of the lower orders were also believed to be especially prone to riot and seditious unrest. But the defects of the males were thought to stem not so much from nature as from nurture: the ignorance in which they were reared, the brutish quality of life and conversation in the peasant's hut or the artisan's shop, and their poverty, which led to envy.[1]

With the women the disorderliness was founded in physiology. As every physician knew in the sixteenth century, the female was composed of cold and wet humors (the male was hot and dry), and coldness and wetness meant a changeable, deceptive, and tricky temperament. Her womb was like a hungry animal; when not amply fed by sexual intercourse or reproduction, it was likely to wander about her body, overpowering her speech and senses. If the Virgin Mary was free of such a weakness, it was because she was the blessed vessel of the Lord. But no other woman had been immaculately conceived, and even the well-born lady could fall victim to a fit of the "mother," as the uterus was called. The male might suffer from retained sexual juices, too, but (as Doctor François Rabelais pointed out) he had the wit and will to control his fiery urges by work, wine, or study. The female just became hysterical.* In the late seventeenth century, when vanguard physicians were abandoning humoral theories of personality in favor of more mechanistic notions of "animal spirits" and were beginning to remark that men suffered from emotional ills curiously like hysteria, they still maintained that the female's mind was more prone to be disordered by her fragile and unsteady temperament. Long before Europeans were asserting flatly that the "inferiority" of black Africans was innate, rather than the result, say, of climate, they were attributing female "inferiority" to nature.[2]

The lower ruled the higher within the woman, then, and if she were given her way, she would want to rule over those above her outside. Her disorderliness led her into the evil arts of witchcraft, so ecclesiastical authorities claimed; and when she was embarked on some behavior for which her allegedly weak intellect disqualified her, such as theological speculation or preaching, that was blamed on her disorderliness, too. The rule of a queen was impossible in France by the Salic law, and mocked by the common proverb "*tomber en quenouille.*" For Pastor John Knox it was a "monstrous regimen," "the subversion of good order . . . all equitie and justice," whereas the more moderate Calvin "reckoned it among the visitations of God's anger," but one that should be borne, like any tyranny, with patience. Even a contemporary defender of queenship, John Aylmer, still had to admit that when he thought of the willfulness of women, he favored a strong role for Parliament. As late as 1742, in the face of entomological evidence to the contrary, some apiologists pretended that nature required the rule of a King Bee.[3]

What were the proposed remedies for female unruliness? Religious training that fashioned the reins of modesty and humility; selective education that showed a woman her moral duty without enflaming her undisciplined imagination or loosing her tongue for public talk; honest work that busied her hands; and laws and constraints that made her subject to her husband.[4]

In some ways, that subjection was gradually deepening from the sixteenth to the eighteenth centuries as the patriarchal family streamlined itself for more efficient property acquisition, social mobility, and

---

* Female medical practitioners also accepted the theory of the "wandering womb" and provided remedies for female hysteria. See *A Choice Manual of . . . Select Secrets in Physick . . . Collected and Practised by . . . the Countesse of Kent* (London, 1653), pp. 114, 145; *Recueil des Remedes . . . Recueillis par les Ordres Charitables de . . . Madame Fouquet* (4th ed.; Dijon, 1690), pp. 168–89; Jean de Rostagny, *Traité de Primerose sur les erreurs vulgaires de la medecine* (Lyon, 1689), p. 774; Angélique Du Coudray, *Abrégé de l'art des Accouchemens* (Paris, 1759), p. 173.

preservation of the line, and as progress in statebuilding and the extension of commercial capitalism were achieved at a cost in human autonomy. By the eighteenth century, married women in France and England had largely lost what independent legal personality they had formerly had, and they had less legal right to make decisions on their own about their dowries and possessions than at an earlier period. Propertied women were involved less and less in local and regional political assemblies. Working women in prosperous families were beginning to withdraw from productive labor; those in poor families were increasingly filling the most ill-paid positions of wage labor. This is not to say that females had no informal access to power or continuing vital role in the economy in these centuries; but the character of those relations was in conflict.[5]

Which side of the conflict was helped by the disorderly woman? Since this image was so often used as an excuse for the subjection of women, it is not surprising to find it opposed by one strain in early feminist thought, which argued that women were *not* by nature more unruly, disobedient, and fickle than men. If anything it was the other way around. "By nature, women be sober," said the poet Christine de Pisan, "and those that be not, they go out of kind."* Women are by nature more modest and shamefaced than men, claimed a male feminist, which is demonstrated by the fact that women's privy parts are totally covered with pubic hair and are not handled by women the way men's are when they urinate. Why, then, did some men maintain that women were disorderly by nature? Because they were misogynists—vindictive, envious, or themselves dissolute.[6]

These claims and counterclaims about sexual temperament raise questions not merely about the actual character of male and female behavior in preindustrial Europe, but also about the varied uses of sexual symbolism. Sexual symbolism, of course, is always available to make statements about social experience and to reflect (or conceal) contradictions within it. At the end of the Middle Ages and in early modern Europe, the relation of the wife—of the potentially disorderly woman—to her husband was especially useful for expressing the relation of all subordinates to their superiors, and this for two reasons. First, economic relations were still often perceived in the medieval way as a matter of service. Second, the nature of political rule and the newer

---

* Some female writers from the sixteenth to the early eighteenth centuries, such as Marguerite de Navarre, Madame de Lafayette, Aphra Behn, and Mary de la Rivière Manley, did not accept this view. Although they did not portray women as necessarily more lustful than men, they did give females a range of sexual appetites at least equal to that of males.

problem of sovereignty were very much at issue. In the little world of the family, with its conspicuous tension between intimacy and power, the larger matters of political and social order could find ready symbolization.*

Thus, Jean Calvin, himself a collapser of ecclesiastical hierarchies, saw the subjection of the wife to the husband as a guarantee of the subjection of both of them to the authority of the Lord. Kings and political theorists saw the increasing legal subjection of wives to their husbands (and of children to their parents) as a guarantee of the obedience of both men and women to the slowly centralizing state— a training for the loyal subject of seventeenth-century France or for the dutiful citizen of seventeenth-century England. "Marriages are the seminaries of States," began the preamble to the French ordinance strengthening paternal power within the family. For John Locke, opponent of despotic rule in commonwealth and in marriage, the wife's relinquishing her right of decision to her husband as "naturally . . . the abler and stronger" was analogous to the individual's relinquishing his natural liberties of decision and action to the legislative branch of government.[7]

Indeed, how could one separate the idea of subordination from the existence of the sexes? Gabriel de Foigny's remarkable fictitious land of Australie (1673), a utopia of hermaphrodites, shows how close the link between the two was perceived to be. The Australian, in whom the sexes were one, could not understand how a conflict of wills could be avoided within the "mutual possession" of European marriage. The

---

* The English characterization of a wife's killing of her husband as petty treason rather than as homicide may be an early example of the kind of symbolism being described here. Petty treason appeared as a crime distinct from high treason in the fourteenth century, and lasted as such till the early nineteenth century. It included the killing of a master by his servant, a husband by his wife, and a prelate by a secular cleric or religious. As Blackstone presents the law, it seems to differ from earlier Germanic practice, which treated the murder of *either* spouse by the other as an equally grave crime. The development of the concept and law of treason was closely connected with the development of the idea of sovereignty. J. G. Bellamy, *The Law of Treason in England in the Later Middle Ages* (Cambridge, Eng., 1970), pp. 1–14, 225–31; William Blackstone, *Commentaries on the Laws of England* (Oxford, 1770), Book IV, chap. 14, including note t.

The use of male/female as an expression of social relationships (master/servant, sovereign/subject, and the like) is not the only kind of sexual symbolism in early modern Europe, though it is the basis for discussion in this essay. Eric Wolf considers male/female as an expression of the relationships public/domestic and instrumental-ordering/expressive-ordering in "Society and Symbols in Latin Europe and in the Islamic Near East," *Anthropological Quarterly* 42 (July 1968): 287–301. For an attempt at a very broad theory of sexual symbolism, see Sherry B. Ortner, "Is Female to Male as Nature Is to Culture?" in Michelle Zimbalist Rosaldo and Louise Lamphere, eds., *Woman, Culture, and Society* (Stanford, Calif., 1974), pp. 67–87.

French traveler answered that it was simple, for mother and child were both subject to the father. The hermaphrodite, horrified at such a violation of the total autonomy that was the sign of complete true "men," dismissed the European pattern as bestial.[8]

The female's position was used to symbolize not only hierarchical subordination but also violence and chaos. Bruegel's terrifying *Dulle Griet*, painted during the occupation of the Netherlands by Spanish soldiers, makes a huge, armed, unseeing woman, Mad Meg, the emblem of fiery destruction, of brutal oppression and disorder. Bruegel's painting cuts in more than one way, however, and shows how female disorderliness—the female out of her place—could be assigned another value. Next to Mad Meg is a small woman in white on top of a male monster; it is Saint Margaret of Antioch tying up the devil. Nearby other armed women are beating grotesque animals from Hell.[9]

Bruegel's Margarets are by no means alone in preindustrial Europe. In hierarchical and conflictful societies that loved to reflect on the world-turned-upside-down, the *topos* of the woman-on-top was one of the most enjoyed. Indeed, sexual inversion—that is, switches in sex roles—was a widespread form of cultural play in literature, in art, and in festivity. Sometimes the reversal involved dressing and masking as a member of the opposite sex—the prohibitions of Deuteronomy 22, Saint Paul, Saint Jerome, canon law, and Jean Calvin notwithstanding.[10] Sometimes the reversal involved simply taking on certain roles or forms of behavior characteristic of the opposite sex. Women played men; men played women; men played women who were playing men.

It is the uses of sexual inversion, and more particularly of play with the image of the unruly woman in literature, in popular festivity, and in ordinary life, that will be the subject of the rest of this essay. Evidently, the primary impulse behind such inversion in early modern Europe was not homosexuality or disturbed gender identity. Although Henri III expressed special wishes of his own when he and his male "mignons" masked as Amazons in the 1570's, and although the seventeenth-century Abbé de Choisy, whose mother had dressed him as a girl through adolescence, had special reasons for using a woman's name and wearing female clothes until he was thirty-three,[11] still most literary and festive transvestism at this time had a wider psychosexual and cultural significance than this.

Anthropologists offer several suggestions about the functions of magical transvestism and ritual inversion of sex roles. First, sexual disguise can ward off danger from demons, malignant fairies, or other powers that threaten castration or defloration. Second, transvestism and sexual reversal can be part of adolescent rites of passage, either to suggest the marginality of the transitional state (as when a male initiate is likened to a menstruating woman) or to allow each sex to obtain something of the other's power (as in certain initiation and marriage customs in early Greece). Third, exchange of sex can be part of what Victor Turner has called "rituals of status reversal," as when women in certain parts of Africa usurp the clothing, weapons, or tasks of the superior males and behave in lewd ways to increase the chance for a good harvest or to turn aside an impending natural catastrophe. Finally, as James Peacock has pointed out, the transvestite actor, priest, or shaman can symbolize categories of cosmological or social organization. For instance, in Java the transvestite actor reinforces by his irregularity the importance of the categories high/low, male/female.

However diverse these uses of sexual inversion, anthropologists generally agree that they, like other rites and ceremonies of reversal, are ultimately sources of order and stability in a hierarchical society. They can clarify the structure by the process of reversing it. They can provide an expression of, and a safety valve for, conflicts within the system. They can correct and relieve the system when it has become authoritarian. But, so it is argued, they do not question the basic order of the society itself. They can renew the system, but they cannot change it.[12]

Historians of early modern Europe are likely to find inversions and reversals less in prescribed rites than in carnivals and festivities. Their fools are likely to escape the bounds of ceremony,[13] and their store of literary sources for inversion will include not only the traditional tales of magical transformation in sex, but also a variety of stories in which men and women *choose* to change their sexual status. In addition, there are comic conventions and genres, such as the picaresque, that allow much play with sexual roles. These new forms offered increased occasions and ways in which topsy-turvy could be used for explicit criticism of the social order. Nevertheless, students of these festive and literary forms have ordinarily come to the same conclusion as anthropologists regarding the limits of symbolic inversion: a world-turned-upside-down can only be righted, not changed. To quote Ian Donaldson's recent study *Comedy from Jonson to Fielding*: "The lunatic governor . . . , the incompetent judge, the mock doctor, the equivocating priest, the hen-pecked husband: such are the familiar and recurrent figures in the comedy of a society which gives a general assent to the necessity of entrusting power to its governors, judges, doctors, priests, and husbands."[14]

I would like to argue, on the contrary, that comic and festive inversion could *undermine* as well as reinforce that assent through its connections with everyday circumstances outside the privileged time of carnival and stage-play. Somewhat in contradistinction to Christine de Pisan and the gallant school of feminists, I want to argue that the image of the disorderly woman did not always function to keep women in their place. On the contrary, it was a multivalent image that could operate, first, to widen behavioral options for women within and even outside marriage, and, second, to sanction riot and political disobedience for both men and women in a society that allowed the lower orders few formal means of protest. Play with the unruly woman is partly a chance for temporary release from the traditional and stable hierarchy; but it is also part of the conflict over efforts to change the basic distribution of power within society. The woman-on-top might even facilitate innovation in historical theory and political behavior.

II

Let us begin with a review of the major types of sexual inversion we find in literary sources—sources sober and comic, learned and popular. Then we will consider the disorderly woman in more detail. What kinds of license were allowed through this turnabout? First of all, we have stories of men who dress as women to save themselves from an enemy or from execution, to sneak into the opponent's military camp, or to get into a nunnery or women's quarters for purposes of seduction. In all of these cases, the disguise is not merely practical but exploits the expected physical frailty of women to prevent harm to the male or to disarm his victim. A more honorable trickery is ventured by Pyrocles in Sidney's *Arcadia*, by Marston's Antonio, and by d'Urfé's Céladon, for they dress as brave Amazons or as a Druid priestess in order to have access to the women they wish to woo. Here no more than in the first case does the inversion lead to criticism of social hierarchy. Rather Pyrocles is rebuked by his friend for "his effeminate love of a woman," for letting his "sensual weakness" rebel against his manly reason.

Only with the male fool or clown do we find literary examples of male transvestism serving to challenge order. In the seventeenth-century *commedia dell'arte*, a black-faced Harlequin dolls himself up as a ridiculous Diana, goddess of the chase, replete with crescent-moon ruff, fancy clothes, and a little bow. The result is so absurd that not only are boundaries between high and low effaced, but, as William Willeford has suggested, reality itself seems to dissolve.[15]

The stories, theater, and pictorial illustration of preindustrial Europe offer many more examples of women trying to act like men than vice versa, and more of the time the sexual inversion yields criticism of the established order. One set of reversals portrays women going beyond what can ordinarily be expected of a mere female; that is, it shows women ruling the lower in themselves and thus deserving to be like men. We have, for instance, tales of female saints of the early Church who lived chastely as male monks to the end of their lives, braving false charges of fathering children and withstanding other tests along the way. Five of these transvestite ladies appear in Voragine's *Golden Legend*, which had wide circulation in manuscript and printed editions in both Latin and the vernacular.[16]

Other uncommon women changed their roles in order to defend established rule or values associated with it. Disguised as men, they prove fidelity to lovers whom they wish to marry or, as in the case of Madame Ginevra in Boccaccio's tale, prove their chastity to doubting husbands. Disguised as men, they leave Jewish fathers for Christian husbands and plead for Christian mercy over base Jewish legalism. Disguised as men, they rescue spouses from prison and the family honor from stain. For example, in *The French Amazon*, one of Mademoiselle l'Héritier's reworkings of an old French tale, the heroine maintains her father's connections with the court by fighting in the place of her slain and rather incompetent twin brother. She, of course, ultimately marries the prince. Along with Spenser's Britomart, Tasso's Clorinda, and others, the French Amazon is one of a line of noble women warriors, virtuous viragos all, magnanimous, brave, and chaste.[17]

To what extent could such embodiments of order serve to censure accepted hierarchy? They might reprove by their example the cowardice and wantonness of ordinary men and women. But they used their power to support a legitimate cause, not to unmask the truth about social relationships. By showing the good that could be done by the woman out of her place, they had the potential to inspire a few females to exceptional action and feminists to reflection about the capacities of women (we will see later whether that potential was realized), but they are unlikely symbols for moving masses of people to resistance.

It is otherwise with comic play with the disorderly woman, that is, inversion that can be expected of the female, who gives rein to the lower in herself and seeks rule over her superiors. Some portraits of her are so ferocious (such as Spenser's cruel Radagunde and other vicious viragos) that they preclude the possibility of fanciful release from, or criticism of, hierarchy. It is the same with those tales, considered humorous at the time, that depict a savage taming of the shrew, as in the fabliau of *La Dame escoillée*, where the domineering lady is given a counterfeit but painful "castration" by her son-in-law, and in the sixteenth-century German cartoon strip *The Ninefold Skins of a Shrewish Woman*, which are stripped off one by one by various punishments. The legend of the medieval Pope Joan also has limited potential for mocking established order. As told by Boccaccio, it is a hybrid of the transvestite saint and the cruelly tamed shrew: Joan wins the papacy by her wits and good behavior, but her illicit power goes to her head, or rather to her womb. She becomes pregnant, gives birth during a procession, and dies wretchedly in the cardinals' dungeon.[18]

There are a host of situations, however, in which the unruly woman is assigned more ambiguous meanings. For our purposes we can sort out three ways in which the multivalent image is used. First, there is a rich treatment of women who are happily given over to the sway of their bodily senses or who are using every ruse they can to prevail over men. There is the wife of Bath, of course, who celebrates her sexual instrument and outlives her five husbands. And Rabelais' Gargamelle—a giant of a woman, joyously and frequently coupling, eating bushels of tripe, quaffing wine, joking obscenely, giving birth in a grotesque fecal explosion from which her son Gargantua somersaults shouting "Drink, drink." Then the clever and powerful wife of the *Quinze joies de mariage*—cuckolding her husband and foiling his every effort to find her out, wheedling fancy clothes out of him, beating him up, and finally locking him in his room. Also Grimmelshausen's Libuschka, alias Courage, one of a series of picaresque heroines—fighting in the army in soldier's clothes; ruling her many husbands and lovers; paying them back a hundredfold when they take revenge or betray her; whoring, tricking, and trading to survive or get rich. Husband-dominators are everywhere in popular literature, nicknamed among the Germans St. Cudgelman (Sankt Kolbmann) or Doktor Siemann (she-man). The point about such portraits is that they are funny and amoral: the women are full of life and energy, and they win much of the time; they stay on top of their fortune with as much success as Machiavelli might have expected for the Prince of his political tract.[19]

A second comic treatment of the woman out of her place allows her a temporary period of dominion, which is ended only after she has said or done something to undermine authority or denounce its abuse. When the Silent Wife begins to talk and order her husband about in Ben Jonson's *Epicoene*, she points out that women cannot be mere statues or puppets; what her husband calls "Amazonian" impudence in her is simply reasonable decorum.* When the Woman-Captain of Shadwell's comedy puts aside her masculine garb and the sword with which she has hectored her jealous and stingy old husband, she does so only after having won separate maintenance and £400 a year. The moral of the play is that husbands must not move beyond the law to tyranny. In *As You Like It*, the love-struck Rosalind, her tongue loosed by her male apparel and her "holiday humor," warns Orlando that there is a limit to the possession he will have over a wife, a limit set by her desires, her wit, and her tongue. Though she later gives herself to Orlando in marriage, her saucy counsel cannot be erased from the real history of the courtship.

The most popular comic example of the female's temporary rule, however, is Phyllis riding Aristotle, a motif recurring in stories, paintings, and household objects from the thirteenth through the seventeenth centuries. Here Aristotle admonishes his pupil Alexander for his excessive attention to a certain Phyllis, one of his new subjects in India. The beautiful Phyllis gets revenge before Alexander's eyes by coquettishly persuading the old philosopher to get down on all fours and, saddled and bridled, carry her through the garden. Here youth overthrows age, and sexual passion, dry sterile philosophy; nature surmounts reason, and the female, the male.[20]

Phyllis' ambiguous ride brings us to a third way of presenting the woman-on-top, that is, where the license to be a social critic is conferred on her directly. Erhard Schoen's woodcuts (early sixteenth century) portray huge women distributing fools' caps to men. This is what happens when women are given the upper hand; and yet in some sense the men deserve it. Erasmus' female Folly is the supreme example

* The ambiguities in *Epicoene* were compounded by the fact that the Silent Wife in the play was a male playing a female, that is, a male actor playing a male playing a female. Professional troupes, of course, always used males for female parts in England until the Restoration and in France until the reign of Henri IV. See J. H. Wilson, *All the King's Ladies. Actresses of the Restoration* (Chicago, 1958) and Léopold Lacour, *Les premières actrices françaises* (Paris, 1921).

of this *topos*. Stultitia tells the truth about the foibles of all classes and defends the higher folly of the Cross, even though paradoxically she's just a foolish gabbling woman herself.[21]

These varied images of sexual topsy-turvy—from the transvestite male escaping responsibility and harm to the transvestite fool and the unruly woman unmasking the truth—were available to city people who went to the theater and to people who could read and afford books. They were also familiar to the lower orders more generally in both town and country through books that were read aloud and through stories, poems, proverbs, and broadsheets.[22]

In addition, popular festivals and customs, hard though they are to document, show much play with switches in sex roles and much attention to women-on-top. In examining these data, we will notice that sexual inversion in popular festivity differs from that in literature in two ways. Whereas the purely ritual and/or magical element in sexual inversion was present in literature to only a small degree, it assumed more importance in the popular festivities, along with the carnivalesque functions of mocking and unmasking the truth. Whereas sexual inversion in literary and pictorial play more often involved the female taking on the male role or dressing as a man, the festive inversion more often involved the male taking on the role or garb of the women, that is, the unruly woman—though this asymmetry may not have existed several centuries earlier.

The ritual and/or magical functions of sexual inversion were filled in almost all cases by males disguised as grotesque cavorting females. In sections of Germany and Austria, at carnival time male runners, half of them masked as female, half as male, jumped and leaped through the streets. In France it was on St. Stephen's Day or New Year's Day that men dressed as wild beasts or as women and jumped and danced in public (or at least such was the case in the Middle Ages). The saturnalian Feast of Fools, which decorous doctors of theology and prelates were trying to ban from the French cathedrals in the fifteenth and sixteenth centuries, involved both young clerics and laymen, some of them disguised as females, who made wanton and loose gestures. In parts of the Pyrénées at Candlemas (February 2), a Bear Chase took place* involv-

---

* Though evidence for the Candlemas Bear Chase is fullest and clearest from the French and Spanish Pyrénées, there are suggestions that it was more widespread in the Middle Ages. In the ninth century, Hincmar of Reims inveighed against "shameful plays" with bears and women dancers. Richard Bernheimer has argued for the connection between the bear hunt and the wild-man hunt, performed in several parts of Europe, and this has been confirmed by Claude Gaignebet, who relates it further to the popular play of Valentin and Ourson. Bruegel represented this game in an engraving and in his painting of the Battle of Carnival

ing a lustful bear, costumed hunters, and young men dressed as women and often called Rosetta. After an amorous interlude with Rosetta, the bear was killed, revived, shaved, and killed again.[23]

In England, too, in Henry VIII's time, during the reign of the Boy Bishop after Christmas some of the male children taken from house to house were dressed as females rather than as priests or bishops. The most important English examples of the male as grotesque female, however, were the Bessy and Maid Marian. In the northern counties, a Fool-Plough was dragged about the countryside, often on the first Monday after Epiphany, by men dressed in white shirts. Sword dances were done by some of them, while old Bessy and her fur-clad Fool capered around and tried to collect from the spectators. Maid Marian presided with Robin Hood over the May games. If in this capacity she was sometimes a real female and sometimes a disguised male, when it came to the Morris Dance with Robin, the Hobby Horse, the dragon, and the rest, the Marian was a man. Here again the Maid's gestures or costume might be licentious.[24]

All interpreters of this transvestism see it, like the African example mentioned earlier, as a fertility rite—biological or agricultural[25]— embedded into festivities that may have had other meanings as well. In the European context the use of the female garb was especially appropriate, for it drew not merely on the inevitable association of the female with reproduction, but on the contemporary definition of the female as the lustier sex. Did it also draw on other features of sexual symbolism in early modern Europe, e.g. the relation of the subordinate to the superior? Did it (as with our transvestite Harlequin of the *commedia dell'arte*) suggest to peasants or city folk the blurring or reversing of social boundaries? Perhaps. When we see the roles that the woman-on-top was later to play, it is hard to believe that some such effect was not stimulated by these rites. In the urban Feast of Fools, in any case, the fertility function of the transvestism was already overshadowed by its carnivalesque derision of the celibate priestly hierarchy.

Along with these instances of festive male transvestism, we have some scanty evidence of a more symmetrical switch. During the Twelve Days of Christmas or on Epiphany, mummers and guisers in northern England, the Scottish Lowlands, and northern France might include

and Lent: a male, masked and dressed as a female, holds out a ring to the wild man. See R. Bernheimer, *Wild Men in the Middle Ages* (Cambridge, Mass., 1952), pp. 52–56; C. Gaignebet, "Le combat de Carnaval et de Carême de P. Bruegel (1559)," *Annales. Economies, Sociétés, Civilisations 27* (1972): 329–31.

men *and* women wearing the clothes of the opposite sex. At Fastnacht in fifteenth-century Nuremberg men dressed as women and women as men, and the same was the case at Shrovetide in sixteenth-century England and perhaps at Mardi Gras in early modern France. Possibly here too there is some old relation to fertility rites, but the exchange may well be connected with the more flexible license of carnivalesque inversion. At least in the case of "goose-dancing" at Eastertime on the Scilly Islands in the mid-eighteenth century, we know the license was used to tell the truth: "the maidens are dressed up for young men and the young men for maidens: thus disguised they visit their neighbours in companies, where they dance, and make jokes upon what has happened on the island; when everyone is humorously told their own without offense being taken."[26]

The truth-telling of Europe's male festive societies was much less gentle than that of the Scilly geese. These organizations were the Kingdoms and Abbeys of Misrule[27] discussed in the previous essay. (In England and Scotland we have Lords of Misrule and Abbots of Unreason, though the exact character of their bands remains to be studied.) Among other roles in town and countryside, the Abbeys expressed the community's interest in marriages and their outcome much more overtly than the cavorting Bessy or Rosetta. In noisy masked demonstrations—charivaris, scampanete, katzenmusik, cencerrada, rough music, and the like—they mocked newlyweds who had not produced a baby soon enough and people marrying for the second time, especially when there was a gross disparity in age between bride and groom. Indeed, any local scandal might be made the target for their pots, tambourines, bells, and horns.

The unruly woman appeared in the Abbeys' plays in two forms. First as officers of Misrule. In rural areas, these were usually called Lords and Abbots; in the French cities, however, they took all kinds of pompous titles. Among these dignitaries were Princesses and Dames and especially Mothers: we find Mère Folle in Dijon, Langres, and Chalon-sur-Saône; Mère Sotte in Paris and Compiègne; and Mère d'Enfance in Bordeaux. In Wales, though I know of no female festive titles, the men who conducted the *ceffyl pren*, as the local rough music was called, blackened their faces and wore women's garb.[28] In all of this there was a double irony: the young villager who became an Abbot, the artisan who became a Prince directly adopted for their Misrule a symbol of licit power; the power invoked by the man who became Mère Folle, however, was already in defiance of natural order—a dangerous and vital power, which his disguise made safe for him to assume.

The unruly woman not only directed some of the male festive organizations; she was sometimes their butt. The village scold or the domineering wife might be ducked in the pond or pulled through the streets muzzled or branked or in a creel.[29] City people from the fifteenth to the eighteenth centuries were even more concerned about husband-beating, and the beaten *man* (or a neighbor playing his part) was paraded through the streets backward on an ass by noisy revelers. In the English Midlands the ride was known as a Skimmington or a Skimmety, perhaps from the big skimming ladle sometimes used by women in beating their husbands. In northern England and Scotland, the victim or his stand-in "rode the stang" (a long hobbyhorse), and a like steed was used in the *ceffyl pren* in Wales. In some towns, effigies of the offending couple were promenaded. In others, the festive organization mounted floats to display the actual circumstances of the monstrous beating: the wives were shown hitting their husbands with distaffs, tripe, sticks, trenchers, water pots; throwing stones at them; pulling their beards; or kicking them in the genitalia.[30]

With these last dramatizations, the Misrule Abbeys introduced ambiguities into the treatment of the woman-on-top, just as we have seen in the comic literature. The unruly woman on the float was shameful, outrageous; she was also vigorous and in command. The mockery turned against her martyred husband. And the message of the urban carnival was mixed: it both exhorted the henpecked husband to take command and invited the unruly woman to keep up the fight.

Real women in early modern Europe had less chance than men to initiate or take part in their *own* festivals of inversion. To be sure, a female fool named Mathurine flourished at the courts of Henri IV and Louis XIII and, dressed as an Amazon, commented on political and religious matters; but there is no sign of festive organizations for young women. Confraternities for young unmarried women, where they existed at all, stayed close to religious devotion. Queens were elected for special occasions, such as Twelfth Night or Harvest, but their rule was gentle and tame. The young May queens in their flowers and white ribbons begged for money for dowries or for the Virgin's altar, promising a mere kiss in return. Some May customs that were still current in early modern Europe, however, point back to a rowdier role for women. In rural Franche-Comté during May, wives could take revenge on their husbands for beating them by ducking the men or making them ride an ass; wives could dance, jump, and banquet freely without permission from their husbands; and women's courts issued mock decrees. (In nearby Dijon by the sixteenth century, interestingly enough, Mère Folle and her Infanterie had usurped this revenge from the women; May was the one month of the year when the Misrule Abbey would charivari a man who had beaten his wife.) Generally, May—Flora's month in Roman times—was thought to be a period in which women were powerful, their desires at their most immoderate. As the old saying went, a May bride would keep her husband in yoke all year round. And in fact marriages were not frequent in May.[31]

In Nuremberg it was at carnival time that women may have assumed some kind of special license in the sixteenth and seventeenth centuries. Illustrated proclamations in joking pompous language granted every female with "a wretched dissolute husband" the right to deny him his freedom and to beat him till "his asshole [was] roaring." Another decree, issued by Foeminarius, the Hereditary Steward of Quarrel and Dispute Valley, gave three years of Privileges to the suffering Company of Wives so that they might rule their husbands: they could bear arms, elect their own mayor, and go out and entertain as they wished while their spouses could buy nothing or drink no wine or beer without the wives' permission. And, of course, the men did all the housework and welcomed any bastards that the wives might bear.[32]

III

The relationship between real marriages and May license, between real pregnancy and Fastnacht games returns us to the question posed earlier in this paper. What were the overall functions of these festive and literary inversions in sex roles? Clearly they filled in part the role attributed to them by anthropologists and historians of literature: they afforded an expression of, and an outlet for, conflicts about authority within the system; and they also provided occasions by which the authoritarian current in family, workshop, and political life could be moderated by the laughter of disorder and paradoxical play. Accordingly, they served to reinforce hierarchical structure.

Indeed, in the early modern period, up to the late eighteenth century, the patriarchal family is not challenged as such even by the most searching critics of relations between the sexes. The late seventeenth-century feminists François Poullain de La Barre and Mary Astell believed the submission of the wife to her husband not to be justified by any natural inferiority of females, but to be necessary nonetheless. As Astell said, "There can be [no] Society great or little, from Empires down to private Families, without a last Resort, to determine the Affairs of that Society by an irresistible sentence. . . . This Supremacy must be fixed somewhere." The best they could imagine was an impossible hermaphroditic utopia or a primitive state of equality between the sexes, now irrevocably lost (perhaps the experience of festive role-reversals at least helped keep this egalitarian dream alive, as Victor Turner has suggested in another connection). The best they could hope for and recommend, like Shadwell's Woman-Captain, were ways to prevent husbandly tyranny: better education for women or a better choice of marriage partners. The only countermodel for the family they had come to recognize by the mid-eighteenth century was the equally hierarchical one of matriarchy.[33]

Thus, this study does not overturn the traditional theory about rites and festivities of inversion; but it does hope to add other dimensions to it. Rather than expending itself primarily during the privileged duration of the joke, the story, the comedy, or the carnival, topsy-turvy play had much spillover into everyday "serious" life, and the effects there were sometimes disturbing and even novel. As literary and festive inversion in preindustrial Europe was a product not just of stable hierarchy but also of changes in the location of power and property, so this inversion could prompt new ways of thinking about the system and reacting to it.

Let us begin with a historical reflection about the family. Europeans of the fifteenth to eighteenth centuries found it remarkably difficult to conceive of the institution of the family as having a "history," of changing through time. Its patriarchal form went back either to the Garden of Eden, where the woman's subjection to the man was at least a gentle one, or to the first moment in human history, when monogamous marriage set mankind off from the promiscuous horde. Political forms might follow each other in a predictable cyclical fashion; economic, religious, and cultural systems might change along with them (as Vico thought). But the family stayed the same. To be sure, curious sexual customs were noted in the New World, but they were used merely to satirize European abuses or dismissed as products of savagery or degeneration. Play with the various images of woman-on-top, then, kept open an alternate way of conceiving family structure.* Ultimately, when the

---

* The Amazons play a role, for instance, in Thomas Hobbes' remarkable theoretical discussion of dominion within the family. As is usual in his period, he insists that it must be vested in one person only; but "whereas some have attributed the dominion to the man only, as being of the more excellent sex; they misreckon in it. For there is not always that difference of strength, or prudence between the man and the woman, as that the right can be determined without war." In commonwealths, the conflict is settled by law, which for the most

Jesuit Lafitau found an order in the strange family patterns (matrilineal and matrilocal) that he had observed among the Iroquois and heard about in the Caribbean, he was able to refer back to legends of the Amazons and to the Lycians, whom he had read about in Herodotus. Lafitau's new theory of "gynaecocracy," as he called the matriarchal stage, was published in 1724 in his *Moeurs des sauvages ameriquains, comparées aux moeurs des premiers temps*. It owed something to the unruly woman.[34]

Play with the exceptional woman-on-top, the virtuous virago, was also a resource for feminist reflection on women's capacities. Although she did not argue that men and women should change the separate offices to which God had ordained them, nevertheless Christine de Pisan was glad to use examples of ancient female conquerors, stock figures in the legends about Amazons and in the stories and proverbs about women's rule, to show that "in many women there is . . . great courage, strength, and hardiness to undertake all manner of strong things and to achieve them as did . . . great men and solemn conquerors." Subsequent writers on "Women Worthies" almost always included some viragos, readily incorporating Joan of Arc into the company. By the early eighteenth century, speculation about virtuous Amazons could be used not only to praise the wise rule of contemporary lawful queens (as it had been already in Elizabeth I's day), but also to hint at the possibility of a wider role of citizenship for women.[35]

Furthermore, the exceptional woman-out-of-her-place enriched the fantasy of a few real women and might have emboldened them to exceptional action. Marie Delcourt has argued convincingly that Joan of Arc's male garb, to which she clung obdurately to the end, was not the product of mere practical military considerations, but was inspired by the example of the transvestite saints of the *Golden Legend*. The unusual seventeenth-century mystic Antoinette Bourignon started her career by fleeing from an impending marriage in the clothes of a male hermit. Among her later visions was that of humankind created originally as androgynous, a state of whole perfection to which it would return at the resurrection of the dead. The Recusant Mary Ward,

---

part decides for the father. But in the state of nature, the decision is made by those who generate the children. It may be made by contract. "We find in history that the Amazons contracted with the men of the neighboring countries, to whom they had recourse for issue, that the issue male should be sent back, but the female remain with themselves: so that the dominion of the females was in the mother." Where there is no contract, the dominion lies with the mother—that is, in the absence of matrimonial laws, with the only person who knows who the true parents are and who has the power to nourish the child. *The Leviathan*, Second Part, chap. 20.

founder of an innovating unenclosed teaching order for women with no male superior but the pope, was taking the Jesuits as her model but may also have received encouragement from traditions of sexual inversion. Galloping over the countryside in the vain effort to reconvert the English to Holy Mother Church, she and the members of her Company struck observers as "apostolic Amazons."[36]

Two of these women ultimately went to prison; the third narrowly escaped arrest. The virtuous virago could be a threat to order after all. But what about the majority of unexceptional women living within their families? What could the woman-on-top mean to them?

Girls were brought up to believe that they ought to obey their husbands; and boys were brought up to believe that they had the power of correction over their wives. In actual marriage, subjection might be moderated by the common causes of economic support, to which they both contributed, of sexual need, of childrearing, or of shared religious interest. It might be reversed temporarily during the lying-in period, when the new mother could boss her husband around with impunity. And subjection might be aggravated by the husband's repeated beatings of his wife. Some women accepted these arrangements. Some women got around them by sneaky manipulations that made their husbands fancy themselves the sole decision-makers. Still other wives rebelled, told their husbands to go to the devil, badgered them, thrashed them. Many circumstances might produce a wife of the third type. Here I wish only to speculate that the ambiguous woman-on-top of the world of play made the unruly option a more conceivable one within the family.[37]

Ordinary women might also be disorderly in public. In principle, women could pronounce on law and doctrine only if they were queens, had unusual learning, or fell into an ecstatic trance. Virtually never were they to take the law into their own hands. In fact, women turn up telling off priests and pastors, being central actors in grain and bread riots in town and country, and participating in tax revolts and other rural disturbances. In England in the early seventeenth century (so Thomas Barnes has discovered), a significant percentage of the rioters against enclosures and for common rights were female. In Calvinist Edinburgh in 1637, the resistance to Charles I's imposition of the Book of Common Prayer was opened by a crowd of "rascally serving women" at Saint Giles' Church, who drowned out the Dean's reading, threw stools at the Bishop of Edinburgh, and when evicted, stoned the doors and windows. The tax revolt at Montpellier in 1645 was started by women, led down the streets by a virago named la Branlaïre, who shouted for death for the tax-collectors who were taking the bread from their children's mouths.[38]

There are several reasons for this female involvement that we cannot consider here, but part of its background is the complex license accorded the unruly woman. On the one hand, she was not accountable for what she did. Given over to the sway of her lower passions, she was not responsible for her actions; her husband was responsible, for she was subject to him. Indeed, this "incapacity" was embodied in varying degrees in English law and in some French customary law. In England, in most felonious acts by a married woman to which her husband could be shown to be privy or at which he was present, the wife could not be held entirely culpable. If indicted, she might be acquitted or receive a lesser sentence than he for the same crime. In Normandy and Brittany, the husband might have to answer for her crimes in court, and everywhere the *sexus imbecillus* might be punished less severely. The full weight of the law fell only on the ruling male. Small wonder that the husbands sometimes thought it safer to send their wives out to do the rioting alone. And small wonder that the Star Chamber grumbled in 1605 that some women who had torn down enclosure fences were "hiding behind their sex."[39]

On the other hand, sexual inversion also gave a more positive license to the unruly woman: her right as subject and as mother to rise up and tell the truth. When a great pregnant woman at the front of a crowd curses grain-hoarders or cheating authorities, the irreverent Gargamelle is part of her tradition. When Katherine Zell of Strasbourg dares to write an attack on clerical celibacy in the 1520's and claims "I do not pretend to be John the Baptist rebuking the Pharisees. I do not claim to be Nathan up-braiding David. I aspire only to be Balaam's ass, castigating his master," then Dame Folly is part of her tradition.[40]

It turns out, however, that Dame Folly could serve to validate disobedient and riotous behavior by men, too. They also could hide behind that sex. Much has been written by historians on the ideals, traditions, symbols, and solidarities that legitimated the numerous rural and urban uprisings of early modern Europe. Among these traditions was the carnival right of criticism and mockery, which sometimes tipped over into real rebellion. In 1630 in Dijon, for instance, Mère Folle and her Infanterie were part of an uprising in masquerade against royal tax officers. In fact, the donning of female clothes by men and the adopting of female titles for riots were surprisingly frequent, beginning (so our still scanty data suggest) in the seventeenth century. In many of these disturbances, the men were trying to protect traditional rights against change; in others, it was the rioters who were pressing for innovation. But in all cases, they were putting ritual and festive inversion to new uses.

So in the Beaujolais in the 1770's, male peasants blackened their faces and dressed as women and then attacked surveyors measuring their lands for a new landlord. Later, when the police agents came, the peasants' wives knew nothing, and said the attackers were "fairies" who came from the mountains from time to time.* Among the market women who marched to Versailles in October 1789, it is very likely there were men in female garb. And in 1829–30, the "War of the Demoiselles" took place in the Department of Ariège in the Pyrénées. The peasants dressed themselves in long white shirts, suggesting women's clothes, wore women's hats, and defended their much-needed rights to wood and pasturage in the forests, then being threatened by a new Forest Code.[41]

In England we find the same thing. In 1451, in the wake of Cade's rebellion, blackfaced "servants of the Queen of the Fairies" broke into the Duke of Buckingham's park in Kent and took his bucks and does. In 1629, "Captain" Alice Clark, a real female, headed a crowd of women and male weavers dressed as women in a grain riot near Maldon in Essex. In 1641, in the dairy and grazing sections of Wiltshire, bands of men rioted and leveled fences against the king's enclosure of their forests. They were led by men dressed as women, who called themselves "Lady Skimmington." In May 1718, Cambridge students followed "a virago, or man in woman's habit, crowned with laurel" to assault a Dissenting meeting house. Two years later, laborers in Surrey rioted in women's clothes, and at mid-century country men disguised as women tore down the hated tollbooths and turnpike gates at the Gloucestershire border. In April 1812, "General Ludd's Wives," two weavers dressed as women, led a crowd of hundreds to smash steam looms and burn a factory at Stockport.[42]

In Wales and Scotland, too, there were uprisings in female disguise. The *ceffyl pren*, with its blackfaced transvestite males, gave way in the 1830's and 1840's in west Wales to the Rebecca riots against the detested

---

* The association of these costumed figures with "fairies," which was also made in a few other riots, adds another dimension to political transvestism. Fairy beliefs were still strong in rural Europe in the eighteenth century, having originated from diverse traditions, including one that associated them with the spirits of the dead. Fairies might assume male or female form, might have various sizes and shapes, and might dress in different ways; but they all had a spiritual power that could be used on human beings either malevolently or benevolently. Female and fairy combine their power in these riots to help the peasants. See K. M. Briggs, *The Fairies in Tradition and Literature* (London, 1967), and Keith Thomas, *Religion and the Decline of Magic* (London, 1971), pp. 606–14.

turnpike tolls and other sources of agrarian complaint. They were led by one "Rebecca" and noisy men in women's clothes. And in 1736 in Edinburgh, the Porteous Riots, which were sparked by a hated English officer, oppressive customs laws, and resistance to the union of Scotland with England, were carried out by men disguised as women and with a leader known as Madge Wildfire.[43]

Finally, in Ireland, where old stories told of the ritual killing of the king at Samhain by men dressed as animals and as women, and where the funeral wakes involved fertility rites with women dressed as men, we have the most extensive example of disturbances led by men disguised as women. For about a decade, from 1760 to 1770, the White-boys, dressed in long white frocks and with blackened faces, set themselves up as an armed popular force to provide justice for the poor, "to restore the ancient commons and redress other grievances." They tore down enclosures, punished landowners who raised the rents, forced masters to release unwilling apprentices, and fought the gouging tithe-farmers mercilessly. Those who opposed their rule they chastised and ridiculed. They sometimes said they acted under "sanction of being fairies," and a favorite signature on their proclamations was Sieve Outlagh (or Sadhbh Amhaltach)—"Ghostly Sally." Ultimately they were suppressed by the armed might of the gentlemen and magistrates, but not before they had left a legacy for the Molly Maguires and the Ribbon Societies of the nineteenth century.[44]

The female persona was only one of several folk disguises assumed by males for riots in the seventeenth and eighteenth centuries, but it was quite popular and widespread. Our analysis of sexual symbolism and of the varieties of sexual inversion should help us understand why this was so. In part, the black face and female dress were a practical concealment, and readily at hand in households rarely filled with fancy wardrobes. More important, however, were the mixed ways in which the female persona authorized resistance. On the one hand, the disguise freed men from full responsibility for their deeds and perhaps, too, from fear of outrageous revenge upon their manhood. After all, it was mere women who were acting in this disorderly way. On the other hand, the males drew upon the sexual power and energy of the unruly woman and on her license (which they had long assumed at carnival and games)—to promote fertility, to defend the community's interests and standards, and to tell the truth about unjust rule.

The woman-on-top was a resource for private and public life in the fashions we have described only so long as two things were the case:

176

first, so long as sexual symbolism had a close connection with questions of order and subordination, with the lower female sex conceived as the disorderly lustful one; second, so long as the stimulus to inversion play was a double one—traditional hierarchical structures *and* disputed changes in the distribution of power in family and political life. As we move into the industrial period with its modern states, classes, and systems of private property, and its exploitation of racial and national groups, both symbolism and stimuli were transformed. One small sign of the new order is the changing butt of domestic charivaris: by the nineteenth century, rough music in England was more likely to be directed against the wife-beater than against the henpecked husband, and there are signs of such a shift in America and even in France.[45]

The woman-on-top flourished, then, in preindustrial Europe and during the period of transition to industrial society. Despite all our detail in this essay, we have been able to give only the outlines of her reign. Variations in sexual inversion from country to country or between Protestants and Catholics have been ignored for the sake of describing a large pattern over time. Cultural play with sex roles intended to explore the character of sexuality itself (Where did one sex stop and the other begin?) has been ignored to concentrate on hierarchy and disorder. The timing and distribution of transvestite riots, and the nature of play with sex roles before the fourteenth century, need to be investigated. (Is it not likely that there were female transvestite rituals in areas where hoeing was of great consequence? Can the unruly woman have been so much an issue when sovereignty was less at stake?) The asymmetry between male and female roles in festive life from the fifteenth through the eighteenth centuries remains to be explored, as do some of the contrasts between literary and carnivalesque inversion. What has been established are the types of symbolic reversal in sex roles in early modern Europe and their multiple connections with orderliness in thought and behavior. The holiday rule of the woman-on-top confirmed subjection throughout society, but it also promoted resistance to it. The Maid Marian danced for a plentiful village; the Rosetta disported with the doomed old bear of winter; the serving women of Saint Giles threw stools for the Reformed Kirk; Ghostly Sally led her Whiteboys in a new kind of popular justice. The woman-on-top renewed old systems, but also helped change them into something different.

Notes

1. Pierre Grosnet, *Les motz dorez De Cathon en francoys et en latin . . . Proverbes, Adages, Auctoritez et ditz moraulx des Saiges* (Paris, 1530/31), f. F. vii^r. Claude de Rubys, *Les privileges franchises et immunitez octroyees par les roys . . . aux consuls . . . et habitans de la ville de Lyon* (Lyon, 1574), p. 74. Christopher Hill, "The Many-Headed Monster in Late Tudor and Early Stuart Political Thinking," in C. H. Carter, ed., *From the Renaissance to the Counter-Reformation, Essays in Honour of Garrett Mattingly* (London, 1966), pp. 296–324.

2. Laurent Joubert, *Erreurs populaires au fait de la medecine* (Bordeaux, 1578), pp. 161ff. François Poullain de La Barre, *De l'excellence des hommes contre l'egalité des sexes* (Paris, 1675), pp. 136ff., 156ff. Ilza Veith, *Hysteria, The History of a Disease* (Chicago, 1965). Michael Screech, *The Rabelaisian Marriage* (London, 1958), chap. 6. Thomas Sydenham, in his important *Epistolary Dissertation to Dr. Cole* (1681), connects the delicate constitution of the woman with the irregular motions of her "animal spirits" and hence explains her special susceptibility to hysteria. Winthrop Jordan, *White over Black. American Attitudes toward the Negro, 1550–1812* (Chapel Hill, N.C., 1968), pp. 11–20, 187–90.

3. Heinrich Institoris and Jacob Sprenger, *Malleus Maleficarum* (ca. 1487), trans. M. Summers (London, 1928), Part 1, question 6: "Why it is that Women are chiefly addicted to Evil Superstitions." Florimond de Raemond, *L'histoire de la naissance, progrez et decadence de l'hérésie de ce siècle* (Rouen, 1623), pp. 847–48, 874–77. Fleury de Bellingen, *L'Etymologie ou Explication des Proverbes françois* (La Haye, 1656), pp. 311ff. James E. Phillips, Jr., "The Background of Spenser's Attitude toward Women Rulers," *Huntingon Library Quarterly* 5 (1941–42): 9–10. [John Aylmer], *An Harborowe for Faithfull and Trewe Subiects, agaynst the late blowne Blaste, concerning the Government of Wemen* (London, 1559). J. Simon, *Le gouvernement admirable ou la République des Abeilles* (Paris, 1742), pp. 23ff. John Thorley, in *The Female Monarchy. Being an Enquiry into the Nature, Order and Government of Bees* (London, 1744), still finds it necessary to argue against those who cannot believe in a queen bee (pp. 75–86).

4. See, for instance, Juan Luis Vives, *The Instruction of a Christian Woman* (London, 1524), and François de Salignac de la Mothe Fénelon, *Fénelon on Education*, trans. H. C. Barnard (Cambridge, 1966).

5. P. C. Timbal, "L'esprit du droit privé," *XVIIe siècle* 58–59 (1963): 38–39. P. Ourliac and J. de Malafosse, *Histoire du droit privé* (Paris, 1963), 3: 145–52, 264–68. L. Abensour, *La femme et le féminisme avant la Révolution* (Paris, 1923), Part 1, chap. 9. Alice Clark, *The Working Life of Women in the Seventeenth Century* (London, 1919; reprint 1968). E. Le Roy Ladurie, *Les paysans de Languedoc* (Paris, 1966), pp. 271–80 and *Annexe 32*, p. 859.

6. Christine de Pisan, *The Boke of the Cyte of Ladyes* (a translation of *Le Tresor de la Cité des Dames*, 1405; London, 1521), f. Ee i^v. Henry Cornelius Agrippa of Nettesheim, *Of the Nobilities and Excellencie of Womankynde* (translation from the Latin edition of 1509; London, 1542), f. B iv^{r-v}.

7. Jean Calvin, *Commentaries on the Epistles of Paul The Apostle to the Corinthians*, trans. J. Pringle (Edinburgh, 1848, 1: 353–61 (1 Cor. 11: 3–12). William Gouge, *Domesticall Duties*, quoted in W. and M. Haller, "The Puritan Art of

Love," *Huntington Library Quarterly* 5 (1941–42): 246. John G. Halkett, *Milton and the Idea of Matrimony* (New Haven, 1970), pp. 20–24. Gordon J. Schochet, "Patriarchalism, Politics and Mass Attitudes in Stuart England," *Historical Journal* 12 (1969): 413–41. Catherine E. Holmes, *L'éloquence judiciaire de 1620 à 1660* (Paris, 1967), p. 76. Ourliac and de Malafosse, *Droit privé*, 3: 66 ("*L'époque des rois absolus est aussi celle des pères absolus.*") John Locke, *The Second Treatise of Government*, ed. T. P. Peardon (Indianapolis, Ind., 1952), chap. 7, par. 82; chap. 9, pars. 128–31.

8. [Gabriel de Foigny], *Les avantures de Jacques Sadeur dans la découverte et le voyage de la terre australe* (Amsterdam, 1732), chap. 5, especially pp. 128–39.

9. Robert Delevoy, *Bruegel* (Lausanne, 1959), pp. 70–75.

10. Deut. 22: 5; 1 Cor. 11: 14–15. Saint Jerome, *The Letters of Saint Jerome*, trans. C. C. Mierow (London, 1963), 1: 161–62 (Letter 22 to Eustochium). Robert of Flamborough, *Liber Penitentialis*, ed. J. F. Firth (Toronto, 1971), Book 5, p. 264. (I am grateful to Carolly Erickson and Stephen Horowitz for the last two references.) Jean Calvin, "Sermons sur le Deutéronome," in *Ioannis Calvini opera quae supersunt omnia*, ed. G. Baum, E. Cunitz, and E. Reuss (Brunswick, 1863–80), 28: 17–19, 234 (hereafter cited as *Calvini opera*). Vern Bullough, "Transvestites in the Middle Ages," *American Journal of Sociology* 79 (1974): 1381–94.

11. Pierre de l'Estoile, *Mémoires-journaux*, ed. Brunet et al. (Paris, 1888–96), 1: 142–43, 157, 180. François-Timoléon de Choisy, *Mémoires*, ed. G. Mongrédien (Paris, 1966), pp. 286–360. Bullough's "Transvestites in the Middle Ages," which I have read as this essay goes to press, also discusses male cross-dressing in social rather than in psychopathological terms, that is, in terms of the higher and lower qualities assigned to male and female traits: males who dress as women have a temporary or permanent desire for status loss (p. 1393). I think this is accurate as a very preliminary formulation. My essay shows the *varied* functions of role inversion and transvestism as well as the gains in power and the options they brought to males.

12. Max Gluckman, *Order and Rebellion in Tribal Africa* (New York, 1963), Introduction and chap. 3. Victor Turner, *The Forest of Symbols, Aspects of Ndembu Ritual* (Ithaca, N.Y., 1967), chap. 4 *Idem, The Ritual Process. Structure and Anti-Structure* (Chicago, 1968), chaps. 3–5. Gregory Bateson, "Culture Contact and Schismogenesia," *Man 35* (Dec. 1935): 199. J. C. Flügel, *The Psychology of Clothes* (London, 1930), pp. 120–21. Marie Delcourt, *Hermaphrodite. Myths and Rites of the Bisexual Figure in Classical Antiquity* (London, 1956), chap. 1. James Peacock, "Symbolic Reversal and Social History: Transvestites and Clowns of Java," in Barbara Babcock-Abrahams, ed., *Forms of Symbolic Inversion* (forthcoming). See also Rodney Needham's discussion of symbolic reversal and its relation to classification in his introduction to E. Durkheim and M. Mauss, *Primitive Classifications*, trans. R. Needham (Chicago, 1972), pp. xxxviii–xl.

13. William Willeford, *The Fool and His Scepter* (Evanston, Ill., 1969), especially pp. 97–98.

14. Ian Donaldson, *The World Upside-Down, Comedy from Jonson to Fielding* (Oxford, 1970), p. 14.

15. Stith Thompson, *Motif-Index of Folk Literature* (rev. ed.; Bloomington, Ind., 1955–58), K310, K514, K1321, K1836, K2357.8. Sir Philip Sidney, *The New*

Arcadia, Book I, chap. 12. Honore d'Urfé, *Astrée* (1609–19). John Marston, *The History of Antonio and Mellida* (1602). Willeford, *The Fool*, pp. 58–62.

16. Delcourt, *Hermaphrodite*, pp. 84–102. John Anson, "Female Monks: The Transvestite Motif in Early Christian Literature," forthcoming in *Viator* (I am grateful to Mr. Anson for several bibliographic suggestions). The transvestite saints appearing in Voragine's *Golden Legend* are St. Margaret, alias Brother Pelagius (Oct. 8); Saint Pelagia, alias Pelagius (Oct. 8); Saint Theodora, alias Brother Theodore (Sept. 11); Saint Eugenia (Sept. 11); and Saint Marina, alias Brother Marinus (June 18). See also Bullough, "Transvestites," pp. 1385–87.

17. Thompson, *Motif-Index*, K3.3, K1837. A. Aarne and Stith Thompson, *The Types of the Folktale* (2d rev. ed.; Helsinki, 1964), 88A, 890, 891A. Giovanni Boccaccio, *Decameron*, Second Day, Story 9. William Shakespeare, *The Merchant of Venice*, Act II, scenes 4–6; Act IV, scene 1. M. J. L'Héritier de Villandon, *Les caprices du destin ou Recueil d'histoires singulieres et amusantes. Arrivées de nos jours* (Paris, 1718), *Avertissement* and tale "L'Amazone Françoise." Celeste T. Wright, "The Amazons in Elizabethan Literature," *Studies in Philology* 37 (1940): 433–45. Edmund Spenser, *The Faerie Queen*, Book III, Canto 1.

18. Spenser, *Faerie Queene*, Book V, Cantos 4–5; Wright, "Amazons," pp. 449–54. "The Lady Who Was Castrated," in Paul Brians, ed. and trans., *Bawdy Tales from the Courts of Medieval France* (New York, 1972), pp. 24–36. David Kunzle, *The Early Comic Strip. Narrative Strips and Picture Stories in the European Broadsheet from 1450 to 1825* (Berkeley and Los Angeles, 1973), pp. 224–25. Giovanni Boccaccio, *Concerning Famous Women*, trans. G. G. Guarino (New Brunswick, N.J., 1963), pp. 231–34.

19. Chaucer, *The Canterbury Tales*, "The Wife of Bath's Prologue." François Rabelais, *La vie très horrifique du Grand Gargantua, père de Pantagruel*, chaps. 3–6. Mikhail Bakhtin, *Rabelais and His World* (Cambridge, Mass., 1968), pp. 240–41. *Les quinze joies de mariage*, ed. J. Rychner (Geneva, 1963). Harry Baxter, "The Waning of Misogyny: Changing Attitudes Reflected in *Les Quinze Joyes de Mariage*," Lecture given to the Sixth Conference on Medieval Studies, Western Michigan University, Kalamazoo, Michigan, 1971. H. J. C. von Grimmelshausen, *Courage, The Adventuress and the False Messiah*, trans. Hans Speier (Princeton, 1964). Johannes Janssen, *History of the German People at the Close of the Middle Ages*, trans. A. M. Christie (London, 1896–1925), 12: 206, n. 1. Kunzle, *Early Comic Strip*, p. 225. *Mari et femme dans la France rurale* (catalogue of the exhibition at the Musée national des arts et traditions populaires, Paris, September 22–November 19, 1973), pp. 68–69.

20. Ben Jonson, *Epicoene*, Act IV. See Donaldson, *World Upside-Down*, chap. 2, and Edward B. Partridge, *The Broken Compass* (New York, 1958), chap. 7. Thomas Shadwell, *The Woman-Captain* (London, 1680). William Shakespeare, *As You Like It*, Act III, scenes 2, 4, Act IV, scene 1. For an interesting view of Shakespeare's treatment of Katharina in *The Taming of the Shrew*, see Hugh Richmond, *Shakespeare's Sexual Comedy* (Indianapolis, Ind., 1971), pp. 83–101. Henri d'Andeli, *Le Lai d'Aristote de Henri d'Andeli*, ed. M. Delboville (Bibliothèque de la Faculté de Philosophie et Lettres de l'Université de Liège, 123; Paris, 1951). Hermann Schmitz, *Hans Baldung gen. Grien* (Bielefeld and Leipzig, 1922), Plate 66 (reproduced here as Plate 11). K. Oettinger and K.-A. Knappe, *Hans Baldung Grien und Albrecht Dürer in Nürnberg* (Nuremberg, 1963), Plate 66. Kunzle, *Early Comic Strip*, p. 224.

21. *Erasmus en zijn tijd* (Catalogue of the exhibition at the Museum Boymans— van Beuningen, Rotterdam, October–November 1969), nos. 151–52. See also no. 150, *The Fools' Tree* (ca. 1526), by the "Petrarch-Master" of Augsburg, reproduced here as Plate 10. Willeford, *The Fool*, Plate 30, drawing by Urs Graf. Erasmus, *The Praise of Folly*. See also Dame Folly leading apes and fools in H. W. Janson, *Apes and Ape Lore in the Middle Ages and Renaissance* (London, 1952), pp. 204–8 and Plate 36.

22. See, for instance, John Ashton, ed., *Humour, Wit and Satire in the Seventeenth Century* (New York, 1968; republication of the 1883 ed.), pp. 82ff. John Wardroper, ed., *Jest upon Jest* (London, 1970), chap. 1. Aarne and Thompson, *Folktale*, 1375, 1366A. Kunzle, *Early Comic Strip*, pp. 222–23.

23. S. L. Sumberg, *The Nuremberg Schembart Carnival* (New York, 1941), especially pp. 83–84, 104–5. Maria Leach, ed., *Funk and Wagnalls Standard Dictionary of Folklore, Mythology and Legend* (New York, 1949–50), "Schemen." Jean Savaron, *Traitté contre les masques* (Paris, 1608), p. 10. M. du Tilliot, *Mémoires pour servir à l'histoire de la Fête des Foux* (Lausanne and Geneva, 1751), pp. 8, 11–12. Arnold Van Gennep, *Manuel du folklore français* (Paris, 1943–49), 1.3: 908–18. Violet Alford, *Pyrenean Festivals* (London, 1937), pp. 16–25. Compare the Pyrénées Bear and Rosetta with the Gyro or grotesque giant woman, played by young men on Old Candlemas Day in the Orkney Islands (F. M. McNeill, *The Silver Bough* [Glasgow, 1961], 3: 28–29). Curt Sachs, *World History of the Dance* (New York, 1963), pp. 335–39.

24. Joseph Strutt, *The Sports and Pastimes of the People of England* (new ed.; London, 1878), pp. 449–51, 310–11, 456. C. L. Barber, *Shakespeare's Festive Comedy* (Princeton, 1951), p. 28. Leach, *Dictionary of Folklore*, "Fool Plough," "Morris."

25. Leach, *Dictionary of Folklore*, "Transvestism." Willeford, *The Fool*, p. 86. Van Gennep, *Manuel*, 1.8: 910. Alford, *Festivals*, pp. 19–22. Sachs, *Dance*, pp. 335–39.

26. Henry Bourne, *Antiquitates Vulgares; or the Antiquities of the Common People* (New-castle, 1725), pp. 147–48. McNeill, *Silver Bough*, 4: 82. Roger Vaultier, *Le Folklore pendant la guerre de Cent Ans* (Paris, 1965), pp. 93–100. J. Lefebvre, *Les fols et la folie* (Paris, 1968), p. 46, n. 66. A. Holtmont, *Die Hosenrolle* (Munich, 1925), pp. 54–55. Donaldson, *World Upside-Down*, p. 15. Van Gennep, *Manuel*, 1.3: 884. Strutt, *Sports*, p. 125.

27. For full documentation and bibliography on this material, see Chap. 4, "The Reasons of Misrule," and E. P. Thompson, "'Rough Music': Le Charivari anglais," Annales ESC 27 (1972): 285–312.

28. P. Sadron, "Les associations permanentes d'acteurs en France au moyen-age," *Revue d'histoire de théâtre* 4 (1952): 222–31. Du Tilliot, *Mémoires*, pp. 179–82. David Williams, *The Rebecca Riots* (Cardiff, 1955), pp. 53–54. Willeford, *The Fool*, pp. 175–79.

29. See Chapter 4, "The Reasons of Misrule," n. 34. J. W. Spargo, *Juridical Folklore in England Illustrated by the Cucking-Stool* (Durham, N.C., 1944). McNeill, *Silver Bough*, 4: 67.

30. In addition to the sources given in n. 28, see Hogarth's illustration of a Skimmington Ride made about 1726 for Samuel Butler's *Hudibras* ("Hudibras encounters the Skimmington").

31. Enid Welsford, *The Fool, His Social and Literary History* (London, 1935), pp.

153–54. Van Gennep, *Manuel*, 1.4: 1452–72, 1693–94. Lucienne A. Roubin, *Chambrettes des Provençaux* (Paris, 1970), pp. 178–79. Chap. 4, "The Reasons of Misrule," n. 13. Jean Vostet, *Almanach ou Prognostication des Laboureurs* (Paris, 1588), f. 12ʳ⁻ᵛ. Erasmus, *Adagiorum Chiliades* (Geneva, 1558), col. 135, "Mense Maio nubunt malae." Gabriel Le Bras, *Etudes de sociologie religieuse* (Paris, 1955), 1: 44. On the women's revenge at Saint Agatha's day in the Savoie, see A. Van Gennep, "Le culte populaire de Sainte Agathe en Savoie," *Revue d'ethnographie* 17 (1924): 12.

32. Kunzle, *Early Comic Strip*, pp. 225, 236.

33. Poullain de La Barre, *De l'excellence des hommes*, Preface, especially his discussion of Saint Paul. *Idem, De l'égalité des deux sexes* (Paris, 1676), pp. 16–22. Mary Astell, *Some Reflections upon Marriage* (4th ed.; London, 1730), pp. 99–107. An early example of the primitive golden age theory and male usurpation is found in Agrippa, *Nobilitie and Excellencie*, f. G iʳ⁻ᵛ. Turner, *Ritual Process*, chap. 5 (cited in n. 12).

34. Jean Calvin, *Commentaries on Genesis*, trans. J. King (Edinburgh, 1847), 1: 172 (Gen. 3: 16). Giambattista Vico, *The New Science*, trans. T. G. Bergin and M. H. Fisch (Ithaca, New York, 1968), nos. 369, 504–7, 582–84, 671, 985–94. Vico describes changes in the father's authority over his sons and in the character of the wife's dowry, but monogamous marriage and paternal power remain throughout. J. F. Lafitau, S.J., *Moeurs des sauvages ameriquains, comparees aux moeurs des premiers temps* (Paris, 1724), 1: 49–90. Anticipating Bachofen's work on matriarchy of a century later, Lafitau's theory of "ginécocratie" does not develop fully the notion of a matriarchal stage for all societies. He speculates that the Iroquois may have originated in Greece and the Mediterranean islands. On the uses of the New World for Old World thought, see Margaret Hodgen, *Early Anthropology in the Sixteenth and Seventeenth Centuries* (Philadelphia, Pa., 1964), and J. H. Elliott, *The Old World and the New* (Cambridge, 1970), chaps. 1–2.

35. Christine de Pisan, *Cyte of Ladyes*, ff.Ff vʳ–Hh iiʳ. Thomas Heywood, *Gynaikeion, or Nine Bookes of Various History, concerninge Women* (London, 1624). Discussion of the Amazons by Pierre Petit in *De Amazonibus Dissertatio* (2d ed.; Amsterdam, 1687) and by Claude Guyon in *Histoire des Amazones anciennes et modernes* (Paris, 1740) tries to find plausible arguments to account for their bravery and successful rule. Both men insist they really existed. The Cartesian Poullain de La Barre did not use them in his arguments for women's entering the magistracy (*De l'églité*, pp. 166 ff.). By the time Condorcet and Olympe de Gouges make a plea for the full citizenship of women in the early years of the French Revolution, the argument is being waged in terms of rights.

36. Delcourt, *Hermaphrodite*, pp. 93–96. Salomon Reinach, *Cultes, mythes et religions* (Paris, 1905), 1: 430, 453–56. M. C. E. Chambers, *The Life of Mary Ward, 1585–1645* (London, 1882). Mademoiselle de Montpensier, one of the leaders of the Fronde and victor in the siege of Orléans, may have drawn some inspiration from Jeanne d'Arc.

37. On the husband's power of correction over the wife, see William Blackstone, *Commentaries on the Laws of England* (Oxford, 1770), Book I, chap. 15; and Ourliac and de Malafosse, *Droit privé*, 3: 133, 140 (cited in n. 5). Evidence here comes from examination of diaries, criminal cases, and the records of the

Geneva Consistory. See, for instance, Nicolas Pasquier's letter to his daughter describing the maneuvers within his own marriage in Charles de Ribbe, *Les familles et la société en France avant la Révolution* (Paris, 1874), 2: 85–87. On wives being beaten, *Journal de Gilles de Gouberville pour les années 1549–1552*, ed. A. de Blangy (Rouen, 1982), 32: 195 (tavernkeeper's wife sends two women over to the Sire de Gouberville for help as her husband has almost killed her through beating). On women telling off their husbands, AEG, PC, 1st ser., no. 1202; 2d ser., no. 1535. For women beating their husbands, in addition to charivaris against them, see a case of 1712, ultimately brought to the Parlement of Pairs, against the wife of a merchant gold-beater, who insulted and beat her husband (E. de la Poix de Fréminville, *Traité de la police generale des villes, bourgs, paroisses et seigneuries de la campagne* [Paris, 1758]).

Alison Klairmont has described the woman's privileges during lying-in in an unpublished seminar paper at the University of California. Italian birth-salvers (that is, trays used to bring women drinks during labor and the lying-in) dating from the late fifteenth and sixteenth centuries were decorated with classical and Biblical scenes showing women dominating men (Victoria and Albert Museum; the Louvre). (I am grateful to Elizabeth S. Cohen and Susan Smith for this information.)

38. E. P. Thompson, "The Moral Economy of the English Crowd in the Eighteenth Century," *Past and Present* 50 (Feb. 1971): 115–17. Olwen Hufton, "Women in Revolution, 1789–96," *Past and Present* 53 (Nov. 1971): 95 ff. My colleague Thomas Barnes has kindly shown me several cases involving women tearing down enclosures, which he has examined in connection with his study of the Star Chamber. See also the excellent article by Patricia Higgins, "The Reactions of Women," in Brian Manning, ed., *Politics, Religion and the English Civil War* (London, 1973), pp. 179–222. John Spalding, *The History of the Troubles and Memorable Transactions in Scotland and England from 1624 to 1648* (Edinburgh, 1828), 2: 47–48. S. R. Gardiner, *The Fall of the Monarchy of Charles I, 1637–1649* (London, 1882); 1: 105–12. Le Roy Ladurie, *Les paysans*, p. 497. J. Beauroy, "The Pre-Revolutionary Crises in Bergerac, 1770–1789" (paper presented to the Western Society for the Study of French History, Flagstaff, Arizona, March 14–15, 1974), describes the important role of women in the May 1773 grain riots in Bergerac.

39. Margaret Ruth Kittel, "Married Women in Thirteenth-Century England: A Study of Common Law" (unpublished Ph.D. dissertation, University of California at Berkeley, 1973), pp. 226–33. Blackstone, *Commentaries* (1770), Book IV, chap. 2; Book I, chap. 15. Ourliac and de Malafosse, *Droit privé*, 3: 135–36. For advice on this matter, I am grateful to John M. Beattie of the University of Toronto, author of a forthcoming essay on "The Criminality of Women in Eighteenth-Century England," to appear in the *Journal of Social History*. Carol Z. Wiener discusses the ambiguities in the responsibility of married women for certain felonies and trespasses in England in the late sixteenth and early seventeenth centuries in an interesting article entitled "Is a Spinster an Unmarried Woman?" (forthcoming in the *American Journal of Legal History*). She speculates that the description of certain married women indicted for riot and other crimes in the Hertfordshire Quarter Sessions as "spinsters" may have been a legal fiction in order to require the women to accept responsibility for their acts.

On how husbands and wives jointly manipulated their diverse roles for their mutual benefit, see N. Castan, "La criminalité familiale dans le ressort de Parlement de Toulouse, 1690–1730," in A. Abbiateci *et al.*, *Crimes et criminaité en France, 17e–18e siècles* (Cahier des Annales, 33; Paris, 1971), pp. 91–107. Harvard Law School, Ms. 1128, no. 334, *Page vs. Page*, Nov. 13, 1605 (communicated by Thomas Barnes).

40. Roland Bainton, "Katherine Zell," *Medievalia et Humanistica*, n.s., 1 (1970): 3.

41. Henri Hours, "Les fayettes de Saint Just d'Avray. Puissance et limites de solidarité dans une communauté rural en 1774," prepared for a forthcoming issue of the *Bulletin de l'Académie de Villefranche* (manuscript kindly shown me by M. Hours).

On the background to the economic difficulties of the peasants in the Ariège and their relation to forest use, see Michel Chevalier, *La vie humaine dans les pyrénées ariégeoises* (Paris, 1956), pp. 500–517. Sources on the uprising: *Gazette des Tribunaux* 5, nos. 1432–1433, March 14–16, 1830, pp. 446–47, 450–51; M. Dubédat, "Le procès des Demoiselles: Resistance à l'application du code forestier dans les montagnes de l'Ariège, 1828–1830," *Bulletin périodique de la société ariégeoise des sciences, lettres et arts 7*, no. 6 (1900); L. Clarenc, "Le code de 1827 et les troubles forestiers dans les Pyrénées centrales au milieu du XIXe siècle," *Annales du Midi* 77 (1965): 293–317. A new study of this uprising by John Merriman is soon to appear: "The Demoiselles of the Arièpe, 1829–1830," in John M. Merriman, ed., *1830 in France* (forthcoming).

42. F. R. H. Boulay, *Documents Illustrative of Medieval Kentish Society* (Ashford, Eng., 1964), pp. 254–55. William A. Hunt, "The Godly and the Vulgar: Religion, Rebellion and Social Change in Essex, England, 1570–1688" (Harvard University, 1974). Eric Kerridge, "The Revolts in Wiltshire Against Charles I," *The Wiltshire Archaeological and Natural History Magazine* 57 (1958–60): 68–71. Historical Manuscripts Commission, *Report on the Manuscripts of . . . the Duke of Portland* (London, 1901), 7: 237–38 (reference kindly communicated by Lawrence Stone). Surrey Quarter Sessions, sessions roll 241, Oct. 1721 (kindly communicated by John M. Beattie of the University of Toronto). *Ipswich Journal*, Aug. 5, 1749 (kindly communicated by Robert Malcolmson, Queen's University, Kingston, Ont.). A. W. Smith, "Some Folklore Elements in Movements of Social Protest," *Folklore* 77 (1967), 244–45. "Memorial of the Inhabitants of Stockport and Vicinity" (Public Record Office, HO 42/128). I am grateful for this reference to Robert Glen, who discusses this episode in his doctoral dissertation "The Working Classes of Stockport During the Industrial Revolution" (University of California, Berkeley, in progress).

In an article written many decades ago, Ellen A. MacArthur said that men dressed as women formed part of a very large female demonstration in August 1643, beating on the doors of Parliament to present petitions asking for peace with Scotland and the settlement of the Reformed Protestant religion ("Women Petitioners and the Long Parliament," *English Historical Review* 24 [1909]: 702–3. The recent work of Patricia Higgins, based on close study of many contemporary sources, does not take very seriously the contemporary claim that "some Men of the Rabble in Womens Clothes" mixed in the crowd. See "The Reactions of Women" (cited in n. 38), pp. 190–97.

43. Williams, *Rebecca Riots*. Thompson, " 'Rough Music,' " pp. 306–7. Daniel

Wilson, *Memorials of Edinburgh in the Olden Time* (2d ed.; Edinburgh and London, 1891), 1: 143–45. Sir Walter Scott, *The Heart of Midlothian*, chap. 7.

44. G. F. Dalton, "The Ritual Killing of the Irish Kings," *Folklore* 81 (1970): 15–19. Vivian Mercier, *The Irish Comic Tradition* (Oxford, 1962), pp. 49–53. Arthur Young, *Arthur Young's Tour in Ireland, 1776–1779*, ed. A. W. Hutton (London, 1892), 1: 81–84; 2: 55–56. W. E. H. Lecky, *A History of Ireland in the Eighteenth Century* (New York, 1893), 2: 12–44. L. P. Curts of Brown University and Robert Tracy of the University of California at Berkeley have given me assistance on these Irish matters. I am grateful to Professor Brendon Ohehir of the University of California at Berkeley for his deciphering of Lecky's reading of the Whiteboy signature and for his translation of it. The Irish personal name behind the English rendering "Sally" meant "Goodness" or "Wealth."

45. Thompson, "'Rough Music,'" especially pp. 296–304. For examples of charivaris against wife-beaters in France in the early nineteenth century, see Cl. Xavier Girault, "Etymologie des usages des principales époques de l'année et de la vie," *Mémoires de l'Académie Celtique* 2 (1808): 104–6 (mentions charivari *only* against men who beat their wives in May; Girault lived in Auxonne, not far from Dijon, where the May prohibition was in effect in the sixteenth century); J. A. Du Laure, "Archeographe au lieu de La Tombe et de ses environs," *Mémoires de l'Académie Celtique* 2 (1808): 449 (mentions charivaris only against wife-beaters and against neighbors who do not go to the wife's aid; La Tombe is in the Seine-et-Marne); Van Gennep, *Manuel*, 1.3: 1073 (Van Gennep also gives examples of the older kind of charivari against the beaten husband, p. 1072).

An example from the American colonies is found in J. E. Culter, *Lynch-Law* (London, 1905), pp. 46–47: a group of men in Elizabethtown, New Jersey, in the 1750's called themselves Regulars and went about at night with painted faces and women's clothes, flogging men reported to have beaten their wives. I am grateful to Herbert Gutman for this reference.

7 The 'Cruel Mother': Maternity, Widowhood, and Dowry in Florence in the Fourteenth and Fifteenth Centuries

Christiane Klapisch-Zuber

In Florence, men *were* and *made* the "houses." The word *casa* designates, in the fourteenth and fifteenth centuries, the material house, the lodging of a domestic unit, and it is in this sense that many documents of a fiscal, legal, or private nature use the term. But it also stands for an entire agnatic kinship group. The *casa* in this case designates all ancestors and living members of a lineage, all those in whose veins the same blood ran, who bore the same name, and who claimed a common ancestor—an eponymic hero whose identity the group had inherited.[1]

"Houses" were made by men. Kinship was determined by men, and the male branching of genealogies drawn up by contemporaries shows how little importance was given, after one or two generations, to kinship through women. Estates also passed from one generation to another through men. Among the goods that men transmitted jealously, excluding women from ownership as far as they could, was the material house, which they "made" also, in the sense that they built it, enlarged it, and filled it with children who bore their name. The Florence of the early Renaissance, the Florence of the great merchants and the first humanists, was not a tenderly feminine city. Family structures and the framework of economic, legal, and political life remained under the control of level-headed males, bastions of solidarity, and family values were inspired by a severely masculine ideal.[2]

In these *case*, in the sense of both physical and the symbolic house, women were passing guests. To contemporary eyes, their movements in relation to the *case* determined their social personality more truly

Originally published as "Maternité, veuvage et dot à Florence," *Annales, E.S.C.* 38, no. 5 (1983): 1097–1109. A first version of this essay was presented at the colloquy at Sénanque organized by Georges Duby in July 1981 on the topic "Maisons et sociétés domestiques au Moyen Age"; it was later revised for the workshop "La femme seule," held 1980–82 at the Centre de Recherches Historiques. The version here is reprinted from Christiane Klapisch-Zuber, *Women, Family and Ritual in Renaissance Italy* (University of Chicago Press, 1985). © The University of Chicago Press. Reprinted with permission.

than the lineage group from which they came. It was by means of their physical "entrances" and "exits" into and out of the "house" that their families of origin or of alliance evaluated the contribution of women to the greatness of the *casa*.[3] The marriage that brought a woman out of the paternal house and lineage, the widowhood that often led to her return, these incessant comings and goings of wives between *case* introduced a truly indeterminate quality in the ways they were designated: since reference to a male was necessary, a woman was spoken of in relation to her father or her husband, even when they were dead. It is clear that the mere reference to the name of the lineage into which she was born or into which she married situated a woman much more clearly than the place where she was living at the moment. Women, then, were not permanent elements in the lineage. Memory of them was short. An important woman, a benefactress for her kin, for example, would eventually be known under her own name and brought to people's attention; but the family chronicler or the amateur genealogist would feel obliged to explain *why*, since the process fit so poorly within their definition of kinship. Thus Paolo Sassetti, noting in his journal the death of a female relative in 1371, writes, "Let special mention be made here, for we considered her to be like a beloved mother, and in all of her works she has been and was among the beloved women who have gone forth from our house."[4] As one who had both "come into" and "gone out of" the house, this exceptional "mother" must have stood out for her fidelity to the family into which she was born. Equally worthy of "special mention" but marked with the seal of the lineage's disapproval were the women who usurped an inheritance and persuaded a husband on his deathbed to disinherit his own kin.[5] More often, the family chroniclers keep the memory of an alliance with a certain lineage, but forget, a few generations after the marriage, the given name of the woman on whom the alliance was built.

The determination of a woman's identity thus depended on her movements in relation to the "houses" of men. The corollary was that upper-class Florentines found females who remained in their house of birth just as intolerable as females who lived independently. "Honorable" marriages were what regulated the entries and exits of the wives, and the normal state, the state that guaranteed the honor of the women and the "houses," could be no other than the married state. Any woman alone was suspect. An unmarried woman was considered incapable of living alone or in the absence of masculine protection without falling into sin.[6] Even if she were a recluse and lived a holy life,[7] even if she retired to a room on the upper floor of the paternal house,[8] she placed the family honor in jeopardy by the mere fact of her celibacy. The convent was the only way out, although terrible doubts about the security of the cloister continued to torment her parents.[9] Among the "best people," therefore, families did not include females over twenty years of age who were not married.[10]

The widow's solitude was hardly less suspect. Although the Church advised the widow with a penchant for chastity not to remarry and to practice the related virtues of *mater et virgo*, secular society did not set much store by her chances of remaining chaste.[11] The problem of where the widow was to live became crucial in such a case, for she was a threat to the honor not only of one family but of two. Given that a wife must live where her father or her husband lived (since they were the guarantors of her good conduct and her social identity), where should a wife be when she lost her husband?

ON THE DWELLING PLACE AND THE VIRTUE OF DOWERED WIDOWS

Theoretically, a widow had some choice in the matter. She could live in her husband's family, by her children's side; she could live independently without remarrying, but near her children; or, finally, she could remarry and leave the first family that had received her. But in practice a widow, if young, was barred from the second option and found herself subjected to contradictory pressures that prevented her from quietly choosing between the other two possibilities. Young widows were in fact the target of a whole set of forces struggling fiercely for control of their bodies and their fortunes.

The statistics of the *catasto* show that widows in 1427 were much more numerous in the general population than widowers (13.6 percent and 2.4 percent, respectively). In Florence these percentages doubled (25 percent and 4 percent).[12] Widowers tended to be older men (14 percent of the age classes of 70 years old and older were widowers), for men remarried promptly up to a late age. Definitive widowhood came much earlier for women: at 40—that is, at an age at which they might still give children to their new husband—18 percent of Florentine women appear in the census as widows, and at 50, nearly 45 percent do so. Furthermore, according to the statistics on couples drawn from family diaries, two-thirds of the women who became widows before

20 found a new husband, one-third of those widowed between 20 and 29, but only 11 percent of those widowed between 30 and 39—when their numbers grow. We might conclude that after 40 they no longer had much chance of remarrying, while from 75 to 100 percent of all men up to 60 years of age took another wife.[13] Even if they hoped for remarriage, then, widows' liberty of choice was singularly limited by their age.

The social group to which they belonged added other constraints. According to the statistics on households, it was easier, in 1427, for a widow to live independently in the city than in the country. In Florence itself, nearly 14 percent of the heads of household were at that time widows, as opposed to 4 percent who were widowers. The difference between the two was smaller in rural areas: 7.6 percent widows and 4.4 percent widowers. What is more, among wealthy Florentines the probability of a widow's living alone collapses: 2 percent of the 472 wealthiest households (which represent less than 5 percent of all Florentine households) were headed by a woman (an even lower percentage than in the country), and rich widows who lived really autonomously were the exception at the upper levels of urban society.[14]

Since it is strikingly obvious that a widow's ability to live alone or simply to head the household of her minor children was correlated to her wealth, we need to raise questions concerning the processes that tied her fate to that of the family estate. By processes I mean legal mechanisms as well as individual and collective behavior that affected the widow or motivated her decisions.

It was of course the dowry that tangled the threads of a woman's fate. In principle, the dowered goods that a wife brought her husband were attached to her for life: they had the double function of providing for the expenses of the household and, when the household dissolved at the husband's death, of providing for the surviving wife.[15] Since she could not inherit her father's estate, which went to her brothers,[16] a woman looked to her dowry to assure her subsistence: she could "keep her estate and her honor" before transmitting to her children, male and female, the dowry she had received at marriage. This lovely scheme was unfortunately often belied by the facts. Every widowhood threatened the economic equilibrium the domestic group had achieved during the father's lifetime. If the widow was 40 years old or older, the difficulty of finding her a new husband discouraged her own parents from intervening. It was up to her husband's heirs to persuade her to remain with them and not to "leave with her dowry" to live independently. What is more, her husband would do his utmost, on his deathbed, to encourage her to give up any such idea. He would agree to assure her a lifetime income and supplementary advantages, over and above the income from her own estate, if she would remain under his roof, and he would make his heirs swear to show her all consideration and to consult her in the management of the holdings in which her dowry would continue to be sunk.[17] All of this was not unique to Florence, or to Italy.[18] Clearly, well-off Florentines did succeed in dissuading their wives from flying with their own wings, since there were very few rich and elderly widows who lived independently. If a widow, however, did not get along with her husband's heirs and preferred her freedom, she had no claims other than to her dowry. The suits initiated by widows to regain their dowry show that the heirs did not always see matters her way. In the fifteenth century, however, widows had the law and judicial institutions on their side: if they were not discouraged from the start, they ended up by taking back what they had brought to their marriage.

Finally, if the heirs—who were not always her own children—did not want to keep her under their roof or give her back her dowry, the Florentine widow could fall back on the *tornata*, a right of refuge in her family of birth. It was the obligation of her close kin or their heirs to receive her and assure her board and lodging.[19] In the fifteenth century, some Florentines, anxious to assure shelter to the widows of their blood after the extinction of their male descendants, provided in their will that one of their houses be devoted to "taking in, in the future, all of our women 'gone out' [of the house] and widowed, and assuring them the *tornata*." Thus, veritable old people's homes for family members were created, in which women rejected by their family by marriage could end their days honorably, knowing they could count on the solidarity of those of their blood even unto the next generation.[20]

These arrangements attest to an anxiety among men—who were deeply committed to maintaining the honor of their "house"—at the thought that a woman of their kin might not be included in a familial group. Even when old, a widow represented a threat to the reputation of good families. Since she had tasted the pleasures of the flesh, she was considered prone, like the hideous merry widow portrayed in Boccaccio's *Corbaccio*, to fall into debauchery.[21] If the heirs let their material interests pass before defense of their honor, the widow's kin, their allied family, felt sufficient responsibility toward her to take her back under their charge—not always without recriminations. Piero di Bernardo Masi, a coppersmith, gave solemn instructions to his progeny, in 1512, to take all precautions to avoid what had happened to his own father and to get guarantees for the dowries they gave their daughters. For fifteen years—until she died—his father had had to maintain at his own expense a sister whose husband had left her penniless.[22]

In this game, a married woman embodied stakes that were fully revealed only if she was widowed young. Early widowhood revived the claims of the widow's family of birth on the goods brought as a dowry. As these were irrevocably attached, by law, to the physical person of the woman for the duration of her life, widowhood forced her own kin to use her as a pawn by making her "come out" of her husband's family. When she remarried, her family could join a new circle of affines. By the remarriage of a widow of their blood, Florentines affirmed that they had never totally relinquished control over the dowries that they had given their daughters or their sisters.[23] At the same time, they claimed a perpetual right to the women's bodies and their fertility. Marriage alliance did not obliterate blood kinship; it did not signify a definitive break between the wife and her family of origin. When the widow returned to her family of birth and once again became part of its matrimonial strategies, the family took back cards it had already played, with every intention of making the most of a second deal of social prestige bought by the conclusion of a new alliance.

As soon as the husband had been buried and the funeral ceremonies had ended, the wife's kin came to claim her if she was young. They brought her back to their own house: such is "the custom of Florence," Paolo Sassetti says in 1395,[24] and a contemporary asserts that it was less than honorable for the widow to leave before the ceremony, but that it was understood as proper and accepted by all that she do so immediately afterward.[25] The right of families of birth to take back their widows was stronger than the desires the deceased had expressed in his will. The Sassetti "extracted" (the verb *trarre* is used) a sister in 1389, a niece of this same Paolo, and they remarried her promptly, even though she had "three little boys of very young age," for whom her husband had named her guardian and of whose inheritance she had been named coadministrator. But, Paolo Sassetti says, "as we had to remarry M[adonn]a Isabetta, she could not, and we did not want her to, take on this guardianship, and she renounced it 7 December 1389." The maternal uncles then took over responsibility for their sister's sons.[26]

THE WIDOW'S DEFECTION AND THE ABANDONMENT OF CHILDREN

A departure like Madonna Isabetta's constituted a double threat: to the children of the couple broken up by the death of the father, and to the children of a previous marriage. If their mother or their stepmother left them abruptly for a second marriage, their economic situation underwent a much more brutal shock than when an aged widow demanded her dowry in order to retire where it suited her. The heirs could put many an obstacle in the way of an older widow, for she would find less support from her own kin than if they had decided to remarry her. Remarriage was an honorable objective—so honorable, in fact, that long delays in the restitution of the dowry were frowned upon. For this reason testators who left minor children and a young widow made every effort to stave off the danger by including many dissuasive stipulations. Giovanni Morelli, in devoting many pages of his *Ricordi* (around 1400) to the fate of the widow after her husband's death, testifies to his own dread of leaving his heirs and their guardians the frightening obligation of a sudden restitution of a dowry.[27] That possibility also explains the recurring advice in Florentine writings that the sums demanded for dowries be kept within reasonable limits. Otherwise their restitution would jeopardize the children's future.[28] Since an inflationary movement inexorably carried urban dowries upward in the fourteenth and fifteenth centuries, these repeated appeals have an almost desperate tone. Nothing could be done about it, however; contemporaries saw the size of a dowry as an indicator of their social status, and they were little inclined to receive a dowry that was less than "honorable."[29] Testators set up barriers to keep a dowry from ebbing from their house toward the house that had given and was taking back the widow, but they could do little to counter the perverse effects of the dotal system in a society in which patrilineal transmission of estates tended to dominate.[30]

"Give a thought, reader," writes one hard-pressed guardian, "of the expenses that have fallen to me in order to satisfy the widows so that they will not abandon their children, especially Neri's widow, who was 25 years old."[31] The remarriage of a widow cast the shadow of a second threat: the abandonment of the children. In fact, the children belonged to the lineage of their father.[32] Thus, boys all their life and girls until their marriage resided with their agnatic kin. Statistics on households, like the daily events chronicled in family journals, show that children rarely stayed for long periods with their maternal kin. If the latter did take them in, they were paid for the children's keep, or they took on management of the children's estates, since children had no rights to goods that belonged to a lineage not their own. Children who followed their remarried mother were even rarer.[33] The documentation shows that arrangements permitting a widow to establish the children of her first marriage (also with payment of their keep) under the roof of the second husband were usually provisional.[34] Although the stepmother was a very familiar figure in Florentine households, the stepfather was practically unknown.

When a widow left a house in order to remarry, she left with her dowry but without her children. In 1427, many of the tax declarations deplore the abandonment of orphans whose mother had "left the family, taking away her dowry," leaving her husband's heirs in the charge of guardians and of paternal kin.[35] The Florentine family journals, too, overflow in the fourteenth and fifteenth centuries with such situations, brutally initiated by the departure of a widow. The paternal kin had to take charge of orphans "of whom it can be said that they are orphaned on both the father's and the mother's side," one Florentine orphan reiterates, "since it can well be said of those who still have a mother that they have none, given the way she has treated them and abandoned them."[36] Giovanni di Niccolaio Niccolini left four orphaned children in 1417, and his uncle Lapo notes bitterly that the widow "left the house [with her dowry of 900 *fiorini*] and left her children on the straw, with nothing."[37] When Bartolo di Strozza Rucellai's mother remarried, he threw himself, with his brothers, on the mercy of the tax officials, declaring, "See what a state we are in, without a father and, one could also say, without a mother, having no one else on earth, abandoned by everyone."[38]

Young widows would certainly have to have had singular tenacity and a good deal of courage to resist the contradictory pressures of their two families. Umiliana dei Cerchi, at the beginning of the thirteenth century, who hoped to live out her life in holy seclusion,[39] and Tancia, the daughter of the notary ser Giovanni Bandini, who wanted to enter a convent in 1450,[40] came into conflict with the desires and the maneuvers of relatives eager to bed them down with new husbands. Umiliana had her way (she was subsequently beatified), but Tancia failed (she was to remain an anonymous housewife). Some women— extraordinarily few—seem to have succeeded in their desire for independence, though there is no way of knowing how widespread this desire might have been.[41] Often, widows really did want to remarry.[42]

Nevertheless, what contemporary reports emphasize above all is the irresolution of widows, and they leave an impression of widows' abject submission to the demands of their kin. Widows had few legal weapons, their whole upbringing had inculcated docility in them, and only in exceptional circumstances could they avoid remarriage if their relatives had decided in favor of it.[43] The widow of Barna di Valorino Ciurianni, to the immense displeasure of her stepsons, "leaves the house with her dowry" the minute her husband was in the ground, probably with remarriage in mind, since she was young. In spite of her promises to Barna and the advantages assured her in his will, she left her twelve-year-old son in the charge of his half brothers.[44]

Manno di Cambio Petrucci's narration, in 1430, of the days following the death of his father, who was carried off by the plague, offers a striking example of the anguish to which a widow could be subjected when her brothers wanted her to remarry.[46] We see her here at the age of thirty-four torn between her aunt—probably sent by her family—and her children and stepchildren, who beg her to remain with them. "Madonna Simona," Manno, the eldest of her stepchildren implores her, "your own children are here. We will treat them as our brothers and you, Madonna Simona, as our mother. Alas! our mother, I beg of you and throw myself at your mercy, for you know our situation. Left without father or mother, if you do not come to our aid we will go headlong into ruin." The widow, however, bowed to her family's wishes: "I will do what my family decides," she says, and Manno adds, "for Madonna Pipa, her aunt, had done her job well overnight." It is a poignant tale, and one in which the children's dismay at the threat of being abandoned is expressed in protestations of respect and fidelity. The children avoid frankly broaching the question of what was most at stake in the conflict, however: the dowry that they might have to give back. Manno admits as much once the break was irreversible: "If Madonna Simona had agreed to remain with us, we would not have had to sell our things at half their price, wasting our substance so that we could give her back some of her dowry."[45]

"GOOD MOTHERS" AND "CRUEL MOTHERS"

When one famous orphan, Giovanni Morelli, became an adult, he accused his mother (who remarried when he was three years old) of having been "cruel" to him and to his brothers, though he does say the epithet was prompted by the Evil One in a moment of doubt and despair.[46] But what did a man of the fifteenth century mean by this accusation? Did it perhaps signify an affective abandonment, a case in which a mother would leave young children who needed her "love" and her "maternal" care? This is the way we spontaneously understand the situation today.[47] The texts of the time suggest this meaning, but they emphasize, perhaps even more strongly, the financial debacle, the ruin that the remarried widow left behind her. The "cruel mother" was the woman who left her young children, but it was above all the mother who "left with her dowry." There is no better evidence of this than this same Giovanni Morelli, who lived a good part of his childhood and adolescence in his stepfather's house, brought up by the very mother whom he nevertheless accuses of having "abandoned" him.[48] The abandonment was economic as much as affective, and what abandoned children complained of explicitly was the financial implications of their mother's remarriage. The mother who deserted the roof under which her children lived placed the interests of her own lineage and her own family above her children's interests, and that is why she was stigmatized. The clearest reproaches on the part of children or children's guardians rarely dwell on anything other than this consequence of remarriage.

The positive image, that of the "good mother," shows *a contrario*, the range of functions that the "cruel mother" who left to remarry failed to fulfill. There is truly no "good mother" who is not "both mother and father." This is the widow who refuses to remarry, no matter how young she might be, "in spite of the objurgations of her entire family," "so as not to abandon her children," "in order not to lead them to ruin," and who is both "a father and a mother for her children."[49] Just like the father, she assured, by her stability, a transmission that was first and foremost a transmission of material goods, without which there was no family. "Remaining," "staying," "living with" her children, bequeathing them the wealth that was theirs—such was the primary paternal obligation in a system of residence and transmission of patrimony organized by patrilineal filiation. The virtues of an exceptional mother are from this point of view all manly virtues.

The widow qualified as a "good mother" was also one who devoted herself to the upbringing of her children with firmness and discipline.[50] Perhaps she could not compete with the father on the terrain of pedagogy. She could not offer a boy all the models of behavior that a father offered his sons, and her inexperience in public and political life constituted a vexing handicap. Her culture was often limited, and worse yet, she was unable to transmit to her sons the values and the spiritual heritage of the lineage, to talk to them of "what happened to their ancestors and of their actions, of those from whom they had received gifts and services and those by whom they had been badly used, of who was their friend in need and, conversely, the vendettas they had engaged in and of recompenses given to those to whom they were obliged."[51] A uniquely maternal upbringing had lacunae and was necessarily incomplete. Nevertheless, if undertaken with constancy and rigor, it could be comparable to the education administered by a father. When widowhood precluded other choices, the "good mother" was an acceptable substitute for the father. The "love" she bore her orphaned children took its full value from its masculine connotations.

Conversely, the bad mother, the "cruel mother," violated the values and the interests of her children's lineage when she showed too much docility toward her family of birth. In this she demonstrated the traditional vices of woman in exaggerated form. "Inconstant," "light," "flighty," she swings from one family to the other, she "forgets" her children and the husband she has just buried to seek pleasure in the bed of a second husband; she shifts shamelessly between the rigid structures of the contending masculine lineages. There is no doubt that the growing misogyny and mistrust of women at the dawn of the Renaissance were reinforced by structural contradictions that made it difficult to combine dotal system with patrilinearity. Among jurists, moralists, and those who reflected on the family, stereotypes presented woman as avid and capricious, eager to appropriate male inheritances for herself or other women, without pity for her children, whom she abandoned the moment she was widowed; a creature inconstant in her family loyalties, of immoderate attachments and inordinate sexuality, insatiable, and a menace to the peace and honor of families.[52] In short, a creature intent on destroying the "houses" that men had constructed.

The tensions caused by the problem of the autonomy or the remarriage of widows did not simply blacken the image of woman in the collective consciousness. They also generated positive but contradictory images of women to serve the opposing interests of the lineage that gave and the lineage that received the wife. The image of the mother loyal to her children countered that of the sister or the daughter faithful to her blood relatives; the wife attentive to the interests of her household contrasted with the woman who remembered her own lineage; the good mother who nearly equaled a father was the counterpart of the good daughter, nearly as good as a son. Even more than the somber image of the concupiscent widow or the "cruel mother," this ambivalence, this double and deep-rooted source of qualities appreciated in women provoked masculine resentment of them for their "inconstancy." No woman was perfect: a man attached to only one woman would be perpetually disappointed with her. Only the male sex, backed up by the law and by the structure of society and the family, could boast of perfection that was seen primarily as fixity and permanence.

Few contemporaries grasped the reasons for these tensions and tried to look beyond their lineage-inspired and antifeminist prejudices. One, however, puts a fine defense of remarried widows into the mouth of a young Florentine. In the *Paradiso degli Alberti*, written around 1425 by Giovanni Gherardi of Prato,[53] a courtly discussion arises among a group of people of polite society.[54] The problem posed is whether paternal love or maternal love is the better. One young man argues heatedly that mothers are not worth much since, contrary to fathers, they abandon their children. In any event, as they are inferior beings, their love could not possibly be as "perfect" as that of men. One young woman "of great wit and of most noble manners" is then charged by the women to respond to him. She cleverly turns his arguments against him by placing herself in his logic: since women are less "perfect" than men, they must obey men and follow them; and "since [women] cannot take their children, nor keep them with them, and they cannot remain alone without harm, especially if they are young, nor remain without masculine protection, it is almost perforce that mothers see themselves constrained to choose the best compromise. But it is not to be doubted that they think constantly of their children and remain strongly attached to them in spite of this separation."[55]

In this demonstration the young woman throws back to her male interlocutor the very contradictions in which he—along with the whole society of his time—let himself be trapped. For how could the "honor" and the "status" of a lineage be increased by taking back a woman and her dowry in order to give them elsewhere, without offending the honor and the standing of the *familia* to which she had given children? How could such a family reassert its rights over the person and the wealth of a woman without depriving another family of those rights? How could the separation of mother and child be avoided when the mother's identity was always borrowed and the child could belong only to his paternal kin? How could a woman be reproached for her docility before men when society denied her economic and legal autonomy?

But the young woman's words go farther. When she evokes the mother's attachment to her children—an attachment that the males of her time either failed to express, rejected, or sublimated into "paternal love," according to whether they stood on one side or the other of the dowry fence—our clever Florentine exposes the mechanisms by which a society that manipulated woman and the wealth attached to her attempted to prove its own innocence by reinforcing the image of the insensitive and destructive female.

Notes

1. D. Herlihy and C. Klapisch-Zuber, *Les Toscans et leurs familles: Une étude du catasto florentin de 1427* (Paris: Presses de la Fondation Nationale des Sciences Politiques, 1978), 532ff.
2. See R. C. Trexler, *Public Life in Renaissance Florence* (New York: Academic Press, 1980).
3. Thus several tables drawn up by genealogists of the fifteenth and sixteenth centuries categorize women under *uscite* and *entrate* according to lineage.
4. Archivio di Stato, Florence (henceforth abbreviated ASF), *Strozziane*, 2d ser., 4, Ricordanze di Paolo Sassetti (1365–1400), fol. 34 (11 February 1371). Dates are given in modern style.
5. Ibid., fol. 68ᵛ (24 September 1383); ASF, *Strozz.*, 2d ser., 13, Ricordanze di Doffo di Nepo Spini, fol. 83 (7 July 1434).
6. In the *catasto* of 1427 there are only 70 unmarried women among the 1,536 female heads of household in Florence.
7. On the suspicion that greeted *pinzochere* (women who took the habit of third order nuns to live in communities or, worse, alone), see below, note 22, and R. Davidsohn, *Storia di Firenze* (Italian trans., Florence, 1965), 6:66ff. On Church attitudes concerning *pinzochere*, see R. C. Trexler, *Synodal Law in Florence and Fiesole 1306–1518* Studi e Testi no. 268 (Vatican City, 1971), 121–22, 142. On the various forms of religious life for women, in community or in seclusion, see the works of A. Benvenuti-Papi, esp. "Penitenza e penitenti in Toscana: Stato della questione e prospettive della ricerca," *Ricerche di storia sociale e religiosa* nos. 17–18 (1980): 107–20; R. Pazzelli and L. Temperini, eds., *Prime manifestazioni di vita comunitaria maschile e femminile nel movimento francescano della penitenza* (Rome, 1982), 389–450.
8. On women who were nuns *in casa*, see Herlihy and Klapisch-Zuber, *Les Toscans*, 153–55 and 580. In Florence, thirty such women made a declaration to the *catasto* in their own name, but many more were part of a family. (In Arezzo, four out of eleven *suore in casa or pinzochere* declared their wealth independently.) See below, note 39, on Umiliana dei Cerchi.
9. R. C. Trexler, "Le célibat à la fin du Moyen-Age. Les religieuses de Florence," *Annales, E.S.C.* 27 no. 6 (1972): 1329–50.
10. Among Florentine women who belonged to the age group of 20–24 years of age, 92 percent were married; the proportion is even higher among the wealthier classes.
11. See J. Kirshner, *Pursuing Honor while Avoiding Sin: The Monte delle Doti of Florence*, Quaderni di *Studi Senesi* 41 (Milan, 1978), 7, n. 22; A. Burguière, "Réticences théoriques et intégration pratique du remariage dans la France

d'Ancien Régime, XVII–XVIII s.," in J. Dupâquier et al., eds., *Marriage and Remarriage in Populations in the Past* (London, 1981), 43. On popular treatment of remarriage, see J. Le Goff and J.-C. Schmitt, eds., *Le charivari* (Paris and The Hague, 1981). See also "De la vie des veuves," in E. C. Bayonne, ed. and trans., *Oeuvres spirituelles de J. Savonarole* (Paris, 1879–80), 5–51.

12. Herlihy and Klapisch-Zuber, *Les Toscans,* appendix V, tables 1 and 2.

13. For comparative data on the problem of remarriage and its implications for fertility, see Dupâquier et al., eds., *Marriage and Remarriage.*

14. Many widows who made independent declarations of their worth to the *catasto* of 1427 in reality lived in their children's household but took this opportunity to have their rights to their personal estate recognized (see Herlihy and Klapisch-Zuber, *Les Toscans,* 61).

15. M. Bellomo, *Ricerche sui rapporti patrimoniali tra coniugi* (Milan, 1961), 61ff.

16. And, in the absence of brothers, to the agnates of the intestate father, up to three-quarters of the total estate. A daughter could inherit only in the absence of agnates to a stipulated degree of consanguinity. (For examples of how this right was put into effect and how it affected lineage ties, see R. Bizzochi, "La dissoluzione di un clan familiare: I Buon-delmonti di Firenze nei secoli XV e XVI," *Archivio storico italiano* 140, no. 511 [1982]: 3–45.) See *Statuta populi et communis Florentiae (1415),* (Fribourg, 1778–81), 1:223ff. A father could, of course, leave more to his daughters in his will; for example, ser Alberto Masi left one-third of his estate to his two brothers and the other two-thirds to his two daughters (ASF, *Manoscritti,* 89, fol. 15).

17. See the example cited in Herlihy and Klapisch-Zuber, *Les Toscans,* 557, n. 21 (year 1312). For another example: Barna Ciurianni stipulates that his widow share in all of the revenue of the family and that she "be in all things honored as it is appropriate, and [that she be] trustee, with Valorino [her son], without having to give accounts" (ASF, *Manoscr.* 77, fol. 19, 1380). Giovanni Niccolini, who died in 1381, left his wife a share in the administration of his estate, with his children, as long as she lived with them, and, after ten years, if she wanted independent widowhood without taking back her dowry, he left her the profits from a farm, or half of the latter if she preferred to take back her dowry—the choice that the widow seems to have preferred after 1382 (C. Bec, ed., *Il libro degli affari proprii di casa de Lapo Niccolini de' Sirigatti,* Paris, 1969, 62ff.). See also the case of Matteo Strozzi in 1429 (ASF, *Strozz.,* 5th ser., 12, fol. 25).

18. See M. T. Lorcin, "Retraite des veuves et filles au couvent: Quelques aspects de la condition féminine à la fin du Moyen-Age," *Annales de Démographie historique* (1975), 187–204; Lorcin, *Vivre et mourir en Lyonnais à la fin du Moyen Age* (Paris, 1981), 65–73.

19. On the right to support and on the *tornata* see *Statuta,* 1:135, 223–25.

20. Conflict with the male heirs could result from the *tornata*: see ASF, *Strozz.,* 5th ser., 1750, Ricordanze di Bartolomeo di Tommaso Sassetti, fols. 181 and 154v. For examples of these houses for retirement within the family, see ASF *Strozz.,* 5th ser., 12, Ricordanze di Matteo di Simone Strozzi, fol. 25 (1429), and *Strozz.,* 5th ser., 15, fol. 96 (the will of Matteo's widow in 1455) and fol. 97 (1464); ASF, *Conventi soppressi,* 83, 131, fol. 100 (1548). See also Biblioteca Centrale Nazionale, Florence (henceforth abbreviated BNF), Magliab. VIII, 1282, fol. 122^v (1367).

21. A debauchery that was all the more repugnant because it was hidden behind

the state of *pinzochera* and because the widow opened her door to mendicant friars, "great consolers of widows" (Giovanni Boccaccio, *Corbaccio*. ed. P. G. Ricci, Classici Ricciardi, 44, [Turin, 1977], 71–72).

22. ASF, *Manoscr.* 88, fol. 160ᵛ.

23. On the remarriage of widows and the recycling of their dowry or their dower, see G. Duby, *Le chevalier, la femme et le prêtre* (Paris, 1981), 88, 96, 283.

24. ASF, *Strozz.*, 2d ser., 4, fols. 74ff.

25. BNF, *Panciatichi*, 120, fol. 156 (1377). Here the widow leaves "although she had four children and she was pregnant and she failed to pay him honor in the church." In the same manner the Bolognese mason, Gasparre Nadi, notes that the neighborhood gossiped a good deal when a widow went to a second husband too quickly (*Diario bolognese*, ed. C. Ricci and A. Bacchi della Lega, Bologna, 1886, 47).

26. ASF, *Strozz.*, 2d ser., 4, fols. 74, 103.

27. Giovanni di Pagolo Morelli, *Ricordi*, ed. V. Branca, (2d ed. (Florence, 1969), 213–23.

28. Ibid., 211. L. B. Alberti, *I Libri della famiglia*, ed. R. Romano and A. Tenenti (Turin Einaudi, 1969), 135–36. A study by Julius Kirshner, to be published, clarifies changes in attitudes regarding the remarriage of widows, which eventually, in 1415, introduced a notable change in the statutes.

29. See Kirshner, *Pursuing Honor.*

30. See "The Griselda Complex", in Klapisch-Zuber, *Women, Family and Ritual*, 213–46.

31. Bonaccorso Pitti, *Cronica*, ed. A. Bacchi della Lega (Bologna, 1905), 200.

32. There is one case that is a tragicomic example of belonging to the father's lineage: a pregnant woman is widowed, her family "retracts" her after the husband's burial but sends her back to the husband's lineage until the child is born. When this happens, the family takes her back to remarry her (ASF, *Acquisti e Doni*, 8, Ricordanze di Jacopo di Niccolò Melocchi fol. 56 [1517]). See also the squabbles of the Minerbetti family: one of them quarrels with his brothers to marry a woman whom he leaves pregnant when he dies. The mother sees her newborn baby whisked off by her brothers-in-law; then her own family has the baby snatched from his nurse. It takes a court decision to get him restored to his paternal uncles, who, when all is said and done, return him to his mother (Biblioteca Laurenziana, Florence, *Acquisti*, 229, fol. 69 (1508).

33. One exception, notable because it is so well known, is that of Giovanni Morelli and his young brothers and sisters, who lived with their maternal grandparents for seven or eight years after their mother's remarriage (see below, note 49).

34. Antonio Rustichi remarried his widowed sister in 1418, and he reached an agreement with his new brother-in-law that the children of the first marriage who accompanied their mother, would renounce all claim to the dowry, probably in compensation for the expenses of their upbringing, assumed by the stepfather (ASF, *Strozz.*, 2d ser., 11, fols. 12ᵛ, 13ᵛ).

35. As examples: in the Pisan countryside the three heirs of Giovanni di Biagio, ranging from 1 to 7 years of age, were abandoned by their mother (Archivio di Stato, Pisa, *Ufficio dei Fiumi e Fossi*, henceforth abbreviated UFF, 1542, fol. 400); so were the two daughters, aged 9 and 12 years old, of Giovanni di

Corsetto (UFF, 1559, fol. 580), and the two children of Battista di Giovanni Guideglia, 3 and 10 years old (UFF 1538, fol. 479).

36. ASF, *Strozz.*, 2d ser., 15, Ricordanze di Cambio di Tano and di Manno di Cambio Petrucci, fol. 64ᵛ (1430).

37. Bec, ed., *Il libro degli affari proprii*, 135.

38. Cited in F. W. Kent, *Household and Lineage in Renaissance Florence* (Princeton, 1977), 36. We might also cite the case of Bernardo di Stoldo Rinieri, who lost his father in 1431 and whose mother remarried eight months later, leaving him with his two young sisters when he was 3 years old (ASF, *Conventi soppressi*, 95, 212, fol. 150).

39. "Vita S. Humiliane de Cerchis," by Vito da Cortona, *Acta sanctorum*, May, IV, col. 388. For Umiliana's life, see also A. Benvenuti-Papi, "Umiliana dei Cerchi: Nascita di un culto nella Firenze del Dugento," *Studi francescani* 77 (1980): 87–117.

40. ASF, *Conv. soppr.*, 102, 82, fol. 15.

41. D. Herlihy has focused on widows' desire for independence and on the role that the new autonomy brought by their widowhood allowed them to assume in urban society. See his "Mapping Households in Medieval Italy," *Catholic Historical Review* 58 (1972): 14; "Vieillir à Florence au Quattrocento," *Annales, E.S.C.* 24 no. 6 (1969): 1342ff. For a discussion of these positions, see Kirshner, *Pursuing Honor*, 8 and n. 23.

42. This is the case with the anonymous widow cited by Vespasiano da Bisticci in his *Vite di uomini illustri del sec. XV*, ed. L. Frati (Bologna, 1892), 3:261, who, "desiring to remarry and take back her dowry, which was great," left her four young children with their paternal grandmother. See also below, note 46.

43. Some mothers must have ended up by regaining the children from whom they had been separated, like the widow Minerbetti cited in note 31, but for one case of this sort, how many scenarios must there have been in which the mother seems to fall in line without the slightest complaint—or at least, with no complaint that succeeds in piercing the thick cloak of male narration of their behavior.

44. ASF, *Manoscr.* 77, fol. 19. She had married Barna in 1365, when he was 43 years old, and had been widowed less than three years before.

45. ASF, *Strozz.*, 2d ser., 15, fols. 61ᵛ–65.

46. Morelli, *Ricordi*, 495. See especially L. Pandimiglio, "Giovanni di Pagolo Morelli e le strutture familiari," *Archivio storico italiano* 136, nos. 1–2 (1978): 6. R. C. Trexler, in *Public Life in Renaissance Florence*, chap. 5, gives a long analysis of the case of Morelli and (particularly p. 165, n. 27) sees one of the reasons for the abandoning of children by their mother in her desire "to establish her *persona*." The fact that the wife's kin in most cases take the initiative in encouraging her departure seems to me to contradict this hypothesis.

47. See the debate about maternal love prompted by E. Badinter's book, *L'amour en plus* (Paris, 1980) and the colloquy of the Société de Démographie historique in November 1981 devoted to the theme "Mothers and Wet Nurses."

48. As noted by Pandimiglio, "Giovanni Morelli e le strutture familiari," 6. For relations with the maternal grandmother, see also the *ricordanze* of Morello Morelli, Giovanni's brother, in ASF, *Carte Gherardi*, Morelli, 163.

49. Giovanni Rucellai, cited in Kent, *Household and Lineage*, 40, n. 64, and in G. Marcotti, *Un mercante fiorentino e la sua famiglia nel sec. XV* (Florence,

1881), 49, 59–60. "Memorie di Ser Cristofano di Galgano Guidini da Siena," ed. C. Milanesi, *Archivio storico italiano* 4 (1843): 25–30. BNF, *Panciatichi*, 134, Memorie Valori, fol. 4 (1438).

50. Donato Velluti found in his mother the equivalent of a father, since his father was "nearly continually absent" on business (*Cronica domestica*, ed. I. Del Lungo and G. Volpi, Florence, 1914, 119–20).

51. Such are some of the merits of a paternal upbringing, as enumerated by G. Morelli, *Ricordi*, esp. p. 269. Conversely, the wife who harangues her husband continually about the great actions of her own lineage is a stock figure in contemporary literature (as in Boccaccio, *Corbaccio*, 46, 61)—a figure perhaps linked to the social hypergamy of men common at the time.

52. The statutes of the city of Pisa in the middle of the twelfth century accuse mothers of manifesting an "impietatem novercalem" (stepmotherly impiety) toward their children rather than their "maternum affectum" (maternal affection) when they take back their dowry and their *antefactum*, and the female sex is frequently qualified by jurists as "genus mulierum avarissimum atque tenacissimum promptius . . . ad accipiendum quam ad dandum" (most avaricious female sex, much more tenacious . . . in receiving than in giving) (texts cited by D. Herlihy in "The Medieval Marriage Market," *Medieval and Renaissance Studies* 6 (1976): 27, nn. 58–59). Let me note once more Boccaccio's *Corbaccio* as the most complete broadside on the vices and misdeeds of women, the root of which is sensuality and greed.

53. Giovanni Gherardi da Prato, *Il Paradiso degli Alberti*, ed. A. Lanza (Rome, 1975), 179–84.

54. The debate on the preeminence of paternal love is a commonplace one that runs from the preachers to Alberti, who classes it among scholastic stylistic exercises (see L. B. Alberti, *I libri della famiglia*, 349).

55. For the masculine argument, see Herlihy and Klapisch-Zuber, *Les Toscans*, 558 n. 22. What the young woman has to say—which occupies three times the space of the young man's argument—astonishes the master of ceremonies: "Per nostra donna, per nostra donna vergine Maria, che io non mi credea che le donne fiorentine fossono filosofe morali e naturali né che avvessono la rettorica e la loica così pronta come mi pare ch'abbino!" (By our Lady, by our Lady the Virgin Mary, I had no idea that Florentine women were moral and natural philosophers, nor that they had such ready rhetoric and logic as it seems to me they have!). He then gives the victory to the ladies (*Il Paradiso degli Alberti*, 183–84).

Witchcraft and Fantasy in Early Modern Germany

Lyndal Roper

In January 1669, Anna Ebeler found herself accused of murdering the woman for whom she had worked as a lying-in-maid. The means were a bowl of soup. Instead of restoring the young mother's strength, the soup, made of malmsey and brandy in place of Rhine wine, had increased her fever. The mother became delirious but, as the watchers at her deathbed claimed, she was of sound mind when she blamed the lying-in-maid for her death. As word spread, other women came forward stating that Ebeler had poisoned their young children too. The child of one had lost its baby flesh and its whole little body had become pitifully thin and dried out. Another's child had been unable to suckle from its mother, even though it was greedy for milk and able to suck vigorously from other women: shortly after, it died in agony. In a third house, an infant had died after its body had suddenly become covered in hot, poisonous pustules and blisters which broke open. The baby's 7-year-old brother suffered from aches and pains caused by sorcery and saw strange visions, his mother suffered from headaches and the whole household started to notice strange growths on their bodies. And a fourth woman found her infant covered with red splotches and blisters, her baby's skin drying out until it could be peeled off like a shirt. The child died most piteously, and its mother's menstruation ceased. All had employed Ebeler as their lying-in-maid. Anna Ebeler was interrogated six times and confessed at the end of the second interrogation, when torture was threatened. She was executed and her body burnt on 23 March 1669—a 'merciful' punishment practised in place of burning in the humane city of Augsburg. She was aged 67. Just two months had elapsed since she was first accused.[1]

From Lyndal Roper, *Oedipus and the Devil* (Routledge, 1994), 199–225. ©Lyndal Roper. Reprinted with permission.

Anna Ebeler was one of eighteen witches executed in Augsburg. As many more were interrogated by the authorities but cleared of witchcraft; others faced religious courts and yet further cases never reached the courts. Augsburg saw no witch-craze. Unlike its south German neighbours, it executed no witch before 1625 and its cases tended to come singly, one or two every few years after 1650.[2] Witchcraft of an everyday, unremarkable kind, the themes of the cases can tell us a great deal about early modern psyches. For Ebeler's crimes were not unusual. It was typical, too, that of her accusers all except one should have been women, and that her victims were young infants aged up to about six weeks and women who had just given birth.

One dominant theme in witch-trials in Augsburg is motherhood. Relations between mothers, those occupying maternal roles and children, formed the stuff of most, though not all, witchcraft accusations in the town.[3] To this extent, early feminist works which focused on birth and midwives in their explanations of witchcraft were making an important observation.[4] But though the trials were concerned with the question of motherhood they were not, it seems to me, male attempts to destroy a female science of birth nor were they concerned with wresting control of reproduction from women. What is striking is that they were typically accusations brought by mothers, soon after giving birth, against women intimately concerned with the care of the child, most often the lying-in-maid and not the midwife.

Many investigations of witchcraft proceed by trying to explain why women should be scapegoated as witches or what other conflicts may have been at the root of the case—conflicts involving issues with which we are more comfortable, such as struggles over charity, property or political power. However, I want to argue that the cases need to be understood in their own terms by means of the themes they develop. As historians, I think we may best interpret them as psychic documents which recount particular predicaments. Witchcraft cases seem to epitomize the bizarre and irrational, exemplifying the distance that separates us from the past. What interests me, however, is the extent to which early modern subjectivities are different or similar to ours. I shall argue that unless we attend to the imaginative themes of the interrogations themselves, we shall not understand witchcraft. This project has to investigate two sides of the story, the fears of those who accused, and the self-understanding of people who in the end, as I shall argue, came to see themselves as witches.

Our perplexity in dealing with witchcraft confessions derives in part from their epistemological status. In a profession used to assessing documents for their reliability, it is hard to know how to interpret documents which we do not believe to be factual. But witchcraft confessions and accusations are not products of realism, and they cannot be analysed with the methods of historical realism. This is not to say that they are meaningless: on the contrary, they are vivid, organized products of the mind. Our problem is not that early modern people had a different ontology to our own, believing in a world populated by ghosts who walked at night, devils who might appear in the form of young journeymen, severed arms carrying needles or wandering souls inhabiting household dust. Rather, all phenomena in the early modern world, natural and fantastic, had a kind of hyper-reality which resided in their significance. Circumstantial details were ransacked for their meaning for the individual, and for what they might reveal about causation and destiny. Causation, which could involve divine or diabolic intervention in human affairs, was understood in terms both moral and religious. Consequently, we need to understand confessions and accusations as mental productions with an organization that is in itself significant. This means analysing the themes of witchcraft not to tell us about the genealogy of magical beliefs—the approach taken by Carlo Ginzburg in his recent book[5]—but to tell us about the conflicts of the actors.

In the cases I have explored, witchcraft accusations centrally involved deep antagonisms between women, enmities so intense that neighbours could testify against a woman they had known for years in full knowledge that they were sending her 'to a blood bath' as one accused woman cried to her neighbours as they left the house for the chancellery.[6] Their main motifs concern suckling, giving birth, food and feeding; the capacities of parturient women's bodies and the vulnerability of infants. This was surprising, at least to me: I had expected to find in witchcraft a culmination of the sexual antagonism which I have discerned in sixteenth- and seventeenth-century German culture. The idea of flight astride a broom or pitchfork, the notions of a pact with the Devil sealed by intercourse, the sexual abandonment of the dance at the witches' sabbath, all seemed to suggest that witchcraft had to do with sexual guilt and attraction between men and women, and that its explanation might lie in the moralism of the Reformation and Counter-Reformation years, when Catholics and Protestants sought to root out prostitution and adultery, shame women who became pregnant before marriage and impose a rigorous sexual code which cast the women as Eve, the temptress who was to blame for mankind's fall.[7]

Some of the cases I found certainly dealt with these themes, but the primary issue in what we might term a stereotypical case of witchcraft was maternity. The conflicts were not concerned with the social construction of gender but were related much more closely to the physical changes a woman's body undergoes when she bears children.[8] While these clearly have a social meaning and thus a history, the issues were so closely tied to the physical reality of the female sex and to sexual identity at the deepest level that they seemed to elude off-the-peg explanations in terms of female roles and gender conflict. The stuff of much of the accusations made by the mothers was not femininity or genital sexuality, but was pre-Oedipal in content, turning on the relationship to the breast and to the mother in the period before the infant has a sense of sexual identity.[9] The primary emotion of the witchcraft cases, envy, also originates in this early period of life.[10] Witchcraft accusations followed a pattern with a psychic logic: the accusations were made by women who experienced childbirth and their most common type of target was a post-menopausal, infertile woman who was caring for the infant. Often, as in the case we have just explored, she was the lying-in-maid.

Here it might be objected that witchcraft interrogations and confessions cannot be used to give us insight into early modern psychic life in this way. They are stereotyped products, it might be argued, not of those interrogated but of the minds of the interrogators. These men wanted to know about witches' sabbaths, sex with the Devil and cannibalism and they forced this information out of the women using leading questions and even outright promptings, resorting to torture to gain the confession they needed to convict the woman. However, such an objection does not recognize the cultural attitude to pain nor its place in the dynamic of interrogation in early modern society. Witches were women who could not feel pain as normal women could. They were unable to weep and they did not sense the witch-pricker's needle.[11] A measure of physical pain, so the interrogators believed, was a process of the body which enabled the witch to free herself from the Devil's clutches, weakening her defences against the admission of guilt. The amount of pain had to be finely judged by the executioner, a scientist of the body. Using his knowledge of the victim's frailty, and in consultation with the council, he calculated the precise grades required at each stage of the process (from exhibition of the equipment, stretching on the rack without attaching weights, through to attaching weights of increasing size) so that the witch's integral, diabolic personality might be stripped away by the application of pain to uncover the truth.[12] Like a kind of medicine of salvation, it assisted her travail to return to the Christian community in contrition so that she might die in a state of grace. Torture was part of an understanding, shared by the witch and her persecutors, of the interrelation of body and soul: the skin of the outer person had to be flayed away to arrive at psychological truth. Those who did not crack under torture were set free despite the seriousness of the accusations against them, because they were said to have proven their innocence: they lacked a diabolic interiority of this kind.

Pain had a religious significance too. By experiencing the pain of flagellation, or participating in the procession of the Twelve Stations of the Cross, a ritual which reached its final form in the Counter-Reformation in Augsburg,[13] one could come closer to Christ by physical imitation of His sufferings. Maternity involved pain. Mary herself had borne Jesus in suffering, and the seven swords of grief piercing the suffering Madonna were a powerful Baroque image. Luisa Accati has written of the importance of the Madonna in agony to Baroque understandings of both Marian piety and motherhood.[14] Soothsayers told of spells in which they appealed to 'the suffering of Mary as she lay on her martyr-bed of straw'.[15] The witch, the woman whose capacity to feel pain was impaired, was thus an unmaternal woman, alienated from the realm of pain so manifestly experienced by the new mothers who accused her of sorcery. Devoid of maternal affection, the witch was incapable of feeling pity for her victims.

Moreover, the system of confession also rested on a measure of collusion between witch and questioner. The witch had to freely affirm her confession after it had been given, in the absence of torture. This was a requirement of the Imperial Law Code of Charles V of 1532, and it was certainly not honoured all over the empire.[16] But in a place like Augsburg which did not experience mass witch-hunts, the credibility of the phenomenon of witchcraft rested on the ultimate truth-telling of the witch. Witches could and did modify their confession: so, for instance, Anna Ebeler, who had confessed to having sex with the Devil a countless number of times, insisted at the last that she had only rarely had diabolic intercourse, a disclaimer incorporated in her final public condemnation. Witches were commonly supposed to have renounced God, Jesus, Mary and the saints, but Ebeler was able to maintain that she had never forsworn the Virgin, who had comforted her during diabolic assaults, and that she had never desecrated the Host as she had earlier confessed she had.[17] Another who firmly denied that she was a witch was not described as such in her denunciation, even though she was executed for having used witchcraft.[18]

This freedom was in some sense apparent rather than real: witches who confessed and then revoked their confession embarked on a long and hideous game of cat and mouse with their interrogators, as they were reinterrogated and tortured until their narrative was consistent. But interrogators knew when a confession was simply a result of torture or its fear, and they noted this. Crucial to their own understanding of their task was the belief that, by repetition and forcing the culprit to describe and redescribe the minutiae of the crime, checking with witnesses, the truth would eventually be uncovered. That truth took on a kind of talismanic quality, as the witch was forced to tell and retell it in up to ten sessions of questioning, making it consistent. Her statements were then read out in full to the assembled council before condemnation could be agreed; a summary of her crimes was recorded in the Council's Punishment Book and read out before her execution; and this material formed the basis for the broadsheets and pamphlets that were written about the case.[19] The reiteration fixed the details until there could be no doubt about the narrative. It was a truth which the witch herself freely acknowledged and for which she alone had provided the material. For despite the power of the stereotypes in the witch's confession, these do not explain the particular inflections individual witches gave to them, as they described how they went to a sabbath that was held just by the gallows outside Augsburg, or how the Devil appeared to them in a long black coat, dressed for all the world like a merchant.[20]

There is a further collusive dynamic at work in interrogation, that between witch and torturer. Torture was carried out by the town hangman, who would eventually be responsible for the convicted witch's execution. Justice in the early modern period was not impersonal: the act of execution involved two individuals who, by the time of execution, were well acquainted with each other. Particularly in witch-trials, torture and the long period of time it took for a conviction to be secured gave the executioner a unique knowledge of an individual's capacity to withstand pain, and of their physiological and spiritual reactions to touch. In a society where nakedness was rare, he knew her body better than anyone else. He washed and shaved the witch, searching all the surfaces of her body for the tell-tale diabolic marks—sometimes hidden 'in her shame', her genitals. He bound up her wounds after the torture. On the other hand, he was a dishonourable member of society, excluded from civic intercourse and forced to intermarry among his own kind. His touch might pollute; yet his craft involved him in physically investigating the witch, a woman who if innocent was forbidden him. He advised on the mode of execution, assessing how much pain the witch might stand, a function he could potentially exploit to show mercy or practise cruelty.[21] In consequence, a bond of intense personal dependence on the part of the witch on her persecutor might be established. Euphrosina Endriss was greatly agitated when a visiting executioner from nearby Memmingen inspected her. She pleaded that 'this man should not execute her, she would rather that Hartman should execute her, for she knew him already'.[22]

Once the torturer's application of pain had brought the witch to confess, she knew she faced execution, and she knew her executioner. In the procedure of interrogation itself, carried out in the presence of council interrogators, scribes and executioner, there is an unmistakable sado-masochistic logic, as the witch, in response to pain, might reveal details of her crimes only to deny them subsequently; or as she proffered scattered scraps of information about diabolic sex only then to tantalize her questioners with contradiction or silence. In this sadistic game of showing and concealing, the witch forced her persecutors to apply and reapply pain, prising her body apart to find her secret. Once it was found, she might herself identify with the aggressor: so, at the conclusion of her final confession as a witch, when it was plain she faced death, Anna Ebeler fell at her persecutors' feet in tears, asking for a merciful execution. 'She begged my lords for forgiveness for what she had done wrong. She thanked them for granting her such a good imprisonment and treatment.'[23] Masochism, however, has its twin in sadism. Even in death, the resolution of the game, the witch herself was believed able to retaliate against her tormentor. One hangman found his hands suddenly crippled after he executed two witches in 1685, and his colleague had to execute the third. Just before Barbara Fischer was executed, so one chronicler noted, a powerful rainstorm struck as if everything must drown: this witch, the writer observed, had shown no signs of contrition.[24] At every stage, the trial progressed through a combustion of sadism, retaliation and masochism, in which each actor might in fantasy veer from persecutor to victim to tormentor.

How can the historian make use of material generated in such circumstances? In spite of the geographical specificity and precision of detail we noted earlier in the confession material, witchcraft confessions certainly do possess a stereotypical aspect. There are elements, like the diabolic pact, the sabbath, the powder the Devil gave them to do harm, which appear in most confessions. But the basic psychic images of any society are usually the stuff of cliché. It is their commonness which makes these images seem banal, yet enables them to give form to inchoate, shared terrors and common predicaments. It is undoubtedly true that the pressures of interrogation and pain caused accused witches to shape their accounts of their own emotions and present a narrative of their psychic worlds in a particular way—the language of witchcraft forced them to present the Devil as their seducer and the ultimate cause of their fall. But narratives in which people try to make sense of their psychic conflicts usually involve borrowing from a language which is not at first the individual's own. We might say that coming to understand oneself can involve learning to recognize one's feelings in the terms of a theory, psychoanalytic or diabolic, which one might not originally have applied to oneself, and it can also entail a kind of violence.

What was the substance of the witches' crime? The grief and terror of the witnesses concentrated on the bodies of those who were the victims of witchcraft. Their bodies bore the signs of their martyrdom. As one mother put it, her dead child was covered in sores so that he looked like a devotional image of a martyr.[25] Strange signs were seen: nipples appeared all over the body of one infant, erupting into pussy sores. The legs of another were misshapen and bent.[26] Repeatedly, witnesses stress the physical character of the victim's agony, incomprehensible suffering which cannot be alleviated by the onlookers or by the mother, and which excite hatred, revenge and guilt feelings in part because of the sufferer's innocence. In emotionally-laden language, the witnesses describe the 'piteous' way a child died, and their own failure to get the child to thrive. It is in this collective world of gossip and advice that the rumours of witchcraft first began, in the grief and guilt of the mother at the loss of the tiny baby, and as the women around them sought to identify the cause of this inexplicable, unbearable suffering. Such gossip could be deadly. It was her employer's tongue, her 'wicked gob' as Barbara Fischer put it, using the term applied to animals' mouths, which caused one lying-in-maid to retaliate against her maligner by poisoning her.[27]

The themes of the injury are not only pitiful but frightening. These terrors circle around nourishment and oral satisfaction, evoking powerful pre-Oedipal feelings. The breast, milk and nourishment were its key images. The food the witch gave the mother was sprinkled with white or black diabolic powders or the soups she was fed were poisonous, and these of course influenced the milk the infant received in a very immediate way. Attacks on the mother's food were thus attacks on her infant as well. When the witch killed, she often used poison, perverting the female capacity to nourish and heal. So one grand-mother was interrogated three times and tortured because her young grandson suspected witchcraft when he felt queasy after drinking an aniseed water tonic she had given him.[28] The witch could be a kind of evil mother who harmed instead of nourishing her charge. The flow of nourishment could be disrupted so that the child dried out and died. In one case, the witch was accused of literally reversing the flow of the maternal fluids, herself sucking the infant dry and feeding on it. Its mother described how

its little breasts had been sucked out so that milk had been pressed out from the child's little teats contrary to nature, . . . and from this time on the child had lost weight so that it looked as if hardly a pound of flesh remained on it.[29]

Another baby was found to be covered with a myriad of tiny teats as if it had become a mere drinking vessel for the thirsty witch; yet another baby's teats produced 'a little drop of white watery liquid'.[30] The signs that sorcery was afoot were clearly written on the infant's body. Its skin dried out for lack of fluid, or else erupted in sores as if evil fluids within its body were forcing their way out. Its entire little body might become 'red and blue, all mixed up, and rigid and hard, like a plank of wood'.[31] The infant might be unable to drink from its own mother, yet when given to another woman, be 'so hearty in sucking that it made her weep'.[32] (These themes could also emerge in cases which did not correspond to the classic accusation against a maid: so Regina Schiller denied that she had had sex with the Devil. He had tried to seduce her but instead 'had come to her breasts, and had tried to give her a little powder so that she could harm people, especially children'.[33] Here, too, a woman was thinking of herself as a witch who was the possessor of a poisonous breast, harming children, again working the images of pre-Oedipal nourishing rather than exploring fantasies of sex with the Devil.) In all these cases, the infant's feeding had been disrupted so that no satisfactory nourishing could take place and the relation between mother and child was destroyed. Feeding had been reversed and the infant's young rosy flesh was wasting away while the old witch thrived.

These beliefs rested on a whole economy of bodily fluids. A post-menopausal woman, the old witch was in a sense a dry woman who, instead of feeding others well, diverted nourishment to her own selfish ends. Older widows were believed to have the power to ruin young men sexually, and youths were warned against marrying such women because they were sexually ravenous, and would suck out their seed, weakening them with their insatiable hunger for seminal fluid and contaminating them with their own impurities.[34] The old witch's fluids did not flow outwards. Often her magic was directed against fertility, making women barren.[35] As was well known, witches could not weep, and old widows could neither menstruate nor suckle children. Instead, so the science of demonology explained, she was nourishing the Devil. The warts for which the executioner searched her naked body were the diabolic teats on which the Devil sucked. Witches were also believed to communicate without confessing, and to secrete the Host in their mouths, taking it home to trample upon and dishonour. In doing so they were not only misusing holy food but maltreating a child, the infant Jesus whose saving death provided the Bread of salvation, squashing him and making him suffer pain. This motif is clearly taken from the older myth of Jewish ritual murder, the belief that Jews were stealing the Host and torturing it to make it bleed, and that they stole Christian children so that they could use their blood in secret rituals.[36] Yet even this hoary fantasy was incorporated into the fabric of daily life: Anna Schwayhofer confessed to this crime in the apocalyptic year 1666, and described how, housewife to the fingertips, she had afterwards swept the crumbs of the desecrated Host off the floor of her lodgings with a broom.[37]

Witches were women who did not feed others except to harm them. Failed exchanges of food typified a witch's interactions with her neighbours. So one woman, suspected of being a witch, offered two sisters who lived in her house a dish of Bavarian carrots. Yet this was a two-edged peace offering. The woman insisted the sisters eat the food, and sat with them until it was all consumed. One of the two was pregnant, and the dish made her ill.[38] The witch said the food would strengthen the child within her, yet this wish for the child's health actually meant its opposite. Like the fairies of fairytale who are not invited to the baptism, the old woman's evil 'wishes' for the infant's future blighted its life. And this could happen in a trice, even without the witch's intention: Maria Gogel explained how 'if a person ate plain milk, peas, meat or cheese, and chanced upon a child and merely said "Oh, what a beautiful child" immediately it is bewitched'.[39]

Witches' other means of harming was by 'trucken', pressing down on the infant or its mother. The verb may also refer to the effort of pushing down in labour. In witchcraft it is used in at least three different contexts: to describe the way the Devil forces one woman to do evil, the smothering of an infant, and a mysterious kind of oppression felt by the woman who has just given birth. Georg Schmetzer's wife complained of feeling that something was coming to her at night, lying on her and pressing her so that she suffered from pain down one side. She suspected the lying-in-maid of coming to her bed in the evening and lying on top of her—a fear strengthened by the maid's unorthodox suggested remedy for her backache that she should undress and lie on top of her in a kind of all over massage.[40] Anna Maria Cramer believed a witch was coming to her at night and lying on her, pressing down on her pregnant body.[41] Another woman heard a mysterious voice crying 'druckdich Madelin, druckdich' (be pressed down, Maggie, be pressed down) and she felt something trying to bite her neck. Her lying-in-maid Euphrosina Endriss was finally brought to confess that she had 'pressed' the baby she carried about with her, squashing its skull so that it died.[42] The themes here do not appear to be directly sexual. Rather, what is described is a kind of heavy, deadly embrace, again typified by an ambiguous mixture of love and hatred which might kill the infant with a kind of excess of maternality. The mother's feelings have more to do with extreme depression, immobility and passivity. In all these cases, the mother seems to suffer from a kind of lassitude, unable to move or act to protect herself and her child beyond screaming for help—she cannot fight back, and the oppressive sensation of smothering symbolizes her inaction and the diffuse nature of the threat to herself and her child, causing harm not from within her own body but in a kind of anonymous pressure from without. As with the disturbances of nourishment, the violence is indirect, its source unclear and retaliation impossible.

Why should it have been motherhood which engendered these murderous antagonisms between women? Mothers in the early modern period spent the first few weeks of their child's life 'lying in', recuperating from the birth. These six or so weeks were set apart from normal life as the woman retreated into the lying-in-room, resting in the bed from which the husband would be banished. There she was the centre of the house, and there, lying in bed, she would entertain her female friends who had supported her during the birth, holding a women-only birth party with wine and delicacies to celebrate her delivery. If she could afford it, she would employ a lying-in-maid, whose job it was to care for both mother and child. During this period when her life was predominantly lived in the world of women, she could not leave the house and some believed her to be under the power of the Devil.[43] Evil influences might make their presence felt; ghosts might appear. At the end of this time she would go to church for the ceremony of purification or churching, which marked her return to marital co-habitation and public life, and the lying-in-maid would be dismissed. Today the attendant psychic conflicts of this period of the mother's life might be described as relating to the loss of the pregnant state and the ending of the unity of mother and child. Together with the incessant demands on time and energy that the new infant makes, these might be related to maternal depression and to a mixture of feelings towards the infant which may extend to anger, envy or even to wishing harm to the child.

What seems to emerge from these cases, however, is a different set of historically formed psychic mechanisms for dealing with this predicament. The time of separation of mother and child was clearly marked in ritual terms.[44] The mother's re-entry into society as a single being, uncontaminated by what can—if she bears a male child—seem to be the bisexuality of pregnancy, was celebrated in churching, a ritual which remained an important ceremony despite the Reformation's attempt to curtail it. These few weeks were also full of danger for mother and child. According to English figures, a woman had a 6 to 7 per cent chance of dying in childbed, and while this figure may seem low, it was an ever-present terror, doubtless added to by the stories passed around by her women visitors.[45] In the first few weeks of life the child was at its most delicate, as feeding had to be established, either with the mother, a wetnurse or else by hand. Interestingly, it was during this period or else immediately after the lying-in-maid's departure that the child began to ail. But instead of seeking the source of her ills in post-natal depression, within herself, as we would, the mother's anxieties about the child's fate and her own ability to nourish it were directed outwards, so that harm to either mother or baby was believed to have been caused by another. Here we might make use of what Melanie Klein says about splitting, which allows intolerable feelings of hostility and malice to be projected on to another, so that the mother recognizes only benevolence in herself, projecting the evil feelings about herself on to the 'other' mother.[46] The lying-in-maid was thus destined for the role of the evil mother, because she could be seen to use her feminine power to give oral gratification to do the reverse—to suck the infant dry, poison the mother and her milk and, in the most extreme form of witch fantasies, to kill, dismember and eat the child at the witches' sabbath. At a time when the new mother's experience of giving birth and caring for an infant might raise memories of her own infancy, recalling the terrifying dependence on the maternal figure for whom she may have experienced unadmitted, intolerable feelings of hatred as well as love, there was another person playing the maternal role to hand. We might say that during the new mother's period of feeling complete inertia, 'pressed down upon', she finally gained the strength to retaliate, resolving her state by accusing the witch of harming her child. In this sense, so far from being a simple expression of misogyny, early modern society can be said to have taken the fears of the mother seriously, supporting her search for the culprit instead of describing her as suffering from post-natal depression or attributing a kind of madness to her—women today may attempt to use the defence of post-partum psychosis to argue that they were not legally responsible for crimes committed during the first few weeks after giving birth.

The lying-in-maid was almost over-determined as the culprit, should witchcraft be suspected. Old, no longer capable of bearing a child herself and widowed, she was a woman who housed alone and was a transitory member of the households of others. No longer at the heart of a bustling household of her own, she was a hired member of the family for whom she worked, privy to the most intimate physical secrets of the bodies of those she tended. An interloper, she was never accorded a real place of her own—one even had to share a cramped bed with a servant which was so narrow that she fell out of it in the night.[47] The lying-in-maid undermined the settled hierarchies of the household at a time when the new baby's arrival overturned the workshop's rhythm. For the six to eight weeks after the mother had given birth, she alone carried out the duties of a mother, dandling, washing and swaddling the baby, and caring for its mother, giving her nourishing soups. Just as she had no place in the house she might call her own, so also her work life left her humiliatingly dependent on others: on the midwife, who trained her, recommended her and from whom she might hear of her next job; on her employer, the mother, who might choose not to re-employ her and who could blacken or enhance her reputation by gossiping with other mothers about her. She lacked the midwife's qualifications and official status as an employee of the council, nor did she have the luxury of the midwife's official retainer to tide her over slack periods. Often, it was her very insecurity which was turned against her. One woman who went down on her knees to plead with her accusers only made them the more convinced that something was amiss; frightened people were likely to be caught in the Devil's snares.[48]

But she was also invested with awesome power. She had her particular recipes for strengthening soups, she had her methods for bringing up young infants, she 'alone cared for the child, and it was in no one's hand but hers' as one lying-in-maid accused of witchcraft put it.[49] She was strong at a time when the new mother was ill and weakened, and she was fulfilling her tasks. The new mother, sleeping alone in the marital bed, was not 'mistress of the household' in sexual terms: old, infertile and unhusbanded as the lying-in-maid was, she represented a double threat to the mother, standing both for the mother's own future and sometimes representing a sexual threat as well. If the husband were 'up to no good', the lying-in-maid, who in many cases had borne illegitimate children, might be suspected.[50]

The lying-in-maid dealt with the waste products of the body, she had access to the afterbirth and to cauls and she had the care of the infant's body.[51] One lying-in-maid was accused of purloining the afterbirth, burning it at night under her bed in a bid to harm mother and child, and it was only with great difficulty that she managed to persuade the judges that she had merely been attempting to clean a pewter bowl.[52] Another was foolish enough to accuse the midwife of hiding a baby's caul. Taking the 'little net' to the child's father in the hope of gaining a handsome tip for her trouble, she not only antagonized the midwife but led people to suspect that she had her own nefarious purposes for the caul.[53] Through the waste products of the body, things invested with their owner's power—hair, nails, afterbirth—the sorcerer could control the individual to whom they had belonged. These substances could be used to direct the emotions, causing the bewitched person to fall in love, and they could be used to harm. In this cosmology, emotions were highly sensitive to manipulation of the body. Emotions, like physical pains, could be the result of external events and could readily be ascribed to other people, their source sought outside rather than in the self.

As any mother knew, to antagonize a lying-in-maid was to court disaster. 'I gave her good words until she left the house', so one young mother said.[54] Many of the witnesses mention the time when the lying-in-maid was 'out of the house', a phrase which captures the element of menace the maid was thought to represent. Only then might an accusation be safely made, because then the maid could not revenge herself by bewitching the child. (One seer refused to help an ailing child until the maid had gone: then she succeeded in restoring its rosy flesh, but it began to waste away again when the maid returned shortly after to collect money she was owed.)[55] So fraught was the moment of the maid's departure that her formal relinquishing of responsibility could also become a test of whether the child had thrived. One woman repeated the ambiguous rhyme she had spoken on parting from the child:

> My dear little treasure, now you are well recovered
> Look master and mistress
> Now I depart from the child
> Whatever may happen to him now
> I will not be held to blame[56]

Such a jingle, with its careful divestment of responsibility, has a menacing tone. It is a double-edged wish. An attempt to free the speaker of blame, it carries the implied threat that something *will* happen to the infant, and it prophylactically points the finger at someone else, by implication the mother, who now assumes the maternal role alone. Indeed, harm often came to the child after the lying-in-maid had departed. 'It was the first night . . . that the lying-in-maid was out of the house', one mother remembered, that strange things began to happen; it was just after the maid had left, another mother noted, when her child had suddenly sickened.[57] Something of the uncertain nature of the relationship between mother and lying-in-maid is caught in the way one maid kept referring to the presents she had received, listing them and naming their giver, in a fruitless attempt to determine the relationship as one of goodwill—yet even the mothers she thought had valued her care were now willing to testify against her conduct.[58] Her behaviour was always indeterminate, its meaning open to a subsequent hostile reinterpretation.

Above all, it was the lying-in-maid's maternal role which placed her in the role of suspect. Sometimes this might lead to straightforward conflicts over upbringing—Euphrosina Endriss was blamed for mollycoddling a child, giving it too many warm cushions.[59] Midwives and mothers suspected maids of bathing the child in water that was too hot, or of swaddling its limbs too tightly so that it might become deformed.[60] Injuries inflicted in the first few weeks of the infant's life might not manifest themselves for years: the failure of one child to speak, harm to one girl's reproductive organs, were all blamed on the lying-in-maid.[61] 'Why must it always be the lying-in-maid who is to blame?' asked one accused woman.[62] A woman who could not be trusted, a woman unable to bear children herself, she was tailor-made for the role of the ultimate evil mother. The very intensity of the bonds between her and the child, as the person who enjoyed a primary attachment to the baby in its first weeks of life, were also the reason to suspect her. As with all witchcraft, it was the powerful ambivalence of feeling

217

which nourished witchery: witchcraft was to be feared not from those indifferent to you, but from those whose relationship was close and whose intimate knowledge of your secrets could be turned to harm. Consequently, every good wish a suspected woman might make for the health and well-being of an infant was charged with its opposite. So one young mother feared the frequent visits the lying-in-maid made to her infant's cradle, standing over it. She later discovered a knife underneath its crib.[63]

And the lying-in-maid had a motive: envy. Envy was the motor of witchcraft as seventeenth-century people understood it. One of the seven deadly sins, it was a feeling which could have material force. It is also an emotion which, according to Melanie Klein, first develops in the early months of an infant's life and is deeply connected to feelings of love and hate. Envy involves wishing harm towards an object. In the logic of sorcery, where emotions might be externalized on to things outside the person and where feelings had active force, the emotion itself was the wellspring of injury. Circumstances conspired to make the lying-in-maid appear a likely sufferer from envy and hatred. As seventeenth-century people saw it, she was poor and single; her employer had a workshop and was comfortably off. Infertile herself, she tended a mother who was surrounded by the love, attention and presents of other women, and who had a baby. By contrast her own children had been conceived illegitimately or had died in infancy. So Barbara Fischer had been raped by her stepfather twenty years before she found herself accused of witchcraft. The child of their relationship had died just a few days after birth. At the time, she had begged the council to let her marry, blaming her stepfather's refusal to let her wed for her own fall into sin with him. But the council had punished her by confining her inside the house for her shame, and, two decades later, she explained her fall into witchcraft as the consequence of not being allowed to marry and become a mother.[64] Interestingly, her diabolic lover appeared to her in the form of a journeyman dyer, the trade her stepfather had followed. Admission of the envy she felt for the mother she tended was, in her case as in many others, the first step in her interrogation towards a full confession.[65] The witch, too, fully believed that to feel envy for a woman was to wish to harm her, and in this emotional world, where things were invested with meaning, emotions could also act directly. Anna Schwayhofer explained she had summoned the Devil when, conscious of her own sins, she despaired of God's mercy: she had taken communion without confession, and she felt 'great envy, resentment and enmity to various persons'.[66]

To this point I have been exploring the psychic world of those who made the accusation, arguing that it is best understood as invoking deep emotions from the early period of the mother's own infant life. She and those around her are able to crystallize her own ambivalence towards her infant by projecting intolerable feelings on to the lying-in-maid. I am not arguing that this always happened: in the vast majority of cases, the childbed was concluded happily and the maid was dismissed with mutual goodwill. But I am claiming that the social organization of mothering practices allowed this to happen, so that a certain kind of psychic dramatic script was available should things go wrong.

But the witch herself had an understanding of her own behaviour. Its main element concerned her own admission of envy. This was the breaking point which then catapulted her into a range of other confessions about the Devil. These form a distinct layer of testimony, elicited under torture and often given with a considerable degree of reluctance. In other contexts, however, where children were not the target of malice, the Devil could be a dominant theme: so the young Regina Schiller baffled authorities all over southern Germany for over a decade with her bizarre physical contortions and extravagant confessions, telling the authorities about her lurid pacts with the Devil and showing the written contract for so many years and so many days, the number indicated with little strokes of blood because she could not count so far.[67]

By contrast, the witches whose fates we have considered here were chary of admitting even to flying or attending the witches' sabbath, and when they did so they presented themselves as outsiders, women who hung at the edges of the wild assemblies, without finding friends among the fellow witches. One witch recalled that the others came from elsewhere, they wore masks and spoke with accents she could not understand, and they were well dressed, not of her class. She did not dance, and at the feast, few people sat at her table.[68] This was certainly a means of cutting down their involvement and guilt and yet the strong sense of being outsiders which their words convey suggests that the fantasies mirrored their current experience of isolation, socially marginal and shorn of friends who might succour them. Their relations with the Devil were distant and unsatisfactory. Even when conviction was a certainty, these accused witches still tried to minimize the extent of their sexual involvement with the Devil, Dorothea Braun insisting at the last that, contrary to her earlier confessions, she had never had sex with the Devil and had always resisted him; Anna Ebeler saying that she had told the Devil she was too old for such things; Anna

Schwayhofer firmly denying that intercourse had ever taken place.[69] Indeed, Braun presents the Devil as a kind of peremptory employer, a master whose whims she was condemned never to satisfy. She was too slow learning the craft, she explained, and so the Devil beat her.[70] Their accounts usually give only the merest description of the Devil—he came as a journeyman, or dressed in black, he was a disembodied arm—and they try to argue that their bodies remained intact. Diabolic invasion presents a taboo from which they wanted to shield themselves. But genital sexuality is seldom their own explanation of what they do, even though the sexual narrative would excuse their deed with the culpability of Eve. Instead, dirt and degradation feature. This is most evident in the names of their diabolic lovers, which had names such as Hendirt, Gooseshit and the like, names which combine animality with excrement.[71] Common to almost all is the acknowledgement of the feeling of hatred and the sense of being deserted by God, exiled from the community of fellow Christians. Yet their deeds are projected on to the Devil: he whispers what they should do, he gives them the powder, he forces them to harm the children. In this way their hostile emotions (apart from the first feelings of hatred) could be projected on to the Devil and dissociated from themselves, in a kind of splitting characteristic of witchcraft at every level.

But if I am right that witchcraft could involve conflicts between women that have to be understood in psychic terms, we still need to explain why such conflicts were open to expression through witchcraft at a particular historical moment. After all, even in the town we have been considering here, there were witchcraft cases which followed this pattern or drew on these motifs for only a little over a century, and they were concentrated in the years from 1650 to 1700. After 1700, we can notice a dramatic inversion of the pattern. Now, children rather than their mothers became the objects of suspicion. Between 1724 and 1730, thirty-one child witches were locked up,[72] while after the death of one suspected witch in custody in 1699, no older women were condemned.[73] This reversal suggests to me that the dynamics of much witch-hunting have to be sought in the relationship between mother and child which, after a certain point, switched to the child rather than its mother. I suspect that witch-hunting in the seventeenth century must in part be related to the idealization of motherhood in Baroque society. This is not simply a matter of misogyny: after all, it was because the state took the fears and accusations of suffering mothers seriously that cases could be prosecuted. Germany in the later seventeenth century was a society recovering from the ravages of the Thirty Years'

War. In Augsburg, the population had halved: small wonder that people feared attacks on fertility.[74] Here the widow played a double role. On the one hand, attacks on old, post-menopausal women are a staple of misogynist tract from the late sixteenth century onwards. But on the other, the widow, I have been suggesting, was merely the mother's mirror image, a woman who could be the repository of all the fears about evil mothers. Maternal hostility and fears about evil mothers could not easily be expressed directly in a society where Mary was revered by both Catholics and Protestants, and where the image of the suffering Madonna was ubiquitous. Hence, too, the tendency in folk-tale to populate a story with evil stepmothers who alone can represent the bad mother, keeping pure the image of the good, dead mother.[75] Here it is no coincidence that this period also saw a dramatic increase in executions of the ultimate evil mother, the woman who commits infanticide: such women had to be executed. This rise occurred from the early seventeenth century onwards, even though the Imperial Law Code of 1532 had paved the way for such executions three genera-tions before. Together with witchcraft, this accounted for the vast bulk of women executed in Augsburg in the seventeenth century.[76] The themes of much witchcraft, I would argue, are to be found not in a simple sexual antagonism between men and women, but in deeply conflicted feelings about motherhood. At this level, we can talk about misogyny: one trouble with modern psycho-analysis, I think, as with seventeenth-century witchcraft, is that in the end, a mother, or a figure in a maternal position, is made responsible for our psychic ills.

What I have been trying to do here is to explore the themes of early modern witchcraft not so much in order to explain that phenomenon, but in order to see, in the one area where we do have detailed docu-mentation, whether early modern subjectivities were radically differ-ent from our own. That is, I have been asking whether and how there is a history of mind and emotion. It might be objected that I have used psychoanalytic categories in order to explore past mental phenomena, and to that extent, my argument is circular, but I think this conceptual difficulty is inherent in the productive use of ideas. One current problem is whether a body of theoretical work like psychoanalysis, designed in a particular historical period, can possibly do justice to the mental lives of people in quite a different time. It is certainly true that psychoanalytic theory can be used to reduce all symbolic worlds to the same meaning, so that everything speaks of phallologocentrism, or betrays the Oedipal complex. I do not think testimony should be read reductively in this way. In the material I was reading, basic psychic conflicts which did not accord with what I expected to find were emerging from witness statements. It seems to me that there are some primary areas of attachment and conflict—between those in maternal positions and children—which are pretty fundamental to human existence, but the form those conflicts may take and the attitude societies adopt to them may change.[77] This, it seems to me, is the territory of the historian. If historians declare the effects of primary emotions of this kind to be unknowable, they will be condemning us to use of a 'common-sense' model of psychological explanation which makes no sense at all because it leaves out of the account the extent to which irrational, deep and unconscious feeling can determine human action—and it is hard to see how any history of witchcraft or even of religion can be satisfactory without exploring this dimension.

Notes

1. Stadtarchiv Augsburg (hereafter cited as StadtAA), Urgichtensammlung (hereafter cited as Urg.), 28 Jan. 1669, Anna Ebeler.
2. StadtAA, Stafbücher des Rats, 1563–1703. For the indispensable, pathbreaking study of witchcraft in Bavaria, see Wolfgang Behringer, *Hexenverfolgung in Bayern. Volksmagie, Glaubenseifer und Staatsräson in der Frühen Neuzeit*, Munich 1987, pp. 431–69: there is one unclear case from 1563; one woman died under arrest in 1591 (p. 157), and another in 1699 (Strafbuch des Rats, 1654–99, 24 Sept. 1699, Elisabeth Memminger). See also Bernd Roeck, *Eine Stadt in Krieg und Frieden. Studien zur Geschichte der Reichsstadt Augsburg zwischen Kalenderstreit und Parität* (Schriftenreihe der Historischen Kommission bei der Bayerischen Akademie der Wissenschaften 37), Göttingen 1989, esp. vol. 1, pp. 113–16, 445–54; and vol. 2, pp. 539–52 on the witch-trial of 1625; and on the cases of 1654, see Wolfgang Wüst, 'Inquisitionsprozess und Hexenverfolgung im Hochstift Augsburg im 17. und 18. Jahrhundert', *Zeitschrift für Bayerische Landesgeschichte*, 50, 1987, pp. 109–26. On witch-hunting in the region as a whole, H. C. Erik Midelfort, *Witch Hunting in Southwestern Germany 1562–1684. The social and intellectual foundations*, Stanford, Calif. 1972.
3. Three of those executed were lying-in-maids, and a fourth was a failed midwife. Four of those heavily suspected were lying-in-maids and most were expelled from the town on other pretexts. Other cases were closely related. One executed witch killed her own child, another committed incest with her own son who later died, while a third had worked as a childminder. In seven further cases, themes were borrowed from the same paradigm: the executed witches had harmed children for whom they were in some sense responsible.
4. Barbara Ehrenreich and Deirdre English, *Witches, Midwives and Nurses. A history of women healers*, New York and London 1973. See also, for a survey of feminist views of witchcraft, Dagmar Unverhau, 'Frauenbewegung und historische Hexenverfolgung', in Andreas Blauert (ed.), *Ketzer, Zauberer, Hexen*,

Die Anfänge der europäischen Hexenverfolgungen, Frankfurt am Main 1990. Recently it has been argued that witchcraft accusations were an attempt to destroy a female science of birth control: Gunnar Heinsohn and Otto Steiger, *Die Vernichtung der weisen Frauen. Beiträge zur Theorie und Geschichte von Bevölkerung und Kindheit* (Part A, Hexenverfolgung, Kinderwelten, Menschenproducktion, Bevölkerungswissenschaft), Herbstein 1985. However, the cases the authors cite are actually about hostility to children, not about birth control: see, for example, pp. 149–56. For a critique of the Heinsohn-Steiger thesis, see Robert Jütte, 'Die Persistenz des Verhütungswissens in der Volkskultur. Sozial- und medizinhistorische Anmerkungen zur These von der 'Vernichtung der weisen Frauen', *Medizinhistorisches Journal*, 24, 1989, pp. 214–31. David Harley has argued that there is little evidence for the importance of midwives among those executed in England: 'Historians as Demonologists: the myth of the midwife-witch', *Social History of Medicine*, 3, no. 1, 1990, pp. 1–26; and for a similar argument, Peter Kriedte, 'Die Hexen und ihre Ankläger. Zu den lokalen Voraussetzungen der Hexenverfolgungen in der frühen Neuzeit—Ein Forschungsbericht', *Zeitschrift für historische Forschung*, 14, 1987, pp. 47–71, 60. While it may be true that the absolute figure of midwives accused or executed was small, they are none the less a recognizable occupational group in the German evidence where only a few other work patterns may be discerned. Their significance might be better related to the involvement of mothers, lying-in-maids and others connected with the care of mothers and infants.

5. Carlo Ginzburg, *Ecstasies. Deciphering the witches' sabbath*, trans. Gregory Roberts, London 1990 (first published in Italian 1989): interestingly, one of the effects of Ginzburg's brilliant analysis is that women's predominance as victims in the witch-hunt tends to slip from the explanation.

6. StadtAA, Urg., 15 July 1650, Ursula Neher, testimony Sabina Stoltz, 29 July 1650. Anna Ebeler screamed that her persecutors were sending her 'to the butcher's slab', 'to the raven stone': StadtAA, Urg., 28 Jan. 1669, Anna Ebeler, testimony of Catharina Mörz, and Anna Ebeler, 24 Jan. 1669.

7. See, on the sexual themes of images of witchcraft, Charles Zika, 'Fears of Flying: Representations of witchcraft and sexuality in early sixteenth-century Germany, *Australian Journal of Art*, 8, 1989–90, pp. 19–48; and on the themes of witch fantasy and their historical elaboration, Richard van Dülmen, 'Imaginationen des Teuflischen. Nächtliche Zusammenkünfte, Hexentänze, Teufelssabbate', and Eva Labouvie, 'Hexenspuk und Hexenabwehr. Volksmagie und volkstümlicher Hexenglaube', both in Richard van Dülmen (ed.), *Hexenwelten. Magie und Imagination vom 16.–20. Jahrhundert*, Frankfurt am Main 1987; Robert Rowland,' "Fantasticall and Devilishe Persons": European witchbeliefs in comparative perspective', in Bengt Ankarloo and Gustav Henningsen (eds), *Early Modern European Witchcraft: Centres and peripheries*, Oxford 1990. On the project of sexual regulation in sixteenth-century Germany, Lyndal Roper, *The Holy Household. Women and morals in Reformation Augsburg*, Oxford 1989; and R. Po-Chia Hsia, *Social Discipline in the Reformation, Central Europe 1550–1750*, London 1989, pp. 122–73.

8. See Estela V. Welldon, *Mother, Madonna, Whore. The idealization and denigration of motherhood*, London 1988, for an illuminating attempt to deal with the issues of female psychosexual identity.

9. John Demos has also noticed the importance of pre-Oedipal themes in Salem witchcraft: *Entertaining Satan. Witchcraft and the culture of early New England*, Oxford 1982, esp. pp. 116ff, 179ff.

10. Melanie Klein, 'Envy and Gratitude' (1957), in *idem, Envy and Gratitude and Other Works 1946–1963*, London 1975.

11. See, for example, StadtAA, Urg., 20 Dec. 1685, Euphrosina Endriss, 6 March 1686, final observation that Endriss had often looked as though she were going to cry but not a single tear escaped from her; Urg., 28 Jan. 1669, Anna Ebeler: at the interrogation of 11 March 1669, Ebeler noted that the Devil had not allowed her to cry properly, but, as the scribe noted, she then began to cry heartily and to pray the Lord's Prayer, the Ave Maria, and deliver a 'beautiful' extempore confession. Urg., 11 Feb. 1666, Anna Schwayhofer, 15 March 1666, interrogators noted that she apparently felt no pain from the thumbscrews, a fact which the executioner explained by saying this was a mild form of torture. The executioner pricked a suspicious looking mark on Anna Elisabeth Christeiner but it disappeared, strong proof, he thought, of the Devil's work: Urg., April 1701, fourth interrogation, 3 Aug. 1701.

12. See Edward Peters, *Torture*, Oxford 1985; on the executioner, often a key figure in the generation of a witch-hunt, Helmut Schuhmann, *Der Sharfrichter, Seine Gestalt—Seine Funktion* (Allgäuer Heimatbücher 67), Kempten 1964; Ch. Hinckeldy, *Strafjustiz in alter Zeit*, Rothenburg 1980; Werner Danckert, *Unehrliche Berufe. Die verfemten Leute*, Munich 1963; Franz Irsigler and Arnold Lassotta, *Bettler und Gaukler, Dirnen und Henker, Aussenseiter in einer mittelalterlichen Stadt*, Cologne 1984, pp. 228–82. The duration of torture might also be measured by the time it took to say particular prayers, a technique which tacitly invoked divine assistance against diabolic power: see, for example StadtAA, Urg., 30 June 1650, Barbara Fischer, for the use of the Miserere and Lord's Prayer. In some Bavarian trials, torture becomes part of an almost physical struggle against the Devil's power: see Michael Kunze, *Highroad to the Stake*, trans. William E. Yuill, Chicago, Ill. and London 1987; and Wolfgang Behringer 'Hexenverfolgung als Machtspiel', R. Po-Chia Hsia and B. Scribner (eds), *History and Anthropology in Early Modern Europe. Papers from the Wolfen-habüttel conference 1991*, forthcoming. Kathy Stuart has researched the role of executioners and dishonourable people in Augsburg in the early modern period, and she has a great deal to say about the executioner as an expert on the body and its capacity to withstand pain, knowledge which also made his skills as a healer greatly valued: Kathy Stuart, 'The Boundaries of Honor. "Dishonorable people" in Augsburg 1500–1800', Ph.D. diss., Yale University 1993.

13. Louis Châtellier, *The Europe of the Devout. The Catholic Reformation and the formation of a new society*, Cambridge 1990, p. 150.

14. Luisa Accati, 'The Larceny of Desire: The Madonna in seventeenth-century Catholic Europe', in Jim Obelkevich, Lyndal Roper and Raphael Samuel (eds), *Disciplines of Faith. Studies in religion, politics and patriarchy*, London 1987.

15. StadtAA, Urg., 2 July 1590, Anna Stauder. I have developed the theme of parallels between spells and Counter-Reformation religiosity in "Magic and the Theology of the Body: Exorcism in sixteenth century Augsburg', in Charles Zika (ed.), *No Other Gods Except Me: Orthodoxy and religious practice in Europe 1200–1700*, Melbourne 1991.

16. *Die peinliche Gerichtsordnung Kaiser Karls V. von 1532*, 4th edn, ed. A. Kaufmann, Munich 1975, arts no. 48–58, pp. 50–6.

17. StadtAA, Urg., 28 Jan. 1669, Anna Ebeler, interrogations 28 Jan. to 23 March 1669; Verruf, 32 March 1669; and Strafbuch Des Rats, 23 March 1669, pp. 312–14.

18. She also denied intercourse with the Devil. StadtAA, Urg., 20 Dec. 1685, Euphrosina Endriss, 4 March 1686, and condemnation, 16 March 1686; Strafbuch des Rats, 1654–99, pp. 557–8.

19. The procedure is described in Staatsbibliothek München, Handschriftenabteilung, Cgm 2026, fos 1 v-5 r. For pamphlets describing the cases, see, for example, *Warhaffter Sumarisch: aussführlicher Bericht vnd Erzehlung. Was die in des Heyligen Röm. ReichsStatt Augspurg etlich Wochen lang in verhafft gelegne zwo Hexen/benandtlich Barbara Frölin von Rieden/vnnd Anna Schäflerin von Etringen . . .* , Augsburg 1654; Relation Oder Beschreibung so Anno 1669 . . . von einer Weibs-Person . . . , Augsburg 1669.

20. StadtAA, Urg., 28 Jan. 1669, Anna Ebeler, interrogation 6 March 1669; Strafbuch des Rats, 1654–99, 7 Feb. 1673, Regina Schiller, pp. 390ff.

21. In 1587 the 'evil custom' of allowing the hangman to carry out torture unsupervised had to be explicitly abolished in Augsburg: Behringer, *Hexenverfolgung in Bayern*, p. 158.

22. StadtAA, Urg., 20 Dec. 1685, Euphrosina Endriss, report of Hans Adam Hartman, 5 Feb. 1686: Hans Adam Hartman, executioner of Donauwörth, was the son of the Augsburg executioner Mattheus Hartman who had been crippled in both hands (see below).

23. 'bitt in fine nochmalen fuessfellig vnd mit Weinen vmb Ein gnedig urthel, vnd Meine herrn vmb verzeihung, wass sie vnrechts gethan. bedankt sich auch dass man ihr so ein gute gefangnuss vnd tractament zukommen lassen', StadtAA, Urg., 28 Jan. 1669, Anna Ebeler, testimony of 21 March 1669. Anna Schwayhofer also concluded her final testimony by saying this was the confession by which she wanted to live and die, 'confessing also, that she was a heavy, yes, the greatest sinner, and therefore she would gladly die, only begging hereby for a merciful judgement': Urg., 11 Feb. 1666, Anna Schwayhofer, interrogation 31 March 1666. On sadism and masochism see Joyce McDougall, *Plea for a Measure of Abnormality*, London 1990 (1st edn, French 1978); Sigmund Freud, 'Three Essays on the Theory of Sexuality', in *On Sexuality* (Pelican Freud Library 7), trans. James Strachey, ed. Angela Richards, London 1977; idem., 'The Economic Problem of Masochism (1924)', in *On Metapsychology* (Penguin Freud Library 11), trans. James Strachey, ed. Angela Richards, London 1984.

24. Staatsbibliothek München, Handschriftenabteilung, Cgm 2026, fols 64^v–65^r, 61^r.

25. StadtAA, Urg., 11 Feb. 1666, Anna Schwayhofer, testimony of Margaretha Höcht, 19 Feb. 1666.

26. StadtAA, Urg., 15 July 1650, Ursula Neher, testimony of Susanna Custodis, 11 July 1650.

27. 'nur vmb Jhres bösen Maules Willen', StadtAA, Urg., 14 June 1650, Barbara Fischer.

28. StadtAA, Urg., 13 May 1654, Anna Zoller.

29. StadtAA, Urg., 15 July 1650, Ursula Neher, testimony of Sabina Stoltz, 11 July

1650. See also Urg., 25 Jan. 1695, Barbara Melder, testimony of Judith Wolf, 23 Feb. 1695 who saw Melder, the suspected witch, suck her baby's breast.

30. StadtAA, Urg., 15 July 1650, Ursula Neher, testimony of Anna Erhardt, 29 July 1650: at the time, she interpreted this naturalistically and only considered sorcery when Stoltz and Vetter accused Neher.

31. 'am ganzen leiblen ganz roht vnd blaw durcheinander, auch ganz stärr vnd hart, wie ein holz', StadtAA, Urg., 11 Feb. 1666, Anna Schwayhofer, testimony of Hans Adam Sperl, 19 Feb. 1666.

32. 'da habe das kind so herzhafft angefallen vnd von Ihr getrunken dass sie Köfppin sich geJammert vnd dorüber Weinen müssen', StadtAA, Urg., 28 Jan. 1669, Anna Ebeler, testimony of Anna Maria Kopf, 13 Feb. 1669.

33. 'Er ihr zu den Prüssten khomben, vnd ein pulverlin geben wollen, damit den Leüthen, vnd sonderlich Khinder zuschaden', StadtAA, Strafbuch des Rats, 1654–99, 7 Feb. 1673, p. 390, Regina Schiller.

34. See Fredericus Petrus Gayer, *Viereckichtes Eheschätzlein. Da ist: Die vier Gradus der Eheleute*, Erfurt, Johann Beck 1602, esp. fos C iii[r] ff. on widows' lust, D vii[v] ff. and E ii[v] where the writer warns that young men who marry old widows are likely to pine and die in their youth before their elderly wives do, because these old widows have concentrated impurities in them (presumably owing to the cessation of menstruation) and even have impure, poisonous breath.

35. See, for example, Emmanuel Le Roy Ladurie, *Jasmin's Witch. An investigation into witchcraft and magic in south-west France during the seventeenth century*, trans. Brian Pearce, London 1987, pp. 25, 43, 59–60: in rural communities in particular, the hostility to fecundity also involves destruction of the earth's fertility.

36. See R. Po-Chia Hsia, *The Myth of Ritual Murder. Jews and magic in Reformation Germany*, New Haven, Conn. and London 1988.

37. StadtAA, Urg., 11 Feb. 1666, Anna Schwayhofer, interrogation 19 March 1666.

38. StadtAA, Urg., 11 Feb. 1666, Anna Schwayhofer, testimony of Anna Corona Cramer, 19 Feb. 1666; 25 Feb. 1666, Anna Maria Cramer; testimony Anna Maria Cramer and Anna Corona Cramer, 13 March 1666; and interrogations.

39. StadtAA, Urg., 15 July 1650, Ursula Neher, testimony of Maria Gogel, 29 July 1650.

40. StadtAA, Urg., 20 Dec. 1685, Euphrosina Endriss, testimony of Georg Schmetzer, 24 Dec. 1685.

41. StadtAA, Urg., 11 Feb. 1666, Anna Schwayhofer, testimony of Anna Corona Cramer, 19 Feb. 1666; 25 Feb. 1666, Anna Maria Cramer; testimony Anna Maria Cramer and Anna Corona Cramer, 13 March 1666.

42. StadtAA Urg., 20 Dec. 1685, Euphrosina Endriss, testimony of Magdelena Hornung, 24 Dec. 1685.

43. On churching, see Susan C. Karant-Nunn, 'A Women's Rite: Churching and the Lutheran Reformation', Hsia and Scribner (eds), *History and Anthropology*, forthcoming. See also, for example, *Andreas Osiander d. A. Gesamtausgabe*, eds Gerhard Müller and Gottfried Seebass, Gütersloh 1975–, vol. 5, Brandenburg–Nuremberg church ordinance 1533, p. 128: women who have just borne children should be instructed by the pastor and preacher that they are not under the power of the Devil, as had previously been believed: 'das sie nicht in gewalt des teueffels sein, wie mans bisshere nicht on sundern nachteyl der gewissen darfür gehalten und groeblich daran geyrret hat'.

44. For an excellent account of these rituals in England, see Adrian Wilson, 'The Ceremony of Childbirth and its Interpretation', in Valeries Fildes (ed.), *Women as Mothers in Pre-Industrial England*, London and New York 1990.
45. Patricia Crawford, 'The Construction and Experience of Maternity in Seventeenth-Century England', in Fildes (ed.), *Women as Mothers*.
46. See, for example, Melanie Klein, 'Envy and Gratitude' (1957), 'Some Theoretical Conclusions Regarding the Emotional Life of the Infant' (1952), 'On Identification' (1955), in *idem, Envy and Gratitude and Other Works*.
47. StadtAA, Urg., 28 Jan. 1669, Anna Ebeler, testimony of Anna Maria Schmuckher, 1 Feb. 1669.
48. StadtAA, Urg., 28 Jan. 1669, Anna Ebeler, testimony of Benedict Widenmann, 24 Jan. 1669.
49. StadtAA, Urg., 20 Dec. 1685, Euphrosina Endriss, pre-trial testimony of Endriss, 4 Dec. 1685.
50. For example, Ursula Neher, StadtAA, Urg., 15 July 1650; Barbara Fischer, Strafbuch des Rats, 1615–32, p. 397, 13 May 1623; tried as a witch in 1650.
51. On the different ways men and women used sorcery and bodily products, see Ruth Martin, *Witchcraft and the Inquisition in Venice, 1550–1650*, Oxford 1989; Ingrid Ahrendt-Schulte, 'Schadenzauber und Konflikte. Sozialgeschichte von Frauen im Spiegel der Hexenprozesse des 16. Jahrhunderts in der Grafschaft Lippe', in Heide Wunder and Christina Vanja (eds), *Wandel der Geschlechterbeziehungen zu Beginn der Neuzeit*, Frankfurt am Main 1991; Roper, 'Magic and the Theology of the Body'.
52. StadtAA, Urg., 15 July 1650, Ursula Neher, and testimony Hans and Jacobina Vetter, 11 July 1650.
53. StadtAA, Urg., 28 Jan. 1669, Anna Ebeler.
54. 'immerdar guete worth gegeben, biss Sie aus dem haus kommen', StadtAA, Urg., 29 Jan. 1669, Anna Ebeler, testimony of Eleonora Schmidt, 1 Feb. 1669.
55. StadtAA, Urg., 15 July 1650, Ursula Neher, testimony of Sabina Stoltz, 29 July 1650.
56. StadtAA, Urg., 20 Dec. 1685, Euphrosina Endriss, qu. 47, and testimony of Georg Schmetzer, 4 Dec. 1685: 'mein Schäzle du bist wohl auf, sehet Herr und Frau, iezo gehe ich Von dem Kind, es geschehe ihm was da wolle, so will ich entschuldiget sein'. The next day, the child began to sicken.
57. StadtAA, Urg., 28 Jan. 1669, Anna Ebeler, testimony of Juditha Schorr, 13 Feb. 1669; Euphrosina Hayd, 1 Feb. 1669.
58. StadtAA, Urg., 29 Jan. 1669, Anna Ebeler, and interrogation, 19 Feb. 1669.
59. StadtAA, Urg., 20 Dec. 1685, Euphrosina Endriss, qu. 50.
60. StadtAA, Urg., 15 July 1650, Ursula Neher, testimony of Jacobina Vetter, 29 July 1650; testimony of Susanna Custodis, 11 July 1650.
61. StadtAA, Urg., 15 July 1650, Ursula Neher; testimony of Adam Schuster, 11 July 1650; testimony of Anna Erhardt, 29 July 1650.
62. 'was die kellerin vmb solche sachen red vnd antwort geben', StadtAA, Urg., 28 Jan. 1669, Anna Ebeler, interrogation, 19 Feb. 1669, qu. 49.
63. StadtAA, Urg., 11 Feb. 1666, Anna Schwayhofer, testimony of Euphrosina Sperl, 19 Feb. 1666: the knife was her husband's but it had been moved.
64. StadtAA, Strafbuch des Rats, 1615–23, 13 May 1623, p. 397; and notes of 19 Oct. 1624, 30 Aug. 1625, 22 Nov. 1625, 29 Jan. 1626; Urg., 10 May 1623,

Barbara Fischer; Strafbuch des Rats, 1633–53, 23 July 1650, fo. 337^{r-v}; Urg., 14 June 1650, Barbara Fischer.

65. StadtAA, Urg., 14 June 1650, Barbara Fischer, see interrogation of 20 June 1650.

66. 'gegen vnderschidlichen Personen grossen Neid, grollen vnd feindtschafft getragen', StadtAA, Urg., 11 Feb. 1666, Anna Schwayhofer, interrogation, 31 March 1666; and see also Urg., 28 Jan. 1669, Anna Ebeler, throughout. On enmity and exclusion from community, see David W. Sabean, *Power in the Blood*, Cambridge 1984, pp. 31–60; for a strict Lutheran interpretation of confession and enmity, *Andreas Osiander d. A Gesamtausgabe*, vol. 7, p. 663, Kirchenordnung Pfalz-Neuburg 1543, no absolution to be granted if someone still bears enmity. On the role of envy and hatred in the bringing of witchcraft accusations see Heide Wunder, 'Hexenprozesse im Herzogtum Preussen während des 16. Jahrdunderts', in Christian Degn, Hartmut Lehman and Dagmar Unverhau (eds), *Hexenprozesse. Deutsche und skandinavische Beiträge* (Studien zur Volkskunde und Kulturgeschichte Schleswig-Holsteins 12), Neumünster 1983, esp. pp. 188–9; Robin Briggs, *Communities of Belief. Cultural and social tensions in early modern France*, Oxford 1989, pp. 7–65, 83–105.

67. Staats- und Stadtbibliothek Augsburg, 2o Cord Aug. 288, Schilleriana; Strafbuch des Rats, 1654–99, 7 Feb. 1673, Regina Schiller, pp. 390ff.

68. StadtAA, Urg., June 1625, Dorothea Braun, interrogation, 22 Aug. 1625.

69. StadtAA, Urg., June 1625, Dorothea Braun, statement, 18 Sept. 1625; Urg., 28 Jan. 1669, Anna Ebeler, interrogation, 23 Feb. 1669. Urg., 11 Feb. 1666, Anna Schwayhofer, interrogation, 26 March 1666; and Strafbuch des Rats, 1654–99, 15 April 1666, pp. 235–6.

70. StadtAA, Urg., June 1625, Dorothea Braun, interrogation, 22 Aug. 1625. An older witch also tried to teach her to fly on a cat, but the cat refused to carry her!

71. 'Hennendreckele': StadtAA, Strafbuch des Rats, 1633–53, 23 July 1650, Barbara Fischer, fo. 337^{r-v}; 'Gänsdreckh', Strafbuch des Rats, 1654–99, 18 April 1654, Anna Schäffler, pp. 4–7.

72. Behringer, *Hexenverfolgung in Bayern*, p. 466; Stadt- und Staatsbibliothek Augsburg, 2o Cod Aug. 289, Acta puncto maleficii et tentationis diabolicae.

73. Wolfgang Behringer has noted a general rise in cases of child witches from the last quarter of the seventeenth century onwards. See his 'Kinderhexenprozesse. Zur Rolle von Kindern in der Geschichte der Hexenverfolgungen', *Zeitschrift für historische Forschung*, 16, 1989, pp. 31–47. StadtAA, Strafbuch des Rats, 1654–99, p. 722, Elisabeth Memminger: since she was considered to have been a witch, her corpse was publicly carted out and buried under the gallows. There were two further similar cases: Christina Haber, a lying-in-maid, was interrogated and tortured, 12 Dec. 1699, but eventually let out on recall: Strafbuch des Rats, 1654–99, p. 725. Anna Maria Christeiner and her daughter were accused of abducting and harming children, Verbrecherbuch, 1700–1806, p. 31, 20 Aug. 1701; Urg., 3 Aug. 1701. They were severely tortured but eventually freed on recall. By contrast, a case of 1700 to 1703 concerns the plight of the daughter of Hans Georg Groninger, a suspected girl witch aged 14 in 1702, who ate lice and her own excrement: Stadt-und Staatsbibliothek Augsburg, 2o Cod Aug. 289, Acta puncto maleficii et tentationis diabolicae; StadtAA, Urg., 17 May 1702, Regina Groninger.

74. Barbara Rajkay, 'Die Bevölkerungsentwicklung von 1500 bis 1648', in Gunther Gottlieb *et al.* (eds), *Geschichte der Stadt Augsburg*, Stuttgart 1985; Roeck, *Eine Stadt in Krieg und Frieden*, vol. 2, pp. 775–85, 880–9.

75. Bernd Roeck argues that Marian devotion was a line of division between the two confessions, but his evidence from baptismal registers also shows that while Catholics favoured the name 'Maria' for girls, the most popular name choice among Protestants was 'Annamaria'. This name choice combined the names of both the mother of Jesus and her mother, suggesting the centrality of Marian ideals and motherhood to Protestant understandings of womanhood. Protestants also strongly favoured the names 'Maria' and 'Regina' (associated with the Queen of Heaven): Roeck, ibid., vol. 2, pp. 847, 862–5. See the rich paper of Marina Warner, 'The Absent Mother, or Women Against Women in the Old Wives' Tale', inaugural lecture, Tinbergen Professor, Erasmus University, Rotterdam 1991.

76. StadtAA, Strafbücher des Rats. Between 1633 and 1699 nine women were punished for this offence, six of whom were executed while a further six women and two men were suspected of the crime.

77. For a different, path-breaking use of psychoanalysis to study witchcraft in New England, see Demos, *Entertaining Satan*. Demos notes the importance of maternal themes in witchcraft material (pp. 181, 198–206) but then goes on to argue that since mothers are almost universally responsible for the care of children, the prevalence of witchcraft is best explained by general child-rearing practices among early New Englanders which resulted in a weak ego structure and a tendency to engage in a good deal of projective behaviour. He uses psychoanalysis, linked with attention to child-rearing practices, to construct a general pathology of New England society: I am using it rather to elucidate particular conflicts between people and illuminate psychic functioning in a manner which does not derive psychic meaning reductively from child-rearing practices. On psychic creativity, see Joyce McDougall, *Plea for a Measure of Abnormality; Theatres of the Body: A psychoanalytic approach to psychosomatic illness*, London 1989; and *Theatres of the Mind: Illusion and truth on the psychoanalytic stage*, New York 1985. A similar emphasis on projective identification is to be found in Evelyn Heinemann, *Hexen und Hexenangst. Eine psychoanalytische Studie über den Hexenwahn der frühen Neuzeit*, Frankfurt am Main 1986.

Part III. **Gender and Genre**

Diana Described: Scattered Woman and Scattered Rhyme

Nancy J. Vickers

The import of Petrarch's description of Laura extends well beyond the confines of his own poetic age; in subsequent times, his portrayal of feminine beauty became authoritative. As a primary canonical text, the *Rime sparse* consolidated and disseminated a Renaissance mode. Petrarch absorbed a complex network of descriptive strategies and then presented a single, transformed model. In this sense his role in the history of the interpretation and the internalization of woman's "image" by both men and women can scarcely be overemphasized. When late-Renaissance theorists, poets, and painters represented woman's body, Petrarch's verse justified their aesthetic choices. His authority, moreover, extended beyond scholarly consideration to courtly conversation, beyond the treatise on beauty to the after-dinner game in celebration of it. The descriptive codes of others, both ancients and contemporaries, were, of course, not ignored, but the "scattered rhymes" undeniably enjoyed a privileged status: they informed the Renaissance norm of a beautiful woman.[1]

We never see in the *Rime sparse* a complete picture of Laura. This would not be exceptional if we were considering a single "song" or even a restricted lyric corpus; gothic top-to-toe enumeration is, after all, more appropriate to narrative, more adapted to the "objective" observations of a third-person narrator than to those of a speaker who ostensibly loves, and perhaps even addresses, the image he describes. But given an entire volume devoted to a single lady, the absence of a coherent, comprehensive portrait is significant.[2] Laura is always presented as a part or parts of a woman. When more that one part figures

From *Critical Enquiry*, 8/2 (1981), 265–78. ©The University of Chicago Press. Reprinted with permission. An early version of this paper was shared with the University Seminar on Feminist Inquiry at Dartmouth College; I sincerely appreciate the time, attention, and suggestions of its members. I am particularly indebted to Richard Corum, Jonathan Goldberg, Katherine Hayles, Marianne Hirsech, David Kastan, Stephen Orgel, Esther Raskin, Christian Wolff and Holly Wolff for their contributions.

in a single poem, a sequential, inclusive ordering is never stressed. Her textures are those of metals and stones; her image is that of a collection of exquisitely beautiful disassociated objects.[3] Singled out among them are hair, hand, foot and eyes: golden hair trapped and bound the speaker; an ivory hand took his heart away; a marble foot imprinted the grass and flowers; starry eyes directed him in his wandering.[4] In terms of qualitative attributes (blondness, whiteness, sparkle), little here is innovative. More specifically Petrarchan, however, is the obsessive insistence on the particular, an insistence that would in turn generate multiple texts on individual fragments of the body or on the beauties of woman.

When the sixteenth-century poet Joachim Du Bellay chose to attack the French propensity for Italianizing, his offensive gesture against the Petrarchans (among whose number he had once prominently figured) culminated in just this awareness: in his final verses he proposed to substitute the unified celebration of female beauty for the witty clichés of Petrarchan particularization:

> De voz *beautez* je diray seulement,
> Que si mon oeil ne juge folement,
> Vostre *beauté* est joincte egalement
> A vostre bonne grace:
> ....
> Si toutefois Petrarque vous plaist mieux,
> ....
> Je choisiray cent mille nouveautez,
> Dont je peindray voz plus grandes *beautez*
> Sur la plus belle Idee.

("Contre les Petrarquistes," ll. 193–96, 201, 206–8)

Of your *beauties* I will only say that, if my eye does not mistakenly judge, your *beauty* is perfectly joined to your good grace: . . . But if you still like Petrarch better . . . I will choose a hundred thousand new ways to paint your greatest *beauties* according to the most beautiful Idea.[5]

Du Bellay's opposition of "beauties" and "beauty" suggests the idiosyncratic nature of Petrarch's depiction of woman as a composite of details. It would surely seem that to Petrarch Laura's whole body was at times less than some of its parts; and that to his imitators the strategy of describing her through the isolation of those parts presented an attractive basis for imitation, extension, and, ultimately, distortion. I will redefine that strategy here in terms of a myth to which both the

Rime and the Renaissance obsessively return, a myth complex in its interpretation although simple in its staging. As a privileged mode of signifying, the recounting of a mythical tale within a literary text reveals concerns, whether conscious or unconscious, which are basic to that text.[6] It is only logical, then, to examine Petrarch's use of a myth about seeing woman in order to reexamine his description of a woman seen. The story of Actaeon's encounter with the goddess Diana is particularly suited to this purpose, for it is a story not only of confrontation with forbidden naked deity but also with forbidden naked femininity.

In the twenty-third *canzone*, the *canzone* of the metamorphoses, Petrarch's "I" narrates a history of changes: he was Daphne (a laurel), Cygnus (a swan), Battus (a stone), Byblis (a fountain), Echo (a voice), he will never be Jove (a golden raincloud), and he is Actaeon (a stag). He has passed through a series of painful frustrations, now experiences a highly specific one, and will never be granted the sexual fulfillment of a god capable of transforming himself into a golden shower and inseminating the object of his desire. His use of the present in the last full stanza, the Actaeon stanza, is telling, for it centers this *canzone* on the juxtaposition of what the speaker was and what he now is: "Alas, what am I? What was I? The end crowns the life, the evening the day."[7] The end also crowns the song, and this song paradoxically abandons its speaker in the form of a man so transmuted that he cannot speak:

> I' segui' tanto avanti il mio desire
> ch' un dì, cacciando sì com' io solea,
> mi mossi, e quella fera bella et cruda
> in una fonte ignuda
> si stava, quando 'l sol più forte ardea.
> Io perché d'altra vista non m'appago
> stetti a mirarla, ond' ella ebbe vergogna
> et per farne vendetta o per celarse
> l'acqua nel viso co le man mi sparse.
> Vero dirò; forse e' parrà menzogna:
> ch'i' senti' trarmi de la propria imago
> et in un cervo solitario et vago
> di selva in selva ratto mi trasformo,
> et ancor de' miei can fuggo lo stormo.
>
> (*RS*, 23. 147–60)

I followed so far my desire that one day, hunting as I was wont, I went forth, and that lovely cruel wild creature was in a spring naked when the sun burned most strongly. I, who am not appeased by any other sight, stood to gaze on her, whence she felt shame and, to take revenge or to hide herself, sprinkled water in my face with her hand. I shall speak the truth, perhaps it will appear a lie, for I felt myself drawn from my own image and into a solitary wandering stag from wood to wood quickly I am transformed and still I flee the belling of my hounds.

Petrarch's account of Actaeon's story closely follows the subtext that obviously subtends the entire *canzone*—Ovid's *Metamorphoses*. Actaeon is, as usual, hunting with friends. At noon, he stumbles upon a grove where he sees Diana, chaste goddess of the hunt and of the moon, bathing nude in a pool.[8] In the *Metamorphoses* she is surrounded by protective nymphs, but Petrarch makes no mention of either her company or of Actaeon's. He thus focuses the exchange on its principal players. Actaeon is transfixed (a stance Petrarch exaggerates), and Diana, both in shame and anger, sprinkles ("spargens") his face ("vultum") and hair ("comas") with water. Although in the *Rime sparse* Diana is significantly silenced, in the *Metamorphoses* she utters, "Now you can tell ["narres . . . licet"] that you have seen me unveiled ["posito velamine"]—that is, if you can tell ["si poteris narrare"]."[9] Diana's pronouncement simultaneously posits telling (description) as the probable outcome of Actaeon's glance and negates the possibility of that telling. Her vengeful baptism triggers a metamorphosis: it transforms Actaeon from horn to hoof into a voiceless, fearful stag (*Metamorphoses* 3. 193–98). It is at this moment that Petrarch, with his characteristic use of an iterative present, situates his speaker: No other sight appeases me; "I am transformed"; "I flee."[10] The speaker *is* Actaeon, but, more important, he is a self-conscious Actaeon: he knows his own story; he has read his own text; he is defined by it and even echoes it in articulating his suffering. What awaits him is annihilation through dismemberment, attack unto death by his own hounds goaded on by his own devoted friends.

Seeing and bodily disintegration, then, are related poles in the Ovidian context that Petrarch brings to his text; they also are poles Ovid conjoins elsewhere. Actaeon's mythological antitypes in dismemberment, Pentheus and Orpheus, are both textually and experientially linked to his story.[11] His is the subtext to their suffering; he is the figure for their pain. In *Metamorphoses* 3. 708–33, Pentheus gapes with "profane eyes" upon the female celebrants of the sacred rites of Bacchus, and they, urged by his mother (the woman who sees him), tear his body limb from limb: "Let the ghost of Actaeon move your heart," he pleads, but "she [his mother] knows not who Actaeon is;

and tears the suppliant's right arm away." In *Metamorphoses* 11. 26–27, Orpheus is so grief stricken at having irrevocably lost Eurydice by turning back to look at her that he shuns other women; falling victim to an explosion of female jealousy, he is dismembered and scattered, "as when in the amphitheatre . . . the doomed stag is the prey of dogs."

All three men, then, transgress, see women who are not to be seen, and are torn to bits. But the Orpheus-Actaeon analogy is particularly suggestive, for in the case of Orpheus, seeing and dismemberment are discrete events in time. The hiatus between them, the extended reprieve, is a span of exquisite though threatened poetry, of songs of absence and loss. Petrarch's "modern" Actaeon is in that median time: he is fearful of the price of seeing, yet to be paid, but still pleased by what he saw. The remembered image is the source of all joy and pain, peace and anxiety, love and hate: "Living is such heavy and long pain, that I call out for the end in my great desire to see her again whom it would have been better not to have seen at all" (*RS*, 312. 12–14). Thus he must both perpetuate her image and forget it: he must "cry out in silence," cry out "with paper and ink," that is to say, write (*RS*, 71. 6, 23. 99).

It is especially important to note that the productive paralysis born of this ambivalence determines a normative stance for countless lovesick poets of the Petrarchan generations. As Leonard Barkan has recently shown, "From that source [Petrarch] Actaeon's story becomes throughout the Renaissance a means of investigating the complicated psychology of love."[12] When Shakespeare, for example, lends a critical ear to Orsino in his opening scene to *Twelfth Night*, we hear what was by 1600 the worn-out plaint of a languishing lover caught precisely in Actaeon's double bind:

Curio:	Will you go to hunt, my lord?
Orsino:	What, Curio?
Curio:	The hart.
Orsino:	Why, so I do, the noblest that I have.
	O, when mine eyes did see Olivia first,
	Methought she purg'd the air of pestilence!
	That instant was I turn'd into a hart,
	And my desires, like fell and cruel hounds,
	E'er since pursue me.

(Act 1, sc. 1, ll. 16–23)

Subsequent imitation, no matter how creative or how wooden, bears witness to the reader's awareness of and the writer's engagement in the practice of "speaking" in Actaeon's voice. A reassessment of Petrarch's use of Actaeon's fate to represent the status of his speaking subject, then, constitutes a reassessment of not just one poetic stance but of many. When we step back from the Petrarchans to Petrarch, the casting of the poet in this role (and, by extension, the beloved in that of Diana) is less a cliché than a construct that can be used to explain both the scattering of woman and of rhyme in his vernacular lyric. Here the "metaphor of appearance," so central to the volume, is paired with the myth of appearance: the fateful first perception of Laura—an image obsessively remembered, reworked, and repeated—assumes a mythical analogue and mythical proportion.[13] What the reader must then ask is why that remembrance, like the rhyme ("rimembra" / "membra" [remember / members]) that invokes it, is one of parts: "Clear, fresh, sweet waters, where she who alone seems lady to me rested her lovely body ["membra"], gentle branch where it pleased her (with sighing I remember)" (*RS*, 126. 1–5).[14]

Although traces of Diana are subtly woven into much of the imagistic texture that progressively reveals the composite of Laura, only one text refers to her by name:

> Non al suo amante più Diana piacque
> quando per tal ventura tutta ignuda
> la vide in mezzo de le gelide acque,
>
> ch'a me la pastorella alpestra et cruda
> posta a bagnar un leggiadretto velo
> ch'a l'aura il vago et biondo capel chiuda;
>
> tal che mi fece, or quand' egli arde'l cielo,
> tutto tremar d'un amoroso gielo.
>
> (*RS*, 52)

Not so much did Diana please her lover when, by a similar chance, he saw her all naked amid the icy waters,

as did the cruel mountain shepherdess please me, set to wash a pretty veil that keeps her lovely blond head from the breeze;

so that she made me, even now when the sky is burning, all tremble with a chill of love.

This simple madrigal based on the straightforward equation of the speaker's pleasure at seeing Laura's veil and Actaeon's pleasure at seeing Diana's body has, of late, received lengthy and suggestive comment. Giuseppe Mazzotta, in an analysis centered on Petrarch's "language of the self," reads it in relation to a reversibility of "subject and object."[15]

John Freccero places Petrarch's use of the "veil covering a radiant face" motif within its traditional context (Saint Paul to Dante), that of a "figure for the relationship of the sign to its referent." He concludes that Laura's "veil, bathed in the water like the naked goddess seen by Actaeon, functions as a fetish, an erotic signifier of a referent whose absence the lover refuses to acknowledge." That act of substituting the veil for the body, previously linked by Freccero to the Augustinian definition of idolatry, ultimately associates the fragmentation of Laura's body and the "non-referentiality" of Petrarch's sequence:

> One of the consequences of treating a signifier as an absolute is that its integrity cannot be maintained. Without a principle of intelligibility, an interpretant, a collection of signs threatens to break down into its component parts. . . . So it is with Laura. Her virtues and her beauties are scattered like the objects of fetish worship: her eyes and hair are like gold and topaz on the snow, while the outline of her face is lost; . . . Like the poetry that celebrates her, she gains immortality at the price of vitality and historicity. Each part of her has the significance of her entire person; it remains the task of the reader to string together her gemlike qualities into an idealized unity.[16]

Freccero's analysis departs from a position shared by many contemporary Petrarch critics—that of the centrality of a dialectic between the scattered and the gathered, the integrated and the disintegrated.[17] In defining Petrarch's "poetics of fragmentation," these same critics have consistently identified as its primary figure the particularizing descriptive strategy adopted to evoke Laura.[18] If the speaker's "self" (his text, his "corpus") is to be unified, it would seem to require the repetition of her dismembered image. "Woman remains," as Josette Féral has commented in another context, "the instrument by which man attains unity, and she pays for it at the price of her own dispersion."[19]

Returning to *Rime sparse* 52, some obvious points must be made: first, this text is read as an emblem of Petrarchan fragmentation; and second, it turns on a highly specific analogy ("I am pleased by Laura's veil as Actaeon was pleased by Diana's nakedness"; "My fetish equals Diana's body"). It is the analogy itself that poses an additional problem. While the enunciation of "I" 's fetishistic pleasure through comparison with Actaeon's voyeuristic pleasure might appear incongruous, it is both appropriate and revealing.

The Actaeon—Diana story is one of identification and reversal: Actaeon hunts; Diana hunts; and their encounter reduces him to the status of the hunted.[20] This fated meeting, this instant of midday recognition, is one of fascination and repulsion: it is a confrontation with difference where similarity might have been desired or even expected. It is a glance into a mirror—witness the repeated pairing of this myth with that of Narcissus (*Metamorphoses* 3. 344–510)—that produces an unlike and deeply threatening image.[21] Perceiving that image is, of course, prohibited; such a transgression violates proscriptions imposed on powerless humans in their relation to powerful divinities. Similarly, such a transgression violates proscriptions imposed upon powerless men (male children) in relation to powerful women (mothers):[22] "This is thought," writes Howard Daniel, "to be one of many myths relating to the incest mechanism—punishment for an even accidental look at something forbidden."[23] The Actaeon—Diana encounter read in this perspective re-enacts a scene fundamental to theorizing about fetishistic perversion: the troubling encounter of a male child with intolerable female nudity, with a body lacking parts present in his own, with a body that suggests the possibility of dismemberment. Woman's body, albeit divine, is displayed to Actaeon, and his body, as a consequence, is literally taken apart. Petrarch's Actaeon, having read his Ovid, realizes what will ensue: his response to the threat of imminent dismemberment is the neutralization, through descriptive dismemberment, of the threat. He transforms the visible totality into scattered words, the body into signs; his description, at one remove from his experience, safely permits and perpetuates his fascination.

The verb in the *Rime sparse* that places this double dismemberment in the foreground is determinant for the entire sequence—*spargere*, "to scatter." It appears in some form (most frequently that of the past-participial adjective "*sparso, -i, -a, -e*") forty-three times; nineteen apply specifically to Laura's body and its emanations (the light from her eyes, the generative capacity of her footsteps) and thirteen to the speaker's mental state and its expression (tears, voice, rhymes, sighs, thoughts, praises, prayers, hopes). The uses of *spargere* thus markedly gravitate toward "I" and Laura. The etymological roots of the term, moreover, virtually generate Laura's metaphoric codes: "I" knows that the outcome of seeing her body is the scattering of his; hence he projects scattering onto her through a process of fetishistic overdetermination, figuring those part-objects in terms of the connotations of "scattering": *spargere*, from the Latin *spargere*, with cognates in the English "sprinkle" and "sparkle" and in the Greek σπείρω—"I disseminate." Laura's eyes, as in the sequence of three *canzoni* devoted exclusively to them (*RS*, 71–73), are generative sparks emanating from the stars; they sow the seeds of poetry in the "untilled soil" of the poet (*RS*, 71. 102–5), and they sprinkle glistening drops like clear waters. Her body parts metaphorically inseminate; his do not: "Song, I was never the cloud of gold that once descended in a precious rain so that it partially quenched the fire of Jove; but I have certainly been a flame lit by a lovely glance and I have been that bird that rises highest in the air raising her whom in my words I honor" (*RS*, 23. 161–66). Desire directed in vain at a forbidden, distant goddess is soon sublimated desire that spends itself in song. That song is, in turn, the celebration and the violation of that goddess: it would re-produce her vulnerability; it would re-present her nakedness to a (male) reader who will enter into collusion with, even become, yet another Actaeon.[24]

Within the context of Petrarch's extended poetic sequence, the lady is corporeally scattered; the lover is emotionally scattered and will be corporeally scattered, and thus the relation between the two is one of mirroring. "I," striking Actaeon's pose, tells us that he stood fixed to see but also to mirror Diana-Laura ("mirarla").[25] He offers to eliminate the only source of sadness for the "lovely eyes," their inability to see themselves, by mirroring them (*RS*, 71. 57–60). And he transforms the coloration of the lady's flesh into roses scattered in snow in which he mirrors himself (*RS*, 146. 5–6). The specular nature of this exchange explains, in large part, the disconcerting interchangeability of its participants. Even the key rhyme "rimembra/membra" reflects a doubling: twice the *membra* are his (*RS*, 15 and 23); once those of the lost heroes of a disintegrating body politic, a dissolving mother country (*RS*, 53); and twice hers (*RS*, 126 and 127). In reading the Diana-veil madrigal cited above, Mazzotta demonstrates this textual co-mingling, pointing out that Diana's body, in the first tercet, is completely naked ("tutta ignuda") in a pool of icy waters ("gelide acque") but, by the last line, her observer's body is all atremble ("tutto tremar") with a chill of love ("un amoroso gielo"). Mazzotta goes on to note that male/female roles often alternate in Petrarch's figurations of the speaker/Laura relationship: he is Echo to her Narcissus, Narcissus to her Echo; she is Apollo to his Daphne, Daphne to his Apollo, and so on.[26] The space of that alternation is a median one—a space of looks, mirrors, and texts.

Actaeon sees Diana, Diana sees Actaeon, and seeing is traumatic for both. She is ashamed, tries to hide her body (her secret), and thus communicates her sense of violation. Her observer consequently knows that pleasure in the sight before him constitutes transgression; he deduces that transgression, although thrilling (arousing), is threatening (castrating). Their initial communication is a self-conscious look; the following scenario fills the gap between them: "I . . . stood to gaze on her, whence she felt shame and, to take revenge or to hide herself, sprinkled water ["mi sparse"—cf. Ovid, "spargens"] in my face with her hand[s]. I shall speak the truth" (*RS*, 23. 153–56). She defends herself and assaults him with scattered water; he responds with scattered words: "You who hear in scattered rhymes the sound of those sighs with which I nourished my heart during my first youthful error, when I was in part another man from what I am now" (*RS*, 1. 1–4). Water and words, then, pass between them; hands and transparent drops cannot conceal her but do precipitate a metamorphosis, preventing a full sounding of what was momentarily seen. Threatened rhymes try to iterate a precious, fleeting image, to transmute it into an idol that can be forever possessed, that will be forever present.

But description is ultimately no more that a collection of imperfect signs, signs that, like fetishes, affirm absence by their presence. Painting Laura in poetry is but a twice-removed, scripted rendering of a lost woman (body → introjected image of the body → textual body), an enterprise by definition fragmentary. "I" speaks his anxiety in the hope of finding repose through enunciation, of re-membering the lost body, of effecting an inverse incarnation—her flesh made word. At the level of the fictive experience which he describes, successes are ephemeral, and failures become a way of life.

> Quella per cui con Sorga ò cangiato Arno,
> con franca povertà serve ricchezze,
> volse in amaro sue sante dolcezze
> ond' io già vissi, or me ne struggo et scarno.
>
> Da poi più volte ò riprovato indarno
> al secol che verrà l'alte bellezze
> pinger cantando, a ciò che l'ame et prezze,
> né col mio stile il suo bel viso incarno.
>
> Le lode, mai non d'altra et proprie sue,
> che'n lei fur come stelle in cielo sparte,
> pur ardisco ombreggiare, or una or due;
>
> ma poi ch'i' giungo a la divina parte,
> ch' un chiaro et breve sole al mondo fue[,]
> ivi manca l'ardir, l'ingegno et l'arte.
>
> (*RS*, 308)

She for whom I exchanged Arno for Sorgue and slavish riches for free poverty, turned her holy sweetness[es], on which I once lived, into bitterness, by which now I am destroyed and disfleshed [I destroy and disflesh myself].

Since then I have often tried in vain to depict in song for the age to come her high beauties, that it may love and prize them, nor with my style can I incarnate her lovely face.

Still now and again I dare to adumbrate one or two of the praises that were always hers, never any other's, that were as many as the stars spread [scattered] across the sky;

but when I come to her divine part, which was a bright, brief sun to the world, there fails my daring, my wit, and my art.

This text organizes itself upon a sequence of oppositions which contrast fullness (presence) with emptiness (absence). The speaker has exchanged Arno (Florence, mother country) for Sorgue (Vaucluse, exile); riches (although slavish) for poverty (albeit free); sweetness for bitterness; a body for dismemberment; and union for separation. The speaker's rhymes point to a past place (a body of water, "Arno") and to two present, though fruitless ("indarno"), activities—he is at once stripped of flesh ("me ne . . . scarno") and would give flesh to her ("incarno"). He acknowledges his inability to re-create Laura's absent face, and yet he maintains that he still tries, "now and again." Her praises (that is, his poems) are but images he "dare[s] to adumbrate," shadows "scattered," like their source, across the sky. Daring, wit, and art cannot re-present her to him, but they can evoke her parts "one by one" and thus generate an exquisite sequence of verse (*RS*, 127. 85–91 and 273. 6). For it is in fact the loss, at the fictional level, of Laura's body that constitutes the intolerable absence, creates a reason to speak, and permits a poetic "corpus." As Petrarch's readers have consistently recognized, Laura and *lauro*, the laurel to crown a poet laureate, are one.[27]

Petrarch's poetry is a poetry of tension, of flux, of alternation between the scattered and the gathered. Laura's many parts would point to a unity, however elusive, named Laura; the speaker's ambivalent emotions are spoken by a grammatically constant "io." In the space of exchange, the only space the reader is given, permutation is possible; each part of her body can produce each aspect of his positive/negative reactions. A given text can expand any combination; infinite variety spawns infinite verse. Petrarch's particularizing mode of figuring that body, the product of a male-viewer/female-object exchange that extends the Actaeon/Diana exchange, thus reveals a textual strategy subtending his entire volume: it goes to the heart of his lyric program and understandably becomes the lyric stance of generations of imitators.

And yet such praise carries condemnation with it because it implies at least two interdependent consequences. First, Petrarch's figuration of Laura informs a decisive stage in the development of a code of beauty, a code that causes us to view the fetishized body as a norm and encourages us to seek, or to seek to be, "ideal types, beautiful monsters composed of every individual perfection."[28] Petrarch's text, of course, did not constitute the first example of particularizing description, but it did popularize that strategy by coming into fashion during the privileged early years of printing, the first century of the widespread diffusion of both words and images. It is in this context that Petrarch left us his legacy of fragmentation. And second, bodies fetishized by a poetic voice logically do not have a voice of their own; the world of making words, of making texts, is not theirs. The status of Laura's voice, however, resists easy or schematic characterization. Once dead, it should be noted, she can often address her sleeping, disconsolate lover; while she is alive, direct discourse from her is extremely rare. Her speech, moreover, undergoes a treatment similar to that of her body in that it ranks high on the list of her exquisitely reified parts: "and her speech and her lovely face and her locks pleased me so that I have her before my eyes and shall always have wherever I am, on slope or shore" (*RS*, 30. 4–6).

Rime sparse 23, the *canzone* of the metamorphoses, strikingly dramatizes the complexity of both citing and stifling Laura's voice. Although each of its transformations repeats an Ovidian model, only three stress the active participation of the Lady. In the first she lifts the speaker's heart out of his chest, utters two exceptional sentences, and ultimately turns him (like Battus) into a stone; next, she reduces him (like Echo) into a repetitive voice; and finally, she transforms him (like Actaeon) into a stag. The Ovidian models are telling in that they all either limit or negate a voice: Mercury says to Battus, "Whoever you are, my man, if anyone should ask you about some cattle, say that you have not seen them" (*Metamorphoses* 2. 692–94); Juno says to Echo, "That tongue by which I have been tricked shall have its power curtailed and enjoy the briefest use of speech" (*Metamorphoses* 3. 366–67); and Diana says to Actaeon, "Now you are free to tell ["narres . . . licet"] that you have seen me unveiled—if you can tell ["narrare"]" (*Metamorphoses* 3.192–93).[29]

The first model permits speech, but insists that it not be true, and, when disobeyed, denies it; the second, by reducing speech to repetition, eliminates its generative capacity; and the third, through irony, does away with it altogether. In Ovid's retelling of that third encounter, Diana is the only person to speak once Actaeon has had his first glimpse of her: "*narrare*" is her word; she pronounces it; she even repeats it. Although she cannot (would not?) prevent him from seeing, she can prevent him from telling. Consequently, that Petrarch erases both her speech and the verbal object of her interdiction (*narrare*) from his own narration is significant. A review of the evolution of the Diana/Actaeon sequence of *Rime sparse* 23, a text at many points explicit in its verbal echoing of Ovid, shows that "I shall speak ["dirò"] the truth" initiates the primary and final versions of line 156: two intermediate variants read "I tell ["narro"] the truth."[30] What that rejected present, *narro*, affirms, in a mode perhaps too obvious to be acceptable even to Petrarch, is that his speaker as Actaeon does precisely what Diana forbids: "'Make no word of this,'" said the "powerful Lady" of a preceding stanza (*RS*, 23. 74, 35). Not only does Petrarch's Actaeon thus nullify Diana's act, he repeats her admonition in so doing; by the time we arrive at the end that "crowns" his song, her speech has been written out and his has been written in. To the measure that he continues to praise her beauties, he persists in inverting the traditional economy of the mythical exchange; he persists in offending her: "Not that I do not see how much my praise injures you [the eyes]; but I cannot resist the great desire that is in me since I saw what no thought can equal, let alone speech, mine or others'" (*RS*, 71. 16–21).

Silencing Diana is an emblematic gesture; it suppresses a voice, and it casts generations of would-be Lauras in a role predicated upon the muteness of its player.[31] A modern Actaeon affirming himself as poet cannot permit Ovid's angry goddess to speak her displeasure and deny his voice; his speech requires her silence. Similarly, he cannot allow her to dismember his body; instead he repeatedly, although reverently, scatters hers throughout his scattered rhymes.

Notes

1. On this "thoroughly self-conscious fashion," see Elizabeth Cropper, "On Beautiful Women, Parmigianino. *Petrarchismo*, and the Vernacular Style," *Art Bulletin* 58 (1976): 374–94. Cropper shares many of the observations on Petrarchan descriptive technique outlined in the following paragraph (see pp. 385–86). I am indebted to David Quint for bringing this excellent essay to my attention.
2. Description is, of course, always fragmentary in that it is by nature enumerative. Petrarch, however, systematically avoids those structures that would mask fragmentation. On enumeration and the descriptive text, see Roland Barthes, *S/Z* (Paris, 1970), pp. 120–22.
3. For lengthy discussions of these qualities of Petrarchan descriptions, see Robert Durling, "Petrarch's 'Giovene donna sotto un verde lauro,'" *Modern*

Language Notes 86 (1971): 1–20, and John Freccero, "The Fig Tree and the Laurel: Petrarch's Poetics," *Diacritics* 5 (Spring 1975); 34–40.

4. On Petrarch's role in the popularization of this *topos*, see James V. Mirollo, "In Praise of '*La bella mano*': Aspects of Late Renaissance Lyricism," *Comparative Literature Studies* 9 (1972): 31–43. See also James Villas, "The Petrarchan Topos 'Bel piede': Generative Footsteps," *Romance Notes* 11 (1969): 167–73.

5. Italics and translation mine.

6. For a recent summary and bibliography of the place of myth in the Renaissance text, see Leonard Barkan, "Diana and Actaeon: The Myth as Synthesis," *English Literary Renaissance* 10 (1980).

7. *Petrarch's Lyric Poems: The "Rime sparse" and Other Lyrics*, trans. and ed. Robert M. Durling (Cambridge, Mass., 1976), *canzone* 23, ll. 30–31; all further references to the *Rime sparse* will be included in the text with poem and line number in parentheses and with Durling's translation. For recent analyses of *Rime sparse* 23, see Dennis Dutschke, *Francesco Petrarca: Canzone XXIII from First to Final Version* (Ravenna, 1997), and Albert J. Rivero, "Petrarch's 'Nel dolce tempo de la prima etade,'" *Modern Language, Notes* 94 (1979): 92–112.

8. For an extremely useful comparison of the Ovidian and Petrarchan narrations of this scene, see Dutschke, *Francesco Petrarca*, pp. 200–209. On the relationship between midday and sexuality in the myth, see Nicolas J. Perella, *Midday in Italian Literature: Variations on an Archetypal Theme* (Princeton, N.J., 1979), pp. 8–9.

9. Ovid, *Metamorphoses*, ed. and trans. Frank J. Miller, 2 vols. (1921; London, 1971), bk. 3, ll. 192–93; all further references to the *Metamorphoses* will be included in the text with book and line number in parentheses. The quotations from this work are based upon but do not entirely reproduce Miller's edition.

10. On the use of the present tense in relation to Actaeon, see Durling's introduction to *Petrarch's Lyric Poems*, p. 28.

11. On the association of Actaeon and Orpheus, see ibid., p. 29. On Actaeon and Pentheus, see Norman O. Brown, "Metamorphoses II: Actaeon," *American Poetry Review* 1 (November/December 1972): 38.

12. Barkan, "Diana and Actaeon," p. 335. On the use of this myth in medieval lyric, see Stephen G. Nichols, Jr., "Rhetorical Metamorphosis in the Troubadour Lyric," in *Mélanges de langue et de littérature médiévales offerts à Pierre Le Gentil, Professeur à la Sorbonne, par ses collègues, ses élèves, et ses amis*, ed. Jean Dufournet and Daniel Poirion (Paris, 1973), pp. 569–85.

13. See Giuseppe Mazzotta, "The *Canzoniere* and the Language of the Self," *Studies in Philology* 75 (1978): 277.

14. The connection between these verses and the Diana /Actaeon myth is noted by Durling, *The Figure of the Poet in Renaissance Epic* (Cambridge, Mass., 1965), p. 73. See also my "Re-membering Dante: Petrarch's 'Chiare, fresche et dolci acque,'" *Modern Language Notes* 96 (1981): 8–9

15. See Mazzotta. "The *Canzoniere*," pp. 282–84.

16. Freccero, "The Fig Tree," pp. 38–39.

17. See, e.g., Durling, introduction to *Petrarch's Lyric Poems*: Freccero, "The Fig Tree"; and Mazzotta, "The *Canzoniere*."

18. For the phrase "poetics of fragmentation," see Mazzotta, "The *Canzoniere*," p. 274.

19. Josette Féral, "Antigone or *The Irony of the Tribe*," trans. Alice Jardine and Tom Gora, *Diacritics* 8 (Fall 1978): 7. I am indebted to Elizabeth Abel for calling this quotation to my attention. See also Durling, introduction to *Petrarch's Lyric Poems*, p. 21, and Mazzotta, "The *Canzoniere*," p. 273.

20. See Barkan, "Diana and Actaeon," pp. 320–22, and Brown, "Metamorphoses II," p. 40.

21. See Barkan, "Diana and Actaeon," pp. 321, 343; Brown, "Metamorphoses II," p. 39; Durling, introduction to *Petrarch's Lyric Poems*, p. 31; and Mazzotta, "The *Canzoniere*," pp. 274, 282.

22. This myth has often been used to point to relationships of power through play on the words *cervus/servus, cerf/serf* (stag/slave); see Barkan "Diana and Actaeon," p. 328. The identification of Diana with women in political power is perhaps best exemplified by the frequent representation of Elizabeth I as Diana; see Barkan, pp. 332–35.

23. Howard Daniel, *Encyclopedia of Themes and Subjects in Painting*, s.v. "Actaeon" (London, 1971). Daniel's point is, of course, supported by the tradition identifying Actaeon's hounds with the Law, with his conscience: "Remorse, the bite of a mad dog. Conscience, the superego, the introjected father or animal: now eating us even as we ate him" (Brown, "Metamorphoses II," p. 39); see also Perella, *Midday in Italian Literature*, p. 42. On Actaeon as "unmanned" or castrated, see Barkan, "Diana and Actaeon," pp. 350–51.

24. See Daniel, "Actaeon." On the casting of the male spectator (reader) in the role of the voyeur, see also John Berger, *Ways of Seeing* (New York, 1977), pp. 45–64, and Laura Mulvey, "Visual Pleasure and Narrative Cinema." *Screen* 16 (Autumn 1975): 6–18. On women conditioned by patriarchal culture to see themselves as "sights," see Jessica Benjamin, "The Bonds of Love: Rational Violence and Erotic Domination," in *The Future of Difference*, ed. Hester Eisenstein and Alice Jardine (Boston, 1980), p. 52, and Berger, *Ways of Seeing*, pp. 46–51.

25. I am, of course, alluding to the etymological associations and not the definition of the verb *mirare* ("to stare").

26. Mazzotta, "The *Canzoniere*," pp. 282–84. See also Durling, introduction to *Petrarch's Lyric Poems*, pp. 31–32.

27. For recent analyses of the play on Laura */lauro*, see François Rigolot, "Nature and Function of Paronomasia in the *Canzoniere*," *Italian Quarterly* 18 (Summer 1974): 29–36, and Marga Cottino-Jones, "The Myth of Apollo and Daphne in Petrarch's *Canzoniere*: The Dynamics and Literary Function of Transformation," in *Francis Petrarch, Six Centuries Later: A Symposium*, ed. Aldo Scaglione (Chapel Hill, N.C., 1975), pp. 152–76.

28. Cropper, "On Beautiful Women," p. 376.

29. On the Diana /Actaeon myth and "the danger of losing the poetic voice," see Mazzotta, "The *Canzoniere*," p. 278; see also Durling, introduction to *Petrarch's Lyric Poems*, p. 28.

30. See Dutschke, *Francesco Petrarca*, pp. 196–98.

31. For the problem of women writing within the constraints of the Petrarchan tradition, see Ann R. Jones, "Assimilation with a Difference: Renaissance Women Poets and Literary Influence," *Yale French Studies* no. 62 (October 1981); on the impact of another masculine lyric tradition on women poets, see Margaret Homans, *Women Writers and Poetic Identity: Dorothy*

Wordsworth, Emily Brontë and Emily Dickinson (Princeton, N.J., 1980), pp. 12–40.

Laura Mulvey comments on the silencing of women in her rereading of a different medium, film: "Woman then stands in patriarchal culture as signifier for the male other, bound by a symbolic order in which man can live out his phantasies and obsessions through linguistic command by imposing them on the silent image of woman still tied to her place as bearer of meaning, not maker of meaning" ("Visual Pleasure," p. 7).

10 Literary Fat Ladies and the Generation of the Text

Patricia Parker

> To play with mimesis is thus, for a woman, to try to recover the place of her exploitation by discourse, without allowing herself to be simply reduced to it. It means to resubmit herself—inasmuch as she is on the side of the "perceptible," of "matter"—to "ideas," in particular to ideas about herself that are elaborated in/by a masculine logic, but so as to make "visible," by an effect of playful repetition, what was supposed to remain invisible: the cover-up of a possible operation of the feminine in language. . . . One must assume the feminine role deliberately, which means already to convert a form of subordination into an affirmation, and thus to begin to thwart it.
>
> (Luce Irigaray)

Much of this essay will have to do with walls or partitions; so we begin with a rhetorical partition, a division of the subject into parts. The first, which might be called "The Body in Question," comes in several sections and is perhaps appropriately by far the largest. The concluding will be a kind of appendage under the rubric of "The Genitive, or Jinny's Case" and "The Vocative, or the Story of O." The Postscript—which goes beyond the Renaissance instances primarily foregrounded here—takes this story into the subsequent history of linkages between female copia, of body and of word, and the copiousness of texts.

First, the question of "fat ladies." We will begin with a woman called Rahab, the redeemed harlot of Jericho from the biblical Old Testament. No record of the conquest of Jericho by Joshua (whom, in Milton's words, the Gentiles Jesus call) indicates that she was physically fat. She was simply the harlot associated with the walls at the entrance to the Promised Land. Her name in Hebrew, however, means "wide" or "broad."[1] Her conversion from the heathen to the Israelite cause involves a turning from letting in men to letting in men—a prelude to the final act of the story in which, as the song goes, the walls come tumbling down. As a figure thus associated both with walls and with discrimination, with taking in the *right* men, she becomes in the biblical tradition of which she is a part a principal Old Testament figure for the Church. The Church figured as female is that other redeemed harlot who in the space between the First and Second Coming of another Joshua, Christ—that is, between the disappearance and final triumphant return of the Master of Creation, Time and History—expands or dilates in order, so to speak, to take in more members, before that ultimate apocalyptic end. One of the iconographic embodiments of this female figure—ambiguously recalling both Mary the Mother and the harlot Mary Magdalene—is the figure most often called *Mater Misericordiae* and pictured as opening her cloak wide enough to encompass the gathered members of the Church or the Body of Christ.

The name of Rahab in Hebrew ("broad, wide") was translated into Latin by the Church Fathers as *dilatio* or dilation, and her opening and expansion in that crucial meantime or threshold period before Apocalypse became known technically as the "dilation of Christendome," a phrase used repeatedly by St Thomas More and others in the Renaissance for the period of spreading or widening through the "dilation of the Word," the crucial activity of that interim of deferred Judgment or Second Coming in which a promised end is yet postponed. "Dilate" comes to us from the same Latin root as Derrida's "*différance*" and involves—commonly throughout Renaissance usage in several languages—that term's curious combination of difference and deferral, dilation, expansion, or dispersal in space but also postponement in time. The dilation of Rahab or of the Church, then, involves symbolically two orifices: expansion to take in a multiplicity of members (as in Donne's sexual pun in the Sonnet on the Church as she who is—he is addressing Christ her Master—"most trew, and pleasing to thee, then / When she's embrac'd and open to most men"); and the propagation, through the mouth, of the Word, again an activity not unexpectedly linked with a Church figured as symbolically female, since one of the oldest topoi of misogyny is the fabled inability of women to keep that particular orifice shut. There is, as Lee Patterson has recently reminded us, at least one recorded instance of the view that Christ revealed himself to women immediately after his Resurrection because he knew that women would spread the word.[2]

This particular figure—of Rahab, understood as dilation, expansion, and deferral, and used as a figure for the space and time of language, discourse, and history before a Master's apocalyptic return—is the figurative fat lady who first interested me when I started to think about romance and about its characteristic association with such dilation or potential vagrancy (or often simply its dilatory refusal to come to a "point").[3] But it was only much later that I began to discover how pervasive and multivalent this entire complex of "dilation" in the Renaissance actually was and how frequently associated with figures of the feminine. This is a link which arises out of romance itself. Spenser used the term "dilate" both for the dilation of history before its deferred apocalyptic (or "sabbath") ending and for the activity of narrating or telling tales, including by implication the dilatory expansion of his own poem; but he also associates this expansion with a dangerous female temptress or enchantress in a canto which is perhaps not by accident the fattest, most dilated canto in the entire poem—a dilation specifically linked with the "gate" of a "Dame" called "Excesse" ("No gate, but like one, being goodly dight / With boughes and braunches, which did broad dilate / Their clasping armes, in wanton wreathings intricate," *The Faerie Queene*, II. xii. 53–5). Overcoming this temptress and the dilated body of the text in question becomes the quest of the knight of Temperance, in a version of what Marvell calls the contest between Resolved Soul—here, the male knight—and the potentially distracting ensnarements of Created Pleasure, the bower of Acrasia. His project, we might say, is to bring this dilated "matter" (with the possibility of a pun on both *materia* and *mater* as in Hamlet's "Now, mother, what's the matter?") to a "point." Though this knight does not use his sword, the word "point" (which designates in so many Renaissance English puns at once "end," sword, and their phallic counterpart) is Spenser's own in the very canto opening which projects the knight's victory over this "matter" in advance even of his setting out ("And this brave knight . . . / Now comes to *point* of that same perilous sted, / Where Pleasure dwelles in sensual delights," II. xii. 1–3). The subtext for the whole is Odysseus' victory over the feminine enticements and enchantments of Circe, pointedly, in that dilated and dilatory text, with his sword; and the victory which in the *Odyssey* only proleptically prefigures the homecoming or closure of the entire narrative is here only too easily converted into a figure for this canto's ending, the coming to a point of another strikingly dilated text.

This association of the dilation of romance narrative with the figure or body of a female enchantress is, moreover, extended in the debate over romance itself as a Circean, female (or even effeminate) form, particularly in the later stages of the Renaissance. Thomas Nashe's *Anatomy of Absurdity* (1589), for instance, combined a satire on women and those who praised them with an attack on the authors of romance. Both were conceived of as potentially corrupting, or leading astray, the will, as making it into a kind of Prodigal Son who might never return to his father.[4] The very popularity of the story of the Prodigal Son in Elizabethan England—of his errancy and prodigality but also of his eventual, repentant return—became, as Richard Helgerson points out, a chief exemplum for the potential vagrancy of the literary activity itself, and of the suspect effeminacy of poets. When Sir Philip Sidney replies to the attacks on romance, as on poetry, in his celebrated *Defence*, by saying that "he knows men that even with the reading of *Amadis de gaule*... have found their hearts moved to the exercise of courtesie, liberalitie, and especially courage," he uses the word "men" pointedly as a counter to the attackers' association of poetry with the feminine.[5] The polemic against the Italianization of Englishmen in the work of one of these opponents of romance—Roger Ascham's *The Schoolmaster* (1570), which follows the model of Vives in its attack and characterizes romances as nothing but bold bawdry— is, in fact, inseparable from a polemic against the romance's corrupting and enervating effect, with the implication that the reader of such texts is cast as an endangered Odysseus whose only moly is a humanist countertraining in virtue and in more canonical reading—the preoccupation, precisely, of the schoolmaster.

Certainly it is this plot of reformation or return from such enchantments—or a turning away from them to something higher or more serious—which is the burden of the figure of the Prodigal Son in which one Elizabethan reader casts himself. John Harington, translator of Ariosto's *Orlando furioso*, first finds in Ariosto's portrayal of Rogero's enticement by the Circe-like Alcina (a source for Spenser's Acrasia) "the very picture of the Prodigal Son spoken of in the scripture, given over to all unthriftiness, all looseness of life and conversation," and then discerns a link between such prodigal vagrancy and his own pursuits. He writes as follows of coming to the place in his translation of the *Furioso* where Melissa reproves Rogero for his dalliance with Alcina (for which the model is Mercury's reproof of Aeneas for his dalliance with Dido rather than getting on with the higher task of establishing the Roman empire): "straight I began to think that my tutor, a grave and learned man, and one of very austere life, might say to me in like sort, 'Was it for this that I read Aristotle and Plato to you and instructed you so carefully both in Greek and Latin, to have you now become a translator of Italian toys?' "[6] Such indulgence in romance was a form of dilatoriness or dalliance, preventing all such latter-day Aeneases from getting on with the business more proper to them.

Just as important a preface to our subject—and to the role of particular dilated female bodies in particular Renaissance texts—are a number of influential subtexts that a Renaissance poet or playwright would have inherited for the narrative topos of overcoming a female enchantress or obstacle en route to completion and ending. Here, where such female figures are linked with a threat to the execution of closure or accomplishment, the appropriate motto would seem to be not *Cherchez la femme*—or a certain way of understanding the question "Is there a woman in this text?"—but rather what we might dub *Ecrasez la femme*, ways of mastering or controlling the implicitly female, and perhaps hence wayward, body of the text itself.[7] The first of these subtexts—already suggested in the opening reference to Rahab, the redeemed harlot whose name is *dilatio* and who stands as a figure for the dilated space of deferred judgment and ending—is the Bible, which is filled with figures for the space and time of such extension (the forty-day space between the announcement of judgment and its execution in the stories of Noah's Flood or Jonah's mission to Nineveh; the space of respite or temporary reprieve from death granted to Hezekiah; the holding back of time itself in the staying of the sun in Joshua, and so on). The reprieve granted to Adam and Eve, the "remnant" of Noah and his family after the almost final closure of the Flood—these and other such reprieves extend both text and time, widening or increasing the space between beginning and end which in Genesis threatens to be very contracted indeed. A structure of deferral inhabits even the Bible's own end or last word, the Book of Apocalypse or Revelation. There, ending is linked to the stripping or overcoming of a female figure, the Whore of Babylon, by the now at last returned Master, Christ. But the final lines end in the still-deferred and still-anticipatory mode of an apostrophe, invocation, or vocative, "Even so, come, Lord Jesus" (Revelation 22), a retreat from a vision of Ending into the ambiguous space before that ending (the model, perhaps, of a similar retreat at the end of Spenser's *Faerie Queene*). What looks like *the* end is, in this quintessential book of endings, presented as still put off or deferred, still yet to come. The New Testament, like the Old, however, is filled with warnings that this deferral of ending must not lull its hearers into the assumption that the promised end will never come. The crucial thing about deferral in its biblical context, then, is that its days are finally numbered, that all time is ultimately borrowed time. The structure of deferred ending remains resolutely teleological—waiting for the return of a delayed but finally coming Master.

The second major subtext for the association of specifically female figures with such dilation or delay is the *Odyssey* already referred to, where Calypso, the enchantress at whose dwelling we first glimpse the latent hero, has a name which means "covering," the very opposite of apocalypse or uncovering, and where Odysseus' mastery of Circe with his sword may be by implication a sort of narratively retroactive liberation from the covering and latency of Calypso's cave, just as it is an anticipation of homecoming to Penelope.[8] Penelope herself, keeping her suitors suspended by the stratagem of weaving and unweaving, while the suitors act like swine, is clearly a subtler or displaced counterpart of Circe, whose spells turn men *into* swine. It is perhaps no accident, then, that subsequent tradition tended to conflate or confuse these three female figures—Calypso, Circe, Penelope—since bringing the story to its ending here involves overcoming the implicitly female body of the romance narrative itself. We might remember, by way of parenthesis, that in Roland Barthes the properly narrative desire to reach an ending and the properly hermeneutic desire to penetrate a text's meaning are countered by the desire to linger or dilate. In Ariosto's *Orlando furioso*, a Renaissance text remarkable for its metafictional sophistication in these matters, one of the principal figures for ending is the overcoming of an enchantress who recalls both Circe and the Whore of Babylon; stripping her bare is termed "reading her pages" in the way they should be read.[9]

It is easy to move from this second subtext to the third—Virgil's influential *Aeneid*—because it is the latter's combination of Odyssean or romance dilatoriness with Iliadic or epic haste which makes it the progenitor of so many Renaissance hybrids, or epic-romances. Virgil's poem, moreover, seems almost to be commenting, in what we would now call self-reflexive fashion, on the differing tendencies and gender associations of both epic and romance: the resolutely teleological drive of epic in its repeated injunctions to "break off delay" (*rumpe moras*) and the Odyssean or romance delaying tactics which make it the long poem it is and which disrupt or postpone the end promised from the beginning. Once again, it is the female figures—Dido, Allecto, Amata, Juno (and their agents)—who are the chief perpetrators of delay and even of obstructionism in relation to the master or imperial project of the completion of the text. Jupiter, the text's meta-authorial presence, is also the guarantor or at least the Olympic patron of ultimate closure.

By making the *Aeneid* a principal subtext of his romance *Cymbeline*, Shakespeare provides an implicit reading of Virgil's poem in precisely such terms. In *Cymbeline* the Queen, like Juno in the *Aeneid*, can delay the fated ending but cannot indefinitely forestall or finally alter it; and a character representing Jupiter descends from the meta-authorial skies in that play's final act to announce why the promised ending has been so long deferred, which is to say, in view of this romance play's massively complicated movement to its own point of revelation or recognition scene, why the play itself has lasted as long as it has.

These influential texts—and their female obstructors—already, then, forge a link between such female figures and the extension or dilation of the text in order to defer its end or "point." But the even more specific link we need to explore before moving on to particular dilated *bodies* in a number of Renaissance and other texts is the rhetorical tradition of the dilation of discourse, and specifically its dilation through "partition," through the multiplication of partitions or rhetorical dividing walls. It is this towards which we need to turn before focusing on the identification of such dilation with corpulent bodies of various kinds, and the significance of their appearance in particular texts.

Erasmus's *De Copia* is here the readiest source not just for this rhetorical tradition but for its dual concerns. The preoccupation of this massively influential text is not only how to expand a discourse—to make its "matter" or *materia* respond to the rhetorical counterpart of the command to Adam and Eve to "increase and multiply"—but also how to control that expansion, to keep dilation from getting out of bounds, a concern repeated in the countless Renaissance rhetorical handbooks which both teach their pupils how to amplify and repeatedly warn them against the intimately related vice of "Excesse" (the same name, we might remember, as Spenser's dilating "Dame"). Dilation, then, is always something to be kept within the horizon of ending, mastery, and control, and the "matter" is always to be varied within certain formal guidelines or rules.

The rhetorical figure of walls or partitions, from that part of Cicero's *Topics* where a discussion of physical "walls" is juxtaposed with a definition of oratorical "partition," involves the dividing of a discourse, like a body, into "members"—a tradition which Shakespeare reveals he knows only too well when, in the Pyramus and Thisbe play of *A Midsummer Night's Dream*, he has Demetrius punningly call the mechanical playing the character of Wall the "wittiest partition that ever I heard discourse" (V. i. 161–8).[10] In the related art of preaching, the principal method of proceeding was to divide and open up a closed or difficult scriptural text so that it might "increase and multiply," be dilated upon by the preacher so as to dilate and spread abroad the Word. In the words of Donne, summing up the entire tradition of the *ars praedicandi*, "Through partition or division, the Word of God is made a Sermon, that is, a Text is dilated, diffused into a Sermon." And this rhetorical dilation by partition was to be used by preachers of the Word in precisely that period of the "dilation of Christendome" before Apocalypse, before the final apocalyptic end both of that "wall of partition" spoken of in Ephesians (2:14) and of discourse itself.[11]

This tradition of rhetorical *dilatio*—with its references to the "swelling" style or its relation to the verbal "interlarding" produced through an excessive application of the principle of "increase"—provides its own links between fat bodies and discoursing "at large," between the size of a discourse and the question of body size. Ascham's *Schoolmaster* treats of the use of "epitome" in reducing the inflated bulk of an oration through the example of the need to put an "overfat" and "fleshy" style on a diet, as Cicero himself did in order to rid himself of "grossness." Though fat is not gendered as female in this passage from Ascham, it most definitely is in anti-Ciceronian contrastings of a more effeminate Ciceronian or Asiatic style—linked with "bignesse" as well as prodigality—to the more virile Attic. Erasmus's *Ciceronianus* (1528) speaks of seeking in vain in Ciceronian eloquence for something "masculine" and of his own desire for a "more masculine" style. Ciceronian *copia* in these discussions is both effeminate and the style of a more prodigal youth, to be outgrown once one had become a man: "I used to imitate [Cicero]," writes Lipsius; "but I have become a man, and my tastes have changed. Asiatic feasts have ceased to please me; I prefer the Attic." A similar contrast, with the appropriate shift of symbolic locus, informs the opposition of fat and effeminating Egypt to lean and virile Rome in Shakespeare's *Antony and Cleopatra*.[12]

This specifically rhetorical tradition of amplified textuality and dilated middles is joined by and easily combined with a whole host of other resonances of "dilation" in the Renaissance, which we can only briefly touch on here, but must at least mention, since they too figure frequently in the imaging of postponed ending or "increase" in the texts of our exemplary fat ladies. One is the Neoplatonic tradition of *dilatio* as the dilation or Emanation of Being, its procession out from and its crucial return to the Source or One. For not only is this one Western example among many of what Derrida repeatedly wants to distinguish from "différance" (since deferral or dilation in this tradition is contained within the horizon of ending, a simple detour between Origin and End); it also provides Spenser with the crucial authority for the final "putting downe" of the upstart Goddess Mutabilitie (as well as the specter of endlessness, perhaps) by Jupiter's female agent Nature, who has clearly been reading her Ficino. A second, related meaning is as a synonym for temporality, for the mediate or earthly as distinguished from the eternal, simultaneous, or immediate—hence the easy identification of dilation, as of the female, with the body of both time and the world, or creation itself. A third is the sense of dilation as the puffing up of pride, as in the warning in an English translation of Erasmus's *Adages* that "we dylate not our selves beyond our condition and state," or the "dilation" of Satan, progenitor of sin, in Milton's *Paradise Lost* ("Collecting all his might dilated stood"; IV. 986).[13]

Still another use of "dilation" occurs in the context of propagation or generation, the postponing of death through natural increase, one of the principal arguments against the premature closure of virginity and a meaning crucial to the potential identification of the rhetorical tradition of "increase and multiply" with the more fruitful dilation of another kind of "fat lady"—the pregnant female body, promising even as it contains and postpones the appearance of an "issue." The generational joins the rhetorical and hermeneutic here through the fact that the command to "increase and multiply" which stands behind this kind of dilation ("Two joyned can themselves dilate") has its rhetorical counterpart in the tradition of the copia of discourse. Augustine in the *Confessions* has a whole chapter devoted to "increase and multiply" (XIII. xxiv) in the sense of the interpreter's opening and fruitful extension of a closed or hermetic scriptural text, what the rhetorical tradition would call "dilating or enlarging of a matter by interpretation." But this "matter" and its enlarging also easily joined with *mater*. Obstetrical descriptions in the Renaissance frequently start with a reminder of the divine command to "increase and multiply" and see the "mouth" of the *matrix* or womb as "an orifice at the entrance into the which may be dilated and shut." Dilation as the "opening" of a closed text to make it "increase and multiply" and to transform its brevity into a discourse "at large," then, joins dilation as both sexual and obstetrical "opening" and the production of generational increase.[14]

There are, to complete this Renaissance catalogue, two other signal contexts for dilation, which in fact often appear together as figures for the postponed ending of a text. The first is the judicial one—the tradition of Essoins or "dilatory pleas" which Hamlet, in a play very much concerned with postponement or deferral, calls "the law's delay," a means of putting off judgment or execution. Hamlet's complaint against the "law's delay" comes in the middle of the very soliloquy of hesitation or doubt ("To be or not to be"), with both its "consumma-tion / Devoutly to be wish'd" and its hesitation to rush to that conclu-sion. And "dilatory pleas" as a means of putting off an ending easily participate in a crossing of legal with other contexts of judgment or consummation. At the end of Chaucer's *Canterbury Tales*, for example, the Parson, speaking of the apocalyptic "day of doom," describes it as that one "juggement" before which "there availeth noon essoin," a reminder that, in the biblical tradition out of which he speaks, dilation as delay is circumscribed finally by a telos, that the putting off of ending here is finally only temporary. The appearance of such a refer-ence in the Parson's Tale (which has been frequently described as the *Tales*' culminating Book of Apocalypse or Revelation) may suggest retrospectively that all of the impressive *copia* or "God's plenty" of *The Canterbury Tales* up to that ending has been a form of "essoin" or "dilatory plea," including the text of that female figure, the Wife of Bath, whose copious discourse or dilated textual body puts off the Parson's concluding text, who announces "My joly *body* shall a tale tell," whose motto is "increase and multiply," and who herself turns to her own quite different purposes the sermon art of the dilation of discourse. As one recent reading of this excessive "Dame" puts it, Alisoun of Bath ameliorates the harsh polarizations of apocalyptic judgment and eschatology and opens up a space of dilation in which what we have come to call literature can have its place. Her "increase," however, is verbal rather than generational, and from this more judg-mental perspective, as a form of sterility or fruitless activity, it is finally preempted by the teleological framework in which there is no—or no longer—"essoin."[15]

The final context for "dilation" is an erotic one within a specific mas-culinist tradition—the putting off of coitus or consummation which Andreas Capellanus describes as a feminine strategy in the art of love, a purportedly female plot in which holding a suitor at a distance creates the tension of a space between as well as an intervening time. By the time of Eve's "sweet reluctant amorous delay" in Book IV of *Paradise Lost*, "dilation" in this sense was almost a *terminus technicus* for the erotics of prolongation, a tradition still current in Addison's reference to "women of dilatory Tempers, who are for spinning out the Time of Courtship." Its focus on the hymen as a dividing wall or partition, moreover, made it easily conflatable with both the rhetorical tradition of the dilation of discourse by "partition" and the intervening "partition wall" of Ephesians 2. This amorous dilation is a frequent part of the plot of wooing or courtship in Shakespeare, in examples almost too numerous to name. But this plot of feminine dilation or delay is rarely linked, by critics of Shakespeare, with the temporal and rhetorical dilation of the plays themselves, though in *A Midsummer Night's Dream* (to take just one example) the erotic consummation promised in the play's opening scene is deferred for a time and space which coincides with that of the play as a whole and which is achieved only when a "partition" or wall associated both with the hymen and with the rhetorical "partition of discourse" is finally put "down,"[16] just as in *The Comedy of Errors* the wall of partition which prolongs the play's various romance-like "errors" by delaying the final recognition scene is associated with the intervening body of a much-dilated female.

This brings us, then, to our first Renaissance "fat lady," the comically dilated body of the kitchen wench in *The Comedy of Errors*, the early play of Shakespeare that is most closely allied to romance. This play extraordinarily combines the dilation of discourse through partition with the figure of Apocalypse (and what delays it) from Ephesians 2, where the coming of Christ breaks down the "wall of partition" between men, anticipating the final, apocalyptic removal of all walls or partitions. It is, indeed, set in Ephesus. The *Comedy* begins with a dilation or deferral of judgment and execution: Egeon, asked to "dilate at full" (I. i. 122) the narrative of his life, is granted a temporary reprieve from "doom" (I. i. 2) which then becomes the whole space and time of "error" in the play itself, culminating in an extraordinary concentration of allusions to the biblical Apocalypse, to the end, that is to say, of this meantime space of deferral, or *dilatio patriae*. The whole of the play, then, becomes an analogue of a space of dilation which does, however, finally come to an end.

In the play's own middle (the third act out of five), we encounter a wall of partition, which keeps the sets of twins from precipitating too early that final recognition scene and thus putting an end to the errors prematurely at that point. The figure who guards this wall and keeps the partition intact is a wondrous fat lady, the opposite (if we might exploit the play's own highly concentrated biblical echoes) of "Knock, and it shall be opened unto you." She is so fat that she is spherical, like the globe itself: "I could find out countries in her," says Dromio (III. ii. 114–15), as he proceeds to do just that. And she is described in a pun which connects "grease" and "grace"—a tradition that seems to have as one of its origins commentaries such as St Bonaventure's on that "grace" which dilates the heart as "oil" dilates the flesh and that is still going strong as an all too easy English-Irish pun in the washer-women scene of Joyce's *Finnegans Wake*.[17] This "wench" is "swart" like the Bride in the biblical Song of Songs, and decked with comic versions of the precious stones of the New Jerusalem whose Master is to return to his betrothed in the Book of Apocalypse. Her description, in fact, ambiguously combines both female versions of the world at once, recalling both the Whore of Babylon and the redeemed harlot, Rahab, and the Church: the phrase applied to her ("a very reverent body," one of whom it is not permitted to speak without saying "Sir-reverence") nicely applies to both Church and whore. This Circean "witch" (III. ii. 144), however, is also, as the scene puts it, a "wondrous fat marriage." We are reminded that she too awaits the return of her betrothed—an event that will occur with the final return of a figure called earlier, in a clear echo of the New Testament passages on the delay of Apocalypse, a "tardy master" who is "at hand" but not yet come (II. i. 44). This female "mountain of mad flesh" (IV. iv. 154) appears in the midst of a comedy which is itself a "farce" in the etymological sense of fattened or "stuffed." But if her dilated body stands in some sense as a figure for the dilation (and "errors") of *The Comedy of Errors*, she is finally to be referred to her proper Master, or returned "betrothed." Perhaps significantly, then, this fat lady (variously called Luce/loose/"light" and Nell/anell) never clearly appears on stage or is permitted, *in propria persona*, to speak: she is only described in her globe-like rotundity. We might remember in this regard that the other text from Ephesians that is crucial to this play set in Ephesus is "Wives submit unto your husbands," the text of the proper hierarchy of female and male. For the play includes not just echoes of this Pauline and other New Testament passages on that end and marriage, including the apocalyptic marriage which will put an end to error or "harlotry," but repeated play on the proverbial Latin tag *respice finem*, or "look to the End," as it moves from this dilated female figure and her "partition wall" to its own ending.

The question of "fine" or end also dominates our second fat lady—the figure of the pregnant woman, that visually dilated *mater* whom Lisa Jardine has linked, in her massiveness of body or "grossesse," not just with copious fertility but with a threatening female sexuality as well.[18] Here we might consider two Shakespearean instances, both in relation to the question of closure. One is the pregnant "gossip" and votaress whose swelling body, "rich" with its contents, is described by Titania in *A Midsummer Night's Dream*:

> Full often hath she gossip'd by my side,
> And sat with me on Neptune's yellow sands,
> Marking th'embarked traders on the flood;
> When we have laugh'd to see the sails conceive
> And grow big-bellied with the wanton wind;
> Which she, with pretty and with swimming gait,
> Following (her womb then rich with my young squire),
> Would imitate, and sail upon the land
> To fetch me trifles, and return again,
> As from a voyage, rich with merchandise.
> But she, being mortal, of that boy did die.　　(II. i. 125–35)

The passage presents, in C. L. Barber's phrase, a picture of a female-centered world, of "women who gossip alone, apart from men and feeling now no need of them, rejoicing in their own special part of life's power." The pregnant votaress is almost literally an image of dilation or swelling (in the sense, at least, of "Women grow by men," as the Nurse puts it in *Romeo and Juliet*, I. iii. 95). And the "grand" style associated with rhetorical dilation or "swelling" is described by Quintilian in precisely the image used here of swelling sails ("Greek keels, even the little ones, know well their ports; let ours usually travel under fuller sails, with a stronger breeze swelling our canvas").[19] But the votaress is also an image of that dilation as only temporary, ending in an "issue" like all pregnancy or "travail," and in her case even more definitively, in death. In this regard, she figures by metonymy much of what happens to the female—as to a temporary dilation and delay—in *A Midsummer Night's Dream*, which begins with the deferral of consummation, deviates into a topsy-turvy middle space of female rebellion, and ends with the proper marital hierarchy. For the child she bears in her own "big-bellied" body is the changeling which will finally be taken away from Titania when that unruly and separatist female—holding off from her own master's bed—is finally mastered by Oberon and this "issue" passes from the world of the mother to that of the father.[20] What, then, in Barber's phrase, might have seemed an autonomous female-centered world turns out to have been only a dilative detour en route to that end, like pregnancy itself in the patriarchal economy enunciated by Theseus in which it is the father who provides the imprinting form ("To you your father should be as a god; / One that compos'd your beauties; yea, and one / To whom you are but as a form in wax, / By him imprinted," I. i. 47–50). Like the dilative copia of the entire play, ending when the hymen or partition preserving another kind of female separateness is finally "down," the swelling of the pregnant or "big-bellied" votaress is only *pro tempore*.

The other Shakespearean "fat lady" in this regard—as a dilative means to a patriarchal end—might be the "Doctor She" of *All's Well That Ends Well*, a play whose teleological title belies the fact that it too depends upon extension and delay, upon the opening of a space both for a female plot and for what its character of "Parolles" ("many words" rather than one) calls a "more *spacious* ceremony" and "more *dilated* farewell" (II. i. 50–7). The play right from its beginning links the generative imperative to "increase and multiply"—the generation of issue through the inflation or "blowing up" of virgins (I. i. 119ff.)—with the putting off of ending through the increase of a copious supply of intermediate words (II. ii). Making the champion of the former and representative of the latter kind of "increase" or "blowing up" the character of Parolles or "words" draws attention to the extending of the play itself, which depends not only on such intermediate *paroles* but on the "putting off" of erotic consummation (II. iv. 43; IV. ii. 34; V. iii. 212–17) and on a series of such displacing farewells. The fact that the play does finally reach an end, if a famously problematic one, provides in gross a repetition of the structure of that smaller scene within it devoted to the theme of "putting off" through words (II. ii), which ends with "things may serve long, but not serve ever" (II. ii. 58–9).

The space opened up to "increase" between the heavy sense of ending at the beginning of *All's Well* and its final end or "fine" is the space of a particular female plot: the working of Helena, the heroine and "Doctor She" whose conversion of her husband's seemingly final "sentence" or doom (III. ii. 61) into her own version of "increase and multiply" in the bed-trick finally makes her pregnant according to the demand. In the language of the whole comic scene on "putting off"—which finally, however, does come to an end—Helena's accomplishment of this "increase" and her pregnancy as the answer to the play's concluding riddles makes her its female embodiment of that "bountiful answer that fits all questions" (II. ii. 15) or that "answer of most monstrous size that must fit all demands" (II. ii. 32–3). Her dilated body—"blown up" on the same night as the merely inflated or puffed-up Parolles is deflated or blown down—is the fulfillment of the whole opening exchange between them on the subject of "increase." But, even in a play which seems to give a space to the achievement of a woman whose pregnancy is the sign of her triumph and achievement, this very "increase" has again to do with the production of an "issue," and with the winning of a recalcitrant husband, to whom the heroine then willingly submits. His noble family expands or extends itself just far enough to contain the exogamous detour her inclusion represents.

The other obvious Shakespearean "fat lady" is ostensibly no lady at all—old Jack Falstaff, whose corpulence, in the *Henriad*, in some sense embodies Prince Hal's delay, a Prodigal Son plot in which the completed movement of reformation and return to the father takes not one but two long and prodigally copious plays to effect. This "hill of flesh" (*1H4*, II. iv. 243) "lards the lean earth as he walks along" (*1H4*, II. ii. 109). But he is even more tellingly imaged in the series of hierarchized oppositions we have already encountered. His fat body is specifically a "*globe* of sinful continents" (*2H4*, II. iv. 285). The second and completing half of the two plays also evokes in both comic and more serious contexts that "Jordan" to be crossed before entrance into the Promised Land, before its own culminating "Jerusalem." It is, we remember, the Chief Justice, representative of both the father and the Law he evades, who warns Falstaff that his "waste"—manifested in his expanding waist—is "great" (*2H4*, I. ii. 141). And the Hal who from the beginning of the two extended plays forecasts to the audience that his own tarrying and prodigality, with this "fat rogue" and the other "tattered prodigals," will be of only a "holiday" or temporary nature, ends that promise of reformation with an echo of the text in Ephesians on redeeming the time ("Redeeming time when men think least I will"; *1H4*, I. ii. 217), leaving Falstaff with the other "Ephesians" or "boon companions" as the counterpart of the unredeemed Ephesus before the "partition" between Old and New is crossed.[21]

Falstaff in these plays, as Hal puts it, is "my sweet creature of bumbast" (*1H4*, II. iv. 327) in both punning senses—the padding that stuffs a body out and its verbal equivalent. His fat is linked not just with "harlotry" (*2H4*, II. iv. 41)—including perhaps that of Mistress Quickly's malapropped "harlotry players" (*1H4*, II. iv. 395)—but with verbal *copia* as well, with that "throng of words" (*2H4*, II. i. 112) which, even in these two prodigally copious plays, "cannot," as Falstaff says of himself, "last forever" (*2H4*, I. ii. 214). Falstaff's own decision to repent his wasted life (with more punning on his expanded waist or girth) is, we might note, accompanied by references to his dwindling size, as if this movement to closure, reformation, and repentance involved a literal relation between the body of this prodigal play and its physically fat emblem (*1H4*, III. iii. 1–2: "Bardolph, am I not fall'n away vilely since this last action? Do I not bate? Do I not dwindle?").

Falstaff himself is, of course, not a woman but a man. But he actually appears as a fat lady in *The Merry Wives of Windsor*. When he does, in a scene of transvestitism which perhaps suggests what Fal-staff has all along been missing, explicit embodiment is given to his effeminate associations throughout the other plays in which he figures. Here, as a "fat woman," he takes refuge in the chamber associated with an "Ephesian" Host (IV. v. 18) and "painted about with the story of the Prodigal" (IV. v. 7–8). And the play links references to "Fat Falstaff" with figures of "mirth . . . so larded with . . . matter" and of recounting "at large" (IV. vi. 14–18). In *Henry IV, Parts 1* and *2*, fat itself is compared to the image of the pregnant earth, filled with wind (Falstaff punningly attributes his great size to his "sighs" or wind). Falstaff's fat is repeatedly associated with the copiousness or dilation of discourse, with avoiding the summons of the law through various counterparts of the "dilatory plea," and with the wombs and tongues of women ("I have a whole school of tongues in this belly of mine, and not a tongue of them all speaks any other word but my name. . . . My womb, my womb, my womb undoes me"; *2H4*, IV. iii. 18–23).

But his expanded "waste" is a womb which in a sense never delivers the "issue" and which is therefore left behind in what, after all, is the drama of a return to the father, or genealogical succession. Falstaff's belly full of tongues links him, as do his tavern hostesses, Mistress Quickly and Doll Tearsheet, with the proverbially unstoppable female tongue. But Hal, in his only temporary prodigality and delay, merely "studies his companions / Like a strange tongue," in order to master or "gain the language," so, "like gross terms" (with Falstaff visibly the grossest), he can "cast" them "off" in "the perfectness of time" (*2H4*, IV. iv. 68–78).[22] If, in seasonal terms, Falstaff's fatness suggests the autumnal plenty of "martlemas" before the coming of winter (*2H4*, II. ii. 97), in genealogical and political terms, he is, together with the languages or "tongues" to be gained by the young prince, finally a sign of the prodigiousness and teleology of mastery. Though technically androgynous, Falstaff ends up, in this movement to kingship which banishes and effectively "kills" him, subject to that law of categorization in which, in relation to the exclusively male, even the androgyne remains on the side of the female. And "banish plump Jack, and banish all the world" (*1H4*, II. iv. 479–80) leaves fat Falstaff, in relation to the fabled leanness of a king descended from a "John of *Gaunt*," in the same textual space, so to speak, in this movement to ending, as that of the globular Nell in *The Comedy of Errors*.

As the "fat woman of Brainford" (*Wives*, IV. ii. 75), Falstaff is not only a harlot or "quean" but a Circean "witch" as well (IV. ii. 172). The fact, however, that this figure associated both with "fat" and with a Ciceronian copia of words is not actually female but effeminized male is in itself revealing. The gendered oppositions at work here—the ones that produced another Renaissance text entitled "Women are words, men deeds," which goes on to treat not of wordy women but of the monstrous third possibility of wordy men, including by implication what Greene called the "babbling" of poets—are by no means stable.[23] The opposition male/female often masks anxieties surrounding the figure of the feminized or effeminate male, just as in the misogynist diatribes against the female tongue the generative power inhabiting and generating the very discourse of misogyny often becomes the female loquacity which is its animating subject.

Male anxiety about the feminization of the verbal body and *copia* of a text which delays arrival at its own point or ending is by no means restricted to the images hovering around the figure of the fat, and transvestite, Falstaff. Dilatory, fat Falstaff, that "globe of sinful continents," and Hamlet, that "distracted globe," both appear in plays whose evocations of Apocalypse call to mind the end of the "globe" itself. Critics recoil, as Maurice Charney observes, from the notion of a corpulent Hamlet, though the slender Burbage who had earlier played Prince Hal was considerably fatter by the time he played the Prince of Denmark, and though there may be more than sweat, inactivity, or indolence involved in Gertrude's reference to her disturbingly prodigal son as "fat, and scant of breath" (V. ii. 287ff.) in the duelling scene. To propose the soliloquizing prince as a fat *lady* would presumably be even more repugnant. Yet some of the same figures—including the traditional association between wordiness and idleness, or the meaning of *dilatio* as melancholic *tarditas*—are clearly operating in this other play in the Shakespeare canon which matches the *Henriad* for sheer copiousness and length, and in which fat is associated explicitly with delay ("the fat weed / That roots itself in ease on Lethe wharf," I. v. 32–3ff).[24] Hamlet compares his own delay and Polonius- or Osric-like wordiness to the impotence and proverbial wordiness of the harlot or whore in one of the many soliloquies castigating himself for "tardiness" (III. iv. 106) in bringing his task to completion ("I . . . / Must like a whore unpack my heart with words, / And fall a-cursing like a very drab," II. ii. 583–6). We might also remember that it is the impotent Polonius who ironically utters the anti-Ciceronian formula "Brevity is the soul of wit" in a scene where he is incapable of bringing his narrative to a point or "consequence" (II. i. 51); or that the kind of effeminate wordiness associated with the courtier Osric is in a similar context in the *Henriad* specifically referred to as indulgence in "holiday and *lady* terms" (*1H4*, I. iii. 46).

In the traditional opposition of genders in which "Women are words, men deeds," Hamlet's comparison of his verbal and deedless delay to the impotent anger of a "drab" sets up a link between his entire period of inactivity and delay and womanish wordiness, in contrast to such one-dimensional emblems of masculinity as Laertes and the aptly named Fort-in-bras. It may be such subtle linkages within the play that Joyce picked up when he incorporated into *Ulysses* the theory that Hamlet was in fact a woman as well as a production of the play with an actress in the role, or that still enable it to be a question, in contemporary productions, of whether Hamlet is predominantly masculine or feminine—Richard Burton's virile or John Neville's effeminate prince. In a plot movement which recasts the political teleology of the *Henriad* in a more tragic key, the Hamlet who can in his delaying phase only like a "whore" unpack his heart with words incorporates ultimately both dilatory Falstaff and the leaner Hal, who in his movement to kingship asserts control over the tongues and styles he has mastered. For at the point of the famous turn in the later play when the Prince of Denmark tells of his revised commission, sending Rosencrantz and Guildenstern to their deaths under the king's seal, there are brought into focus three such purposeful and end-directed messages: the "dilated articles" (I. ii. 38) of the reigning king's earlier commission sent to put an "end" to a troublesome business (II. ii. 85); that same Claudius's second commission to the King of England "*Larded* with many several sorts of reasons" (V. ii. 20) but controlled by the telos of a particular message or point; and finally, in a marked turn from his earlier delay, the revised commission in which Hamlet too now masters the techniques of dilation used to "interlard" a more pointed purpose or end (V. ii. 38–43)—an act which prompts Horatio's ambiguous "Why, what a king is this!" (V. ii. 62).[25] Undirected and pointless dilation, without "consequence"—the feminized Hamlet impotent to do more than utter "words, words, words." (II. ii. 192)— yields finally, that is to say, to a sense of an ending which gives us in the emblematic form of a duelling scene the literal and fatal "point" which puts an end to all.

There is one final fat lady we will consider here, not from Shakespeare, but rather from Ben Jonson. Jonson signals his own familiarity with the tradition of rhetorical dilation and its link with the extending of time in an evocatively bad pun in the Cary-Morison Ode, about a character whose life was simply undistinguished temporization or prolongation ("What did this stirrer," he asks, but "*die late?*").[26] The Jonsonian fat lady I wish to exhibit is the pig woman Ursula from *Bartholomew Fair* (1614), who stands in some sense as a symbol for the fatness of the Fair and its fabled "enormities," and thus also by extension for the world, and whose associations with swine make her part of the sisterhood of Circe (as well as another instance of the prodigality of the Prodigal Son). As the Schoolmaster in this play says to the play's own Prodigal Son, who only too enthusiastically would get lost in the Fair's "enormities," this fat woman is "all vanity": "The fleshly woman (which you call Ursula) is above all to be avoided, having the marks upon her of the three enemies of man, the world as being in the Fair; the devil, as being in the fire; and the flesh, as being herself" (III. vi. 30–3). She is not only fat but perpetually in heat, and her body seems to image not just this gross animal sexuality, but its female original in Eve. "I am all fire and fat," she herself is made to say; "I shall e'en melt away to the first woman, a rib again" (II. ii. 46–8)—as if she were a kind of latter-day, much-expanded version of the initial "enormity" brought into the world by Adam's rib and dilated through the principle of "increase and multiply," which also applies (as Donne notes in one of his sermons) to sin, or the body of Leviathan. Like Falstaff, indeed, she is very like a whale ("They'll kill the poor whale and make oil of her"; II. v. 114–15).[27]

Ursula's enormity thus makes her a principal target of the judgment in this play of a character fittingly called "Adam" Overdo, whose first name links him explicitly to the founding father, and who, like Christ, promises to appear at the Second Coming, in a version of the Last Judgment. Her booth at the fair—"the very womb and bed of enormity"—recalls the traditional stage entrance to Hell in the Moralities. The "pig" she is coterminous with revives an ancient slang term in Latin and in Greek for the female genitals. As the "sow of enormity" (V. vi. 51) in a play full of gaps and holes, she is "the celebrant of the open orifice," both gaping mouth and womb.[28] Her grossness is more than once an object of misogynist fantasy, of the fear that in this "quagmire" or "bog" a man "might sink . . . and be drowned a week, ere any friend he had could find where he were" (II. v. 83–5). In a play whose copia is generated by the increase and multiplication of vernaculars or mother tongues, the implicit "Hail Ursula full of grease" which hovers around the figure of this "mother," whose pigs are symbols not just of female sexuality but of birth, makes her, as a daughter of Eve, a kind of profane or "harlot" counterpart to Eve's corrective, Mother of God.

As with Shakespeare's Nell, her grease punningly echoes grace (there is, indeed, another female character in the play whose name *is* "Grace" and who is Adam's to bestow), and as with Nell her dilation is linked with the dilation, or copiousness, of discourse: her language is said to be "greasier" than her pigs. She is, however, also joined in this by her overbearing judges, and their own tendency to verbal dilation or rhetorical amplitude—by the Schoolmaster's bloated speech, filled with classic instances of *amplificatio*; by Rabbi Busy, whose repetitious rhetoric evokes the notorious dilation of the often seemingly endless Puritan sermon; and by Adam "Overdo" himself, whose oratorical style, with his fatuously rotund circumlocutions, explicitly recalls all of the traditional excesses of rhetorical amplitude.[29] This Jonsonian fat lady, that is, appears in a play whose own verbal copia is generated from representatives of both the *ars praedicandi* and the Ciceronian rhetorical tradition.

In a sense, neither fat Ursula nor her attackers in this play (who also include the figure of Puritan attackers on the "enormities" of the plays and the stage) emerges unscathed. But what is interesting here, again, is that the fat lady in question is brought under control as the play itself proceeds—a movement associated explicitly with the shrinking of Ursula's body size (as in "I'll stay the end of her now; I know she cannot last long; I find by her similes she wanes apace," II. v. 122–3). Like the greatly expanded body of the play itself—generated in characteristically ambivalent Jonsonian fashion by the puffing up of pride, as by variations on the refrain of increase and "multiply ye," and an extremely varied yet masterfully controlled matter or *materia*—this particular *mater* ("mother of the pigs," "mother of the bodies," and "Body of the Fair") cannot last forever. Reminiscent both of Virgil's female discord Allecto and of the fat *Mère* of Mardi Gras or "Fat Tuesday" before it yields to the leanness of Lent.[30] This carnivalesque Discordia, large as the play itself, yields ultimately to a more austere shaping; and a "Jordan" of passing—like Falstaff's, a pisspot—is once again associated with her dwindling.

Rabbi Busy, in the end, is finally put down by the puppet Dionysius, whose name recalls the patron of theaters. The extreme representative of Puritan opposition to the theaters is put in his place by a puppet in a gesture which seems a kind of grotesque version of the biblical prophecy that in the Apocalypse or final Recognition Scene of history there will be neither male nor female, whatever the more hierarchical relation of the sexes in the meantime ("It is your old stale argument against the players, but it will not hold against the puppets; for we have neither male nor female amongst us," V. vi. 88–90). Dionysius pulls up his garments to reveal that puppets are innocent because they are sexless, a transformation into the language of gender of Sir Philip Sidney's earlier defense of poetry as that which neither "affirmeth" nor "lieth." And yet Ursula herself, whatever carnivalesque overturning she has occasioned, is finally subordinated within a hierarchy which still ends with an "Adam," even though he has been counseled to leave his other name of "Overdo," and to invite one and all to a slightly more chastened feast, neither the leanness of the Puritan nor the enormity of the Fair. In the Apocalypse there may be neither male nor female, but here the hierarchy of the middle or mean-time is one that is only too familiar: the play's *copia* is controlled, at last, and it ends with an address to the judgment and authority of the king, ruler and patriarch at once.

One of the chief concerns of the tradition that portrays women as unflappable talkers is how to master or contain such feminine mouthing. In the different terms we have traced, this control of female speech resembles the provision of shaping and closure to the potentially endless movement of dilation or, in the specific case of the fat lady who is the only temporarily dilated, pregnant woman, the production of an issue within a patriarchal economy of increase. The supposed copiousness of the female tongue, epitomized in the admission of Shakespeare's Rosalind ("I am a woman . . . I must speak"),[31] or in the open mouth of Mopsa in Sidney's *Arcadia* ("her mouth O heav'nly wide!"), has its textual counterpart in the danger of losing the thread of a discourse and never being able to finish what was begun, the specter of endlessness or inability to come to a point which hovers around the edges of all these characterizations of a female speech as "penelopes webb . . . [that] never makes an end."[32] A Renaissance text actually called *Penelope's Web*,[33] by Robert Greene, is literally generated out of the "prattle" of Penelope's garrulous Nurse and her maids ("setting their hands to the Web, and their eares to hir talke," p. 62) as their nightly untwisting of this famous unfinished textile makes the labor of weaving potentially "endlesse" (p. 194) and defers indefinitely the moment of choosing among the suitors. Their "endlesse Web" is finally abandoned only at the point of the return of the absent master Ulysses, when their "discourse" is at the same time "broken off" (p. 233) and when, in dialectical fashion, the "foolish prattle" (p. 208) or female chatter which had provided up to this point the generative power of the text is ended on the night dedicated to the wifely virtue of "Silence."

Female speech or mouthing, however, is not only in this misogynist tradition the representative of the infuriating opposite of Silence but—as with the two orifices with which we began—inseparable from the vice opposed to the corresponding virtue of Chastity, as both are ranged against Obedience. Not only is the link between garrulity and unbridled sexuality expressed in such utterances as the husband's complaining "I could neither governe her tongue, nor—" in the anonymous *Curtaine Lecture* (1637) devoted to the fabled talkativeness of women; but the extremes of the effort of containment are traceable in such instances as the figure of *Garrulitas* in emblem books like Alciati's or Whitney's (the violated Procne/Philomel seen as a woman who, even with her tongue cut out, managed somehow to tell her tale),[34] or the instrument of containment and discipline known as the brank or "Scold's Bridle" (Figure 1), quite clearly, in what it encloses and restricts, a kind of chastity belt for the tongue.

It is this question—of a feminine speech potentially out of control, and of a linking of these two female orifices—which brings us finally to our last partition: the question of the Genitive or "Jinny's case" and the Vocative, or the story of "O," the figure whose shape brings us back full circle to the fat ladies of our title. Both figures—genitive and vocative—are suggested by a single scene from Shakespeare's *Merry Wives of Windsor* (IV. i), the same play in which Falstaff appears as a fat woman and is roundly cast out. It is a strange (and to the rest of the play seemingly irrelevant) scene of grammatical instruction, in which the mother of a schoolboy asks that her son be put through his lessons by the schoolmaster; and it is an exchange in which it is very much a question of the relation between humanism (with its pedagogical economy of men and boys)[35] and an extravagantly errant female speech, the female in question here being that seemingly

FIG. 1. Scold's bridle

270

irrepressible producer of malapropisms, Mistress Quickly, a garrulous old woman and the play's principal go-between.

The subject of "case" is present in this scene throughout, as one would expect in a lesson on grammar,[36] but "Jinny's case" occurs only when Mistress Quickly gives evidence of a particularly improper misunderstanding of the lesson she witnesses from the outside. "What is your genitive case plural, William?" asks the schoolmaster, and William dutifully replies, in the lesson's properly catechistic mode, "Genitive case . . . *horum, harum, horum*" (IV. i. 59–61). "Vengeance of Jinny's case! Fie on her!" breaks in Mistress Quickly. "Never name her, child, if she be a whore." "Genitive case," in Quickly's mistranslation, slides into "Jinny's case," the case of the "Virginia"/"Jinny"/"Jenny" who is the feminine counterpart of "Jack," simply the stock name of the female. And "case" clearly (here, as elsewhere in Shakespeare, or in Freud, in the "Theme of the Three Caskets," or in female "cases" of various kinds) is the code term for female genitalia, as in our contemporary slang phrase "the family jewels." "Case" is also linked elsewhere in Shakespeare with the legal case, as when Cloten in *Cymbeline*, mounting his attack on the seemingly inviolate Imogen, determines "I will make / One of her women lawyer to me, for / I yet not understand the case myself" (II. iii. 73–5). In other words, in order finally to understand that case (a familiar enough pun in Shakespeare's bawdy), he will find himself a female go-between, thus opening up a space or plot which might link the pursuit of such a "case" to the legal and erotic language of the dilatory plea.

"Case," however, is also never far from the question of romance, in a literary as well as an erotic sense; and when we come upon the observation, in Helgerson's *Elizabethan Prodigals*, that "Humanism inhabited the masculine and misogynistic world of school and state; romance 'had rather to be shut in a lady's casket,'"[37] we might begin to see some link between Quickly's errors and the characteristic errancy of romance as the humanists' particular version of Pandora's Box. We have already remarked the tension between humanism and the enticements both of women and of romance. Both work directly on the will, leading a young man into wanton living. It may be no accident, then, that the schoolboy in this very scene from *Merry Wives* bears Shakespeare's own name of "Will" (indeed, in a play which calls attention elsewhere to textuality, "Will Page"); for the school here is on a holiday, and the boy in this impromptu scene of masterly instruction is, one senses, very much a potential Prodigal Son. The focus of the lesson is the humanist pedagogical method of a fixed system of translation—out of Latin into English and then from English back into Latin again (it is, indeed, her inability to comprehend the Latin of the lesson that leads to Mistress Quickly's errant "Jinny's case").[38] But when "will" appears earlier in this same play, not as proper name but as the potentially vagrant faculty itself, it is also in a context of translation: "He hath studied her will, and translated her will—out of honesty into English" (I. iii. 49–50). It is English, the vernacular or "mother" tongue, which here (outrageously, as the vehicle of Mistress Quickly) tempts Will into a kind of lazy vagrancy, into a prodigality of synonyms or sideways sliding from English to yet more English (synonyms being also one of the principal means of verbal dilation), in lines in which Will is only at the schoolmaster's sharp reproof brought back to Latin or the *sermo patrius*. "What is *lapis*, William?" asks the schoolmaster, expecting the dutiful return of the translated back into its paternal origin or father tongue. "A pebble," replies William, sliding laterally out of honesty into the sexual double entendre which is the province of the untutored Mistress Quickly herself.

"Jinny's case," nowhere mentioned in the humanist grammars, is thus in some sense here the "mother tongue." Mistress Quickly's case—described elsewhere as "so openly known to the world" (*2H4*, II. i. 31)—is generative, through both the vagaries of her indefatigable mouth and her uneducated female ear. Indeed, Jinny's case (to adopt a punning line from *Cymbeline*) is to have a "vice" (but also, punningly, a potentially different "voice") in her "ear," which interrupts or transforms the message, just as Quickly, ignorant of the master tongue, can only mangle or deform it.

"Jinny's case," in this scene from *Merry Wives*, would thus appear to be subversive of the entire system of instruction, a dangerous supplement to the closed humanist economy of "translation." And yet, like the genitive case itself, it remains enclitic or dependent on something else. The genitive (despite or perhaps because of its associations with both gender and the generative) is always grammatically related to another, "as source, possessor, or the like," says the *OED*.[39] And the case of Jinny here (*horum, harum, horum*) is also to belong to another. Mistress Quickly both interrupts and ultimately defers to the Master. When Quickly herself pronounces "Vengeance of Jinny's case!" it is not clear—precisely because of the ambiguous grammatical construction—whether this vengeance is a vengeance of Jinny's case *on* something else or a plague on Jinny's own case. In the familiar misogynist tradition with which we began, the genitive/generative space of female speech or loquaciousness is traditionally often simply nagging, or at least some form of pursuit of a "master" ear, and like the dilation of textuality is still from this perspective dependent on that end. Thomas Greene points out, in an essay which argues against the anachronistic reading of an endless Derridean "différance" into Renaissance texts, that it is precisely dilation or dissemination *without* return to a source which haunted Erasmus and the humanists who followed his magisterial example.[40] Copia is to be controlled, and one wonders if this final closing of the case, so to speak, might relate as well to the enclosure of the dilated textual bodies we have had occasion to treat. "Jinny's case" is always possessed by something it depends upon; and old woman Quickly remains throughout not just a deviant and loquaciously digressive female but (like the character who is literally a "Page" in this play) simply an instrument or go-between.

This brings us finally to the story of "O," which appears in this same scene of Quickly's aberrant translations, and which as a figure of both open mouth and open female "case" already appears in the mouth of Quickly's counterpart, the garrulous Nurse of *Romeo and Juliet* ("O, he is even in my mistress' case, / Just in her case. . . . / Stand up, stand up, stand, and you be a man. / For Juliet's sake, for her sake, rise and stand; / Why should you fall into so deep an O?"; III. iii. 84–90). The story of "O" in Shakespeare, as in other Renaissance texts, is one which includes both a round space (like the world) and a zero or nothing—including that "nothing" which lies "between maid's legs," as Hamlet puts it (*Hamlet*, III. ii. 119–21). "What is the focative case, William?" asks the old schoolmaster in the scene of instruction from *Merry Wives*, thus by his own Welshing of English sliding into the vernacular as into the obscene. "O—*vocativo*, O," replies William, hesitatingly suspended for lack of an immediate answer in the father tongue—only to be reminded by this parody humanist that "focative is *caret*." "*Caret*" in this mangled Latin means "is missing." But Quickly's ear hears the everyday garden-variety "carrot" and hastens to pronounce it a "good root," obscenely transferring the Latin "is missing" into the slang for penis, but also echoing an earlier scene when the Latin *pauca verba* (or "few words") is also translated into the vegetative tongue, as "Good worts" (I. i. 121). If "few words" are valued as "good words," then the feminine mouth which produces by contrast a throng of words is the kind of copiousness produced by this "nothing," the copious "O" produced by that female deficiency or lack.

The sexual double entendres for what is missing here are clearly too tangled for the present occasion to follow through to their enticing conclusions, but in the context William's "O" is not only an unwitting *example* of the vocative, and clearly related somehow to the female space designated throughout as "oman" (rather than as "woman"), but also schoolboy Will Page's hesitation or delaying of the required answer: "O" here, that is to say, designates (and unwittingly fills by embodying) that seemingly empty space of stalling for time with a figure ("O") which elsewhere in Shakespeare variously figures the globe (this "little O, th' earth," in *Antony and Cleopatra*), a "nothing" or cipher (in *King Lear*), and the space of playing, the round globe of the stage itself (as in the "wooden O" of the Prologue to *Henry V*).

The vocative, or apostrophe, remarks Jonathan Culler in the course of a well-known essay on the subject, is associated with mouthing and with voice (and with poetry itself, perhaps, as in Auden's "poetry is / A way of happening, a mouth").[41] But it is also frequently a subject of embarrassment, a temporary turning from which one might want to turn away in turn. "Apostrophes are forbidden on the funicular," writes Wallace Stevens, in a line Culler uses for the epigraph for his essay, presumably because there is, on the funicular, no turning back. "Apostrophes are vorbidden in the vernacular," we might malaprop this line, falling in with the errant language of Mistress Quickly. The figure of "O" which figures the open mouth or the voice—the figure of the vocative which Culler describes as so frequently "repressed or excluded"—may be our final mouthy fat lady, at least in a story of "O" in which that space finally does come to an ending. The Page, as we noted, is one of the several bearers of messages, or go-betweens, in *Merry Wives*, a play which repeatedly calls attention to textuality and puns on the name of the veiled Mistress Page.[42] And the schoolboy *Will* Page, after all, in this scene—when temporarily caught out, at a loss to finish the lesson of the Master—produces in embarrassment a stalling "O," whose principal invocation or call is a call for (more) time.

POSTSCRIPTUM

Since [women] have such a copia verborum, or plenty of words, it is a pity they should not put it to some use.

(Addison, 1713)

Censor the body and you censor breath and speech at the same time . . . More body, hence more writing.

(Hélène Cixous)

In the texts we have looked at, the dilation and control of a copiousness figured as female might at the highest level of generalization be
seen as the gendered counterpart of what Steven Mullaney and other
recent interpreters of representation in the Renaissance have characterized as a "rehearsal"—an allowed expansion or proliferation of the
alien, multiform, and multilingual in order finally to dramatize the
very process of its containment, the limiting structures of authority
and control.[43] Each of the texts we have seen would need, in a more
detailed treatment than is possible here, to be situated in its own historical specificity in order to gauge the politics as well as the gender
politics negotiated through this textual body's figurings and
refigurings. Certainly by the time of Donne's version of Rahab as the
Church who is "open" to most men, or Jonson's richly ambivalent
generation of the "enormities" of the Fair and its enormous female
emblem, we can begin to see at work a specifically post-Reformation
shifting of the ambivalences of this female figure toward the type of
the Whore of Babylon that in another contemporary version of the
Protestant imagination created the very unreverent body, as well as
"enormity," of a pregnant female Pope, the Whore of Babylon made
palpable and present in the flesh.[44]

To follow through the reasons for the shifting relation between such
textual bodies and the generation, and body, of a given text would take
more space and more specific historical investigation than the present
context allows. But we might do worse than to stay a bit longer within
the textual traces of this figure and the complex of "dilation" we have
remarked. In the oral form in which this essay was first presented,
its aligning of fat female bodies, or female loquacity, with fatty texts
elicited a series of instances of such an alignment in periods later than
the Renaissance, including the punning "fluent mundo"—world and
mouth or *Mund*—of the "Fat girl, terrestrial" who appears as muse-
figure in that very unapocalyptic (or "eucalyptic") poet Wallace
Stevens, producer of the hyperbolically redundant "Fat! Fat! Fat! Fat!"
Others included the fat lady at the end of Salinger's *Franny and Zooey*,
and the one in the story by Flannery O'Connor significantly called
"Revelation," whose name is "Ruby," who tends an "old sow" in a "pig
parlor," and who hears from "Mary Grace" that she is both "saved" and
"from hell."[45]

It is also striking to turn from the texts and tradition we have traced
to recent French discussions of *écriture féminine*, which reproduce the
misogynist topoi of unending female speech and multiple "tongues" in
a celebratory and, as Elaine Showalter puts it, "utopian" mode, or to

275

encounter the multiple "O's" in Monique Wittig's *Les Guérillères* or the description of women's speech, in Luce Irigaray, as "dilatable."[46] The rhetorical tradition of dilation here outlined is one on the whole forgotten to us, though when Roland Barthes wrote of the extending strategies of the classical novel he had recourse to the figure of the narrative's dilatory and dilated "espace dilatoire"—perhaps self-consciously, considering that he also wrote a much lesser-known "Aide-mémoire" to the terminology of ancient rhetoric, including *partitio* and *divisio*. The tradition of narrative romance, developing into the novel, gave us after all Richardson's *Pamela*, a "dilated novel" in the sense of the shorter novella form extended, and a heroine whose seductive disclosures and prodigious textuality recontextualize the stereotypical female case in which the "Closets of Womens thoughts are always open; and the depth of their hearts [provided with] a string that reacheth to their Tongues," whatever other case may temporarily be closed.[47] We might remember that Richardson's heroine derives her name from the same *Arcadia* as the one which gives us the "O" of Mopsa's mouth, its orality recast in a more contemporary written mode.

It is certainly remarkable how much of the tradition we have traced through the Renaissance survives into later periods, after the apparent eclipsing of a more self-conscious rhetorical tradition. Pope, whose *Dunciad* provides extraordinary instances of this continuance, speaks elsewhere of *amplificatio* as the "spinning wheel" of bathos, in a distant echo of the feminine distaff of Penelope. Fielding, that novelist who swallowed earlier romance tradition virtually whole, devotes a prominent chapter of *Joseph Andrews* to the question "Of Divisions in Authors," noting that "common readers imagine, that by this art of dividing, we mean only to *swell* our works to a much larger *bulk* than they would otherwise be extended to." He remarks its use not only in Homer and Virgil but also in Milton, who "went originally no farther than ten [books]; 'till being *puffed up* by the praise of his friends, he put himself on the same footing with the Roman poet." The instance makes explicit an alignment between the puffing up of pride and the puffing up of texts which Milton himself may be more subtly noting in linking the "dilation" of Satan with the rhetorical dilation of his own epic, product of the desire for fame, that last infirmity of noble minds. In another direction, we might ponder the fact that Mary Shelley, in writing of the monstrous and out-of-control in *Frankenstein*, reflects upon how she came to "dilate upon so very hideous an idea," or consider the figure of the tale-telling housekeeper of the gothic *Melmoth the Wanderer* (1820), a "witch" or "Sibyl" whose body seems to increase in size with her incredible tale ("when interrogated on the subject of the story, she rose at once into consequence,—her figure seemed *frightfully dilated, like that of Virgil's Alecto*, who exchanges in a moment the appearance of a feeble old woman for that of a menacing fury").[48]

The underground link between sexual opening and the opening of a closed or difficult text also continues well beyond the Renaissance, in texts such as an early eighteenth-century one which introduces its explication and dilation of a scriptural verse with "Now to draw our Discourse to a Head, after we have thus *opened the Case*." A virulent piece of misogyny roughly contemporary with it provides in a single paragraph a truly extraordinary concentration of the entire complex we have outlined—including the opening of a text and the open "O" of vagina and mouth—in a satire against women which begins with one "whose Sins are as big as her body":

My Lady F . . . one whose *Proportion* puts us in Mind of her *Excellencies*, and he who means to *board* her must put off his Doublet and *Swim*, its being of the same *Size* with a *Fish-Pond*. Yet it is *ten* to *one* if he escape *sinking*; since she is somewhat of Kin to *Goodwin Sands*, having swallow'd up Abundance of whole Families. . . . It is a very hard Matter to know, whether she be a Lady, or a *Leviathan*. Sure no *Weapon* but that of a *Goliah* can *fit* her. . . . And he who will *please* her . . . must convert a *Weaver's Beam* into a *D–l–e* [Dildoe]. . . . I believe the *Parson* too is puzzled; to interpret the barrenness of My Lady S——. She gives him the *opening* of many a hard *Text*. . . . Her *Mouth*, like Mopsa's, is *O Heavenly wide*; . . . her *Tail* being of the same *Size*.[49]

Changes in the semiotics of body size are subtly tied to other economies and exigencies of representation, including those linked to the shifting figure of the body politic, as recent work on the body and its representations has made clear.[50] But as part of the continuation of this assimilation of body and text, we need to remark how persistent is the link between textuality and female bodies, whether fat or talkative or both. Though the texts we have considered are male-authored ones, the collocation seems to depend not so much on that fact as on the existence and adoption of a form which involves a combination and double movement of textual expansion with closure or "point."[51] A text like Ann Radcliffe's *Mysteries of Udolpho*, for example, depends for its considerable size not only on the garrulity of its lower-class women but also on the separation of the heroine from their hysteria and pointlessness. Jane Austen's *Emma* might similarly be read in a way which would take David Miller's category of the "narratable" in Austen even more specifically back through questions of gender and the female tongue, beginning with the relation between the unbearable loquacity and diffusiveness of Miss Bates and the trajectory which takes Emma through so much "error" or wandering to the traditional marital end. We might also consider the talkative and ample Flora Finching of Dickens's *Little Dorrit,* whose prattle never leads anywhere, or the simultaneously loquacious and fat gossip-writer Henrietta Stackpole of Henry James's *Portrait of a Lady.* James would provide a particularly telling study in this regard, perhaps nowhere more importantly than in *The Golden Bowl.* For that late novel features both the full-figured Fanny Assingham, whose "amplitude of person" is matched by a verbal amplitude which generates so much of the text, and her husband, whose "leanness of person" is joined by a dislike of "waste" and who "edit[s], for economy" the "play" of his wife's mind as he does her redundancies—avatars together, perhaps, of the particularly Jamesian project of bringing the more undisciplined form of the novel, that "loose baggy monster," under greater control.

There are many directions this complex would lead to, including, closer to the present, the "overfed" and "flabby" mother of John Osborne's *Look Back in Anger* or the overweight "Mom" of Philip Wylie's immensely popular *Generation of Vipers,* "all tongue and teat and razzmatazz"—both contemporary novels which reproduce the topoi of more ancient misogynist tradition. Or the female "Mouth" of Beckett's *Not I,* one of the many late Beckett texts preoccupied with the postponing of ending. The anxieties of effeminization we have traced, together with the motive of controlling the female tongue, would also take us to Freud and the text of psychoanalysis—the "talking cure" named and generated through the historic case of the multilingual "Anna O." But perhaps the text that comes most easily to mind is the one generated by yet another Penelope, the rambling and unpointed monologue of Joyce's Molly Bloom. The refusal of closure in "Penelope," *Ulysses'* open-ended ending, seems to reflect Joyce's overall refusal of closure, what Ernst Bloch, in a passage full of anxieties of form equal to the anxiety critics have felt before Molly's sexual and verbal openness or the effeminacy of Bloom ("the new womanly man"), characterizes negatively as "a mouth without Ego, drinking, babbling, pouring it out."[52] The unpointed monologue of the figure who makes her appearance in "Notes and Early Drafts" as a *perragorda* or "fat bitch" continually both evokes and postpones images of the Last Judgment, in ways that prefigure the never accomplished "Bockalips" and recurrent Scheherazade of *Finnegans Wake.* "Stately plump" and garrulously evasive of narrative point (though not, in

Joyce's patriarchal economy, of phallic ones), this modernist Penelope might imagine the way that wayward women and wayward and copiously fattened texts continue to figure and refigure each other still.

Notes

This essay, first presented at Stanford University in 1983, has in subsequent versions benefited from comments from audiences at Cornell and Princeton Universities, the University of Chicago, the University of Wisconsin at Milwaukee, the Academy of Literary Studies, and the Association of Canadian University Teachers of English. It has also had the good fortune of comments and suggestions from Walter Swayze, Eve Kosofsky Sedgwick, Terry Castle, Mary Nyquist, David Quint, Diana de Armas Wilson, Maria di Battista, Patricia Meyer Spacks, Jennifer Brady, and, in its final version, David Riggs.

1. On Rahab in the Hebrew Bible, see Judith Baskin, "The Rabbinic Transformations of Rahab the Harlot," *Notre Dame English Journal*, 11, 2 (April 1979), pp. 141–57.
2. For Rahab as *dilatio*, see Jean Daniélou, *From Shadows to Reality: Studies in the Biblical Typology of the Fathers*, trans. Dom Wulstan Hibberd (London, 1960), pp. 250ff. For the "dilation of Christendome," see St Thomas More, *Comfort against Tribulation* (1529), III, weeks 1213/2, And, for "différance," see Jacques Derrida, *Marges de la philosphie* (Paris, 1972), pp. 1–29; trans. Alan Bass as *Margins of Philosophy* (Chicago, 1982), pp. 1–27. The Donne sonnet cited is Holy Sonnet 179. On women's spreading of the word, see Lee W. Patterson, " 'For the Wyves love of Bathe': Feminine Rhetoric and Poetic Resolution in the *Roman de la Rose* and the *Canterbury Tales*," *Speculum*, 58, 3 (1983), p. 664, citing the *Liber Lamentationum Matheoluli*. Unless otherwise noted, all italicization in the text is mine.
3. In *Inescapable Romance: Studies in the Poetics of a Mode* (Princeton, NJ, 1979), esp. pp. 54ff. For Hamlet's "mother" and "matter," below, see Margaret W. Ferguson, "*Hamlet*: letters and spirits," in Patricia Parker and Geoffrey Hartman (eds), *Shakespeare and the Question of Theory* (New York and London, 1985), p. 295.
4. St Jerome, who repented of his own attraction towards rhetoric, interpreted the swine's food in the Parable of the Prodigal Son as "the song of the poets, prophane philosophy, and the verbal pomp of the rhetoricians." On Jerome and other patristic commentary on the Prodigal Son parable, see Bernard Blumenkranz, "Siliquae Porcorum: L'exégèse médiévale et les sciences profanes," *Mélanges d'histoire du Moyen Age dédiés à la mémoire de Louis Halphen* (Paris, 1951), pp. 11–17, and Richard Helgerson, *The Elizabethan Prodigals* (Berkeley and Los Angeles, 1976), p. 55, together with Helgerson's overall discussion of the importance of the parable for Renaissance English literary men.
5. On Sidney and the attack on poetry as not fit for men, see Walter J. Ong, SJ, "Latin Language Study as a Renaissance Puberty Rite," in his *Rhetoric, Romance, and Technology* (Ithaca, NY, 1971), pp. 130ff. The text used in all

subsequent citations from Ascham is *The Schoolmaster* (1570), ed. Laurence V. Ryan (Ithaca, 1967).

6. See Sir John Harington (trans.), *Orlando furioso* (1591), sig. Mm iii and Sig. ¶ viii–viii^v (UMEES, Reel 194), with Helgerson, *Elizabethan Prodigals*, pp. 38–9.

7. See Mary Jacobus, "Is There a Woman in This Text?," *New Literary History*, 14, 1 (Autumn 1982), pp. 117–41. I use "subtext" here in the sense of an informing predecessor text. See Thomas M. Greene, *The Light in Troy: Imitation and Discovery in Renaissance Poetry* (New Haven and London, 1982), pp. 18–31.

8. I am, of course, aware that Calypso comes chronologically later than Circe in the homecoming journey of Odysseus. But the *narrative* order moves from Calypso, and an initial latency, to the victory over Circe. The *Odyssey* is traditionally characterized as a romance or *romanzo* in Renaissance discussions of the form.

9. See Ariosto, *Orlando furioso*, VII. 74. 1–4; Parker, *Inescapable Romance*, pp. 30–1; and Roland Barthes, *S/Z: Essai* (Paris, 1970). There is clearly an important difference between closural forms in the Bible, even with its open-ended ending, and the *Odyssey*, where we are told within the text that Odysseus, after reaching home and Penelope, will one day set out again. But the conflation within later literary, and specifically romance, tradition of temptress figures from both texts suggests the perceived links between the trajectory of "homecoming" in both.

10. See Desiderius Erasmus, *De Copia*, in *Collected Works of Erasmus*, vol. 24, ed. Craig R. Thompson (Toronto, 1978); the warnings against "Excesse" in, for example, Henry Peacham's *The Garden of Eloquence* (1593 edn), ed. William G. Crane (Gainesville, Florida, 1954). For the "wall" or *paries* and Cicero's *Topics*, see T. W. Baldwin, *William Shakespere's Small Latine and Lesse Greeke*, 2 vols (Urbana, 1944), vol. II, p. 110. The link between weaving and the dilation of discourse, as of the play, in *A Midsummer Night's Dream*, might be most succinctly conveyed through the fact that the name of "Bottom" the "Weaver" comes from that "bottom" of thread which Francis Bacon, in *The Advancement of Learning* (II. xviii. 8), has recourse to as a figure for "rhetoric" as having to do with discoursing "at large," and the attendant need to avoid "proxility" ("as skeins or bottoms of thread, to be unwinded at large when they come to be used"). Though the relation between Bottom's name and the play's constant playing on the dilation and partition of discourse has not been discussed, the link with "bottom of thread" both in relation to weaving and in relation to phallic "point" has. See Wolfgang Franke, "The Logic of *Double Entendre* in *A Midsummer-Night's Dream*," *Philological Quarterly*, 58 (1979), pp. 284, 287ff. For further discussion of *A Midsummer Night's Dream* in relation to its incorporation of the language of rhetoric, see Patricia Parker, *Literary Fat Ladies* (London: Methuen, 1987), pp. 97–125.

11. See *The Sermons of John Donne*, ed. George R. Potter and Evelyn M. Simpson, 10 vols, vol. V (Berkeley and Los Angeles, 1959), p. 56; and the discussion of the *ars praedicandi* tradition in John S. Chamberlin, *Increase and Multiply* (Chapel Hill, NC, 1976), and Patterson, " 'For the Wyves love of Bathe'," p. 675.

12. See Ascham, *The Schoolmaster*, pp. 106–14; Erasmus, Epistle 899, quoted in Izora Scott, *Controversies over the Imitation of Cicero* (New York, 1910), vol. II, p. 84, and, for the reference to "bignesse," Cornwallis's essay "Of Vanity" (1601), both cited in George Williamson, *The Senecan Amble* (Chicago, 1951),

pp. 19 and 106. For Lipsius, see Morris W. Croll, "'Attic Prose' in the Seventeenth Century," *Studies in Philology*, 18 (April 1921), p. 98.

13. See, respectively, Ficino's use of *dilatio* in his translation of Plotinus' Fifth *Ennead*, with his translation of *Enneads*, 6:7.2,3; *De immortalitate animorum*, I.iii;v.x; and *De vita coelitus comparanda*, ch. 1; John Erskine Hankins, *Source and Meaning in Spenser's Allegory* (Oxford, 1971), p. 291; Parker, *Inescapable Romance*, pp. 54–6; Hugh Latimer's sermon of 1552 on the Lord's Prayer, where he remarks that heaven, unlike earth, is a place where God's will is done "without dilation"; Richard Taverner's 1539 English translation of the *Adages* of Erasmus; and Milton, *Paradise Lost*, IV. 986.

14. See Herbert of Cherbury's "Ode upon a Question Mov'd" ("So when one wing can make on way / Two joyned can themselves dilate, / So can two persons propagate"). For the obstetrical tradition, as well as the use of the term "dilation" for the sexual opening of a woman, see *The Works of Aristotle, the Famous Philosopher*, in the reprint edition by Arno Press (New York, 1974), pp. 10, 81. For "dilating or enlarging of a matter by interpretation," see John Smith's *Mysterie of Rhetorique Unvail'd* (1657), under "Paradiastole or *distinctio*." Audrey Eccles' *Obstetrics and Gynaecology in Tudor and Stuart England* (Kent, Ohio, 1982), pp. 28 and 40, also cites passages on the "opening of the cervix in Copulation . . . and in childbirth."

15. The language of legal "dilation" still continues in Hobbes's *Leviathan* (I. xiv: "the not decreeing Execution, is a decree of Dilation," its "deferring till another time"). I am indebted here to the reading of the ordering of the *Canterbury Tales*, of the Wife of Bath as putting off the Parson's Tale, and of the link with literature in Lee Patterson's "'For the Wyves love of Bath'," pp. 676ff.

16. For the tradition of erotic dilation or putting off, see Andreas Capellanus, *De Arte Honeste Amandi*; and Addison, *Spectator*, 89 (1711), with Patterson, "'For the Wyves love of Bath'," p. 671n. on Andreas' substitution of *dilatio* for the *mora* of Ovid's *Ars amatoria*. The "Wall" between the lovers which must be "down" in the play of Pyramus and Thisbe in *A Midsummer Night's Dream* is linked by a series of obscene double entendres to the hymeneal wall, and the imagery there draws on the traditional typological assimilation of Ephesians' "wall of partition" to the "wall" of Canticles 2:9. For this assimilation see, for example, *The Sermons of John Donne*, ed. Potter and Simpson, vol. II (Berkeley and Los Angeles, 1955), pp. 108, 110–11. In *A Midsummer Night's Dream*, Hippolyta is identified with the erotic delay: C. L. Barber, in *Shakespeare's Festive Comedy* (Princeton, NJ, 1959), p. 125, provides a formulation indicative of the continuance of this gendered tradition: 'Theseus looks towards the hour with masculine impatience, Hippolyta with a woman's happy willingness to dream away the time." The edition used for all citations from Shakespeare is *The Riverside Shakespeare*, ed. G. Blakemore Evans (Boston, Mass., 1974).

17. See St Bonaventure's Sermon no. 6 (*De verbo incarnato*) in *Opera theologica selecta*, ed. Quaracchi (Florence, 1964), vol. V, esp. pp. 309ff.

18. See Lisa Jardine, *Still Harping on Daughters* (Brighton, 1983), p. 131.

19. See Barber, *Shakespeare's Festive Comedy*, p. 137; and Quintilian, *Institutio oratoria*, XII. x. 37, in the Loeb translation.

20. For discussion of *A Midsummer Night's Dream* in relation to the Aristotelian tradition of the female as "a vessel" and rhetorical *dispositio*, see Parker, *Literary Fat Ladies*, p. 123.

21. See Ephesians 5: 16 and Hal's "Redeeming time when men think least I will" (*1 Henry IV*, I. ii. 217). One particularly suggestive scene for the association of fat Falstaff with the copious dilation of discourse and lean Hal with its corrective is Act II, scene iv of *Henry IV, Part 1*, where Falstaff's expanding tall story of proliferating thieves yields to comic invective on Hal's thinness ("you starveling, you eel-skin") when the amplified tale is in danger of being exposed (and finally is by Hal's contrastingly brief "plain tale").

22. For a fascinating reading of this mastery of languages in the *Henriad* in these terms, see Steven Mullaney, "Strange Things, Gross Terms, Curious Customs: The Rehearsal of Cultures in the Late Renaissance," *Representations*, 3 (Summer 1983), pp. 53–62. On the feminization of Falstaff within the *Henriad* itself, see Gayle Whittier, "Falstaff as a Welshwoman: Uncomic Androgyny," *Ball State University Forum*, 20, 3 (Summer 1979), pp. 25–35.

23. The text of "Women are words, men deeds" is from Thomas Howell's *Devises* (1581). For Robert Greene on "babling Poets," see *Penelope's Web*, in Robert Greene, *The Life and Complete Works in Prose and Verse*, ed. Alexander B. Grosart, 15 vols (New York, n.d.), vol. V, p. 158. All subsequent references are to this edition. For stimulating discussions of the inhabiting of male or misogynist discourse with the female loquacity that is its subject, see Patterson, "'For the Wyves love of Bathe,'" pp. 660ff.; R. Howard Bloch, "Medieval Misogyny," *Representations*, 20 (Fall 1987), pp. 1–24; and, for the later case of Milton, Jim Swan, "Difference and Silence: John Milton and the Question of Gender," in Shirley Nelson Garner *et al.* (eds), *The (M)other Tongue* (Ithaca, NY, 1985), pp. 142–68.

24. See Maurice Charney, *Style in Hamlet* (Princeton, NJ, 1969), pp. 88, 94, 100, 104; and for a contemporary assimilation of wordiness and idleness, Francis Bacon, *Advancement of Learning*, II. xxiii. 6 ("words and discourse abound most where there is idleness"). For *dilatio* as *tarditas* or *accidia/melancholia*, see Reinhard Kuhn, *The Demon of Noontide* (Princeton, NJ, 1976), p. 40 n.2. For links between Falstaff and Hamlet, see G. R. Hibbard, "*Henry IV* and *Hamlet*," in *Shakespeare Survey*, 30, ed. Kenneth Muir (Cambridge, 1977), pp. 1ff.

25. Hamlet's "interlarding" in the revised commission makes use of the amplifications and embellishments he has learned ("many such-like as's of great charge," V. ii. 43), and does so in order to substitute for Claudius' commission an equally pointed message—of death. The assimilation of Hamlet at this point to a "king" is underscored both by Horatio's double reference in "Why, what a king is this!" (V. ii. 62) and by the fact that Hamlet uses his father's seal for the kingly commission. It is at this point in the play, after his return from England, that critics of *Hamlet* traditionally see the former delay replaced by a new sense of purpose and end. The effeminating associations of mere railing are conveyed elsewhere in Shakespeare by the appellation of Thersites as "Mistress Thersites" in *Troilus and Cressida* (II. i. 36). I have departed from the Riverside text for the "dilated articles," above, because the Q2 "delated" chosen by the Riverside editor is, as the gloss notes, a variant of "dilated."

26. The line is from Jonson's Pindaric Ode "To the Immortall Memorie, and Friendship of that Noble Paire, Sir Lucius Cary and Sir H. Morison." I have treated this pun and its evocativeness within the Ode in greater detail in "Deferral, Dilation, Différance: Shakespeare, Cervantes, Jonson," in Patricia

Parker and David Quint (eds), *Literary Theory / Renaissance Texts* (Baltimore, 1986), pp. 198–203.

27. The edition used in all references to *Bartholomew Fair* is that of *The Complete Plays of Ben Jonson*, ed. G. A. Wilkes, based on the edition of C. H. Herford and Percy and Evelyn Simpson (Oxford, 1982), vol. IV. For Donne, see his sermon no. 3 (on Psalm 38: 4, "For mine iniquities are gone over my head, as a heavy burden, they are too heavy for mee"), in *The Sermons of John Donne*, ed. Potter and Simpson, vol. II, pp. 95–118. In a way directly significant for the complex we have been tracing, this sermon also contains reference to the "wall of partition" of Ephesians 2, and the multiplication or "increase" of sin made possible by the proliferation of "partitions," in the midst of a sermon which, in self-conscious fashion, is itself constructed according to the *ars praedicandi* principles of dilation by partition.

28. See, respectively, Jackson I. Cope, "*Bartholomew Fair* as Blasphemy," *Renaissance Drama*, 8 (1965), p. 129, on the echoes of Judgment Day; R. B. Parker, "The Themes and Staging of *Bartholomew Fair*," *University of Toronto Quarterly*, 39 (1969–70), p. 294, on Ursula's booth and "Hell"; Peter Stallybrass and Allon White, *The Politics and Poetics of Transgression* (Ithaca, NY, 1986), pp. 44ff., on the symbolics of the pig and on Ursula as "the celebrant of the open orifice" (p. 64). I am grateful to David Riggs for his comments and suggestions here.

29. For the extraordinary exploitation in this play of all the resources of rhetorical *copia* and *amplificatio*, see Jonas Barish, *Ben Jonson and the Language of Prose Comedy* (Cambridge, Mass., 1960), pp. 188–219; and Eugene M. Waith's introduction to the Yale Ben Jonson edition of *Bartholomew Fair* (New Haven and London, 1963), pp. 3ff.

30. For these identifications, see, respectively, Cope, "*Bartholomew Fair* as Blasphemy," p. 144, and R. B. Parker, "Themes and Staging," p. 297.

31. *As You Like It*, III. ii. 249–50.

32. See *Fifty-Five Enigmatical Characters, All Very Exactly Drawn to the Life* (London, 1665), p. 33.

33. Robert Greene, *Penelope's Web*, in *The Life and Complete Works*, vol. V, the edition to which all parenthetical page references in the text refer.

34. See *A Curtaine Lecture* (London, 1637), attributed to Thomas Heywood, p. 17; Alciati, *Emblemata* (London, 1551), p. 78; and Geoffrey Whitney, *A Choice of Emblemes* (Leyden, 1586), p. 50. For further discussion of the misogynist topos of the garrulity of women, see Parker, *Literary Fat Ladies*, pp. 104–10.

35. On this male pedagogical economy, dominant in spite of more minor humanist encouragements of the education of women, see Ong, "Latin Language Study as a Renaissance Puberty Rite," pp. 113–41.

36. Play on "case" is ubiquitous in the Renaissance, as in Ben Jonson's *The Case is Altered*. For the bawdy and bodily associations of grammatical "case," see Roland Barthes, "L'Ancienne Rhétorique: Aide-mémoire," *Communications*, 16 (1970), p. 174. The nominative case was understood as the *casus rectus* or "erect" case from which others deviated or declined. See J. B. Greenough *et al.* (eds), *Allen and Greenough's New Latin Grammar* (New Rochelle, NY, 1983), p. 209. On Mistress Quickly's "case" as "so openly known to the world" and the legal/sexual "case," see Parker, *Literary Fat Ladies*, pp. 106–7.

37. Helgerson, *Elizabethan Prodigals*, p. 42, quoting John Lyly, *Euphues*, ed. Morris

W. Croll and Harry Clemons (1916; repr. New York, 1964), p. 200.

38. For this economy of translation, from father tongue, through English, and back to father tongue, see, for example, Roger Ascham, *The Schoolmaster*, pp. 15, 83. John Brinsley's later text, *A Consolation for Our Grammar Schooles* (1622), makes it clear as well how intimately tied this translative economy would become to the marginalizing and even eliminating of competing tongues as part of an imperial project to enforce the study of English ("that all may speake one and the same language"), since it was directed especially to "all those of the inferiour sort, and all ruder countries and places; namely Ireland, Wales, Virginia, with the Sommer Islands." The model here is of a translation from and back to the *sermo patrius* in which there is to be no difference between the paternal original and the dutiful copy ("and to turne or reade the same, out of the Translation into good Latine . . . so as in most, you shall hardly discerne, whether it be the Authors Latine or the Scholars"; p. 52).

39. *The Womens Sharpe Revenge* (London, 1640), a reply to the misogynist author of the Juniper and Crabtree lectures, puns on "gender" and "generation" (pp. 16–17) and, in remarking that its opponent is "quite out in all the Cases" in his attack on women, observes of his mistake in the genitive: "In the Genetive, by making us to be loose, lascivious, wanton, wilfull, inconstant, incontinent, and the Mothers of misbegotten Children" (p. 19).

40. Thomas M. Greene, "Erasmus' 'Festina lente': Vulnerabilities of the Humanist Text," in *The Vulnerable Text* (New York, 1986), pp. 1–17. For one Renaissance passage which explicity engages the problem of having "no certain end," see Richard Hooker, *Of the Laws of Ecclesiastical Policy* (London, 1907), Book I, p. 200.

41. See Jonathan Culler, "Apostrophe," in *The Pursuit of Signs* (Ithaca, NY, 1981), pp. 135–54.

42. The emphasis on "page," "letter," "post," and printed text is insistent throughout *Merry Wives*. See for example the exchange on the identical "letters" sent to Mistress Page and Mistress Ford (II. i. 70–9); the various go-betweens who act as bearers of messages; the "postmaster's boy" (V. v. 199) who substitutes for Ann Page at the end; and the Page ("Robin") who "will carry a letter twenty mile as easy as a cannon will shoot point-blank twelve score" (III. ii. 32–4). Play on "Page" and "page" is not exclusive to Shakespeare. See Nashe's preface to the "Pages" in *The Unfortunate Traveller* and Margaret W. Ferguson, "Nashe's *The Unfortunate Traveller*; The 'Newes of the Maker' Game," *ELR* (Spring 1981), pp. 166ff.

43. See Mullaney, "Strange Things, Gross Terms, Curious Customs," pp. 40–67; and Stephen Greenblatt, "Invisible Bullets: Renaissance Authority and its Subversion," *Glyph*, 8 (1981), pp. 40–61.

44. On the figure of the female and outrageously pregnant Pope Joan, see C. A. Patrides, *Premises and Motifs in Renaissance Thought and Literature* (Princeton, NJ, 1982), pp. 152–81.

45. See "Bantams in Pine-Woods" and, for "fluent mundo," the end of *Notes Toward a Supreme Fiction* (x). On Stevens as a "eucalyptic" (another term involving covering) rather than "apocalyptic" poet, see the marvelous study by Eleanor Cook, "Directions in Reading Wallace Stevens: Up, Down, Across," in Chaviva Hošek and Patricia Parker (eds), *Lyric Poetry: Beyond New Criticism*

(Ithaca, NY, 1985), pp. 298–309. For "Revelation," see Flannery O'Connor, *The Complete Stories* (New York, 1979), pp. 48–50.

46. See Elaine Showalter, "Feminist Criticism in the Wilderness," *Critical Inquiry*, 8 (1981), pp. 179–206; and Luce Irigaray, *This Sex Which is Not One*, trans. Catherine Porter (Ithaca, NY, 1985), p. 111. Annie Leclerc speaks in *Parole de femme* of the need to "invent a language that is not oppressive, a language that does not leave speechless but that loosens the tongue"; Hélène Cixous's *Vivre l'orange* (Paris, 1979) is written in French and English, but includes Portuguese, German, and Italian in a proliferation of mother tongues. See Dianne Hunter, "Hysteria, Psychoanalysis, and Feminism: The Case of Anna O.," in Shirley Nelson Garner *et al.* (eds), *The (M)other Tongue* (Ithaca, NY, 1985), p. 114.

47. See Roland Barthes, *S/Z* and "L'Ancienne Rhétorique: Aide-mémoire." The passage on the "Closets of Womens thoughts" is from the description of "Aspertions laid upon Women" (pp. 44–5) in the response of Ester Sowernam (pseud.), in *Ester hath hang'd Haman* (London, 1617), to the famous misogynist tract by Joseph Swetnam. The continuation into the eighteenth century of the masculinist tradition of feminine erotic dilation or holding off is suggested by such instances as Jeremy Collier's remark in "Of Whoredom," that "difficulty and danger heighten the success, and make the conquest more entertaining," in *Essays upon Several Subjects*, 3rd edn (London, 1720), vol. III, pp. 114–15.

48. See, respectively, Pope's *Peri Bathous or The Art of Sinking in Poetry* (1727), ch. 8, on amplifiers "but for which, the tale of many a vast romance, and the substance of many a fair volume might be reduced to the size of a primmer"; Henry Fielding, *Joseph Andrews*, Book II, ch. 1; Mary Shelley's Introduction to *Frankenstein*; and Charles Maturin, *Melmoth the Wanderer* (1820; Lincoln, Neb., 1961), p. 18. I am grateful to Susan Wolfson and Terry Castle for these last two references. For Milton, see my "Dilation and Delay: Renaissance Matrices," *Poetics Today*, 5, 3 (1984), pp. 526–7.

49. The two cited texts are Mordecai Moxon, *The Character, Praise and Commendation of a Chaste and Virtuous Woman, in a Learned and Pious Discourse Against Adultery* (London, 1708), p. 7; and *News from the New-Exchange: or, the Common-wealth of Ladies: Drawn to the Life, in their several Characters and Concernments*, 2nd edn (London, 1731), pp. 7–12.

50. See, most recently, the essays in *Representations*, 14, special issue, *Sexuality and the Social Body in the Nineteenth Century* (Spring 1986), in particular the essay by Catherine Gallaher entitled "The Body Versus the Social Body in the Works of Thomas Malthus and Henry Mayhew."

51. I am indebted in what follows to various readers and hearers of the oral version of this essay; on Radcliffe and Austen, to Eve Kosofsky Sedgwick; on Henrietta Stackpole, to Deborah Esch; on Beckett and Joyce, to Maria di Battista and Jennifer Levine. The reference to David Miller below is to the highly suggestive discussion of Austen in his *Narrative and its Discontents* (Princeton, NJ, 1981). On Freud, Breur, and the multilingual Bertha Pappenheim, see Dianne Hunter, "Hysteria, Psychoanalysis, and Feminism: The Case of Anna O.," pp. 89ff.

52. See Ernst Bloch, as cited by Georg Lukács, "Realism in the Balance" (1938), reprinted in *Aesthetics and Politics* (London, 1977), p. 38.

Margaret Cavendish and the Romance of Contract

Victoria Kahn

> All things by war are in a Chaos hurl'd
> But love alone first made,
> And still preserves the world.

(Alexander Brome)

In histories of early modern political thought, the rise of theories of contractual obligation has always played an important role; and yet the usual histories construe contract in an overly narrow way, focusing on the canonical works of writers such as Hobbes, Locke, and Rousseau in which contract is imagined as a social and political agreement between equal parties to set up a sovereign. In these modern histories, contract theorists offer a simple theory of motivation, according to which the parties to the contract are moved by rational self-interest; the consent of the governed is defined in opposition to coercion; and erotic passion is irrelevant to the production of "calculating and calculable" citizens.[1] And, while some historians and feminist critics have challenged these fictions of contract theory[2]—in some cases by directing us to the widespread use of the marriage contract as a metaphor for the hierarchical, inequitable political relations of sovereign and subject—they have for the most part been content to offer a reinterpretation of the canonical texts of political theory. As a result of this narrowly focused discussion, much of what is interesting and complicated in this history has been lost sight of—not least of all the role of narrative and of the passions in motivating contractual obligation.

In the following pages I suggest that we can enrich our understanding of seventeenth-century debates about contractual obligation if we turn to some of the neglected literary texts of the period: specifically, contemporary prose romance dramatizes the paradoxical coexistence

From *Renaissance Quarterly*, 50 (1997), 526–66. Reprinted with permission. The version printed here has been shortened and amended by the author for this collection.

of coercion and consent that is at the heart of theories of contractual obligation. In recent years, historians and literary critics have made us aware of the political uses of romance during the reign of Charles I and the Protectorate. Yet while these scholars have shown how the adventures and set debates of prose romance allegorize the trauma of civil war, they have given short shrift to the passion of romantic love and its role in debates about contractual obligation.[3] Similarly, historians who have analysed the rhetoric of the passions and interests in contemporary debates about obligation have focused on self-interest, greed, or acquisitiveness rather than on erotic love.[4] I would like to suggest, in contrast to both these approaches, that in the 1640s and 1650s the romance plot of love and adventure explicitly engages contemporary theories of contract by helping the reader both to imagine and to ask questions about a political subject who consents to be contractually bound. Margaret Cavendish's short prose romance, "The Contract", provides an exemplary illustration of the inseparability of romance and contract in seventeenth-century English political debate. In so doing, it contributes to a revised history of seventeenth-century accounts of political obligation, one that integrates literary as well as political works, and which attends to the political dimension of literary genre.[5]

"The Contract" (published in 1656 in a volume entitled *Natures Pictures*) tells the story of a young woman who, orphaned at birth, is betrothed in childhood by her uncle and guardian to the son of a friend.[6] The contract of the title is thus a marriage contract. At issue from the outset are the conditions that make a contract binding; of particular concern is the relationship of contract to consent. To the proposed contract, the uncle of the lady answers that "he was very willing, if [his niece] were of years to consent", and proceeds to agree to the contract in the expectation that she will ratify it when she comes of age. The son and prospective husband at first urges his father "not to marry him against his affections". Then, torn between allegiance to his father and his own desires, he "seemed to consent, to please his father". "Then were they as firmly contracted as the priest could make them, and two or three witnesses to avow it." Some years later, when the young lady comes of age, the young man (now become a duke) falls in love with another woman and marries her. News of this breach of the original contract reaches the uncle, who decides to bring his niece to the city to educate her and present her at court. She meets the Duke at a masque and they fall in love. The question the narrative then seeks to answer is whether and under what conditions the original contract is valid, given the fact that the Duke subsequently entered into a new marriage contract, with the added complication that the uncle of the lady is arranging a new marriage contract for his niece. As Cavendish was well aware, these are questions that were crucial not only for men and women entering into marriage contracts, but for all adult male citizens who were being asked to consent to the new Cromwellian government.

In the following pages I argue that Cavendish's romance is both a commentary on contemporary gender relations and on contemporary debates about political obligation, and that these two commentaries are entwined in important ways. In taking up what contemporary manuals of casuistry and "domestick oeconomie" called a "matrimoniall case", Cavendish dramatizes a range of concerns that were also central to contemporary political debate—and were likely to be so understood by contemporary readers. As we will see, Cavendish uses the language of romance both to argue for a more equitable contractual relationship between husband and wife, and to present an account of political obligation that is based on love rather than on filial obedience, wifely subordination, or a Hobbesian account of self-interest. In romance Cavendish finds an alternative motive for political contract, an alternative account of interest, and thus, indirectly, an argument for allegiance to Charles II.

Yet, if the arguments about gender and political obligation are mutually implicated in the language of romance, they are also at odds with each other (how intentionally it is difficult to tell). For, such an emphasis on romance seems to grant more importance to the ongoing consent and affection of the partners to a contract than do royalist or Hobbesian conceptions of contract—both of which involve an initial, but irrevocable act of consent. Thus, in striking contrast to previous royalist writers, who had used the analogy between the marriage contract and the political contract to justify absolute sovereignty, Cavendish's emphasis on "true romance" threatens to undo the hierarchical, inequitable relationship between the contracting parties—not only husband and wife, but also sovereign and subject. Although such an equitable relationship in marriage might be desirable even to a royalist, it could never be the basis of a subject's oath of allegiance to an absolute sovereign. In her critique of the marriage contract, the royalist Cavendish ironically draws near to the parliamentarians' theory of an original and revocable contract between the people and their ruler.

A reading of "The Contract" will allow us to see not only the role of prose romance in constructing arguments for political obligation, but also the inextricability of passion and interest, coercion and consent, categories that too often figure as antithetical in traditional accounts of contract. In confounding the distinction between rational self-interest and romantic love, between a legalistic model of contract and the "discipline" of the passions, "The Contract" exposes the obstacles confronting any analysis of obligation based primarily on the calculation of self-interest. Cavendish's romance thus provides a vivid illustration of the way in which the language of contract is a contested concept or "node of stress" in seventeenth-century English politics and culture—a point where the proto-liberal language of contract, consent, and rational self-interest intersects with the languages of coercion, casuistry, and the passions.[7]

POLITICAL CONTRACT AND THE MARRIAGE CONTRACT

Readers of "The Contract" in the 1650s would have been disposed to understand Cavendish's tale in political terms for at least three reasons. First, the marriage contract was a charged metaphor for political obligation in the seventeenth century. Second, the marriage contract was itself an occasion of conflicts of authority and allegiance in this period. And, third, the civil war, regicide, and new Cromwellian government posed a series of casuistical dilemmas involving the subject's allegiance to the sovereign that echoed debates about political contract and the marriage contract. In order to understand the full implications of Cavendish's revisionary romance, we need to recover the political connotations of contract in these three contexts.

In seventeenth-century England, as on the continent, the language of political contract emerged in part in response to a breakdown of traditional forms of political allegiance. Contract was one answer to the problem of political obligation for a culture newly sceptical of the claims of tradition, reason, and natural law, a world in which the passions and the interests threatened to run rampant.[8] Most familiar to us is the Hobbesian solution, according to which fear of violent death serves as the impetus for the rational calculation of self-interest. This calculation in turn leads us to contract with others to set up an absolute sovereign—a sovereign who has the power to coerce us to obey. Hobbes seems to have agreed with Machiavelli at least in this respect: if you must choose, it is better to be feared than loved.

But there was another, more widely disseminated model of political contract in the seventeenth century, one based on the marriage contract. This was a model of contract that preserved an older sense of status and natural hierarchy while simultaneously addressing contemporary arguments for the voluntary nature of political obligation. According to this model, the relationship between subject and sovereign was not based on fear or coercion but on love and unadulterated consent: the best analogy for sovereignty was the affectionate relationship of marriage. If in the first, Hobbesian model, contract responds to and reconfigures the passions and the interests, construed as the baser elements of human nature, in the second model, it is ostensibly not base human nature but the most elevated affections which underwrite the contract of political obligation.

Precisely because marriage in the seventeenth century was understood to be a natural political relationship involving the sovereignty of husband over wife, the marriage contract was an important ideological weapon in Stuart propaganda for absolute monarchy. While emphasizing mutuality, such an analogy did not preclude inequality; in fact, one could say that the point of the analogy was to naturalize and romanticize absolute sovereignty by making it seem that the subject, like the wife, was both naturally inferior and had consented to such inferior status out of affection. Yet, while such a contract was originally predicated upon consent of the governed (or the wife), once it had been agreed to, the contract was irrevocable. Accordingly, the royalist Henry Ferne described the king as "sponsus Regni [bridegroom of the realm], and wedded to the kingdom by a ring at his Coronation", and he used the analogy to argue that resistance to the king was as illegitimate as divorce: "what our Saviour said of their light and unlawfull occasions of Divorse [sic], *non suit ob initio*, it was not so from the beginning, may be said of such a reserved power of resistance, it was not so from the beginning."[9]

It quickly became clear that this analogy could work both ways: devised at first to justify royal absolutism, the analogy between marriage and sovereignty could also be inverted to suggest that the king was the wife of his subjects and so subservient to their wills.[10] In his *Observations upon some of his Majesties late Answers and Expresses* (1642), the parliamentarian Henry Parker remarked that the analogy between king and husband, along with that of king and father, was an imperfect "similitude": "for the wife is inferiour in nature, and was created for the assistance of man ... but it is otherwise in the State betwixt man and man." The only way to restore the citizens' rightful position as husbands was either to abandon or implicitly to reverse the gender analogy by making king subservient to his people.[11] Accordingly, in *Jus populi* (1644), Parker inverted the analogy by comparing the king to the wife rather than the husband: "*Man* (saies the Apostle) *was not made of the woman, but the woman of the man*: and this is made an argument why the woman should pay a due subjection to man"; so, Parker argued, "*Princes were created by the people, for the peoples sake, and so limited by expresse Laws as that they might not violate the peoples liberty.*"[12]

As these quotations suggest, well before Hobbes elaborated his fiction of an original political contract, the language of the marriage contract was appropriated by both royalists and parliamentarians in their debate over the conditions of legitimate sovereignty. For both, in contrast to Hobbes, love rather than fear was the ostensible key to lasting political union; for both, the hierarchy of the marriage relationship had important (if diametrically opposed) political implications. Precisely because of this difference, as Shanley has noted, parliamentarians eventually abandoned the metaphor of the marriage contract altogether, correctly perceiving that it was deleterious to their argument for contractual obligation predicated not only on consent but also on equality.[13]

In the seventeenth century, the marriage contract was not only a vexed metaphor for political obligation; it could itself occasion conflicts of allegiance. In particular, the moral and legal status of marriage contracts *per verba de praesenti* and *de futuro* was a frequent topic of discussion.[14] This was no doubt in part because there was genuine confusion about the relative weight of canon and common law in disputed cases; but it was also because spousal contracts and the state of marriage were themselves the locus of casuistical dilemmas. All commentators agreed that parents arranging for the marriage of their children should ask their consent; they also agreed that children should not act against the wishes of their parents. Almost by definition, then, marriage contracts posed questions regarding the relation of coercion and consent, conflicts regarding obedience to one's own conscience and to one's superior, whether one's father or husband. Even in cases where no parents were involved, it was not always clear how to define consent or how to distinguish clearly between a promise to marry and the act itself. As Keith Thomas has noted, "Next to politics and religion, the most persistent source of cases of conscience [in the seventeenth century] was to be found in the domestic sphere" (1993: 46).

Readers of "The Contract" in the 1650s would not only have recognized it as a domestic case of conscience concerning the validity of spousal contracts *de futuro*; they would also have had in mind the casuistical dilemma brought about by the change of regime. Of particular relevance in this context is the engagement controversy (1649–52), when parliament sought to secure allegiance to the new government of Cromwell after the execution of Charles I. The statement of engagement, which was eventually required of all male citizens aged 18 or over, gave rise to a fast and furious pamphlet war debating the legitimacy of declaring allegiance to the new government when one had previously sworn obedience to the king. Thus, like the Duke's breach of the original marriage contract, the engagement presented its would-be subscribers with a case of conscience—of conflicting moral allegiances and legal obligations. Of particular concern to the pamphleteers were the conditions that would allow one to argue that an earlier oath was invalid or still binding. Casuistical concerns of another sort entered into the debate as well, for parliamentarians were anxious that those who declared allegiance not engage in any sort of equivocation by—in Cavendish's words—*seeming* to consent.[15]

The royalist Cavendish, who was married to one of Charles I's most important financial backers and military commanders, Sir William Cavendish, was certainly aware of the drama of the engagement and the more general crisis of royalist ideology precipitated by the civil war.[16] Although she and her husband were in exile on the continent in the late 1640s and 1650s (first in Paris, then in Rotterdam and Antwerp), Cavendish travelled to England in 1651 and remained until 1653, attempting to negotiate with Parliament on behalf of her husband's sequestered estates. When these negotiations failed and Cavendish applied to the Council of State for a pass to return to Antwerp in 1653, she was asked to take the engagement but refused to do so.[17] This experience, along with her exile and her failure to secure her husband's estates, could only have made her more acutely aware of the costs—both personal and financial—of allegiance to the king.

Finally, Cavendish may also have confronted the issues of allegiance and engagement through her acquaintance with Thomas Hobbes, whom Sir William had patronized in the 1630s (Hobbes dedicated *The Elements of Law* to him) and with whom the Cavendishes associated during their exile in Paris. Notoriously, *Leviathan* was read by contemporaries as a contribution to debates about the legitimacy of the new government and the nature of political contract. Although in her *Philosophical Letters* of 1664 Cavendish asserts that she did not read those parts of *Leviathan* that discussed politics (a subject inappropriate for women), she went on in the same letter to give some of her opinions on government; and in a later letter she briefly alluded to contemporary debates about political obligation, criticizing those who "endeavour to cut between command and obedience to a hairs breadth".[18] Here too Cavendish signalled her awareness of the political case of conscience confronting her compatriots in England.

POLITICS AND THE GENRE OF ROMANCE

For both formal and historical reasons, romance was an obvious choice of genre for Cavendish as she thought about commenting on the contemporary crisis of political obligation. In theme and plot, mid-seventeenth-century romance (whether in the form of masque, pastoral drama, or prose narrative) involved the politically charged issues of coercion and consent, force and desire. Not only do we find idealizing fictions characterized by simplified characterization, the ethical extremes of good and evil, a tendency towards allegory, and a plot often modelled on the quest; increasingly during the civil war years and the Protectorate we find as well a concern with the moral conflicts of passion and interest that confronted royalists and parliamentarians alike. These conflicts are dramatized, on the one hand, through casuistical debate and, on the other, through the narrative of love and adventure, including the effort on the part of hero or heroine to overcome some kind of sexual barrier (in Northrop Frye's formulation: the innocent heroine brings the truculent hero to heel).

Of particular relevance for a revised history of contract is the way in which the traditional romance plot of love and adventure both represents the contingent realm of fortune, to which parliamentary rational models of contract were also trying to respond; and presents the contingent adventures of the romance narrative as the vehicle of the ultimate reconciliation of coercion and consent, pleasure and virtue, destiny and choice. In the course of the narrative, characters who were originally coerced into a marriage contract come to love each other "of their own free will", and contingency is simultaneously cancelled and preserved in that illusion of self-determination. Here we begin to see why prose romance has traditionally been associated with the assimilation (and hence decline) of the formal discipline of casuistry and the rise of a new ideal of autonomous moral character; we also begin to see how romance could contribute to the "disciplining" in the Foucauldian sense of a political subject, who internalizes coercion in the form of her very own passions.[19] These themes and formal devices would be put to good use by Cavendish in her own prose romance about the drama of coercion and consent in England of the 1650s.[20]

But there were political reasons as well for Cavendish's choice of romance. As lady-in-waiting to Queen Henrietta Maria, Cavendish would have been aware not only of the prominence of the marriage contract in contemporary political debate, or of a more general "politics of love" at the Caroline court.[21] She would also have been aware of the specific prominence of the genre of romance in court entertainments, both in England and in the Parisian court in exile.[22] Charles was known for his love of chivalric romance, as Henrietta Maria was for her love of pastoral romance. For both, romance was a powerful vehicle of political allegory, serving not only to transmute the language of interest into one of love and affection but also to justify contemporary domestic and foreign affairs.[23]

Romance was equally important to royalist propaganda during the civil war. In these years, supporters of the king were particularly interested in using the romance narrative of love and adventure both to stage and to deny any significance to the crisis of the civil war. This is the case with Sir Richard Fanshawe, who translated Guarini's pastoral romance, *Il Pastor fido* (The Faithful Shepherd) and dedicated it to the future Charles II. *Il Pastor fido* must have attracted Fanshawe not only because it begins with a coerced vow (or, as Fanshawe translates, "contract") which is broken off only to be re-established as a "happy Royall Marriage", but also because it tells a story of a faithfulness which endures in the face of deception and misfortune.[24] In one sense the plot serves both to represent the trials and tribulations of the suffering prince and to deny that they could have any possible effect on his constancy;[25] in another sense, the plot dramatizes the royalists' fantasy that the relation between sovereign and subject could never be one of simple coercion, but will always—also—be one of affection and consent. The contingency of the romance plot is thus the narrative equivalent of the ideological message that we consent, of our own free will, to be coerced: by a series of apparently fortuitous events and individual choices, the protagonists bring about the marriage that has been decreed by an oracle even before the opening of the play.[26] Similarly, Fanshawe implies, if the relation between sovereign and subject must be conceived of as contractual, it should not be imagined as the Hobbesian or parliamentary contract of equal parties, but rather the marriage contract of husband and wife.

Fanshawe's gloss on *Il Pastor fido* foreshadows the 1650s and 1660s, which saw the appearance of a form of romance narrative that was neither chivalric nor pastoral, but closer to the Greek romances of Heliodorus, "a form that allowed for adventure and coincidence but not for the improbably supernatural "marvels" of the old chivalric narratives".[27] Here, too, romance was very often construed as a vehicle of royalist ideology—although, the message was no longer the celebration and justification of domestic and foreign policy of the 1630s but rather (as with Fanshawe's "faithful shepherd") the depiction of the "travails" of the royal protagonists and their ability to withstand the vagaries of fortune through strength of character. Crucially important for the revival of this form of romance narrative were the translations of French romances by Madeleine de Scudéry, de la Calprenède, and others: whereas the contemporary romances of English authors such as William Sales and Percy Herbert stressed the aptness of romance adventures to allegorize the political upheavals of the civil war, the French works satisfied the reader's desire both for "strange actions" and for the analysis of the passions and development of character, in part through casuistical debate. Such an emphasis, Annabel Patterson has suggested, provided "a role, both in political life and in the new literature, for women", and may have contributed to the popularity of these romances with female readers.[28] Margaret Cavendish undoubtedly had some familiarity with these popular romances in France and with their English translations; as we will see, her own romantic critique of romance involves a similar emphasis on character, casuistry, and women's agency.

CONTRACT V. ROMANCE: THE CASE OF HOBBES

Committed royalists such as Davenant and Fanshawe were not the only ones thinking about the relationship of romance to political obligation in the middle decades of the seventeenth century: at the same time that Charles's supporters were elaborating a rhetoric which used the language of the marriage contract to imply irrevocable consent and the language of married love and of romance to obfuscate the elements of self-interest and coercion in politics, Hobbes was developing a different view of political obligation. Central to Hobbes's discussion was an unsentimental view of contract, shorn of the romantic fictions so prominent in the royalist camp. *Leviathan* can serve as an illustration of one sort of argument Cavendish and other royalists were at pains to combat; it can also help us to see what was at stake in Cavendish's attempt to argue against the new government by reforming romance from within.

In *Leviathan* Hobbes argued for a model of sovereignty based on the consent of the contracting parties "to conferre all their power and strength upon one Man, or upon one Assembly of men, that may reduce all their Wills, [by plurality of voices] unto one Will".[29] Yet, infamously, in Hobbes's analysis, a covenant without force cannot possibly be binding: "The bonds of words [he writes in *Leviathan*] are too weak to bridle mens ambition, avarice, anger, and other Passions, without the feare of some coercive Power" (*L* 14. 196). Thus, while no government is legitimate without the consent of the governed, consent is perfectly compatible with coercion in Hobbes's analysis. Contracts that are coerced by fear are not, for all that, less binding: "Feare and Liberty are consistent" (*L* 21. 262).

Yet, as these quotations suggest, if the power of coercion is a condition of absolute sovereignty, it is also an argument for the legitimacy of de facto political power. Since "the end of Obedience [to the sovereign] is Protection", the covenant may be broken when the sovereign no longer has the ability to protect his subjects (*L* 21. 272). Conversely, the government that does have the power to protect us is the one that deserves our allegiance. This was precisely the argument that defenders of the oath of engagement made about Cromwell's new government—which helps explain why royalists were less than pleased with *Leviathan*. For while the goal of *Leviathan* is to provide a logically compelling model of absolute sovereignty and irrevocable contract, the exception to this rule of irrevocability is the right of self-defence consistently invoked by parliamentary critics of the king.

Before turning to Cavendish's romance, it is important to stress that Hobbes's model of contract is explicitly presented as a demystified account of political obligation—one predicated on the rational calculation of interests. He represents his opponents—whether parliamentarians or royalist supporters of episcopacy—as incapable of sound reasoning. It is well known that Hobbes attributed this incapacity in part to familiarity with classical literature; less well known is his belief that the vainglory and enthusiasm of his contemporaries were also the result of reading "romances". Thus, for example, in a discussion of the imagination in *Leviathan*, Hobbes implied that the reading of romances fuelled the ambition of those who fought in the civil war: "Compound imagination" occurs "when a man compoundeth the image of his own person, with the image of the actions of an other man; as when a man imagins himself a *Hercules*, or an *Alexander*, (which happeneth often to them that are much taken with reading of Romants) it is a compound imagination, and properly but a Fiction of the mind."[30]

If romance contributes to the self-aggrandizing fantasies of parliamentarians and royalists, it also describes the delusions of the "Kingdome of Darknesse" in book 4 of *Leviathan*. Here Hobbes blames heathen poets and philosophers, among others, for the current spiritual darkness, arguing that the "ghosts" and "faeries" of ancient poets are based on "false, or uncertain Traditions, and faigned, or uncertain History" (*L* 44. 629)—precisely the charges brought against medieval romance by its critics. Similarly, he describes the images and idols worshipped by pagans as "meer Figment[s], without place, habitation, motion, or existence, but in the motions of the Brain" (*L* 45. 665), and remarks further on "A man can fancy Shapes he never saw . . . as the Poets make their Centaures, Chimaeras, or other Monsters never seen" (*L* 45. 669). Such fictions are politically dangerous when their fictive quality is masked and when claims are made for their validity or efficacy that pose a threat to the absolute authority of the sovereign. In *Leviathan* the Roman Catholic Church (and the English Presbyterians) are the chief promulgators of such ideological fictions and Hobbes's task is to demystify these fictions as romance and as ideology.

ROMANCE AND CONTRACT: THE CASE OF CAVENDISH

Cavendish was also concerned to demystify romance ideology, but unlike Hobbes her aim was to reform romance from within. As she stated in the preface to *Natures Pictures* (the volume in which "The Contract" appeared), her goal was to use romance's representation of the passions in order to quench passion or, at the very least, to redirect erotic passion to political obligation:

Though some of these Stories be Romancical, I would not be thought to delight in Romances, having never read a whole one in my life; and if I did believe that these Tales should neither benefit the Life, nor please the Mind, more than what I have read in them, did either instruct or satisfie me; or that they could create Amorous thoughts in idle brains, as Romances do, I would never suffer them to be printed, and would make Blots instead of Letters. But Partiality persuades me otherwise; and I hope that this Work will rather quench Passion, than enflame it. . . .

Simultaneously declaring and denying the romance elements of the stories that follow, Cavendish alerts us to her dialectical critique of the genre most prominently associated with the court and with royalist political propaganda from the 1630s to the 1660s. In "The Contract", she does not oppose romance and contract in the Hobbesian manner; but neither does she simply conflate them in a royalist politics of love. In the process of making what appears to be a traditional royalist argument for the role of love in securing political obligation, Cavendish parodies not only the Hobbesian picture of the passions and the interests, of power seeking after power, but also the excesses of court life; even more important, she uses romance to revise the absolutist model of the marriage contract and, in so doing, suggests a critique of the royalist argument for political contract as well.[31]

Cavendish's intention to reform romance is apparent early on in "The Contract": the uncle keeps his young charge away from "courts, masques, plays, [and] balls", and forbids her to read "romancies", substituting instead moral philosophy and history. She in turn adopts a Jonsonian strictness about the masque of life. Examined by her uncle for her opinion of "the riches and gallantry of the city" (8) in one of the many such scenes of casuistical debate, she replies:

as I pass by, I please my eye, yet no other ways than as senseless objects; they entice me not to stay, and a short view satisfies the appetite of the senses, unless the rational and understanding part should be absent; but to me they seem but moving statues. (9)

Thus, while the lady is herself a beautiful orphan who is described in the language of allegorical romance, she is saved from the vanity of court spectacle by virtue of her own discriminating judgement. It is this moral superiority, Cavendish suggests, which produces a suitably Spenserian victory when the lady does finally attend a masque at court with her uncle: "pressed . . . to the wars of vanity, where Cupid is general", she strikes the assembled courtiers with "amaze".

Although the masque itself is criticized for its superficial display, it is also the occasion of "true romance", for it is here that the lady and the Duke meet and fall in love. It is also here that the uncle meets the elderly Viceroy to whom he hopes to marry his niece. These events then motivate the rest of the plot, for the newly amorous Duke must extricate himself from his current marriage; the lady must negotiate her conflicting allegiances to her uncle and her new love; and the uncle must be convinced that the new marriage contract he is negotiating on his niece's behalf with the elderly Viceroy is invalid. One thing is clear: a contract that was originally broken for lack of consent begins to be validated through romance, specifically romantic love.

Cavendish then develops her views about the relationship of contract to consent, morality and "nice scruples" to love, in a number of exemplary scenes. These scenes amount to a kind of anatomy of contract, specifically in relation to the passions and interests which contract is intended to reconfigure or represent. In simultaneously stressing the importance of consent and its irrelevance, these scenes suggest that precisely this contradiction is the heart of the royalist argument about irrevocable political contract; at the same time, they dramatize Cavendish's attempt to use the conventions of romance to reconcile coercion and consent in an argument for political obligation that is modelled on romantic love. In the end, however, "The Contract" also illustrates the paradox of using the passions to respond to arguments for the engagement and political obligation which are based on the rational calculation of self-preservation—that paradox, that is, of using the passions to provide a securer foundation for contract. As Hobbes himself had noted in making fear of violent death a cornerstone of his commonwealth, the passions are themselves a source of interest; and as he acknowledged in the conclusion to *Leviathan*, the interest of self-preservation may ultimately give rise to the same sorts of casuistry and broken contracts that the original contract was designed to avoid. The final scene of "The Contract" shows us that the same is true of "true love".

In the first exemplary scene (really two in quick succession), both the lady and her uncle see contract as an agreement that is based on love and consent. Thus, in trying to persuade his niece to marry the Viceroy, the uncle resorts to persuasion rather than coercion. Although the lady suspects her uncle's "design" to marry her against her affections, the uncle initially has no such intention. Instead, he urges the lady to put aside passion and to marry "a discrete and sober man" (19–20), and he tells the Viceroy that "he could not force [his niece's] affection", although he would try "to get her to consent to marry" (20). When he then tries to persuade the lady of the Viceroy's virtues, she protests that they are ill-suited—for he is old and she is young, he will be jealous and she will be restrained "like a prisoner" (22). Obviously, the partner she has in mind is one who will be like her in age as well as station; the contract she envisions is one that will preclude coercion both before and during the marriage. Nevertheless, at the end of this scene, she reiterates that she is "bound in gratitude and duty to obey" her uncle's will, thereby calling attention not only to the case of conscience posed by the uncle's proposed contract but also to the difficulty of making consent a meaningful act in the context of a relationship that is hierarchical and inequitable (23).

Shortly after this, the lady experiences pangs of conscience about replying to the Duke's love-letter, both because her uncle would disapprove if she responded and because the Duke would think her "malicious" if she did not. This case of conscience is explicitly "resolved" by an appeal to her own experience of "charity and love", which persuade her the Duke "speaks the truth" when he claims her indifference will kill him: "I would be loath to murder him with nice scruples [about replying to his letter], when I am neither forbade by honour nor modesty, religion nor laws. Well, I will adventure, and ask my uncle pardon when I have done" (24). In her reply to the Duke, the lady similarly conflates conscience and love: "if you have wars with your conscience, or fancy, or both, interrupting the peace of your mind, as your letter expresses, I should willingly return to your side, and be an arbitrator; yet the fates have determined it otherwise" (25). In these and other scenes in which the lady both acknowledges and casuistically evades the authority of her uncle, Cavendish seems to be suggesting that conscientious consent is required for a contract or any other "law" (including the moral law) to be binding.[32] And that consent is figured as love.

In the second exemplary scene, by contrast, the Duke describes the original marriage contract in terms of a model of political obligation that is hierarchical, inequitable, and irrevocable, and to which consent is irrelevant. He does so in response to the news that the lady has been betrothed to the Viceroy after all. Here and in the following episode, we see the narrative explicitly take up the central question of the engagement controversy: under what conditions is a contract no longer binding? Although the match was arranged "without the young Lady's consent", "the uncle told her afterwards, she must prepare herself to be the Viceroy's bride; and, said he, if you consent not never come near me more" (28). We know that she does tacitly consent because, immediately after this, the Duke who has heard of the match appears in the lady's chamber to protest, and she responds that if she were to disobey her uncle she would prove herself "a traitor to gratitude" (29). The

Duke then argues that the original marriage contract between the two of them is still in effect:

you cannot want an owner whilst I live, for I had, nor have no more power to resign the interest I have in you, than Kings to resign their crown that comes by succession, for the right lies in the crown, not in the man, and though I have played the tyrant, and deserved to be uncrowned, yet none ought to take it off my head, but death, nor have I power to throw it from myself, death only must make way for a successor. (29)

Contrary to what we might expect, the Duke is not claiming that the original contract is now valid because his consent has finally been secured, but that it has continued to be valid regardless of his consent. Thus, in describing his situation, he draws an analogy between his condition and that of the absolute monarch himself who remained sovereign even when he was a tyrant. The implication seems to be that, as Hobbes argues in *De corpore* and *Leviathan*, contracts are legally binding as long as the contracting parties are in a position to perform their obligations (whether they do or not). The application of the analogy to contemporary politics is obvious: Charles I was king and deserved his subjects' allegiance by virtue of his office. What complicates this reading is that the motive for the Duke's argument is his passionate love for the lady. To focus on the domestic drama is to see that it is passion that is figured as sovereign, and that the Duke now defends the marriage contract because he is in love and it is thus in his interest to do so.

That Cavendish believes love is a more powerful basis for obligation than coercion and self-preservation is dramatically illustrated by the third scene, a parody of the Hobbesian account of contract, which mediates between the lady's emphasis on consent and Duke's insistence on its irrelevance. In this scene, the Duke confronts the Viceroy at swordpoint and insists that he swear in writing not to marry the lady. When the Viceroy very reasonably asks why, the Duke informs him that "she is my wife, and I have been married to her almost nine years" (31). The Duke thus argues that the Viceroy's contract is invalid because of a prior existing contract. It is not the force of logic that persuades the Viceroy, however, but mere brute force: not until the Duke tells him "If you do not [swear], you shall die a violent death", does the Viceroy agree (31). The scene reads as a textbook illustration of the question at the heart of the engagement controversy—the question of whether one can break a prior contract (and sign a new one) for reasons of self-preservation. Whereas Hobbes had answered in the affirmative and had used such arguments to justify the legitimacy of de facto political power, Cavendish strikingly uses the argument for engagement to justify a prior contract and the status quo ante. Here, too, what the scene with the Viceroy appears to illustrate for Cavendish is that contracts based on fear and self-interest are weaker than those based on love, for they will always be broken when the contracting party is threatened with force. In marked contrast to the nascent view that a person pursuing his own interest becomes "transparent and predictable", and that "interest will not lie", Cavendish shows us that interest—at least the interest of self-preservation—is the source of inconstancy.[33] The Viceroy is forced to "unswear" his recent oath to marry the lady, with the result that the earlier oath of engagement between the Duke and the lady is reaffirmed—and thus, indirectly, the earlier oath of obedience to the king.

While in the encounter between the Duke and the lady the Duke argues that contracts are binding even without consent and the episode with the Viceroy shows that contracts may be broken for reasons of self-preservation, in both cases these arguments are in the service of preserving the original engagement of the Duke and the lady, one now infused with true love. The final scene of "The Contract", however, seems to dramatize some of the problems of granting the affections such a role by linking the royalist interest in true romance with the engagers' worst fears of royalist deception and manipulation.

In this last scene the Duke and the lady have consented to marry, but the Duke must still extricate himself from his current marriage. Accordingly, the lady and the duke decide "to conceal their agreement . . . , and to cover it by the Duke's *seeming dissent*"—a phrase that echoes his "seeming consent" to the first contract at the very beginning of the narrative (37). Lest he seem to have deliberately contracted to marry two women, the lady agrees to pretend to sue for his hand in court. This way the Duke can seem to be "coerced" by justice to consent to the original contract. What is politically troubling about this final scene is the obvious casuistry involved in the lady's pleading before the judges—not casuistry in the sense of a case of conscience, for the Duke and the lady appear to have no scruples at all about their mock suit, but casuistry in the sense of equivocation and deceit—of romance, we might say, in the sense of improbability and fiction.

First, the lady insists that she was "married" to the Duke according to common law (if not canon law), and that her legal status as a minor is irrelevant now that she has consented to the marriage as an adult.[34] She then argues in Hobbesian fashion that the Duke was old enough to consent when the original contract was made and "if a coward make a promise through distracted fear, laws that carry more terrors, than the broken promise [carries] profit, will make him keep it,"

for a promise must neither be broken upon suspicion, nor false construction, nor enticing persuasions, nor threatening ruins, but it must be maintained with life, and kept by death, unless the promises carry more malignity in the keeping them, than the breaking of them. (39)

As a result, the Duke's "vows" to his current wife could only be "love's feignings, [rather] than really true": "for where right is not, truth cannot be" (40). Affection, the lady argues, cannot itself be the basis of a new marriage contract when an old bond is still in force; to the contrary, it will instead be a cause of "feigning", including the pretense of freedom to contract a new marriage; yet "he cannot be free, unless he hath my consent, which I will never give" (40).

The lady then protests that (unlike the Duke) she is incapable of deceit:

And for dissembling, I have not had time enough to practice much deceit; my youth will witness for me, it is an art, not an inbred nature, and must be studied with pains, and watched with observation, before any can be master thereof. And I hope this assembly is so just, as not to impute my innocent simplicity to a subtle, crafty, or a deceiving glass, to show the mind's false face, making that fair, which in itself is foul. (41)

Yet that is precisely what the trial is designed to do: to make the Duke's past foul behaviour seem fair—or fairer than it might otherwise seem—through the artful dissembling of his knowledge of the validity of the prior contract and of his desire to be rid of his present wife. And part of her casuistry is to invoke the Hobbesian argument for the validity of covenants made for reasons of fear, although the motive for the trial is that the contract is now motivated by love.

This casuistical sacrifice of love to the law only in order to enforce "the law of the heart" is then replayed by the Duke, who confesses that in his licentious youth he

sought pleasure more than virtue: but experience hath learned me stricter ways, and nobler principles, insomuch as the reflection of my former actions, clouds all my future happiness, wounds my conscience, and torments my life; but I shall submit to what your wise judgements think fit. (42)

The Duke portrays himself as a "wounded conscience"—a common phrase from casuistical manuals and treatises concerning political obligation—not because he is faced with a conflict of allegiances (as in the engagement controversy) but rather because his wayward passion and infidelity have been revealed to him by the law. A few lines later, the lady reiterates the fiction that passion forced the Duke to break his prior vow, when she urges that the court "excuse the faults of the Duke, since he was forced by Tyrant Love to run in uncouth ways" (43). And yet, as the reader knows, the law that reveals the wounded conscience is also the instrument that reconciles "pleasure" and "virtue". Not surprisingly, when the court rules that the lady is his "lawful wife", he "willingly submit[s]", thereby making his legal destiny his choice (43).

One way to read this last scene is as Cavendish's final attempt to rebut arguments such as Hobbes's and the engagers': whereas in *Leviathan*, irrevocable political contract is predicated on consent and validated by coercion, for Cavendish such coercion will, ideally, always be staged, since the real relationship between contracting parties is not only one of consent, but also of true love. This argument has obvious gender implications as well: just as the lady in the trial scene recalls the enterprising, independent-minded heroine of Shakespearean comedy—a woman such as Rosalind or Portia who is capable of acting in her own interest—so the contract she defends is one that fulfils her own desires just as much as her husband's.

This fiction of satisfied desire has potentially revolutionary implications. As we have seen, romance in Cavendish's work is the motor and motive of narrative: the narrative of coming to understand one's obligations as willed—not as a matter of self-preservation but of fantasy, desire, and self-fulfilment. Yet, to the extent that self-fulfilment requires the greater equality—to adopt Eve's oxymoron in *Paradise Lost* (bk. 9, l. 823)—of the contracting parties (in the first instance husband and wife, but also sovereign and subject), it threatens not only the traditional understanding of the marriage contract but also the royalist's use of the marriage contract as a justification of political subordination and absolute sovereignty. After all, it is not the wife but the husband who "willingly submit[s]" at the end of the trial, a gesture (however feigned) which recalls the pejorative analogy between obedient and effeminized subjects that parliamentarians such as Henry Parker had used to argue against absolute sovereignty (see above, p. 291). Intentionally or not (or perhaps both, given her characteristically ambivalent claims for the equality of the sexes), Cavendish's defence of a more equitable marriage contract may in the end bring her closer to parliamentary critics of the king than she would have liked.[35]

Specifically, in making the lady's marriage contract the central issue of her romance, Cavendish implies not only that women are the representative political subjects but also that they are the representative dissenters.[36] For, in narrating a story in which a marriage contract is ultimately validated by the true love of the contracting parties, Cavendish suggests a mutuality between subject and sovereign that is potentially at odds with the irrevocable contract she seeks to justify. In using romance to justify the "marriage contract' of subject and sovereign, she exposes the illogic at the heart of the royalist marriage/sovereignty analogy, for she shows almost in spite of herself that true romance is as much a justification of personal and political divorce as it is of marriage.

Yet, other aspects of the final trial scene of "The Contract" are at odds with the radical political possibilities I have just sketched. In particular, the obvious casuistry of the lady and the Duke leaves us with a feeling of discomfort reminiscent of Shakespeare's problem plays—a feeling of the incompatibility of law and romance, coercion and consent, both in the domestic and the political spheres. This incompatibility is illustrated by the fact that the fictions of the final scene—that love is tyrannical and contracts are binding without consent—are at odds with the implicit argument of earlier episodes according to which contract is a vehicle of true romance. In the end Cavendish's romance justification of sovereignty dramatizes some of the same problems we observed in *Leviathan*. For to the extent that she emphasizes the consensual aspect of romance, she runs the risk of justifying parliamentary critics of absolute sovereignty; and, to the extent that she sees romance as a figure of coercion, she runs the risk of apologizing for de facto political power.[37]

There are other ways as well in which true romance is contaminated by coercion and dissembling at the end of "The Contract". As we have seen, for the Duke "the wounded conscience" is less a matter of principle than of psychology; it does not involve an application of moral judgement but an experience of guilt. Yet this psychologizing of conscience is not a move that inspires confidence in the Duke's reformed character, since we know that he is acting the part of the penitent rake for the benefit of his judges. This dissembling then seems to call into question the resolution of the plot. In particular, our discomfort with the Duke's "conversion" and his marriage to the lady is aggravated by the fact that the elderly Viceroy makes what appears to be a purely expedient proposal at the last moment to the Duke's first wife—"since the law has given away your husband, I will supply his place" (43)—and by the fact that the new marriages seem likely to be as unsatisfactory as the old.

These darker elements invite an alternative reading of the end of "The Contract". According to this reading, the final trial scene is less of a simple rebuttal of Hobbes and the engagers than an adaptation of their arguments concerning the power of self-interest. In this light, the collusion of the Duke and the lady appears as a commentary on the difference between the reign of Charles I and the Protectorate—in which the law can never be infused with romance but must instead be casuistically manipulated by royalists. In such a world, Cavendish may be suggesting, true romance must be supplanted by the problem play.[38]

This instability of genre, which we might describe thematically as an uncertainty about the relationship between coercion and consent, passion and interest, returns us to the relationship of the marriage contract to political contract. For, as I have already suggested, not the least of the "problems" that the final scene stages is the very incompatibility of Cavendish's critique of the marriage contract with her royalist argument for allegiance to the king—the incompatibility, that is, of the more radical gender argument and the argument for traditional political obligation. What I would now like to stress is that this incompatibility reappears within Cavendish's representation of marriage as well. For example, although the lady demonstrates great resourcefulness in winning over the Duke and satisfying her own desires, nothing in the plot suggests that her marriage will challenge the conventional hierarchical relation of husband and wife. As she remarks earlier in response to her uncle's plans to marry her to the Viceroy, "you give your power, authority, and commands, with my obedience, away; for if my husband and your commands are contrary, I can obey but one, which must be my husband" (22). And, as she remarks somewhat later to the Duke, "it is an unheard of malice to me . . . nether to own me yourself, nor let another": self-ownership is apparently not a permanent option for women in this text (29). It is precisely for this reason, I suggest, that the plot of "The Contract" is taken up with the dilatory space of debating the conditions of contract rather than with married life itself: focusing on the time before marriage allows the lady some degree of autonomy, however unrepresentative of the married state that lies before her. It may also be for this reason that Cavendish protests in the preface to *Natures Pictures* that she never read "a whole [romance]" in her life: it is not good for women to have romances end, for romantic closure is antithetical to female independence.[39]

As "The Contract" illustrates, in mid-seventeenth-century England romance is a vehicle for debates about the proper role of coercion and consent in establishing political obligation. If, as Sheldon Wolin has argued, Hobbes saw himself as the hero of a new kind of epic, combatting the Kingdom of Darkness with the weapon of "right method",[40] Cavendish imagined herself as the heroine of a new kind of philosophical romance—a chaste "She-Anchoret" (the title of one of the other works in *Natures Pictures*) pronouncing on the central political and philosophical issues of the day. Like Hobbes, Cavendish was concerned to describe a model of obligation that is both irrevocable and consensual; unlike Hobbes, I believe, she was eager to justify the original oath of allegiance to Charles I. To Hobbes's motives of fear and self-preservation, Cavendish opposes romantic love as a stronger foundation for irrevocable contract. In the process, she also appropriates and revises the language of interest. Ideally, she suggests, self-interest need not underwrite a Hobbesian account of life as nasty, brutish, and short: for, in Cavendish's hands, romantic love is both a passion (one might even say, a form of coercion) to which we readily consent; and an interest which allows us to be faithful to our contractual obligations, even in the face of threats to our self-preservation.[41] In contrast to William Cavendish, who sacrificed his interest to the king's and whose love was unrequited,[42] Margaret Cavendish suggests that passion and interest may together underwrite the contract of political obligation, and that honour and loyalty may not be incompatible with "politic designs".

While apparently at odds with such ostentatiously demystified accounts of contract as Hobbes's *Leviathan*, Cavendish's prose romance helps us to see the languages of romance and contract may be related, and often inextricable, approaches to formulating a theory of political obligation. In fact, one might say that romance amounts to an internalization of the Hobbesian theory of contract, according to which we consent to be coerced; whereas in Hobbes's account coercion takes the form of the sovereign's power of the sword, in Cavendish coercion takes the form of our very own passions: we are coerced, in short, by ourselves. One might even argue that such coercion amounts to a disciplining, in the Foucauldian sense, of the political subject who paradoxically experiences such constraint as the most authentic—because most inward and self-imposed. Such a reading would make the projected marriage compatible with the argument for allegiance to the king; but, as we have seen, in Cavendish's hands romance is also at odds with the demands of political absolutism since it dramatizes the instability of the passions, the necessarily figurative dimension of any so-called "binding" contract.[43]

In dramatizing the intersection of romance and contract, Cavendish's work contributes to a revised history of theories of political obligation in the seventeenth century.[44] Not only does "The Contract" illustrate the general principle that seventeenth-century political debate was often carried out in terms of competing uses of the same literary genre.[45] It also suggests that romance was particularly well suited to staging the problematic coexistence of coercion and consent, passion and interest, in contemporary theories of contract. This is no doubt in part because, as Hobbes feared, the world of politics is itself "concerned with the imaginary and the fantastic", with " 'lived' remance".[46] But Cavendish takes us one step further: if the legalistic language of contract exposes romance as a matter of interest and calculation, romance simultaneously reveals the fictional and affective dimension of contract. This is as true of political contract as of the marriage contract: in both cases, as Cavendish shows, contract is predicated on and fosters a kind of pretence, even dissimulation. In *Patriarcha*, Filmer made a related point when he argued that the notion of the original contract was a ridiculous fiction.[47] Cavendish suggests, with considerably more sympathy, that contract is one of the seventeenth century's most powerful forms of romance.

Notes

1. The phrase is from Tully 1988: 12. On contract, see Gough 1957, Gierke 1950, and Cassirer 1946: chap. 13. As Gierke notes, theories of social contract are often a prelude to or fused with theories of political contract, the act which establishes the sovereign power (1950: 107–11). For a critique of Gierke's ahistoricism, which nonetheless shares the assumptions I mention, see Höpfl and Thompson 1979.
2. See e.g. Herzog 1989, Pateman 1988, Elshtain 1981, Shanley 1979, and Saccamano 1992 for an astute reading of the social contract in Rousseau.
3. Patterson 1984: chap. 4, offers an excellent account of Renaissance romance theory and the varieties of romance available to writers in the later sixteenth and early seventeenth centuries. On royalist romance, see in particular Potter 1989, Smith 1994, Patterson 1984, and Salzman 1984.
4. See Hirschman 1977 and Gunn 1969.
5. Corns 1992, Patterson 1984, Potter 1989, Norbrook 1984, Salzman 1984,

Sharpe 1987, 1989, Smith 1994, and Worden 1981, 1990, among others, have made important contributions to this revised history.

6. The text of "The Contract" is cited from Cavendish 1992. The following quotations are taken from p. 4; hereinafter cited in the text.

7. In using the term "discipline", I mean to invoke and complicate Foucault's distinction between law and discipline, between a "juridico-discursive" model of power, "centered on . . . the statement of the law and the operation of taboos", and a new method of power, "whose operation is [ensured] . . . not by law but by normalization" (1980*a*: 82, 85, 89). According to Foucault, the legal notion of contract is characteristic of the juridico-discursive model of power (1980*b*: 91–2), whereas our most intimate experiences of pleasure and of the passions are the locus of power in the disciplinary model. Pateman correctly notes in contrast to Foucault that "law and contract, obedience and contract, go hand in hand, but it does not follow that contract is concerned only with law and not also, in Foucault's terminology with discipline, normalization, and control" (1998: 16). I borrow the term "node of stress" from Crane 1993.

8. On scepticism about natural law in relation to contract and to new models of statecraft, see, among others, Tuck 1993, Herzog 1989, and the review article by Miller 1995. On the emerging language of interest, see Hirschman 1977 and Gunn 1969.

9. Henry Ferne, *Conscience Satisfied: That there is no warrant for the Armes now taken up by Subjects . . .* (Oxford, 1643), 12; cited in Shanley 1979: 81. On the relation between the marriage contract and the sexual contract, see Pateman 1988: 3–7, 54, 90.

10. Shanley also makes this point (1979: 82–5).

11. Parker's *Observations* are reprinted in Haller 1934: vol. 2; I quote here from Parker's pagination, 185.

12. Henry Parker 1644: 1–2. Milton, in the famous "Preface to Parlament" appended to the second edition of *The Doctrine and Discipline of Divorce*, argued the case for divorce by referring to the parliamentary argument for government by consent.

13. Consent, of course, also has an important role to play in Hobbes's theory, according to which we consent to be coerced by the sovereign, as I discuss below. Crucially, however, in Hobbes's model the sovereign is not a party to the contract, and so there is no relationship of mutual consent between subject and sovereign.

14. For the common distinction between spousal contracts *de futuro* (promises to marry at some future time), and *de praesenti* (an exchange of vows that constitutes marriage in the present moment, preferably but not necessarily according to canon law, with witnesses and solemnization in Church), see Swinburne 1985. On marriage contracts, see also Houlbrooke 1984: chap. 4; Ingram 1987: chaps. 4–6. All the major casuists of the seventeenth century (William Perkins, William Ames, Joseph Hall, Robert Sanderson, and Jeremy Taylor) discussed "matrimonial cases".

15. On the arguments pro and contra engagement, see Skinner 1972 and Wallace 1964 and 1968.

16. On the crisis of royalist ideology, see Corns 1992: chap. 4, including a discussion of "the interrelatedness of Cavalier as lover and loyalist" (77); on loyalism and loyalism, see Wallace 1968.

17. Grant 1957: 132.

18. Cavendish moved to France with the court of Henrietta Maria in 1643. Sir William Cavendish went into exile in 1645 after being defeated by the Parliamentary army at Marston Moor in 1644. Cavendish's life is summarized by Moira Ferguson in Wilson and Warnke 1989. Fuller biographical accounts are offered by Mendelson 1987 and Grant 1957. In *The Life of . . . William Cavendish* Cavendish recounts a number of conversations between her husband and Hobbes. See also *Philosophical Letters* (1664), 47, 492. The first part of this text offers a commentary on chapters 1–6 of *Leviathan* and parts of Hobbes's *Elements of Philosophy*. The phrase quoted comes from p. 492.

19. For two stimulating recent discussions of the development of the early modern notion of character, see Leites 1988 and Tully 1988. On the connection between casuistry and the novel, see also Starr 1971. For a related discussion of contract in the context of the novel, see Armstrong 1985. Armstrong argues that contract declined as a model for political relationships because of contradictions in the theory, but had a different fate in the novel, where the social contract lived on as the sexual contract; the female gendering of subjectivity through the novel in turn had important political consequences.

20. I borrow the catalogue of the formal and thematic features of romance as a genre in part from Frye 1957.

21. See Sharpe 1987, Veevers 1989, and Butler 1984. According to Sharpe, Charles I's tastes did not preclude "political debate and discussion" and "love was the metaphor, the medium, through which political comment and criticism were articulated in Caroline England" (1987: 39). In discussing the politics of love in the 1630s, both Sharpe and Butler have emphasized that "marriage was the ultimate relationship of equals in love" (Sharpe 1987: 288); but as I have argued above, marriage was a favourite metaphor for royalist politics because it emphasized hierarchy as well as mutuality, subordination as well as consent.

22. On Charles's "political reasons for developing his own image in romance terms", see Patterson 1984: 166–76; Potter 1989: chap. 3.

23. In the 1630s, both critics and supporters of the Crown saw romance as a particularly royalist genre: the genre favoured by court patronage but also the genre of royal behaviour. In addition to Potter 1989: chap. 3, see Patterson 1984: chap. 4; Sharpe 1987: 95–6. For examples of the republican use of romance, see Smith 1994: 246–9.

24. In the list of characters, Silvio is described as "contracted to Amarillis". See also Fanshawe 1647: 210 ("compact") and 211 ("contract").

25. See Bakhtin on the Greek "adventure novel of ordeal", in which "from the very beginning, the love between the hero and heroine is not subject to doubt; this love remains *absolutely unchanged* throughout the entire novel" (1981: 89). Bakhtin remarks on the relevance of this "chronotope" to seventeenth-century romance (1981: 96).

26. There is, of course, a gender dimension to this argument, for it is only the female protagonist whose yielding to a final kiss is described as "a willing No; an Act / mixt of Conquest and Compact" (Fanshawe 1647: 209–10). For a discussion of an analogous moment in *Paradise Lost*—the scene in which Eve is led away from the pool by Adam (bk. 4, ll. 488–9)—see Rogers 1996.

27. Patterson 1984: 184.

28. For a discussion of the greater realism of character in French romance and its relation to what I have been calling casuistical debate, see Smith 1994: 241–6. For the "decidedly feminist impulse" of French romances, see Patterson 1984: 186–9.

29. References to Hobbes's *Leviathan* are to chapter and page number, as here; *L* 17. 227.

30. My attention was drawn to this passage by Smith, who discusses Hobbes's antipathy to romance (1994: 159–60). In his "Answer to Davenant", Hobbes also criticized the improbable fictions of romance. Grant writes that in 1650 Davenant "sent Newcastle a printed copy of the famous preface, bound together with Hobbes's equally famous reply"; Margaret discussed Davenant's *Gondibert* in her *Sociable Letters* (Grant 1957: 114).

31. See Salzman 1984: 240, on the opposition between English prose romances and the Hobbesian picaresque of power seeking after power. Sharpe 1989, echoes Salzman, arguing that "the rogue tradition and the anti-romance were the mode of a new society of commerce, interest and experimental science and philosophy" (1989: 264). Much of Cavendish's work complicates this distinction, since it uses romance to rehabilitate romance as a genre capable of addressing the new society of commerce, interest, etc.

32. While the lady declares that when she is married she will be obedient to her husband (22), love in these scenes licenses disobedience, specifically disobedience to her uncle's rules for her conduct.

33. On the maxim "interest will not lie", see Hirschman 1977: 50 and *passim*.

34. Canon law would have upheld the validity of the Duke's current marriage, which had already been consummated, rather than the *de futuro* spousal contract of a minor which, as Swinburne argues, is not binding without the adult consent of both parties.

35. Rogers 1996 makes a related argument about the "anti-authoritarian, republican" implications of Cavendish's shift from the scientific theory of Hobbesian, mechanist atomism to vitalism. See also Leslie (unpublished paper), who discusses the political implications of another of Cavendish's short prose romances, "Assaulted and Pursued Chastity", and comes to conclusions similar in some respects to my own.

36. See Jordan 1990: 308: "Eve as *femina* must obey the reduced and deribbed Adam as *vir*, her fallible yet absolute governor. Hers is therefore the position of the quintessential political subject, forever bound conscientiously to honor divine law and also assiduously to obey her human superior."

37. Catherine Gallagher has argued that Cavendish's many comparisons between political absolutism and her own "empire of the mind" suggest that writing was "a compensatory withdrawal [into] . . . the domain of subjectivity": commenting on a passage in *Sociable Letters* where Cavendish remarks that because women are not legal citizens of the commonwealth, they cannot be subjects, Gallagher writes, "much in Cavendish's texts suggests that the absolutist desire, the desire to be the sovereign monarch, itself derives from a certain female disability: not from her inability to be a monarch but from her inability to be a full *subject* of the monarch. Of the two available political positions, subject

and monarch, monarch is the only one Cavendish can imagine a woman occupying" (1988: 27). In "The Contract", however, Cavendish uses the royalists' own analogy of the marriage contract to political contract not to withdraw into a domain of subjectivity but rather to comment on parliamentary as well as sexual politics.

38. On the prominence of tragicomedy in royalist literature of the 1650s, see Potter 1989, who describes it as "the dramatic manifestation of romance"; and Smith 1994: 76–87. The genres of romance and tragicomedy were often linked in the sixteenth and seventeenth centuries.

39. In this respect, "The Contract" conforms to the formal characteristics Patricia Parker has ascribed to romance in Parker 1979. On the advantage to women of prolonging the negotiations of the spousal contract, see Iwanisziw, who argues that the "liminal state of "espousal" . . . conferred a certain sexual agency upon women along with the property rights of an unmarried woman. And it is this matrix of sexual agency, material properties and legal rights that creates the romantic plots of early modern English pastoral tragicomedies:" (1994: 248).

40. Wolin 1970: 22.

41. See pp. 30 and 36 of "The Contract" for use of "interest" to describe love or passion.

42. In *The Life of William, Duke of Newcastle* (n.d.), Margaret Cavendish portrays her husband as a gentleman and soldier, one whose devotion to Charles I and Charles II was uncontaminated by considerations of personal self-interest: "He never minded his own interest more than his loyalty and duty, and upon that account never desired nor received anything from the Crown to enrich himself, but spent great sums in his Majesty's service." The duke's old-fashioned values of honour and loyalty in the midst of the civil war are explicitly contrasted to those who have "politic designs", which "tend more to interest than justice"; in contrast to the self-serving courtiers surrounding Charles II, William Cavendish loved the king more than his "wife, children, and all his posterity" (*Life*, 93, 129, 135).

43. As Hume was to write some eighty years later in his essay, "Of the Original Contract", any acquiescence or consent that is truly voluntary is also, precisely for that reason, precarious (1875: i. 446).

44. It may also contribute to a feminist critique of contract theory, although this point is obviously beyond the scope of this essay.

45. Smith 1994, among others, offers a compelling and richly illustrated argument to this effect.

46. Smith 1994: 235 makes this point about Hobbes's fear and the accuracy of his insight into the fictional dimension of politics.

47. See Filmer 1991: 21: "The ambition of one man, sometimes of many, or the faction of a city or citizens, or the mutiny of an army, both set up or pulled down princes. But they have never tarried for this *pretended* orderly proceeding of the whole multitude", i.e. government set up by contract (emphasis added). See also in the same volume *The Anarchy of a Limited or Mixed Monarchy*, 132, 139–40, and 153, where Filmer criticizes Hobbes's "platonic monarchy": "The book hath so much of fancy that it is a better piece of poetry than policy."

References

Armstong, Nancy (1985). *Desire and Domestic Fiction*. Oxford.

Bakhtin, M. M. (1981). *The Dialogic Imagination*, ed. Michael Holquist, trans. Caryl Emerson and Michael Holquist. Austin, Tex.

Boscobel: or The History of His Sacred Majesties Most Miraculous Preservation after the Battle of Worcester 3 Sept. 1651. London, 1660.

Butler, Martin (1984). *Theatre and Crisis, 1632–42*. Cambridge.

Cassirer, Ernst (1946). *The Myth of the State*. New Haven.

Cavendish, Margaret (1992). *The Description of the New Blazing World and Other Writings*, ed. Kate Lilley. Washington Square, New York.

—— (n.d.). *The Life of William, Duke of Newcastle*, ed. C. H. Firth, 2nd edn. London.

—— (1656). *Natures Pictures drawn by Fancies Pencil to the Life*. London.

—— (1662). *Plays written by the thrice Noble . . . Lady Marchioness of Newcastle*. London.

—— (1664*a*). *Philosophical Letters*. London.

—— (1664*b*). *CCXI Sociable Letters*. London.

Corns, Thomas (1992). *Uncloistered Virtue: English Political Literature, 1640–1660*. Oxford.

Crane, Mary Thomas (1993). *Framing Authority: Sayings, Self, and Society in Sixteenth-Century England*. Princeton.

Eagleton, Terry (1990). *The Ideology of the Aesthetic*. Cambridge, Mass.

Elshtain, Jean Bethke (1981). *Public Man, Private Woman: Woman in Social and Political Thought*. Princeton.

Fanshawe, Richard (trans.) (1647). *Il Pastor Fido or the Faithful Shepherd*. London.

Filmer, Robert (1991). *Patriarcha and Other Writings*, ed. Johann P. Sommerville, Cambridge.

Foucault, Michel (1980*a*). *The History of Sexuality*, i. *An Introduction*, trans. Robert Hurley. New York.

—— (1980*b*). *Power/Knowledge*, ed. Colin Gordon. New York.

Frye, Northrop (1957). *The Anatomy of Criticism*. Princeton.

Gallagher, Catherine (1988). "Embracing the Absolute: The Politics of the Female Subject in Seventeenth-Century England", *Genre*, 1:24–39.

Gierke, Otto (1950). *Natural Law and the Theory of Society*, trans. Ernest Barker. Cambridge, 1934; 1950.

Gough, J. W. (1957). *The Social Contract: A Critical Study of its Development*, 2nd edn. Oxford.

Grant, Douglas (1957). *Margaret the First: A Biography of Margaret Cavendish, Duchess of Newcastle*. Toronto.

Gunn, J. A. W. (1969). *Politics and the Public Interest in the Seventeenth Century*. London.

Haller, William (1934). *Tracts on Liberty in the Puritan Revolution, 1638–1647*, 3 vols. New York.

Herzog, Don (1989). *Happy Slaves: A Critique of Consent Theory*. Chicago.

Hill, Christopher (1964). *Society and Puritanism*. London.

Hirschman, Albert O. (1977). *The Passions and the Interests*. Princeton.

Hirst, Derek (1990). "The Politics of Literature in the English Republic", *The Seventeenth Century*, 5: 133–55.

Hobbes, Thomas (1975). *Leviathan*, ed. C. B. Macpherson. Harmondsworth.

Höpfl, Harro, and Thompson, Martyn P. (1979). "The History of Contract as a Motif in Political Thought", *American Historical Review*, 84: 919–44.

Houlbrooke, Ralph A. (1984). *The English Family, 1450–1700*. London and New York.

Hughes, Christopher (1995). "Romance, Probability, and Politics in England, 1650–1720", Ph.D. diss., Princeton University.

Hume, David (1875). "Of the Original Contract", in *Essays, Moral, Political, and Literary*, ed. T. H. Green and T. H. Grose, 2 vols., 443–60. London.

Ingram, Martin (1987). *Church Courts, Sex and Marriage in England, 1570–1640*. Cambridge and New York.

Iwanisziw, Susan B. (1994). "The Place of Women in Early Modern English Closet Drama", Ph.D. diss., University of Pennsylvania.

Jonsen, Albert R., and Toulmin, Stephen (1988). *The Abuse of Casuistry*. Berkeley and Los Angeles.

Jonson, Ben (1970). *Selected Masques*, ed. Stephen Orgel. New Haven and London.

Jordan, Constance (1990). *Renaissance Feminism*. Ithaca, NY and London.

Leites, Edmund (1988). "Casuistry and Character", in Edmund Leites (ed.), *Conscience and Casuistry in Early Modern Europe*, 119–33. Cambridge and Paris.

Leslie, Marina. "Evading Rape and Embracing Empire in Margaret Cavendish's *Assaulted and Pursued Chastity*", unpublished paper.

McKeon, Michael (1987). *The Origins of the English Novel, 1600–1740*. Baltimore.

Mendelson, Sara Heller (1987). *The Mental World of Stuart Women*. Brighton.

Miller, Peter (1995). "Statecraft and Culture in Early Modern Europe", *The Historical Journal*, 38: 161–73.

Milton, John (1957). *Complete Poems and Major Prose*, ed. Merritt Y. Hughes. Indianapolis.

——(1959). *The Doctrine and Discipline of Divorce*, vol. ii in *Complete Prose of John Milton*, ed. Ernest Sirluck, 8 vols. New Haven.

Norbrook, David (1984). *Poetry and Politics in the English Renaissance*. London and Boston.

Parker, Henry (1644). *Jus Populi*. London.

Parker, Patricia A. (1979). *Inescapable Romance: Studies in the Poetics of a Mode*. Princeton.

Pateman, Carole (1988). *The Sexual Contract*. Stanford, Calif.

Patterson, Annabel M. (1983). "*Paradise Regained*: A Last Chance at True Romance", *Milton Studies*, 17: 187–208.

—— (1984). *Censorship and Interpretation*. Madison.

Potter, Lois (1989). *Secret Rites and Secret Writing: Royalist Literature, 1641–1660*. Cambridge.

Rogers, John (1996). *The Matter of Revolution: The Poetics of Agency and Organization in the Age of Milton*. Ithaca, NY and London.

Saccamano, Neil (1992). "Rhetoric, Consensus, and the Law in Rousseau's *Contract Social*", *Modern Language Notes*, 107: 730–51.

Salzman, Paul (1984). *English Prose Fiction, 1558–1700*. Oxford.

Sandy, Amelia (1996). "Secret Agents: Politic Ideology and Jacobean Romance", Ph.D. diss., Princeton University.

Scudéry, Madeleine de (1652). *Ibrahim*, trans. Henry Cogan. London.

Shanley, Mary Lyndon (1979). "Marriage Contract and the Social Contract in Seventeenth-Century English Political Thought", *Western Political Quarterly*, 32: 79–91.

Sharpe, Kevin (1987). *Criticism and Compliment: The Politics of Literature in the England of Charles I*. Cambridge.

—— (1989). *Politics and Ideas in Early Stuart England*. London and New York.

Skerpan, Elizabeth (1992). *The Rhetoric of Politics in the English Revolution, 1642–1660*. Columbia, Mo.

Skinner, Quentin (1972). "Conquest and Consent: Thomas Hobbes and the Engagement Controversy", 79–98 in G. E. Aylmer (ed.), *The Interregnum: The Quest for Settlement*, New York.

Smith, Nigel (1994). *Literature and Revolution in England, 1640–1660*. New Haven and London.

Spenser, Edmund (1924). *The Faerie Queene*, in *Spenser's Poetical Works*, ed. J. C. Smith and E. de Selincourt. Oxford.

Spingarn, J. E. (1957). *Critical Essays of the Seventeenth Century*, 3 vols. Oxford, 1906; rpt. 1957.

Starr, George (1971). *Defoe and Casuistry*. Princeton.

Swinburne, Henry (1985). *A Treatise of Spousals, or Matrimonial Contracts: wherein all the Questions relating to that Subject are ingeniously Debated and Resolved* (London, 1686), facsimile rpt., vol. iii in *Marriage, Sex, and the Family in England 1660–1800*, ed. Randolph Trumbach, 44 vols. New York and London.

Thomas, Keith (1993). "Cases of Conscience in Seventeenth-Century England", in John Morrill, Paul Slack, and Daniel Wolff (eds.), *Public Duty and Private Conscience in Seventeenth-Century England*, 29–56. Oxford.

Tuck, Richard (1993). *Philosophy and Government, 1572–1651*. Cambridge.

Tully, James (1988). "Governing Conduct", in Edmund Leites (ed.), *Conscience and Casuistry in Early Modern Europe*, 12–71. Cambridge and Paris.

Veevers, Erica (1989). *Images of Love and Religion: Queen Henrietta Maria and Court Entertainments*. Cambridge.

Wallace, John M. (1964). "The Engagement Controversy 1649–1652: An Annotated List of Pamphlets", *Bulletin of the New York Public Library*, 68: 384–405.

315

Wallace, John M. (1968). *Destiny his Choice: The Loyalism of Andrew Marvell*. Cambridge.

Wilson, Katharina M., and Warnke Frank (1989). *Women Writers of the Seventeenth Century*. Athens, Ga.

Wolin, Sheldon (1970). *Hobbes and the Epic Tradition of Political Theory*. Berkeley and Los Angeles.

Worden, Blair (1981). "Classical Republicanism and the Puritan Revolution", in Hugh Lloyd-Jones, Valerie Pearl, and Blair Worden (eds.), *History and Imagination: Essays in Honor of H. R. Trevor-Roper*, 182–200. New York.

——(1990). "Milton's Republicanism and the Tyranny of Heaven", in Gisela Bock, Quentin Skinner, and Maurizio Viroli (eds.), *Machiavelli and Republicanism*, 225–46. Cambridge.

12 Surprising Fame: Renaissance Gender Ideologies and Women's Lyric

Ann Rosalind Jones

In Renaissance iconography, fame is a woman: a winged figure herald-ing present and future reknown. Ronsard, in his 1555 *Hymne* to Henri II, writes of "La Fame qui vole et parle librement,/ et qui sujette n'est à nul commandement" (ll. 341–42). But in Renaissance gender ideol-ogy, fame was not *for* women. Ronsard's figure of free-speaking liberty is diametrically opposed to the social ideal of woman as it was con-structed by early modern writers on feminine conduct. In the dis-courses of humanism and bourgeois family theory, the proper woman is an absence: legally, she vanishes under the name and authority of her father and her husband; as daughter and wife, she is enclosed in the private household. She is silent and invisible: she does not speak, and she is not spoken about.

I am going to analyze this ideological climate in some detail, in order to suggest how problematic the notion of literary fame was for women writing in the Renaissance. I might call what I am doing the study of pre-poetics: of the conditions necessary for writing at all, and of the ways those conditions shape the lyrics of sixteenth-century women writers. In this period, when public eloquence was becoming the central requirement for masculine careers, when training in oration and written argument was essential for men managing cities, for ambassadors and advisors to princes, for courtiers and poets, prohibi-tions against women's speech seem to have intensified. Ruth Kelso, a historian of Renaissance gender doctrines, conjectures that women may have been on the receiving end of a cultural guilt complex: as men turned more and more to secular, civic ambitions, the residual Chris-tian virtues of humility and retirement from the world were displaced onto women (25, 26).[1] Two writers on education provide an illustra-tive contrast. Juan Luis Vives, writing for the teachers of men in *De*

From Nancy K. Miller (ed.), *The Poetics of Gender* (Columbia University Press, 1986), 74–95. © Columbia University Press. Reprinted with permission.

Tradendis Disciplinis (1516), celebrates rhetoric as a training system for all mental capacities and professional positions:

Rhetoric is of the greatest influence and weight. It is necessary for all positions in life. For in man the highest law and government are at the disposal of will. To the will, reason and judgment are assigned as counsellors, and the emotions are its torches. Further, the emotions of the mind are enflamed by the sparks of speech. So, too, the reason is impelled and moved by speech. Hence it comes to pass that, in the whole kingdom of the activities of man, speech holds in its possession a mighty strength, which it continually manifests. (181)

Lionardo Bruni, some years earlier, wrote a letter-essay to a noble-woman, defining what an elite education for a woman should be: *De Studiis et literis* (c.1405). Bruni was more liberal than many men who wrote on education, but he expressly prohibited the study of rhetoric to women. He wrote to Baptista di Montefeltro, the about-to-be-married countess to whom he directed his tract:

subtleties of Arithmetic and Geometry and not worthy to absorb a cultivated mind . . . and the great and complex art of Rhetoric should be placed in the same category. My chief reason is the obvious one, that I have in view the cultivation most fitting to a woman. To her neither the intricacies of debate nor the oratorical artifices of action and delivery are of the least practical use, if indeed they are not positively unbecoming. Rhetoric in all its forms—public discussion, forensic argument, logical fencing, and the like—lies absolutely outside the province of woman. (126)

Bruni excludes rhetoric because it belongs to the public realm, the sphere of law, politics, and diplomacy, which was firmly defined as off-limits to women. Certain women of the high nobility, such as Anne de Beaujeu, recognized that the wives of princes played highly visible and articulate roles, but exceptions of this kind were not acknowledged by humanists reinforcing the long-standing public/private dichotomy in their writing on contemporary sex roles. Writers aiming advice at fathers and husbands in lower ranks limited women's exposure to language and learning even further. They opposed the frivolous and potentially dangerous pleasures of poetry and philosophy to the sober, useful work assigned to the daughters and wives of the petty gentry and urban merchant class. Giovanni Bruto typifies this counteraristocratic move in his *L'Institutione di una fanciulla nata nobilmente*, published in a French translation in Anvers in 1555. Bruto dedicated this tract to the daughter of a Genoese shipping magnate, whom he clearly wanted to prevent from aspiring to the courtly accomplishments and the elite cultural training of women above her station. He opposes domestic virtue to public ambition; he links literary fame to lascivious self-indulgence. He begins with a transvaluation of historical categories, rewriting the reputations of classical heroines such as Sappho and Diotima:

They, I say, never got so much fame by their learning as they did defame, for their unhonest and loose living. And I suppose there is no man of reason and understanding, but had rather love a Mayden unlearned and chaste, than one suspected of dishonest life, though never so famous and well learned in philosophy.[2] (B8ᵛ)

He goes on to set up a pair of antithetical images that appear throughout Renaissance attacks and defenses of women who write:

how far more convenient the Distaffe and Spindle, Needle and Thimble, [are] for [maids] with a good and honest reputation, then the skill of well using a pen or writing a lofty verse with diffame dishonor, if in the same there be more erudition than virtue. (C2ʳ)

The spindle and distaff versus the pen, private decency versus infamous verse: these oppositions aren't self-evident. Why should learning and writing be equated with immorality and dishonor? Bruto's assumption that learning and chastity are mutually exclusive points to the concern—the obsession, in fact—that underlies the great majority of Renaissance pronouncements on women's speech and fame: female sexual purity. The link between loose language and loose living arises from a basic association of women's bodies with their speech: a woman's accessibility to the social world beyond the household through speech was seen as intimately connected to the scandalous openness of her body. By leaving the confines of domestic privacy, a woman exposed herself to dangers of both visual and verbal kinds. To be seen and to be engaged in conversation were equally potentially transgressive.

An early instance of this body/speech analogy appears in Francesco Barbaro's 1513 essay on *The Duties of a Wife*. Barbaro repeats a Roman anecdote about a noble matron who withdrew her bare arm from the sight of a man who had praised it: "Ah, but it is not public," she said. Like most Italian humanists who cited Roman texts, Barbaro approves of this one; and he goes on to make its implicit assumptions explicit: "It is proper that the speech of women never be made public; for the speech of a noblewoman can be no less dangerous than the nakedness of her limbs" (205). This equation between women's bodies and women's speech depends upon a further assumption: women's onlookers and hearers are always men. The threat envisioned by male social theorists comes from an audience that is always presumed to be masculine. The body-speech link is made more bluntly in a popular tag quoted by the English translator of an Italian treatise on jealousy, (Benedetto Varchi, *The Blazon of Jealousie*, 1615). Richard Toste's summing up of marital common sense suggests that racy speech in a woman is worse than an actual sexual lapse:

> Maides must be seene, not heard, or selde, or never,
> O may I one such wed, if I wed ever.
> A Maid that hath a lewd Tongue in her head,
> Worse than if she were found with a Man in bed. (Stallybrass, fn. 18)

It is clear in Shakespearean comedy that verbal challenges from women were perceived as sexual challenges as well (see, on this subject, the witty coda to Lisa Jardine's chapter on the representation of shrews in Elizabethan and Jacobean drama, "Scolding or Shrewing Around?").[3] And the equation between women's chat and women's sexuality also surfaces in etiquette books such as Stefano Guazzo's *Civil Conversation* (1574; English trans. 1581). When the leading speaker in Guazzo's dialogue announces that he will now discuss "la conversatione delle donne," his listener assumes that he means men's sexual relationships with prostitutes, with the kind of women who play at "the game of embraces" ("con le quali si giuoca alle braccia" [1:290]). The confusion is symptomatic: the man takes "conversation," like the modern word "intercourse," to have two meanings. Among men it is civil, that is, public, civilizing; between men and women, it is carnal.

At court, where women were habitually seen and heard, as the onlookers and the admiring chorus for men's self-display, the tension between public accessibility and private chastity was acute. Even in the idealizing atmosphere of Castiglione's *Courtier*, the speeches of male characters register the strain arising from the contradictory requirements imposed on the court lady, or *donna di palazzo*: to demonstrate courteous affability but also to be pure in manners and body. Giuliano de' Medici recommends that feminine speech balance a "ready livelieness of wit" against "sober and quiet manners"; the female courtier must compensate for being entertainingly witty (*arguta*) by also being unfailingly modest (*discreta*). She must, Giuliano says, "keepe a certain mean very hard, and come just to certain limits" (343). The admitted delicacy of this balance confirms that, in a woman, verbal fluency and bodily purity are understood to be contrary conditions.

By the early seventeenth century, remarks on women's speech suggest that an intensification of prohibitions was underway, particularly in England, where the Protestant focus on marital duties intensified surveillance over daughters and wives. Richard Brathwaite, in *The English Gentlewoman* (1631), hints at a certain frustration at the difficulty of controlling his countrywomen's speech:

To enter into much discourse . . . with strangers argues lightness or indiscretion: what is said of maids may properly be applied to all women: *They should be seen and not heard.* . . . women's tongues are held their defensive armor, but in no particular detract they more from their honor than by giving too much scope to that glibbery member. (78)

He expands the classical *topos* of the teeth as a natural fence for the tongue into an elaborate image of repression and containment:

What restraint is required in respect of the tongue may appear by that ivory guard or garrison with which it is impaled. See how it is doubly warded, that it may with more reservancy and better security be restrained! (88)

The belief that women's speech opened them to irresistible sexual temptation, that articulateness led to promiscuity, produced a related set of prohibitions against women's being spoken *about*. Men's eyes and men's tongues were assumed to share the power to define and possess a feminine object. Wives especially were warned of the indecency of worldly fame. Orazio Lombardelli, writing to his young wife in 1574, declared, "Being known to many men is not a sign of moral health. And acquiring a nickname, . . . like being sung about in songs, are signs of too much desire to be seen" (*Dell 'Uffizio della Donna Maritata*, 27–28). Robert Greene attributes similar ideas to two classical authors to the same effect (*Penelope's Web*, 1601):

The wise and learned man Euboides, whose sayings have ever been counted as oracle, was of this opinion, that the greatest virtue in a woman is to be knowne of none but her husband: alleging the saying of Argius, that the praise of a woman in a strange mouth is nothing else but a secret blame. (E4ʳ)

The injunction to silence and invisibility was laid upon all women, married or not. Thucydides was much quoted: "The most praiseworthy woman is she whose praises are kept within the walls of the private house" (in Tasso, 2)[4] and Aristotle's distinction between the sexes—"Silence is the virtue of woman as eloquence is of the man" (in Tasso, 3)—was used as a basis for paradoxical commands. Barbaro concludes his commentary on women's speech by declaring, "Women should believe that they have achieved the glory of eloquence if they will honor themselves with the outstanding ornament of silence" (*De Re Uxoria*, 206). This sounds like nonsense; it is. But it is also a logical outcome of the reasoning through which Renaissance gender theory produced the ideal woman. She was distinguished by what she did not do, or, equally important, by what men did not do to her: she was unseen, unheard, untouched, unknown—at the same time that she was obsessively observed. This must be what is meant by saying that women occupy a negative position in culture.

More precisely, I have been describing the *assignment* to women of a negative position in culture. But there is a difference between being the subject *of* discourse and being a subject *in* discourse. No system of sexual opposition allows its participants to speak freely, but the poetic collections of Renaissance women show that they did not simply accede to the silencing logic of their culture. Those who submitted entirely, of course, are not available for reading; those who wrote did so through a range of responses to the interdiction against going public. None of the three poets I am going to discuss rebelled outright against the idealization of the silent woman. Rather, they carried out a sort of *bricolage* with social dictates, enacted a partial obedience toward them, earned the right to fame through a series of subtle appropriations and reshufflings of prevailing notions of feminine virtue. A pose of deference and of self-effacement before the masculine right to fame could act as a scaffolding for various countermoves: a woman poet could promote her own reputation; she could weave a class-based model of the good bourgeois daughter into a defense for women's poetic practice; she could disarm and surround potential male critics by drawing them into a system of cooperative or dialogic authorship. More open challenges to the exclusion of women from humanist claims to fame occurred during the sixteenth century, but I am concerned less with heroines here than with canny compromisers, whose responses to their male contemporaries reveal how *situational* women's writing was, and to what extent it needs to be understood as an adaptation to the gender ideologies reigning in the *pre*-texts of literary culture. Renaissance women poets, given their enforced location outside public discourse, worked their ways into them more often by indirection than by confrontation.

It is important not to overestimate the room for maneuver available to women. One thing that sets their anxiety of authorship[5] apart from the anxiety of later women writers is the absolute centrality of men as writers and as readers in the sixteenth-century literary system. Every woman poet recognized the necessity of winning men over to her side as mentors and as critics. The enormous feminine audiences for romances and novels of the eighteenth and nineteenth centuries did not exist in the 1500s: women were advised to read religious and moral tracts rather than contemporary poetry, which was considered trivial or risky for them. And although women poets occasionally open or close their collections with appeals to women readers, it is very rare to find them acknowledging or taking encouragement from other women poets. Their models and their judges are men, and they do not count on a sympathetic reading. Two Ovidian heroines appear throughout the love poetry of Italian women writing in the Cinquecento: Philomel and Echo, figures of feminine speechlessness that might be taken as emblems of the isolated woman poet in an era of literary prohibitions. Philomel, whose tongue was cut out by the rapist Tereus, nonetheless wove her story into a tapestry of her own devising; Echo, made mute in punishment for her connivance with Jove, could only repeat the tag ends of phrases uttered by the ever-elusive Narcissus.[6]

PERNETTE DU GUILLET: SELFLESSNESS AS SELF-SERVICE, OR FAME THROUGH DEMURRAL

It may be better to be Echo than to be entirely inaudible, however. And the case of Pernette du Guillet shows that echoing may be a cover for forays into new verbal territory. Pernette, writing in Lyon in the early 1540s, adopted a stance of selfless discipleship to Maurice Scève. The publishing circumstances of her *Rymes* suggest that she avoided acting on any public ambition herself; it was left to her husband to publish her poems after her death in 1545. She claims in several poems that her one goal is to lose herself entirely by being transformed into her model and mentor. In her fifth epigram, for example (in which she writes "CE VICE MUERAS" as an anagram of Scève's name), she promises him, "Je tascheray faire en moy ce bien croitre,/ Qui seul en toy me pourra transmuer" (I shall try to increase in myself that good/Which alone will be capable of transforming me into you) (Epigram 5, ll. 3–4). Imitation here is metamorphosis into the Other. Pernette continues to deny any desire for an independent poetic voice; in Epigram 6 she announces that she is incapable even of contributing to Scève's fame, that is, of reciprocating the poems he has composed in praise of her, unless he lends her the skill to write exactly as he does: "Preste moy donc ton eloquent sçavoir/ Pour te louer ainsi que tu me loues" (ll. 9–10). The echo-writing she envisions here sounds less like imitation than ventriloquism: the disciple hopes to become her master's voice.

But there is a subtle ploy of fame-claiming and fame-bargaining going on here. In that last line, "So that I may praise you as you praise me," Pernette points to her own fame as the topic of Scève's massive poetic output; it has been his poems in her praise that set this exchange of compliments in motion. Thus fame leads to fame: being spoken about obliges Pernette to speak in return. The praises of the master poet are invoked as a justification for the responses of the disciple. By appealing to a notion of gender-free reciprocity, the woman poet makes her writing look like the fulfillment of a courteous obligation rather than a transgression of gender boundaries. Pernette's enactment of selfless modesty is actually a strategy of self-defense.

In a later poem, the pose of self-effacement before the male poet's reputation frames an extraordinary fantasy of gender transgression. Pernette's *Elégie* 2 is a rewriting of the Actaeon myth, in which the woman poet takes on the death-dealing powers of the goddess Diana and directs them toward the erotic and verbal domination of the male poet.[7] Pernette imagines herself bathing naked in a fountain. Singing a poem and playing the lute, she would lure her lover toward her, but she would deflect his embrace by splashing him with "l'eau pure de la clere fontaine," turning him not into a "Cerf" (deer) but a "serf," (slave) a "serviteur" acknowledging her total "puissance" over him. The narrative ends with Pernette's renunciation of this divine power to transfix the man. She sacrifices her desire to enslave him, "à l'asservir," in a gesture of homage to his fame. She defers to Apollo, the Muses and his public audience, taking on the role of one reader among many:

> Laissez le aller les neuf Muses servir,
> Sans le vouloir dessoubz moy asservir . . .
> Laissez le aller, qu'Apollo je n'irrite,
> Le remplissant de Deité profonde,
> Pour contre moy susciter tout le Monde,
> Lequel un jour par ses escriptz s'attend
> D'estre avec moy et heureux, et content.

> (ll. 47–54, 59–60)

> Let him go, to serve the nine Muses,
> Without wanting to enslave him to myself . . .
> Let him go, let me not anger Apollo,

Filling him full of deep godly power,
To stir up the entire world against me,
That world which hopes one day through his writing
To be, along with me, both fortunate and happy.

But her performance throughout the elegy is far less humble than this expiatory final gesture. *She* represents and controls the scene of seduction, *she* invents the pun that turns the poet into a deer and into her slave, she attributes to *herself* the power of sending the poet back to his vocation. After thirty-eight lines of erotic aquatics, she cannot finally disappear into the anonymous group identity that she claims at the end of the poem. The movement of the elegy toward this apparently modest conclusion, however, may make possible the surfacing, the de-repression, of its central fantasy. Pernette finally neutralizes her transgression of gender laws—her role as seductress and literalizer of Neoplatonic metaphors of devoted service—through a ritual of self-sacrifice or self-erasure. But the elegy's framework of socially endorsed modesty simultaneously supports an experimental vision of sexually and verbally active femininity.

CATHERINE DES ROCHES: HOUSEHOLD BARGAINS, OR CLASS LOYALTY AS THE RIGHT TO WRITE

The enabling fiction of self-abnegation before a male mentor has something in common with a broader tactic adopted by another French woman, writing in Poitiers twenty years after Pernette: Catherine Des Roches, the daughter in a mother-daughter pair who published joint collections of poems in 1578 and 1583. Catherine Des Roches appropriated a class-based definition of feminine virtue as a support for her writing: she aligned herself with bourgeois writers celebrating the practical activity of the domestic woman against the frivolous and presumably decadent dilettantism of the aristocratic lady. This was a line of argument that had begun as early as Leon Battista Alberti's *Della Famiglia* (1433–34) and was extended in a careful distinction made by Jacques Du Bosc in his *L'Honneste Femme* (1632). Du Bosc is sympathetic to many womanly refinements, but he limits them to the childless noblewoman: "It should not be thought that in this portrait of the accomplished lady we intend to paint a mother of a family who is expert in giving orders to her servants and who has the duty of caring for her children. Music, history, philosophy and other such exercises are more appropriate to our picture than those of a good housewife" (178). Des Roches, by identifying herself with solidly useful household work, with the spinning that was the constant task of the poor and middle-class family woman, applies for a compensatory license to write.

A first instance of this identification with antiaristocratic class ideals comes in her paraphrase of a popular Renaissance text, the Old Testament portrait of the virtuous woman, whose "price is far above rubies" (*Proverbs*, 31). Des Roches's "La femme forte descritte par Salomon" is a fascinating modernization of the Hebrew ideal of the hard-working, all-providing wife and mother. This was an active and a practical ideal, and Des Roches emphasizes both these qualities in her expansion of the Biblical text. The Old Testament basis for the eight-line passage below is a mere two lines in the King James version: "She girdeth her loins with strength, and strengtheneth her arms." Des Roches enlarges this statement into a critique of the physical inactivity of aristocratic women by praising the active force of the housewife. In common with writers such as Alberti, she eroticizes domestic energy: the housewife is beautiful in her strength:

> Vous la verriez parfois r'accourcir sa vesture,
> Troussée proprement d'une forte ceinture,
> Et revirer apres ses manches sur les bras
> Qui paroissent charnus, poupins, douïllets et gras:
> Car il ne faut penser que la delicatesse
> Se trouve seulement avecques la paresse.
>
> (*Oeuvres*, 149)

> You'd see her at times pin up her gown,
> Neatly bound in with a sturdy belt,
> And then roll up her sleeves on her arms,
> Which look plump and rosy, tender and full:
> For it's wrong to believe that delicacy
> Co-exists only with laziness.

Her concluding couplet has a combative, critical ring:

> La femme ménagère est plus belle cent fois
> Que ne sont ces Echo qui n'ont rien que la voix.

> The housewifely woman is a hundred times lovelier
> Than these mere Echos who have only a voice.

It is clear here that Des Roches is asserting class independence from aristocratic notions of feminine beauty and reticence in feminine discourse. By speaking as the good bourgeois daughter, she claims and celebrates a counteridentity in the process of being formed against the presumed self-indulgence of higher-ranking women. She demonstrates her loyalty to two histories simultaneously: she appears to serve the men of her class, as she serves the marital theory of the Old Testament by translating it into French.

But the confidence, even the aggressiveness, of this paraphrase takes on a different cast in a sonnet, "A ma quenoille" (To my distaff), in which Des Roches balances concessions to domestic imagery against a claim to public space as a writer. This is a complicated poem, full of repetitions and retractions, because it carries out a complicated strategy. Des Roches is so hesitant to admit any desire for fame that she speaks *around* its possibility. The first quatrain of the sonnet depends upon negation and periphrasis. The desire for a literary reputation is dismissed as a vain search after ephemera:

> Quenoille, mon souci, je vous promets et jure
> De vous aimer tousjours, et jamais ne changer
> Vostre honneur domestic pour un bien etranger,
> Qui erre constamment et fort peu de temps dure.

> Distaff, my care, I promise and swear
> I'll love you forever, and never forswear
> Your homely glory for an outside desire,
> Which wanders forever and lasts but a day.

But this dismissal of a poetic career goes hand in hand with two emblems of the writer's trade. Des Roches appeals to the distaff for permission and protection; she transforms the conventional household emblem into a shelter against insult and infamy, the criticism that she assumes will follow upon her use of ink and paper:

> Vous ayant au costé, je suis beaucoup plus seure
> Que si encre et papier se venoient à ranger
> Tout à l'entour de moy, car pour me revanger
> Vous pouvez bien plustost repousser une injure.

> With you by my side, I am safer by far
> Than if ink and paper joined in a circle
> In my defense; for, to protect me,
> You are abler by far to push back an attack.

This is highly defensive vocabulary. If fame is only indirectly named in the poem, the necessity of combatting hostile responses is not; "revanger" means to protect oneself through counterattack, and "repousser" has equally military connotations. Des Roches writes with a clear eye to the resistance her role as a poet is certain to stir up.

In the sestet, she protects herself by setting up an elaborate equilibrium between the male-defined symbol of feminine industry and her counteremblem of woman as writer. The cajoling intimacy in her appeal to the distaff foregrounds the difficulty of reconciling sixteenth-century demands for housewifely modesty with the guilty desire to write:

> Mais quenoille m'amie il ne faut pas pourtant
> Que pour vous estimer, et pour vous aimer tant
> Je delaisse du tout cest'honneste coustume
> D'escrire quelque fois; en escrivant ainsi
> J'escris de vos valeurs, quenoille mon souci,
> Ayant dans la main le fuzeau, et la plume. (152)

> But distaff, my love, it's surely not the case
> That because I admire you and love you so much,
> I must leave off entirely my virtuous habit
> Of writing at times; for when I do write,
> I write of your value, distaff, my care,
> With the spindle and the pen together in my hand.

Des Roches's promise of unfailing loyalty to womanly virtues is, then, the first step in a propitiatory maneuver. This spinner wants to write, so she disguises her ambition as homage to the ideologically sanctified spindle, the "fuzeau" of her final line. The coordinating conjunction of her last line supports the balancing act toward which she has been working all along: the spindle *and* the pen, not either/or but both/and. This is Des Roches's way past the enforced choice between domestic virtue or writerly publicity. Her love poem to the emblem of housewifely routine earns her access to a feminine pen, which acquires a new respectability through its juxtaposition with the unimpeachable "quenoille." Tight class loyalty (and a certain complicity with masculine fantasy) makes possible a loosening of gender rules. This daughter of the bourgeoisie expands those rules to include herself as writer.

TULLIA D'ARAGONA: NEGOTIATING CELEBRITY, OR FAME AS A MULTI-PARTY CONTRACT

The ingratiating compromise worked out by Catherine Des Roches takes on a more dramatic and expanded form in the collected poems of an Italian courtesan, Tullia d'Aragona. I offer her as a final instance of women's claims to fame because her collection of *Rime* (Venice,

1547) exposes the structure and the processes of fame in a way that few Renaissance texts, by women or by men, do. As a courtesan, Tullia d'Aragona was an admittedly public woman, a sexual professional whose capital consisted in successfully manipulated display: spectacular appearances in processions and at banquets, a high intellectual style. Her reputation, on which she based the high fees that distinguished the courtesan from the common prostitute, depended on a male clientele, the Venetian and Florentine literati and courtiers with whom she traded sexual favors in return for literary recognition. Her set of poems reveals rather than conceals the negotiations and exchanges through which Renaissance writers—perhaps all writers—construct a reputation for themselves.

Throughout the *Rime* Tullia collects and preserves poetic praise in the form of verse epistles, the letters of recommendation through which she and her interlocutors build up a group identity assembled through laudatory dialogues. The *Rime* are composed of 105 poems. Forty-nine are by Tullia; thirty-nine of these are sonnets addressed to men whom she names both in her titles and in the poems themselves. The middle section of the collection is a long eclogue written for Tullia by her old ally, Girolamo Muzio: "La Tirrhenia," in which the nymph of the title is given charisma through the enumeration of her admirers, recognizable as contemporary writers, professionals and noblemen, encoded in Muzio's pastoral pseudonyms. The third section of the book consists of fifty-five poems by men, addressed to Tullia by acquaintances she had cultivated throughout fifteen years of elite literary coteries in Rome, Ferrara, and Venice. What is going on in this multiauthored collection? It is clearly not the product of a unique, originary voice; it is, rather, a carefully organized collaboration, designed as a set of testimonials to Tullia's beauty and eloquence.

How did she acquire this dossier, and why did her contributors oblige? Many of her sonnets are transparent requests for *laude*, poems of praise, and although she regularly deprecates her own lyric competence, she often promises a praise-poem in return. A case in point: writing to Benedetto Varchi, she begins with a eulogy of his "high, immortal worth" and complains that her melancholy and bad fortune prevent her from rising to his "high knowledge and sweet song." But she suggests, in her conclusion, that even dying of grief would be bearable if Varchi wrote a poem in her honor:

> Ma s'a me pur così convien finire
> La penna vostra al men levi il mio nome

Fuor degli artigli d'importuna morte.

But if I must die in this way,
Let your pen [wing] at least raise my name
Above the weapons of relentless death.

(Sonnet 22, p. 8a)

In her sixth sonnet, written to Cosimo de' Medici (who had saved her from prosecution for breaking the sumptuary laws of Florence, which required that courtesans wear a yellow-bordered veil), she makes a similar shift: her posture of helplessness again gives way to a strategy of self-commemoration. Claiming that Cosimo's virtues surpass her ability to praise him, she asks the Muses to produce a eulogy in her stead. But this self-effacement suddenly turns into a claim of authorship, after all. In her final line, Tullia adopts a literary-historical perspective on her own performance, naming herself and her setting in place and time from the third-person perspective of a posthumous biographer: "Cosi dicea la Tullia in riva d'Arno" (Sonnet 6, p. 4a: "Thus spake Tullia, on the banks of the Arno").

Tullia's determination to textualize her own name, to be the subject as well as the author of her poems, orchestrates many of the echo poems in the first section of the *Rime*. These paired *proposte/risposte* sonnets share the same rhyme scheme: one by a man to Tullia, one by her in return (or one by her, followed by a man's response). Typically, the topic of these duets is fame itself. One pair opens with a sonnet by Antonio Grazzini ("Il Lasca"); he describes Tullia as a figure of international renown in order to argue that only she can formulate compliments worthy of her reputation. In response, she tells him that his celebration has revived and rejuvenated her, to the extent that she can now praise him in return. The stakes in this exchange are new: they are not the claim to private passion through which a male poet wins public fame. What circulates in the dialogue is not desire or even flirtation but a familiar lexicon of literary terms: sheets of paper, styluses and style, the penning of praise. Tullia, the woman poet, is addressed, precisely, *as* a woman poet by "Il Lasca"; and in spite of the intimacy suggested by the juxtaposition of the two poems, the exchange foregrounds the reputation-swapping that is the real business of Tullia's *Rime*, romanticized in gestures toward erotic pairing—gestures which also serve the reputation-building of men in Tullia's sociotextual circuit.

IL LASCA
Se'l vostro valor Donna gentile
Esser lodato pur dovresse in parte,

Vopo sarebbe al fin vergar le carte
Col vostro altero, et glorioso stile.
Dunque voi sola a voi stessa simile,
A cui s'inchina la natura, et l'arte
Fate di voi cantando in ogni parte
TULLIA, TULLIA suonar da Gange a Thile.
Si vedrem poi di gioia et maraviglia
Et di gloria, et d'honore il mondo pieno
Drizzare al vostro nome altare, et tempi.
Cosa che mai con l'ardenti sue ciglia
Non vide il Sole rotando il Ciel sereno.
O ne gli antichi, o ne moderni tempi.

LA TULLIA

Io, che fin qui quasi alga ingrata, et vile
Sprezzava in me cosi l'interna parte,
Come un fior che tosto invecchia, et parte
Da noi ben spesso nel piu bello Aprile.
Hoggi, LASCA gentil non pur a vile
Non mi tengo (merce de le tue carte)
Ma movo anchor la penna ad honorarte,
Fatta in tutto a me stessa dissimile.
Et, come pianta, che suggendo piglia
Novo licor da l'humido terreno,
Manda fuor frutti, e fior, benche s'attempi,
Tal'io potrei, si nuovo mi bisbiglia
Pensier nel cor di non venir mai meno,
Dar forse anchor di me non bassi essempi.

[LASCA]

If your high worth, gentle lady,
Had to be praised, if only in part,
Yours would be the task of covering paper
With your lofty and famous style (stylus).
Thus you alone equal to yourself,
To whom nature and art bow down,
You yourself make, singing everywhere,
TULLIA, TULLIA echo from the Ganges to Thule.
Then we will see the world, filled with
Joy and wonder, with your glory and honor,
Raise up altars and temples to your name—
Something the sun, with his burning brows,
Has never seen as he wheels through the calm sky,
Either in ancient or in modern times.

[TULLIA]

I, who till now, like a weak and lowly weed
Have scorned my inner self,
Like a flower, which suddenly ages and leaves
Us in the midst of the loveliest April,
Today, gentle LASCA, I no longer
See myself as vile, thanks to your poem,
But I raise my pen again, to honor you,
Transformed entirely from my former self.
And, as a plant, drawing up new moisture
From the dampened earth,
Sends forth fruits and blossoms, even though it grows older,
So may I, since a new thought whispers
In my heart that I need never decay,
Produce again, perhaps, not unworthy
Examples of what I can do.

(Sonetti di diversi alla signora Tullia
con le risposte di lei, pair 5, p. 18a)

Most Renaissance lyric collections included poems written in praise of their author, but Tullia's *Rime* take this representation of mutual admiration to an extreme: of 105 poems, only 49 are hers. She was not interested in assembling a self-enclosed oeuvre, but in gathering distinguished men into an affirmative chorus. Their willingness to participate in this "polylogue" calls for analysis. I would argue that Tullia's collection substitutes an improving fiction for the realities of a courtesan's life and the rivalry among her clients. In the *Rime*, potential rivals are transformed into flattering mirrors for each other; Tullia is a channel through which her interlocutors emerge as members of a masculine elite constructed within the group text. She makes herself the medium through which each man takes on some of the luster of his fellows. This idealized version of male bonding becomes explicit in Muzio's eclogue, in which he lists Tirrhenia's admirers and their accomplishments one after another. As the list gets longer, each of its members takes on greater and greater éclat. The process ends when the shepherd Dametas crowns Tirrhenia with a garland woven of the famous "souls" who have sung her praises (ll. 211–15). The gesture records for posterity both the woman and the men who attest to her desirability—and to each other's erotic connoisseurship. Rather than denying her desire for fame, or disarming male readers with a display of class solidarity, Tullia absorbs her critics into her text and fixes them in postures of admiration.

Fame of this kind, the erotic starring role in a cast of many men, was certainly not permissible to a married noblewoman like Pernette or to a middle-gentry daughter like Catherine Des Roches. Tullia's assembling of a group portrait was a consequence of her position as a socially saturated, public figure. She did not challenge the assumption that verbal forwardness in a woman went hand in hand with sexual forwardness; she profited from it. (The *Rime* were published four times in her lifetime, and they won her publishers for a later philosophical dialogue and a verse romance.) And precisely by going after fame so single-mindedly, she demystified the whole issue of poetic reputation. Fame is never the simple result of independent merit or aesthetic autonomy. The solitary poet goes unread; the famous poet is socially constituted, invented through the gaze, the commentary, the assessment of others. It is no accident that two of the best known women poets of the Renaissance, Louise Labé and Veronica Franco, were notorious before they were famous. For a woman who entered the realm of poetic publicity inevitably had to break the rules of gender decorum.

But I hope I have shown that the rules could be bent as well as broken. Prohibitions on women's intercourse with the literary world were not as paralyzing as they were intended to be. Their effect was not to silence women but to provoke them into complex forms of negotiation and compromise. I would characterize Pernette, Catherine Des Roches, and Tullia d'Aragona as subversive conformists; without directly opposing social interdictions, they nonetheless took oblique paths toward fame. Pernette backed into it. Her denial of her own ambition and her deference toward her mentor increased the likelihood that her poems would be published. (Good girls sometimes get away with surprisingly gross disobedience.) Des Roches, more positively, made an alliance with the men of her class, an alliance through which she earned more than they perhaps bargained for. As an expert in calculated concession, she proved that a woman can be loyal to more than one cause at a time. Tullia, finally, affirmed the sexual suspicion that underlay Renaissance gender ideology: the woman of many words may indeed be a woman of little chastity. But she refused the double standard. Men are equally involved, she demonstrated, in the group exchange of poetic reputation-building. Altogether, this trio suggests that women's writing in the Renaissance needs to be read for resistance and invention as well as sociotextual constraint. For men and women, fame was not the same. Women claimed it in intricate and indirect ways: they spun safety nets for themselves from the loose ends of masculine discourse, they composed poems that record rather than harmonize the tensions they confronted in a cultural context that demanded women's silence. Reading such poets consequently requires an ear open to the half-said, the quickly withdrawn, the manipulation of masculine rituals of self-eternalization.

"Fame," in English, comes from the Greek root *phanei*, to speak and to be spoken about. The two were linked through prohibition in the ideologies aimed at women in early modern Europe. How, then, do we now read a woman who could be condemned in 1550 as unworthy of hearing precisely because she wanted to be heard? Prepoetically, by necessity. Women are spoken of; they speak to. The "of" and the "to," the context and the audience, must be the starting-points for any understanding of sixteenth-century women's writing.

Notes

1. For a general argument that the Renaissance disempowered women, with a focus on courtly love as ideology in Italy, see Kelly-Gadol (139–64). A more optimistic view, stressing class differentials, urban flexibility, and reformed religion as benefits for women, is Davis (65–95). See also the introduction to Ferguson et al. for an overview of economic and ideological changes, especially as they affected Englishwomen.
2. Compare the remark of Thomas Powell, aiming at the upwardly mobile fathers of merchant and professional families in London. In *The Art of Thriving*, he writes of middle-class daughters: "Instead of Song and Musick, let them learne Cookery and Laundry. And in steade of reading Sir Philip Sidney's Arcadia, let them read the grounds of good Huswifery. I like not a Female Poëtesse at any hand" (114–15).
3. Lisa Jardine (121–40).
4. Torquato Tasso quotes but also, atypically, questions Thucydides in his *Discorso della virtù femminile, e donnesca*.
5. I borrow this term, which I use less psychologically but similarly as a way of describing women writers' confrontation with the cultural restriction of writing to men, from Sandra Gilbert and Susan Gubar, *The Madwoman in the Attic*.
6. Gaspara Stampa calls on Philomel (and her sister Procne) in her *Rime* (Venice, 1554), Sonnet 173. Veronica Franco mentions both in her *Terze Rime* (Venice, 1575), 3, ll. 25–27. Tullia d'Aragona aligns herself with the Ovidian victim in one of her best-known sonnets, "Qual vaga Philomela" ("Like the Longing Philomel"), *Rime*, 28. References to Echo occur in Stampa (*Rime*, 152) and in Franco (*Terze Rime*, 3, ll. 16–18). The conduct-book writer, Robert Cleaver, appeals to the Echo myth with very different intentions: "as the echo answereth but one word for many, which are spoken to her, so a Maid's answer should be in a single word" (A *Godly Forme of Houshold Government* [London, 1588], p. 94).
7. For an early analysis of this elegy, see Perry, 259–71. I am indebted to Lawrence Lipking for his observation that Pernette further reverses gender roles in this

poem by making herself the agent through whom Apollo is filled with divinity—in contrast to the Sybil, who was traditionally on the receiving end in this process (Poetics of Gender colloquium, Columbia University, November 1984).

Works Cited

Alberti, Leon Battista. *Della Famiglia* (*Libro Secondo*). Turin: Einaudi, 1972.

Aragona, Tullia d'. *Rime della Signora Tullia d'Aragona, et di diversi a lui.* Ed. Enrico Celani. Venice, 1547; repr. Bologna: Romagnoli Dall'Acqua, 1891, 1968.

Barbaro, Giovanni. *De Re Uxoria.* Paris, 1513, 1533. Trans. in *The Earthly Republic: Italian Humanists on Government and Society.* Ed. Benjamin Kohl et al. Philadelphia: University of Pennsylvania Press, 1978.

Brathwaite, Richard. *The English Gentlewoman.* London, 1631.

Bruni d'Arezzo, Lionardo. "Concerning the Study of Literature: A Letter Addressed to the Illustrious Lady, Baptista Malatesta." In *Vittorino da Feltre and Other Humanist Educators.* Ed. William Harrison Woodward. New York: Columbia University, Teachers College Press (Classics in Education, no. 18), 1963.

Bruto, Giovanni. *L'Institutione di una Fanciulla nata nobilmente.* Anvers, 1553. Trans. Thomas Salter, as *A Mirrhor mete for all Mothers, Matrones and Maidens, intituled the Mirrhor of Modestie.* London, 1579.

Castiglione, Baldessar. *Il Libro del Cortigiano.* Venice, 1528; repr. Turin: UTET, 1964. Ed. Bruno Maier. Trans. Sir Thomas Hoby, *The Book of the Courtier.* London, 1561; repr. London: H. M. Dent, 1974.

Cleaver, Robert. *A Godly Forme of Houshold Government.* London, 1588.

Davis, Natalie Zemon. "City Women and Religious Change." In *Society and Culture in Early Modern France.* Stanford: Stanford University Press, 1975.

Du Bosc, Jacques. *L'Honneste Femme.* Paris, 1632.

Du Guillet, Pernette. *Rymes.* Ed. Victor Graham. Geneva: Droz, 1968.

Des Roches, Madeleine and Catherine. *Les Oeuvres de Mes-Dames des Roches de Poetiers, mère et fille.* Paris, 1578.

Ferguson, Margaret; Quilligan, Maureen; and Vickers, Nancy, eds. *Rewriting the Renaissance: The Discourses of Sexual Difference in Early Modern Europe.* Chicago: Chicago University Press, 1986.

Gilbert, Sandra M., and Gubar,Susan. *The Madwoman in the Attic: The Woman Writer and the Nineteenth-Century Literary Imagination.* New Haven: Yale University Press, 1979.

Greene, Robert. *Penelope's Web.* London, 1587; 2nd ed., 1601.

Guazzo, Stefano. *La Civil conversatione del signor Stefano Guazzo.* Venice, 1575. London, 1581. (Trans. George Pettie). Repr. London: Constable, 1925. Ed. Edward Sullivan.

Jardine, Lisa. *Still Harping on Daughters: Women and Drama in the Age of Shakespeare.* Totowa, N.J.: Barnes and Noble, 1983.

Kelly-Gadol, Joan. "Did Women Have a Renaissance?" In *Becoming Visible: Women in European History*. Ed. Renate Bridenthal and Claudia Koonz. Boston: Houghton Mifflin, 1977; repr. in *Women, History, and Theory: The Essays of Joan Kelly*. Chicago: University of Chicago Press, 1985.

Kelso, Ruth. *Doctrine for the Lady of the Renaissance*. Urbana and Chicago: University of Illinois Press, 1956, 1978.

Lombardelli, Orazio. *Dell'Uffizio della Donna Maritata: Capi Centottanta*. Florence, 1585.

Perry, T. A. "Pernette du Guillet's Poetry of Love and Desire." *Bibliothèque d'humanisme et Renaissance* (1973), vol. 35.

Powell, Thomas. *The Art of Thriving, or the plaine Path-way to preferment*. London, 1635.

Ronsard, Pierre de. "Hymne du treschrestien Roy de France Henry Il de ce nom." *Les Hymnes de 1555, Oeuvres complètes*. Ed. Paul Laumonier. Paris; Droz, 1935, vol. 8.

Tasso, Torquato. *Discorso della virtù femminile, e donnesca*. Venice, 1582.

Toste, Richard, trans., *The Blazon of Jealousie*. London, 1615. Quoted by Peter Stallybrass in "The Body Enclosed," fn. 18, in Ferguson et al., eds., *Rewriting the Renaissance*.

Vives, Jean Luis. *De Tradendis Disciplinis (The Transmission of Knowledge)*. Trans. Foster Watson. Totowa, N.J.: Rowman and Littlefield, 1971.

Part IV. **Women's Agency**

13 Women on Top in the Pamphlet Literature of the English Revolution

Sharon Achinstein

There was much gender trouble in the pamphlet literature of the English Revolution, and that gender trouble was often expressed through sexual satire. Radical sects in particular bore the brunt of much of this satire. "Unnatural" sexual acts were commonly depicted in this literature, like the woodcut of the public masturbation of "Adamite" men on the title-page of *A New Sect of Religion Decried, called ADAMITES* (1641), which, though it served the reader's voyeuristic pleasure also served to delegitimize the sects by ridicule. Ranting rites were said to include group sex, public sado-masochism, and female erotic behavior; one such depiction of a Ranter church service in a pamphlet from 1650, entitled *The Ranters Ranting*, shows a woman kneeling to kiss a brother's buttocks, while naked women and men—with woodcuts crudely depicting the men's erections—dance around a fiddler.[1] Such pornographic attacks on radical sects expressed fears about radicals who threatened to "turn the world upside down," and who appeared to destroy the effects of civilization and its rule of propriety, starting, of course, in the bedroom.

Sexual satire was a means to delegitimize, demonize, and scapegoat "Others" in the Civil War period—the radical sects for example—but such sexual satire served other purposes as well. For example, Royalists often represented Parliament as a woman, whether as a sick female, as a bewitching temptress, as a whore, or as a sexually ravenous beast.[2] The bawdy image used by Royalists of "Mistress parliament" offered a counter-offensive to the Whore of Babylon imagery applied to Henrietta Maria by the Parliamentary pamphleteers.[3]

The "Mistress parliament" genre and the attacks on women in the radical sects may be understood in the tradition of *charivari*. Natalie Davis has examined this "women on top" tradition in the folk rituals, the *charivaris* of early modern France, in which women temporarily

From *Women's Studies*, 24 (1994), 131–63. © 1994 Gordon and Breach Science Publishers SA. Reprinted with permission.

take on the superior position in community festivities.[4] The "woman on top" both temporarily suspends—and perhaps questions—'natural' social order, and the rites also suppress that questioning by finally reinstating proper gender roles. The *charivari* tradition of woman on top has been read as a discourse about male anxiety, either an anxiety with psychological roots, or one arising from a social, structural crisis.[5] The *charivari* with its reversal of gender roles is a pressure-valve release for gender anxiety in particular and for social anxiety in general.[6]

Attacks on women in public seem endemic to revolution. Social crisis seems to arouse fears about gender de-differentiation, as Rene Girard explains in *Violence and the Sacred*: "one of the effects of the sacrificial crisis [a crisis in the community which results in the search for a scapegoat] is a certain feminization of the men, accompanied by a masculinization of the women."[7] Much of the work of historians of anti-feminine activity in early modern England take this functionalist approach. In treating the phenomenon of the scold, for instance, Susan Amussen argues that a surge in legal prosecutions against unruly women "reflected the anxiety of those in authority about the potential for disorder," a disorder that came about because of rapid population growth, social mobility, increases in poverty and vagrancy, and economic crisis during the years 1540–1640. Looking at court records from Norfolk, Amussen explains that scolding women disappeared from the courts when these factors stabilized: "Scolding ceased to be a problem when disorder ceased to be an obsession."[8] In the same vein, David Underdown finds the preoccupations with unruly women such as scolds and witches were cultural responses to social change, that people expressed fears about economic dislocation in the form of gender oppression. "The preoccupation with scolding women during the century 1560–1660," Underdown concludes, "can . . . be seen as a by-product of the social and economic transformation that was occurring in England during that period—of the decline in habits of good neighbourhood and social harmony that accompanied the spread of capitalism."[9] In these accounts, attacks on women are seen as responses to *something else*, and that something else is structural, social, economic—not necessarily political. Yet when Bulstrode Whitelocke recounted the actions of women petitioning Parliament in 1649, he used the language of the scold to suit his political purpose of dismissing the women: "some hundreds of women attended the house with a petition on the behalf of Lilburne and the rest; it was reproachful, *almost scolding,* and much to the effect with former petitions for them" (italics added).[10]

Where does politics fit in? The relation between such fears about gender identity and political crisis has been examined in the research on pornography and anti-feminine iconography of the French Revolution. Using the work of Girard, as well as the psychoanalytic concept of the Oedipal complex, Lynn Hunt has argued that the French Revolution was a "gender drama" in which the body of the French Queen played a critical role in establishing the masculine ideology of republicanism.[11] The anti-woman narratives were allegories pointing to something other than actual women, as Lynn Hunt suggests: "through their rejection of [Marie Antoinette] and what she stood for, republican men could reinforce their bonds to one another."[12] Women in these texts were "signs" of—or allegories pointing to—male ideological concerns. For the English Revolution, Susan Wiseman has similarly argued that in the pornographic pamphlets written by republican men, the appearance of women was used as a means to critique patriarchal political theory; thus again, stories involving women are really stories about men.[13]

In this line of thinking, images of women are signs through which men express their desires and their fears, political ideologies and psychological needs. My own thinking has led me to see this account of structural misogyny or allegorical displacement as only part of the story. What if the English Revolutionary attacks on women were not merely allegories but were also literal attacks on women, on how women were behaving; what if the attacks were not emblems for something else but were attacks on women in public? Carole Pateman has argued that the Lockean political theory that triumphed at the end of the seventeenth century definitively separated the men who can rationally contract into a civil fraternity from the women who cannot because of their prior, and natural, subjection. She calls this triumph the "sexual contract." Women and women's rights were thereby excluded from the emergent political social contract.[14] But there is evidence from English Revolutionary writing that women themselves were seeking a role in the public sphere, both in religious and in political circles. From this evidence, we may conclude that these women, in their bid for a public role, were challenging claims about their prior or natural subjection and displaying a potential for feminine rationality. The controversy over the inclusion of women in leadership in the sects was one occasion for debate concerning women's roles and capabilities.[15] There are many instances in which we find such occasions, where women's appearances in public offer us instances of unprecedented autonomy and authority during the English Revolutionary period, especially in the exercise of their rationality.

"Women-on-top" social explanations that do not take into account political meanings miss some of what is going on in the English Revolutionary pamphlet literature. Sexual satires on women expressed concerns about women's equality and about the roles women were actually taking in public. In the sexual satires of the English Revolution, writers cast gender hierarchies against unstable political hierarchies and confronted the threat of gender equality. In Thomas Jordan's conservative ballad, "The Rebellion," for example, we find a world-turned-upside-down vision of anarchy in the many voices of the people, and that upside down world reflects anxieties about political, as well as social, order:

> Come Clowns, and come Boys, come Hoberdehoys,
> Come Females of each degree
> Stretch out your Throats, bring in your Votes,
> And make good the Anarchy;

Jordan, a "popular" city poet who, after the Restoration, became the official poetic propagandist of the Lord Mayor of London, expresses fears about the unruly lower orders and women. His ballad not only takes alarm at improper social hierarchy, but also worries about the political power the lower orders have: votes.

> Then thus it shall be, says *Alse*,
> Nay, thus it shall be, says *Amie*,
> Nay, thus it shall go, says *Taffie*, I trow,
> Nay, thus it shall go, says *Jenny*.

Each vote contradicts the other, and those voting are women. Public disagreement is the only observable feature of this new regime; we don't even know what the issue is.

> Speak *Abraham*, speak *Hester*,
> Speak *Judith*, speak *Kester*,
> Speak tag and rag, short coat and long:
> Truth is the spell that made us rebel,
> And murder and plunder ding dong;
> Sure I have the truth, says *Numphs*,
> Nay, I have the truth, says *Clem*,
> Nay, I have the truth, says reverend *Ruth*,
> Nay, I have the truth, says *Nem*.[16]

The song mixes "common" materials, "tag and rag," and the ballad refrain, "ding dong," to make light of the serious threat of popular rule, led by the likes of Abraham, Judith, and Ruth. By these biblical names, we see that at least some of these giddy anarchists are Puritans; they certainly indicate that women are taking political power. These voices are predominantly female ones—Judith, Amie, Taffy—"women on top." The poem points to the language in which such rebellion is expressed: "tag and rag," *not* the acceptable language of politics found among educated men. The moral of the piece—"Thus from the Rout who can expect/Ought but confusion?"—is exemplified by making the popular voices express open political conflict with no apparent reasons. Political power is being asserted by those who do not belong in the public sphere and this includes women.

The conclusions drawn by social historians of anti-feminine proceedings have not adequately accounted for the very real political content of the revolutionary attacks on women; the sense that what was wrong was not that women were provoking or signifying a general or even a particular kind of social disorder, but that they were voting, speaking out in public spaces, voicing religious truths, challenging authority in ways that were not wholly irrational or "other," but that were politically recognizable. Many pamphleteers, both Royalist and anti-Royalist, both monitored, and balked at, this potential revolution for women. In this essay, I suggest that the sexual contract Pateman describes may be understood in the context of Interregnum political culture; that the Interregnum be seen as a pivotal moment in which women's place in the political life of the nation was being considered and that the attempt to exclude women was *a response to* their vivid participation in the public sphere. This essay considers pamphlets in which women are represented as taking part in activities of the public sphere traditionally assigned to males: specifically, in the business of political activity and religious leadership. It challenges the social historians' account where the trope of the "women on top" primarily reflects male anxieties about social and economic order; rather it explores the dislocations in gender ideologies that were brought about by the presence and participation of women in politics and religion during the English Revolution.

1. WOMEN AND POLITICS (OR SEX?) IN PUBLIC

During the civil war period, women were struggling to participate in public activity like never before. On the military side, in 1643, as the staunch Royalist Lady Bankes launched a successful defense of Corfe

Castle in Dorset, and was later praised for exhibiting a "constancy and courage above her sex," the pro-Parliamentary Brilliana Harley defended her own besieged country estate, displaying what one admirer called "masculine bravery."[17] We have heard much about women participating in the religious sects, and their move to center stage both as prophets and as petitioners to Parliament brought much contemporary comment then, as well as giving "her-stories" to modern feminist historians, examples of women breaking the traditional codes of silence and moving into the public sphere.[18] Phyllis Mack, for example, has demonstrated in her exhaustive study of Quaker women that the practice of religion offered women temporary liberation from rigid gender roles.[19]

In the sphere of politics, however, the picture is less clear as historians have examined the activities of religious women rather than their political counterparts. Though the distinction between religious and political spheres scarcely exists in the seventeenth century, I take "political" in its narrow sense, meaning activities specifically to do with formal institutions of politics. Wives often agitated on behalf of their imprisoned husbands or for the release of their sequestered estates.[20] These women represented landed nobility on down the social scale to city women. Yet, since their first petitions in 1642, they also expressed broader political concerns: petitioning for peace, freedom of trade, the rectification of imprisonment laws, and other political issues. One striking example reveals the many meanings of such women's appearance in public. In spring 1649, several hundred women from the middling sort petitioned Parliament for the release of the Leveller leader John Lilburne and his associates. Between three and five hundred women, it was reported, came out to submit a petition to Parliament; the petition reportedly contained 10,000 women's signatures. Because there was exhaustive coverage of the event in the press, we may begin to gauge some ways in which women's public participation was received. Parliament had imprisoned Lilburne, William Walwyn, Richard Overton, and Thomas Prince for their accusations that the Rump was showing tyrannical tendencies and for their opposition to Cromwell's tough military policy in Ireland. As the Commonwealth regime struggled for legitimacy in its first moments, Lilburne and his associates offered vocal resistance, as spokesmen for the Leveller party, a group loosely committed to entertaining rights for all 'free-born Englishmen.' Largely drawing support from the Army, and comprised of people from the lesser gentry and middling sort, the Levellers pressed for expanded manhood suffrage, the "fundamental rights of all Englishmen," toleration of religion in the name of *salus populi*, and presented petitions demanding constitutional reform, including the *Agreements of the People*, documents that gave birth to the Leveller party.[21]

The Levellers did not advocate a women's franchise. However, within the Leveller movement women had a place; wives of Leveller leaders helped to drum up support, and several of the Leveller pamphlets addressed men and women alike.[22] In their petitioning before Parliament, nonetheless, the women supporting the Levellers demanded participation. Though Parliament rejected their petition in 1649 without allowing it entrance inside the walls of the building, the newsbooks of the time gave the women a hearing, with at least six papers reporting the content, and even the precise language, of the women's appeals. The women's voices were represented with an astonishing completeness in these contemporary newsbooks, and this contemporary comment tells us something about the reception of women taking political roles in public: even if Parliament would give them no quarter, the women's actions were newsworthy. Their words deserved reproduction and dissemination and were of interest to a reading public. When Bulstrode Whitelocke recalled the incident, he used traditional misogynistic language of scolding, yet many representations in the press attempted a more transparent representation; the Parliamentary journals across the political spectrum—from pro-Rump to conservative army to pro-Leveller—gave surprisingly complete accounts of the incident and reproduced at length the precise language of the women's petition.[23] From a comparison between the text of the women's petition and these newspaper accounts, it is clear that in many cases the newswriters worked from copies of the petition. In one case, a pro-Rump but anti-Leveller paper, the journalist sprinkled his own editorial comment following each section of this transcription of the women's demands: after the women's soliciting that "Parliament would set themselves cordially and sensibly to remove the burthens of the people, and settle this Common-wealth upon foundations of true freedom," the editor injected his own commentary in italics, "*That is as much to say, let women weare the breeches.*"[24] For women to be acting in an advisory way to Parliament and to be demanding "true freedom" was tantamount to wearing breeches, taking on men's roles. Yet other newspapers reported the women's language without such editorializing. Though it is tendentious to draw conclusions from this silence, nonetheless, the lack of negative commentary in many journals tells us that women's voices were being allowed to have an audience in public.[25]

The public sphere of print was being used to represent women, even if they could not be represented in Parliament.

The women petitioners themselves, however, followed a logic of gender equality, asking for the same fundamental rights as the Leveller men had. Along with their suits to release the Leveller men, they appealed to the "foundations of true freedom," mentioning their "native liberties." They also articulated that, as women, they were entitled to a prevailing interest in national affairs: "that we have an equal share and interest with men in the Common-wealth, and it cannot be laid waste (as now it is)."[26] It is significant that only one paper chose to reproduce these words; the most forthrightly "feminist" assertions of women's equal political interest were left out of the other accounts. Perhaps this wasn't deemed newsworthy because they were not articulating precise demands; or perhaps the editor found these ideas too startling to reproduce, too radical even for radicals. The women justified their political petitioning often in maternal or matronly language, often referring to their starving children, their husbands' loyalty to the Commonwealth, and their men's brave acts of citizenry on its behalf and made clear that they were speaking under extraordinary circumstances: "We are over-prest, so over whelmed in affliction, that we are not able to keep in our compasse, to be bounded in the custom of our Sex; for indeed wee confesse it is not our custome to addresse our selves to this House in the publike behalf."[27] Yet, citing biblical precedents like Jael and Deborah and secular historical exemplars from British history, the 1649 women's petition went on not merely to defend their husbands and their families, but to articulate Leveller thought. Rather than choose the role of the ecstatic prophetess—one sometimes acceptable way for women to express opinions in public— or to detach themselves from familial structures, these women chose the discourse of rational political debate that was being established in the political culture of the time.

In their second petition, submitted in early May 1649, the women reasserted their inclusion in political process and based their argument for that inclusion on grounds of natural equality:

Since we are assured of our creation in the image of God, and of an interest in Christ equal unto men, as also of a proportionable share in the freedoms of this commonwealth, we cannot but wonder and grieve that we should appear so despicable in your eyes as to be thought unworthy to petition or represent our grievances to this honourable House. Have we not an equal interest with the men of this nation in those liberties and securities contained in the *Petition of Right*, and other the good laws of the land? Are any of our lives, limbs, liberties, or goods to be taken from us more than from men, but by due process of law and conviction of twelve sworn men of the neighborhood? And can you imagine us to be so sottish or stupid as not to perceive, or not to be sensible when daily those strong defences of our peace and welfare are broked down and trod underfoot by force and arbitrary power?[28]

The women demanded that they be taken seriously, that they were not "sottish" and "stupid," not lacking in mental capability to know when they were being treated unfairly, and insisted on their counting in the rational sphere of public affairs. In 1653, they went so far as to state their "undoubted right of petitioning . . . we claim it as our right to have our petitions heard; you having promised to govern the nation in righteousness."[29] Such assertions regarding women's capabilities and rights made possible, and authorized, their unusual speaking positions. Rather than accepting the traditional argument about women's natural inferiority or adopting the defensive posture of a prophet, these women were enacting their rationality in public, using the same rhetoric as men had done.

What these women found unbearable was Parliament's response: one of neglect, dismissal, and belittlement. For in response to their first petition, Parliament's Sergeant-at-Arms was commanded by the speaker to send the women home. The newsbooks all report his words: "That the matter you petition about, is of an higher concernment then you understand, that the House gave an answer to your husbands; and therefore that you are desired to go home, and looke after your owne business, and meddle with your huswifery."[30] According to Parliament's spokesman, women's business was different from "our business"; political matters "of an higher concernment" than women could understand. Women do not belong in politics because their interests are elsewhere, in the business of "huswifery," and because they have fallible understandings. One Parliamentary newsbook added a flourish: "It is fitter for you to be washing your dishes, and meddle with the Wheele and distaffe," consigning women to the domestic duties of the private sphere.[31] One Royalist newspaper reported on Parliament's rejection of the women with glee, snidely accusing the MPs of "unmannerly" behavior in "repulsing" the women. This account follows a logic of paternalistic protectionism of the women: Parliament was not treating its women right. However, the women returned with a petition that resisted their exclusion from the sphere of politics on the grounds that the domestic sphere could *not* be a refuge from political engagement: "Would you have us keep at home in our houses, when men of such faithfulness and integrity as the four prisoners, our friends, in the Tower, are fetched out of their beds?"[32]

Though Parliament clearly excluded the women, the Parliamentary newsbooks did not. After hearing the Sergeant at arms, reported one paper, the women "very civilly all went away," as if the author of the account seeks to reassure readers of the moral sobriety of these petitioners.[33] The extent and accuracy of the record in the Parliamentary press of these women's demands are remarkable, and to me denotes that the women were taken very seriously indeed as political agents. The contrast with Royalist coverage is striking and tells us that taking women seriously was controversial. In the Royalist response, there was a refusal to admit any political content in these women's actions. Royalist papers chose instead to view these women in light of contemporary women's sectarian roles, calling the women petitioners "Religious Charmers" and "holy sisters," when in fact they took on no religious personae to authorize their appeal.[34] Moreover, Royalist comment on the incident turned their political action into a sexual matter, a ruse common to anti-sectarian fare. The newsbook *Mercurius Elencticus* presented the incident as follows: "it seems the fairest of those [women] which this day came with a Petition to the house in the behalf of John Lilburne etc. could not prevail . . . for although they had put on their best Petticoats and set their Eyes in a posture of temptation, and woo'd hard on all hands to beget compassion toward their dear bretheren in bondage, yet long was it before any one would listen to the sugared Notes of these Religious Charmers."[35] In this account, women's political action is represented as a sexual seduction. Among the women, only the "fairest" have come to plead, and they have dressed up in "their best Petticoats" in order to be physically attractive. Their demands are seen as "wooing," as the women adopt "a posture of temptation," using feminine wiles, "sugared Notes," to secure their ends, which are sexual rather than political in interest. And their methods of political petitioning are feminine, "charming," appealing to the senses, rather than convincing to the mind by the properly rational language of political persuasion.

The participation of Leveller women in politics was represented by Royalists as a sexual threat. That sexual threat expressed fears in a number of ways. The women's demands are a libertine—advocating liberty of sexuality—extension of the Leveller demands for "liberty." Attacking the women, then, could be a figural means of attacking their husbands' politics. The royalist newsheet *Mercurius Pragmaticus*, which reported on the demonstration of Leveller women who protested against Parliament over Lilburne and Overton's imprisonment in 1649, called these four or five hundred women petitioners a "Meek-hearted Congregation of *Oysterwives*," slander that labelled these women prostitutes.[36] Women who defended "Levelling" men could only be libertines or prostitutes by this logic.

But female presence in public was also a threat in and of itself. The Leveller women were accused by Royalists of having "strange visions on their backs," in a convergence of a religious and sexual posture, yet, as the archroyalist author John Crouch warned the Army leader Fairfax in 1649, such women were not completely disenfranchised: "Holoferness Fairfax look to thy head." The author warns of the assassinating power of these women, "for Judith is a-coming; the women are up in arms, and vow they will tickle your Members, your heads stands too ticklish, where they do."[37] These women were dangerous to leaders like Fairfax, and their political power is represented as *sexual* in nature, with the double entendre of "members" referring both to M.P.s and to the male sexual organs over which these women (who are spuriously given prostitutes' names—Ruth Turn-up, Doll Burn-it, and sister Wagtail) exert control.

Further, the threat of these women was not just a scapegoating or an "othering," but rather a threat that could infiltrate ordinary society. A Royalist pamphlet has Hugh Peter, the radical Parliamentary Army chaplain, fictively report: "I went to New-England, and here I saw a blessed sight, a world of wild women and men lying round a fire, in a ring, stark naked,"—typical anti-sectarian fare. Yet the character continues with a warning to those at home: "If this custom should come up in London (as I see no reason but it may, *if the State will vote it*) then every woman may have her belly-full, and it would be a certain cure for cuckolds and jealousie, and so the City would lose nothing by this Thanksgiving" (italics added).[38] Illicit sex could be voted in with new legislation. It is true that Parliaments were interested in revising laws concerning marriage and divorce throughout the Interregnum, yet the real threat here is that women could gain power through the political process of voting.[39]

In the pamphlet literature of the English Revolution, women seemed to be voting in sex all over the place. In *The Parliament of Ladies* (1647), a pamphlet written by the republican Henry Neville, women have taken over the business of governance and are converting the political sphere into the domestic sphere, passing legislation so that women are allowed to have two husbands each in order to satisfy their sexual needs. The names of these women, Mrs Tattle-well, Mistris Dorothy

Do-Little, Bridget Boldface, Tabitha Tear-sheet, Anne Ever-cross, Rachel Rattlebody draw upon the tradition of the woman-in-public-as prostitute.[40] The women in the 1646 anonymous Royalist tract *The Parliament of Women* are depicted on the title page woodcut of the pamphlet sitting in parliament around a table on which parchment and a pen are ready. They are ready to write legislation, to take political action. They are dressed as women (not as women-in-men's clothing, as the women in the *querelle* tracts often were) in caps and with covered heads, ruffs and long, simple dresses: modest images, quite different from the "Man-Woman" depicted on the title-page of the 1620 pamphlet *Hic Mulier* with her hair cut short, wearing a man's hat and plume, and dressed in rich finery, or on the frontispiece of *Haec-Vir*, also 1620, appearing with short hair, a man's hat, spurs, dagger, and pistol.[41] In the *Parliament of Women*, rather, the women are clearly presented as modestly-dressed *women*.

In *The Parliament of Women*, rather than committing crimes against gender identity, their danger is in their inhabiting the sphere of politics. One of them presides at the head of the table from a throne-like chair. We have a list of the "merrie laws" by the women, "newly enacted." And they are: "To live in more ease, pomp, pride, and wantonness; but especially that they might have superiority and domineer over their husbands." Power over husbands, however, was represented as sexual domination over husbands: "with a new way found out by them to cure old or new Cuckolds, and how both parties may recover their credit and honesty again."[42] This pamphlet draws upon the early modern pamphlet war against women, the *querelle* as it has been called, and extends the theme of women's insubordination to intrude upon the realm of politics.

What is the meaning of this kind of sexual slander against voracious women passing laws to give themselves more sex? The antifeminine pamphlet literature of the English Revolution raises questions about the interrelationships of sexual discourse and public political discourse. There are several possible interpretations of this interrelationship. In part, the representations of sexually voracious or unruly women are conventional, misogynistic responses to the appearance of women in public, and they affirm a long tradition of conflating woman in public with prostitutes, dating back at least to humanists in Italy and followed through in England in the *querelle des femmes*, the pamphlet war on women.[43]

But there is a new twist in these English Revolutionary representations. The danger was not that women were becoming more man-like, donning men's clothes, or more feminine, sexually voracious; rather, their danger was *where* they were and *what* they were doing: in public, at the lectern, in politics, not under their husband's control. When pamphlet writers during the English Revolution imagined women in public they did not express a fear of *conflation* of private and public spheres, or a de-differentiation of sexual identities. Women's engagement with a public life was being criticized not solely on traditional grounds of their natural propensity—that women were becoming Amazons, madwomen, or prostitutes. Their involvement in public was dangerous because it put them where they were not supposed to be—in public—doing what they were not supposed to do—taking on religious or political authority. The sexual slander is not merely a sign of political trouble, a sign that points allegorically elsewhere; rather, it speaks a political content in and of itself.[44] During the English Revolution, much of the writing against women was really about women: a consideration of what role they could play inside and outside the family, in the Churches, and in politics.

Images of female sexual superiority or potency, from attacks on Ranters on up to attacks on Henrietta Maria, who was thought to rule over Charles, exemplify this anxiety about women's autonomy from and power over men. And women's power was recognized as a threat arising not from individuals, but from a class. One newspaper reported a network of women were being roused to support the Leveller women's petition of 1649, that, "copies of the Petitions were sent to all parts about London, &c. To desire that all those women that are approvers thereof should subscribe it (which accordingly many did), and delivered in their Subscriptions to certain women appointed in every Ward and Division to receive the same."[45] Women in groups were asserting kinds of independence and autonomy that exposed and challenged the workings of the gender system. They did not always agree with their husbands on political points. Henry Neville's pamphlet *An Exact Diurnal of the Parliament of Ladies* (1647) charges Royalist leaders with being fomenters of "divisions between the *Ladies* and their *Husbands*."[46] Another satirical pamphlet from the same year represents a "Parliament of Ladies" where a "rattle-head lady" disagrees with a "round-head lady," but the two are counseled by their companion members of this feminine counter-Parliament to make peace with one another and to "unite against a common enemy, their husbands."[47] With women becoming powerful, with their politics and religion even disrupting the private sphere, these pamphlets warned that men had better watch out.

351

2. WOMEN AND RELIGIOUS AUTHORITY IN PUBLIC

There is debate amongst feminist historians over the degree to which seventeenth-century women were expressing notions of female emancipation in their religious activism.[48] It is true that women in the sects upset patriarchalist gender roles. During the revolutionary period, it has been argued, sectarian women were seen to challenge traditional feminine roles by their merging of gender roles in ecstatic prophecy and by their participation in church. These challenges created unique anxieties for patriarchal social order in which the man was the leader and the voice of the household, itself a model of order for the state.[49] Susan Wiseman has argued that the anti-feminine pamphlets of the 1640s and 1650s critique the situation "*consequent* on the breakdown of agreement in the masculinist ordering of society and respond to the competing rhetorics of patriarchal and populist political theory."[50] How did writers appeal to gendered categories in order to assert and to buttress ideological arguments concerning the nature, scope, and limits of women's involvement with the institutions of religious and political authority?

With religious toleration a major issue that divided Parliamentarians, women's active participation, whether preaching or pursuing separatist religious groups, became an occasion for voicing opposition to toleration for the sects. The Presbyterian minister Dr. Daniel Featley's catalogue of sectaries. *The Dippers Dipt* (1645), features a beautiful frontispiece engraving, "The Description of the severall sorts of Anabaptists," with its central panel illustrating naked men and naked women being baptised in a river under the watchful eye of the devil. A description of these rites follows in the text: "they strip themselves stark naked, not only when they flocke in great multitudes, men and women together to their *Jordans* to be dipt" (203). Featley offers the Baptists' credo which justifies their sexual license: "*but all that are of their society are so knit one to the other, that they are all one body, as well as one spirit,*" and recounts one especial baptism when a group of dippers "had no sooner instild this doctrine into the weaker Sex, but two maids at *Sanctogall*, immediately after their second Baptisme, made ship-wrack of their virginity; and a third dashing at the same rock, and being called into question by the Magistrate for her incontinency, professed that shee out of her pure conscience did it; that is, played the Whore" (204). The images of women sectaries played upon pre-existent gender anxieties, as well as exposed new ways in which women threatened men's authority. In representing sectarian women as sexually potent, anti-sectarians responded to the threat of equality between the sexes. If all consciences were equally "pure," then women could take control of their sexuality in revolutionary ways.[51] If separate sects were tolerated, parish unity would be fragmented and individuals could pursue voluntary choices apart from traditional structures of authority: the family, the church.[52] The separatist case seemed especially troubling with respect to women.

Equality of conscience was a difficult doctrine to maintain at the same time as maintaining rigid gender hierarchies. Puritan notions of marriage were based on the idea of spiritual equality, yet the sects seemed to take this too far, according to many Presbyterians. Some Puritan ideals of marriage seemed to allow the equality of sorts inside the household, but not outside it.[53] Daniel Cawdrey, in *Family Reformation Promoted* (1656), made no distinctions between the duties husbands and wives owe to each other, what he called the "mutual duties" of a marriage based on choice of a "fit helper," which included sexual parity, "due benevolence," "mutual love"; the aim of both husband and wife was to "study to please one another."[54] Yet such a puritan doctrine could also be thoroughly patriarchal in its political meaning, as Keith Thomas has argued.[55] It was when women sought certain kinds of autonomy outside of the household—preaching, acting in politics—that they ran into trouble.

Women's public religious activity was frequently represented as a ruse to hide their wanton sexual behavior. The charges of impropriety were a way for writers to express condemnation of women's decisions to carry on religious activity outside the house. In the anonymous royalist pamphlet, *A Strange Wonder or A Wonder in A Woman* (1642), women use religious pretences to cover up their lewdness. This pamphlet draws upon the stereotype of the innate hypocrisy of women: "Of all WHORES there is no WHORE to a Holy WHORE, which when she turns up the White of her Eye, And the Black of her Tail when she falls flat on her Back, According as the Spirit moves her, The Fire of her Zeale, Kindles such a Flame, that the Divell cannot withstand her, Besides she can fit a man with such a Cloake for her Knavery she can cover her Lust with Religion, O! These Lasses that can rise and get them ready by Six a Clock in the Morning to go to *Christ* Church, And then in the Afternoone to go to Saint *Amholing* O! how they listen for that *Tinckl tinckl* bell that raises them in a morning to a stirring exercise."[56] The so-called religious woman is lewd, a manipulator, and a liar; she is able to take advantage of her gullible husband to obtain her sexual pleasures outside the household. This pamphlet implicitly recognizes that in a Puritan household women do have power over, or at least equal to, their husbands. What provokes these speculations about her sexual desires, though, is her action of *leaving* the household to go to church, here perhaps even to a Catholic service. The only way to explain her abandonment of her proper domestic sphere is by claiming she seeks to fulfil her sexual desire. There can be no other reason.

Sex is the reason many women were portrayed as leaving their households. The Royalist poet Robert Heath represents a "She white linnen Saint" who seeks illicit sex with another member of the congregation inside an empty church:

> Out you unhallow'd whore! is this the way
> To enter heav'n at thy streight gate I pray?
> D'you sanctifie your Cuckold dormant? must
> Your mother Church be bawd to goatish lust?
> Yet goes she in and sitting prays and hears
> With as observing eies, attentive ears
> The Lecture, as the holiest Matron there.

Heath insists that the motivation for this woman's public religious activity is to obtain sex, and the poem is critical of what he perceives as this woman's sexual hypocrisy: she seems religious, but she is filled with "goatish lust." Yet the poetic language here makes a suggestive analogy between this woman's sexual receptiveness that is represented by a vaginal image, "thy streight gate," and her religious receptiveness that is represented through other orifices: she "hears/With as observing eies, attentive ears." The implied correspondence is between her vagina and her other orifices: what goes in one must be going in the other. If the woman is open to receiving a "lecture," she must be open to receiving sex.

The poetic language here forces us to see that this woman's choice to pursue active participation in non-traditional religiosity threatens to expose her to seductions that are both religious and sexual. As the poem goes on to describe a meeting of these religious women, it mocks their religious discussion for being overly concerned with sexual conduct:

> Such strange disputes here controverted be
> Would puzzle a Scotch-lay-Presbyterie.
> Whether that *Bigamie* been't as lawful now
> As 'twas 'tofore? Speak Sister *Ruth*! We know
> You have two husbands now, besides that one

Who next stands fairly in election.
Truly and verily, I professe you may,
How should the Church be built up else, I pray?
Her doctrine *Hannah* did approve, and doubt
Whether not in the Church as well as out
Women might speak? the Priest resolv'd they should
Speak out as much as often as they would,
But never in.[57]

The scene presents as preposterous the idea of a theological discussion among women. Though the women imitate male modes of rational activity, asking questions about religious doctrine, these "strange disputes," are unrecognizable in the male world of religious conversation, even in a "Scotch-lay-Presbytery." In this Anglican male fantasy, because the women's religious receptivity can only be thought of as sexual interest, women's questions about orthodoxy focus on sexual habits. These women seek in doctrine a way to make lawful their sexual desires, to make lawful having more than one husband. The language of sexual desire is the only conceivable language these "receptive" women could partake in, as it is preposterous that they have any other theological concern. In Heath's poem we see the concern with how women may participate in non-traditional religion at all. The answer is, only as sex. The last line however raises the question, Where is women's religious activity to be sanctioned? The answer is not *in* Church, but *out* of it. The correspondence between sexual and religious receptivity is a logic of inside/outside: *In* church makes their bodies liable to penetration, threatens their chastity.

Women's bodily imperatives—their appetites for sex or for food—are seen as their primary motives in many pamphlets that consider the activity of women taking part in religious leadership in public. In the anonymous anti-sectarian *A Discoverie of Six Women Preachers* (1641), Anne Hempstall, for example, is said to have spoken for two hours to women who came from far away. The author is amazed at her power to attract listeners and quick to explain that power in terms of physical appetite: another woman preacher had promised a "good fat pig" after her sermon. According to this author, the women's "thoughts were bent more upon the strong water bottle" than on the Lord.[58] Liquor was often blamed for the activities of women preachers, as in *A Dialogue Betweene Sacke and Six* (1641), in which the two types of ale vie for precedence. "Six" boasts of "the enabling of six women to preach devoutly up and downe the City . . . by virtue of this heavenly potion, in regard their husbands cannot sufficiently preach to them at home."[59]

In *A Discoverie of six Woman Preachers*, the author blames the women's husbands for the misbehavior of their wives, on the title-page asserting that Pauline injunction to keep women silent: "Let your women keepe silence in the Churches, for it is not permitted unto them to speake, but they are commanded to be under obedience, as also saith the Law. And if they will learne any thing, let them aske their husbands at home: for it is a shame for women to speake in the Church."[60] Women do not belong in the public sphere of religion as vocal participants.

This Pauline argument against women speaking in public was invoked not solely in relation to the question of women's speech in church. It was also used by pro-Parliamentary newspapers against the Leveller women petitioning to Parliament in 1649. "Paul tells women that it is not fit . . . nor civill for Women to prate in Congregations of men, and to aske their Husbands at home," the author castigates, "we shall have things brought to a fine passe, if women come to teach the parliament how to make Lawes." What's wrong here is that women were breaking the Pauline injunction—this time by speaking out in the political sphere. Women weren't solely to blame however; men weren't exerting proper control over their wives at home. The journalist draws this conclusion after transcribing—with accuracy no less—the women's plea that Parliament follow due process. There the reporter once again jumps in: "It can never be a good world, when women meddle in State matters. If their tongues must be pratling, they may finde other talke, And their Husbands are to blame, that have no fitter imployment for them."[61] Relying upon notions of the natural talkativeness of women, this journalist makes the leap from what is said about women's conduct in church to what women may say in politics. And the message of the pamphlet is mixed; by reporting the women's speech with a degree of accuracy, the newsbook takes their words seriously, worthy of inclusion in a public sphere of political reporting. Yet he also seeks to condemn and silence the women on patriarchalist grounds. These contradictory messages reveal the complexity of responses to women acting in politics in the English Revolutionary period.

3. WOMEN'S RATIONALITY IN THE PUBLIC SPHERE

Although in the anti-sectarian *A Discoverie of Six Women Preachers* the women are driven by their bodily needs for sex, ale, and food, their deficiencies are conceived as mental: "Thus have I declared some of the female Academyes, but where their University is I cannot tell, but I suppose that Bedlam or Bridewell would be two convenient places for them, is it not sufficient that they may have the Gospell truly and sincerely Preached unto them, but that they must take their Ministers office from them?"[62] The women have trespassed onto the male sphere of intellectual activity, the Academy and the pulpit, and threaten to annex these territories. The more appropriate social space for these women, according to this author, is gaol or the madhouse.

Michel Foucault's study of insanity in the early modern period, *Madness and Civilization*, posits one possible understanding of the opposition between the social spaces for reason and nonreason. By designating what was mad, Foucault has argued, humans also designated what was to be rational, and in developing social spaces in which to confine the insane, they placed the realms of insanity and rationality in an oppositional dialectic. With the advent of hospitals for the insane, Foucault argues, "confinement hid away unreason . . . but it explicitly drew attention to madness, pointed to it . . . organized it . . . at a distance, under the eyes of reason that no longer felt any relation to it."[63] In claiming that women, by virtue of their sexuality, were mentally insufficient, that their "irrational" or overly-physical nature was their prime motivation of action, interregnum pamphleteers construed an inverted image of a rational public sphere. Women's voices belonged to an inverted world, a world of sexual—rather than political or religious—desire, a world against which a rational world might be positioned. Women's interest in a public life could thus only be represented as an expression of their physical natures. Against this interpretation, however, the polemicists were insisting that what was madness in one sphere, however, might be proper behavior for another: the women would be acting properly as long as they stayed at home.

Yet these women, rather than staying within the family, were portrayed as disrupting public places, specifically transgressing the Pauline injunction to women's silence in church. These polemicists were apparently beginning to take what women had to say seriously—seriously enough to record it and to refute it in terms that sought to eliminate women's participation in debate. The debate in most separatist congregations, where the number of women was greater than men, was the question of how women were to be involved in church leadership.[64] Even the powerful pamphleteer and sectarian defender Katherine Chidley was barred by her own church from office.[65] The controversial role played by women within Quakerism represents the extreme, liberal end of the spectrum for women's voices. Quakers, who afforded women more autonomy and authority than other sects, were known for disrupting official rituals, whether in church or in society. Their "quaking," as well as their resistance to ordinary dress codes, their refusal of hat honor, bowing or curtseying to superiors, and their repudiation of inauthenticity of all kinds, have been understood by historians to express social protest and a critique of rank.[66] A striking instance of such an act of defiance seems to have taken place in May 1652, when, in the middle of a sermon at Whitehall chapel, a woman, naked from the waist up, appeared in the crowd. The preacher Peter Sterry, an Independent and member of the Westminster Assembly, explains why he did not speak out against the woman, but rather settled on having her removed from the church: "I was in the midst of my Sermon, when I saw at one end of the Chapell a great disturbance among the people, with a sudden fear. I cast my eye on the other end, where I saw in the midst of the crowd a Woman as I guest by her head bare to the middle of her back, the rest of her being hid from my sight in the throng. Hereupon I turned to the disturbed people to quiet them, by telling them, that there was no danger, that it was a mad-woman onely."[67] For a woman to intrude into a public space in this way could only denote non-sense, madness.

Yet a listener to the sermon, one David Brown, was not satisfied with the minister's response. He asked the minister to condemn the woman, whom he deemed *not* to be insane, but rather to be a member of a radical sect. Brown, a writing master, was a Scottish immigrant to London and had been associated with separatist churches since the 'teens all the way through the 'fifties.[68] Even from his Independent position, however, he opposed the woman's actions, not on the grounds of the woman's irrationality, but because of her religious politics. As Brown saw it, this was "a bold woman of about 30 years old, sober in her speech,"—he thus emphasized her control over her own actions, her sense—who "came in a most Strumpet-like posture, mocking you, and that your Sermon of the Ressurrection, and all that honourable Congregation . . . that Strumpet-like woman, who durst be so bold in out-facing shame, even on the Lords day in the forenoon and midst of your Sermon, to come in such a posture which is a shame to expresse, and publickly offer such a vile disgrace, provocation, contempt, yea and (as it were) a defyance to God, his ordinances and people."[69] For Brown, the woman was not mad; rather, she was making a sincere and coherent gesture of protest. David Brown wanted the minister to be sure to address this woman as a self-motivated agent, in control of her actions, not mad, in order to condemn improper religious behavior.

Brown saw the actions of this woman as requiring harsh measures: he criticized Sterry, who, in "so eminent a place, and upon so urgent an occasion, [could] be so negligent in the discharge of that your duty," pleading to the minister to take this women's nakedness seriously: "you . . . are by your silence and negligence the instrumentall cause that all of her mind and faction are not only waxed more audacious, outrageous and numerous, but likewise doe think themselves to be more confirmed and allowed, thus by outfacing authority to proceed in their wickednesse."[70] There were others who were of "her mind and faction," others committed to the same principles and party, who needed to be stopped. The threat of this woman sectary was as a public threat to religious order, not dismissable as a kind of insane "other." The naked woman, "sober in her speech," constituted a danger, according to Mr. Brown, and she needed to be contained. Brown wished to see her quite literally shut up, charging his Minister, "it was your duty so to have confirmed that their worthy act of removing her, that you should have given them charge likewise by vertue of your own Ministerial charge, to have kept her close and safe from any escape, untill the matter had been exactly tryed, and so much the rather, that the like in our dayes at least, never occurred."[71] Foucault's narrative of the rise of public institutions in which to house and contain the mad only helps us so far here. Brown does not claim the naked woman belongs in Bedlam. Rather, he calls for a public inquiry, a treatment of the woman as an autonomously driven creature, asking for a confinement not to discipline and exclude her as a madwoman, but to investigate and to try her. Above all, he was asking Sterry for a rational censure of her public actions, and he expressed that request in the public sphere of the press. Brown viewed that the woman was capable of rational political action, and it was precisely for these actions that she must be stopped—by a rational, public response. I take his response to be a significant "advance" for women in that there is no argument made against this woman's actions based on her mental incapacity—her insanity—or her natural deficiency of reasoning powers—her natural subjection. Rather, Brown insists she be treated as a fully autonomous, rational creature.

Their expression of autonomy and their use of reason in public were among those feminine activities attacked by anti-sectarians. In his catalogue and diatribe against the sects, *Gangraena* (1646), the Presbyterian Thomas Edwards combined an anti-tolerationist polemic with a record of the activities of the sects. Edwards was a great list maker and seems to have tracked down every possible instance of non-orthodox religious behavior he could find; the book itself was an enormous publishing success, requiring a second and a third part and numerous reprints. Edwards was concerned that unauthorized groups—the lower and artisan classes and women—were entering into the sphere of religious authority. Edwards explains, "Among all the confusion and disorder in Church matters both of opinions and practices, and particularly of all sorts of Mechanicks taking upon them to preach and baptize, as Smiths, Taylors, Shoomakers, Pedlars, Weavers, &c. there are also some women-Preachers in our times, who keep constant Lectures, preaching weekly to many men and women."[72] After naming several of these women, Edwards goes on to describe a meeting presided over by a Lace-woman in London, in Bell-Alley in Coleman Street, that was witnessed by "a godly Minister" who gave Edwards his report. This was Mrs. Attaway, the most notable woman preacher in London, who began her career as a General Baptist. From 1645 until 1646 in Coleman Street, there was a public weekly sectarian lecture— Edwards estimates a thousand were in attendance—organized by women that followed the format of conventional puritan lectures.[73] The scene Edwards describes at one meeting, according to one witness, was one of female disorder, an inversion of the sober, silent religious conduct that should become women.

That witness testified that "there was such laughing, confusion, and disorder at the meeting that [he] professed he never saw the like: he told me the confusions, horror, and disorder which he saw and heard there, was unexpressible, and so he left them." Yet when it comes to reporting what actually happened at the meeting, the Minister's account is careful to detail the action regarded as "confusions": women entering into religious discussion. A company exhorts the Lace-woman (Attaway) to speak, which she does reluctantly, and her speech, a half an hour prayer, followed by a reading of a biblical text: "when she had read the Text, she laboured to Analyze the Chapter as well as she could, and then spake upon the Text, drawing her Doctrines, opening them, and making two uses, for the space of some three quarters of an hour: when she had done she spake to the company, and said, if any had any thing to object against any of the matter delivered, they might speak, for that was their custome to give liberty in that kinde (but though there was a great company both of men and women) yet no man objected, but all held their peace." Finally, a second woman criticizes Attaway's interpretation, offering another reading, however, "speaking non-sense all along . . . jumbling together some things": rationality and order have disintegrated. As Attaway "fell upon concluding all with prayer," some in the congregation wished her to be quiet, "praying God to stop her mouth."

What is in the account to justify the Minister's complaint that in this meeting were "confusions, horror, and disorder . . . unexpressible"? What seems to have upset the visiting Minister was the intellectual conflict between the two women in interpreting the Bible and that Attaway went on so long. What caused the horror was to have witnessed women participating in religious discussion, women who disagreed in public: truly a horror indeed for an anti-sectarian Presbyterian who sought to stamp out religious disagreement at all; and to see women fomenting it broke both the rules against discord and against women's speech in church. The report seems complexly working out the problem of women's public speech in religious matters: Attaway's speech is represented with a degree of sobriety and respect; the second woman's speech appears as "nonsense" and "jumbled." Were both women's speech in public nonsense, or was only one woman's speech in public nonsense, the other's sense? Or were both women by voicing bad doctrine, speaking, "confusions, horror, and disorder . . . unexpressible"? In the account of the naked woman and of the meeting at Coleman Street, there are mixed signals. There is disparity between Brown and Sterry over whether the naked woman should be taken as a rational creature. There is ambiguity in the understanding of women's rationality in the account reported to Edwards of the women's religious meeting. These contradictory and ambiguous responses, however, reveal to us that the understanding of women's rational nature was far from settled during this period; that women were by some attributed with rationality and that the problem was where and how it should be expressed.

4. WOMEN AND THE PUBLIC SPHERE

It has been argued that the Puritan notion of marriage and the ideas of spiritual equality promoted by Puritans as well as by the sects represented a threat to patriarchy in general. The shift to a Protestant ideal of marriage accounts for some of this anxiety about women's power in and out of the household. Since the Royalist political position was to justify social order by patriarchy, any disruption in the family was perceived as a threat to the state.[74] It is true, women acting in politics and religion were represented as disrupting family relations.

Yet the female prophets and women petitioners were portrayed as disrupting public places, not family places. The naked woman, "sober in her speech," was a threat to the Independent Mr. Brown, who wished to have her contained and tried, in a manner exemplary to others of her "faction," her religious associates. Such potent women, as well as those who threatened sexual ravenousness or intellectual overreaching, were entering dangerously into the new public sphere. In the political pamphlets, enemies of women's participation accused sexually potent women of threatening to overturn laws, of bringing the bedroom into matters of state. In the religious pamphlets, women were accused of taking part equally in sex with men and introducing nonsensical discourses in religion, visibly disrupting religious ritual, not only as ecstatic prophets or as naked protesters, but also as interpreters and explicators of Scripture. According to these polemicists, they brought sexuality, and what was called irrationality, into the public sphere. But, as Brown and the newspapers report, women also threatened to bring feminine reason and autonomy into the public sphere. Thinking about women was complex and contradictory. Even a revolutionary group such as the Levellers excluded women in their quest for the "fundamental rights" of Englishmen. Many of the radical political and religious movements intended no emancipation of women from traditional structures of authority, allowing them no leadership in separatist churches.[75] Those who stopped women's mouths were as often from the revolutionary side, and their particular task was to legitimize their own political and religious activities, to protect the rights of their own politicians and ministers to speak, and one means to do this was by discrediting the women.[76] That discrediting, however, helped to shape the character of the public sphere which they were beginning to define. In examining the responses to women's voices and their public actions in political and religious realms, we see in what ways women were given or denied access to the emerging discourses of the public sphere.

One place women's rationality, autonomy, and authority were visible was in the press. As I have argued elsewhere, an important outcome of the English Revolution was the development of a notion of a public sphere, in which political negotiations were to take place which included the public. During the English Revolution, many of the revolutionaries defined for themselves a public sphere as equivalent to the audience for print.[77] The explosion of printing after the lapse of censorship in 1641 contributed to turning citizens into political actors, though of course printing did not cause England's revolution.[78] What printing did, however, was to be a forum for many political discussions that reached a wide audience of readers outside of formal political institutions. People were taking sides in a civil war, and they were increasingly thirsty for information, war news, and opinions. The swell of pamphlets in the press indicates that many ordinary citizens were willing to buy news, and thus to participate in the political life of the nation.[79] Impetus for publication also came from opinion-makers, those writers and politicians who were increasingly concerned with persuading the people to side with their political views. Women, by their inclusion as a topic for debate in the press, were becoming part of that political life.

Who read the English revolutionary publications? Evidence of readership of such ephemera is hard to obtain; since more people could read than could write in seventeenth-century England, many readers left no written record of their reading habits. There were, of course, economic limitations to readership, with the typical cost of a pamphlet or chapbook a cheap 2d–6d.[80] Yet the price need not have deterred readers; news pamphlets and ballads were often read aloud in public, shared, or passed around from one person to another. Historians estimate that 30% of adult males could read; the figures were considerably higher in London, where 60% of adult males were literate. Press runs for an individual pamphlet would range from five hundred to fifteen hundred copies, and the number of a popular genre such as almanacs produced annually for the Stationers' Company in the 1660s ran between 300,000 to 400,000, or one for every four families.[81]

We might see that the English Revolutionary press contributed to the "structural transformation of the public sphere," as Jürgen Habermas has called it, in which power came to be constructed not out of adherence to the authority of special persons, but was constituted by the conditions of public discussion.[82] The "public sphere" emerged in early modern Europe, Habermas explains, "in which private people, come together to form a public, readied themselves to compel public authority to legitimate itself before public opinion." As a consequence of this transformation, power came to be constructed not out of adherence to the authority of special persons, but through the conditions of public discussion. Habermas stresses the means of political discussion through which private people came together as a public, the "public use of their reason," and the forums for that use, the press, the coffeehouse, the salon.[83] Habermas has assigned a more recent date—the late eighteenth century—to the formation of the public sphere in England, in which participatory political processes and the media, along with social and cultural institutions, coalesced to make it possible for the public to become the basis for politics; this public sphere is set against the "intimate sphere" of the newly developing bourgeois family. Although the Habermasian scheme has been criticized for its basis in an unreflective notion of "reason" and by feminist scholars who have pressed Habermas to reconstruct an "unthematized gender subtext," the concept is relevant to analysing the writing of the English Revolution, to exploring a cultural milieu in which the material conditions were in place for affordable, accessible printing, and an intellectual climate of public debate: all these might be said to anticipate Habermas' scheme by a century or so.[84] In his emphasis on the rational basis of the public sphere, Habermas explores the rise of its ideology in England by a focus on Hobbes and Locke. Yet the meanings of the public sphere may be charted not through the explicit "ideology" of the political theorists of the age, but through the equally ideological rhetoric, the images, and the satiric attacks of the time. The consideration of the public roles of women in the pamphlet press may have been one means to shape the character of the public sphere. By analyzing such reactions, we see how rationality becomes established as the predominant means of expression in the public sphere and understand women's relation to it. In exploring reactions to women we can begin to reconstruct what was meant by "rational" and see that the estimation of women's capabilities and decisions about the roles they were to play contributed to the fashioning of the public sphere in England.

If one of the triumphs of the English Revolution was the development of an idea of the public sphere as the location for political activity, we need to understand how this construct involved women, and whether women were excluded by the kinds of images and stereotypes we have been examining here. Were these very stereotypes a means of working out how women were to be included or excluded? Are there differences in the ways women could express autonomy and authority in religious and political realms? Many of these negative images of women's roles in public helped to express and to consolidate the need for differences between public and private spheres. Yet some representations of women by the press—in their petitioning, for example—were less negative, and gave women voices they were denied in formal politics. Further work needs to explore more fully the relationship between attacks on women acting in explicitly public ways and the development of a rationalist discourse that was to constitute the public sphere.

This essay is a perilous attempt to synthesize research findings on women in the English Revolution. My unanswered question is, Can we see a coherent statement, detect a prevailing logic of the sex system, in the range of responses to women in public? Was the English Revolution an "advance" for women? I admit from the start that my evidence is skewed towards the literary, and thus the conclusions I draw are partial, perhaps deeply suspect to the historian trained on county and court records. Literary sources are always a shaky ground on which to build history. But literary representations help us understand the visions, the perceptions, the ideologies, and the self-understandings of a society. David Underdown, writing on literary representations of the scold, claims that "the endless reiteration of such commonplaces [as found in misogynistic pamphlet literature] would surely have been unnecessary had there not been uneasy feelings that too many such [unruly] families existed."[85] I agree. Both the structural meanings of these representations and the precise political content matter. If the concern over these women during the period 1560–1660 may be seen as a sign of structural social crisis, then I wish to revise this explanation, suggesting that the political crisis in which women were taking on new roles needs to be taken into account. It is precisely at the moment when English citizens were engaging in conflict over political ideologies that we see a preoccupation with the institutions of marriage and the family. This domestic arena was undergoing transformation not only because of social and economic changes, not only because of the ideological challenges, the threats to political order, established by anti-monarchists in the English Revolution, but also because of women's activities in the public sphere. Both from the left and from the right, the obsession with unruly women reveals deep engagement with the construction of a public sphere, and these literary representations offer us a way to understand how women on top signified a political reality.

Notes

I would like to thank Barbara Newman, Steve Pincus, and Wendy Wall for their relevant suggestions and comments on an earlier version of this essay.

1. *The Ranters Ranting* (1650). All original sources are published in London. For an analysis of this and other pornographic political prints, see Tamsyn Williams, " 'Magnetic Figures': Polemical Prints of the English Revolution," in

Lucy Gent and Nigel Llewellyn, eds., *Renaissance Bodies: The Human Figure in English Culture, c.1540–1660* (London: Reaktion, 1990). 86–110; and, for the political implications of this "porno-political rhetoric," see Susan Wiseman, "'Adam, the Father of all Flesh,': Porno-political Rhetoric and Political Theory in and After the English Civil War," in James Holstun, ed., *Pamphlet Wars: Prose in the English Revolution* (London: Frank Cass, 1992), 134–157.

2. *The Disease of the House, or the State Mountebank administering physick to a sick Parliament* (1649); *Mercurius Melancholicus* No. 36 (1–8 May 1648); *Mistris Parliament Her Gossiping* (1648); *Mistris Parliament Presented in her Bed . . . in the Birth of her Monstrous Offspring, the Child of Deformation* (1648). See Lois Potter, ed., "The *Mistress Parliament* Political Dialogues," *Journal of Analytic and Enumerative Bibliography* 1 (1987), 101–170.

3. Lois Potter, *Secret Rites and Secret Writing: Royalist Literature, 1641–1660* (Cambridge: Cambridge University Press, 1989), 132.

4. Natalie Z. Davis, "Women on Top," in *Society and Culture in Early Modern France* (Stanford: Stanford University Press, 1977), 124–151. For England, see Peter Burke, *Popular Culture in Early Modern Europe*, (New York: Harper and Row, 1978), 199–202.

5. Taking a psychoanalytical approach to "woman on top" literature, Mary Russo in, "Female Grotesques: Carnival and Theory," in Teresa de Lauretis, ed., *Feminist Studies/Critical Studies* (London: Macmillan, 1986), 217, argues that "women and their bodies, certain bodies, in certain public framings, in certain public spaces, are always already transgressive—dangerous and in danger." Similarly, the anthropologist Suzanne Dixon argues, that "An autonomous mother or sexual partner is a woman to be feared. Yet a woman is intended to be a mother and a sexual partner, so in their right places these are seen as essentially female roles," in "Conclusion—The enduring Theme: Domineering Dowagers and Scheming Concubines," in Barbara Garlick, Suzanne Dixon and Pauline Allen, eds., *Stereotypes of Women in Power: Historical Perspectives and Revisionist Views* (New York: Greenwood Press, 1992), 213. My interest here is not in the psychoanalytic substrate of such anti-feminine expressions, but in the political and cultural work they do.

6. There has been debate with respect to class over the cultural meanings of the tradition of *charivari* in England, whether such rituals evince a withdrawal of the upper classes from popular culture, as in Burke, *Popular Culture*, 207–243; for an opposing view, see Martin Ingram, "Ridings, Rough Music and the 'Reform of Popular Culture' in Early Modern England," *Past and Present* 105 (1984), 79–113.

7. Rene Girard, *Violence and the Sacred*, trans. Patrick Gregory (Baltimore: The Johns Hopkins University Press, 1977), 141.

8. Susan Dwyer Amussen, *An Ordered Society: Gender and Class in Early Modern England* (Oxford: Basil Blackwell, 1988), 141.

9. David Underdown, "The Taming of the Scold: the Enforcement of Patriarchal Authority in Early Modern England," in A. Fletcher and J. Stevenson, eds., *Order and Disorder in Early Modern England* (New York: Cambridge University Press, 1985), 126.

10. Bulstrode Whitelock, *Memorials of the English Affairs*, 4 vols. (Oxford: Oxford University Press, 1853), III, 20.

11. Lynn Hunt, "The Many Bodies of Marie Antoinette: Political Pornography and

the problem of the Feminine in the French Revolution," in Lynn Hunt, ed., *Eroticism and the Body Politic* (Baltimore: The Johns Hopkins University Press, 1991), 126; and Lynn Hunt, *The Family Romance of the French Revolution* (Berkeley: University of California Press, 1992). Sarah Maza, writing about attacks on Marie Antoinette in the pre-Revolutionary decade, concludes that the affair helped to consolidate the iconography that would exclude women from the public political sphere, that "the overlapping of female sexual and political activity had become a central metaphor for political decay," in "The Diamond Necklace Affair Revisited (1785–1786): The Case of the Missing Queen," in Lynn Hunt, ed., *Eroticism and the Body Politic*, 76.

12. Hunt, "The Many Bodies," 126. In a similar vein, Joan B. Landes has argued that "the Republic was constructed against women, not just without them," in *Women and the Public Sphere in the Age of the French Revolution* (Ithaca: Cornell University Press, 1988), 12, allowing that the mobilization of women during the French Revolution created a gender crisis that was "solved" by the exclusion of women from the public sphere. For criticism of this position, see Keith Baker, "Defining the Public Sphere in Eighteenth Century France: Variations on a Theme by Habermas," in Craig Calhoun, ed., *Habermas and the Public Sphere* (Cambridge: MIT Press, 1992), 181–211.

13. Susan Wiseman, " 'Adam, the Father of all Flesh'."

14. Carole Pateman, *The Sexual Contract* (Stanford: Stanford University Press, 1988), 77–96.

15. Patricia Crawford, *Women and Religion in England, 1500–1720* (New York: Routledge, 1993), 146; Claire Cross, " 'He-goats before the flocks': A Note on the Part Played by Women in the Founding of Some Civil War churches," *Studies in Church History*, 8 (1972), 195–202.

16. Thomas Jordan, "The Rebellion," in *Rump: Or an Exact Collection . . . 1639 to Anno 1661*, facs. ed. (London: Henry Brome and Henry Marsh, 1874), Vol. 1. 291–5.

17. Antonia Fraser, *The Weaker Vessel: Woman's Lot in Seventeenth-Century England* (London: Methuen, 1985), 184.

18. See, for example, the following essays: Keith Thomas, "Women and the Civil War Sects," *Past and Present*, 13 (1958), 42–62; Christine Berg and Philippa Berry, " 'Spiritual Whoredom': An Essay on Female Prophets in the Seventeenth Century," in *1642: Literature and Power in the Seventeenth Century*, ed. Francis Barker (Colchester: University to Essex, 1981), 37–54; Phyllis Mack, "Women as Prophets during the English Civil War," *Feminist Studies* 8:1 (1982); Ellen A. McArthur, "Women Petitioners and the Long Parliament," *English Historical Review*, 24 (1909), 698–709.

19. Phyllis Mack, *Visionary Women: Ecstatic Prophesy in Seventeenth-Century England* (Berkeley: University of California Press, 1992), 49. Patricia Crawford examines the experiences of, and reactions to, women in radical religion during the English Revolution in *Women and Religion*, 119–184.

20. Patricia Higgins, "The Reactions of Women, with special reference to women petitioners," in Brian Manning, ed., *Politics, Religion and the English Civil War* (London: Edwin Arnold, 1973), 179–224.

21. William Haller, *Liberty and Reformation in the Puritan Revolution* (New York: Columbia University Press, 1955), 262. On Lilburne, see also Christopher Hill, *Puritanism and Revolution* (London: Mercury Books, 1962); M. A. Gibb, *John*

Lilburne the Leveller (London: Lindsay Drummond, 1947). On the social composition of the Leveller movement, see, G. E. Aylmer, "Gentlemen Levellers?" in Charles Webster, ed., *The Intellectual Revolution of the Seventeenth Century* (London: Routledge and Kegan Paul, 1974), 101–8.

22. Keith Thomas, "The Levellers and the Franchise," in G. E. Aylmer, ed., *The Interregnum: The Quest for Settlement* (London: Macmillan, 1972), 57–78. Leveller pamphlets specifically including women are Richard Overton, *The Bull Baiting of the Great Bull of Bashan* (1649); *The Large Petition of the Levellers* (1648).

23. *Perfect Occurrences . . . Proceedings of the Councell of State: And other Moderate intelligence from . . . Lord Generall Fairfax's army*, Numb. 121 (20–27 April 1649) ed. Henry Walker E529 (21); *England's Moderate Messenger*, Numb. 1 (23–30 April 1649); *Impartiall intelligencer*, Numb. 8 (18–25 April 1649) E529 (20); *Continued Heads of Perfect Passages in Parliament*, Numb. 23 (20–27) April 1649). The petition was printed as *To the Supreme Authority of this Nation* (1649) E551 (4).

24. *Continued Heads of Perfect Passages in Parliament*, Numb. 23 (20–27 April 1649).

25. On the spread of newspapers during the civil war period, see Joseph Frank, *The Beginnings of the English Newspaper, 1620–1660* (Cambridge: Harvard University Press, 1961); Frederick S. Siebert, *Freedom of the Press in England, 1476–1776* (Urbana: University of Illinois Press, 1952), 166–176; C. Blagden, "The Stationers' Company in the Civil War Period," *The Library*, fifth series, 13:1 (1958), 1–17; Potter, *Secret Rites and Secret Writing*, 1–37.

26. *To the Supreme Authority of this Nation*, 4; also verbatim in *England's Moderate Messenger*, numb. 1 (23–30 April 1649).

27. *England's Moderate Messenger*, Numb. 1 (23–30 April 1649).

28. *A Petition of women, Affecters and Approvers of the Petition of Sept. 11, 1648* (5 May 1649), in A. S. P. Woodhouse, *Puritanism and Liberty* (Chicago: University of Chicago Press, 1974), 366–67.

29. *Unto every individual member of Parliament: the . . . Representation of . . . women . . . on behalf of Mr John Lilburne* (1653), 669f (17), cited in Higgins, 216.

30. *Perfect Occurrences* (20–27 April 1649).

31. *Continued Heads of Perfect Passages* (20–27 April); the Royalist *Mercurius Elencticus* (24 April–1 May 1649) also reported that Parliament had "biden them go home and wash their dishes."

32. *A Petition*, 367.

33. *Perfect Occurrences* (20–27 April 1649).

34. *Mercurius Elencticus, Communicating the Unparallel'd Proceedings*, no. 1 (24 April–1 May 1649), 3.

35. *Mercurius Elencticus* 1 (24 April–1 May 1649), 6.

36. *Mercurius Pragmaticus* (23–30 April 1649), A2; *Mercurius Pragmaticus* (24 April–1 May 1649), Qqq3v.

37. John Crouch, *Man in the moon, Discovering a World of Knavery under the Sun* (April 1649–Jun 1650), 11.

38. *Hosanna: Or, A song of Thanks-giving* (1649), 6.

39. An interesting question is, why did negotiations about marriage legislation become an emblem for political disorder, and why were *women* represented

as the advocates of it? On the "puritan sexual revolution" as evidence of the reality of the English Revolution, see Christopher Hill, *The World Turned Upside Down* (Harmondsworth, Middlesex: Penguin, 1975), 306–323. On the long background to puritan legislation to reform marriage and sexual relations, see Keith Thomas, "The Puritans and Adultery: the Act of 1650 Reconsidered," in David Pennington and Keith Thomas, eds., *Puritans and Revolutionaries* (Oxford: Clarendon Press, 1978), 257–82, who demonstrates that reform in marriage laws "had been in gestation for over a century" (272). Both of these accounts of puritanism and its discontents on the marriage front are interested in what the overturning of traditional sexual order has to do with the structural, long-term crisis that culminated in the English Revolution, and they are less interested in what the debate over marriage laws had to do with gender. The marriage problem as Hill and Thomas, as well as Lawrence Stone, *The Family, Sex, and Marriage in England, 1500–1800* (New York: Harper and Row, 1979) see it, is really about relations between men; that is, the reform of marriage whether through legislation or through ideologies of love, helped to regulate property, to consolidate male authority, and to impose the patriarchy that accompanied the rise of the bourgeois state. My approach here shifts attention away from what the concern over marriage had to do with regulating these male relations, and towards thinking about the problem as a problem of male/female relations. See Sherry Ortner, "The Virgin and the State," *Feminist Studies* 4:3 (1978), 19–36.

40. Henry Neville, *The Parliament of Ladies: With their Laws Newly enacted* (1647). For an analysis of this idiosyncratic and complicated pamphlet that takes into account Neville's republicanism, see Susan Wiseman, " 'Adam, the Father of all Flesh.' "

41. In K. Henderson and B. McManus, *Half Humankind: Contexts and Texts of the Controversy About Women, 1540–1640* (Urbana: University of Illinois Press, 1985).

42. *The Parliament of Women* (1646), t.p.

43. Women in public are accused of being prostitutes in the case of attacks on women humanists, according to Anthony Grafton and Lisa Jardine, "Women humanists: Education for What?" in *From Humanism to the Humanities* (Cambridge: Harvard University Press, 1986), 39–43. See also Peter Stallybrass for an account and description of the process of making women private, domestic, and contained in "Patriarchal Territories: The Body Enclosed," in Margaret W. Ferguson, Maureen Quilligan and Nancy J. Vickers, eds., *Rewriting the Renaissance: The Discourses of Sexual Difference in Early Modern Europe* (Chicago: University of Chicago Press, 1987), 123–142.

44. As Rachel Weil argues in her examination of the relationship between slander and pornography in Restoration England, the language of sexual slander is not merely a sign of political conflict, but expresses it, for example, the meaning of tyranny, in, "Sometimes a Scepter is Only a Scepter: Pornography and Politics in Restoration England," in Lynn Hunt, ed., *The Invention of Pornography: Obscenity and the Origins of Modernity, 1500–1800* (New York: Zone Books, 1993), 145.

45. *Continued Heads of Perfect Passages in Parliament*, Numb. 23 (20–27 April 1649).

46. Henry Neville, *An Exact Diurnall of the Parliament of Ladyes* (1647), 5–6.

47. *The Parliament of Ladies, or divers Remarkable passages of Ladies in Spring-garden; in Parliament Assembled* (1647), 6.

48. Higgins, "The reactions of Women," argues that women were beginning to emancipate themselves through their political actions in the civil war period; Mack, in *Visionary Women*, 185, explains, "self-transcendence, not self-expression, was the ultimate goal of Quaker worship."

49. According to Rachel Trubowitz, "the sects inadvertently helped women to abandon their traditional duties as wives or mothers and to define themselves instead as independent thinkers and preachers," in, "Female Preachers and Male Wives: Gender and Authority in Civil War England," in James Holstun, ed., *Pamphlet Wars: Prose in the English Revolution* (London: Frank Cass, 1992), 118. Mack, *Visionary Women*, would disagree with precisely this line of thinking; she argues, rather, that women's prophecy was an extension of their roles as mothers and wives. The classic study of patriarchalism in England is Gordon Schochet, *Patriarchalism and Political Thought* (Oxford: Basil Blackwell, 1975).

50. Susan Wiseman, "'Adam, the Father of all Flesh,'" 148.

51. Margaret W. Ferguson, in "A Room Not Their Own," in Clayton Koelb and Susan Noakes, eds., *The Comparative Perspective on Literature: Approaches to Theory and Practice* (Ithaca: Cornell University Press, 1988), 93–116, explores in what ways do womens' written and published works in the Renaissance, particularly those of humanist women, sanction "a certain disobedience and freedom of speech for women; in so doing . . . implicitly interrogate the idea of woman as the property of men: both, indeed show women taking possession of their bodies," 111.

52. Murray Tolmie surveys the rise of separatism in *The Triumph of the Saints: The Separate Churches of London, 1616–1649* (New York: Cambridge University Press, 1977), 33. The argument for individualism is also voiced by Christopher Hill, *Society and Puritanism in Pre-Revolutionary England* (London, 1964).

53. The development of an affective and spiritual model of marriage is presented by Stone, *The Family, Sex, and Marriage in England*; its application to English Renaissance literature is worked out by Mary Beth Rose, *The Expense of Spirit: Love and Sexuality in English Renaissance Drama* (Ithaca; Cornell University Press, 1988); the position that there was a new Puritan model of marriage is critiqued by Kathleen M. Davies, "The sacred condition of equality: How original were Puritan doctrines of marriage?" *Social History* 5 (1977), 563–80. Puritan women had a tradition of marked independence, and the more sober women, the matrons and the godly—not the visionaries—maintained that tradition, according to Cross, "'He-Goats before the Flocks,'" 195–202.

54. Daniel Cawdrey, *Family Reformation Promoted* (1656), 92, 93, 96, 97.

55. Thomas, "Women and the Civil War Sects," 42–62.

56. I. H., *A Strange Wonder or A Wonder in A Woman . . . a plaine discription of many mad tricks and flights lately performed by a Zealous sister which was overcome with the Spirit* (1642), 2–3, 4.

57. Robert Heath, *Clarastella: Together with Poems Occasional* (1650), H5–6.

58. *A Discoverie of Six Women Preachers* (1641), t.p., 2.

59. *A Dialogue Betweene Sacke and Six* (1641), A4.

60. *A Discoverie of Six Women Preachers*, t.p. Paul: 1 Timothy 2. 11–12.

370

61. *Continued Heads of Perfect Passages* (20–27 April 1649).

62. *A Discoverie of Six women Preachers*, 5.

63. Michel Foucault, *Madness and Civilization: A History of Insanity in the Age of Reason*, trans. Richard Howard (New York: Vintage, 1973), 70. For a critique of Foucault and reassessment of the history of madness in England, see Michael MacDonald, *Mystical Bedlam: Madness, Anxiety and Healing in Seventeenth-Century England* (Cambridge: Cambridge University Press, 1981).

64. Crawford, *Women and Religion in England*, 143, 146.

65. Tolmie, *The Triumph of the Saints*, 22.

66. Mack, *Visionary Women*, 152; Christopher Hill, *The World Turned Upside Down* (Harmondsworth, Middlesex: Penguin, 1975), 231–41.

67. David Brown, *The Naked Woman, or a Rare Epistle sent to Mr. Peter Sterry, Minister at Whitehall* (1652), 16.

68. Tolmie, *The Triumph of the Saints*, 13.

69. *The Naked Woman*, 9–10.

70. *The Naked Woman*, 7.

71. *The Naked Woman*, 9, 7.

72. Thomas Edwards, *The First and Second Part of Gangraena* (1646), 29, 30, 31.

73. Tolmie, *The Triumph of the Saints*, 81. Tolmie states the lectures were not formally authorized by the London congregation; but Patricia Crawford, *Women and Religion in England*, 135, states that they were.

74. Amussen, *An Ordered Society*, 63; see also Schochet, *Patriarchalism and Political Thought*, 54–55.

75. Mack, *Visionary Women*, 72. Even the radical Gerrard Winstanley, the "communist" Digger leader attacked the Ranters on the grounds of their gender equality. See Winstanley, *A Vindication of Those, Whose Endeavors is only to Make the Earth a Common Treasury* (1649), in George H. Sabine, ed., *The Works of Gerrard Winstanley* (Ithaca: Cornell University Press, 1941), 400.

76. Thomas reminds us, in "Women and the Civil War Sects," 52, that Quakers and other sects were "notoriously patriarchal," and that spiritual equality was "to remain strictly spiritual only"; what is interesting for us here is the perception that sectarian families were inverted.

77. Achinstein, *Milton and the Revolutionary Reader* (forthcoming, Princeton University Press, 1994).

78. E. Eisenstein's *The Printing Press as an Agent of Change* (Cambridge: Cambridge University Press, 1985), and her seminal article, "The Advent of Printing and the Problem of the Renaissance," *Past and Present*, 45 (1969), 1989, have aroused debate over the deterministic path of print; T. Rabb and E. Eisenstein, "Debate: The Advent of Printing and the Problem of the Renaissance: A Comment," *Past and Present* 52 (1971), 135–144. For general printing patterns, literacy, and distribution, see Margaret Spufford, *Small Books and Pleasant Histories: Popular Fiction and its Readership in Seventeenth-Century England* (Cambridge: Cambridge University Press, 1985).

79. Richard Cust, "News and Politics in Early Seventeenth Century England," *Past and Present* 112 (1986), 60–90; F. J. Levy, "How Information Spread, 1540–1640," *Journal of British Studies* 21 (1982), 11–34; Folke Dahl, "A Short-title Catalogue of English Corantos and Newsbooks, 1620–1642," *The Library*, 4th series 19 (1939), 44–98. Carolyn Nelson and Matthew Seccombe, eds.,

British Newspapers and Periodicals, 1641–1700 (New York: Modern Language Association of America, 1987) is indispensable for the study of these materials.

80. M. Spufford, *Small books*, 93. On the spread of popular literature, see B. Capp, "Popular Literature," in B. Reay, *Popular Culture in Seventeenth Century England* (New York: St. Martin's Press, 1985), 198–243; C. J. Sommerville, "On the Distribution of Religious and Occult Literature in Seventeenth-Century England," *The Library*, 5th ser. 29 (1974), 221–25.

81. Cyprian Blagden, *The Stationers' Company: A History, 1497–1959* (Stanford: Stanford University Press, 1960), 188; Spufford, *Small Books*, 100. On the extent of literacy during the revolutionary period, see David Cressy, *Literacy and the Social Order* (Cambridge: Cambridge University Press, 1980): Margaret Spufford, "First Steps in Literacy," *Social History* 4 (1979), 407–35.

82. Jürgen Habermas. *The structural Transformation of the Public Sphere: An Inquiry into a Category of Bourgeois Society*, tr. T. Burger (Cambridge: MIT Press, 1989).

83. Habermas, *The Structural Transformation of the Public Sphere*, 25–26, 27, 42–43. See also, Keith Baker, "Politics and Public Opinion under the Old Regime: Some Reflections." in Jack R. Censer and Heremy D. Popkin, eds., *Press and Politics in Pre-Revolutionary France* (Berkeley: University of California Press, 1987), 204–46; and, for England, see David Zaret, "Religion, Science, and Printing in the Public Sphere in Seventeenth Century England," in Craig Calhoun, ed., *Habermas and the Public Sphere* (Cambridge: MIT Press, 1992), 212–235; and Steve Pincus, " 'Coffee Politicians Does Create': Coffeehouses in Restoration Political Culture," *Journal of Modern History*, forthcoming.

84. See Calhoun, ed., *Habermas and the Public Sphere*, especially essays by Moishe Postone, Nicholas Garnham, Michael Schudson, and Nancy Fraser. For feminist criticism of Habermas, see Nancy Fraser, "What's Critical about Critical Theory? The Case of Habermas and Gender," in Mary Lyndon Shanley and Carole Pateman, eds., *Feminist Interpretations and Political Theory* (University Park, PA: Pennsylvania State University Press, 1991), 253–277, 254; and Carole Pateman, "Feminist Critiques of the Public/Private Dichotomy," in *The Disorder of Women: Democracy, Feminism, and Political Theory* (Stanford, CA: Stanford University Press, 1989), 122–123.

85. David Underdown, "The Taming of the Scold," 118.

La Donnesca Mano

Fredrika Jacobs

In the congenial arts I see us still obliged to renounce sculpture and even painting . . . The "decency" that excludes us from studying the human form, everything in our ethos opposes our progress . . . Thus we are limited to music, dance and banal versifying. Meager resources, which lead nowhere.

(Mme Louise d'Epinay, 1771)

Is an image reflective of its maker and does it reveal something about the individual who produced it? Leonard da Vinci's well-known aphorism, "Every artist paints himself [*ogni dipintore dipinge se*]" suggests it does. In fact, examples of the reflexivity of art are not hard to find in early critical writings. Giorgio Vasari's description of frescoes in the church of Santa Maria Nuovo, Florence, illustrates the point. Accepting as fact the story of Andrea del Castagno's purported murder of a rival painter, Vasari claims the "malignant" Castagno unwittingly "painted himself with the face of Judas Iscariot, whom he resembled in both appearance and deed."[1] Although this example implies a one-to-one relationship between the artist and the subject he paints, reflexivity was also perceived in the artist's style. In essence style was viewed as a type of signature which, among other things, disclosed the gender of the maker. Accordingly, critics scrutinized images and objects for signs of strength and vigor (*ardito, furioso, pugnato, virile*, etc.) or indications of timidity and excessive care (*arrendevole, stento, tenero, feminile*, etc.). Not unexpectedly, these critical terms carried qualitative weight. Looking back at the cinquecento, the seventeenth-century critic Carlo Cesare Malvasia compared the style of the Bolognese painter Elisabetta Sirani (1638–65) to those of her forebears. Sirani,

From Fredrika Jacobs, *Defining the Renaissance Virtuosa: Women Artists and the Language of Art History* (Cambridge University Press, 1997), 85–122. © Fredrika H. Jacobs. Reprinted with permission.

whose style is described as "*virile*" and "*grande*", "never left in her work signs of timidity and flattery, which is characteristic of the weaker sex [non lasciò mai una certa timidità e leccatura propria del debile sesso]".[2]

Over and above the contention that style is gendered, Malvasia's observation makes clear three points. First, masculine style is more commendable than feminine style. Second, feminine style typically reveals a female hand. Third, the gender of the style, like that of *virtù*, is not necessarily determined by sex. Just as Malvasia sees virility in Sirani's style, so des Ferrante Carli, for example, view the paintings of Guido Reni as "womanly, Flemish, washed out and without force [da donna, fiaminga, slavata, senza forza]".[3] But despite the equivocal relationship of a gendered style to the artist's sex, one thing was certain. Within the semantic values of the critic's terminology, the concept of femininity was an effective rhetorical weapon.

According to Ficino, from the inspired *furor* of the *homo melancholis* comes the breath of life that vivifies art.[4] So defined, Platonic *furor* was designated by sixteenth-century art-theorists as the inventive means to the desired aesthetic end, *la bella maniera*, and thus tailored to the values of *l'arte del disegno*. In something akin to a mathematical equation, the *furor* of the mind was added to the *furia* and *fierezza* of the hand. Combined, they imparted to the visible form a "quickness and liveliness of movement that eliminates any and all signs of labor and affectation [prontezza e fierezza di moto senza stento e affatatione].[5] Since, as Federico Zuccaro argues, "spirit is that *vivezza* and *fierezza di moto* in the glance and gesture," *furia* as a sign of decorum (or movement) corresponds to a transcendental reality.[6] In this respect, *furia* is associated closely with grace (*grazia*) and, at its highest level, is a hallmark of genius.[7]

Ideally and in practical terms, the *furor* of conception would not be lost nor diminished as it progressed from a labor of the spirit to a material product produced by the hand and presented to the eye. To insure that this was indeed the case, Francisco de Hollanda urged artists to place the "idea or concept . . . most quickly in execution before it is lost or diminished by some perturbation." Because any loss of "that divine furor and image that it bears in the *fantasia*" would inevitably reveal a weakness of talent, or *ingegno*, de Hollanda designated the quill pen the best instrument for this task.[8] Giorgio Vasari had argued the same point. "Pen or other drawing instruments or charcoal" are well suited to the "furor dello artefice," since they allow the artist to "express hastily" the spirit of an idea as it "occurs to him." These notations—

schizzi, bozze, macchie—are an essential part of *disegno* in the broadest sense of the word. Not only do they reveal a learned hand: a "facilità del disegnare" that promotes "buona forma i disegni";[9] they define the art of drawing as a creative and cognitive process which, because of its conceptual basis and in keeping with a metaphorical system that connects the creative process to God's plan of creation, grants the artist a form of divinity. It is this nexus that ties *furia* to *grazia* and, by extension, to genius.

But the convergence of learned hands and concepts (*mani sapeva e concetti*) was not possible for all artists. Thus, Vasari advises anyone who "feels himself not strong enough" to visualize his own ideas to "try with all possible diligence [diligenza] to copy from life" as well as after masterpieces of art.[10] This method of making, however, carried a warning. Any "lingering too long" over a work "takes away all the good that facility [facilità] and grace [grazia] and boldness [fierezza] might do." In fact, "effort and labor [stento e fatica] . . . make things appear hard and crude; besides which, too much study" often "spoils" an image.[11] "It appears very often in sketches [bozze], born from a moment in the fury of art [nascendo in un subito dal furore dell'arte], that a man's conception is expressed in a few strokes, while, on the contrary, effort and too great diligence [lo stento e la troppa diligenza] detract from the force and judgment" seen in works by excellent masters. Indeed, "whoever knows that the arts of design . . . are similar to poetry knows that, as the poems dictated by poetic furor are good and true and better than those that are labored, so the works of men excellent in design are better when they have been made at one stroke by the force of that furor [forze di quel furore]."[12]

Such prohibitions against too evident labor (*stento*) stand as warnings against the stylistic and mimetic affectation (*affettatione*) that can arise from painstaking diligence (*diligenza*) and assiduity of study (*l'assiduità dello studio*). They also point to a theoretical shift. Whereas Leon Battista Alberti believed that the perception of beauty on which the Idea depends is grounded in the observation and experience of nature, Vasari, Lomazzo, Armenini, Zuccaro, and others considered the Idea in more metaphysical terms. As the connection of *furor* and *grazia* in both a spiritual and stylistic sense suggests, the Idea that is "born" in the creative mind is of a purer and more perfect kind than that rooted solely in material reality.[13] Although all Renaissance theorists shared the goal of advancing art to ever higher levels of excellence, the shift in focus from the sensible to the conceptual necessitated changes in practice. This, in turn, required the development of a critical language that would allow writers to differentiate the origins and quality of works of art. And this fostered what may best be described as a symbiotic view of art, a view that made an artist's sex a factor of critical consequence.

According to theorists and critics, the finished product provides in its style insight into the process by which it came into being. In other words, the first visible notation of a composition has a perceptible impact on the completed image. This is true when the image, to use Armenini's words, records an Idea "which seems to be born in the mind" and drawn "velocemente" as well as when it is a painstaking working out of figures and compositions.[14] The finished image is, therefore, inseparable from the process. This necessarily makes it indivisible from its maker. Stated succinctly, art is self-reflexive.

As sixteenth-century writers began increasingly to review the relative merits of theory and practice in recognition of the qualitative differences among works by different artists, a two-tiered structure of critical evaluation took shape. In essence, this system distinguishes the *artista* from the *artigiano* and, ultimately, the inspired *pittore* from the proficient *pittrice*. It does so through the selective and systematic contextual application of critical terms which, not surprisingly, were structured into oppositional pairs: *affettatione—sprezzatura, ritrarre— imitare*, and so forth. Certain words—*furia, sprezzatura, grazia, imitare, invenzione*—recognize in a work the skilled hand and creative mind of the artist. Other words—*affettatione, stento, diligenza, ritrarre*— acknowledge the well-practised but often uninspired hand and mind of the craftsman. As more and more critics assessed the merits of specific artists—both male and female—these terms absorbed current notions about gender. Works by men, who by reason of being male are susceptible to creative melancholia, typically evince the *fierezza* and *sprezzatura* of inspired *furor*. Works by women, who are "naturally" resistant to melancholy and physically fragile, often display not only the *troppa diligenza* of labored study but also reveal the "delicacy" and even the "affectation" of the feminine touch.

There are, of course, exceptions. A woman can sometimes rise above her femaleness, and a man sometimes falls to fill the void left by her ascension. In either case, an exception is a contradiction in terms and, as such, in no way alters perceptions of gender difference or changes the positive and negative values associated respectively with masculinity and femininity.[15] Indeed, by stressing the singularity of the masculine female (or oddity of the effeminate male) essentialist notions are reenforced. Thus, typically and at best, woman's work, because of an attention to detail, a preference for geometric pattern, a predilection for ornament, and a certain preciosity, was said to reveal *la donnesca mano*. Accordingly, Malvasia observed in portraits by the hand of Lavinia Fontana a certain "gentleness, diligence, and delicacy [gentili, diligenti e teneri]." And, "no less precious, as having come from the hand of a woman, are those few altarpieces by her seen in some of our churches."[16] Luigi Lanzi was to pick up where Malvasia had left off. Fontana's works, he claims, exhibit "without a doubt a certain feminine patience [femminil pazienza]."[17] Similar descriptive terms are used for works by other sixteenth-century *pittrici*. According to Paolo Morigia, Fede Galizia's works are marked by "delicacy" and, in the case of her portrait of Ercole Ferraro's wife Camilla, betray in their attention to detail "diligenza grandissima."[18] Agostino Santagostino agreed. Galizia's portrait of Morigia, he claims, was "made with her usual diligence."[19] When these statements are read against earlier comments, such as Franco Sacchetti's satirical equation of woman's skill in portraiture with her application of cosmetics or Boccaccio's contemporaneous labeling of the latter of these activities as woman's attempt to overcome with "diligence" her "unfitness," the negative implications of *diligenza* are all too evident.[20]

This is not to say that critics never saw *diligenza* in a man's, indeed a master's, works.[21] According to Vasari, "In the attitude of each [the figures of Christ and John the Baptist in Raphael's *Madonna of the Goldfinch*] is a certain childlike simplicity that is wholly lovely, besides that they are so well colored and executed with such great diligence [tanta diligenza] that they appear as living flesh rather than worked by color and design; the Madonna likewise has an air truly full of grace and divinity."[22] This passage, like many in Raphael's *vita*, stresses the importance of hard work but equally emphatically makes the point that it is not sufficient in itself. Innate talent is essential. Vasari's remarks about Sofonisba Anguissola make the same point. "With diligence and readiness [con diligenza e prontezza]" she creates images "that truly seem alive [che paiono veramente vive]" and thus evinces "more study and . . . greater grace than any other woman [più studio e . . . miglio grazia che altra donna]."[23] As the phrase "more than any other woman" discloses, the Cremonese *virtuosa* is exceptional among *artiste femminile*. In fact, excluding assessments of Anguissola's art, descriptions of Renaissance women's works, whether written in the late sixteenth or early twentieth century, never rescue *diligenza* with a string of positive aesthetic terms. Rather than neutralize a negative with a positive, as Vasari did by connecting Sofonisba's *diligenza* to her *prontezza*, critics have emphasized the negative by making it feminine. The strategy has been long-lived and effective.

In 1929, for example, Adolfo Venturi professed his ability to distinguish the hand of Marietta Robusti not only from that of her father but also from those of her brothers and other members of the Tintoretto workshop. Certain passages in *The Baptism of Christ*, *The Miracle of Saint Agnes*, and *The Virgin in Glory with Saints George and Cecilia*, he states, display a "sentimental femininity, a woman's grace that is strained and resolute [femminilità affettiva, una grazia mulierbre che si sforza e si determina]."[24] More recently, Vera Fortunati Pietrantonio has continued to voice the party line. Sounding remarkably like Nicola Pio and P. A. Orlandi, who in 1724 and 1753, respectively, noted that Lavinia Fontana "succeeded in things sweet [cosi dolce]," she observed that Fontana's early devotional panels were created "with somewhat oversweet familial sentiment."[25]

Equally typical, but worse and certainly more direct in its condemnation, *la donnesca mano* was said to lay bare artistic deficiencies. "The things of Lavinia," argued Giuseppe Maria Mazzolari, "do not have the excellence and valor to be found in such things by great men because they are, after all, by a woman who has left the usual path and all that which is suitable to their hands and fingers."[26] Baglione was more specific. Fontana's large-scale *istoria* in San Paolo fuori le Mura, Rome, which illustrates *The Martyrdom of Saint Stephen*, 1603–4, was "unsuccessful". The *pittrice*, he contends, was quite simply incapable of meeting the awesome challenges of a monumental multifigural composition, which, as is well known, can only be produced by those endowed with "grand'ingegno." He therefore advised the artist to limit herself to painting portraits, "à quali col inclinava."[27]

Accepting the premise that the finished work reflects the manner in which it is made, comments such as these imply that women artists worked slowly and with painstaking care. Whether or not this is the case is impossible to tell. Drawings by Renaissance women are, to say the very least, rare. Although more than two dozen drawings have been attributed to Fontana, few have been given to Anguissola, and none have been securely established as the work of any other female hand. Of the identified drawings, a majority are portraits, which, by the very nature of portraiture, makes them replications of the visible rather than expressions of the conceptual. And as finished drawings rather than notational sketches, they naturally evince greater *assiduità dello studio* than *forze di . . . furore*. But does this necessarily translate into works made with obvious diligence? According to Pliny, at least one woman, who "painted chiefly portraits"—Marcia—worked with great speed. In fact, "no artist worked more rapidly than she did."[28] Given the analogies drawn between ancient and Renaissance women artists, Marcia's example should have provided early critics with the all-important precedent for recognizing a woman's *facilità*—but it did not. Whereas Malvasia, in 1678, was to compare Elisabetta Sirani's "virile" handling of the brush to Marcia's "speed . . . in painting," earlier writers refrained from making such comparisons.[29] The contention that a woman's work is marked by *pazienza* and *diligenza* was never really contested. Images, however, can be more eloquent than critical praise.

Although it is true that some of Sofonisba Anguissola's portraits of members of the Spanish court and royal family are so formal as to appear rigid, they must be seen as reflections of decorum rather than considered as evidence of a lack of technical and stylistic ease, or *disinvoltura*. Certainly, her drawings and paintings of family members, unfettered by courtly convention, exhibit, as both Vasari and Cavaliere note, a lively *vivezza*.[30] Baglione's attack on Fontana's *istorie* seems likewise to reflect inequitable critical selection. Unfortunately, her *Martyrdom of Saint Stephen* was destroyed by fire on 16 July 1823, making it impossible to read Baglione's censure of it in light of the actual image. But another monumental work painted a few years earlier, *The Vision of Saint Hyacinth*, 1599, in the church of Santa Sabina in Rome, raises real questions about the objective value of the critic's denunciation (Figures 1 and 2).[31] Seen *in situ*, the altarpiece, particularly the figure of the enraptured Hyacinth, gives visible expression to the essence of *furia* as both an impassioned state of mind and as an ideal aesthetic. Calculated but not contrived, the saint's body and limbs are symmetrically and three-dimensionally counterposed, reaching out of and extending into the pictorial space. As an example of a form arranged in a complex contrapposto, the figure of Hyacinth exhibits a balanced blending of *difficultà* and *facilità*. Indeed, Fontana's figure fits neatly the classical view expressed by Andrea Gilio which defines decorum as "that proportion, correspondence or conformity that style has with subject."[32] As such, it resists the frankly decorative energies that are often apparent in similar centrifugally inflected figures.[33] Detail is neither abundant nor precise, and "preciosity" is nowhere visible. The painting, unified by repetitions and modulations of color that subtly reenforce the shared *grazia* and *furia* of form and sentiment, is a masterful example of perspicuous formal devices placed in the service of a transcendental subject. If we accept Sir Joshua Reynold's later definition of the artistic genius as one who extends his

379

FIG. 1. Lavinia Fontana, *The Vision of Saint Hyacinth*, 1599. Ascoli Chapel, church of Santa Sabina, Rome. (Photo: author.)

"attention at once to the whole," then Baglione's criticism of Fontana must be seen to be biased. Opinions expressed by others support this conclusion.[34]

Baldinucci calls *The Vision of Saint Hyacinth* a "miracle" "for having come from a woman's hand [per uscire da mano donnesca]," and even Baglione concedes that it has good coloring and is "just about the best work she made."[35] Others were more effusive in their praise of the *pittrice* and her altarpiece. Giambologna, a friend of the Fontana

FIG. 2. Lavinia Fontana, *The Vision of Saint Hyacinth*, 1599. Detail.
Ascoli Chapel, church of Santa Sabina, Rome. (Photo: author.)

family, forwarded to the painter in a letter dated I January 1599 his assessment of a smaller version of the image. Above all, he marvels at Fontana's capacity to achieve naturalism in a picture depicting "the most holy of mysteries" and admires her ability to convey 'great majesty" in a "small painting."[36] Moreover, he wants to "let [Fontana] know that in Florence no painter, neither great or small, has failed to stop to see it and that it has astounded and amazed everyone."

When the large-scale and final version of the image reached Santa Sabina in Rome it evoked a similar response. As Giambologna had done, Rosato Rosati, secretary to the cardinal of Ascoli and a longtime friend of the painter, informed Fontana of the altarpiece's reception.[37] In a letter of 4 March 1600, he professes his personal elation on viewing the work. His joy, he claims, is shared by all who enter the Ascoli Chapel. The altarpiece, he writes, "astounds all of Rome." Viewing Fontana's *Vision of Saint Hyacinth in situ*—that is, flanked by Federico Zuccaro's frescoes depicting scenes from the saint's life—apparently intensified his appreciation of the work. In comparison to Fontana's painting, Zuccaro's frescoes are, says Rosati, "an affront [smaccato]" (Figure 3). "If I were him, I'd whitewash them."

FIG. 3. Federico Zuccaro, *Scenes from the Life of Saint Hyacinth*, 1599/1600. Ascoli Chapel, church of Santa Sabina, Rome. (Photo: author.)

In contrast to Baglione's remarks about Fontana's *Martyrdom of Saint Stephen*, which subscribe to widely held truths concerning the general relationship of an artist's sex to her style, those by Giambologna and Rosati concerning *The Vision of Saint Hyacinth* suggest that the sex–style relationship was somewhat elastic. Women can excel and men can fail, or, more typically, a person of one sex can evince the abilities characteristic of the other. This, according to C. Torre, was the case with Fede Galiza, "a woman it is true, but a prodigious amazon of painting."[38] If Torre's aside implies a slippage from the oxymoronic to the androgynous, Paolo Pino explained the phenomenon in more explicit terms by drawing an analogy between female painters and stories he has heard of hermaphrodites.[39] But such elasticity has its limits. Although a woman can distinguish herself by acting (or painting) like a man, and, conversely, a man can debase himself by acting like a woman, that which deserves commendation does not change. A good style is always masculine, or *virile*. This necessarily makes a so-called feminine style less than good. Pino also makes this point. Following his reference to hermaphrodite-like female artists, he condemns the "uomo effeminato" as "a vituperative thing."[40]

All of this needs to be seen in the context of a critical language rife with gender-based evaluative oppositions and associations. Castiglione, whose ideas on manners were incorporated into mannerist theory, provides a logical starting point.

This excellence which is opposed to affectation [affettazione] and which at the moment we are calling "nonchalance" [sprezzatura], besides being the real source from which grace springs, brings with it another ornament which, when it accompanies any human action however small, not only reveals at once how much the person knows who does it, but often causes it to be judged much greater than it actually is, since it impresses upon the minds of the onlookers the opinion that he who performs well with so much facility [facilmente] must possess even greater skill than this, and that, if he were to devote care and effort [studio e fatica] to what he does, he could do it far better.[41]

Applied to the artistic process, Castiglione's comments concerning *studio e fatica* came to be understood as the capacity to strike a carefully balanced equilibrium between hard work and seemingly effortless technique, or *sprezzata disinvoltura*. Images displaying *disinvoltura* enable the viewer to see the challenges in the process of making—such as foreshortening, variation in figural pose, gesture, and type, the ordering of parts within the whole—yet simultaneously blind the viewer to the efforts demanded by these challenges. Making the difficult appear easy thus is deemed a defining mark of a truly *miracoloso* and *sopra humano* talent. Because practice, once considered the source of theory, was now both its justification and realization, these terms spawned an associative oppositional pairing of others.

One of these pairs was *ritrarre* and *imitare*. As Vincenzo Danti explained and others corroborated, this pair, while not exactly antithetical, acknowledges nonetheless a qualitative difference in style similar to that of *affettazione* and *sprezzatura*. The former (*ritrarre*) replicates meticulously and without alteration, thereby leaving the imperfect flawed. It demands *diligenza* and *pazienza*. The latter (*imitare*) is the process of imitating with an eye to perfecting any and all weaknesses inherent in the model. It requires *facilità* and *sprezzatura*. In terms of portraiture, the difference between these mimetic methods is, as Armenini states, the difference between *mediocre ingegno* and true, unqualified *ingegno*.[42] Nonetheless, imitation must be seen as a logical extension of replication. Copying what the eye sees prepares the hand to render that which the mind conceives. In other words, when it was conjoined with innate ability and thus not an end in itself, *studio e fatica* paved the way for *sprezzata disinvoltura*.

Academicians not only codified these theoretical terms into a pedagogical unity, they devised a practical course of study that would guarantee their perpetuation. Women, however, lacked full access to the newly established institutions that reviewed theoretical precepts as part of a program of *perfezionamento artistico*. Even an artisans' confraternity restricted the activities of female *confratelli*. The Roman Confraternity of San Giuseppe, which would in later years be known as the Congregazione dei Virtuosi del Pantheon, can serve as an example. Following her marriage to the architectural draughtsman Francesco da Volterra, Diana Scultori moved to Rome in 1575, secured a papal privilege for making and marketing her prints, and, together with her husband, joined the Confraternity of San Giuseppe. Diana's membership allowed her to participate only in religious services and in the process of dowering young girls.[43] Francesco, by contrast, was permitted full involvement in all professional and governing activities. Clearly, participatory privileges for women were limited.

The limitations imposed on women may be seen as one factor contributing to the establishment of informal *scuole* in which both instructors and pupils were female. According to Dionigi Atanagi, a group of ladies met regularly in the Venetian home of Irene di Spilimbergo in order to converse, play music, and draw. It was in this environment that Campaspe Giancarli extended to Irene artistic instruction.[44] A similar situation reportedly existed in Naples. At the request of "some ladies," Mariangiola Criscuolo ran a "scuola" for artistically talented girls.[45] Moderata Fonte's conclusion to *Il merito delle donne*, 1600, reveals the effects of segregation. Like Christine de Pizan before her, Fonte creates a space for women apart from the world of men. Although Fonte's female society discusses at length the merits of women and ennumerates in detail the defects of men, when the assembled ladies came at last to listing "the best lawyers, the best doctors, the best writers, [and] the best artists" of cinquecento Venice, they surrendered all laurels to men.[46] Why? Is this the effect of typological thinking? Is Fonte giving voice to a belief in the concept of a "naturally" constituted man and woman? This seems unlikely, if for no other reason than that by writing a text Fonte was challenging the notion that the very act of self-expression was a violation of the spirit of domesticity and hence a transgression of feminine virtue. Francesco Barbaro spoke for many when he stated that women "should think that they shall obtain the glory of eloquence, if they adorn themselves with the famous ornament of silence."[47] But not all women were receptive to Barbaro's injunction. Certainly, Fonte was not silent. Neither were the nearly forty Renaissance women who chose the painter's brush or sculptor's chisel as their instrument for self-expression. To varying degrees, every one of them challenged the notion of femininity touted in the proliferation of emblems, like that in Andrea Alciati's *Emblematum libellus*, 1542, based on Plutarch's *Conjugalia praecepta* (142.31.C): "Phidias made Aphrodite of the Eleans with one foot on a tortoise to typify for women keeping at home and keeping silent. For a woman ought to do her talking through her husband .. [for] she makes a more impressive sound through a tongue that is not her own" (Figure 4).[48] But a female challenge to the male-dominated "profession of gentlemen" did not necessarily mean overcoming the feminine. Art critics rarely acknowledged a female capacity to conceive *invenzioni* and never recognized a woman's ability to visualize *fantasie*. Similarly, all were reluctant to state that *la donnesca mano* can shed *femminilità affettiva*. Clearly, the sex of the artist matters.

Sixteenth-century writers devising the rhetoric and form of the new discipline of art history—Giorgio Vasari, Alessandro Lamo, Gian Paolo Lomazzo, Paolo Pino, and others—were the same writers intent upon codifying aesthetic values and evaluating artists according to canonical standards. Although they could not ignore the female presence, they

F I G. 4. Andrea Alciati, from *Emblematum libellus* (Paris, 1542), no. 106. (Photo: Biblioteca Apostolica Vaticana, Vatican City.)

could define it. By describing style in relationship to practice and by then comparing it with the theoretical ideal of *la bella maniera*, early critics found an effective means of advancing typological difference. Social restrictions insured the accuracy of their critical suppositions. Unwelcomed in *academie*, Renaissance women artists were forced to make do with existing structures of study or invent alternatives. They did both. Artists like Marietta Robusti and Fede Galizia worked in the family *bottega*. Diana Scultori, who, together with her brother Adamo, learned the art of engraving from her father, ultimately settled for limited participation in the Confraternity of San Giuseppe. Amilcare Anguissola, recognizing artistic potential in his fourteen-year-old daughter Sofonisba, sent her and her sister Elena to study with Bernardino Campi. Lucrezia Quistelli gained access to the works of Alessandro Allori, while Irene di Spilimbergo, who received some instruction from Campaspe Giancarli, studied works by Titian. Mariangiola Criscuolo, the daughter and sister of painters, reportedly established her own school. But regardless of which path the female artist chose as her route into the professional art world, she encountered barriers, the effects of which were duly noted by critics.

"It is against propriety for [women] to draw from the nude," Gian Lorenzo Bernini noted in 1665: "the best advice one can give them is to choose only the best examples to copy.[49] If earlier critics are to be believed, Bernini's recommendation was an established modus operandi. Renaissance women artists kept busy meticulously replicating a person's physical features and studiously reproducing extant images. Properzia De'Rossi, we are told, copied works by Raphael. Sofonisba Anguissola copied those of Bernardino Campi and "colored in oil" drawings by Michelangelo. Lucrezia Quistelli copied works by Alessandro Allori, Marietta Robusti "drew after her father," Irene di Spilimbergo reproduced images by Titian, and Suor Plautilla Nelli's "best works" are "those she derived from others."[50] As noted, critics recognized the effects of these laborious efforts when, with purposeful regularity, they described women's works with words like "patience" and "diligence." Examples are numerous. Borghini, for instance, describes De'Rossi's carved peach stones in the Grassi family crest as having been made with "grandissima patienza" and says that her angel carved in relief for San Petronio exhibits "diligentemente lavorati". Such "patience" and "diligence," says Vasari, marked all of her works with a "delicatissima maniera."

Once again, it is important to remember context. The issue of propriety aside, the advice to copy masterpieces was not directed only at women. Academy curricula as well as numerous illustrations of artists at work, such as Federico Zuccaro's drawing of Florentine artists studying Michelangelo's sculptures in the Medici Chapel, ca. 1564 make clear that copying was a practice recommended to all aspiring artists. But replication is never to be an end in itself. Instead, *ritrarre* is to promote *imitazione*, which in turn is to further the creation and recording of *invenzioni*. Replication is, in other words, the stepping stone enabling the artist gripped by *furor dello artefice* to record his ideas. If an artist fails to go beyond the initial stage of this progressive development— from *ritrarre* to *imitare* and *invenzione*—he is doomed to be inferior, since, says Vasari, "excessive study or diligence tends to produce a dry style," one that is presumably void of *vivezza*. This was held to be equally true of male and female artists. When artists "seek to do no more than copy the manner of their master, or that of some other men of excellence . . . and when they study these things only, they may with time and diligence come to make them exactly the same, but they cannot by these means attain perfection in their art."[51] They will, says Vincenzo Danti, end up with things just as they are, "whether good or bad [ò buono, ò tristo]."

As Vasari's remark, which was made in reference to Mino da Fiesole, demonstrates, it would be preposterous to suggest that only women were said to exhibit in their art the undesirable qualities that result from excessive study. It should be remembered, however, that this and several other examples of references to *pittori* lacking *sprezzatura*, such as Battista Franco, were more than balanced by literally dozens of references to male displays of *disinvoltura*. No such claim can be made about women's work. In the same vein, and as stated earlier in reference to Raphael, it must be stressed that female artists were not alone in exhibiting "diligence," "delicacy," and "sweetness" in their works. In a memorandum dated about 1490, the duke of Milan's Florentine agent distinguished Botticelli's style from that of Filippino Lippi. Botticelli's paintings have "aria virile." Filippino's have "aria più dolce." Although it is true that it is difficult for us to know exactly what the agent meant by "virile" and "dolce," it is also true that he took care to differentiate them in terms of quality. Botticelli's works, which have "aria virile," "are done with the best method." As for Filippino's "aria più dolce," the agent concludes, "I do not think they have as much skill [non credo habiano tanta arte]."[52]

Defining the feminine in style and grounding it in practice challenged the woman artist, to use Hieronimo Mercuriale's words, "to prevail over the conditions of her sex."[53] This was not, according to Filippo Baldinucci, an impossible task. "It is neither impossible nor particularly unusual that the well-trained and talented woman can become marvelous in many areas, when, as occasionally happens, she is removed from those humble duties to which her sex is usually condemned."[54] In 1793, Francesco Maria Tassi was to support this contention. Celebrated are "the many who left behind natural weakness and vanity [naturali debolezze e vanitadi]" in order to study painting.[55] But despite Baldinucci's pronouncement and Tassi's corroboration of it, early critical commentary suggests it was rarely possible for a woman to put aside typical female activities. Indeed, the "humble duties to which . . . [the female] sex is usually condemned," it was thought, accounted for a woman's stylistic *diligenza* and *pazienza* as much as anything else. When, for example, Mazzolari noted Fontana's stylistic deficiencies, he blamed their appearance on the decision of the *pittrice* to leave "the usual path and all that which is suitable to [a woman's] hands and fingers." Pino goes farther. He suggests that such departures are transgressions of natural law. "Art draws the feminine species away from that which is proper to it." A woman's hand, he says, should grasp only "the distaff and the spindle."[56] The metamorphosis of Alciati's 1542 emblematic tortoiselike Venus (Figure 4) into Johann van Beverwijck's 1643 portrait of the artist Anna Maria van Shurman poised on the same creature in front of a house in which a woman sits spinning (Figure 5) gives visual expression to Pino's ideological concerns and demonstrates just how hard it was for a woman to distance herself from her prescribed "humble duties."

At best, Pino's directive insured the continuance of the status quo. At worst, it quashed any chance a woman might have for displaying the *disinvoltura* so admired by critics. Stitching is a painstaking task that can only stifle *sprezzatura*. This, undoubtedly, is one of the reasons behind Caterina Ginnasi's later lament that "the needle and distaff are the mortal enemies of the painter's brush."[57] Even the most valiant attempt to cast the distaff and spindle in a favorable light fails. For example, Atanagi praises Irene di Spilimbergo for choosing to "flee idleness, the principal enemy of [the female] sex," by occupying herself with the needle. It was, he says, a judicious move on her part, for it prepared her for better things. "Departing from the common path followed by other girls," Spilimbergo, who was to be celebrated in dozens of *rime* for having vanquished Minerva with "the needle [l'ago]," soon set aside the needle and reached for the brush. Within six weeks, says

FIG. 5. Johann van Beverwijck, portrait of Anna Maria van Schurman. Frontispiece, *Van de Wtnementheyt des Vrouwelicken Geslachts* (On the excellence of the female sex) (1643). (Photo: author.)

389

Atanagi, she mastered color, foreshortening, *chiaroscuro*, anatomy, and the handling of drapery. He credits the *pittrice*'s prodigious display of painterly proficiency to two factors. First, from the practice of embroidery she had acquired "great patience." Second, this *pazienza* enabled her to copy with "great diligence" "those most perfect things by Titian."[58]

In writings on women's works such critical observations are conspicuous by their omnipresence. In Fede Galizia's *piccoli ritratti* one sees, according to Paolo Morigia, a likeness of the sitter recorded with "diligenza grandissima."[59] Similarly, Ercole Basso notes that "the little picture" by Lavinia Fontana which he owns is "molto diligente" and, "as the work of a woman, praiseworthy."[60] Within the context of cinquecento critical theory it is impossible to read any of these remarks favorably, particularly since terms signifying a mastery of skill—*sprezzatura* and *facilità*—are absent. Indeed, there can be no doubt that *pazienza* and *diligenza*, when unsupported by innate talent, not only go hand in hand with *l'assiduità dello studio* and *stento*, they ultimately betray artistic stasis. "If," says Vasari, "Nature had made [Valerio Vincentino] excellent in *disegno* as well as diligent [diligente] and very patient [pazientissimo] in the execution of his works, [then] he would have surpassed the ancients . . . However, he used to copy the designs of others."[61] There is yet another side to these critical evaluations. Copying (*ritrarre*) figures prominently in the equation of *diligenza* and *stento*. Spilimbergo's *pazienza*, learned with the needle, enabled her to copy diligently works by Titian. That the *troppa diligenza* of sewing and embroidery prepares *la donnesca mano* for the demands of earnest and meticulous copying is, perhaps, best exemplified by Isabella Cattani Parasole.

The few facts known about Parasole's life and career come from Baglione's *Le vite de'pittori, scultori et architetteti*, 1642. Parasole apparently learned the art of intaglio from her husband Lionardo Parasole, Il Norcino, who, we are told, worked first in wood and then switched to the "più difficile" medium of copper. Isabella seems to have limited herself to wood. Baglione credits her with supplying woodcut illustrations to two books. The first book, of "her own invention," contained "diverse patterns for lace and other works for women" and was printed by Francesco Villamena. The second was "a book on herbs by Principe Cesi d'Acquasparte, *letteratissimo Signore*."[62] Of these, the first can be identified with certainty. Published by Lucchino Gargana in Venice in 1600 and dedicated to Gironima Colonna, *Libro della Pretiosa Gemma* is acknowledged on the dedication page as "a collection of works by

Signora Isabella Catanea Parasole." The following year a second *Libro della Pretiosa Gamma* was issued by the same press. It contains the following notice. "In the preceding year I presented . . . the first book of works by Signora Isabella Parasole." Presumably the second, like the first one, is by Parasole's hand. Each book contains twenty designs for *punto reale a reticella*, a combination of open and tight lace patterns, used typically in the making of liturgical vestments (Figure 6).[63]

It is more difficult to identify with precision the second group of works cited by Baglione, "gl'intagli nel Libro dell'herbe del Principe Cesi d'Acquasparte." Federico Cesi d'Acquasparte (1585–1630) was an influential and supporting member of the Accademia del Lincei, an academy dedicated to the study of the natural sciences. A single bound volume, *Fabii Columnae Lyncei di Nardi Antonii Recchi* includes Cesi's *Phytosophicarum Tabulae*, 1628.[64] It is not an illustrated essay. Indeed, only one study among the collected treatises in *Fabii Columnae Lyncei* is illustrated. That one is a study of herbs (Figure 7). As is appropriate to a work of its kind, the illustrations in *Fabii Columnae Lyncei* are precise, recording observable differences in plant structure and surface texture. These images are not decorative but, in keeping with the contemporary interest in the diversity of nature, documentary.[65] It would

FIG. 6. Isabella Parasole, lace pattern, from *Secondo libro della pretiosa gemma delle virtuose donne* (1601). Biblioteca Angelica, Rome. (Photo: Humberto N. Serra, Rome.)

FIG. 7. Isabella Parasole (?), botanical illustration, from *Fabii Columnae Lyncei di Nardi Antonii Recchi*, 1628. Biblioteca Vaticana, Vatican City. (Photo: Biblioteca Apostolica Vaticana, Vatican City.)

be wrong, therefore, to see Parasole at the beginning of a trend, a trend that would associate botanical illustration with the sensible and the beautiful, label it "craft," and ally it with the feminine hand. But having said this, it must be acknowledged that Parasole's move from lace design to studied plant illustration was precisely the kind of move that art history and criticism came to regard as appropriately female. Indeed, the painting of still lifes, like the painting of small devotional images and lifelike (albeit lifeless) portraits, became the proper venue for female talent like that of Fede Galizia.

One of the more interesting discussions of the association between still lifes and "feminine" space is found in an essay in Norman Bryson's *Looking at the Overlooked*.[66] Using Pliny's praise of Piraeicus's paintings of "barbers' shops, cobblers' stalls, asses, eatables and similar subjects" as a point of departure, Bryson reviews representations of the decidedly common in a multiplicity of compositional contexts as well as in various value systems (monetary, aesthetic, etc.). Still lifes of the kind painted by Galizia fall into the category of images represented "frankly and on their own terms. There is no desire to inflate the scene beyond itself" (Figure 8). Caravaggio's famed *Basket of Fruit* also falls within the category of *cose inanimate* (Figure 9). But putting aside the similarity of the blemished fruits and the absence of any indication of place in the images by these two artists, these pictures are, says Bryson, strikingly different. Although they share equally a "historical claim to invention . . . the tone of ambition [visualized in Galizia's painting] is far less strident." Caravaggio injects "into his scenes qualities of the heroic and the extraordinary; mundane space is intensified to the point of theatricality and hyper-reality." By contrast, "Galizia's still-life is much closer to its subject." She "paints from within the same plane of existence as her subject," whereas he "paints his subject from on high." Here, as elsewhere, Bryson is sensitive to hierarchical constructs, including those involving gender. Yet in his comparison of still lifes by Caravaggio and Galizia he lets stand the juxtaposition of presentation and representation, high and low, art and craft. The former comes into being only inside the picture. It does so through the master's artifice. Indeed, as artifice, it is created. The latter already exists. It is merely

FIG. 8. Fede Galizia, *Still Life*, 1602. (Photo: Silvano Lodi Collection, Campione d'Italia, Switzerland.)

FIG. 9. Caravaggio, *Still Life of a Basket of Fruit*, c.1600. Pinacoteca Ambrosiana, Milan. (Photo: Alinari/Art Resource, New York.)

replicated. At the very least, the distinction between presentation and representation points to the continued defining presence of Pythagorean contrarieties, replete with all of its positive and negative associations.

It would be inaccurate to claim that the hierarchies within the history and theory of art: copying versus invention, *diligenza* versus *disinvoltura*, still life versus history painting, and craft versus fine art, were fully realized in sixteenth-century critical discourse. It would, however, be accurate to say that this era sowed the seeds that would later bloom into clear-cut divisions that ultimately distinguished the artist from The Artist and typically reflected gendered notions concerning feminine versus masculine style. Early critics, for example, uniformly describe a woman's style as marked by "tanta pazienza" and "troppa diligenza." In several specific cases, these defining characteristics are tied directly to the needle, distaff, and spindle. And in an even greater number of instances, these tools are described as naturally proper to, yet artistically inhibiting of, *la donnesca mano*. The comparison of Scipione Delfinone with Caterina Cantona suggests that in the final analysis the difference between *ricamtori* and *ricamatrici* comes down to the issue of creating *istoria* replete with "nuova inventione" as opposed to the less difficult task of copying a likeness.[67] Indeed, by awarding Delifinone "the first place" in *ricamo*, Paolo Morigia and Gian Paolo Lomazzo make clear that even in art forms viewed as proper to the female mind and hand, woman remained secondary to man, feminine style the distant runner up to a masculine manner.

As Isabella Parasole's *Libro della Pretiosa Gemma* suggests and Morigia's concluding statement to Caterina Cantona's *vita* makes clear, women of all classes—"donne . . . della prima nobilità, . . . gentildonne, cittadine e artiste"—embroidered.[68] Noting that a majority of Parasole's lace patterns were for *punto reale a reticella* and considering that Cantona's works could be seen in chalice covers, liturgical vestments, and processional banners "ornamenting more than thirty churches" throughout Milan, one can assume that many of these pieces made their way into religious institutions. Such decorative objects were not the only type of art produced by women for churches and convents, nor were lay women the only ones making art works destined for these sites. Of the thirty-seven sixteenth-century women artists named in early texts, twelve were Dominican nuns.[69] Three—Suore Alessandra del Milanese, Felice Lupiccini, and Angiola Minerbetti—are identified as miniaturists.[70] Six—Suore Plautilla Nelli, Prudenza Cambi, Agata Trabalesi, Maria Ruggieri, Tommasa del Fiesca, and "Veronica"—are called painters.[71] Three—Dionisia Niccolini, Maria Angelica Razzi, and Vincenza Brandolini—are said to have "worked in *rilievo*" and modeled devotional terracotta figures.[72] Only Tommasa del Fiesca is referred to as an embroiderer, and only then in a note to Sopriani's *Vite*.[73] Indeed, although early writers indicate that convents were productive art institutions in their own right, providing instruction to novices and selling their works throughout Italy, no author identifies the embroiderer's needle as the instrument proper to *i benedetti mani* of *suore*. While it seems logical that nuns, like their secular sisters, were skilled with *l'ago*, it must also be assumed that the needle was not their sole source of study nor embroidery their preferred medium.

Conventual communities had long provided women with environments conducive to creative endeavors.[74] But such environments had their negative aspects. Opportunities for study were obviously far more limited for women in *clausura* than for either artist-daughters or *gentildonne* living at home. Yet life without men did not necessarily mean an artistic life without male instruction or influence. Just as Properzia De'Rossi copied works by Raphael and Marietta Robusti "drew after" those by Tintoretto, Suor Plautilla Nelli reportedly made "a picture of the Nativity of Christ, copied from one which Bronzino once painted for Filippo Salviati."[75] Moreover, the close affiliation of convents with monasteries, particularly after 1500, when attempts to restrict the liberating effects of Savonarolan reform on conventual communities were especially intense, could work to the advantage of the nun-artist.[76] Whereas both Suor Caterina dei Vigri (1431–36), a Poor Clare and prioress of the convent of Corpus Domini in Bologna, Suor Tommasa del Fiesca (ca. 1448–1534), affiliated first with the Dominican convent of Santi Giacomo e Filippo in Genoa and later transferred with eleven others to assist in the reform of the convent of San Silvestro in Pisa, and the Dominican Tertiary Suor Caterina de'Ricci (1522–87), prioress of the convent of San Vincenzo in Prato, relied on their own mystical visions for artistic inspiration, Suor Plautilla Nelli (1523–87), prioress of the Dominican convent of Santa Caterina da Siena in Florence, had at her disposal a large cache of drawings by Fra Bartolomeo. These drawings were not only inspirational, they were instructive. The inventory drawn up on the Frate's death in 1517 lists "866 loose sheets of drawings, 12 sketchbooks, and an unspecified number of landscape drawings, colored as well as in pen and ink, pasted onto canvas rolls."[77] According to Vasari, Fra Paolino da Pistoia (ca. 1490–1547) was heir to Fra Bartolomeo's drawings.[78] Again according to Vasari, most of these drawings went from the monastery of San Marco to its sister convent Santa Caterina.[79] They did so, says Baldinucci, by way of the convent's prioress and student of Fra Paolino, Plautilla Nelli.[80] That the prioress-painter had at least some of them cannot be doubted.

Plautilla, we are told, was a prolific painter. Vasari lists more works by her hand than does any other critic about any Renaissance woman artist. She painted "large altarpieces [tavole grande]," "small devotional pictures [quadretti]," and miniatures. Her paintings graced "the homes of gentlemen throughout Florence" and adorned not only the walls and altars of her convent, but those of other churches in Florence, Pistoia, and Perugia. Both Fra Serafino Razzi, who walked nine hundred miles around northern Italy in search of documents in Dominican monasteries which he compiled into a biographical history of illustrious Dominicans, and Francesco Bocchi, author of the well-known guidebook *Le bellezze della città di Firenze*, confirm Vasari on this point. They also provide the specific locations of some images mentioned only in passing by the author of the *Vite*. Unfortunately, only two of her many paintings have been securely identified. The first of these is a large work representing the Last Supper. It is reported as hanging originally in Santa Caterina's refectory, a typical location for depictions of this theme. When in 1853 Santa Caterina became the Galleria dell'Accademia, the image was moved to the chapterhouse of the Dominican church of Santa Maria Novella.[81] An early photograph of it, which was taken before 1930, shows it there, obscuring a large section of Andrea di Bonaiuto's fourteenth-century fresco of the life of Saint Peter Martyr. When Bonaiuto's fresco was restored to full view, Nelli's painting was moved. Unfortunately, I have only just learned its current location and therefore have relied on an old photograph as visual documentation of its appearance.[82] From this bit of evidence Nelli appears to have been a competent but not exceptional artist. The composition follows convention, and figural poses as well as gestures adhere to prescribed rhetorical types. Because of these features, and the absence of facial expressions, Nelli's *Last Supper* appears rigid and archaic. Fortunately, another work, a *Lamentation*, can be viewed in the Museo di San Marco in Florence. This makes possible a more accurate assessment of Plautilla Nelli's artistic abilities (Figures 10 and 11).

Like *The Last Supper*, Nelli's *Lamentation* relies on convention. In fact, aspects of its compositional structure are strikingly similar to the recently cleaned *Pietà* by Fra Bartolomeo (Figure 12), although one nineteenth-century source says it is "the invention of the celebrated painter Andrea del Sarto, which was carried out by Plautilla [L'invenzione del celebre pittore Andrea Sarto e di Suor Plautilla la esecuzione]."[83] The most notable likeness is between the Frate's Saints Peter and Paul and the prioress's two standing male figures, who, like those by Fra Bartolomeo, counterbalance one another through their closed and open postures. While it is possible to see this likeness of pose as a reflection of conventional compositional arrangement, the same cannot be said of the standing male figure on the left. Although cropped, the Frate's Peter leans forward so that he hovers over the grieving group surrounding Christ. His right hand, covered by a weighty mantle that sweeps around his entire form in broad and curving folds, clutches his identifying attribute, a key. Plautilla's corresponding figure is more erect. The cloak her figure wears hangs in folds more vertical than encircling, and his shrouded hands hold nothing. Like Fra Bartolomeo's weeping Saint Peter, Suor Plautilla's figure may be related to a figure study by Fra Bartolomeo drawn with black chalk and heightened with white, now in the Museum Boymans-van Beuningen in Rotterdam (Figure 13).

The drawing came to the Boymans-van Beuningen as part of "Volume M," a collection of 201 folios. The title page of Volume M reads in part as follows:

FIG. 10. Suor Plautilla Nelli, *The Lamentation*, 1550s (?). Museo di San Marco, Florence. (Photo: author.)

FIG. 11. Suor Plautilla Nelli, *The Lamentation*, 1550s (?), detail. (Photo: author.)

FIG. 12. Fra Bartolomeo, *Pietà*, 1511–12. Galleria Palatina, Palazzo Pitti, Florence. (Photo: Archivio Fotografico dell'Opificio delle Pietre Dure di Firenze.)

FIG. 13. Fra Bartolomeo, Study for a weeping Saint Peter, 1511–12. Museum Boymans-van-Beuningen, Rotterdam. (Photo: Museum Boymans-van-Beuningen, Rotterdam.)

First Volume of Original Drawings by Fra Bartolomeo of San Marco, secularly called Baccio della Porta from Florence. See Giorgio Vasari, who talks about these drawings at the end of his Life of this famous painter . . . He says that on his death Fra Bartolomeo left these drawings to a nun called Sister Plautilla. a pupil of his, who was in the convent of Santa Caterina opposite San Marco. They remained in the said convent until the year 1727, when they were bought from the nuns to preserve them, . . . [since] for many years [they] were condemned to the inexperience of those Mothers and were wretchedly used for wrapping up coins.[84]

Despite the inaccuracies—Nelli, who was born six years after Fra Bartolomeo's death, could not have been either Fra Bartolomeo's pupil or his direct heir—the title page of Volume M supports the visual evidence. Plautilla Nelli had access to the Frate's drawings.

Nelli's *Lamentation* and Fra Bartolomeo's study provide us with a rare opportunity. Although the copying of men's work by women artists is routinely mentioned and the effects of copying duly assessed, it is, except in this case, impossible to compare influencing and influenced images in light of critical commentary. Here we can do both.

According to Giorgio Vasari,

The best works from [Plautilla's] hand are those she has copied from others, wherein she shows that she would have done marvelous things if she had enjoyed, as men do, advantages for studying, devoting herself to drawing and copying living and natural objects. And that this is true is seen clearly from a picture of the Nativity of Christ, copied from one [by] Bronzino . . . The truth of such an opinion is proved by this, that in her works the faces and features of women, whom she has been able to see as much as she pleased, are considerably better than the heads of the men . . . In the faces of women in some of her works she has portrayed Madonna Costanza de'Doni . . . painting her so well that it is impossible to expect more from a woman who, for the reasons mentioned above, has had no great practice in her art.[85]

Here, Vasari sounds familiar themes. As Boccaccio had done and as Bernini would do, he acknowledges decorum as an issue of consequence. Although the ancient painter Marcia, says Boccaccio, may have been able to choose either "to make men imperfect, or, by making them perfect, forget her maidenly modesty," Nelli could not.[86] She could "copy living and natural things" in only a limited sense. Therefore, to quote Bernini's later advice to women, the best thing for her to do "was to choose only the best examples [of works by others] to copy." Clearly, her options were limited in this regard as well. But although her options were few, drawings by Fra Bartolomeo in her possession were many. Nonetheless, having a rich source of visual material to copy (*ritrarre*) did not mean the prioress was able to imitate (*imitare*) the Frate's style, one in which classicizing idealism subsumes the immediate, personal, and introspective. The *Lamentation* makes this clear.

As it hangs in the Museo di San Marco, Nelli's painting appears quite different from the many contemporary Italian works around it, a majority of which reveal the influence of Fra Bartolomeo. Although the Frate and the best of his followers articulate intimate emotions with an extraordinary subtlety and expansive feeling that speaks universally, the Suor renders grief with an individualized intensity and precision more typically associated with northern Europe. Tears, each one meticulously defined, fall from red-rimmed eyes and streak pallid cheeks. Similarly, whereas Fra Bartolomeo amplifies, complicates, and unifies compositional structure using only the resources that reside in form, Suor Plautilla pushes her figures forward and spreads them across the picture plane in three tiers. To this, she adds copious detail. Stones littering the path to Calvary can be counted, as can the hairs on Mary Magdalene's head and the links in Joseph of Arimathaea's chain. Despite its monumental scale, Plautilla Nelli's painting is not a monumental composition. The *difficultà* of painting an *istoria* is apparent; so too is the *diligenza* that comes from *assiduità dello studio*.[87]

Still, the prioress's *Lamentation* is a moving image. It is true that Plautilla Nelli's painting has stylistic weaknesses, such as the over-crowding of the foreground and the distractions of minutiae. As for the awkward rigidity of Christ's propped-up body, we can, if we accept popular tradition, credit it to her model: the corpse of "a dead nun [una monaca defuncta]."[88] But despite these weaknesses, the work has its strengths. These should not be ignored, nor should the power of the image to affect the viewer be denied. Vasari was right. "In [Nelli's] works the faces and features of women, whom she has been able to see as much as she pleased, are considerably better than the heads of the men." The accuracy of Vasari's observation, which points to Nelli's artistic strengths, is verified by a comparison of the three Marys in the *Lamentation* with the twelve apostles in *The Last Supper*. It is also confirmed by a comparison of the female and male faces within the San Marco painting itself (except that of the youthful John, who displays the same characteristics of sorrow seen in the grieving women). Here, the benefits of direct observation—Nelli's ability "to see as much as she pleased" the faces of women—are clearly visible. Indeed, here observation is combined with the painter's predilection for detail to a positive end. Not only are tearful eyes red, so are noses. Such signs of despair are familiar, the sense of loss inducing them comprehensible. To Nelli's credit, she did not sentimentalize these emotions. In fact, she captured and conveyed the very essence of grief—a commonly experienced sense of despair that ultimately cannot be shared. While outwardly showing signs of sorrow, each of these figures turns within to ease his or her pain.

Despite stylistic qualities that perhaps may be attributed to Plautilla's having had "no great practice in her art," such as her stylized rendering of drapery, there can be no doubt that works by this prolific prioress enjoyed popularity. According to Francesco Bocchi, not only is "the Church [of Santa Caterina] adorned with paintings made by her hand, as one can see, but others have also been sent to various locations with great praise to her name."[89] These "various locations" were private homes as well as religious institutions. Concerning the former, Vasari reports that in the homes of Florentine gentlemen ("gentiluomini di Firenze") "there are so many pictures [by Nelli] that it would be tedious to speak of them all." Thus, he limits himself to two: "A large picture of the Annunciation belonging to the wife of the Spaniard, Signor Mondragone, and another [painting] like it which is owned by Madonna Marietta de'Fedini."[90] Regarding the latter, many a church within and outside of Florence's walls housed a painting made by this Dominican prioress. Vasari and Fra Serafino Razzi identify two non-Florentine locations: Santa Lucia in Pistoia and San Domenico in Perugia.[91] In fact, Plautilla's name, if not her paintings, had traveled far, as Karel van Mander's reference to her in *Het Schilder-Boeck*, 1618, makes clear.[92]

What was so appealing about Plautilla Nelli's work? We might begin to answer this question by asking who was attracted to her images. Here, we have the assistance of Vasari, Razzi, Bocchi, and van Mander. According to these writers, paintings by the prioress were admired and purchased by *gentiluomini*, women, the devout, and northern Europeans. Is there any way to connect this appreciative group to the little bit of visual evidence we have concerning Nelli's style? I suggest that Michelangelo's discourse on Flemish painting as recorded by Francisco de Hollanda provides the needed link. When Vittoria Colonna asked about Flemish painting, which she found "very devout," Michelangelo responded by contrasting the "boldness" and "vigor" of Italian art with the surfeit of detail in northern painting: "the fabrics and masonry, the green grass of the fields, the shadows of trees, and rivers and bridges . . . with many figures on this side and that."[93] Clearly, this description can be applied to Nelli's *Lamentation* just as easily as to a painting by Jan Mostaert or Jan van Scorel. More to the point, this style, says Michelangelo, "will please the devout" and "appeal to women, especially very old and very young women, and also to monks and nuns and to certain noblemen who have no sense of true harmony." If we assume that viewers are attracted to qualities in art that somehow mirror themselves, then what we have here is a definition of feminine taste.[94]

Michelangelo's critique of Flemish painting reflects an Italian bias structured on the conventional juxtaposition of penetrating masculine reason and substance with feminine irrationality and susceptibility to the superficial world of appearance.[95] As the list of miscellanea—fabrics, masonry, grass, trees, rivers, bridges, and numerous figures—indicates, at least a part of Flemish painting's seductive appeal to women, monks, and nuns resides in its copious detail.[96] Nelli's *Lamentation*, filled with meticulously rendered stones, masonry, plants, fabrics, and figures, may be seen as the type of painting Michelangelo devalued. Does this explain van Mander's praise of Plautilla or account for the appearance of her work in convents, monasteries, and the homes of Signora Mondragone and Marietta de'Fedini? I suggest an alternative reason. Rather than credit the appeal of her images to the allure of the sensual and the superficial that are the reported results of an attention to detail, the attraction was in the "blessed hand [benedetta mano]" that put brush to panel. In other words (and with the aphorism "Every painter paints him/herself" in mind) appeal resides not so much in the virtuosity of the maker but rather in her virtue. As Paolo Morigia's admiration of Cantona's "divina mano" suggests, the virtue of the *virtuosa* was of no little consequence. Certainly, Domenici imparts this idea in his life of Mariangiola Criscuolo. "Some ladies who knew the goodness of her life, sent their daughters to her not so much that they should learn the virtuoso application of painting as learn by the good example of her Christian life."[97] At least one of her pupils learned her lessons well. After taking her vows, Luisa Capomazza went on to "make paintings for various chapels in the Church of Santa Chiara" in Naples, although "in drawing, to say the truth [she] is not perfect."[98]

Was Capomazza's reported weakness in drawing a reflection of Criscuolo's own deficiencies, a result of limited opportunities for study, or, in the mid-eighteenth century, was Domenici providing evidence of the continued presumption that women simply did not possess *forze di quel furore?* The question raises a final point about nun-artists and their source of inspiration. Conventual communities were sympathetic to mystical visions. Recording them, it seems, kept many a *benedetta mano* busy. Caterina dei Vigri, Tommasa del Fiesca, and Caterina de'Ricci all had mystical visions which informed their work and that of those around them.[99] In the case of Caterina dei Vigri, poems and prayers sprang from experiences of spiritual ecstasy.[100] Presumably, these entranced visions also provided the prioress of the Poor Clares of Bologna's convent of Corpus Domini with rich source material for her paintings. According to Raffaello Sopriani, this was true of Tommasa del Fiesca.[101] Caterina de'Ricci's work, such as a small devotional *Man of Sorrows* painted for Charles Borromeo, may have come from a similar source. Certainly, Caterina de'Ricci's visions were many—and many were the devout hands that recorded them in word and image. Indeed, the prioress apparently recognized a good thing when she encountered it. According to Fra Serafino Razzi's *Historia de gli Huomni illustri*, 1596, San Vincenzo was home to "many sisters competent in painting." Encouraged by Caterina, nuns expressed their reverence to God and fealty to their superior sister by painting devotional images that ultimately made their way to "tutta Italia" because "they came from the holy monastery where there were one hundred and fifty noble handmaids of God."[102]

Translations of the verbal into the visual seem to have been commonplace in convents. Maria di Reggio, who took her vows in 1508, reportedly led a group of nuns into the woods to pray at a wooden cross erected "in memoria della Passione di Nostro Signore." While gazing at the cross, Maria, with "open eyes" and "in estasi di spirito," saw the suffering and blood-stained Christ. Recovering her senses, she described her vision to her companions. They, in turn, painted it.[103] Lacking any works associated specifically with such mystical visions, it is impossible to assess whether one woman's divine *furor* could metamorphose into another woman's *furor dello artefice*. However, because all sixteenth-century discussions of *furia* and *fierezza* bind the perceiving eye to the visualizing hand, the separation of the mystic from the painter suggests, at least theoretically, that this did not occur. In fact, for one person to visualize the visions of another may be seen as a form of copying and thus susceptible to all the stylistic weaknesses that inhere in the practice. The *furor* of conception, or more properly in these instances perception, must inevitably be lost or diminished as it progresses from an image of the spirit to a marketable material product.

Notes

1. Giorgio Vasari, *Le Opere*, ed. Gaetano Milanesi, Florence, 1906, vol. 2, p. 678. Vasari's discussion of Properzia de' Rossi's carving of *Joseph Fleeing Potiphar's Wife*, *c*.1525–26 (Bologna: Museo di San Petronio) is another example. See Vasari, vol. 5, pp. 73–81. See also "Melancholia: a case study", chapter 4 of Fredrika Jacobs, *Defining the Renaissance Virtuosa*, (Cambridge and New York: Cambridge University Press, 1997), pp. 64–84.

2. Carlo Cesare Malvasia, *Felisina Pittore. Vita de pittore bolognese* [1679] (Bologna: 1841), vol. 2, p. 385.

3. Carli quoted in Philip Sohm, "Gendered Style in Italian Art Criticism from Michelangelo to Malvasia", *Renaissance Quarterly*, 48 (1995), p. 794. The reference to Flemish style in this context echoes Michelangelo. See Franciso de Hollanda, *Four Dialogues on Painting*, trans. Aubrey Bell (London: 1928), p. 15. For an excellent discussion of gendered style applied to schools of painting and techniques (oil versus fresco) see Sohm, pp. 773–98.

4. Marsilio Ficino, *The Book of Life* (Liber de Vita) *Opera Omnia* (Basel: 1576), p. 1365.

5. See, for example, *Scritti d'arte di Federico Zuccaro*, ed. Detlef Heikamp (Florence: 1957), p. 234. As Sohm, p. 790, points out, fresco painting was gendered masculine because "it demands decisiveness and prompt action." The same may be said of drawing. Indeed, while Pietro Testa tried to reconcile rather than polarize *disegno* and *colorita*, gender continued to inform critical language. For a transcription of and commentary on Testa's remarks, see Elizabeth Cropper, *The Ideal of Painting: Pietro Testa's Dusseldorf Notebook* (Princeton: 1984), no. 61.2, pp. 252–3.

6. Zuccaro, p. 234. See also David Summers, *Michelangelo and the Language of Art* (Princeton: 1981), p. 61.

7. The equation of grace with movement and *vivezza* as a sign of artistic excellence was nothing new. See Leon Battista Alberti, *Della pittura*, ed. L. Mallè (Florence: 1950), pp. 89–90.

8. Francisco De Hollanda, *De la pintura antigua por Francisco de Hollanda, versión castellana de Manuel Denis* [1563], ed. E. Tormo (Madrid: 1921), p. 59.

9. Vasari, vol. I, p. 174.

10. Ibid.

11. Ibid., vol. 6, p. 577. This idea was long-lived. See Pliny the Elder, *Natural History* trans. H. Rackham (Cambridge, Mass.: 1956–66), 34.92: Callimachus's "attention to detail knew no limit . . . Also by this artist are the Laconian Dancers, a flawless work, but one in which attention to detail has taken away its charm [*gratiam omnem diligentia abstulerit*]."

12. Vasari, vol. 2, p. 171. This theme runs throughout the *Vite*. For Vasari, vol. 7, pp. 426–8, drawing was an inventive process, one which "fills the mind with good ideas".

13. Prior to the mid-sixteenth century, the term *divino* is, according to Martin Kemp, "From 'Mimesis' to 'Fantasia': The Quattorcento Vocabulary of Creativity, Inspiration and Genius in the Visual Arts", *Viator*, 8 (1977), p. 397, "applied to art or artists in a few spectacular instances—Marsuppini's epitaph for Brunelleschi and the assertions of the divine power of painting

by Alberti and Leonardo—but only Giustiniani fully equates painting with poetic ideals of divine inspiration."

14. Giovambattista Armenini, *De'veri precetti della pittura* (Ravenna: 1586), bk. I, chap. ix, p. 75.

15. For an interesting twist on this, see June Wayne, "The Male Artist as a Stereotypical Female", *Art Journal*, 32 (1973), 414–16.

16. Malvasia, vol. I, pp. 177–8.

17. Luigi Lanzi, *Storia pittorica della Italia* [1789] (Florence: 1968), vol. 3, p. 33.

18. Paolo Morigia, *La nobilità di Milano* [1595] (Milan: 1619), bk. V, chap. iii, p. 467. Attention to detail was believed to have a particular appeal to certain audiences—women and nuns. Michelangelo's denigration of Flemish painting, as reported by de Hollanda, falls into this category.

19. Agostino Santagostino, *L'immortalità e gloria del penello. Catalogo delle pitture insigni che stanno esposto al pubblico nella città di Milano* (Milan: 1671), p. 71.

20. In Sachetti's *Trecento Novelle*, ca. 1390, the sculptor Alberto Arnaldo refutes the contention of other artists that "this art [painting] has grown and continues to grow worse day by day". He argues that excellent painters, "The Florentine women, whose skill in cosmetics corrects the defects of the greatest painter of them all, God", are at work as he speaks. Sacchetti is quoted in Millard Meiss, *Painting at Florence and Siena after the Black Death* (New York: 1951), p. 3. I am grateful to Paul Watson for directing my attention to this citation. For later negative connotations of the relationship between cosmetics and painting, see Jacqueline Lichenstein, "Making up Representations: The Risks of Femininity", *Representations*, 20 (1987), pp. 77–87.

21. The terms *diligens* and *diligenta* were used in ancient art criticism to imply precision, often in terms of the application of some theoretical precept and sometimes in order to contrast a style that reflects a scrupulous adherence to the rules with stylistic subjectivism. See J. J. Pollitt, *The Ancient View of Greek Art: Criticism, History, and Terminology* (New Haven: 1974), pp. 351–7.

22. Vasari, vol. 4, pp. 321–2.

23. Ibid., vol. 6, p. 498, and vol. 5, p. 81.

24. Adolf Venturi, *Storia Dell'arte Iraliana* (Milan: 1901–40) vol. 4, pp. 684–6.

25. Nicola Pio, *Le vite de pittori, scultori et architetti*, ed. Catherine Enggass and Robert Enggass (Vatican City, 1977), p. 206, and P. A. Orlandi, *Abecedario pittorico* (Venice: 1753), p. 334. Pietrantonio's remark is in *The Age of Corregio and the Carracci* (Washington, DC: 1986), p. 132.

26. Mazzolari, as quoted in Malvasia's *vita* of Fontana, vol. I, p. 180. Paolo Pino, *Dialogo della pittura* [1548] (Milan: 1954), p. 36, identifies the suitable tools as the distaff and the spindle (*la conoccha e l'arcolaio*).

27. Giovanni Baglione, *Le vite de'pittori, scultori, architteti ed intagliori. dal Pontificato di Gregorio XIII. del 1572 fina a' tempi di Papa Urbano VIII. nel 1642.* (Naples: 1733), pp. 136–7.

28. Pliny, *Natural History*, 35.148.

29. Malvasia, vol. 2, p. 389.

30. The same dichotomy is visible in Moroni's portraits, as may be seen by anyone looking at those hanging together in the Galleria Palatina, Palazzo Pitti, Florence.

31. Fontana's Santa Sabina altarpiece, like Ottavia Leoni's in Santa Maria

Maggiore, Rome (1598), was clearly influenced by Ludovico Carraci's 1594 painting of this theme, now in the Louvre. See *Ludovico Carraci*, ed. Andrea Emiliani (Bologna: Museo Civico Archeologico–Pinacoteca Nationale, 1993), pp. 87–8, Fontana's composition is her own, differing from Ludovico's formally and in ethos.

32. For Gilio's ideas as they refer to contrapposto, see David Summers, "*Contrapposto*: Style and Meaning in Renaissance Art", *Art Bulletin*, 59 (1977), p. 343.

33. For the rules governing the construction of "la figura piramidale, serpentinata e moltoplicata", see Gian Paolo Lomazzo, *Scritti sulle arte*, ed. Roberto Paolo Ciardi (Florence: 1974), vol. 1, pp. 29–30. Also see John Shearman, *Mannerism* (Harmondsworth, UK: 1967), pp. 165–6; David Summers, "*Maniera* and Movement: The *Figura serpentinata*", *Art Quarterly*, 35 (1972), 269–301; and Summers, 1977, pp. 336–71.

34. There is much extant documentation concerning Fontana's *Vision of Saint Hyacinth*. See Maria Teresa Cantaro, *Lavinia Fontana bolognese "pittora singolare"* (Milan: 1989), pp. 194–5, and 310–12, nos. 5a17–20.

35. Filippo Baldinucci, *Lezione di Filippo Baldinucci* (Florence: 1692), vol. 5, pp. 96–7; Baglione, p. 136. Both statements are reprinted in Cantaro, p. 326, no. 5b13 and p. 323, no. 5b11, respectively.

36. Given Giambologna's description of the work as "a small painting", he must have seen a finished study. According to Cantaro, p. 194, "del bozzetto purtroppo non vi e più traccia". For the full text of Giambologna's letter, see Cantaro, p. 310, no. 5a17.

37. For the full text of Rosati's letter, see Cantaro, pp. 311–12, no. 5a20.

38. C. Torre, *Il Ritratto di Milano* [1714], quoted in Flavio Caroli, *Fede Galazia* (Turin: 1989), p. 21.

39. Pino, p. 36.

40. Ibid.

41. Baldesar Castiglione, *Il Cortegiano* (Florence: 1854), bk. 1, chap. 26, p. 35.

42. Giovambattista Armenini, *De'veri precetti della pittura* (Ravenna: 1586), bk. III, chap. xi, p. 190.

43. For information on Diana Scultori, see Stephania Massari, *Incisori Mantovani del '500, Giovan Battista, Adamo, Diana Scultori e Giorgio Ghisi* (Rome: 1980); *Giulio Romano pinxit et delineavit. Opere grafiche di collaborazione e bottega* (Rome: 1993); Paolo Bellini (ed.), *L'opera incisa di Adame e Diana Scultori* (Vicenza: 1991); Valeria Paganini, "Adamo Scultori e Diana Mantovani", *Print Quarterly*, 9 (March 1992), 72–87.

44. *L'Atanagi da Cagli*, ed. D. A. Tarducci (Cagli: 1904), p. 44.

45. Bernardo de Domenichi, *Vite de'pittori scultori e architetti Napoletani* [1742], 2 vols. (Naples: 1843), vol. 2, p. 350.

46. Moderata Fonte (Modesta dal Pozzo) "Il merito delle donne", in *Donne e società nel seicento: Lucrezia Marinelli e Arcangela Tarabotti*, ed. Ginevra Conti Odoriso (Rome: 1979). Also see Patricia Labalme, "Venetian Women on Women: Three Early Modern Feminists", *Arte veneto*, ser. 5, 197 (1981), 89, and Margaret L. King, *Women of the Renaissance* (Chicago: 1991), pp. 228–32.

47. Francesco Barbaro, *De re uxoria*, 1416, quoted in Constance Jordan, *Renaissance Feminism: Literary Texts and Political Models* (Ithaca, NY: 1990), p. 45.

48. Andrea Alciatus, *Emblemata libellus* (Paris: 1542), p. 106. Also see Alciati,

Emblems in Translation, ed. Peter M. Daly (Toronto: 1985), emblem no. 196. Day publishes four variations of the emblem, from different editions (Paris, 1536; Paris, 1542; Lyon, 1549; and Lyon, 1551). Christian writers could easily meld Plutarch's comment with biblical passages, such as 1 Timothy 2: 11–12.

49. Paul Freart de Chantelou, *Diary of the Cavaliere Bernini's Visit to France*, trans. Margery Corbett (Princeton: 1955), p. 285.

50. For de' Rossi, Quistelli, and Nelli, see Vasari, vol. 5, pp. 78 and 80. Also for Nelli, see Luigi Lanzi, *Storia pittorica della Italia*, [1789], 3 vols. (Florence: 1968), vol. 2, p. 87 and Orlandi, p. 436. For Robusti, see Carlo Ridolfi, *Delle maraviglie dell'arte* (Venice: 1648), vol. 2, pp. 71–2. For Anguissola, see Sandra Perlingieri, *Sofonisba Anguissola: The First Great Woman Artist of the Renaissance* (New York: 1992), pp. 47–8. For Spilimbergo, see Atanagi, 1904, p. 144; Lomazzo, 1974, vol. 1, p. 95; and Giovambattista Zaist, *Note istoriche de'pittori, scultori, ed architetti cremonesi* (Cremona: 1774), pp. 232–3.

51. Vasari, vol. 3, pp. 115–16.

52. Michael Baxandall, *Painting and Experience in Fifteenth Century Italy* (Oxford: 1972), p. 26.

53. Mercuriale's statement, made in reference to Fontana, is in a letter to the duke of Urbino, 18 June 1588. See Cantaro, pp. 308–9, no. 5a13.

54. Baldanucci, vol. 8, p. 208. The statement appears in his introduction to Sofonisba Anguissola: "ma io, che so che non solo non è cosa impossibile, nè anche cosa punto nuova, che un ben coltivato ingegno d'una femmina si renda in ogni facoltà maraviglioso, ogni qual volta, tolto da quelle umili applicazioni, alle quali per lo più vien condennato quel sesso, egli sia posto nella sua libertà."

55. Franceso Maria Tassi, *Vite dei Pittori, scultori e architetti Bergameschi* (Bergamo: 1793), vol. 1, pp. 224–5.

56. Pino, p. 36.

57. Domenici, vol. 3, p. 93.

58. Atanagi, 1904, p. 144.

59. Morigia, bk. V, chap. iii, p. 467.

60. Basso's letter, dated 1585, is quoted in Cantaro, p. 308, no. 5a11.

61. Vasari, vol. 5, p. 379.

62. Baglione, pp. 394–5. Also see Girolamo D'Adda, "A l'essai bibliographique des anciens modèles de lingerie, detelles et tapisseries publiès en Italie aux XVI et XVII siècles", *Gazette des beaux-arts*, 17 (1864), 430–6; Dèsire Guilmard, *Les maitres oenemanistes* (Paris: 1880–1), vol. 1, p. 298; and M. Jourdain, "The Lace Collection of Mr Arthur Blackborne", *Burlington Magazine*, 5 (1904), 557–69. Guilmard, followed by Jourdain, confuses the identity of Parasole with "Lucrezia Romana" as the Florentine Lucrezia Quistelli.

63. I found the book in the Biblioteca Angelica, Rome, I. I. 3. Perhaps Caterina Cantona, the Milanese "Minerva" of her time, used this technique in the many vestments she made for some thirty churches in and around her native city.

64. Biblioteca Vaticano, Barberini M. IV. 28. Since the publication of this book it has come to my attention that the project is most probably an illustrated version of Francisco Hernandez's treatise on Mexican Plant life. See Evelyn Lincoln, on Parasole in *Dictionary of Women Artists*, ed. D. Glaze (London 1997), Vol. 2, p. 1069.

65. See *la natura morta al tempo di Caravaggio*, exhibition catalogue (Naples: 1995).
66. Norman Bryson, *Looking at the Overlooked* (Cambridge, Mass.: 1990), pp. 136–78, especially p. 64.
67. Morigia, bk. V, chap. xviii, pp. 495–6; Lomazzo, 1974, vol. 1, p. 371; and Lomazzo, *Rime* (Milan: 1587), pp. 114–15.
68. Morigia, bk. V, chap. xviii, p. 496.
69. Nineteenth-century authors expanded the list. See, for example, Tommaso Trenta, *Memorie e documenti per servire all'istoria del Ducato di Lucca* (Lucca: 1822), vol. 8, pp. 122–3, for the following additions: Suor Aurlia Fiorentini, "who came to light in 1595"; Suor Lodovica Carli, "che esercitavasi nella pittura decorosamente verso il 1579", Suor Brigida Franciotti, who assumed the habit at San Giorgo in 1532.
70. Paolo Mini, *Discorso della Nobilità di Firenze, e di Fiorentini* (Florence: 1593), p. 108; Giuseppe Richa, *Notizie istoriche delle Chiese Fiorentine devise ne'suoi quartiere* (Florence: 1754–64), vol. 8, p. 283.
71. Fra Serafino Razzi, *Historia de gli Huomini illustri dell'Ordine de'Predicatori* (Lucca: 1596), p. 369, refers to Cambi, Trabalesi, and Ruggieri as "pupils of the Prioress Plautilla" [discepole della prefeta suor Plautilla].
72. Razzi, p. 369; Richa, vol. 8, p. 2823.
73. Raffaello Sopriani, *Vite de pittori, scultori ed architetti Genovesi* [2nd edn. 1674], (Genoa: 1768–9), vol. 1, p. 25, note b.
74. Those headed by Hildegard of Bingen (1098–1179) and Herrade of Landesberg (d. 1195) are two of the better-known medieval examples. One wonders what happened to Ucello's daughter. According to Vasari, vol. 2, p. 217, the painter taught her how to draw. In his notes to the *Vite*, Milanese identifies her as Antonia (1456–91) a Carmelite nun.
75. Vasari, vol. 5, p. 80 and Razzi, p. 369.
76. See Lorenzo Polizzotto, "When Saints Fall Out: Women and the Savonarolan Reform in Early Sixteenth Century Florence", *Renaissance Quarterly*, 47 (1993), 486–525.
77. Chris Fischer, *Fra Bartolomeo, Master Draftsman of the High Renaissance* (Seattle: 1990), p. 12.
78. Vasari, vol. 4, pp. 220–1.
79. Ibid., vol. 4, p. 195.
80. Baldinucci, vol. 2, pp. 289–90. Baldinucci claims Fra Bartolomeo left the drawings directly to Plautilla Nelli—an impossibility, since he died six years before her birth. As Fischer, p. 13, notes, this inaccuracy has been repeated.
81. See Milanese's notes in Vasari, vol. 5, p. 79.
82. Since the writing of this text I have learned that the painting is in the Caserma adjacent to Sta. Maria Novella. My thanks go to Andrée Hayum for this information. In addition there is a *Pentecost*, 1554, in its original location: left transept, San Domenico, Perugia. See padre Serafini Siepi, *Descrizione topologico-istorica della città di Perugia*, ii, (Perugia: 1822), pp. 516–17.
83. P. Vincenzo Marchese, *Memorie dei più insigni, pittori, scultori e architetti domenicani* (Florence: 1854), vol. 2, p. 265.
84. Fischer, pp. 18–19.
85. Vasari, vol. 5, p. 80.

86. Giovanni Boccaccio, *Concerning Famous Women*, trans. G. Guarino (Princeton: 1963), p. 145.
87. According to Richa, vol. 8, p. 283, Nelli "è commendata particolarmente per la diligenza grande".
88. Marchese, vol. 2, p. 266.
89. Francesco Bocchi, *Le bellezze della citta Fiorenza* (Florence: 1591), pp. 8–9.
90. Vasari, vol. 5, p. 79.
91. Vasari (ibid.) describes the Santa Lucia painting as a Madonna and Child with multiple saints. Today this small church exists only as an apartment building at Vita de' Rossi, 3. Razzi, p. 369, also mentions a painting (presumably the same one) at Santa Lucia. He is the source for the San Domenico reference.
92. Carel van Mander, *Den grondt ter edel vry schilder-const* (Amsterdam: 1618), fol. 116a.
93. De Hollanda, 1928, p. 15, and Sohm, pp. 775–6.
94. For the art historical repercussions of this, see Svetlana Alpers, "Art History and Its Exclusions: The Example of Dutch Art", in *Feminism and Art History: Questioning the Litany*, eds. Norma Broude and Mary Garrard (New York: 1982), pp. 183–200.
95. Sohm, pp. 775–84, relates this to the *colorire-disegno* debate. Also see Patricia L. Reilly, "The Taming of Blue: Writing out Color in Renaissance Theory", in *The Expanding Discourse, Feminism and Art History*, eds. Norma Broude and Mary Garrard (New York: 1992), pp. 87–100.
96. For a discussion of the aesthetics of detail, see Naomi Schor, *Reading in Detail: Aesthetics and the Feminine* (New York: 1987).
97. Domenici, vol. 2, p. 350.
98. Ibid., vol. 3, p. 93.
99. Although not an issue addressed by earlier writers on art, the relationship between melancholia, visions, and creativity is one deserving investigation. A point of departure would be the visionary Hildegard of Bingen, who discussed melancholy in relation to gender. See Juliana Schiesari, *The Gendering of Melancholia: Feminism, Psychoanalysis and the Symbolics of Loss in Renaissance Literature* (Ithaca, NY: 1992), pp. 141–59.
100. See Zuan Antonio, *Vita della Beata Catherina Bolognese de lordini de la diva Clare Donne* (Bologna: 1502). The first biography of Caterina Vigri, *Specchio di Illuminazione*, which was written by her close friend Illuminate Bembo in 1469, specifically cites Caterina's visions as a source for her imagery. It was not published until 1787 (*Le Armi necessarie alla battaglia spirituale, oppretta composta da S. Catarina da Bologna alla quale si aggiunge lo Specchio di Illuminatzione sulla vita della medesima santa* (Bologna, 1787)).
101. Sopriani, vol. 1, p. 25.
102. Razzi, p. 369. Also see P. Guglielmo M. Di Agresti, *Santa Caterina De'Ricci*, vol. 1 (Florence: 1963) and vol. 4 (Florence: 1966).
103. Gian Ludovico Masetti Zannini, *Motivi storici della educazione feminile (1500–1650)* (Bari: 1980), pp. 131–2.

15 Guilds, Male Bonding and Women's Work in Early Modern Germany

Merry Wiesner

Though they are featured prominently in studies of medieval urban life, craft guilds have received less attention from early modern historians, who often view them as institutions in decline which were trying unsuccessfully to prevent economic change. This view of the guilds' decay has been successfully challenged in the case of Germany by Mack Walker, who demonstrates that in most medium-sized German cities the time after the Thirty Years War was 'the period probably of their greatest power to impress their values and goals upon the society of which they were components'.[1] These values and goals primarily involved maintaining the local economy and upholding the honour of the guilds. Walker and others have analysed the guild notion of honour quite extensively without noting what is, in my opinion, the most important component of it: this was an honour among *men*, an honour which linked men together with other men and excluded women. Craft guilds became an excellent example of what sociologists and psychologists term 'male bonding'.

Male bonding is a concept rarely used by historians, perhaps owing to the fact that the male group so predominates as a subject of historical study that male bonding appears trans-historical and almost self-evident. In this case, however, the notion of male bonding can prove enlightening and help to explain some of the actions of craft guilds in early modern Germany which are difficult to explain in terms of more standard social, economic, and political factors. It is an even more powerful determinant of the actions of journeymen's guilds, which were a new force in the economy of early modern German cities. I thus use the concept of male bonding to analyse the aims and actions of craft guilds and journeymen's guilds in German cities from the fifteenth to the eighteenth centuries. Though this exploration could go off in many directions, I will focus my dis-

From *Gender and History*, 1 (1989), 125–37. Reprinted with permission.

cussion on two questions: How did the concept of themselves as a group of men determine the way craft and journeymen's guilds defined skilled work and the gender boundaries of work? How did male bonding affect women's access to skilled work and to other forms of economic power?

First a few words on theories of male bonding. The concept was first extensively discussed by Lionel Tiger in his now classic *Men in Groups*. In his words: 'Males consciously create secret groups for the gregarious and efficacious control of political, religious, and/or economic worlds, and for the enjoyment of male company under emotionally satisfying conditions. Such grouping exhibits the culturally learned and socially mediated manifestations of a broad biological feature of the male life cycle.'[2] Tiger's most controversial point is revealed in his use of the word 'biological' to describe the underlying reason for male bonding. He views men's need to associate with other men as stemming from cooperative hunting during prehistoric times, and sees it as so ingrained in the male character as to be practically genetic. All men in all cultures feel the need to bond at certain points in their lives; the only difference is the form those bonds will take. Tiger would even go so far as to say that for certain men, the need to bond with other men is stronger than their sexual needs. (Tiger, I might add, sharply distinguishes between male bonding and male homosexuality, though notes that the former might have a somewhat hidden erotic component.)

Tiger's stress on the trans-cultural, trans-historical nature of male bonding is not accepted by other scholars, who view certain periods as favouring the formation of tighter male groups. To cite just one example that has applications for an analysis of early modern guilds, Ruth El Saffar asserts that males in the sixteenth century are being socialized for the first time in milieus almost entirely without women—milieus that impose discipline and foster male camaraderie at levels previously far less common.[3] She uses professional armies, the universities, and the expanded government bureaucracy as examples of these milieus. This male camaraderie both caused and resulted from men's attempts to disidentify with their mothers, which she and several contemporary psychoanalysts view as the core issue in the establishment of the modern masculine identity.[4] Her sources are primarily literary, and give evidence of a preoccupation with the disordering influence of women. Though one might argue that she overstresses the novelty of all-male milieus in the early modern period—the Athenian gymnasium provides one much earlier example, and the medieval

413

university another—the notion that women are a source of disorder and dishonour is not simply a literary conceit during the period. As we shall see, that idea becomes the basis for craft guild regulations and actions, and is taken up in the late sixteenth century with even more vehemence by the journeymen's guilds.

The earliest guild ordinances in Germany, from the late thirteenth to the early fifteenth centuries, did not regard skilled guild labour as a male preserve. Some of them mention both male and female masters, although it is difficult to tell if these women had been trained independently in all cases or were actually masters' widows. In some guilds the women may have been trained on their own, as the ordinances regulating apprenticeship talk about both boys and girls. Many medieval guilds went to great lengths to make sure that all women who practised their craft were members, subject to the normal rules and paying the normal fees, just as municipal laws required female heads of household to pay taxes.[5] Although it is impossible to tell from prescriptive ordinances just how many women were actually involved in craft work, one study using tax records finds 10–15 per cent of the iron-working shops in Nuremberg to be headed by widows or other women.[6] This, of course, does not count all the women who worked in a male-headed shop, nor is it a trade which was likely to attract high levels of female labour. Other studies indicate that women were even more likely to work in trades such as weaving, needle-making, yarn-spinning and hatmaking, which depended on dexterity rather than strength.[7]

Beginning in the mid-fifteenth century, many crafts expanded their ordinances and began to use more exclusively male language; the words 'female master' and 'girl apprentice' were often simply dropped with no explanation of why this was done. It is dangerous to draw conclusions from this change alone, but in some cases change was accompanied by specific ordinances prohibiting the work of women. Generally restrictions on masters' widows were the first to appear: a widow was allowed to continue operating a shop for only a short period of time, or only if she had a son who could take over; she was not allowed to take on or retain apprentices or journeymen; she could only finish work that had already been begun.[8] These restrictions were followed by limitations on the work female servants could do in a guild shop, which was generally limited to unskilled tasks such as preparing raw materials, cleaning and packing finished goods and cleaning the shop. Guilds which had previously seen high levels of female labour, such as those of weavers, dyers, and small hatmakers (*Baretmachern*), allowed women to produce only lower-priced and lower-quality goods.[9]

When I first examined this gradual exclusion of women from craft guilds, I attributed it to a number of factors—attempts to limit the number of workshops as the economies of various towns declined, conflicts between guilds and city councils over who had the power to control what went on in the shop, inter-guild rivalries, real or fabricated concerns over the quality of products.[10] To these economic and political factors I would now add an ideological one—guild honour. Women were to be kept out of guild shops not only because they had not been formally trained or would work more cheaply, but simply because they were women.

Several historians, most recently Mack Walker, have pointed out that social exclusiveness and a concern for maintaining honour and morality became the hallmarks of craft guilds after the Thirty Years War.[11] He lists a number of qualities that could make an individual 'dishonourable' and therefore not acceptable in a guild—illegitimacy, servile ancestry, parents who had worked as barbers, skinners, millers, shepherds, or linen-weavers.[12] To this list we must add having worked next to a woman or in a guild which still accepted women. To give just one example: in 1649 the Frankfurt hatmakers refused to take on journeymen who had been trained in Fulda, because the hatmakers in Fulda continued to use 'all sorts of female servants, maids, women and embroideresses'. The abbot of Fulda replied that it had long been the custom in Fulda to employ women as assistants, but now, 'since the hatmakers here have been insulted and despised because of this, their children, journeymen and apprentices hindered, and the quality of their work denigrated', he agreed to forbid women to work any longer.[13] Cases involving linen-weavers in Saxony, stonemasons in Frankfurt, and brewers in Munich use similar language.[14]

Why guilds which still allowed female labour should have been judged prima facie dishonourable is an interesting question. Jean Quataert proposes one reason, noting that in their attempts to maintain a monopoly on market production, craft guilds devalued all occupations which maintained their connection with household production. She comments: 'By the end of the Thirty Years' War, household production had become inextricably linked with women's work in the eyes of the threatened craftsmen', who attempted to define both as not really work.[15] The male/female dichotomy eventually became more pronounced than the guild/domestic one, so that in the nineteenth century women who spun, washed, or ironed in their own homes were not considered workers (and thus eligible for pensions according to the German industrial code), while male shoemakers or tailors who worked in their own homes were.[16]

I agree with Quataert, but would add male bonding as another reason why guild work was increasingly seen as 'a learned art and given to men alone'.[17] Not only were women excluded, but connections were explicitly established between men, connections which can be traced in the language of early modern guild ordinances. Whereas medieval guild ordinances often spoke about the duty of masters to uphold decorum (*Zucht*), by the eighteenth century masters were instructed specifically to uphold male decorum (a rather inelegant translation of *Manns-Zucht*). For example, an ordinance for the saddlers in Linz in 1750 reads: 'All city and rural masters shall take great pains to maintain proper male decorum among themselves, and to instruct their apprentices and journeymen in such male decorum . . .'; and one from the same city in 1742 for the bakers: 'This ordinance is proclaimed for the preservation of unity and honourable male decorum [*Ehrbarer Manns-zucht*] among masters, journeymen and apprentices.'[18]

There were limits to the level of male bonding that could be achieved in any craft guild, however, because masters were almost always married and one of their main aims was the support of their families. This was not a constraint on journeymen, however, who were usually unmarried, and the journeymen's guilds which grew up in Germany and elsewhere in Europe in the seventeenth century provide an even better example than craft guilds of strong male groups.

In the expanding economies of medieval cities, journeymen were simply part of the craft guild; they had finished their apprenticeship, and travelled from town to town working for different masters as they improved their skills. They looked forward to the time when they, too, could become masters, marry, and establish their own shop and household. This began to change in the sixteenth century as craft guilds became more restrictive and limited membership to sons of masters or those who married a master's widow or daughter. Many journeymen continued to work for a master all their lives, becoming essentially wage labourers. As their work became proletarianized, they began to think of themselves as a group distinct from the masters rather than as masters-in-training (*Gesellen* rather than *Knechte*) and began to form separate journeymen's associations. Tiger comments that the need to form all-male groups and to prove oneself a 'man among men' is strongest among men feeling 'relatively deprived';[19] given their declining social and economic position, the journeymen certainly fit the pattern here.

Because authorities worried they might provoke social and political unrest, journeymen's associations were illegal in some parts of Europe, so their guilds were secret, and often operated out of alehouses, which automatically excluded respectable women.[20] Tiger notes that 'the male bonding process may constitute a strong inducement to sever family-of-origin ties and circumscribe reproductive-family activity.'[21] Whether an inducement or a consequence, both of these tendencies may be seen among journeymen. Their wanderings often took them from their home towns, and they gained status among themselves according to how many places they had been to and how much of the world they had seen.[22] They also expected one another not to marry, and fervently opposed allowing any married journeymen the right to work.

Journeymen had originally been forbidden to marry in most craft guilds because they were expected to live with a master's family until they could become masters themselves. As their opportunities to become masters diminished in the sixteenth century, one might have expected journeymen's guilds to push for the right to marry. They did in a few cities, but in most they did not.[23] Instead of setting up their own households, they lived in all-male journeymen's hostels and in some cases pressured guilds which had originally accepted married journeymen to forbid them.[24] State authorities trying to promote the free movement of labour in the eighteenth century ordered journeymen to accept their married colleagues and provided stiff punishments for those who did not, but opposition remained strong well into the nineteenth century.[25]

This hostility to married journeymen can be partially explained as an attempt by unmarried journeymen to secure more work places, but the vehemence with which married journeymen and the masters who hired them were attacked hints at something deeper. As their opportunities to become masters or to amass actual capital declined, journeymen became increasingly obsessed by what Andreas Grießinger has nicely called 'the symbolic capital of honour'. Craft guilds had always been concerned about honour, and often demanded higher standards of honour for membership than that required for citizenship or an official position; for example, guilds refused to allow those legitimized after they were born to become members, until they were forced to by imperial ordinances in the eighteenth and nineteenth centuries.[26] Journeymen became the most vigorous guardians of a shop's honour, because they needed to be accepted elsewhere and thus 'their careers were more threatened by the taint of dishonour than an established master's was'.[27]

Because losing his honour meant a journeyman also lost the right to a work place, honour was an economic commodity for him in the same way as his training. At times their concern for honour caused journeymen to do things which worked against their own economic interests, however. They developed elaborate initiation rituals, and achieved high prestige by learning and transmitting these rituals, or by serving as a guild officer, even if the time spent resulted in a loss of wages.[28] They refused to work in the shops of masters who were suspected of moral infractions, though this meant a decline in the total number of work places available.[29] In some cases they refused to work for any master of a guild deemed less than honourable, simply avoiding certain cities in their travels, despite laws which prohibited this and prison sentences enforcing those laws.[30]

Journeymen forced one another to comply with their code of honour by refusing to work next to any journeyman who had broken the code, and reinforced their bonds with each other when they travelled.[31] Journeymen's practice of going from town to town assured that the names of those reprimanded or banned would be known throughout a broad area even if a formal guild did not exist; such banning often lasted for decades.[32] Though their local influence was less than that of craft guild masters, their transient status gave journeymen a great deal of influence throughout the Empire, perhaps more than they had in the centralized states of western Europe.

Not working next to women became an important part of journeymen's notion of honour. Journeymen originally objected to women's work for economic reasons, viewing women as taking work places they regarded as rightfully theirs. During the sixteenth century, women's work also became a political issue for journeymen; as their opportunities to become masters declined, forcing a master's female servants, wife, and daughters out of a shop became one way of demonstrating their power *vis-à-vis* the masters. In order to accomplish this, journeymen began to argue that any shop or guild which allowed female labour was tainted.

Journeymen's attempts to differentiate their work sharply from that of women came at exactly the same time that their actual work situation was becoming more like that of women. No longer was the position of journeyman necessarily simply a stage in the male life cycle; rather it was a permanent state, leaving one dependent on a master for wages. Because journeymen generally had little or no real property or goods, their honour was their most important economic asset, in the same way that it was for women; for women, a loss of honour might also bring economic devastation because of the resultant loss of marital opportunities. Joan Kelly-Gadol has noted that courtiers during the Renaissance became more like women in their dependent status, and so may have been increasingly motivated to limit the independence of their female relatives.[33] Could something similar have been operating here with journeymen, at least on a subconscious level?

Whatever the reasons for their hostility to women's work, journeymen carried this idea with them from town to town, and forced guilds in many towns to prohibit work by female servants for the first time in the seventeenth and eighteenth centuries.[34] As with other parts of their code of honour, they enforced this by refusing to work with any journeyman who had worked next to a woman, forcing guilds in every city to comply. The first attempts by state authorities to compel journeymen to relax their code of honour precipitated a wave of strikes and riots in the 1720s, and an imperial edict of 1772 permitting women to work in crafts had little practical effect.[35] A later Prussian edict again allowing women to work specifically ordered that journeymen were not to be punished or censured for working next to a woman, but this, too, probably had little effect.[36]

Once the notion that women made a *shop* dishonourable took hold among journeymen, it was not very far to the idea that all contact with women was dishonourable, which helps explain their hostility toward marriage and their married colleagues. This is also one reason why they banned any journeyman known to frequent prostitutes or engage in other forms of 'licentious behaviour'; not only was this dishonourable in the same way as any moral infraction, but it also meant that the individual had had contact with a woman. Though prohibitions of contact with prostitutes were certainly not effective everywhere, they did in some cases lead to a journeyman's being barred from work.[37] Combined with the hostility to marriage, this left journeymen with few sexual outlets, making journeymen's guilds a good example of a group in which the need for male bonding was 'functionally equivalent to, and probably more powerful than, the development of a sexual bond'.[38]

During the early modern period, then, skilled work in guild shops was increasingly defined as men's work, and the 'mystery' of any 'craft', the 'secrets of the trade' as something which should not be shared with women. (I put these words in quotes because they are often used interchangeably, though we usually forget the connotations of secrecy when using the word 'craft'.) The craft guilds themselves, and even more the journeymen's guilds which were both part of and in opposition to the craft guilds, became totally male groups.

Of course, the vast majority of those working in guild shops, and certainly the vast majority of masters, had always been male, so one might question whether this was really much of a change. Because so many female artisans were the wives, daughters, widows, and maids of masters, and because their participation in crafts was informal rather than regulated by the formal apprenticeship structure, it is difficult to quantify the effects of the exclusion of women. Nevertheless, one can find evidence that women's work in the crafts was actually declining, and that the goal of an all-male workshop was being achieved.

As crafts gradually imposed restrictions on the rights of widows during the fifteenth and sixteenth centuries, many widows appealed to city councils or other authorities for the right to keep working. In some cases they were allowed, and in others not, though nowhere in Germany did a city council categorically permit widows the right to continue their husbands' shops.[39] Continuing a shop was thus a special privilege based on a council's generosity and the merits of the case, not a widow's right, though, as noted above, 10–15 per cent of guild shops in some cities continued to be run by widows or other women during the sixteenth century. By the seventeenth century, however, some widows began to request the right to give up their shops, even though this ended their children's rights to remain in the guild.[40] As all guilds by this time had very high entrance fees, this also meant that the children would generally be reduced to doing piecework, working as servants or unskilled labourers, or working in an unregulated craft, with very little opportunity of entering the guild again. This affected sons directly, but also daughters, whose rights to pass on a guild membership to their husbands might have been worth more than any cash dowry.

Why would a widow give up her shop and impoverish her children? This was not her free choice, but the result of guild restrictions. Prohibited from utilizing journeymen or apprentices, she could not produce enough even to pay guild fees. A recent study of weavers in Augsburg around 1600 finds that 15 per cent of the master weavers were women, but they employed only 5 per cent of the journeymen and apprentices. As we would expect, tax records indicate that most of these women were very poor.[41] Widows were always vastly over-represented among the 'very poor' in every city.[42]

A more complicated question is why guilds would act against the interests of the widows and children of their own members. One of the main aims of the craft guilds had always been the maintenance of masters' families; numerous ordinances which favoured masters' sons and those who married masters' widows or daughters point out the importance of the familial and social aspects of a mastership in an era before pensions and social security. Preserving the male nature of the guild by restricting widows' rights worked at cross-purposes to this, but in this instance excluding women from skilled work seems to have been judged more important to many guilds. A statistical study of how businesses were passed down among the joiners and corset-makers in Vienna during the Thirty Years War indicates that roughly 10 per cent were handed down to sons, between 12 per cent and 18 per cent to journeymen who married a widow or daughter, and more than 70 per cent were simply purchased by strangers.[43] Christopher Friedrichs' sample of the occupations of brides and grooms in early modern Nördlingen also shows that only a small minority of men married within the same occupation or took the occupation of their bride's father or former husband.[44] Connecting through women was not a typical way of moving from one all-male group to another, nor did marriage 'serve as a mechanism to promote occupational solidarity'.[45]

Just as widows no longer had any real 'rights' to continue operating a shop, they also had no rights to support in the way male members did. Supporting one's guild brothers in times of need was a way of reinforcing trade solidarity, while supporting widows was a way to show the guild's devotional philanthropy, a distinction evidenced by the fact that guilds often supported needy women who were not widows of guild masters, while they never supported nonguild men.[46] Widows asking for support or for special consideration were most successful when they pleaded extreme poverty and need rather than craft ties: 'How heavy and hard the hand of God, himself burdened with the cross, has come down on me, and in what a pitiful situation I find myself after the all-too-sudden death of my late husband, with my young and helpless child still nursing at my breast.'[47]

Journeymen's efforts to force masters' wives, daughters, and female servants out of guild shops also appear to have been quite successful, at least judging by the number of times such restrictions are upheld by city councils.[48] Though this often put the councils in opposition to guild masters, the councils justified their actions by commenting that other cities had already given in to the journeymen, so that they would have to follow suit or risk economic decline from journeymen boycotts. In fact, some cities were even more active in courting journeymen, offering them the right to decide who would be hired in a workshop (the *Schenkwesen*), to draw them away from cities where masters held this right.[49] Given the journeymen's attitude toward women's work, their holding the *Schenkwesen* was not beneficial to women's employment. In 1607, for example, journeymen cord-makers in Frankfurt forced the masters there to stop employing female servants in the shop, and only to use their daughters for finishing and cleaning; in 1701, journeymen book-binders in Nuremberg were able to exclude all women.[50] As noted above, only with the growth of more centralized state power in Germany were laws passed against journeymen; no city had the economic power to do this alone. Women were thus relegated to work outside the craft guilds in the expanding domestic industries or in trades which were not organized as a guild, trades which did not demand a high level of skill.

One might argue that the changes discussed here were not all that significant for women. Weren't craft guilds themselves in decline during this period? Wouldn't journeymen's guilds lose their meaning and eventually disappear with industrialism? What did it matter that women were excluded from a vanishing part of the economy?

There are three ways to answer these objections. First, as Mack Walker has so ably demonstrated, craft guilds remained the most important part of the economy in many cities of Germany, particularly those slow to industrialize, well into the nineteenth century. They determined the economic policies of many towns, and 'bore political and civic factors into economic practice'.[51]

Second, guilds left a tremendous legacy to industrialism. The craft tradition of reserving skilled work for men continued in the artisan shop, and then the factory, as jobs there which were better paid and required some training went to men, leaving the least skilled jobs for women. Gender divisions within the factory thus mirrored those among artisans outside it. Journeymen's guilds also made important contributions to the development of trade unions.[52] One of their less positive contributions was the hostility toward women's work which many trade unions exhibited, though this also had other roots in the industrial economy.

Third, the guild concept of the strongest bonds being those between men had implications far beyond the realm of economics, which has been my main concern here. The guild notion that the workshop was a male preserve gradually became a more generally accepted ideal, predating, as Jean Quataert notes, 'by at least a century the related Romantic notions of separate spheres for males and females'.[53] As R. Po-Chia Hsia has pointed out, 'patriarchal sacred kinship received its inspiration partly from the Old Testament and partly from the social practices of the guilds ... the artisans of the guild community lived in a social world in which an extra familial male corporation, with its ideology of a fictive kinship, a fraternity, reinforced their own positions as heads of households, as fathers and husbands, within the nuclear family'.[54] Though Anthony Black strangely never mentions the masculine nature of guilds, his description of them as 'a seedbed of *fraternity* as a popular belief' is here particularly apt.[55] The male bonds created by craft and journeymen's guilds are in many ways still with us.

Notes

1. Mack Walker, *German Home Towns: Community, State, and General Estate 1648–1871* (Cornell University Press, Ithaca, NY, 1971), p. 76. Richard MacKenney finds that guilds in Venice also played a very prominent and positive role in the sixteenth and seventeenth centuries, adapting to economic change much more readily than previously assumed. He extends his conclusions tentatively to guilds in other cities, and calls for a reassessment of the relationship between guilds and mercantile capitalism. (*Tradesmen and Traders: The World of Guilds in Venice and Europe, c.1250–c.1650* (Barnes and Noble, Totowa, NJ, 1987), pp. 113–25.)

2. Lionel Tiger, *Men in Groups* (Random House, New York, 1969), p. 140.

3. Ruth El Saffar, 'Literary reflections on the "new man": changes in consciousness in early modern Europe', unpublished paper, p. 14.

4. Ibid., p. 20; Ralph Greenson, 'Dis-identifying with the mother: its special importance for the boy', *International Journal of Psychoanalysis* 49 (1968): 370–4; Robert J. Stoller, 'Facts and fancies: an examination of Freud's concept of bisexuality', in *Women and Analysis*, ed. Jean Strouse (Grossman Publishers, New York, 1974), pp. 343–64.

5. Rudolf Wissell, *Des alten Handwerks Recht und Gewohnheit*, 2. Einzelveröffentlichungen der historischen Kommission zu Berlin, 7 (Colloquium, Berlin, 1974), p. 441; Helmut Wachendorf, *Die wirtschaftliche Stellung der Frau in den deutschen Städten des späteren Mittelalters* (C. Trute, Quackenbruck, 1934), pp. 30–2, 57; Benno Schmidt and Karl Bücher, *Frankfurter Amts und Zunfturkunden bis zum Jahre 1612*. Veröffentlichungen der historischen Kommission der Stadt Frankfurt a.M., Vol. 6 (Joseph Baer, Frankfurt, 1914), p. 513; Gustav Schmoller, *Die Strassburger Tucher und Weberzunft, Urkunden und Darstellung* (Karl J. Trübner, Strasbourg, 1879), pp. 40–1.

6. Rainer Stahlschmidt, *Die Geschichte des eisenverarbeitende Gewerbes in Nurnberg von der ersten Nachrichten im 12.–13. Jahrhundert bis 1630*. Schriftenreihe des Stadtarchivs Nürnberg, no. 4 (Stadtarchiv, Nuremberg, 1971), pp. 186–7. Lyndal Roper also finds 10% of the population of Augsburg in a 1539 muster list to be widows, though not all of these ran craft shops. ('Urban women and the household workshop form of production: Augsburg 1500–1550', unpublished paper, p.6.)

7. Wissell, *Des alten Handwerks*, Vol. 2, p. 139; Merry Wiesner, *Working Women in Renaissance Germany* (Rutgers University Press, New Brunswick, NJ, 1986).

pp. 151–85; E. William Monter, 'Women in Calvinist Geneva', *Signs* 6 (1980): 204; Karl Bücher, *Die Berufe der Stadt Frankfurt im Mittelalter* (Teubner, Leipzig, 1914); Annette Winter, 'Studien zur sozialen Situation der Frauen in der Stadt Trier nach der Steuerliste von 1364', *Kurtrierisches Jahrbuch* 15 (1975): 20–5. The only all-female guilds in Germany, those of gold-spinners in several cities and yarnmakers and silk-weavers in Cologne, also demonstrate this trend in women's work. (Margaret Wensky, *Die Stellung der Frau in der stadtkölnische Wirtschaft im Spätmittelalter.* Quellen und Darstellung zur hänsische Geschichte (Böhlau, Cologne, 1981). Natalie Davis finds women most prevalent in the textile and clothing trades in Lyon as well. ('Women in the crafts in sixteenth-century Lyon', in *Women and Work in Pre-Industrial Europe*, ed. Barbara Hanawalt (Indiana University Press, Bloomington, 1986), p. 181.)

8. Munich Stadtarchiv (hereafter MU), Ratsitzungsprotokolle, 1461, fols. 39, 42; 1526; Nuremberg Staatsarchiv (hereafter N), Ratsbücher: 2. fols. 31 (1475), 282 (1479), 318 (1479); 11, fol. 324 (1520); 22, fol. 236 (1544); Frankfurt Stadtarchiv (hereafter FF), Bürgermeisterbücher, 1515, fol. 112b; 1580, fol. 189b; FF, Zünfte, Ugb. D–3 (1527, 1588 and 1596); Nuremberg Stadtarchiv (hereafter NB), QNG, no. 68/11, 506; no. 68/1, 115 (1535); Strasbourg, Archives municipales (hereafter AMS), Akten der XV, 1613, fol. 201b; Memmingen Stadtarchiv (hereafter MM), Zünfte, 451(3), Hutmachem (1613).

9. Restrictions on weavers: Wissell, *Des alten Handwerks*, Vol. 2, p. 441; F. G. Mone. Die Weberei und ihre Beigewerbe vom 14.–16. Jhd.', *Zeitschrift für Geschichte des Oberrheins* 9 (1858): 174. Restrictions on dyers: NB, QNG, no. 68/1, 311; MU, Ratsitzungsprotokolle, 1558, fol. 133; FF, Bürgermeisterbücher, 1590, fol. 201a; AMS, Akten der XV, 1655, fols. 33, 34. Restrictions on small hat makers: NB, QNG: no. 68/III, 1302 (1597); 1303 (1603); MU, Gewerbeamt, no. 1020, 1603 Krämerordnung; MM, Zünfte, 451(3) (1613); AMS, Akten der XV: 1639, fols. 120, 154, 164, 171, 182; 1665, fol. 94.

10. Wiesner, *Working Women*, pp. 161, 168.

11. Walker, *German Home Towns*, p. 89.

12. Ibid., pp. 104–5.

13. FF, Zünfte, Ugb. C–36, Cc (1649–Huter).

14. Wissell, *Des alten Handwerks*, Vol. 2, p. 444; FF, Ugb. C–38, Z (1624); MU, Ratsitzungsprotokolle, 1599, fol. 164.

15. Jean Quataert, 'The shaping of women's work in manufacturing: guilds, households, and the state in central Europe, 1648–1870', *American Historical Review* 90 (1985): 1124. Quataert's conclusions can also help explain why linen-weaving was considered dishonourable in many parts of Germany, and is included in Walker's list noted above, though in most places wool-weaving was a perfectly respectable or even high-status occupation. Walker comments that linen-weaving was dishonourable because it was 'primitive' and had 'suspect rural overtones and connections' (*German Home Towns*, p. 104) while Quataert is more specific: 'Those activities, like linen weaving, that remained closely associated with the household economy never achieved high social value' ('Shaping', p. 1147).

16. Quataert, 'Shaping', p. 1146. This is a good example of the way in which gender can come to take precedence over all other variables, subsuming even those with which it was originally linked.

17. MU, Ratsitzungsprotokolle, 1599, fol. 164.
18. Gerhard Danninger, *Das Linzer Handwerk und Gewerbe vom Verfall der Zunfthoheit über die Gewerbefreiheit bis zum Innungszwang. Linzer Schriften zur Sozial- und Wirtschafts-geschichte*, Vol. 4 (Rudolf Trauner, Linz, 1981), p.75.
19. Tiger, *Men in Groups*, p.198.
20. Rudolf M. Dekker, 'Women in revolt: popular protest and its social basis in Holland in the seventeenth and eighteenth centuries', *Theory and Society* 16 (1987): 347; C. R. Dobson, *Masters and Journeymen: A Prehistory of Industrial Relations 1717–1800* (Croom Helm, London, 1980), p. 38.
21. Tiger, *Men in Groups*, p. 135.
22. Andreas Grießinger, *Das Symbolische Kapital der Ehre: Streikbewegungen und kollektives Bewußtsein deutscher Handwerksgesellen im 18. Jahrhundert* (Ullstein Materialen, Frankfurt, 1981), pp. 67–8.
23. For an example of a city where journeymen did demand the right to marry, see AMS, Akten der XXI, 1620 on.
24. Walker, *German Home Towns*, p. 83; Wissell. *Des alten Handwerks*, Vol. 2, p. 448; Klaus Schwarz, *Die Lage der Handwerksgesellen in Bremen während des 18. Jahrhunderts*, Veröffentlichungen aus dem Staatsarchiv der Freien Hansestadt Bremen, Vol. 44 (Staatsarchiv, Bremen, 1975), p. 38.
25. See, for example, the Imperial Trades Edict of 1731, translated in Walker, *German Home Towns*, p. 448, and a proclamation of Maria Theresa in 1770, reprinted in Wissell, *Des alten Handwerks*, Vol. 2, p. 449.
26. Wissell, *Des alten Handwerks*, Vol. 1, pp. 253–4.
27. Walker, *German Home Towns*, p. 94.
28. Grießinger, *Symbolische Kapital*, p. 451.
29. Wissell, *Des alten Handwerks*, Vol. 1, p. 271; Frank Göttman, *Handwerk und Bundnispolitik: Die Handwerkerbände am Mittelrhein vom 14. bis zum 17. Jahrhundert*. Frankfurter Historische Abhandlungen, no. 15 (Steiner, Wiesbaden, 1977), pp. 153, 280; AMS, Akten der XV, 1628, fols. 152, 164.
30. Wissell, *Des alten Handwerks*, Vol. 1, pp. 269, 272.
31. Ibid., Vol. 1, p. 257.
32. Ibid., Vol. 2, p. 232; Walker, *German Home Towns*, p. 83.
33. Joan Kelly-Gadol, 'Did women have a Renaissance?' in *Becoming Visible: Women in European History*, 2nd edn, ed. Renate Bridenthal, Claudia Koonz and Susan Stuard (Houghton Mifflin, Boston, 1987), p. 196.
34. Wissell, *Des alten Handwerks*, Vol. 2, pp. 448–9; Karl Heinrich Kaufhold, *Das Handwerk der Stadt Hildesheim im 18. Jahrhundert*, Göttinger Beiträge zur Wirtschafts und Sozialgeschichte (Otto Schwarz, Göttingen, 1980), p. 118; NB, Quellen zur Nürnbergische Geschichte, no. 68/III, 1108.
35. Walker, *German Home Towns*, p. 84; Grießinger, *Symbolische Kapital*, passim; Wissell, *Des alten Handwerks*, Vol. 2, p. 445; Beata Brodmeier, *Die Frau im Handwerk*, Forschungsberichte aus dem Handwerk, Vol. 9 (Handwerkswissenschaftlichen Institut, Münster, 1963), pp. 19, 36.
36. Wissell, *Des alten Handwerks*, Vol. 2, p. 445.
37. Ibid., pp. 140, 271; Schmidt and Bücher, *Frankfurter Amts*, p. 280.
38. Tiger, *Men in Groups*, p. 172.
39. FF, Zünfte, Ugb. D–2, F (1506); C–43, L (1600); C–59, Gg, no. 3 and Aa no. 4 (1672); AMS, Akten der XV: 1607, fol. 147; 1610, fols. 146, 156, 198, 225; 1618,

fols. 8, 14, 20, 28, 119; 1617, fols. 84, 144, 247; 1633, fols. 88, 154, 173, 177, 178, 230, 232; MM, Ratsprotokollbücher: 15 September 1556; 8 November 1560. Inger Dübeck has discovered that in Denmark, as well, city governments did occasionally grant widows' privileges against the wishes of a guild. (*Købekoner og Konkurrence* (Juristforbundets, Copenhagen, 1978), pp. 395–404.)

40. MU, Gewerbeamt, no. 2293; AMS, Akten der XV, 1608, fol. 22.

41. Claus-Peter Clasen, *Die Augsburger Weber: Leistungen und Krisen des Textilgewerbes um 1600*. Abhandlungen zur Geschichte der Stadt Augsburg, no. 27 (Muhlberger, Augsburg, 1981), pp. 23, 59.

42. Roper, 'Urban women', p. 6; MU, Steuerbücher (1410–1640). This was also true in English cities, as Diana Willen reports for Warwick, Salisbury, Ipswich and Norwich ('Women in the public sphere in early modern England: the case of the urban working poor', *Sixteenth Century Journal* 9 (Winter 1988): 562) and Mary Prior fox Oxford ('Women and the urban economy: Oxford 1500–1800' in her *Women in English Society, 1500–1800* (Methuen, London, 1985), p. 106). Prior also notes that only a tiny share of masters' widows took on apprentices.

43. Heinz Zatschek, 'Aus der Geschichte des Wiener Handwerks während des 30 jährigen Krieges: Eine soziologische Studie', *Jahrbuch des Verein für Geschichte der Stadt Wien*, 9 (1951), p. 33.

44. Christopher R. Friedrichs, *Urban Society in an Age of War: Nördlingen, 1580–1720* (Princeton University Press, Princeton, 1979), p. 86.

45. Ibid., p. 87.

46. Roper, 'Urban women', p. 9. MacKenney also found this to be true in Venice (*Tradesmen and Traders*, p. 70).

47. FF, Zünfte, Ugb. D–24, L4 (1698).

48. NB, QNG, no. 68/II, 663, 674, 847, 853, 873; no. 68/III, 1093, 1107, 1189; Augsburg Handwercksordnungen, 1550, Nestler and Huter: Wachendorf, p. 63; Martha Howell, *Women, Production and Patriarchy in Late Medieval Cities* (University of Chicago Press, Chicago, 1986), p. 91.

49. Ernst Mummenhoff, 'Frauenarbeit und Arbeitsvermittlung: Eine Episode aus der Handwerksgeschichte des 16. Jahrhunderts', *Vierteljahrsschrift für Sozial- und Wirtschaftsgeschichte* 199 (1926): 157–65.

50. Schmidt and Bücher, *Frankfurter Amts*, pp. 417–20; Wissell, *Des alten Handwerks*, Vol. 2, p. 448. Alice Clark has discovered that journeymen's organizations and their ability to 'bargain advantageously with the masters' had similar effects on women's work in seventeenth-century England (*Working Life of Women in the Seventeenth Century* (Routledge and Kegan Paul, London, 1919), p. 298).

51. Walker, *German Home Towns*, p. 77.

52. The links between journeymen's guilds and trade unions have merited surprisingly little study by labour historians. One of the few works which does examine them is R. A. Lesson, *Travelling Brothers: The Six Centuries' Road from Craft Fellowship to Trade Unionism* (George Allen and Unwin, London, 1979), whose title unconsciously supports my point in this paragraph.

53. Quataert, 'Shaping', p. 1147.

54. R. Po-Chia Hsia, 'Münster and Anabaptists', in *The German People and the Reformation*, ed. R. Po-Chia Hsia (Cornell University Press, Ithaca, NY, 1988), p. 69.

55. Anthony Black, *Guilds and Civil Society in European Political Thought from the 12th Century to the Present* (Methuen, London, 1984), p.31 (my emphasis). Black also notes (p. 55) the connection between guild moral values and city values stressed by both Walker and Hsia.

16 Language, Power, and the Law: Women's Slander Litigation in Early Modern London

Laura Gowing

"A married woman perhaps may doubt whether shee bee either none or no more than half a person", wrote the anonymous author of the first exposition of women's equivocal legal position, *The lawes resolution of womens rights*, in 1632. Legally, women's agency was vested in their husbands: "Women have no voyse in Parliament, they make no lawes, they consent to none, they abrogate none. All of them are understood either married or to be married and their desires are subject to their husband, I know no remedy, though some women can shift it well enough".[1]

For much of the legal practice of early modern England this outline was an accurate one. In particular, while contemporaries observed increased levels of litigation, women's access to this kind of participation in the law was restricted. Technically, married women could not sue cases at the common law: their desires, and their legal authority, were "subject to their husband". But among those who could "shift it well enough" must surely have been the women who fought cases at the church courts. There, married, single and widowed women sued cases in their own names over disputed wills, tithes, and, most often, sex and marriage. In the most popular type of litigation, suits alleging sexual slander, they brought cases up to five times more often than men did. A typical case in London in 1628 involved Magdalen Lewis and Mary Record, neighbours from near Bridewell. The two had fallen out after Magdalen's husband persuaded Mary's lodgers not to go to her wedding feast. Mary interpreted this as a slur on her premarital conduct and, in return, launched an attack on Magdalen's honesty, calling her "a pore sorry thinge a common thinge and one that was familiar with every hattmakers boy", adding "that she had had a bastard by a hattmakers boy before she was married". The slander stuck. Six

From Garthine Walker and Jenny Kermod (eds.), *Women, Crime and the Courts in Early Modern England* (UCL University Press, 1994), 26–74 Reprinted with permission.

months later a witness testified that as Magdalen went about her business "people thereabouts do mocke at her and say that she must goe into poules to try her honesty". Magdalen followed their advice to "goe into poules", bringing a suit against Mary at London's principal church court, the consistory court held in St Pauls.[2]

Such legal recourse was expensive and time consuming, yet Magdalen and Mary were only two of around 230 women suing and defending defamation cases every year in the early seventeenth-century consistory court. The ecclesiastical courts dealt with sexual slander because it imputed spiritual, rather than temporal, sin. Sexual slander had always been sued predominantly by women, and in the early seventeenth century suits for slander were increasing in all courts.[3] But after 1600, the volume of both defamation cases and women litigants increased to such an extent in London that sexual slander accounted for the largest part of the consistory court's business. By 1633, as many as 70 per cent of cases at the court concerned defamation, and 85 per cent of those were sued by women.[4] In a legal system where women's testimonies were rarely accorded the same measure of credit as men's, defamation cases also involved higher numbers of female witnesses than other suits.[5] This essay examines the contexts and meanings of the slander litigation that women fought at the London church courts in the late sixteenth and early seventeenth centuries.[6] Looking first at the language of slander, and then at women's litigation, it examines the ways gender determined ideas of sexual honour, uses of slander, and the effects of insult; how women used the courts, and what kinds of opportunities litigation offered women; and how the particular circumstances and definitions of women that obtained in early modern society both circumscribed women's actions, and provided a base from which they could claim verbal, local, and legal authority.

Ostensibly, defamation was concerned with morality and reputation. Slanderous words attacked immoral behaviour; lawsuits in response to them fought to restore a person's damaged reputation. To historians, the increase in slander litigation has suggested the possibility of tracing a growing popular intolerance of illicit sexuality through the currency of insult; but the evidence of dispute has also shown the extent to which defamation disputes arose from complex local and personal conflicts.[7] For early modern commentators, rising levels of litigation were evidence most of all of the pollution of ideals of neighbourliness by malicious dispute.[8] Slander litigation was far more than a response to dishonour. The battles that were fought out in the words of slander and at the court were complex and heterogenous, and their context was far wider than the incidents retailed to the court. Defamation was also an imaginative enterprise. The words of slander did not echo the view of sexual responsibility that contemporary moralists were endeavouring to enforce. While the homilies, sermons and law of the church stress the culpability of both men and women for illicit sex, the idiom of slander holds women entirely responsible for it, contains no words to condemn male sexual misconduct, and judges men and women by two sets of incommensurable values. Women and men used that idiom to produce personal, creative complaints that used, rather than absorbed, contemporary visions of morality.

The motives and functions behind sexual slander, predominantly targeted at and fought at law by women, cannot be understood without taking gender into account. Women's use of both language and lawsuits was determined by their specific places in the economies of language, law, sex, household and community. In a culture where a host of prescriptions limited women's words, and where women's participation in the law was explicitly restricted, sexual insult and legal action represented particular opportunities. Women in London used those opportunities, in conjunction with a set of established customary and practical powers, to claim a verbal and legal authority that was at once powerful and fragile.

London women's involvement in slander was shaped by their particular situation. The women who fought defamation were mostly married or widowed. Gentlewomen did not bring defamation suits, nor did the poorest women. Most litigants were the wives, daughters and widows of middle-status tradesmen and craftsmen, working in shops or markets, nursing, washing, or in service. Their litigation made London's principal ecclesiastical jurisdiction look like a women's court.[9] Here, the metropolitan experience seems to have been unique: although sexual defamation cases regularly attracted large numbers of women plaintiffs, it was only in London that women's business came to take up so large a part of the court's time.

This might be traced in part to London's demographic situation. With a constantly increasing population, sustained by immigration, the city was characterized by a changing topography and a high degree of mobility.[10] A sample of inhabitants between 1572 and 1640 shows that only one in ten Londoners were living in the parish in which they were born, and three-quarters came from outside London and Middlesex.[11] The daily experience of urban life, with its crowded conditions and fragile boundaries, must have exerted considerable strain, particularly on those women and men new to it, and conflicts over property boundaries and shared resources were frequently at the root of defamation. More generally, most people were living in a community where they had a short personal history, and no family past. Public discussions of past sexual behaviour might provide one forum for the exploration of those gaps and the voicing of anxieties about geographic and economic mobility. The specific conditions of urban gender relations were also likely to influence these women's contact with the courts. Many women were working in shops in the fronts of their houses, in their own alehouses, or selling goods at markets; in the eastern parishes, women married to sailors spent much of their time living and working in a predominantly female world. All these circumstances both increased their public profile and made them more likely to be involved in social dispute.

Slander in London was determined by particular urban circumstances, but it was expressed in a language of insult whose themes are recorded in defamation cases across the country.[12] Central to this language was the word "whore", the focus for a dialogue about the honesty of women. Insults like "base whore", "common whore" or "pocky whore" were used not to denote the actual financial and sexual relations of prostitution, but as a shorthand for a fuller exposition of sexual misconduct. The language of defamation construed the whore as the exact opposite of the honest woman. Defamers accused whores of looking "brazen-faced" and dressing luxuriously. Other slanderers complained of women "nightwalking and daywalking", spending their time on the street instead of in the house, and being proud, insubordinate and immodest. All these proofs of dishonesty were familiar from the literature, sermons and biblical texts that advised women on their rôle and behaviour.[13] But defamers also used rumour, elaboration, and invention to construct their own condemnations, transforming the stock cultural images of whoredom into personal insults. Their language established a set of associations through which the word "whore" could be made a symbol for every kind of female misbehaviour.

As the primary targets of insult, women occupied a very particular place in the negotiation of sexual guilt and honour. Insults of women played on a culpability for illicit sex that was unique to them. The personal, verbal, social and institutional sanctions against "whores" and "bawds" had no counterpart for men. Men were less likely than women to be presented for illicit sex. Men's adultery was never an accepted ground for marital separation, as women's was. And the word "whore" had no male equivalent. Instead, men fought cases over insults like "whoremonger", "pander", or "cuckold", concerning not their own sexuality but that of women for whom they were in some sense responsible. In these insults male sexual behaviour was perceived not through its promiscuity, but through the measure of men's control over women's sexuality. Through the power, simultaneously vague and immense, of the word "whore", sexual honour was imagined entirely through women, and in the language of abuse women's dishonesty was interpreted through its direct and material effects on the whole household. The reputation of the house itself rested on women. In 1613 Anne Gibbons complained of a series of sexual insults directed at her husband but focusing on her: "cuckold", "wittall" and "everyone that passeth by thy house and seeth thy wife saieth there is a whore and there is a bawdye house".[14] Women were at the pivotal centre of the circulation of blame and dishonour for sex: responsibility was channelled entirely through them.

That responsibility made women the natural targets for sexual insult, but it also gave some women an investment in the regulation of sexuality inside and outside their households. Sexual honour was overwhelmingly a female concern, and as much as women were the targets of the regulation of honesty, they made themselves the agents of its definition. Women used the broad and powerful possibilities of the word "whore" in every sort of local and personal conflict. They called other women whores loosely, with little or no further details, as one weapon in disputes about money, goods or territory; and they told circumstantial stories of actual, rumoured or imagined sexual transgressions. It seems that women were using the language of slander to perform a function for which men were more likely to look to official, institutional and legal spheres.

The publicity of defamation was central to its power for women. Insulting other women in the street, they made themselves responsible for the honesty of the whole neighbourhood. Defamations regularly began "Goe you whore" or "away you whore", and defamers referred particularly to the localities notorious for prostitution and bawdy houses, Clerkenwell and Turnmill Street.[15] The spirit behind regulations that confined prostitutes to a particular area outside the city walls acted equally effectively for women insulting each other.[16] Ellen Tilbury's abuse of her neighbour in "angrie and malicious manner" in 1625 was typical: "hang thee whore thou keepest a bawdy house" and "Turnbull Street is a more fitt place for thee than to laie here amongst thy neighbours".[17] In insults like these women assumed a particular responsibility for local honesty, claiming the right to define and enforce the moral character of their neighbourhood.

Within the neighbourhood, women drew on a set of other powers from the realms of custom, tradition and law. Some conventionally female areas of power gave women's words a forceful backing. One of these was pregnancy. As midwives, women's sphere of action in the realm of childbirth extended from practical knowledge about pregnancy, abortion and miscarriage and supervision at the time of labour, to the quasi-legal task of questioning illegitimately pregnant women for the names of their partners at the times when labour pains were supposed to make them most truthful. As neighbours, women assisted in the rituals of childbed and the time of seclusion that followed the birth and ended with the re-entry into a mixed world at the moment of churching.[18] So both professionally and socially they were invested with an access to the truth of the physical experience of pregnancy. In the words and actions of slander women exploited this access to expand upon the results of whoredom. In 1624 Anne Pomeroy claimed to be able to detect loss of virginity at sight. In a kitchen of the Inns of Court, she heard someone call Elizabeth Maskall "maid". She intervened "I warrant she is no mayd, for she hath had a child", and told the others there "doe you all thincke that I have some skill, I cann tell uppon the sight of one whether she be a mayd or no".[19]

More often women proclaimed their skills at noticing the specific signs of pregnancy, defined exactly by one woman's observation of the changes in her neighbour: "her great belly milking of her brests her lookes and shortnes of her coates".[20] Others claimed medical or visionary skills, like Susan Chaddocke of Wapping, who told a neighbour in 1613 that "she had found in the house of Elizabeth Barwicke an urinall And yt she . . . did looke upon the water which was in the same urinall and saied that whose water soever that was they were with child". At this Elizabeth "did take the same urinall and did throw the water which was in it into her parlour chimney saieing unto . . . Susan Chaddocke that she had as much skill as the dog". Susan had recently herself been presented by Elizabeth's father for bastardy, and she took her assertions to Elizabeth's parents and told her father "nowe it was quid pro quo or it was come home by his . . . dore".[21]

More invasive tests of pregnancy included the squeezing of other women's breasts to check for milk.[22] And once children were born it was women who had the first and fullest chances to examine their features for the evidence of dubious paternity. Ellen Fanch, visiting a neighbour in childbed in 1631, was asked about her sister-in-law's

young daughter. She replied "she cared not how they did and further
. . . that Richard Wood didst beget her husbands brothers wife", and "I
will take mine oath that he didst begett [it] and it is like his Children
. . . and I . . . cannot love it".[23] All the knowledge of female bodies with
which women were credited and their authority in the area of childbirth established a source of power that was immensely productive in
the shaping of abuse.

Pregnancy was perceived as the natural punishment of whoredom:
one frequent insult was "if she is not with child, she has deserved to be
so". But women also interested themselves in particular physical, ritual
and communal punishments, both informally and through the law.
Community custom included an established set of symbolic rituals to
punish infringements of sexual rules, and in those rituals women were
prominent. In London there is little evidence of the skimmingtons or
ridings with which disturbers of the sexual order were received in rural
areas.[24] Instead, defamers and their witnesses refer to public rituals that
were in many cases specific to women. Broken windows were supposed
to mark a bawdy house, and some women had their windows broken
to show their whoredom. In 1628 Catherine Ripon was accused of
calling Sibill Brosse whore and breaking both her head and her
windows, in an action that combined the symbolizing of whoredom
with physical violence against the whore.[25] Like the rituals of rough
music recorded in other areas, the banging of basins and pans at
women was used to accuse them of whoredom or scolding, and this
too found its way into the vernacular of defamation. Alice Fullham and
Ellen Alsop called each other "quean" and "bitch" in the street in 1611,
and Alice said to Ellen "a cart and a basen tyng tyng, a cart and a basen
tyng tyng, a cart and a basen if thou wilt not be quiet".[26] Here, as so
often, verbal and sexual incontinence were conflated.

A more personal punishment involved an actual mutilation of the
whore, to make her as visible as she was meant to be. In Stepney in
1618 Alice Squire scratched Katherine Berry's face and said she had
given her a "whores marke". This mark was a slit nose, traditionally
conceived as the injured wife's revenge on her husband's mistress.[27]
Other women threatened the same penalty. In 1619 Joan Hickman
accused her neighbour Joan Bird of "keeping her husband" and threatened to "slitt her nose and marke her for a whore". Witnesses described
this as having "used her pleasure of Joane Bird in speeches", echoing
the familiar phraseology of sexual pleasure in the shape of the plea-
surable verbal revenge for it.[28] Given the way that noses, in early
modern culture, could stand in for phalluses, it is a revenge that looks

like castration.[29] Symbolic actions and threats like these sustained the tradition of this corpus of women's sanctions, encompassing sexual sin in contexts as broad as the neighbourhood and as narrow as the household.

Women's power to punish whoredom was not confined to the communal, informal sphere. Whereas men decided and enforced the temporal and spiritual law's penalties for illicit sex, many women made explicit reference to those punishments and proclaimed their own power to invoke them. Women found guilty of whoredom or bawdry at the sessions were regularly sentenced to be carried in a cart through specified neighbourhoods, and carting proved an institutional punishment that satisfied with its ritual humiliation and local visibility. The church courts had an equally powerful ritual, the penance that adulterers and fornicators were ordered to do in a white sheet, sometimes with a paper proclaiming their sins at their heads, and this furnished an equally fruitful source of insult.

Many defamers linked the two kinds of punishment so their insults called down a whole range of sanctions against the whore. Margery Hixwell and Phoebe Cartwright fell into an argument in Margery's shop in Fleet Street in 1613, and a woman in the shop next door heard Margery say to Phoebe "Thou art a quean and a wrymouth quean and I will make thee do penaunce in a white sheet and I will have thee carted out of the street".[30] Anne Johnson was sitting in her shop selling fruit with Marie Buckle's child in her arms, when Elizabeth Lee came past and

tooke the child and kissed yt sayeing Thow art a pretty child and Marie Buckle did not stand in a white sheete for nothinge, and . . . further that Alice Clerke . . . was a Bawde and she would cause her to be carted for a bawd, which words she . . . spake verie loude.[31]

Such institutional punishments had a clear neighbourhood character. The church courts' penance was staged in the parish church of the offender, and included asking forgiveness of the congregation. Carting brought the offender through selected neighbourhoods connected with her crime. It was these local contexts that gave such punishments their effect and, as in women's use of the idea of neighbourhood honesty to insult "whores", it was the local and communal context that enabled women to claim their part in the male judicial system. Punishments like carting or ordering the penance of a white sheet were the public manifestations of a formal, male legal institution; but in form they were closely related to community rituals in which women could claim more agency.[32] And whereas male constables, churchwardens, and local officials presented women for sexual misconduct to the secular and spiritual courts, the procedures of informal complaint and formal presentment by which discipline was invoked were also open to women. In the words of defamation, some women made an explicit and public claim to the power of local punishment.

This claim found its fullest expression when women were concerned with sexual misconduct not in the neighbourhood, but in the household. While many of the insults exchanged between neighbours or acquaintances used sexual words as a useful weapon rather than an accurate description of misconduct, and many others produced sexual stories from vague rumours, insult also provided a means of complaining publicly about more concrete situations. In one household situation, that of a husband's adultery, slander was particularly useful for women. In the idiom of sexual insult there was one phrase that had meaning only between women and it was used again and again: "thou art my husband's whore". Men were most unlikely to refer to even the potential of sexual relations between their wives and other men. But women complained of their husbands' adultery in long and specific detail, explaining its damages in sexual, emotional and financial terms, and directing the blame always onto other women. Joan Marwent said that Prudence Hosegood was "a base quean and that she kept company with her [Joan's] husband and what he got he spent uppon her and when he came from her he alwaies beat her".[33] In 1632 three men and women testified how, in midsummer of that year, Mary Sadd had come to Horne Alley to find the woman she called her husband's whore. Sara Saunderson, hearing "a greate noise" in the alley, went down "and finding a woeman standing at her husbands house door railing with a great company of people about her she . . . demanded of the woeman what she meant to kepe such a railing at her doore". Mary pointed at the house where Margaret Eddis lodged and replied "I would have the whore out of that house . . . for she is a base whore and a hospitall whore" and said that "her [Mary's] husband pawned her goades and . . . her childrens clothes to maintaine her [Margaret], and that she had rousted her out of one place already, and yf she staied but til tomorrow she would roust her out of this".[34]

Incidents like this reveal the prime concerns of women who suspected their husbands of adultery. Sexual, financial and physical injuries are evaluated with care to explain the disruption of marriage through the consequent disorganization of household consumption. If these women were making allegations they believed to be true, they were engaged in an endeavour with particular significance for women. Although both sexes could, in theory, sue their spouses for adultery at these same courts, women hardly ever did so. In legal practice, it was women's and not men's adultery that was culpable, and this was under-lined in 1650 when women's adultery was made a capital offence. Through defamation, women were able to invoke a public humiliation in response to adultery, and, following the legal system, they directed the blame not toward their husbands but toward other women. Mary Sadd's threats reveal a repertory of specific actions with which this blame could be pursued by women against the women they called their husbands' whores: going to confront them, defaming them in front of landladies, workmates or neighbours, "rousting" them out of lodgings and forcing them to move.

Less specific insults served as fuel for disputes that turn out to have had little to do with sex, where "whore" became a shorthand for much wider grievances. Because the sexual honesty of women had implica-tions for so many other spheres, from their speech to their financial honesty, it easily became the focus for disputes about a whole range of familial and community issues. Most often these disputes were con-cerned very closely with the organization of neighbourhood relations, between houses or within streets. Women's conflicts over children or servants, about shared fences or walls, or neighbourhood resources like water, shifted through defamation into sexual dispute. A typical exchange in 1629 reveals the steps through which this translation of dispute into the realm of the sexual was effected. Elizabeth White heard Rachel Townsend persuading her husband not to pay the debts he owed Elizabeth's husband, and to make Elizabeth instead "take her course by law". Confronting Rachel, she told her "she was a scurvy woman in soe doing"; Rachel responded "I am not so scurvy a woman as you for I never sould my daughters maydenhead for money", and she accused Elizabeth of taking £5 for her daughter's virginity.[35] Rachel transposed the financial issue into another accusation of economic misdealing; in this way, disputes that were fought out between women became focused on the sexual.

The slanderous words that women exchanged in cases like these functioned both as complaint about sexual misconduct and, much more broadly, as one step in wider neighbourhood conflicts. Slander has often been conflated with gossip, understood as a way of regulat-ing behaviour and social relations through the emphasis of group values, consonant with a larger moral system represented in various forms of contemporary culture, custom and law.[36] But the categorizations and condemnations through which slander was effected constituted a project more creative and more disruptive than this interpretation allows. The voicing of sexual slander was far more than a perpetuation of predefined condemnations of women's sexual sin. The word "whore" was used with no reference to the real financial–sexual exchanges of prostitution, and the stories that were woven around it referred to incidents from the concrete to the imaginary. It was used with imagination and elaboration: the words of slander defined with care the exact lines that delineated honesty. Clearly, in many cases, slander worked as a way of calling men or women to account for sexual grievances, and as such it was particularly important for women who had few other avenues of effective response. But slander worked very often against, not in concord with, prescribed moral values; more than normative regulation, it represented a creative offensive. Ostensibly concerned with the detailed mechanics of heterosexuality, slander was also about another kind of relationship, the social ties between women.[37] At this level, the established language of insult operated as a sign for other grievances or disputes, and when women spoke sexual insult they adopted a discourse whose idiom and meaning were already set up to focus on women's sexual faults, and used it towards their own ends. The exchanges of slander represent not normative regulation of heterosexuality, but disruptive interpersonal abuse in a larger social context.

More than sex, slander was about gender. Women who used the language of insult claimed for themselves responsibility for the definition of honest femininity. And, as women's unchastity had implications for their whole character, so defining sexual honesty meant defining womanhood. The constant repetition of the word whore, and its associated terms "jade", "bawd" and "quean", presented femininity through the terms of honesty, distributing blame so as to differentiate men from women and honest women from whores. If, as Judith Butler has argued, we understand gender not as a static division but a definition in progress, mobilized through the repetition of particular acts, sexual slander might productively be read as a set of representations and performances in which women defined honesty and femininity.[38]

In many ways, then, the language of slander offered particular linguistic powers to women, through which they asserted their verbal, physical and legal agency to judge and condemn other women. But such sexually explicit speech had its risks for women. Using sexual insult to prove other women dishonest left slanderers themselves open to charges of impropriety. Incontinence of speech and sexuality were directly linked in contemporary sources. In New England, although not in England, women found guilty of defamation could be punished by ducking in the same way as scolds: women's sexual slander was crime against verbal and social norms.[39]

The dangers of women's speech about sex were particularly apparent when women alleged seduction, assault or rape. Men regularly sued women for their attempts to fix sexual responsibility on them. Even the most conventional forms of such attempts were liable to interpretation as defamation. In 1613 Martha Day was sued by John Cowell for confessing to her midwife that he was the father of her illegitimate child, and for saying as he passed her that "I was his whore". More assertive claims and complaints against men's sexual misconduct were even more liable to prosecution as slander. Many involved complaints against masters, employers and landlords. In 1624 Susan Turton, a servant, protested to a local gentleman about her master's treatment of herself and her fellow servant: "I could not be in quiet for him for he would fynde me out in anie room of the house"; "he would be tousing and mousing[40] of them and urging them to follie and did take upp their clothes and would have had the carnal knowledge of their bodies"; "she was sometymes out of breath to resiste him and [he] did throwe her upon a bed and strived with her by pulling up of her Cloathes".[41] When her master heard of her complaints he sued her for defamation. Dorcas Newton accused her landlord William Garrad of "lying with her against her will in ye malt room at her dwelling house" and of making her pregnant. Her servant testified to hearing her cry out, and her husband brought a suit at common law against Garrad, yet Garrad was able to sue both Dorcas Newton and her servant for slander.[42] The early modern legal system offered most women little recourse against rape, particularly when men's stories were given more credit by economic and social advantage.[43]

The stories that men told about sex automatically received more credit than those of women. Accusations like these by women were pitted against this credit and against all the legal, literary and customary practices of penalizing sexual sin, where only women could be characterized as "whores", where only women were sued for adultery, and where men's honour never involved their sexual behaviour. Some men even defamed women for being "whores" with them, as one man did in 1587: "Thow . . . art an arrant whore, aye and I have lyen with thee and my friende too have lyen with the".[44] Men spoke with a self confidence about their own sexual behaviour that was entirely absent from women's speech. Women talked of their own sexual behaviour from a very different angle. Their references to men's misconduct were not so much insults as complaints that attempted to fix blame upon the men who had dishonoured them. With neither the rhetoric of insult nor the framework of sexual honour on which sexual insults of "whores" depended, women who accused men of sexual sin were redefining the very grounds of slander to insist upon a male culpabilty that was not enforceable in practice.[45]

From women's disputes in the street, I want to turn now to their confrontations in the courts. Like the language of defamation itself, the litigation by which victims complained of slander was a complicated transaction, involving a set of particular and gendered purposes, meanings and results, and functioning in a much broader context of personal and neighbourhood relations and disruptions. When women uttered slanderous words they set in motion a train of consequences that had a place in larger conflicts. After slanderous words were spoken their victims might complain of their abusers to other neighbours, to local gentry or to the clergy. Attempts might be made at informal and formal mediation to resolve the dispute; at the same time the dispute might spread as family, neighbours and friends took sides or repeated the slander. If every other attempt at settlement failed, the case might end up in the church courts.

The pursuit of words like these at law assumed that their effects were so damaging as to require public retraction and apology. The law of defamation posited a direct link between the words of temporal and spiritual slanders and their material effects. What were those effects, supposedly so powerful? Treatises on defamation discuss the various effects of slander on men but say little about its results for women. For men, slander posed a material threat to profession, inheritance, advancement or livelihood, and hence a man's good name was, as John Godolphin wrote, "Equilibrious with his Life".[46] The same kind of effects were understood to apply to women, but women's livelihood and "advancement" were conceived in a much narrower sphere than men's. In these texts women's material livelihood is affected not through their own earnings, but through their marriage prospects: marriage is women's only opportunity for the kind of advancement that makes up men's careers.[47]

At the church courts, witnesses for single women sometimes spoke of "discredit" to "a mayden . . . in the waie of preferment in marriage",[48] but in most cases, the victims were married and the conflation of "chastity" and "virginity" that was assumed by writers on honour could not apply. Instead, plaintiffs and litigants described how husbands might treat suspicion of their wives' infidelity as a threat to their marriage. When Margaret Smith was accused of saying to Anne Fanne "thou art a whore thou hast dishonested my house for I did see Hopkins and thee togither he with his breeches downe", one witness testified that Anne's husband had been so offended he would not let her lie with him and Anne had gone to her mother in the country.[49]

Other people spoke of the broader ways slander might damage women. As sexual behaviour had implications for women's whole characters, so, in theory, sexual insult could affect their whole lives. Witnesses for slandered women assessed the damage in phrases like "[she is] discredited in her reputation and calling to be so evil spoken of"; "upon the speaking of the said words [she] imagined very ill of the producent and she yet doth till she hath cleared herself"; "notwithstanding that [he] was great friends with the producent he did tell his ... wife that he was persuaded that the words about the falling out ... was a bad matter and very suspicious and as yet [he] cannot think well of the producent until she hath cleared herself".[50] The key words are "imagined", "persuaded" and "suspicious", suggesting the way reputation developed: influences and suspicions might be effective through their very imprecision.

In another case one witness attempted, in contrast, a material assessment of damage. In 1590 in Woodford, Essex, Elizabeth Dymsdale was reported to have called Susan More "an arrant whore ... that laye first with the master and then with the man in Mill Lane", and said "there were two dozen men witness to it". A witness to the words estimated the effects on Susan's reputation:

Susan Mores name is by reason of the saide scandalls uttered by Elizabeth Dymsdall as aforesaid spreaded about all the country thereabouts and she is talked about commonly amongst the neighbours, to the great discredit of the producent, And he verily thinketh the producent to have rather given twenty pounds than to have had such a speche goe upon her, as that the said speaches is gonne and doth yet goe and is talked of, for he saieth the producent hath byen taken by the neighbours hereabouts as a very honest woman.[51]

This is an unusually lengthy account of how defamatory speeches were perceived as circulating, damaging as they went. It would have been in the interests of plaintiffs to produce witnesses who could elaborate on the exact damage done by slander, but few did so. The effects of insult,

441

and its relationship to the actual operation of honour, remain elusive; the most substantive result of slander seems to be talk. Anne Pridgen, who sued Christopher Thompson in 1588 for calling her whore "in fleering manner", brought a witness to testify: "foreasmuch as people are commonly given to speake the worste of a woman whome they heere to be evell spoken of she thincketh the good name of Anne Pridgen to be impayred and hurte by the said Thompson".[52] Evil words lead to more evil words, nothing more substantial.

This consistent failure to mark out the exact effects of defamation suggests that more was at stake in litigation than the urge to defend a materially damaged reputation. Historians have tended to stress, through the evidence of slander, an idea of popular honour as both consonant with the standards of ecclesiastical and secular morality, and homogenous across differences of age, geography and class.[53] But the enterprise of defamation was as much about defining honesty as repeating predefined prescriptions: in practice, both women and men worked out codes of sexual honour that served certain purposes.[54] The ideas of honesty and morality that church law, household advice, sermons, or popular literature suggested did not dictate popular morality. They provided, rather, a set of ideals that could be invoked, adapted or transformed in daily life. The imprecisions of the effects of slander suggest the potential for accommodation, negotiation and reproduction of ideas about sex and honourable behaviour. Given this flexibility, the functions and meanings of litigation require a more fluid and complex analysis.

Litigation was in itself a potentially ambiguous response to slander. Some people insisted that it was dishonouring to let an insult go unchallenged. Elizabeth Aldeworth took Christopher Mortimer to court in 1572 for impugning her honesty by saying that she had been "called whore, and prevye whore to yor teth, and ye were gladd to take it quyetlye and put it upp". Elizabeth responded in defence of her record of litigation, saying she had sued a previous detractor to protect her name, and another neighbour intervened to support her.[55] But taking sexual insult to court was hardly consistent with the ideas of women's honour that provided the basis for defining honesty and dishonesty. Perfectly chaste and honourable women should not, technically, have discussed their sexual reputation in court; self-defence against accusations of whoredom could be seen as contributing to dishonour, in perpetuating the discourse about sex. While some women were accused of dishonesty for not pursuing defamation in the courts, others were attacked for being too litigious. One woman defended herself against such suggestions in 1610: "Had I had any more lawe than an honest woman should have?"[56] Clearly the argument about defending modesty by litigation could be used both ways.

Litigation did not provide a predictable, guaranteed result. If the case went to the judge, a final sentence was given which might impose a penance and a repayment of costs on the guilty party. But few slander cases got as far as this. Although most sentences were given in favour of the plaintiff, only one in five to one in three cases even called witnesses, and of these over 80 per cent were settled or abandoned long before their formal conclusion. The church courts always aimed to encourage reconciliation, more than confrontation. Ostensibly, slander suits enabled the regulation of disruptive speech and the reconciliation of dispute. Martin Ingram's work has shown how these functions might serve litigants who sought conciliation.[57] But the contexts of these cases suggest that the relationship between the court's aims and those of their clients might also be a less easy one. If litigants wanted conciliation, there were plenty of opportunities outside the court.[58] Many people mediated their disputes through older neighbours, gentry or ministers, making a formal settlement and sealing it with shared food, drink and forgiveness. Taking a case to court, litigants rejected all these informal methods and set in train instead a series of regular official confrontations between plaintiffs, defendants, witnesses and proctors. Invoking the process of litigation seems more likely to have perpetuated a dispute than to have ended it. It was in the light of this use of the courts to "maintain" local and personal disputes that contemporaries complained of the increase in slander litigation, noting a tendency to "flee to the Law out of malice and make the Courts of Justice maintainers of every small and vaine brabble".[59] Like slanderous speech, litigation could be a stage in the processes of social disruption. Increasingly in the seventeenth century it led not to conciliation, but to the spread of dispute, with defendants and witnesses starting new suits of their own in complex networks of litigation. Slander and its prosecution were occasions, not of regulation or reconciliation, but of disturbance and dysfunction.

The words and legal actions of slander were a familiar part of the fabric of local disputes. Sexual slander litigation was one of the main ways in which women in early modern London found themselves in contact with the courts: in the seventeenth century, even the smaller city parishes of 200 or so households sent one or two cases of defamation a year to the consistory court.[60] Other people were involved in presentments for disciplinary offences, or the different kinds of business that went to the other church courts and the secular law.[61] The mechanics and meanings of litigation and disciplinary justice were common currency in local dispute, and they were recognized as serving particular social purposes. In the exchanges and disputes that fill these records, men and women threaten each other with legal language, talking of citation and prosecution, presentments and defences, standing bail and giving witness; they refer often to other lawsuits in progress amongst other members of the neighbourhood; and they explain the kinds of tensions about friendliness, money or territory that were associated with such litigation. Women insist on their power over institutional sanctions, proclaiming their ability to get other women "carted" or sent to Bridewell; others complain that they have been cited, or presented, or fined "at the suit of" a woman.

As much as legitimate complaint, the processes of disciplinary justice were perceived and discussed as a means of pursuing personal grievances. In the summer of 1621, Ann Yarrington and Ann Croste fought each other through a combination of public rituals and formal actions. In August Ann Yarrington "unhosed" Ann Croste in the street, saying to her "I am shited [punning rudely on cited] to poules [St Pauls] with a shitacon and that at the sute of Ann Croste whoe is my husbands whore". She produced an old handkerchief from her pocket and continued "for this ould handkercher my husband . . . hath occupied her . . . seaven tymes".[62] In such disputes, legal processes were understood to be part of the armoury of weapons for local and personal confrontations. They were particularly significant weapons for women. The men who came to this court were increasingly likely to participate in local and parochial government, to be able to write and to have some form of contact with formal record keeping: but their wives could rarely sign their names, most often worked outside companies and were explicitly excluded from participation in local officialdom. Participation in litigation offered women a rare official, institutional weapon in the daily and occasional conflicts of their local lives.

It also presented the opportunity of establishing a permanent record of their words or actions. Witnesses and litigants at the court told stories of the contested events to a clerk who recorded them at length in an idiom that was partly shaped by court tradition but that also bore traces of the narrator. Once it was written down, they heard it repeated to the court's judge. For most women this was the only time their words would be recorded with such acute attention. It enabled them to rewrite the events of dispute in their own versions, in the context of their involvement. The resulting depositions can be long, detailed and original narratives.[63] Women told stories that focused on their part in the words and acts of dispute, describing the work they were doing, their relationship to the combatants and how they intervened: their statements focused on women's daily lives. They also repeated with care the offensive words of sexual insult, dwelling at length on the details that were meant to play no part in women's speech.

At every level, the occasions involved in defamation made it a verbal and legal process that enabled women to stake some specific claims to authority in the household and the community. While punishment for sexual crimes was enforced through the church courts and by men, women asserted their part through more informal confrontations and penalties. While men's adultery was rarely pursued through the courts as women's was, some women publicized their husbands' behaviour through the words of insult, centring the blame on other women in order to speak at loud and at length about their emotional and financial grievances. In the household, women used the vocabulary of insult to complain of their husbands' adultery; in the broader range of the neighbourhood they used their position as the figurehead of household honour to decide other women's honesty, buttressed by their traditional authority over pregnancy or the informal punishment of "whores". At the courts, litigation provided a way of shifting personal, semi-public disputes into a much broader, official sphere to which women rarely had access. And once at the courts, women were required to repeat in full, in a church, the sexual words of defamatory disputes and to tell personal stories that were preserved in the kind of written record with which early modern women, to our loss, only occasionally came into contact.

Notes

I am very grateful to the participants of the conference for their discussion of this paper, and to Lyndal Roper and Sarah Waters for their help in revising it.

1. T. E., *The lawes resolution of womens rights: or, the lawes provision for women* (London, 1632), pp. 6, 4.
2. Greater London RO DL/C 231 f. 40, Lewis con Record, 24/10/1628. All cases quoted are from the records of the London consistory and archdeaconry courts, held at the Greater London RO (series DL/C) and the Guildhall Library (MS. 9189), between 1566 and 1640, when this series of records ends. For clarity, in quotations from witness depositions I have expanded contractions; the omissions shown are mostly of repetitive legal formulae.
3. For studies of slander elsewhere see J. A. Sharpe, *Defamation and sexual slander*

in early modern England: the church courts at York, Borthwick Papers, 58 (York, 1980); M. Ingram, *Church courts, sex and marriage in England, 1570–1640* (Cambridge, 1987) ch. 10; A. Gregory, Slander accusations and social control in late sixteenth and early seventeenth century England, with particular reference to Rye (Sussex), DPhil thesis, University of Sussex, 1984; J. A. Thompson, "Her good name and credit": the reputation of women in seventeenth-century Devon, PhD thesis, University of Cincinnati, 1987. The situation in London before the Reformation is covered briefly in R. Wunderli, *London church courts and society before the Reformation* (Cambridge MA, 1981); and slander in eighteenth-century London is discussed in A. Clark, Whores and gossips: sexual reputation in London 1770–1825, in *Current issues in women's history*, eds A. Angerman *et al.* (London, 1989), pp. 231–48 and T. Meldrum, Defamation at the church courts: women and community control in London 1700–1745, MSc thesis, London School of Economics and Political Science, 1990. For the particular pattern of gender and defamation shaped by a different sex ratio, see M. B. Norton, Gender and defamation in seventeenth-century Maryland, *William and Mary Quarterly*, third series, 36, 1979, pp. 3–39.

4. DL/C 18 (1618), 22 (1624), 27 (1633).

5. In marriage cases at the consistory court (sued half the time by women), 36 per cent of witnesses were women; in defamation cases, 46 per cent were women, and in those cases fought between women, 60 per cent of witnesses were women. Figures obtained from consistory court deposition books, 1572–1640 (from a total of 5371 witnesses).

6. The set of records I am using, mostly relating to the consistory court but some to the archdeaconry court, runs from 1566 to 1640.

7. Sharpe, *Defamation and sexual slander*, pp. 24–6, 22; Ingram, *Church courts, sex and marriage*, pp. 165–6, 304–306, 313–16.

8. J. March, *Actions for slaunder, or, a methodicall collection under certain grounds of heads, of what words are actionable in the Law, and what not?* (Lodon, 1647), especially p. 4. Legally, spiritual defamation was defined by the element of malice in an imputation: *Auctoritate dei Patris* (1222), quoted in R. H. Helmholz, *Select cases on defamation to 1600* (London, 1985), pp. xxxii–xxxiv.

9. As a lesser London court the commissary, already did in the early sixteenth century, and as the consistory was to continue to do when it resumed business after the Civil War: Wunderli, *London church courts and society*, p. 76; Meldrum, Defamation at the church courts, p. 16.

10. On the experience of London in this period, see I. Archer, *The pursuit of stability: social relations in Elizabethan London* (Cambridge, 1991), ch. 4 and S. Rappaport, *Worlds within worlds: structures of life in sixteenth-century London* (Cambridge, 1989), ch. 3.

11. Calculated from the biographical information given by witnesses at this court, 1572–1640.

12. Many of these themes are common to slanderous language recorded elsewhere in Europe, in New England and in New France: see for comparison P. Burke, The art of insult in carly modern Italy, *Culture and History*, 2 (1987), pp. 68–79; M. B. Norton, Gender and defamation in seventeenth-century Maryland; P. N. Moogk, "Thieving buggers" and "stupid sluts": insults and popular

culture in New France, *William and Mary Quarterly*, third series, 36 (1979), pp. 524–47.

13. For examples of the advice literature, see W. Gouge, *Of domestical duties: eight treatises* (London, 1622); R. Clever, *A godlie form of household government: for the ordering of private families, according to the direction of Gods word* (London, 1598); and one of their principal sources, H. Bullinger *The christen state of matrimonye*, tr. Miles Coverdale (Antwerp, 1541). The best guide to this literature is K. M. Davies, Continuity and change in literary advice on marriage, in *Marriage and society: studies in the social history of marriage*, ed. R. B. Outhwaite (London, 1981), pp. 58–80. The book of Proverbs, in particular Proverbs 6. 12–19, is one of the few sources directly evident in the words of insult: one defamer referred explicitly to the words of Solomon. See DC/C 231, f. 236, Treat con Blyth, 22/10/1628.

14. DL/C 221, ff. 539ᵛ–540, Gibbons con Stronge, 15/11/1613. A wittall is a contented cuckold.

15. I. Archer's map of London bawdy houses shows a concentration around this area: Archer, *The pursuit of stability*, p. 212.

16. On such regulations see R. M. Karras, The regulation of brothels in later medieval England, in *Sisters and workers in the Middle Ages*, eds J. M. Bennett et al. (Chicago, 1989), pp. 97–127.

17. DL/C 230, ff. 16, 17, Banbridge con Tilbie, 27/1/1626.

18. On the female rituals of childbirth, see A. Wright, The ceremony of childbirth and its interpretation, and on women's experience of motherhood, and P. Crawford, The construction and experience of maternity in seventeenth-century England, both in *Women as mothers in pre-industrial England*, ed. V. Fildes (London, 1990), pp. 68–107 & 3–38.

19. Guildhall MS 9189/1, f. 130ᵛ, Maskall con Pomeroy, 6/2/1624.

20. DL/C 630, f. 290ᵛ, Office ad promotionem Layton con Francis, 11/11/1634.

21. DL/C 222, f. 1290, Barwicke con Chaddocke, 19/4/1613; DL/C 221, f. 1319 *et seq.*, Pett con Chaddocke, 21/10/1613.

22. See for example DL/C 630, f. 330ᵛ, Bowles con Heale, 21/1/1634.

23. DL/C 233, f. 229, Wood con Fanch, 18/11/1631.

24. Mocking processions. D. Underdown, The taming of the scold: the enforcement of patriarchal authority in early modern England, in *Order and disorder in early modern England*, cds A. Fletcher & J. Stevenson (Cambridge, 1985), pp. 116–36; M. Ingram, Ridings, rough music and mocking rhymes in early modern England, in *Popular culture in seventeenth-century England* (London & Sydney, 1985), pp. 166–97.

25. DL/C 231, f. 28ᵛ, Brosse con Ripon, 7/7/1628.

26. DL/C 220, ff. 540ᵛ–48ᵛ, Alsop con Fullham, 15/6/1611.

27. See for example the ballad "Have among you good women", *The Roxburghe Ballads* I, no. 146, ed. W. Chappell & J. W. Ebsworth (London & Hertford, 1871–95); DL/C 225, f. 351, Berry con Squire et alios, 16/11/1618.

28. DL/C 226/III, ff. 41–2, Bird con Hickman, 17/11/1619.

29. Syphilis, for example, was perceived as affecting men's penises, but women's noses; many sexual insults go into exact detail about infection and damage.

30. DL/C 221, f. 1189ᵛ, Cartwright con Hixwell, 8/6/1613.

31. DL/C 226/IV, f. 28, Clerke con Lee, 26/1/1620.

32. These different kinds of response existed uncomfortably together, as M. Ingram points out (*Church courts, sex and marriage*, p. 163); nevertheless, they relied on similar kinds of symbolism and were equated by a number of these defamers.

33. DL/C 230, f. 225^v, Hosegood con Marwent, 24/11/1626. Prudence also called Joan a whore, either earlier, or in retaliation: *ibid.*, f. 240^v, Marwent con Hosegood, 6/12/1626.

34. Guildhall MS. 9057/1, f. 12, Eddis con Sadd, 1/12/1632.

35. DL/C 231, ff. 321–2, White con Townsend, 4/2/1629.

36. J. A. Sharpe, *Defamation and sexual slander*, p. 19; M. B. Norton, Gender and defamation in seventeenth-century Maryland, pp. 35–9; R. Thompson, "Holy watchfulness" and communal conformism: the functions of defamation in early New England communities, *New England Quarterly*, 56, 1983, pp. 504–22: pp. 520–22.

37. No London slanders mention homosexuality at all; in the case of men this may have been because sodomy was a temporal more than a spiritual crime, and allegations of it were punishable at the secular courts.

38. J. Butler, *Gender trouble: feminism and the subversion of identity* (London, 1991), pp. 139–41.

39. C. A. Bowler, Carted whores and white shrouded apologies: slander in the county courts of seventeenth-century Virginia, *The Virginia Magazine of History and Biography*, 85, 1977, pp. 411–26: p. 413.

40. Pulling them about, mishandling them.

41. DL/C 229, ff. 89, 90, Holmes con Turton, 3/12/1624.

42. DL/C 232, f. 156^v, Garrad con Newton, 1630 [n.d.]; *ibid.*, f. 286, Garrad con Gilder, 2/2/1630.

43. N. Bashar, Rape in England between 1550 and 1700, in *The sexual dynamics of history*, ed. London Feminist History Group (London, 1983), pp. 28–42.

44. DL/C 213, p. 154, Banbury con Harman, 15/6/1587.

45. See also Norton, Gender and defamation in seventeenth-century Maryland.

46. J. Godolphin, *Reportorium canonicum* (London, 1678), p. 516.

47. Godolphin, *Reportorium canonicum*, p. 517; W. Vaughan, *The spirit of detraction, coniured and convicted in seven circles* (London, 1611), p. 346.

48. DL/C 227, f. 175, Matthewe con Brittanne, 26/10/1620.

49. DL/C 219, ff. 245–6^v, Fanne con Smith, 31/10/1610.

50. DL/C 228, f. 71, Ashley con Gibbes, 8/11/1621; DL/C 214, pp. 95, 83, Holstead con Wharton, 25 and 13/11/1591. "Producent" is the church courts' term for plaintiff, i.e. the woman who was slandered.

51. DL/C 214, pp. 18–19, More con Dymsdale, 12/6/1591. The dispute was continued in a subsequent case, Elizabeth Dymcross con John More (*ibid.*, p. 21), in which Susan's husband was accused of attacking Elizabeth Dymsdale both physically and verbally and she of throwing a pail of burning coals at him.

52. DL/C 213, pp. 432, 445, Pridgen con Thompson, 9 and 12/11/1588. "Fleering" means sneering.

53. Sharpe, *Defamation and sexual slander*, pp. 3, 24–8; S. D. Amussen, *An ordered society: gender and class in early modern England* (Oxford, 1988), pp. 130–31; Ingram, *Church courts, sex and marriage*, pp. 166, 303; R. A. Houlbrooke, *Church courts and the people during the English Reformation, 1520–1570* (Oxford, 1979), p. 87.

54. A. Clark's work on eithteenth-century London shows women defining to a certain extent their own codes of sexual morality: Clark, *Whores and gossips*.

55. DL/C 211/1, f. 105, Aldeworth con Mortimer, 13/11/1572.

56. DL/C 219, f. 174ᵛ, Greenrise con Pinge, 15/6/1610.

57. Ingram, *Church courts, sex and marriage*, pp. 317–18.

58. See J. A. Sharpe, "Such disagreement betwyx neighbours": litigation and human relations in early modern England, in *Disputes and settlements: law and human relations in the West*, ed. J. Bossy (Cambridge, 1983), pp. 167–87.

59. J. March, *Actions for slaunder* (London, 1647), p. 4.

60. Calculated from the books and deposition books for 1631–40, GLRO DL/C 27, 232–35.

61. On involvement in the secular law, see C. Herrup, *The common peace: participation and the criminal law in seventeenth-century England* (Cambridge, 1987), and R. B. Shoemaker, *Prosecution and punishment: petty crime and the law in London and rural Middlesex, c.1660–1725* (Cambridge, 1991), chs 2, 8.

62. DL/C 228, ff. 95ᵛ–96, Croste con Yarrington, 23/11/1621.

63. On these narratives and their meanings see L. Gowing, Women, sex and honour: the London church courts, 1572–1640, PhD thesis, University of London, 1993, pp. 172–207.

17 Finding a Voice: Vittoria Archilei and the Florentine 'New Music'

Tim Carter

In Florence towards the end of the sixteenth century there arose a new school of singing and new styles of solo song that had a profound influence on the course of music in the Baroque era. The so-called 'new music' embraced both opera and chamber song (monody); it emerged in response to a Humanist-inspired interest in the music of Classical Antiquity, to a dissatisfaction with the affective limitations of contemporary compositional techniques (in particular, multi-voice polyphony) and to a sense that music could and should achieve new dramatic, rhetorical, and emotional power in the service of its text.[1] It also reflected a fascination with the virtuoso singer. At the head of these developments were two virtuoso tenors and composers who were both colleagues and rivals among the musicians of the Medici court, Giulio Caccini (1551–1618) and Jacopo Peri (1561–1633). The 'new music' was not exclusively Florentine—important developments in Naples, Rome, and Ferrara also played their part—and it was less the result of a coherent aesthetic programme than of the collusion and collision of ideas and techniques stemming from a number of patrons, poets, composers, and performers. Yet Florence created the hot-house environment in which the 'new music' could take seed and grow before spreading its branches through the rest of Italy and beyond, enmeshing itself firmly in the musical styles and practices of the seventeenth century.

Caccini had been brought to Florence from Rome in 1565 and spent the rest of his life in Medici service, writing theatrical and chamber music, and heading with his wife and daughters a renowned performing group that the Medici had established on the model of the famed *concerto di donne* of Ferrara, an ensemble of women (predominantly) singers performing elaborately embellished works to instrumental accompaniment with which Duke Alfonso II d'Este amazed select visitors to his court. Caccini published two important collections of his music, *Le nuove musiche* ('New songs') in 1602 and *Nuove musiche e nuova maniera di scriverle* ('New songs and a new way of writing them out') in 1614. Both prints attempted through prose description and through musical notation to convey both the details and the flavour of the new styles of singing that Caccini did so much to promote. But such verbal and visual means were ill-equipped to convey the subtleties of an essentially aural phenomenon. So how are we to recover the sounds and silences of a too dim and too distant past?

For all his efforts in and through print to proclaim his status as a composer, Caccini was first and foremost a performer. And inevitably he was associated with other performers whose achievements both influenced and were influenced by him. That composition and performance were intimately related—both processes feeding off each other—is clear from the preface to *Le nuove musiche* and also from Caccini's letters. For example, on 14 February 1596, he sent a new song to Virginio Orsini, Duke of Bracciano, in Rome:

I have composed Your Most Illustrious Excellency's madrigal with those notes which I have recognized and known to be more suitable to express the affect of the words, and [I have] accompanied it also with those *passaggi* which I have imagined might give delight to Your Excellency when you will hear it. And if you were to say to me that you desired that the madrigal should be sung by Signora Vittoria, Your Excellency should know that while I made it, she heard it several times, and I finished it according to her taste. Since I am leaving today for Pisa—and since Your Excellency has still not arrived—I have decided (for the better) to give it to her, so that Your Excellency will not have the chance to hear it [sung] by others, which might also serve me by art, for with the sweetness of her song she makes my works appear what in themselves they are not.[2]

Here we have a typical emphasis on the way in which the 'new music' was designed to 'express the affect of the words', with tasteful *passaggi* (virtuoso embellishments) aimed at delighting the listener. But Caccini's notion that his song was 'made' over a period of time in collaboration with another singer, and completed according to the taste of that singer, is more intriguing: so, too, is his concern that his patron might hear his madrigal sung by the wrong performer. This focuses our attention less on the work as a finished text than on the notion of composition being, in a very real sense, some manner of performance, fulfilled only by a song's realization in sound.

The singer with whom Caccini left his madrigal, and who sang his music so well, was the virtuoso soprano Vittoria Archilei, the prize musical possession of the Medici court.[3] She was one of a number of gifted sopranos in high demand in the late sixteenth and early seventeenth centuries given the new emphasis on virtuoso singing in the north Italian courts of Ferrara, Mantua, and Florence. Like Laura Peverara, Ippolita Recupito, Adriana Basile, and Francesca Caccini—to name only the most obvious—Archilei played a key role in the contemporary musical world, delighting her patrons with the beauties of her voice. Like them, too, she occupied a difficult position within the patriarchal societies of their time. These singers were expected to cultivate the graces and talents of the well-rounded courtier—and could often be regarded and rewarded as such—but they remained servants at the whim of their employer. As women, too, their role as 'courtiers' could easily shift to that of the courtesan—their sex was fair game in the male power-play that made up the politics of prestige—and in both professional and private terms, they were subject to the men (patrons, husbands, sons) that dominated their space and controlled their lives.

Archilei's husband, Antonio, is a rather shadowy figure. Born Antonio Vimercati in Albano in late 1541 or 1542, he moved to Rome at the age of 9 and from his boyhood was employed as a musician by Cardinal Alessandro Sforza dei conti di Santa Fiora (appointed cardinal in 1565, he died in 1581); hence he was occasionally styled Antonio di Santa Fiore, although for an as yet unknown reason he also took the name Archilei at least by 1577. In 1576, if not before, he was known to Cardinal Ferdinando de' Medici—second son of Grand Duke Cosimo de' Medici and resident in Rome during the reign of his elder brother, Grand Duke Francesco—and Ferdinando may well have taken him on as a musician after Cardinal Sforza's death. In 1582 Antonio married Vittoria di Francesco Concarini in Rome: she may have been placed with him as an apprentice singer, which was a standard training strategy of the period.[4] It was, one assumes, a marriage of convenience (engineered by Cardinal Ferdinando?) as with most marriages between musicians at this time: for a patron, the best way of guaranteeing a woman's status and continued services was to have her married to another employee.[5]

Vittoria Archilei performed in Florence in 1584 during the festivities for the wedding of Vincenzo Gonzaga and Eleonora de' Medici, and her virtuosity was paid none-too-veiled homage in a madrigal set to music by Luca Marenzio and published that same year.[6] Her elder son, Ottavio, was born on 26 December 1585; other children included Ferdinando, who was to become a priest, and three daughters, Emilia (buried on 29 August 1597), Maria (a nun in S. Matteo in 1630), and Cleria (employed at court to serve the princesses from 14 April 1607). In 1587 Cardinal Ferdinando de' Medici returned to Florence to take the throne as Grand Duke on the untimely (and suspicious) death of his brother, Francesco (and his second wife, Bianca Capello), and Antonio, and Vittoria also moved there, with a nurse (Archilei may have just given birth) and a pupil (Margherita; probably the same Margherita who became Caccini's second wife). They became closely associated with another musician who had been linked to Cardinal Ferdinando in Rome and who himself moved to Florence around the same time to head the new Grand Duke's musical establishment, Emilio de' Cavalieri (Archilei's daughter Emilia was presumably named after him). Vittoria, Antonio, and Margherita performed in the grandiose festivities for the wedding of Grand Duke Ferdinando and Christine of Lorraine in 1589, and she moved the audience to tears in Cavalieri's *La disperatione di Fileno*, a pastoral entertainment with music staged at court in 1590. Her association with Cavalieri was to cause her problems in the subsequent decade given his fluctuating fortunes at court (he was strongly disliked by his Florentine colleagues). But her skills were well recognized by the Grand Duke: she had a high monthly salary of ten *scudi*, plus four *scudi* from the privy purse (and on his death in 1609, Grand Duke Ferdinando left her an additional pension of twelve *scudi* per month)—Antonio also earned twelve *scudi* a month.

Vittoria and Antonio were back in Rome in the winter of 1593–4. We have accounts (largely from Cavalieri) of her performing in the chief musical circles in Rome, not least before Filippo Neri (i.e. St Philip Neri):

Vittoria was in the room of Messer Filippo [Neri], and [Cardinal] Cusano was also present. She sang a Benedictus, but they wanted to hear *spagnole* and *galanterie*. There were many people there, and in the end Messer Filippo had a priest of the Vallicella dance. He did the *canario* and the *pedrolino*, and Vittoria said to me that he danced stupendously and must practise frequently. Messer Filippo then gave the benediction to several, notably to Vittoria, and so that she would remember him he gave her a good slap and made her promise to come back another time.[7]

It was doubtless during this stay in Rome that Archilei came into contact with the Spanish composer Sebastian Raval, who noted in his *Madrigali a tre voci* (Rome, 1595) that during a recent visit to Rome he had composed many of the pieces therein for 'Signora Vittoria Romana, most excellent musician of the Most Serene Grand Duke of Tuscany', with all the 'artifice and charm' required for such a virtuoso

453

singer (he also dedicated the first madrigal in the book, 'Vezzosetta fanciulla', to her).[8] We have regular notice of Archilei singing in Florence in the late 1590s (in particular, in the annual performance of lamentations in Pisa, where the court traditionally spent Lent). However, she does not seem to have been used for the wedding festivities of Maria de' Medici and Henry IV of France held in Florence in October 1600 and which included the première of the first opera to have survived complete, Jacopo Peri's *Euridice* (to a libretto by Ottavio Rinuccini): Cavalieri was somewhat under a cloud due to competition at court from Giulio Caccini and the lutenist Antonio Naldi, and Archilei appears to have suffered with him. She also seems to have been ill, perhaps losing for a time her most precious possession, her voice.[9]

In November 1601 Antonio and Vittoria were back in Rome, having been sent on loan to Cardinal Montalto. On 11 January 1602 Cavalieri thanked a court secretary for official permission to have Archilei sing in his house in Rome, and on 18 January he reported:

Cardinal Montalto was with [Cardinal del] Monte four days ago, and he said to me: 'I have a thought, this Lent twice a week, to have the litanies sung in my chapel, and so that Signora Vittoria should sing something, I have taken advantage of you . . . for without you, things will go badly'. I replied *alla cortegiana*, without saying either yes or no, but I do not want more troubles.[10]

However, in a letter to Grand Duchess Cristina of 28 January 1602 Archilei reveals herself beset by a number of worries:

Most Serene Madame

I find myself today with the Most Illustrious Signor Cardinal Montalto, in whose house I have landed for that time I have to be here in Rome. It seems to me that I serve the same person as the Most Serene Grand Duke and Your Most Serene Highness given that his Most Illustrious Lordship is so great a friend and servant of your Most Serene house, and since from His Most Illustrious Lordship I receive daily many favours. And with this good opportunity, I would hope through the grace and favour of Your Most Serene Highness to obtain some ecclesiastical preferment for the person of Ferdinando, my son and a vassal of Your Most Serene Highness, since it was you who placed him in this seminary where he is continually advancing himself to make himself worthy in *belles lettres* and in good manners, wishing to be a priest. I beseech you for the love of God that you might do me the favour of allowing me still some little time to be able to stay here serving His Most Illustrious Lordship, for with this I am sure that I will easily obtain what I desire, when, however, will be recommended by the kind hand of Your Most Serene Highness my said son, who, when he has finished his studies, will be able like we ourselves to serve Your Most Serene Highness in everything that he will know he can be good at in serving. Most Serene Lady, I have spent all the years of my youth in the service of the greater rulers of Christendom, and also I believe that I am not among the worst of my profession. Today I find myself in such straits that if by chance my husband should die, not only could I not support my family, but I would have great difficulty in being able to live on my own, since I can say to you truthfully that I have nothing else in this world other than that small dowry left me by the happy memory of my first employer—I attribute this only to my ill fortune and not to any failing on the part of my Most Serene patrons—because all the others who have served during my time, from the least to the greatest, have all been rewarded in some manner, except poor Vittoria [*la povera Vittoria*], who has so exclaimed with her poor voice [*la povera voce*] which has now come to annoy all the world, and it [?she] can scarce any longer be good for such an end. Now finding itself [?herself] old and poor, whence thinking well about its [?my] fate while it [?she] still has a little breath, with the grace and favour of Your Most Serene Highness it [?she] wishes to see whether at this good juncture one can grant it [?her] now at least some little pension for its [?her] son, which will not be difficult so long as with your good grace I might stay here a few months. In the meanwhile, if it will please Your Most Serene Highness that its [?her] salary should continue, so much the greater will be the debt; and if even this will not seem [right] to be granted, in every way it [?she] will remain most satisfied and most content so long, however, as everything follows with all the good grace of the Most Serene Grand Duke and Your Most Serene Highness, to whom, with that greater humility that it [?she] can, it [?she] bows and kisses your gown, praying always to the eternal and great God for your health. From Rome, 28 January 1602.

> Your Most Serene and Most Beneficent Highness's
> Most Humble Servant
> Vittoria Archilei[11]

This sad letter speaks eloquently of the trials and tribulations of a female singer, used and abused by the forces of patronage; as other documents also make clear, Archilei performs and indeed lives only at the behest of her employers, who treat her like a chattel. The letter is difficult to translate, not least because of the confusion caused by Archilei's playing off 'la voce' and 'la Vittoria', giving her voice a true *persona*. But of course, there is no real confusion here: to all intents and purposes, Archilei was her voice and nothing more, and once her voice was in decline (as she seems to suggest here), she had little left.

Vittoria Archilei performed in the festivities for the wedding of Prince Cosimo de' Medici and Maria Magdalena of Austria in October 1608—where the Florentine composer Marco da Gagliano, perhaps out of native pride, said that she surpassed Ippolita Recupito, a virtuoso soprano in the service of Cardinal Montalto and brought to

Florence specially for the occasion[12]—and on 14 February 1611 she took part in a *mascherata* staged at court for which she had also written some of her own music: this is the only notice we have of her as a 'composer'.[13] But she feared competition from younger virtuoso singers such as Adriana Basile: as Cardinal Ferdinando Gonzaga wrote on 16 June 1610, 'Vittoria has not wanted to let herself be heard, having heard that Signora Adriana is in the palace'.[14] Her son Ottavio was always a problem (in 1608, he was arrested for inviting women of ill repute into his carriage), and her husband died in 1612 (he was buried in the Florentine church of S. Michele on 14 November). We have records of her through the 1610s (for example, writing on behalf of her son Ottavio) and taking part in music at court (in what capacity remains unclear). But her career seems to have continued its downward turn. We do not even know her date of death; Giambattista Marino wrote a sonnet 'In morte di Vittoria cantatrice famosa' published in his *Della lira* of 1614;[15] Lorenzo Parigi seems to suggest that she was dead by 1618 (although we have letters from her from 1619); and the Roman commentator Vincenzo Giustiniani speaks of her in the past tense in around 1628. However, the Medici court made one and the same monthly payment to a Vittoria Archilei through to the early 1640s. But even if she was still alive then, she had in effect died with her voice, however many years before.[16] Certainly that was all she was remembered for. According to Giustiniani (*c*.1628), she was 'the famous Vittoria, with whom has almost originated the true method of singing for females'.[17] And the Florentine theorist and composer Severo Bonini said (*c*.1650): 'In this new style sang with singular affect, her chief talent esteemed by each professor of the art, Signora Vittoria Archilei, a Roman citizen but employed by their highnesses of Florence . . . who, having spread forth heavenly glory for herself, then at a late age gave her spirit to God with this eternal fame'.[18]

What chance is there of recovering a voice so lauded in its time? We do in fact have one seeming musical record of an actual performance by her, in Cristofano Malvezzi's print of the music for the spectacular *intermedi* performed with Girolamo Bargagli's comedy *La pellegrina* as the centrepiece of the festivities celebrating the wedding of Grand Duke Ferdinando de' Medici and Christine of Lorraine in 1589.[19] Vittoria Archilei took part in at least four numbers, including the first two of the fifth *intermedio* ('Io che l'onde raffreno', accompanied by an *arciviolata lira* played by Alessandro Striggio plus a lute and chitarrone, and a solo for Archilei and a trio for Vittoria, Antonio, and their pupil Margherita within 'E noi con questa bella'; in both cases the music was by Malvezzi) and the trios (sung with Lucia Caccini and Margherita) interspersed in Emilio de' Cavalieri's final *ballo* at the end of the sixth *intermedio* (the three women also danced and played instruments). Her main contribution to the 1589 *intermedi*, however, took pride of place at the beginning: she sang the very first song 'Dalle più alte sfere' representing the allegorical figure Harmony (accompanied by two chitarroni played by Antonio Naldi and Antonio Archilei, the latter the composer of the music).[20] As she descended on a cloud machine, playing a *leuto grosso*, her voice was clearly intended to invoke the harmony of the spheres now brought into the service of Medici glorification.

Vittoria Archilei's virtuoso song is meticulously notated in the print with full embellishments. To be sure, this is only a representation of a performance; its relationship to how the music actually sounded is surely tenuous, as with all these notated performances that became something of a vogue in music prints of the late sixteenth and early seventeenth centuries.[21] But even as a representation, it is revealing of the kinds of sounds that Archilei was thought to produce. The extensive embellishments and *passaggi* clearly have an emblematic significance—this is Harmony singing—confirming the long-established association between virtuosity and supernatural powers. They reach a peak towards the end of the setting, as the last line of Giovanni de' Bardi's text ('qual voi, nova Minerva e forte Alcide'; 'as you, new Minerva and brave Alcides'), and particularly 'forte Alcide' (i.e. Grand Duke Ferdinando), ring forth in a phenomenal display of vocal expertise. But there is also an alternative, shorter ending to the song, and one that uses embellishments in a slightly different way, with more focused *passaggi* emphasizing echo-effects and more elegant dotted rhythms. We do not know which of these endings Archilei in fact sang (or whether she did both).[22]

This is the kind of performance that Grand Duke Ferdinando must have so much enjoyed from his favourite singer. But its various types of embellishments, especially in the two contrasted endings, seem to reflect different schools of embellished singing, one Roman and the other Florentine. Thus, the short ending seems much more in keeping with the ideas expressed in the preface to Caccini's *Le nuove musiche* (1602): Caccini took objection to ill-used *passaggi* on unaccented syllables as merely 'a kind of tickling of the ears' and sought a more restrained, text-expressive approach to embellishment.[23] We might also find in the shorter ending what Caccini claimed in the dedication of his opera *Euridice* (Florence: Giorgio Marescotti, 1600)[24] was 'the new manner of *passaggi* and *raddoppiate* invented by me, which Vittoria Archilei uses in singing my works now for a long time, a singer of such excellence as is revealed by the clamour of her fame'.[25]

Here, and somewhat typically, Caccini is less generous to Archilei in print than he was in his private correspondence (compare the letter to Virginio Orsini given above). But he was not alone in mentioning her in his dedication. Even though she seems to have been excluded from the 1600 wedding festivities, her name was bandied about by all the protagonists in early Florentine opera (Caccini, Cavalieri, Peri) as, it seems, a weapon in their competitive claims for precedence in inventing a new style of music capable of expressing the text and arousing the emotions. Peri, for example, was careful to note the approval awarded the musical recitative in his first opera (now mostly lost), *Dafne* (1598), by 'that famous lady whom one may call the Euterpe of our age, Signora Vittoria Archilei';[26] Euterpe is, of course, the Muse of lyric poetry. But his argument then takes a significant turn. Archilei

has always made worthy of her singing my musical works, adorning them not only with those *gruppi* and with those long roulades [*giri di voce*] both simple and double which by the liveliness of her wit have now been rediscovered, more to obey the practice of our times than because she judges to consist in them the beauty and force of our singing, but also those delights and graces [*vaghezze, e leggiadrie*] which cannot be written down, and being written down cannot be learned from writings.[27]

There is a great deal between the lines here, mostly reflecting Peri's antagonism towards Giulio Caccini: witness the claims that Archilei had rediscovered 'those *gruppi* and . . . long roulades both simple and double . . . by the liveliness of her wit' (Caccini claimed that they were his invention in the dedication of his own *Euridice*), and that one could not write down and/or learn from such writings anything concerning the art of graceful singing (Caccini had already promised the text on vocal technique that became the preface to *Le nuove musiche*).

More interesting for present purposes, however, is Peri's claim that Archilei does not approve of such embellishments, and uses them only 'to obey the practice of our times'. Indeed, there is evidence to suggest that she preferred a different type of song, one more faithful to the text and which made fewer extravagant technical demands on a voice that, as she was already learning to her cost, was hard-pressed by the contemporary vogue for virtuoso singing. If the songs of Caccini's *Le nuove musiche* reveal one strand of the Florentine 'new music', another is offered by the more serious, less ornate style of composers such as

Peri and the visiting virtuoso Sigismondo d'India, drawing more on expressive techniques developed within the tradition of the polyphonic madrigal. In the preface to his *Le musiche* of 1609, d'India notes his presence in Florence the previous year while preparations were under-way for the festivities celebrating the wedding of Prince Cosimo de' Medici and Maria Magdalena of Austria, when

I myself sang some [of my songs] to Signora Vittoria Archilei, musician of His Most Serene Highness and most excellent above all other singers, who as most intelligent concerning this profession exhorted me to pursue this my manner, saying that she had never heard a style which had such force and which at the same time expounded the conceit [of the text] with such diversity of notes [and] variety of harmony, and with so new a style of embellishment. And not content with the approval for my songs which she also expressed verbally, while the chief singers of the world were rehearsing in the house of Signor Giulio Romano [Caccini] the comedies and entertainments for the wedding of His Highness she also wanted, having rehearsed them herself, to honour them with the sweetness and mellifluousness of her singing.[28]

D'India's 'manner' is described elsewhere in his preface as consisting less of embellishments than of unusual intervals, striking dissonances, and other text-expressive techniques, placing the emphasis more on music's emotional power than on virtuoso display.

Jacopo Peri was strongly influenced by d'India in both stylistic and aesthetic terms.[29] And in the first of his numerous letters to the Mantuan patron Prince (later Cardinal, then Duke) Ferdinando Gonzaga of 11 August 1607 we again find Vittoria Archilei supporting the work of a composer:

Most Illustrious and Most Excellent Lord, My Most Singular Patron

I send back to Your Most Illustrious Excellency the madrigal with the music written by me with love. And if it is of little worth, blame the weakness of my talent, but not the readiness of my soul, for in truth I have never written music to words more readily than to these, because it was commanded to me by you. And I very well know that you have around you most excellent men as well as you yourself [and so] could have done it perfectly in every way, [yet] you deigned to do me this favour. And if some time you will give me something [else] to do, I will receive it as a particular sign of grace, because I do not desire anything but to have the occasion to show myself to be a true and devoted servant, both according to my duty as from the particular inclination that I have to serve you, and I say this sincerely. Finding myself by chance yesterday with Signora Vittoria, I let her hear it, and because it seemed to her appropriate for her voice, since she pressed me for it, I could not fail to give her a copy, hoping that this is by Your Excellency's good grace. I also made the recommendations to the Camerata [= the Accademia degli Elevati] and they send you a thousand thanks, and I with them, [and] with all emotion and reverence we kiss your gown, praying that the Lord God might grant you the summit of his grace. From Florence, 11 August 1607.

Your Most Illustrious Excellency's
Most Affectionate and Most Obliged Servant
Jacopo Peri[30]

The madrigal that turned out to be appropriate for Archilei's voice seems to have been to words by Prince Ferdinando (a sometime poet) or by someone close to him.[31] It may, of course, be lost today. But among the songs included in Peri's collection of songs published as *Le varie musiche* in 1609,[32] there are settings of four poetic madrigals, 'Ho visto al mio dolore' to a text by Alessandro Striggio the younger (the Mantuan librettist of Claudio Monteverdi's first opera, *Orfeo*),[33] 'O durezza di ferro', 'Lungi dal vostro lume', and 'Solitario augellino'. The vocal lines of 'Ho visto al mio dolore' and 'Lungi dal vostro lume' are given in the soprano clef (hence for a female or male soprano voice), and those of the other two songs in the tenor clef. The cleffing may or may not be significant—these songs were often transposed by an octave from soprano to tenor ranges or vice versa—but it is at least tempting to suggest that the madrigal sent to Prince Ferdinando Gonzaga in August 1607 was 'Lungi dal vostro lume' ('Ho visto al mio dolore' was to a text by a Mantuan poet, but it probably dates from 1606 or earlier). This is a remarkably expressive song, with no elaborate embellishments—only a short scale in semiquavers to paint 'venti' and a delicate *passaggio* for the final 'dolore'—but instead relying on lyricism, chromaticism, and dissonances (including a striking chain of parallel sevenths between voice and bass) to make its effect. But whether or not 'Lungi dal vostro lume' was the piece sent to Ferdinando Gonzaga, it is entirely typical of the style that Peri, following d'India, appears to have been cultivating in the second half of the first decade of the new century. It is also a style that seems to have been admired, perhaps even inspired, by Vittoria Archilei.

We do not know whether Archilei now preferred this style of writing simply because her voice was no longer as agile as it had once been, or whether out of a genuine sense that here, and not in Caccini's style of song, lay the true expressive path of the 'new music'. Perhaps, too, the sorry events of the 1600 festivities and their aftermath—with Caccini eventually claiming the limelight for his own singing *donne*—also had their effect. It may well be no coincidence that in an undated sonnet in manuscipt in praise of Archilei, the Florentine poet Ottavio Rinuccini felt it necessary offer Giulio Caccini a gentle reminder of her remarkable abilities as a singer:

Ove scioglie Vittoria a i dolce accenti
la nobil voce, ch'auree corde scote
al vario suon delle soavi note,
Giulio, arrestano il piè fiumi e torrenti.
Piegon' l'orride fronti i monti algenti
ch'il furor' d'Aquilone in van percote
e le fere stupir vedrest' immote
e bei lumi del ciel rotar' più lenti,
ma l'alme, e cori poi, pregio più degno,
ogni terren desìo fugato e spento,
se ne volan' al ciel col suo bel canto,
né più soave per l'ondoso regno
temprò Sirena mai mortal' concento
in verde bosco filomena ha pianto.[34]

(Where Vittoria loosens to the sweet accents | her noble voice, and strikes golden strings | to the varied sound of the mellow notes, | Giulio, rivers and torrents halt their foot. || The freezing mountains bend their fearsome brow | which Aquilon's fury strikes in vain, | and you would see the wild animals fixed in awe, | and the beautiful lights of heaven rotate more slowly. || But souls, and then hearts, a more worthy prize, | with all earthly desire gone and extinguished, | fly to heaven with her beautiful song. || Nor more sweetly in the watery kingdom | did ever a siren temper a mortal harmony[:] | in a verdant wood, Philomel has wept.)

With its references to Archilei's performances in the 1589 *intermedi* (as Harmony and a siren) and perhaps in the now-lost *La disperatione di Fileno* (did Philomel a p p e a r here?)—and also with the overtones of Orphic power—Rinuccini's sonnet transcends conventional poetic conceits to offer a heart-felt tribute to a virtuoso singer whom many felt was the most distinguished of her time. And indeed, for all her own fears about her voice, there was more to Archilei's contribution to musical life in the period than just a striking vocal technique. We have already seen how many composers—Raval, Cavalieri, Caccini, Peri, d'India—acknowledged both publically and privately their debt as composers to her abilities and encouragement. Of all those involved in the remarkable flowering of song in late Renaissance Florence, Vittoria Archilei is perhaps the least known, the one most silenced by the passing of time: she had neither the power nor the medium to preserve the fruits of a lifetime serving 'the greater rulers in Christendom'. But by giving her voice again, we can catch a glimpse both of the creative energies let loose by composers and performers in the Florentine 'new music', and of the place of one woman in a remarkable period in music history.

Notes

This essay is a revision of a paper presented at the conference *Femmes musiciennes aux XVIᵉ et XVIIᵉ siècles*, Centre de Musique Ancienne, Tours, November 1993. It depends largely on the documentation provided in Warren Kirkendale's magisterial *The Court Musicians in Florence during the Principate of the Medici, with a Reconstruction of the Artistic Establishment* ('Historiae musicae cultores' biblioteca, lxi; Florence: Olschki, 1993); Kirkendale assembles documents previously published and a great many newly discovered, if with little of the interpretation attempted here. My text also draws some inspiration from Anthony Newcomb, 'Courtesans, Muses, or Musicians? Professional Women Musicians in Sixteenth-Century Italy', in Jane Bowers and Judith Tick (eds.), *Women Making Music: The Western Art Tradition, 1150–1950* (Urbana and Chicago: University of Illinois Press [London: Macmillan], 1986), 90–115. All translations are my own except where indicated.

1. I discuss the broad significance of these changes in my *Music in Late Renaissance & Early Baroque Italy* (London: Batsford, 1992), *passim*. The term 'new music' is in fact somewhat anachronistic—it derives from a misprision of the title of Giulio Caccini's first book of songs (see below)—although it has become widely used and certainly reflects Caccini's perception of, and ambitions for, his work.

2. Rome, Conservatorio di Musica S. Cecilia, Carteggio Orsini, 106, fo. 109, given in Kirkendale, *The Court Musicians in Florence during the Principate of the Medici*, 132, 264: 'Ho composto il madrigale di V[ostra] E[ccellenza] Ill[ustrissi]ma con quelle note che ho conosciuto, e saputo esser più a proposito per esprimere l'affetto delle parole, et accompagnatolo anco di quei passaggi, ch'io mi sono immaginato che possino dar' gusto a V[ostra] E[ccellenza] quando li sentirà. Et che mi disse che desiderava, che'l madrigale fusse cantato dalla S[igno]ra Vittoria; saprà V[ostra] E[ccellenza] che mentre l'ho fatto ella l'ha udito più volte, e conforme al suo gusto l'ho finito, perché partendo hoggi per Pisa né essendo V[ostra] E[ccellenza] mai venuta, ho preso resolutione (per lo meglio) di darlo a lei, acciò V[ostra] E[ccellenza] non habbia occasione di udirlo da altri, che mi potia ancor' servir per arte, poi ché facendo lei con la dolcezza del suo canto apparir' le cose mie quello, che per si [*recte* se] stesse non sono.' It is not clear whether 'Your Most Illustrious Excellency's madrigal' is actually by Orsini—members of the nobility were often lesser poets—or has just been sent to Caccini by him.

3. Vittoria Archilei and her husband Antonio have biographical entries in Kirkendale, *The Court Musicians in Florence during the Principate of the Medici*, 261–76.

4. Musicians were often required to take young trainees into their households whether or not at a patron's expense: Giulio Caccini did so often in Florence—see Tim Carter, 'Giulio Caccini (1551–1618): New Facts, New Music', *Studi musicali*, xvi (1987), 13–31, at p. 21—as did the *maestro della musica di camera*

of Duke Vincenzo Gonzaga of Mantua, Claudio Monteverdi with the young singer Caterina Martinelli. For these and other examples, see also Stuart Reiner, 'La vag'Angioletta (and others): i', *Analecta musicologica*, xiv (1974), 26–88; John Walter Hill, *Roman Monody in the Circle of Cardinal Montalto* (Oxford: Clarendon Press, 1997), *passim*.

5. Giulio Caccini's two wives, Lucia Gagnolanti and Margherita Benevoli della Scala (for the latter, see below), were both singers of some distinction, and likewise, his daughters Francesca and Settimia were both married to court musicians. Francesca Caccini is to be the subject of a major biography by Suzanne Cusick; for the moment, see eadem, 'Of Women, Music, and Power: A Model from Seicento Florence', in Ruth A. Solie (ed.), *Musicology and Difference: Gender and Sexuality in Musical Scholarship* (Berkeley, Los Angeles and London: University of California Press, 1993), 281–304; '"Thinking from Women's Lives": Francesca Caccini after 1627', in Kimberly Marshall (ed.), *Rediscovering the Muses: Women's Musical Traditions* (Boston: Northeastern University Press, 1993), 206–25. Cusick's remarkable texts are required reading for anyone interested in gender issues in this period. For Settimia Caccini and her husband Alessandro Ghivizzani, see also Kirkendale, *The Court Musicians in Florence during the Principate of the Medici*, 333–46; Tim Carter, 'Intriguing Laments: Sigismondo d'India, Claudio Monteverdi, and Dido *alla parmigiana* (1628)', *Journal of the American Musicological Society*, xlix (1996), 32–69, esp. p. 50 n. 37, on how musician husbands claimed ownership of performing wives, and even authorship of their compositions.

6. 'Cedan l'antiche tue chiare vittorie' in Marenzio's *Il secondo libro de madrigali a sei voci* (Venice: Gardano, 1584); presumably Marenzio was seeking favour from Cardinal Ferdinando de' Medici.

7. Trans. in Claude V. Palisca, 'Musical Asides in the Diplomatic Correspondence of Emilio de' Cavalieri', *The Musical Quarterly*, xlix (1963), 339–55, repr. in idem, *Studies in the History of Italian Music and Music Theory* (Oxford: Clarendon Press, 1994), 389–407, at p. 397. For the original, see Kirkendale, *The Court Musicians in Florence during the Principate of the Medici*, 266.

8. Kirkendale, *The Court Musicians in Florence during the Principate of the Medici*, 272: 'con l'occasione della Sign[ora] Vittoria Romana musica eccellentissima del Serenissimo Gran Duca di Toscana, trovandomi pochi tempi sono in Roma, gli compose molti di questi madrigali a 3 voci, con l'artifitio e vaghezza che potè e richiedeva a simile virtuosa'.

9. A letter of 14 March 1599 to the Grand Duchess suggests that she was (temporarily?) unable to sing for an unspecified occasion, although she says that her husband is working with Jacopo Peri to see what might be performed; see ibid. 267.

10. Ibid. 268: 'Il Cardinale Montalto, fu da Monte quattro giorni sono, et me disse: "io ho pensiero, questa quaresima due volte la settimana; nella mia cappella far cantare le letanie; et poiché la S[igno]ra Vittoria, canti qual cosa; ho fatto capitale de voi . . . poiché senza voi, si farria male"; io le risposi alla cortegiana; senza dir, né sì, né no; ma io non voglio più fatighe'.

11. Ibid. 268–9: 'Ser[enissi]ma Mad[a]ma | Io me ritrovo ogi apresso l'Ill[ustrissi]mo S[ign]or Card[ina]l[e] Mont'Alto, nella qual' casa mi son buttata per quel' tempo che ho da star qua in Roma parendomi di servire la istessa persona del Ser[enissi]mo Gran Duca e di V[ostra] A[ltezza]

463

S[erenissima] per essere S[ua] S[ignoria] Ill[ustrissi]ma tanto amico e servitore di quella Ser[enissi]ma Casa, e perché da S[ua] S[ignoria] Ill[ustrissi]ma io ricevo giornalmente molte gratie e che con questa bona occasione potrei sperare mediante la gratia et favore di V[ostra] A[ltezza] S[erenissima] ottener' qualche bene ecclesiastico in persona di Ferdinando mio figliuolo e creatura di V[ostra] A[ltezza] S[erenissima] per haverlo lei fatto mettere in questo luogo del seminario dove che va tuttavia havanzandosi per farsi meritevole nelle bone lettere e nelli boni costumi, volendo esser' sacerdote. La suplico che per amor' de Idio vogli farmi gratia di concedermi ancora qualche poco tempo da poter' star' qua servendo S[ua] S[ignoria] Ill[ustrissi]ma che con questo io mi assicuro facilmente di ottenere quanto desidero quando però dalla benigna mano di V[ostra] A[ltezza] S[erenissima] gli venghi raccomandato detto mio figliuolo il quale poi quando harrà finito il suo studio come noi medesimi potrà servire V[ostra] A[ltezza] S[erenissima] in tutto quello che conoscerà possi esser buono per servire. Ser[enissi]ma Sig[no]ra, io ho speso tutti gl'anni della mia gioventù in servitio delli magior' principi di Cristianità e anco credo non essere stata delle ultime nella mia professione. Me ritrovo ogi in tal termine che se a sorte mi mancasse il mio marito, non solo non potrei sostentare la mia famiglia ma durarei una gran fatiga a poter viver io sola, potendo dir' veramente di non haver altro in questo mondo che quella poca dote che mi diede la buona memoria del mio primo padrone, attribuendo tutto questo solamente a la mia mala fortuna e non per mancamento alcuno delli miei Ser[enissi]mi padroni, perché tutti gl'altri che anno servito del tempo mio, dal minimo sin'al magiore, tutti sono stati in qualche maniera remunerati, eccetto la povera Vittoria, la quale à esclamato tanto con la sua povera voce che ormai è venuta in fastidio a tutto il mondo e poco più può esser' bona per tal'effetto: retrovandosi ogi mai vecchia e povera, onde che pensando molto bene al fatto suo essendoci ancora un poco di fiato con la gratia e favore di V[ostra] A[ltezza] S[erenissima] vol' vedere in questa bona congentura se puole accomodar' almeno di qualche pensioncella per hora questo suo figliuolo, il che non gli serrà dificile ogni volta che con la sua bona gratia possi stare ancor' qualche mese qua. Nel qual tempo si piacerà all'A[ltezza] V[ostra] S[erenissima] che gli corra la sua provesione tanto magior' sarrà l'obligo; e se anco questo non gli parerà di concederglelo a ogni modo restarà sodisfattissimo e contentissimo ogni volta però che tutto segua con tutta la intiera buona gratia del' Ser[enissi]mo Gran Duca e di V[ostra] A[ltezza] S[erenissima], alli quali, con quella magior' umiltà che pole, se gl'inclina e gli basa la veste pregando sempre l'eterno e magno idio per la loro salute di Roma li 28 di gennaro 1602. | D[i] V[ostra] A[ltezza] Ser[enissi]ma e Benig[nissi]ma | Serva umilissima | Vittoria Archilei.'

12. For these entertainments, see Tim Carter, 'A Florentine Wedding of 1608', *Acta musicologica*, lv (1983), 89–107.

13. Kirkendale, *The Court Musicians in Florence during the Principate of the Medici*, 220, 265. The text was by Ottavio Rinuccini and the music mostly by Jacopo Peri, save four *ottava rima* stanzas which were 'composte musicalmente dall'istesse donne che le cantarono' (Vittoria Archilei and Francesca and Settimia Caccini), a chorus by Marco da Gagliano, and instrumental music by Lorenzo Allegri (see ibid. 220). Archilei's stanza, 'Donne, dal cui sembiante', was sung by her 'con la solita sua grazia, e voce angelica' (ibid. 265).

14. Ibid. 265: 'Vittoria non si è voluta lassar sentire, sentito che hebbe la S[igno]ra Adriana in palazzo'.

15. Given in ibid. 274–5; Kirkendale also gives three poems by Guarini probably in praise of Vittoria Archilei (ibid. 273–4).

16. The situation is remarkably similar to Francesca Caccini, whose supposed 'death' in 1627—shortly after the real death of her first husband, Giovanni Battista Signorini—in fact marked her second marriage to a Lucchese patron and a subsequent career in Lucca; see Cusick, ' "Thinking from Women's Lives" '.

17. Trans. in Carol MacClintock, *Hercole Bottrigari*, *'Il Desiderio . . . '*; Vincenzo Giustiniani, *'Discorso sopra la musica'* (Musicological Studies and Documents, ix; American Institute of Musicology, 1962), 70; for the original, see Kirkendale, *The Court Musicians in Florence during the Principate of the Medici*, 275. It is doubtless significant that Giustiniani also mentions prominently the fact that she was married to Antonio.

18. *Discorsi e regoli sovra la musica et il contrappunto*, given in ibid. 275: 'In questo nuovo stile cantò con affetto singulare, suo principal talento stimato da ciascuno professore dell'arte, la Sig[no]ra Vittoria Archilei per nazzione romana stipendiata da queste altezze di Firenze . . . la quale doppo haver sparso di sé celeste gloria, ormai d'età matura rese lo spirito a Dio con questa eterna fama'.

19. *Intermedi et concerti, fatti per la commedia rappresentata in Firenze nelle nozze del serenissimo don Ferdinando Medici, e madama Christiana di Lorena, gran duchi di Toscana* (Venice: Giacomo Vincenti, 1591); see D. P. Walker (ed.), *Les Fêtes du mariage de Ferdinand de Médicis et de Christine de Lorraine, Florence 1589*, i. *Musique des intermèdes de 'La pellegrina'* (Paris: CNRS, 1963; repr. 1986). For the entertainments in general, see James M. Saslow, *The Medici Wedding of 1589: Florentine Festival as 'Theatrum mundi'* (New Haven and London: Yale University Press, 1996).

20. The music is attributed to Emilio de' Cavalieri in other sources; see Walker (ed.), *Les Fêtes du mariage de Ferdinand de Médicis et de Christine de Lorraine, Florence 1589*, p. xxxvii. Again (compare note 5 above), this may reflect a husband's right to 'own' the music sung by his wife.

21. As I shall be discussing in 'Printing the "New Music" ', in Kate van Orden (ed.), *Music and the Cultures of Print* (New York and London: Garland, forthcoming).

22. The 1591 print has a number of problems as a supposedly 'faithful' documentary record of the 1589 *intermedi*; see the critical apparatus in Walker (ed.), *Les Fêtes du mariage de Ferdinand de Médicis et de Christine de Lorraine, Florence 1589*.

23. This important preface is discussed and translated in H. Wiley Hitchcock (ed.), *Giulio Caccini: 'Le nuove musiche' (1602)* (Recent Researches in the Music of the Baroque Era, ix; Madison: A-R Editions, 1970).

24. Caccini's version of *Euridice* (to the same libretto by Ottavio Rinuccini as set by Jacopo Peri) was printed to pre-empt the publication of Peri's score (which appeared some three months later); Peri's, however, was the one performed during the 1600 festivities, although Caccini managed to insert in that performance some of his own music (specifically, for the female singers under his control). For some of the problems experienced during these festivities, see Tim Carter, *'Non occorre nominare tanti musici*: Private Patronage and Public

Ceremony in Late Sixteenth-Century Florence', *I Tatti Studies: Essays in the Renaissance*, iv (1991), 89–104.

25. 'la nuova maniera de passaggi, e raddoppiate inventati da me i quali hora adopera cantando l'opere mie già è molto tempo, Vittoria Archillei, cantatrice di quella eccellenza, che mostra il grido della sua fama'; trans. in Zygmunt Szweykowski and Tim Carter (eds.), *Composing Opera: From 'Dafne' to 'Ulisse errante'* (Practica musica, ii; Kraków: Musica Iagellonica, 1994), 39. The term 'raddoppiate' ('redoublings') is unclear; one possible meaning is the echo-effects such as are seen in the shorter ending of 'Dalle più alte sfere'.

26. In his preface to *Le musiche . . . sopra 'L'Euridice'* (Florence: Giorgio Marescotti, 1600 [= 1601]), trans. in Szweykowski and Carter (eds.), *Composing Opera*, 29: 'quella famosa, che si puo chiamare Euterpe dell'età nostra, la Signora Vettoria Archilei . . .'.

27. Loc. cit. (trans. adapted): '. . . la quale ha sempre fatte degne del cantar suo le Musiche mie, adornandole, non pure di quei gruppi, e di quei lunghi giri di voce, semplici, e doppi, che dalla vivezza dell'ingegno suo son ritrovati ad ogn'hora, piu per ubbidire all'uso de' nostri tempi, che, perch['ella stimi consistere in essi la bellezza, e la forza del nostro cantare, ma anco di quelle, e vaghezze, e leggiadrie, che non si possono scrivere, e scrivendole non s'imparano da gli scritti'.

28. Sigismondo d'India, *Le musiche da cantar solo* (Milan: Heirs of Simone Tini and Filippo Lomazzo, 1609), preface 'Al cortese lettore': 'Et nel mio ritorno à Firenze io stesso ne cantai alcune alla Signora Vittoria Archilei Musica di quella Sereniss[ima] Altezza, & sopra ogn'altra Cantatrice eccellentissima, la quale come intelligentissima di questa professione mi esortò à seguire questa mia maniera, dicendo non haver' udito stile, c'havesse tanta forza, & che insieme spiegasse il concetto con tal diversità di corde, varietà d'armonia, & con sì nova maniera di passeggiare; & non contenta dei favori ch'anco fece à bocca alle musiche mie, mentre le prime Cantatrici del Mondo in casa del Sig[nor] Giulio Romano si concertavano per le Comedie, & feste delle nozze di quell'Altezza, volse anco concertatole da se honorarle con la dolcezza, & soavità del suo canto'.

29. See the discussion in Tim Carter, *Jacopo Peri (1561–1633): His Life and Works* (Outstanding Dissertations in Music from British Universities; New York and London: Garland, 1989), 216–21.

30. Mantua, Archivio di Stato, Autogr. 6, fo. 45, given in Kirkendale, *The Court Musicians in Florence during the Principate of the Medici*, 214: 'Ill[ustrissi]mo et Ecc[ellentissi]mo Sig[no]r[e] e Padrone mio Singular[issi]mo | Rimando a V[ostra] E[ccellenza] Ill[ustrissi]ma el madrigale con la musica composta da me con amore. E se sarà di poco valore, ne incolpi la debolezza dell'ingegno mio, ma non già la prontezza dell'animo che in vero non ho mai fatto musica sopra parole più volentieri che queste, perché da lei mi vien comandato. E benissimo conosco che havendo appresso di sé huomini eccellentissimi oltre che lei medesima lo poteva fare perfettamente in ogni modo si sia degnata farmi questo favore e se qualche volta mi darà da far qualcosa, lo riceverò per grazia particolare, poi ché non desidero altro che havere occasione di mostrarmele vero e devoto suo servitore, sì per mio debito, come per inclinazione particolare che ho di servirla; e questo lo dico sinceramente. Trovandomi a sorte ieri con la Sig[no]ra Vittoria gnene feci sentire e per[ciò] gli parve

a proposito per la sua voce facendomene instanzia non potrei mancare dargnene copia sperando sia con buona grazia di V[ostra] E[ccellenza]; feci anco le raccomandazioni alla camerata, e gli rendon mille grazie, et io con loro con ogni affetto, e reverenza gli baciamo la veste, pregando il Sig[no]re Dio gli conceda il colmo delle sue grazie di Firenze li xi d'Agosto 1607. | D[i] V[ostra] E[ccellenza] Ill[ustrissi]ma | Aff[ettuosissi]mo et obligat[issi]mo ser[vito]re | Jacopo Peri.'

31. I assume that Peri uses the term 'madrigal' in its specific sense, as a freely constructed lyric poem in seven- and eleven-syllable lines in contrast with fixed forms such as the sonnet, *ottava rima*, *terza rima*, etc.

32. For the music, see Tim Carter (ed.), *Jacopo Peri: 'Le varie musiche' and Other Songs* (Recent Researches in the Music of the Baroque Era, l; Madison: A-R Editions, 1985).

33. The song was first published in Girolamo Montesardo's collection *L'allegre notti di Fiorenza . . . dove intervengono i piu eccellenti musici di detta città: musiche a una, due, tre, quattro, e cinque voci* (Venice: Angelo Gardano & Fratelli, 1608), the contents of which appear to date from Montesardo's visit to Florence in 1606; see Tim Carter, '*Serate musicali* in Early Seventeenth-Century Florence: Girolamo Montesardo's *L'allegre notti di Fiorenza* (1608)', in Andrew Morrogh, Fiorella Superbi Gioffredi, Piero Morselli, and Eve Borsook (eds.), *Renaissance Studies in Honor of Craig Hugh Smyth* (2 vols; Florence: Giunti Barbèra, 1985), i. 555–68.

34. Florence, Biblioteca Nazionale Centrale, Fondo Palatino 249, fo. 136ᵛ, given in Kirkendale, *The Court Musicians in Florence during the Principate of the Medici*, 273.

Bibliography

The following bibliography does not pretend to be comprehensive, and the categories into which it is divided are meant to be helpful rather than discrete. Where an interdisciplinary collection has been cited, the essays in it have not been given individual entries, so the reader is advised that a collection which falls under the heading (for example) of 'Sexuality and the Body' may nevertheless contain essays on literature or art, and vice versa.

Literature and Humanist Learning

Beilin, Elaine, *Redeeming Eve: Women Writers of the English Renaissance* (Princeton: Princeton University Press, 1987).

Benson, Pamela Joseph, *The Invention of the Renaissance Woman: The Challenge of Female Independence in the Literature and Thought of Italy and England* (University Park: Pennsylvania State University Press, 1992).

Brant, Clare, and Purkiss, Diane (eds.), *Women, Texts and Histories, 1575–1760* (London: Routledge, 1992).

Chedgzoy, Kate, Hansen, Melanie, and Trill, Suzanne (eds.), *Voicing Women: Gender and Sexuality in Early Modern Writing* (Keele: Keele University Press, 1996).

Ezell, Margaret, *The Patriarch's Wife: Literary Evidence and the History of the Family* (Chapel Hill: University of North Carolina Press, 1987).

Ferguson, Margaret, Quilligan, Maureen, and Vickers, Nancy (eds.), *Rewriting the Renaissance: The Discourses of Sexual Difference in Early Modern Europe* (Chicago: University of Chicago Press, 1986).

Harvey, Elizabeth, *Ventriloquized Voices: Feminist Theory and English Renaissance Texts* (London: Routledge, 1992).

Henderson, Katherine Usher, and McManus, Barbara F. (eds.), *Half Humankind: Contexts and Texts of the Controversy about Women in England, 1540–1640* (Urbana and Chicago: University of Illinois Press, 1985).

Hendricks, Margo, and Parker, Patricia (eds.), *Women, "Race" and Writing in the Early Modern Period* (London: Routledge, 1994).

Hobby, Elaine, *Virtue of Necessity: Englishwomen's Writings 1646–1688* (London: Virago Press, 1988).

Hull, Suzanne W., *Chaste, Silent and Obedient: English Books for Women, 1475–1640* (San Marino, Calif.: Huntington Library, 1982).

Hutson, Lorna, *The Usurer's Daughter: Male Friendship and Fictions of Women in Sixteenth Century England* (London: Routledge, 1994).

Jardine, Lisa, *Still Harping on Daughters: Women and Drama in the Age of Shakespeare* (Hassocks, Sussex: Harvester Press, 1983).

Jed, Stephanie H., *Chaste Thinking: The Rape of Lucretia and the Birth of Humanism* (Bloomington: Indiana University Press, 1988).

Jones, Anne Rosalind, *The Currency of Eros: Women's Love Lyric in Europe 1540–1620* (Bloomington: Indiana University Press: 1990).

King, Margaret L., *Women of the Renaissance* (Chicago: University of Chicago Press, 1991).

——and Rabil, Albert (eds.), *Her Immaculate Hand: Selected Works by and about the Woman Humanists of Quattrocento Italy* (Binghampton, NY: Medieval and Renaissance Texts and Studies, 1993).

Labalme, Patricia (ed.), *Beyond their Sex: Learned Women of the European Past* (New York: New York University Press, 1980).

Lewalski, Barbara, *Writing Women in Jacobean England* (Cambridge, Mass.: Harvard University Press, 1993).

Migiel, Marilyn, and Schiesari, Juliana (eds.), *Refiguring Woman: Perspectives on the Italian Renaissance* (Ithaca, NY: Cornell University Press, 1991).

Rose, Mary Beth (ed.), *Women of the Middle Ages and the Renaissance: Literary and Historical Perspectives* (Syracuse, NY: Syracuse University Press, 1986).

Rummel, Erika (ed.), *Erasmus on Women* (Toronto: University of Toronto Press, 1996).

Schiesari, Juliana, *The Gendering of Melancholia: Feminism, Psychoanalysis and the Symbolics of Loss in Renaisssance Literature* (Ithaca, NY and London: Cornell University Press, 1992).

Wilson, Katherina M. (ed.), *Women Writers of the Renaissance and Reformation* (Athens and London: University of Georgia Press).

Woodbridge, Linda, *Women and the English Renaissance: Literature and the Nature of Womenkind 1540–1620* (Urbana: University of Illinois Press, 1984).

Religion and Reformation

Bainton, Roland H., *Women of the Reformation from Spain to Scandinavia* (Minneapolis, Minn.: Augsburg Publishing House, 1977).

Berg, Christine, and Berry, Philippa, ' "Spiritual Whoredom": An Essay on Female Prophets in the Seventeenth Century', in Francis Barker (ed.), *1642: Literature and Power in the Seventeenth Century* (Colchester: University of Essex, 1981), 37–54.

Crawford, Patricia, *Women and Religion in England 1500–1720* (New York: Routledge, 1993).

Davis, Natalie, *Society and Culture in Early Modern France* (Stanford, Calif.: Stanford University Press, 1975).

Hannay, Margaret P. (ed.), *Silent but for the Word: Tudor Women as Patrons, Translators and Writers of Religious Works* (Kent, Oh.: Kent State University Press, 1985).

Mack, Phyllis, *Visionary Women: Ecstatic Prophesy in Seventeenth Century England* (Berkeley: University of California Press, 1992).

Roper, Lyndal, *The Holy Household: Women and Morals in Reformation Augsburg* (Oxford: Clarendon Press, 1989).

Thomas, Keith, 'Women and the Civil War Sects', *Past and Present*, 13 (1958), 42–62.

Political Thought

Harris, Barbara J., 'Women and Politics in Early Tudor England', *The Historical Journal*, 33 (1990), 259–81.

Hinds, Hilary, *God's Englishwomen: Seventeenth Century Radical Sectarian Writing and Feminist Criticism* (Manchester: Manchester University Press, 1996).

Jordan, Constance, *Renaissance Feminism: Literary Texts and Political Models* (Ithaca, NY: Cornell University Press, 1990).

Oikin, Susan Moller, *Women in Western Political Thought* (Princeton: Princeton University Press, 1979).

Pateman, Carole, *The Sexual Contract* (Oxford: Polity Press, 1988).

——and Shanley, Mary Lyndon (eds.), *Feminist Interpretations and Political Theory* (Oxford: Polity Press, 1991).

Schochet, Gordon J., *The Authoritarian Family and Political Attitudes in 17th Century England: Patriarchalism in Political Thought* (Oxford: Basil Blackwell, 1975).

Smith, Hilda L. (ed.), *Women Writers and the Early Modern British Political Tradition* (Cambridge: Cambridge University Press, 1998).

Work, Family, and the Law

Brown, Judith C., and Davis, Robert C. (eds.), *Gender and Society in Renaissance Italy* (Longman: 1998).

Cahn, Susan, *Industry of Devotion: The Transformation of Women's Work in England, 1500–1660* (New York: Columbia University Press, 1987).

Clark, Alice, *The Working Life of Women in the Seventeenth Century* (London: Routledge, 1919; rpt. 1968, 1982, 1992).

Cox, Virginia, 'The Single Self: Feminist Thought and the Marriage Market in Early Modern Venice', *Renaissance Quarterly*, 48 (1995), 513–81.

Dean, Trevor, and Lowe, K. J. P. (eds.), *Marriage in Renaissance Italy* (Cambridge: Cambridge University Press, 1997).

Erickson, Amy, *Women and Property in Early Modern England* (London and New York: Routledge, 1993).

Gowing, Laura, *Domestic Dangers: Women, Words and Sex in Early Modern London* (Oxford: Clarendon Press, 1996).

Hafter, Daryl (ed.), *European Women and Preindustrial Craft* (Bloomington: Indiana University Press, 1995).

Hanawalt, Barbara (ed.), *Women and Work in Preindustrial Europe* (Bloomington: Indiana University Press, 1986).

Hufton, Olwen, *The Prospect Before Her: A History of Women in Western Europe*, i. *1500–1800* (London: HarperCollins, 1995).

Kermode, Jenny, and Walker, Garthine (eds.), *Women, Crime and the Courts in Early Modern England* (London: University College, 1994).

Klapisch-Zuber, Christiane, *Women, Family and Ritual in Renaissance Italy*, trans. Lydia G. Cochrane (Chicago: University of Chicago Press, 1987).

Prior, Mary (ed.) *Women in English Society 1500–1800* (London and New York, Routledge, 1985).

Wiesner, Merry E., *Working Women in Renaissance Germany* (New Brunswick, NJ: Rutgers University Press, 1986).

—— *Women and Gender in Early Modern Europe* (Cambridge: Cambridge University Press, 1993).

—— *Gender, Church and State in Early Modern Germany* (Longman: 1998).

Music

Bowers, Jane, 'The Emergence of Women Composers in Italy 1566–1700', in Jane Bowers and Judith Tick (eds.), *Women Making Music: The Western Art Tradition, 1150–1950* (London: Macmillan Press, 1986), 116–67.

Cusick, Suzanne, 'Of Women, Music, and Power: A Model from Seicento Florence', in Ruth Solie (ed.), *Musicology and Difference* (Berkeley: University of California Press, 1993), 281–304.

—— ' "Thinking from Women's Lives": Francesca Caccini after 1627', in Kimberly Marshall (ed.), *Rediscovering the Muses: Women's Musical Traditions* (Boston: Northeastern University Press, 1993), 206–26.

Macneil, Anne, 'The Divine Madness of Isabella Andreini', *Journal of the Royal Musical Association*, 120 (1995), 195–215.

Neuls-Bates, Carol, *Women in Music: An Anthology of Source Readings from the Middle Ages to the Present* (Boston: Northeastern University Press, 1996).

Newcomb, Anthony, 'Courtesans, Muses or Musicians? Professional Women Musicians in Sixteenth Century Italy', in Jane Bowers and Judith Tick (eds.), *Women Making Music: The Western Art Tradition, 1150–1950* (London: Macmillan Press, 1986), 90–115.

Pendle, Karin (ed.), *Women and Music: A History* (Bloomington: Indiana University Press, 1991).

Art History

Broude, Norma, and Garrard, Mary (eds.), *Feminism and Art History: Questioning the Litany* (New York: Harper and Row, 1982).

471

Cropper, Elizabeth, 'On Beautiful Women, Pamigianino, *Petrarchismo*, and the Vernacular Style', *Art Bulletin*, 58 (1976), 374–94.

Fine, Elsa Honig, *Women and Art: A History of Women Painters and Sculptors from the Renaissance to the 20th Century* (Montclair, NJ and London: Allanheld & Schram/Prior, 1978).

Garrard, Mary, *Artemisia Gentileschi* (Princeton: Princeton University Press, 1988).

——'Artemisia Gentileschi's Self-Portrait as the Allegory of Painting', *Art Bulletin*, 62 (1980), 97–112.

——'Here's Looking at Me: Sofonisba Anguissola and the Problem of the Woman Artist', *Renaissance Quarterly*, 47 (1994), 556–622.

Gouma-Peterson, Thalia, and Matthews, Patricia, 'The Feminist Critique of Art History', *Art Bulletin*, 69 (1986), 326–57.

Jacobs, Fredrika H., *Defining the Renaissance Virtuosa: Women Artists and the Language of Art History and Criticism* (Cambridge: Cambridge University Press, 1998).

——'Woman's Capacity to Create: The Unusual Case of Sophonisba Anguissola', *Renaissance Quarterly*, 47 (1994), 74–101.

Schutte, Anne Jacobson, 'Irene di Spilimbergo: The Image of a Creative Woman in Late Renaissance Italy', *Renaissance Quarterly*, 44 (1991), 42–61.

Sohm, Philip, 'Gendered Style in Italian Art Criticism from Michelangelo to Mavasia', *Renaissance Quarterly*, 48 (1995), 759–808.

Sexuality and the Body

Brown, Judith C., *Immodest Acts: The Life of a Lesbian Nun in Renaissance Italy* (Oxford: Oxford University Press, 1986).

Foucault, Michel, *The History of Sexuality*, trans. Robert Hurley (3 vols.; New York: Vintage, 1988–9).

Fradenberg, Louise, and Freccero, Carla (eds.), *Premodern Sexualities* (New York and London: Routledge, 1996).

Goldberg, Jonathan (ed.), *Queering the Renaissance* (Durham, NC: Duke University Press, 1994).

Hillman, David, and Mazzio, Carla (eds.), *The Body in Parts: Fantasies of Corporeality in Early Modern Europe* (New York and London: Routledge, 1997).

Laqueur, Thomas, *Making Sex: Body and Gender from the Greeks to Freud* (Cambridge, Mass.: Harvard University Press, 1990).

Maclean, Ian, *The Renaissance Notion of Woman: A Study in the Fortunes of Scholasticism and Medical Science in European Intellectual Life* (Cambridge: Cambridge University Press, 1980).

Purkiss, Diane, *The Witch in History: Early Modern and Twentieth Century Representations* (London: Routledge, 1996).

Roper, Lyndal, *Oedipus and the Devil: Witchcraft, Sexuality and Religion in Early Modern Europe* (London: Routledge, 1994).

Traub, Valerie, 'The Morphology of the Clitoris', *GLQ: A Journal of Gay and Lesbian Studies*, 2 (1995), 81–113.

—— Kaplan, M. Lindsay, and Callaghan, Dympna (eds.), *Feminist Readings of Early Modern Culture: Emerging Subjects* (Cambridge: Cambridge University Press, 1996).

Turner, James Grantham (ed.), *Sexuality and Gender in Early Modern Europe: Institutions, Texts, Images* (Cambridge: Cambridge University Press, 1993).

Index

Note: Page numbers in italics refer to illustrations, but there may also be textual references on that page. The letters 'fn' refer to footnotes on that page.